msdn

msdn training

Info@dotNetguru.Net
www.mobilelearning.tv
* (Student Kit)

Password

2565A: Developing Microsoft® .NET Applications for Windows® (Visual Basic® .NET)

Test

Olaf Cames

MCSD

Microsoft®

Course Number: 2565A
Part Number: X10-28198
Released: 05/2002

END-USER LICENSE AGREEMENT FOR MICROSOFT OFFICIAL CURRICULUM COURSEWARE -STUDENT EDITION

PLEASE READ THIS END-USER LICENSE AGREEMENT ("EULA") CAREFULLY. BY USING THE MATERIALS AND/OR USING OR INSTALLING THE SOFTWARE THAT ACCOMPANIES THIS EULA (COLLECTIVELY, THE "LICENSED CONTENT"), YOU AGREE TO THE TERMS OF THIS EULA. IF YOU DO NOT AGREE, DO NOT USE THE LICENSED CONTENT.

1. **GENERAL.** This EULA is a legal agreement between you (either an individual or a single entity) and Microsoft Corporation ("Microsoft"). This EULA governs the Licensed Content, which includes computer software (including online and electronic documentation), training materials, and any other associated media and printed materials. This EULA applies to updates, supplements, add-on components, and Internet-based services components of the Licensed Content that Microsoft may provide or make available to you unless Microsoft provides other terms with the update, supplement, add-on component, or Internet-based services component. Microsoft reserves the right to discontinue any Internet-based services provided to you or made available to you through the use of the Licensed Content. This EULA also governs any product support services relating to the Licensed Content except as may be included in another agreement between you and Microsoft. An amendment or addendum to this EULA may accompany the Licensed Content.

2. **GENERAL GRANT OF LICENSE.** Microsoft grants you the following rights, conditioned on your compliance with all the terms and conditions of this EULA. Microsoft grants you a limited, non-exclusive, royalty-free license to install and use the Licensed Content solely in conjunction with your participation as a student in an Authorized Training Session (as defined below). You may install and use one copy of the software on a single computer, device, workstation, terminal, or other digital electronic or analog device ("Device"). You may make a second copy of the software and install it on a portable Device for the exclusive use of the person who is the primary user of the first copy of the software. A license for the software may not be shared for use by multiple end users. An "Authorized Training Session" means a training session conducted at a Microsoft Certified Technical Education Center, an IT Academy, via a Microsoft Certified Partner, or such other entity as Microsoft may designate from time to time in writing, by a Microsoft Certified Trainer (for more information on these entities, please visit www.microsoft.com). WITHOUT LIMITING THE FOREGOING, COPYING OR REPRODUCTION OF THE LICENSED CONTENT TO ANY SERVER OR LOCATION FOR FURTHER REPRODUCTION OR REDISTRIBUTION IS EXPRESSLY PROHIBITED.

3. **DESCRIPTION OF OTHER RIGHTS AND LICENSE LIMITATIONS**

3.1 *Use of Documentation and Printed Training Materials.*

3.1.1 The documents and related graphics included in the Licensed Content may include technical inaccuracies or typographical errors. Changes are periodically made to the content. Microsoft may make improvements and/or changes in any of the components of the Licensed Content at any time without notice. The names of companies, products, people, characters and/or data mentioned in the Licensed Content may be fictitious and are in no way intended to represent any real individual, company, product or event, unless otherwise noted.

3.1.2 Microsoft grants you the right to reproduce portions of documents (such as student workbooks, white papers, press releases, datasheets and FAQs) (the "Documents") provided with the Licensed Content. You may not print any book (either electronic or print version) in its entirety. If you choose to reproduce Documents, you agree that: (a) use of such printed Documents will be solely in conjunction with your personal training use; (b) the Documents will not republished or posted on any network computer or broadcast in any media; (c) any reproduction will include either the Document's original copyright notice or a copyright notice to Microsoft's benefit substantially in the format provided below; and (d) to comply with all terms and conditions of this EULA. In addition, no modifications may made to any Document.

Form of Notice:

© 2002. Reprinted with permission by Microsoft Corporation. All rights reserved.

Microsoft and Windows are either registered trademarks or trademarks of Microsoft Corporation in the US and/or other countries. Other product and company names mentioned herein may be the trademarks of their respective owners.

3.2 *Use of Media Elements.* The Licensed Content may include certain photographs, clip art, animations, sounds, music, and video clips (together "Media Elements"). You may not modify these Media Elements.

3.3 *Use of Sample Code.* In the event that the Licensed Content includes sample code in source or object format ("Sample Code"), Microsoft grants you a limited, non-exclusive, royalty-free license to use, copy and modify the Sample Code; if you elect to exercise the foregoing rights, you agree to comply with all other terms and conditions of this EULA, including without limitation Sections 3.4, 3.5, and 6.

3.4 *Permitted Modifications.* In the event that you exercise any rights provided under this EULA to create modifications of the Licensed Content, you agree that any such modifications: (a) will not be used for providing training where a fee is charged in public or private classes; (b) indemnify, hold harmless, and defend Microsoft from and against any claims or lawsuits, including attorneys' fees, which arise from or result from your use of any modified version of the Licensed Content; and (c) not to transfer or assign any rights to any modified version of the Licensed Content to any third party without the express written permission of Microsoft.

3.5 *Reproduction/Redistribution Licensed Content.* Except as expressly provided in this EULA, you may not reproduce or distribute the Licensed Content or any portion thereof (including any permitted modifications) to any third parties without the express written permission of Microsoft.

4. **RESERVATION OF RIGHTS AND OWNERSHIP.** Microsoft reserves all rights not expressly granted to you in this EULA. The Licensed Content is protected by copyright and other intellectual property laws and treaties. Microsoft or its suppliers own the title, copyright, and other intellectual property rights in the Licensed Content. You may not remove or obscure any copyright, trademark or patent notices that appear on the Licensed Content, or any components thereof, as delivered to you. **The Licensed Content is licensed, not sold.**

5. **LIMITATIONS ON REVERSE ENGINEERING, DECOMPILATION, AND DISASSEMBLY.** You may not reverse engineer, decompile, or disassemble the Software or Media Elements, except and only to the extent that such activity is expressly permitted by applicable law notwithstanding this limitation.

6. **LIMITATIONS ON SALE, RENTAL, ETC. AND CERTAIN ASSIGNMENTS.** You may not provide commercial hosting services with, sell, rent, lease, lend, sublicense, or assign copies of the Licensed Content, or any portion thereof (including any permitted modifications thereof) on a stand-alone basis or as part of any collection, product or service.

7. **CONSENT TO USE OF DATA.** You agree that Microsoft and its affiliates may collect and use technical information gathered as part of the product support services provided to you, if any, related to the Licensed Content. Microsoft may use this information solely to improve our products or to provide customized services or technologies to you and will not disclose this information in a form that personally identifies you.

8. **LINKS TO THIRD PARTY SITES.** You may link to third party sites through the use of the Licensed Content. The third party sites are not under the control of Microsoft, and Microsoft is not responsible for the contents of any third party sites, any links contained in third party sites, or any changes or updates to third party sites. Microsoft is not responsible for webcasting or any other form of transmission received from any third party sites. Microsoft is providing these links to third party sites to you only as a convenience, and the inclusion of any link does not imply an endorsement by Microsoft of the third party site.

9. **ADDITIONAL LICENSED CONTENT/SERVICES.** This EULA applies to updates, supplements, add-on components, or Internet-based services components, of the Licensed Content that Microsoft may provide to you or make available to you after the date you obtain your initial copy of the Licensed Content, unless we provide other terms along with the update, supplement, add-on component, or Internet-based services component. Microsoft reserves the right to discontinue any Internet-based services provided to you or made available to you through the use of the Licensed Content.

10. **U.S. GOVERNMENT LICENSE RIGHTS**. All software provided to the U.S. Government pursuant to solicitations issued on or after December 1, 1995 is provided with the commercial license rights and restrictions described elsewhere herein. All software provided to the U.S. Government pursuant to solicitations issued prior to December 1, 1995 is provided with "Restricted Rights" as provided for in FAR, 48 CFR 52.227-14 (JUNE 1987) or DFAR, 48 CFR 252.227-7013 (OCT 1988), as applicable.

11. **EXPORT RESTRICTIONS**. You acknowledge that the Licensed Content is subject to U.S. export jurisdiction. You agree to comply with all applicable international and national laws that apply to the Licensed Content, including the U.S. Export Administration Regulations, as well as end-user, end-use, and destination restrictions issued by U.S. and other governments. For additional information see <http://www.microsoft.com/exporting/>.

12. **TRANSFER.** The initial user of the Licensed Content may make a one-time permanent transfer of this EULA and Licensed Content to another end user, provided the initial user retains no copies of the Licensed Content. The transfer may not be an indirect transfer, such as a consignment. Prior to the transfer, the end user receiving the Licensed Content must agree to all the EULA terms.

13. **"NOT FOR RESALE" LICENSED CONTENT.** Licensed Content identified as "Not For Resale" or "NFR," may not be sold or otherwise transferred for value, or used for any purpose other than demonstration, test or evaluation.

14. **TERMINATION.** Without prejudice to any other rights, Microsoft may terminate this EULA if you fail to comply with the terms and conditions of this EULA. In such event, you must destroy all copies of the Licensed Content and all of its component parts.

15. **DISCLAIMER OF WARRANTIES. TO THE MAXIMUM EXTENT PERMITTED BY APPLICABLE LAW, MICROSOFT AND ITS SUPPLIERS PROVIDE THE LICENSED CONTENT AND SUPPORT SERVICES (IF ANY) *AS IS AND WITH ALL FAULTS*, AND MICROSOFT AND ITS SUPPLIERS HEREBY DISCLAIM ALL OTHER WARRANTIES AND CONDITIONS, WHETHER EXPRESS, IMPLIED OR STATUTORY, INCLUDING, BUT NOT LIMITED TO, ANY (IF ANY) IMPLIED WARRANTIES, DUTIES OR CONDITIONS OF MERCHANTABILITY, OF FITNESS FOR A PARTICULAR PURPOSE, OF RELIABILITY OR AVAILABILITY, OF ACCURACY OR COMPLETENESS OF RESPONSES, OF RESULTS, OF WORKMANLIKE EFFORT, OF LACK OF VIRUSES, AND OF LACK OF NEGLIGENCE, ALL WITH REGARD TO THE LICENSED CONTENT, AND THE PROVISION OF OR FAILURE TO PROVIDE SUPPORT OR OTHER SERVICES, INFORMATION, SOFTWARE, AND RELATED CONTENT THROUGH THE LICENSED CONTENT, OR OTHERWISE ARISING OUT OF THE USE OF THE LICENSED CONTENT. ALSO, THERE IS NO WARRANTY OR CONDITION OF TITLE, QUIET ENJOYMENT, QUIET POSSESSION, CORRESPONDENCE TO DESCRIPTION OR NON-INFRINGEMENT WITH REGARD TO THE LICENSED CONTENT. THE ENTIRE RISK AS TO THE QUALITY, OR ARISING OUT OF THE USE OR PERFORMANCE OF THE LICENSED CONTENT, AND ANY SUPPORT SERVICES, REMAINS WITH YOU.**

16. **EXCLUSION OF INCIDENTAL, CONSEQUENTIAL AND CERTAIN OTHER DAMAGES. TO THE MAXIMUM EXTENT PERMITTED BY APPLICABLE LAW, IN NO EVENT SHALL MICROSOFT OR ITS SUPPLIERS BE LIABLE FOR ANY SPECIAL, INCIDENTAL, PUNITIVE, INDIRECT, OR CONSEQUENTIAL DAMAGES WHATSOEVER (INCLUDING, BUT NOT**

LIMITED TO, DAMAGES FOR LOSS OF PROFITS OR CONFIDENTIAL OR OTHER INFORMATION, FOR BUSINESS INTERRUPTION, FOR PERSONAL INJURY, FOR LOSS OF PRIVACY, FOR FAILURE TO MEET ANY DUTY INCLUDING OF GOOD FAITH OR OF REASONABLE CARE, FOR NEGLIGENCE, AND FOR ANY OTHER PECUNIARY OR OTHER LOSS WHATSOEVER) ARISING OUT OF OR IN ANY WAY RELATED TO THE USE OF OR INABILITY TO USE THE LICENSED CONTENT, THE PROVISION OF OR FAILURE TO PROVIDE SUPPORT OR OTHER SERVICES, INFORMATION, SOFTWARE, AND RELATED CONTENT THROUGH THE LICENSED CONTENT, OR OTHERWISE ARISING OUT OF THE USE OF THE LICENSED CONTENT, OR OTHERWISE UNDER OR IN CONNECTION WITH ANY PROVISION OF THIS EULA, EVEN IN THE EVENT OF THE FAULT, TORT (INCLUDING NEGLIGENCE), MISREPRESENTATION, STRICT LIABILITY, BREACH OF CONTRACT OR BREACH OF WARRANTY OF MICROSOFT OR ANY SUPPLIER, AND EVEN IF MICROSOFT OR ANY SUPPLIER HAS BEEN ADVISED OF THE POSSIBILITY OF SUCH DAMAGES. BECAUSE SOME STATES/JURISDICTIONS DO NOT ALLOW THE EXCLUSION OR LIMITATION OF LIABILITY FOR CONSEQUENTIAL OR INCIDENTAL DAMAGES, THE ABOVE LIMITATION MAY NOT APPLY TO YOU.

17. LIMITATION OF LIABILITY AND REMEDIES. **NOTWITHSTANDING ANY DAMAGES THAT YOU MIGHT INCUR FOR ANY REASON WHATSOEVER (INCLUDING, WITHOUT LIMITATION, ALL DAMAGES REFERENCED HEREIN AND ALL DIRECT OR GENERAL DAMAGES IN CONTRACT OR ANYTHING ELSE), THE ENTIRE LIABILITY OF MICROSOFT AND ANY OF ITS SUPPLIERS UNDER ANY PROVISION OF THIS EULA AND YOUR EXCLUSIVE REMEDY HEREUNDER SHALL BE LIMITED TO THE GREATER OF THE ACTUAL DAMAGES YOU INCUR IN REASONABLE RELIANCE ON THE LICENSED CONTENT UP TO THE AMOUNT ACTUALLY PAID BY YOU FOR THE LICENSED CONTENT OR US$5.00. THE FOREGOING LIMITATIONS, EXCLUSIONS AND DISCLAIMERS SHALL APPLY TO THE MAXIMUM EXTENT PERMITTED BY APPLICABLE LAW, EVEN IF ANY REMEDY FAILS ITS ESSENTIAL PURPOSE.**

18. **APPLICABLE LAW.** If you acquired this Licensed Content in the United States, this EULA is governed by the laws of the State of Washington. If you acquired this Licensed Content in Canada, unless expressly prohibited by local law, this EULA is governed by the laws in force in the Province of Ontario, Canada; and, in respect of any dispute which may arise hereunder, you consent to the jurisdiction of the federal and provincial courts sitting in Toronto, Ontario. If you acquired this Licensed Content in the European Union, Iceland, Norway, or Switzerland, then local law applies. If you acquired this Licensed Content in any other country, then local law may apply.

19. **ENTIRE AGREEMENT; SEVERABILITY.** This EULA (including any addendum or amendment to this EULA which is included with the Licensed Content) are the entire agreement between you and Microsoft relating to the Licensed Content and the support services (if any) and they supersede all prior or contemporaneous oral or written communications, proposals and representations with respect to the Licensed Content or any other subject matter covered by this EULA. To the extent the terms of any Microsoft policies or programs for support services conflict with the terms of this EULA, the terms of this EULA shall control. If any provision of this EULA is held to be void, invalid, unenforceable or illegal, the other provisions shall continue in full force and effect.

Should you have any questions concerning this EULA, or if you desire to contact Microsoft for any reason, please use the address information enclosed in this Licensed Content to contact the Microsoft subsidiary serving your country or visit Microsoft on the World Wide Web at http://www.microsoft.com.

Si vous avez acquis votre Contenu Sous Licence Microsoft au CANADA :

DÉNI DE GARANTIES. Dans la mesure maximale permise par les lois applicables, le Contenu Sous Licence et les services de soutien technique (le cas échéant) sont fournis *TELS QUELS ET AVEC TOUS LES DÉFAUTS* par Microsoft et ses fournisseurs, lesquels par les présentes dénient toutes autres garanties et conditions expresses, implicites ou en vertu de la loi, notamment, mais sans limitation, (le cas échéant) les garanties, devoirs ou conditions implicites de qualité marchande, d'adaptation à une fin usage particulière, de fiabilité ou de disponibilité, d'exactitude ou d'exhaustivité des réponses, des résultats, des efforts déployés selon les règles de l'art, d'absence de virus et d'absence de négligence, le tout à l'égard du Contenu Sous Licence et de la prestation des services de soutien technique ou de l'omission de la 'une telle prestation des services de soutien technique ou à l'égard de la fourniture ou de l'omission de la fourniture de tous autres services, renseignements, Contenus Sous Licence, et contenu qui s'y rapporte grâce au Contenu Sous Licence ou provenant autrement de l'utilisation du Contenu Sous Licence. PAR AILLEURS, IL N'Y A AUCUNE GARANTIE OU CONDITION QUANT AU TITRE DE PROPRIÉTÉ, À LA JOUISSANCE OU LA POSSESSION PAISIBLE, À LA CONCORDANCE À UNE DESCRIPTION NI QUANT À UNE ABSENCE DE CONTREFAÇON CONCERNANT LE CONTENU SOUS LICENCE.

EXCLUSION DES DOMMAGES ACCESSOIRES, INDIRECTS ET DE CERTAINS AUTRES DOMMAGES. **DANS LA MESURE MAXIMALE PERMISE PAR LES LOIS APPLICABLES, EN AUCUN CAS MICROSOFT OU SES FOURNISSEURS NE SERONT RESPONSABLES DES DOMMAGES SPÉCIAUX, CONSÉCUTIFS, ACCESSOIRES OU INDIRECTS DE QUELQUE NATURE QUE CE SOIT (NOTAMMENT, LES DOMMAGES À L'ÉGARD DU MANQUE À GAGNER OU DE LA DIVULGATION DE RENSEIGNEMENTS CONFIDENTIELS OU AUTRES, DE LA PERTE D'EXPLOITATION, DE BLESSURES CORPORELLES, DE LA VIOLATION DE LA VIE PRIVÉE, DE L'OMISSION DE REMPLIR TOUT DEVOIR, Y COMPRIS D'AGIR DE BONNE FOI OU D'EXERCER UN SOIN RAISONNABLE, DE LA NÉGLIGENCE ET DE TOUTE AUTRE PERTE PÉCUNIAIRE OU AUTRE PERTE**

DE QUELQUE NATURE QUE CE SOIT) SE RAPPORTANT DE QUELQUE MANIÈRE QUE CE SOIT À L'UTILISATION DU CONTENU SOUS LICENCE OU À L'INCAPACITÉ DE S'EN SERVIR, À LA PRESTATION OU À L'OMISSION DE LA 'UNE TELLE PRESTATION DE SERVICES DE SOUTIEN TECHNIQUE OU À LA FOURNITURE OU À L'OMISSION DE LA FOURNITURE DE TOUS AUTRES SERVICES, RENSEIGNEMENTS, CONTENUS SOUS LICENCE, ET CONTENU QUI S'Y RAPPORTE GRÂCE AU CONTENU SOUS LICENCE OU PROVENANT AUTREMENT DE L'UTILISATION DU CONTENU SOUS LICENCE OU AUTREMENT AUX TERMES DE TOUTE DISPOSITION DE LA U PRÉSENTE CONVENTION EULA OU RELATIVEMENT À UNE TELLE DISPOSITION, MÊME EN CAS DE FAUTE, DE DÉLIT CIVIL (Y COMPRIS LA NÉGLIGENCE), DE RESPONSABILITÉ STRICTE, DE VIOLATION DE CONTRAT OU DE VIOLATION DE GARANTIE DE MICROSOFT OU DE TOUT FOURNISSEUR ET MÊME SI MICROSOFT OU TOUT FOURNISSEUR A ÉTÉ AVISÉ DE LA POSSIBILITÉ DE TELS DOMMAGES.

LIMITATION DE RESPONSABILITÉ ET RECOURS. MALGRÉ LES DOMMAGES QUE VOUS PUISSIEZ SUBIR POUR QUELQUE MOTIF QUE CE SOIT (NOTAMMENT, MAIS SANS LIMITATION, TOUS LES DOMMAGES SUSMENTIONNÉS ET TOUS LES DOMMAGES DIRECTS OU GÉNÉRAUX OU AUTRES), LA SEULE RESPONSABILITÉ 'OBLIGATION INTÉGRALE DE MICROSOFT ET DE L'UN OU L'AUTRE DE SES FOURNISSEURS AUX TERMES DE TOUTE DISPOSITION DEU LA PRÉSENTE CONVENTION EULA ET VOTRE RECOURS EXCLUSIF À L'ÉGARD DE TOUT CE QUI PRÉCÈDE SE LIMITE AU PLUS ÉLEVÉ ENTRE LES MONTANTS SUIVANTS : LE MONTANT QUE VOUS AVEZ RÉELLEMENT PAYÉ POUR LE CONTENU SOUS LICENCE OU 5,00 $US. LES LIMITES, EXCLUSIONS ET DÉNIS QUI PRÉCÈDENT (Y COMPRIS LES CLAUSES CI-DESSUS), S'APPLIQUENT DANS LA MESURE MAXIMALE PERMISE PAR LES LOIS APPLICABLES, MÊME SI TOUT RECOURS N'ATTEINT PAS SON BUT ESSENTIEL.

À moins que cela ne soit prohibé par le droit local applicable, la présente Convention est régie par les lois de la province d'Ontario, Canada. Vous consentez Chacune des parties à la présente reconnaît irrévocablement à la compétence des tribunaux fédéraux et provinciaux siégeant à Toronto, dans de la province d'Ontario et consent à instituer tout litige qui pourrait découler de la présente auprès des tribunaux situés dans le district judiciaire de York, province d'Ontario.

Au cas où vous auriez des questions concernant cette licence ou que vous désiriez vous mettre en rapport avec Microsoft pour quelque raison que ce soit, veuillez utiliser l'information contenue dans le Contenu Sous Licence pour contacter la filiale de succursale Microsoft desservant votre pays, dont l'adresse est fournie dans ce produit, ou visitez écrivez à : Microsoft sur le World Wide Web à http://www.microsoft.com

Contents

Module 4: Using Data in Windows Forms Applications

Module 5: Interoperating with Managed Objects

Module 6: Printing and Reporting in Windows Forms Applications

Module 7: Asynchronous Programming

Module 8: Enhancing the Usability of Applications

Module 9: Deploying Windows Forms Applications

Module 10: Securing Windows Forms Applications

Appendix A: Using Filled Shapes and Images

About This Course

This section provides you with a brief description of the course, audience, suggested prerequisites, and course objectives.

Description

Windows Forms is the new platform for Microsoft® Windows® application development, based on the Microsoft .NET Framework. The .NET Framework provides a clear, object-oriented, extensible set of classes that enables developers to develop rich Windows Forms applications. Additionally, Windows Forms can act as the local user interface in a multi-tier distributed solution.

This three-day instructor-led course provides students with the skills required to build Windows Forms applications by using the .NET Framework.

Audience

This course is intended for the intermediate programmer who is responsible for designing and building Windows Forms applications by using the .NET Framework. It is designed for developers who have Microsoft Visual Basic® .NET development skills.

Typically, these individuals perform the following key activities:

- Help with creation of functional specifications
- Design and develop user interfaces
- Create and test prototypes
- Write Windows Forms applications

Student prerequisites

This course requires that students meet the following prerequisites:

- Experience with a .NET Framework language such as Visual Basic .NET

  Microsoft MSDN® Training Course 2559A: *Introduction to Visual Basic .NET Programming with Microsoft .NET* will help students gain basic skills in Visual Basic .NET programming techniques and meet the prerequisites for this course.
- Experience developing applications with Visual Basic 6

Course objectives

After completing this course, the student will be able to:

- Create and populate Windows Forms.
- Organize controls on Windows Forms.
- Create menus in a Windows Forms application.
- Add code to form and control event procedures in a Windows Forms application.
- Create Multiple Document Interface (MDI) applications.
- Use dialogs in Windows Forms applications.
- Validate user input in a Windows Forms application.
- Create and use user controls in a Windows Forms application.
- Create licenses for controls.
- Bind Windows Forms applications to various data sources by using Microsoft ADO.NET.
- Consume XML Web services from Windows Forms applications.
- Use .NET and COM components in a Windows Forms application.
- Call Microsoft Win32® APIs from a Windows Forms application.
- Upgrade Visual Basic 6.0 applications to Visual Basic .NET.
- Print documents in a Windows Forms application.
- Make asynchronous calls to methods from a Windows Forms application.
- Debug a Windows Forms application.
- Incorporate accessibility features in a Windows Forms application.
- Localize a Windows Forms application.
- Add support for help to localize a Windows Forms application.
- Create help files in a Windows Forms application.
- Deploy a Windows Forms application.
- Implement code access and role-based security in a Windows Forms application.
- Add deployment flexibility to applications by using shared assemblies.

Student Materials Compact Disc Contents

The Student Materials compact disc contains the following files and folders:

- *Autorun.exe*. When the compact disc is inserted into the CD-ROM drive, or when you double-click the **Autorun.exe** file, this file opens the compact disc and allows you to browse the Student Materials compact disc.
- *Autorun.inf*. When the compact disc is inserted into the compact disc drive, this file opens Autorun.exe.
- *Default.htm*. This file opens the Student Materials Web page. It provides you with resources pertaining to this course, including additional reading, review and lab answers, lab files, multimedia presentations, and course-related Web sites.
- *Readme.txt*. This file explains how to install the software for viewing the Student Materials compact disc and its contents and how to open the Student Materials Web page.
- *2565A_ms.doc*. This file is the Manual Classroom Setup Guide. It contains a description of classroom requirements, classroom setup instructions, and the classroom configuration.
- *Democode*. This folder contains files that are used in the instructor demonstrations.
- *Flash*. This folder contains the installer for the Macromedia Flash 5.0 browser plug-in.
- *Fonts*. This folder contains fonts that are required to view the PowerPoint presentation and Web-based materials.
- *Inetpubs*. This folder contains files used by the sample Web-based applications in this course.
- *Labfiles*. This folder contains files that are used in the hands-on labs. These files may be used to prepare the student computers for the hands-on labs.
- *Media*. This folder contains files that are used in multimedia presentations for this course.
- *Mplayer*. This folder contains the setup file to install Microsoft Windows Media™ Player.
- *Practices*. This folder contains files that are used in the hands-on practices.
- *Sampapps*. This folder contains the sample applications associated with this course.
- *Sampcode*. This folder contains sample code that is accessible through the Web pages on the Student Materials compact disc.
- *Webfiles*. This folder contains the files that are required to view the course Web page. To open the Web page, open Windows Explorer, and in the root directory of the compact disc, double-click **Default.htm** or **Autorun.exe**.
- *Wordview*. This folder contains the Word Viewer that is used to view any Microsoft Word document (.doc) files that are included on the compact disc.

Document Conventions

The following conventions are used in course materials to distinguish elements of the text.

Convention	Use
Bold	Represents commands, command options, and syntax that must be typed exactly as shown. It also indicates commands on menus and buttons, dialog box titles and options, and icon and menu names.
Italic	In syntax statements or descriptive text, indicates argument names or placeholders for variable information. Italic is also used for introducing new terms, for book titles, and for emphasis in the text.
Title Capitals	Indicate domain names, user names, computer names, directory names, and folder and file names, except when specifically referring to case-sensitive names. Unless otherwise indicated, you can use lowercase letters when you type a directory name or file name in a dialog box or at a command prompt.
ALL CAPITALS	Indicate the names of keys, key sequences, and key combinations—for example, ALT+SPACEBAR.
`monospace`	Represents code samples or examples of screen text.
[ ]	In syntax statements, enclose optional items. For example, [*filename*] in command syntax indicates that you can choose to type a file name with the command. Type only the information within the brackets, not the brackets themselves.
{ }	In syntax statements, enclose required items. Type only the information within the braces, not the braces themselves.
|	In syntax statements, separates an either/or choice.
►	Indicates a procedure with sequential steps.
...	In syntax statements, specifies that the preceding item may be repeated.
. . .	Represents an omitted portion of a code sample.

msdn training

Introduction

Contents

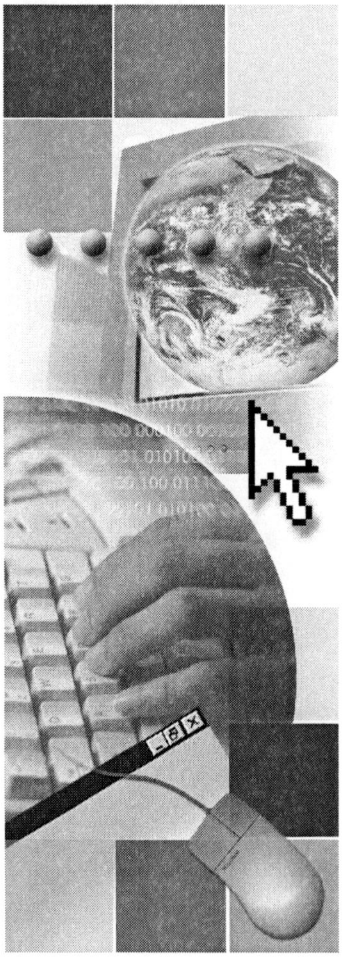

Microsoft

Introduction

- Name
- Company affiliation
- Title/function
- Job responsibility
- Programming and database experience
- Microsoft Visual Basic and .NET experience
- Expectations for the course

Your instructor will ask you to introduce yourself and provide a brief overview of your background, addressing the bulleted items on the slide as appropriate.

Course Materials

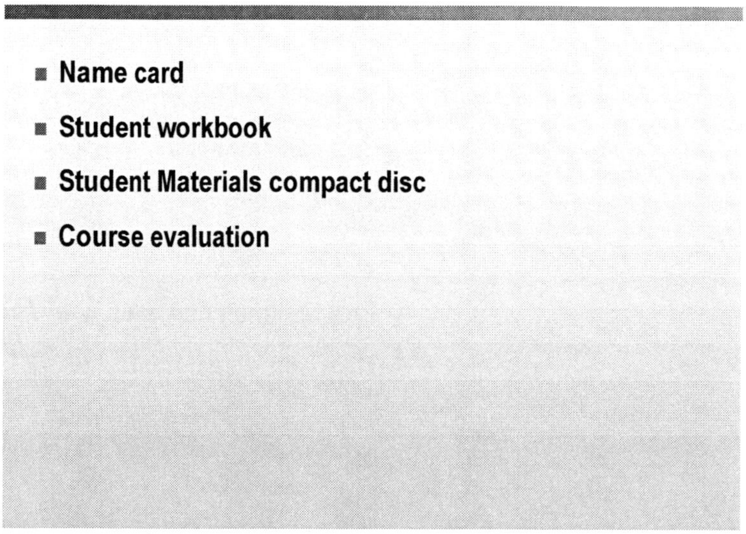

The following materials are included with your kit:

- *Name card.* Write your name on both sides of the name card.
- *Student workbook.* The student workbook contains the material covered in class, in addition to the hands-on lab exercises.
- *Student Materials compact disc.* The Student Materials compact disc contains the Web page that provides you with links to resources pertaining to this course, including additional readings, review and lab answers, lab files, multimedia presentations, and course-related Web sites.

  Note To open the Web page, insert the Student Materials compact disc into the CD-ROM drive, and then in the root directory of the compact disc, double-click **Autorun.exe** or **Default.htm**.

  Important There are starter and solution files associated with the labs in this course. If you perform a default installation, the starter and the solution files install to C:\Program Files\Msdntrain\2565. However, if you install to a different location, you must reset the assembly references in the starter and solution projects.

- *Course evaluation.* To provide feedback on the course, training facility, and instructor, you will have the opportunity to complete an online evaluation near the end of the course.

  To provide additional comments or inquire about the Microsoft Certified Professional program, send e-mail to mcphelp@microsoft.com.

Prerequisites

- **Experience programming with Microsoft Visual Basic**
- **An understanding of the Microsoft .NET Framework**
- **Experience developing applications**
- **Recommended prerequisite course**
  - Course 2559A: *Introduction to Visual Basic .NET Programming with Microsoft .NET*

    -or-
  - Equivalent knowledge

This course requires that you meet the following prerequisites:

- Experience programming with Microsoft Visual Basic .NET
- An understanding of the Microsoft .NET Framework
- Experience developing applications

  –and–
- Completion of Microsoft MSDN® Training Course 2559A, *Introduction to Visual Basic .NET Programming with Microsoft .NET*

  –or–
- Equivalent knowledge

Course Outline

- Module 1: Introducing Windows Forms
- Module 2: Working with Controls Templates
- Module 3: Building Controls (own)
- Module 4: Using Data in Windows Forms Applications

SQL
XML
(Web Store)

Module 1, "Introducing Windows Forms," introduces Windows Forms and controls, which are part of the Microsoft .NET Framework. It explains how to create and populate base forms and inherited forms by using Microsoft Visual Studio® .NET. It also covers organizing controls on a form and creating Multiple Document Interface (MDI) applications. This module is meant mainly to be a review of concepts that you are familiar with but also presents some new concepts, such as how to use Visual Studio .NET tools for organizing controls on a Windows form.

Module 2, "Working with Controls," explains how to code for event procedures associated with different controls. The module covers how to use some of the Windows Forms intrinsic controls in an application. It also explains how to use dialog boxes, validation controls, and menus in a Windows Forms application. The module also includes a section on the controls collection and how to add controls at run time.

Module 3, "Building Controls," describes the options for building your own controls. It explains how to extend the functionality of an existing Windows Forms control, combine multiple existing controls into a composite control, and build a new custom control. It also covers how to add design-time attributes and licensing support to a control.

Module 4, "Using Data in Windows Forms Applications," describes how to bind Windows forms to various data sources by using Microsoft ADO.NET and the Bindings collection. The module also provides an overview of the XML Web services programming model and covers how to create applications that use XML Web services. The module also provides an overview of how to persist data to and read data from files and isolated storage.

Course Outline *(continued)*

- Module 5: Interoperating with Managed Objects
- Module 6: Reporting and Printing in Windows Forms Applications
- Module 7: Asynchronous Programming
- Module 8: Enhancing the Usability of Applications
- Module 9: Deploying Windows Forms Applications
- Module 10: Securing Windows Forms Applications

advanced course 2557

Transaction Incorporates COM+

Module 5, "Interoperating with Managed Objects," explains how to use .NET and COM components in your Windows Forms application. You will also learn how to call Microsoft Win32® APIs in your Windows Forms application. The module also covers upgrading Microsoft Visual Basic 6.0 applications to Visual Basic .NET by using the Upgrade Wizard. – Not recommended – No advantage

Module 6, "Reporting and Printing in Windows Forms Applications," explains how to create reports in a Windows Forms application by using Crystal Reports. The module also covers how to implement printing in a Windows Forms application.

Module 7, "Asynchronous Programming," explains how to use the techniques of asynchronous programming and multithreading to avoid blocking the user interface of an application.

Back to 3 & 2 module →

Module 8, "Enhancing the Usability of Applications," explains how to use the accessibility, Help, and localization features available in the .NET Framework.

Module 9, "Deploying Windows Forms Applications," explains assemblies and the use of strong-named assemblies and the global assembly cache in the .NET Framework. It also covers how to configure and deploy your Windows Forms applications.

Module 10, "Securing Windows Forms Applications," explains how to use the security features in the .NET Framework in Windows Forms applications.

* Dot.Net is unsecure – course is about 3½ yrs old. Better today.

Demonstration: Expense Report Application

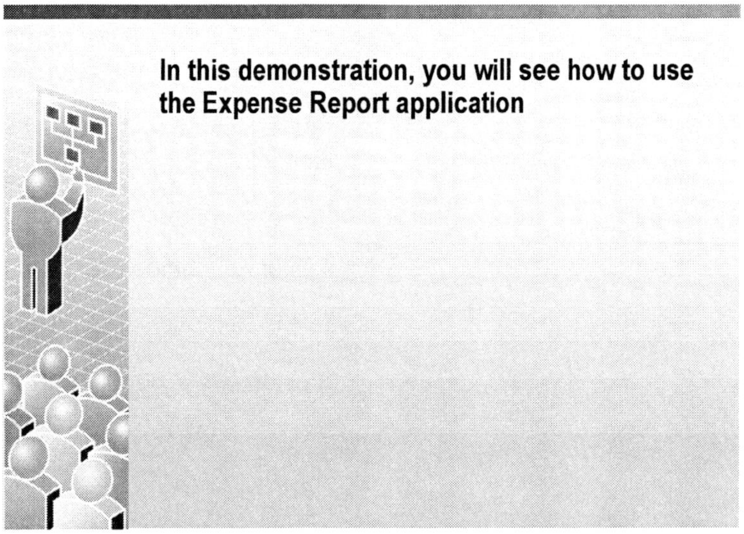

Introduction

In this demonstration, you will see how to use the Expense Report application.

Instructions

> **Note** If you performed a default installation of the course files, *install_folder* corresponds to C:\Program Files\Msdntrain\2565.

► **To run the demonstration**

1. Open the InternalBusinessApp.sln solution file from the *install_folder*\Sampapps\Business Application Shell.
2. Mention that the business expense reporting application consists of two major parts:
   - A Windows Forms-based client application that resides on the user's local computer.
   - An XML Web services component that returns information about existing expense reports and receives and stores information for newly submitted expense reports.

   All users of the application can create, submit, and view their own expense reports. Users who are managers can also view expense reports for their reporting employees and approve or disapprove those reports.

   While disconnected from the network, users can create new reports or view saved reports. Users must be connected to the network to submit reports or retrieve information about reports that do not reside on their local computer.

3. Describe the user interface.

   The user interface of the client application consists of several forms.

   The main control panel form for the Business application will display a **Logon** form in its **Load** event handler.

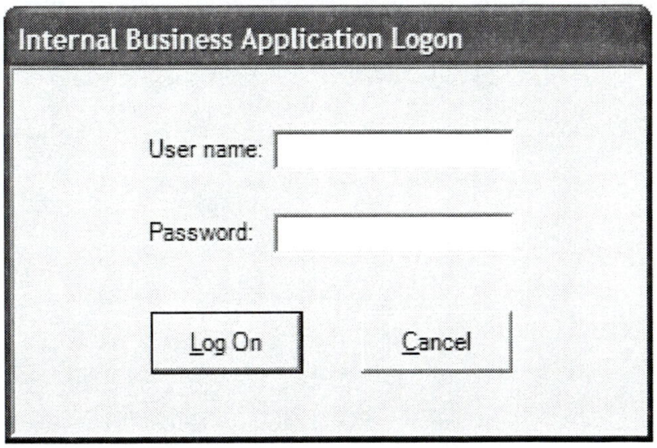

4. Log on to the application. Specify **mario** for the user name and **P@ssw0rd** for the password.

   After the user has successfully logged on, the main control panel form for the Business application appears.

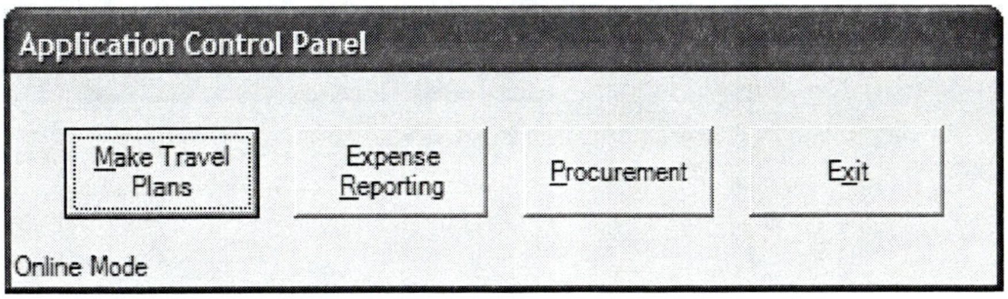

5. Describe the buttons on the main page.

   The **Make Travel Plans** and **Procurement** buttons are just placeholders with no real functionality. Students will work on implementing various parts of the Expense Reporting functionality. The **Exit** button closes the application.

6. Click **Expense Reporting**. Also demonstrate the multithreading feature of the application.

   When the user clicks the **Expense Reporting** button, an Expense Report control panel form appears.

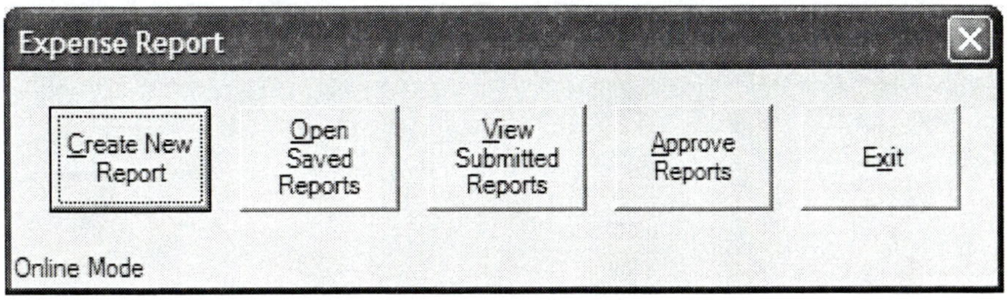

An Expense Report summary form displays a list of reports and summary information.

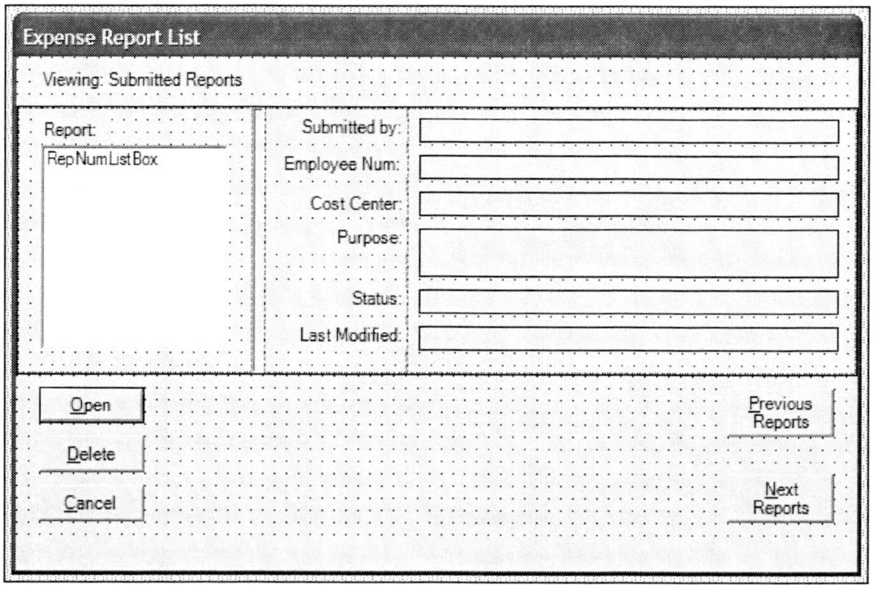

7. Double-click a given expense report in the list.

   When the user double-clicks a given expense report in the list, an **Expense Report Details** screen appears and shows the details for that report.

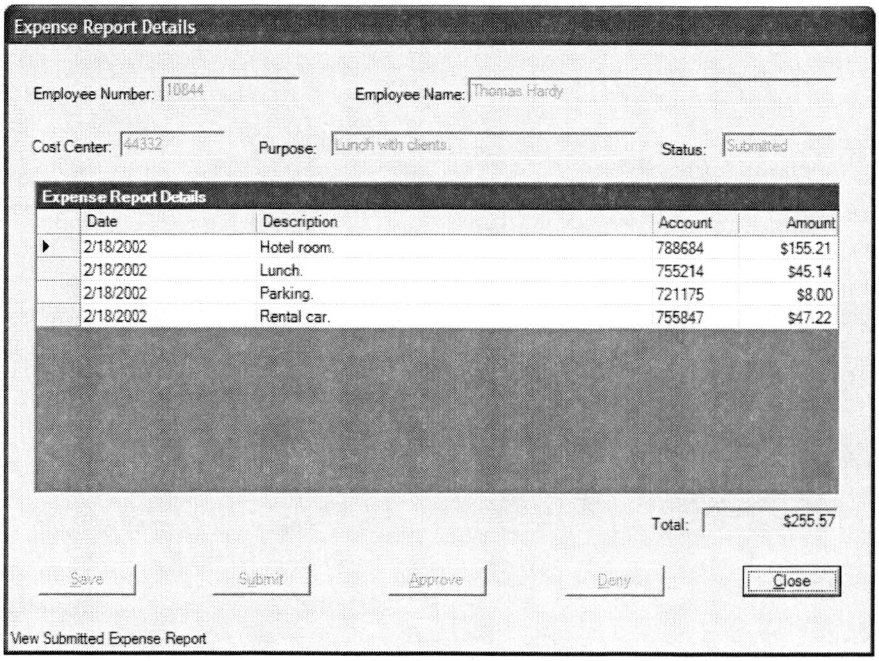

Demonstration: Purchase Order Application

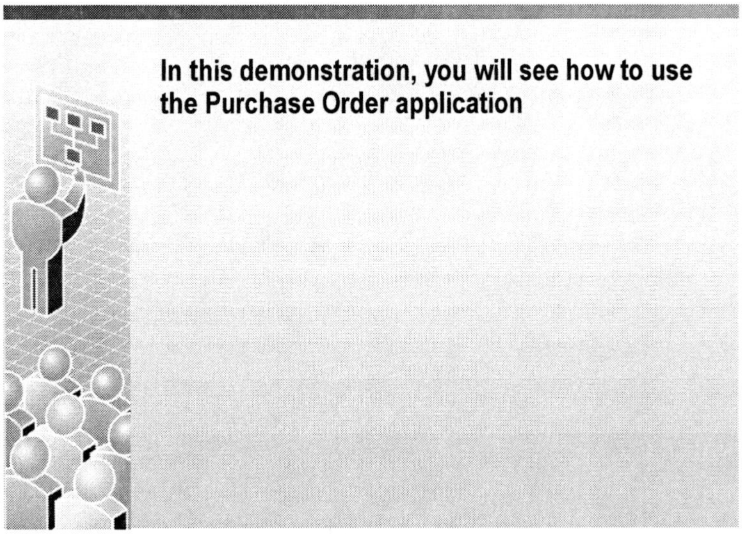

Introduction

In this demonstration, you will see how to use the Purchase Order application.

Instructions

► **To run the demonstration**

1. Open the Purchase Order application from *install_folder*\Sampapps\OrderApplication.
2. Mention that the Purchase Order application consists of:
   - A Windows Forms-based client application.
   - A DataSet containing customer, product, and order information from the Northwind database. The DataSet is stored as a local XML file, and the user can choose to refresh this file when connected to the database. The DataSet is bound to controls in the main form and to a custom composite control.
   - A DataSet containing new order and order detail information that is stored as a local XML file and is used to update the database when connected.
   - A custom composite control that displays product information and exposes properties, methods, and events implemented in the main form.
   - A Crystal Report, bound to the local DataSet, that displays the history of customer orders.
   - Printing abilities that allow users to preview a print document, specify page settings, and print a document.

3. Describe the user interface.

   The user interface of the client application consists of several screens.

   The Logon form is displayed when an employee chooses to refresh data and the **EmployeeID** is unknown. The form is also displayed when the user chooses to change their identity by using the **Option** menu on **MainForm**.

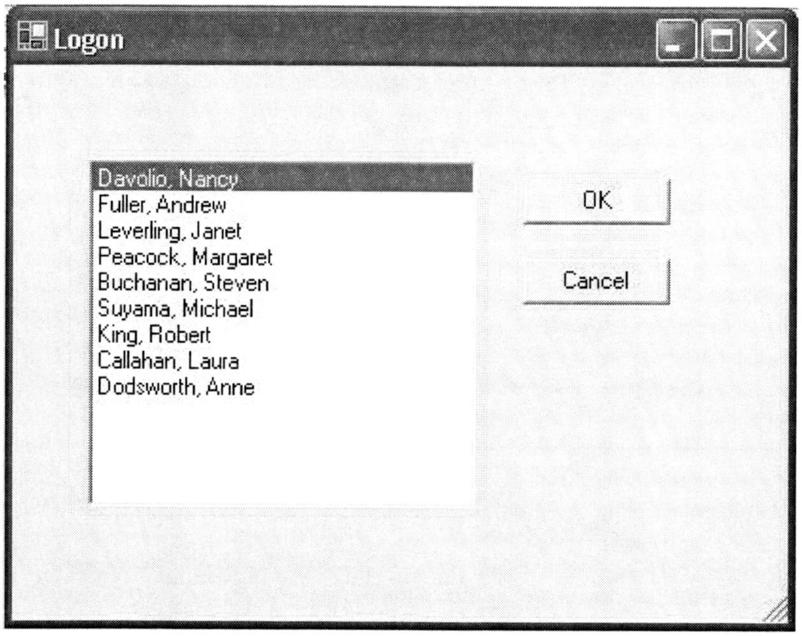

4. Open the Options form.

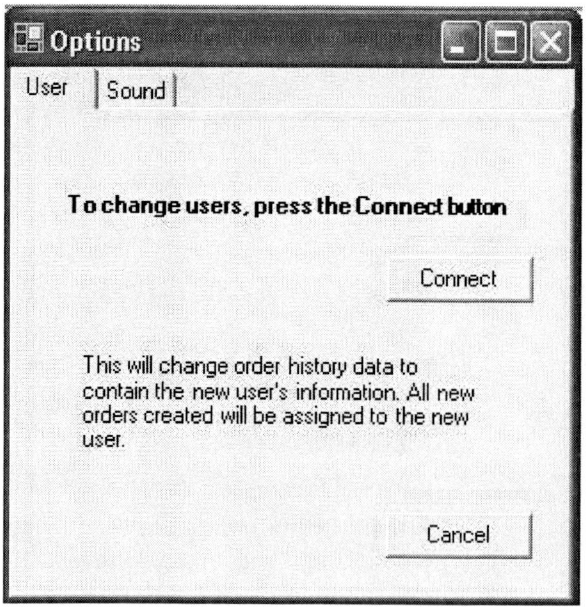

Users can change the employee information of the Purchase Order application and can also turn the sound effects on or off. The Options form includes two tabs: the first is used to change the **EmployeeID**, and the second is used to turn the sound on or off.

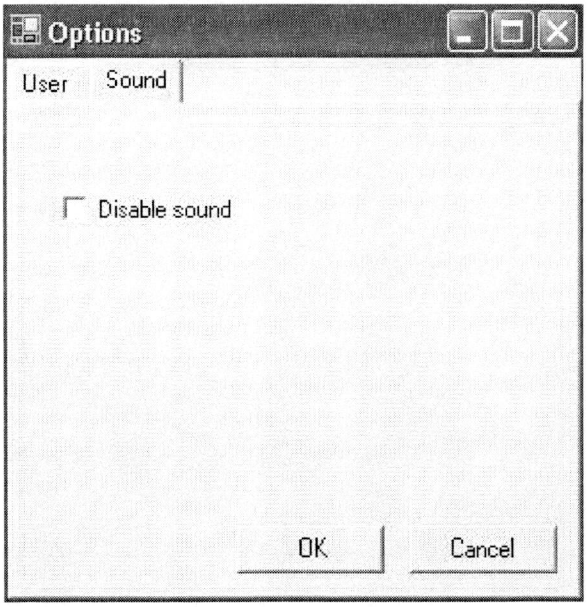

5. On the **View** menu, click **View Unsubmitted Orders** to open the Pending Orders form.

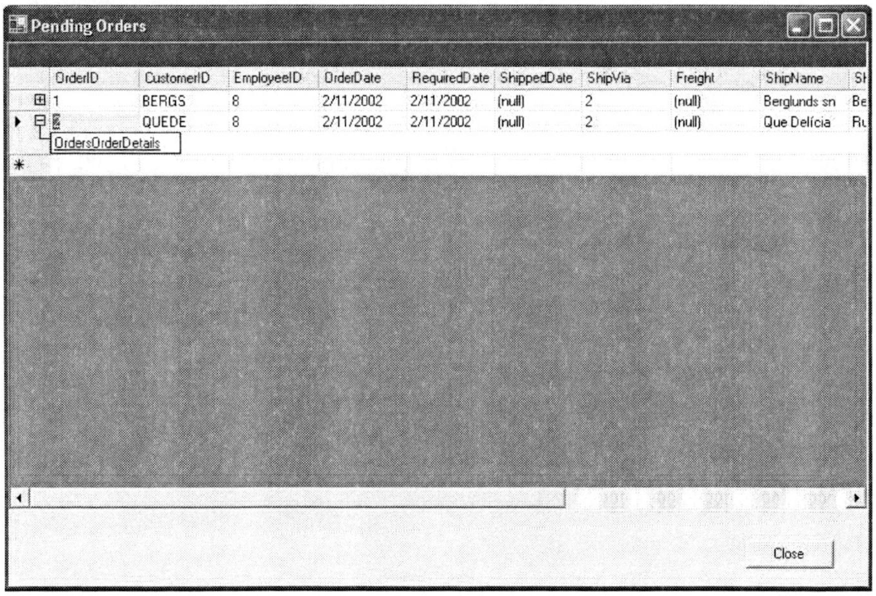

The Pending Orders Form allows users to view and edit orders that have not been submitted. Clicking the **OrdersOrderDetails** link for an order displays the individual order items of a particular order.

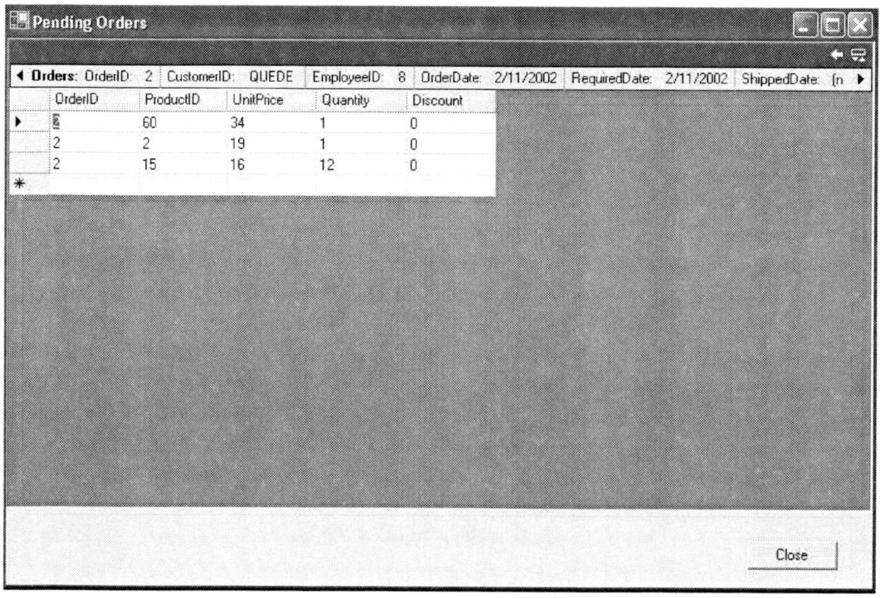

You can navigate from the parent and child tables by using the navigational controls provided by the **datagrid** control. Modifications can be made and are persisted when the Pending Orders form is closed.

In both views, some of the data columns are set to ReadOnly to maintain data integrity.

6. On the **View** menu, click **Submitted Orders** to open the Report History form.

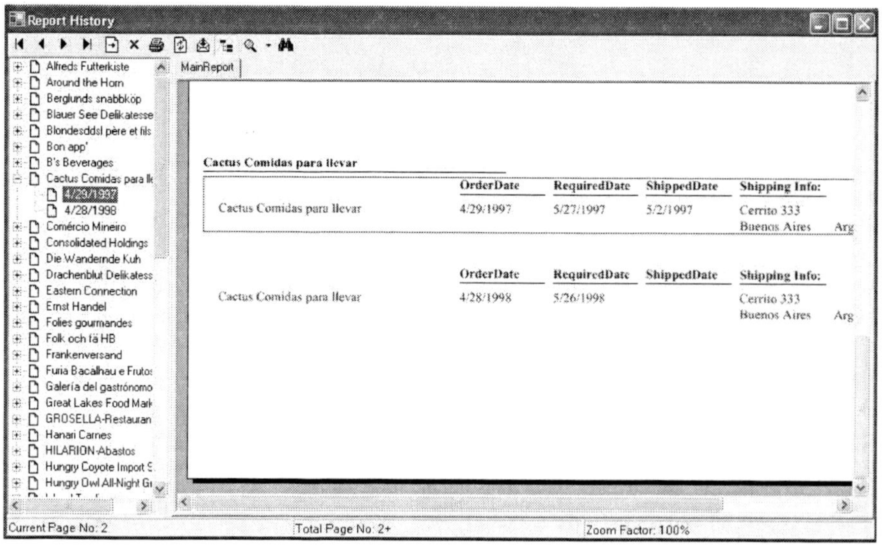

This form uses a Crystal Report Viewer to display all order history for a given employee. Order information is displayed by **CustomerName** and by **OrderDate**. You can also click each order in the report to display order details.

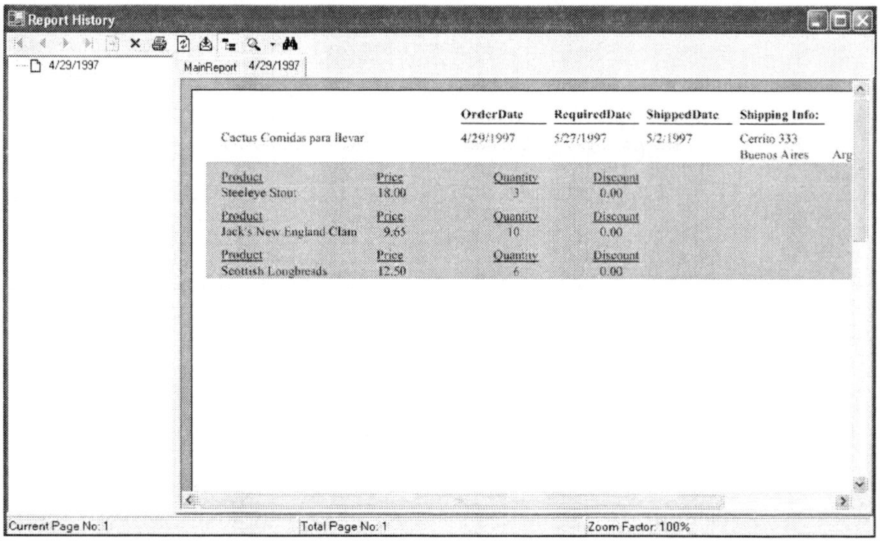

7. Show the print features by clicking the **PrintPreview** button on the toolbar.

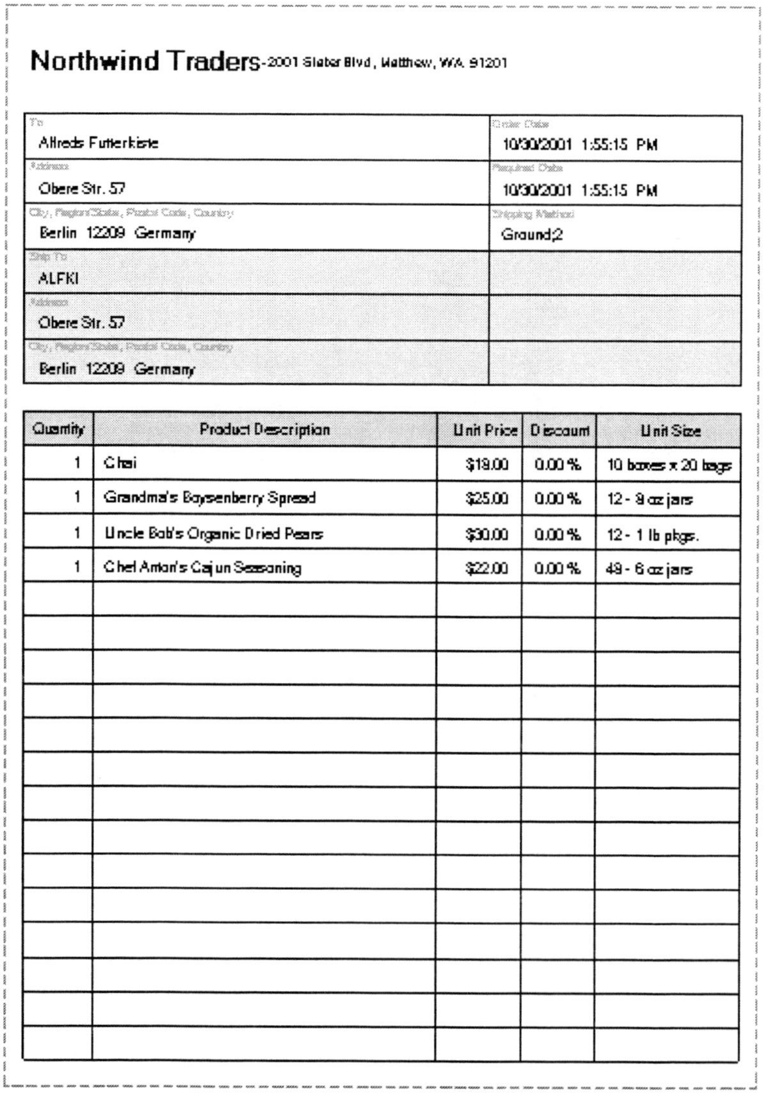

Northwind Traders-2001 Slater Blvd, Matthew, WA 91201

To Alfreds Futterkiste	Order Date 10/30/2001 1:55:15 PM
Address Obere Str. 57	Required Date 10/30/2001 1:55:15 PM
City, Region/State, Postal Code, Country Berlin 12209 Germany	Shipping Method Ground;2
Ship To ALFKI	
Address Obere Str. 57	
City, Region/State, Postal Code, Country Berlin 12209 Germany	

Quantity	Product Description	Unit Price	Discount	Unit Size
1	Chai	$18.00	0.00 %	10 boxes x 20 bags
1	Grandma's Boysenberry Spread	$25.00	0.00 %	12 - 8 oz jars
1	Uncle Bob's Organic Dried Pears	$30.00	0.00 %	12 - 1 lb pkgs.
1	Chef Anton's Cajun Seasoning	$22.00	0.00 %	48 - 6 oz jars

Microsoft Certified Professional Program

11:45 / 1:00

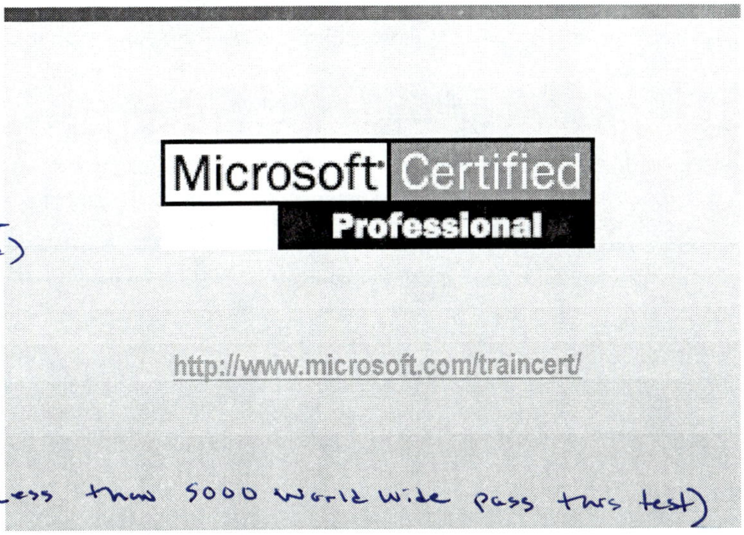

If you pass one course you are MCP (Microsoft Certified)

MCSD for .Net

MCAD for .Net (Less than 5000 world wide pass this test)

Microsoft Training and Certification offers a variety of certification credentials for developers and IT professionals. The Microsoft Certified Professional program is the leading certification program for validating your experience and skills, keeping you competitive in today's changing business environment. The Microsoft Certified Professional program includes the following certifications.

Certification	Description
MCSA on Microsoft Windows 2000	The Microsoft Certified Systems Administrator (MCSA) certification is designed for professionals who implement, manage, and troubleshoot existing network and system environments based on Microsoft Windows 2000 platforms, including the Windows .NET Server family. Implementation responsibilities include installing and configuring parts of the systems. Management responsibilities include administering and supporting the systems.
MCSE on Microsoft Windows 2000	The Microsoft Certified Systems Engineer (MCSE) credential is the premier certification for professionals who analyze the business requirements and design and implement the infrastructure for business solutions based on the Microsoft Windows 2000 platform and Microsoft server software, including the Windows .NET Server family. Implementation responsibilities include installing, configuring, and troubleshooting network systems.
MCSD	The Microsoft Certified Solution Developer (MCSD) credential is the premier certification for professionals who design and develop leading-edge business solutions with Microsoft development tools, technologies, platforms, and the Microsoft Windows DNA architecture. The types of applications MCSDs can develop include desktop applications and multi-user, Web-based, N-tier, and transaction-based applications. The credential covers job tasks ranging from analyzing business requirements to maintaining solutions.

(continued)

Certification	Description
MCDBA on Microsoft SQL Server™ 2000	The Microsoft Certified Database Administrator (MCDBA) credential is the premier certification for professionals who implement and administer Microsoft SQL Server databases. The certification is appropriate for individuals who derive physical database designs, develop logical data models, create physical databases, create data services by using Transact-SQL, manage and maintain databases, configure and manage security, monitor and optimize databases, and install and configure SQL Server.
MCP	The Microsoft Certified Professional (MCP) credential is for individuals who have the skills to successfully implement a Microsoft product or technology as part of a business solution in an organization. Hands-on experience with the product is necessary to successfully achieve certification.
MCT	Microsoft Certified Trainers (MCTs) demonstrate the instructional and technical skills that qualify them to deliver Microsoft Official Curriculum through Microsoft Certified Technical Education Centers (Microsoft CTECs).

Certification Requirements

The certification requirements differ for each certification category and are specific to the products and job functions addressed by the certification. To become a Microsoft Certified Professional, you must pass rigorous certification exams that provide a valid and reliable measure of technical proficiency and expertise.

For More Information See the Microsoft Training and Certification Web site at http://www.microsoft.com/traincert/.

You can also send e-mail to mcphelp@microsoft.com if you have specific certification questions.

Acquiring the Skills Tested by an MCP Exam

Microsoft Official Curriculum (MOC) and MSDN Training Curriculum can help you develop the skills that you need to do your job. They also complement the experience that you gain while working with Microsoft products and technologies. However, no one-to-one correlation exists between MOC and MSDN Training courses and MCP exams. Microsoft does not expect or intend for the courses to be the sole preparation method for passing MCP exams. Practical product knowledge and experience is also necessary to pass the MCP exams.

To help prepare for the MCP exams, use the preparation guides that are available for each exam. Each Exam Preparation Guide contains exam-specific information, such as a list of the topics on which you will be tested. These guides are available on the Microsoft Training and Certification Web site at http://www.microsoft.com/traincert/.

Facilities

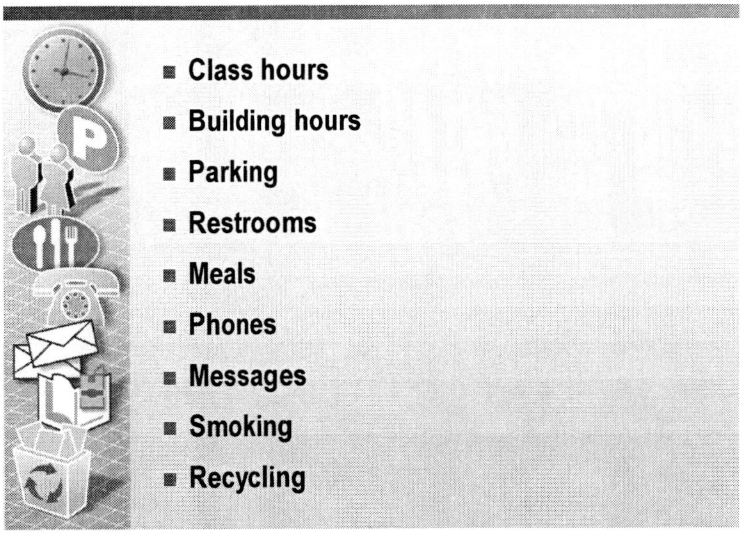
Class hours
Building hours
Parking
Restrooms
Meals
Phones
Messages
Smoking
Recycling

msdn training

Module 1: Introducing Windows Forms

Contents

Microsoft

Overview

- Creating a Form
- Adding Controls to a Form
- Creating an Inherited Form
- Organizing Controls on a Form
- Creating MDI Applications

Introduction

Windows Forms is part of the new Microsoft® .NET Framework, and it uses many new technologies including a common application framework, managed execution environment, integrated security, and object-oriented design principles. In addition, Windows Forms offers full support for quickly and easily connecting to Extensible Markup Language (XML) Web services and building rich, data-aware applications based on the ADO.NET data model. With the new shared development environment in the Microsoft Visual Studio® .NET development system, developers are able to create Windows Forms applications by using any of the languages supporting the .NET platform, including the Microsoft Visual Basic® .NET and Microsoft Visual C#™ .NET development systems.

Two services
XML
Web (channel based service)
Not limited to HTTP TCP

Objectives

After completing this module, you will be able to:

- Create a form and add controls to it.
- Create an inherited form by using Visual Inheritance.
- Organize controls on a form.
- Create Multiple Document Interface (MDI) applications.

ADO.Net
Marketing name from Microsoft

Lesson: Creating a Form

- Windows Forms vs. Web Forms
- How to Create a Form
- How to Set Form Properties
- Form Life Cycle
- How to Handle Form Events
- Windows Form Designer-Generated Code

Introduction

Forms are the basic element of the user interface (UI) in applications created for the Microsoft Windows® operating system. They provide a framework that you can use throughout your application to give it a consistent look and feel. A form in Windows-based applications is used to present information to the user and to accept input from the user.

Forms expose properties that define their appearance, methods that define their behavior, and events that define their interaction with the user. By setting the properties of the form and writing code to respond to its events, you customize the form to meet the requirements of your application. A form is a control derived from the **Form** class, which in turn derives from the **Control** class. The framework also allows you to inherit from existing forms to add functionality or modify existing behavior. When you add a form to your project, you can choose whether it inherits from the **Form** class provided by the .NET Framework, or from a form you have created previously.

This lesson covers the basic concepts of forms and how to add controls to forms.

Lesson objectives

After completing this lesson, you will be able to:

- Describe a form.
- Determine whether to use Windows Forms or Web Forms in a scenario.
- Create a form.
- Set the properties of a form.
- Describe the events and methods in the forms life cycle.

Windows Forms vs. Web Forms

Feature	Windows Forms	Web Forms
Deployment	Can be run without altering the registry	No download required
Graphics	Includes GDI+	Interactive or dynamic graphics require round trips to the server for updates
Responsiveness	Provide the quickest response speed for interactive applications	Can take advantage of the browser's dynamic HTML to create rich UI
Platform	Requires .NET Framework running on the client computer	Require only a browser
Programming model	Based on a client-side, Win32-based message-pump mode	Applications components are invoked via HTTP
Security	Code-based and role-based security	Role-based security

Introduction

When designing applications that involve a user interface, you have two choices: Windows Forms and Web Forms. Both have full design-time support in the development environment and can provide a rich user interface and advanced application functionality to solve business problems. When you have multiple options, it is important for you to know which option to use when.

Windows Forms

Windows Forms are used to develop applications where the client is expected to shoulder a significant amount of the processing burden in an application. These include classic desktop applications for the Microsoft Win32® application programming interface. Examples include drawing or graphics applications, data-entry systems, point-of-sale systems, and games. All of these applications rely on the power of the desktop computer for processing and high-performance content display.

Web Forms

ASP.NET Web Forms are used to create applications in which the primary user interface is a browser. This includes applications intended to be available publicly on the World Wide Web, such as e-commerce applications.

Windows Forms vs. Web Forms

The following table provides a comparison of different application criteria and how Windows Forms and Web Forms technologies address these criteria.

Feature/criterion	Windows Forms	Web Forms
Deployment	Applications can be downloaded, installed, and run directly on the users' computers without any alteration of the registry.	Have no client deployment; the client requires only a browser. The server must be running Microsoft .NET Framework. Updates to the application are made by updating code on the server.
Graphics	Windows Forms include Graphic Design Interface (GDI+), which allows sophisticated graphics to be used for games and other extremely rich graphical environments.	Interactive or dynamic graphics require round trips to the server for updates when used on Web Forms. GDI+ can be used on the server to create custom graphics.
Responsiveness	Windows Forms can run entirely on the client computer; they can provide the quickest response speed for applications requiring a high degree of interactivity.	If you know that users will have Microsoft Internet Explorer 5 or later, a Web Forms application can take advantage of the browser's dynamic HTML (DHTML) capabilities to create a rich, responsive UI. If users have other browsers, most processing (including UI-related tasks such as validation) requires a round trip to the Web server, which can affect responsiveness.
Platform	Windows Forms require the .NET Framework to be running on the client computer.	Web Forms require only a browser. DHTML-capable browsers can take advantage of extra features, but Web Forms can be designed to work with all browsers. The Web server must be running .NET Framework.

(continued)

Feature/criterion	Windows Forms	Web Forms
Programming model	Windows Forms are based on a client-side, Win32-based message-pump mode, in which instances of components are created, used, and discarded by the developer.	Web Forms rely on a largely asynchronous, disconnected model, in which components are loosely coupled to the application front end. Typically, application components are invoked by HTTP. This model may not be suitable for applications that require extreme throughput from the user end or for those with high-volume transactions. Similarly, Web Forms applications may not be suitable for database applications that require high levels of concurrency control (for example, pessimistic locking).
Security	Windows Forms use granular permissions in its implementation of code access security to protect computer resources and sensitive information. This allows careful exposure of functionality, while retaining security.	Web Forms allow you to control the identity under which server application code is executed. Applications can execute code by using the identity of the requesting entity, which is known as impersonation. Applications can also dynamically tailor content based on the requestor's identity or role. For example, a manager could receive access to a site or to content that requires a higher level of security than someone with lesser credentials.

How to Create a Form

- **A base form is created when you create a new project**
- **To create a new form**
  1. Right-click the project in Solution Explorer
  2. Click **Add**
  3. Click **Add Windows Forms**

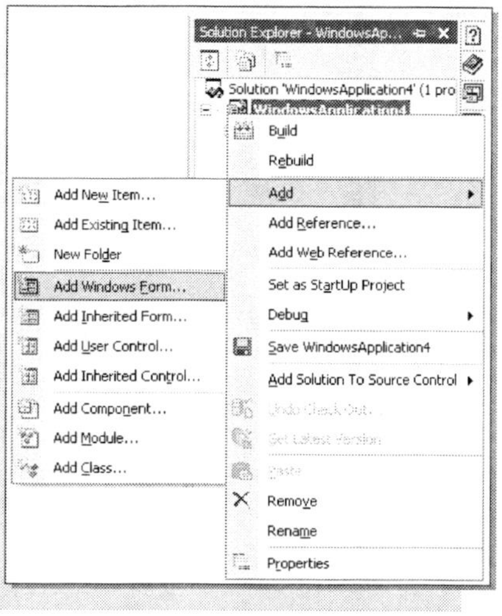

Introduction

In a Windows-based application, the form is the primary element for user interaction. By combining controls and your own actions, you can request information from the user and respond to it.

In Visual Studio .NET, a form is a window used in your application. When you create a new Windows Application project, Visual Studio .NET provides a Designer view that contains a form. The default form contains the minimum elements used by most forms: a title bar, a control box, and **Minimize**, **Maximize**, and **Close** buttons.

Procedure: Creating forms

Most applications require more than one window. You must add a form to your project for every window that your application requires.

To add additional forms to your project:

1. If Solution Explorer is not open, on the **View** menu, click **Solution Explorer**.
2. In Solution Explorer, right-click the project name, point to **Add**, and then click **Add Windows Form**.
3. In the **Add New Item** dialog box, in the **Name** box, type an appropriate name for the form, and then click **Open**.

How to Set Form Properties

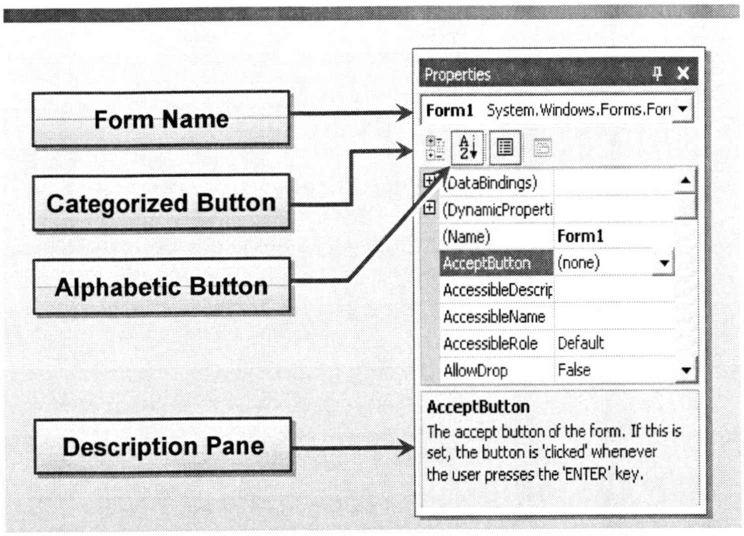

Introduction

When you are building the user interface of a Windows-based application, you must set the properties for the objects that you create.

Common form properties

The following table describes some common form properties that you typically set at design time.

Property	Description	Default setting
(Name)	Sets the name of the form in your project. (This is not the name that is displayed to the user in the caption bar but rather the name that you will use in your code to reference the form.) **Important:** If you change the **(Name)** property of your form, you must set the startup object for your project to the new name or the project will not start up correctly. For more information about how to change the startup object, see Form Life Cycle in this lesson in this module.	Form1 (Form2, Form3, and so on)
AcceptButton	Sets which button is clicked when the user presses the ENTER key. **Note:** You must have at least one button on your form to use this property.	*None*
CancelButton	Sets which button is clicked when the user presses the ESC key. **Note:** you must have at least one button on your form to use this property.	*None*
ControlBox	Determines whether a form displays a control box in the caption bar. The control box can contain the **Minimize** button, **Maximize** button, **Help** button, and the **Close** button.	True
FormBorderStyle	Controls the appearance of the border for the form. This will also affect how the caption bar appears and what buttons appear on it.	Sizable

(continued)

Property	Description	Default setting
MaximizeBox	Determines whether a form has a **Maximize** button in the upper right corner of its caption bar.	True
MinimizeBox	Determines whether a form has a **Minimize** button in the upper right corner of its caption bar.	True
StartPosition	Determines the position of a form on the screen when it first appears.	WindowsDefaultLocation
Text	Sets the text displayed in the caption bar of the control.	Form1 (Form2, Form3, and so on)

Procedure: Setting form properties

You can set form properties either by writing code or by using the Properties window. Any property settings that you establish at design time are used as the initial settings each time your application runs.

To set form properties at design time:

1. If the Properties window is not open, on the **View** menu, click **Properties Window**.
2. In Design view, click the form for which you want to set a property. The name of the form appears in the **Object** list at the top of the Properties window.
3. Use the **Alphabetic**  and **Categorized**  buttons in the Properties window to choose whether to view the form properties alphabetically or by category.
4. In the **Properties** window, click the property that you want to set.

Note When you select a property, a description of the property appears at the bottom of the Properties window, in the Description pane.

5. Type or select the property setting that you want.

Form Life Cycle

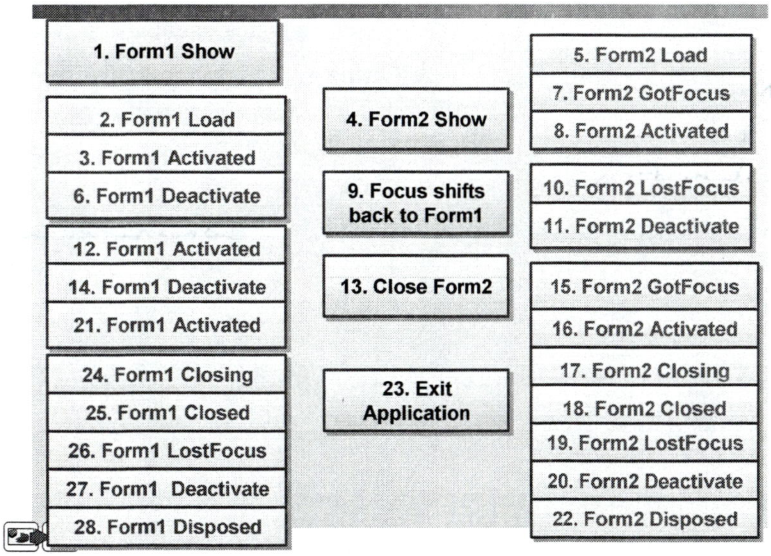

Introduction

After adding the necessary forms to your project and setting the startup form, you must determine which events and methods to use. The entire lifecycle of a form uses several methods and events.

Form events and methods

When the **Show()** method is called, the form events and methods are generally triggered in the following order:

1. Load
2. GotFocus
3. Activated
4. Closing
5. Closed
6. Deactivate
7. LostFocus
8. Dispose()

New

The **Initialize** event is typically used to prepare an application for use. Variables are assigned to initial values, and controls may be moved or resized to accommodate initialization data.

In earlier versions of Visual Basic, the **Initialize** event was used to execute code before a form was loaded. In .NET, initialization code must be added to the form constructor (**Sub New()**) after the call to **InitializeComponent()** as shown in the following example:

```
Public Sub New()
    MyBase.New()
    ' This call is required by the Windows Forms Designer.
    InitializeComponent()
    ' Add your initialization code here
```

Show

The **Show** method includes an implied **Load**; this means that if the specified form is not already loaded when the **Show** method is called, the application automatically loads the form into memory and then displays it to the user. The **Show** method can display forms as modal or modeless.

```
FrmSplash.Show()
```

You can use the **ShowDialog()** method to show a form as a dialog box.

Load

The **Load** event is used to perform actions that must occur before the form displays. It is also used to assign default values to the form and its controls.

The **Load** event occurs each time that a form is loaded into memory. A form's **Load** event can run multiple times during an application's life. **Load** fires when a form starts as the result of the **Load** statement, **Show** statement, or when a reference is made to an unloaded form's properties, methods, or controls.

Activated/Deactivate

When the user moves among two or more forms, you can use the **Activated** and **Deactivate** events to define the forms' behaviors. The **Activated** event occurs when the form is activated in code or by the user. To activate a form at run time by using code, call the **Activate** method. You can use this event for tasks such as updating the contents of the form based on changes made to the form's data when the form was not activated.

The **Activated** event fires when the form receives focus from another form in the same project. This event fires only when the form is visible. For example, a form loaded by using the **Load** statement isn't visible unless you use the **Show** method, or set the form's **Visible** property to **True**. The **Activated** event fires before the **GotFocus** event.

Use the following code to set the focus to a form.

```
FrmSplash.Focus()
```

Deactivate fires when the form loses focus to another form. This event fires after the **LostFocus** event.

Application Boundaries.

Both the **Activated** and **Deactivate** events fire only when focus is changing within the same application. If you switch to a different application and then return to the program, neither event fires.

Important If you need to add code that executes either when the form is being displayed or when the form is being hidden, add the code to the **Activated** and **Deactivate** event handlers instead of to the **GotFocus** and **LostFocus** event handlers.

Closing

The **Closing** event is useful when you need to know how the user is closing the form. The **Closing** event occurs when the form receives a request to close. Data validation can occur at this time. If there is a need to keep the form open (for example, if data validation fails), the closing event can be canceled.

Closed

The **Closed** event occurs when the form is closed and before the **Dispose** event. Use the **Closed** event procedure to verify that the form should be closed or to specify actions that take place when closing the form. You can also include form-level validation code for closing the form or saving data to a file.

Dispose

The .NET Framework does not support the **Terminate** event. Termination code must execute inside the **Dispose** method, before the call to **MyBase.Dispose()**.

```
Public Overrides Sub Dispose(ByVal Disposing As Boolean)

    ' Termination code goes here.
    ' The following code was automatically added by the
'Dispose method.
    MyBase.Dispose(Disposing)
    If Disposing Then
        If Not components Is Nothing Then
            Components.Dispose(Disposing)
        End If
    End If
End Sub
```

The **Dispose** method is called automatically for the main form in an application; you must call it explicitly for any other form.

Hide

The **Hide** method removes a form from the screen without removing it from memory. A hidden form's controls are not accessible to the user, but they are available to the running application. When a form is hidden, the user cannot interact with the application until all code in the event procedure that caused the form to be hidden has finished executing.

If the form is not already loaded into memory when the **Hide** method is called, the **Hide** method loads the form but doesn't display it.

```
frmMyForm.Hide()
```

How to Handle Form Events

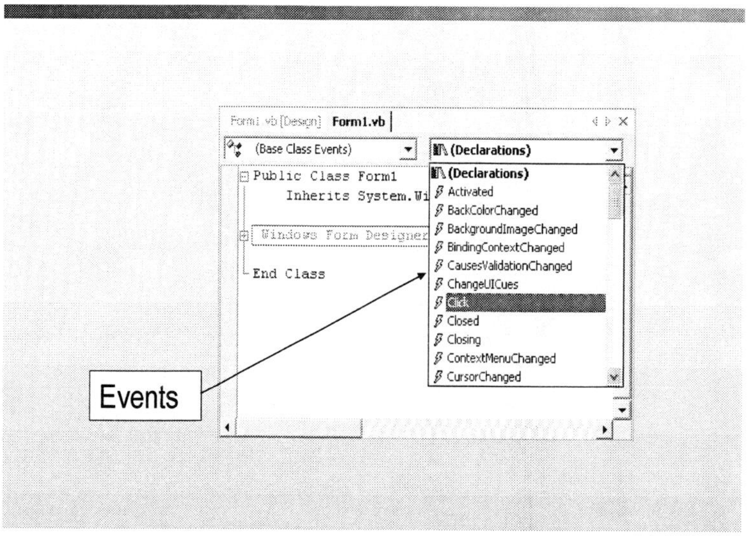

Introduction

An *event handler* is a segment of code that is called when a corresponding event occurs. For example, you can write code in an event handler for the **Activated** event of a form to perform operations such as updating the data displayed in the controls of the form when the form is activated.

The .NET Framework uses a standard naming convention for event handlers. The convention is to combine the name of the object that sends the event, an underscore, and the name of the event. For example, the **Click** event of a form named Form1 would be named **Form1_Click**.

Procedure

To add an event handler:

1. Open the Code Editor for the form for which you want to add an event handler.
2. In the **Class Name** list box, click **(Base Class Events)**. The following illustration shows the **Class Name** list box with **(Base Class Events)** selected.

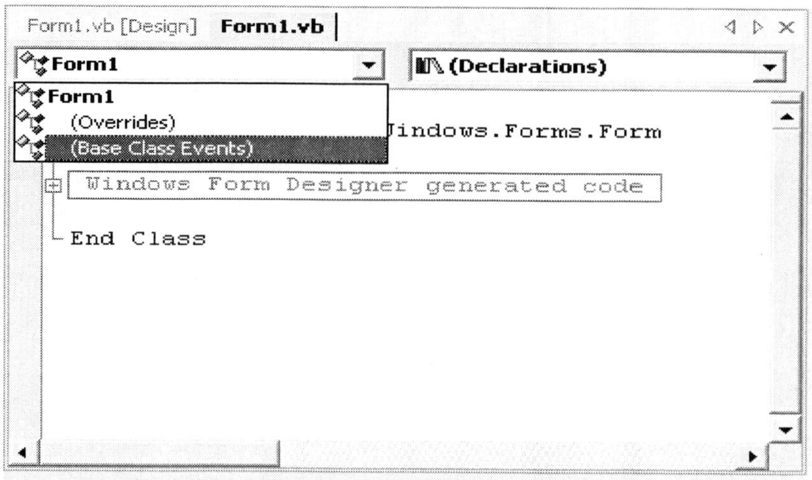

3. Click the drop-down arrow for the **Method Name** list box to view events available for the form. The following illustration shows the **Method Name** list box with form events listed and the **Click** event selected. Notice that the Event icon  to the left of the event name indicates that it is an event.

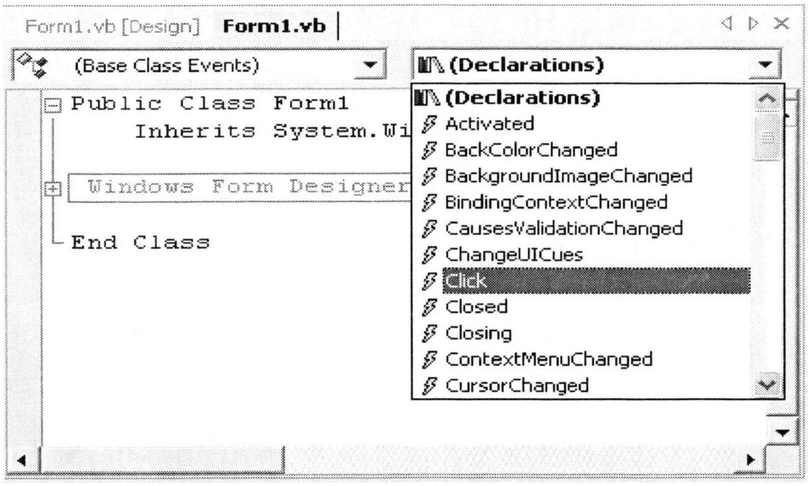

4. Click the event to add the event handler.

You will learn more about using events and event handlers in the .NET Framework in Module 2, "Working with Controls" in Course 2565A, *Developing Microsoft .NET Applications for Windows (Visual Basic .NET).*

Windows Forms Designer-Generated Code

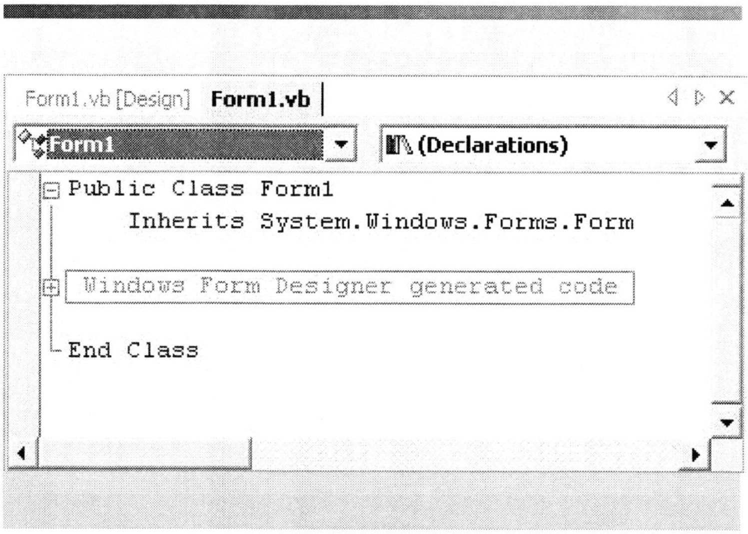

Introduction

When you create a form by using Windows Forms Designer, the Designer generates a lot of code that you would have to write if you were creating a form on your own.

Designer-generate code

If you look at the default code for the form, you will find the following code generated by the Designer.

```
#Region " Windows Form Designer generated code "

    Public Sub New()
        MyBase.New()

        'This call is required by the Windows Form Designer.
        InitializeComponent()

        'Add any initialization after the
InitializeComponent() call

    End Sub

    'Form overrides dispose to clean up the component list.
    Protected Overloads Overrides Sub Dispose(ByVal disposing
As Boolean)
        If disposing Then
            If Not (components Is Nothing) Then
                components.Dispose()
            End If
        End If
        MyBase.Dispose(disposing)
    End Sub

    'Required by the Windows Form Designer
    Private components As System.ComponentModel.IContainer

    'NOTE: The following procedure is required by the Windows
Form Designer
    'It can be modified using the Windows Form Designer.
    'Do not modify it using the code editor.
    <System.Diagnostics.DebuggerStepThrough()> Private Sub
InitializeComponent()
       components = New System.ComponentModel.Container()
       Me.txt

    End Sub

#End Region
```

Parts of the generated code

- InitializeComponent

  This code is used by the development environment to persist the property values that you set in Windows Forms Designer. In previous versions of Visual Basic, this information was not saved as code but as textual statements at the top of the .frm file that were always hidden from the developer.

- Public Sub New()

  This is the class constructor. Although you can put initialization code for the form here, you should put it in the form's **Load** event (unless it absolutely has to be here).

Important Avoid modifying or deleting the Windows Forms Designer-generated code. Modifying or deleting this code can result in errors in your project.

Lesson: Adding Controls to a Form

- How to Add Controls to a Form
- How to Add Menus to a Form
- How to Customize the Controls Toolbox
- Practice: Creating a Form and Adding Controls

Introduction

To create a user interface for an application, you must add controls to a form. This lesson covers adding controls to a form.

Lesson objectives

After completing this lesson, you will be able to:

- Add controls to a form.
- Add menus to a form.
- Customize the Controls Toolbox.

How to Add Controls to a Form

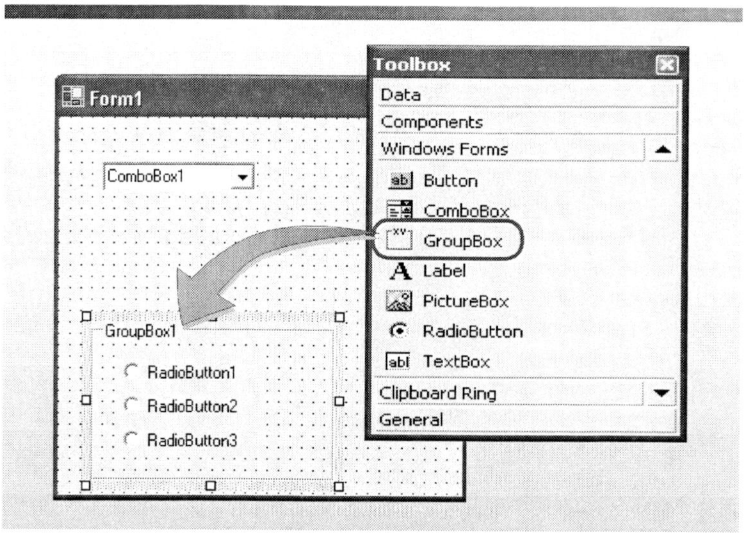

Introduction

Controls are objects that are contained in form objects. Buttons, text boxes, and labels are examples of controls.

Procedure: Adding controls to a form

There are two ways to add controls to a form. The first way allows you to add several controls quickly and then size and position them individually. The second way gives you more initial control over the size and position of the control.

To add controls to a form and then size and position them:

1. If the Toolbox is not open, on the **View** menu, click **Toolbox**.
2. In the Toolbox, double-click the control that you want to add. This places an instance of the control at the default size in the upper left corner of the active object. When adding multiple controls in this manner, they are placed on top of each other.
3. After the controls are added, you can reposition and resize them:
   a. To reposition the control, click the control to select it, and then drag the control to the correct position.
   b. To resize the control, click the control to select it, drag one of the eight sizing handles until the control is properly sized.

To size and position controls while you add them to a form:

1. If the Toolbox is not open, on the **View** menu, click **Toolbox**.
2. In the Toolbox, click the control that you want to add.
3. Move the mouse pointer over the form. The pointer symbol changes to a crosshair.
4. Position the crosshair where you want the upper left corner of the control.
5. Click and drag the crosshair where you want the lower right corner. A rectangle that indicates the control's size and location is drawn on the screen.
6. When the control is correctly sized, release the mouse button. The sized control appears in the correct location on the form.
7. You can reposition or resize the control after you have released the mouse button:
    a. To reposition the control, click the control to select it, and then drag the control to the correct position.
    b. To resize the control, click the control to select it, and drag one of the eight sizing handles until the control is properly sized.

How to Add Menus to a Form

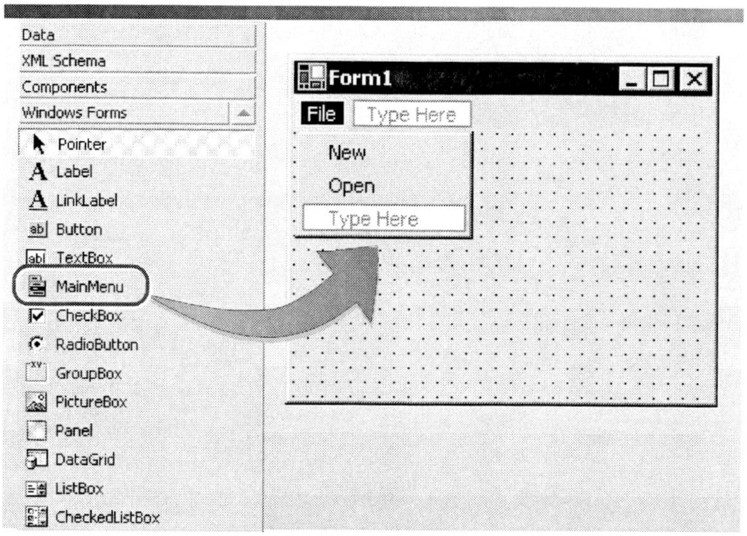

Introduction

Menus provide a structured way for users to access the commands and tools contained in an application. Proper planning and design of menus and toolbars is essential and ensures proper functionality and accessibility of your application to users.

A menu control has many properties such as **Name**, **Caption**, and **Index**.

- The **Name** property identifies the menu control in code.
- The **Index** property identifies controls that share the same name.
- The **Caption** property is the text that appears on the menu bar at run time.

Procedure: Adding menus to a form

To add menus to a form:

1. If the Toolbox is not open, on the **View** menu, click **Toolbox**.
2. In the Toolbox, double-click the **MainMenu** control.
3. In the **Caption** box, on the newly created menu, type the text for the first menu's title. This title will appear on the menu bar.
4. In the **Name** box, in the Properties window, type the name that you will use to refer to the menu control in code.

How to Customize the Controls Toolbox

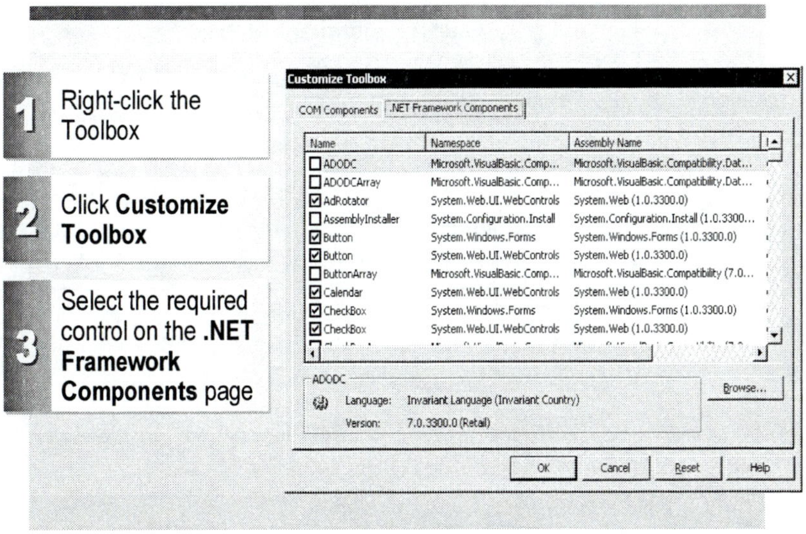

Introduction

The Toolbox displays a variety of items for use in Visual Studio .NET projects. The items available include .NET components, Component Object Model (COM) components, Hypertext Markup Language (HTML) objects, code fragments, and text. The Toolbox contains a variety of controls that you can use to add art work, labels, buttons, list boxes, scroll bars, menus, and geometric shapes to a user interface.

Each control that you add to a form becomes a programmable user interface object in your application. These objects are visible to the user when the application runs, and they operate like the standard objects in any Windows-based application. However, there are some controls that are visible on the Toolbox by default. You must customize the Toolbox to display such controls on the Toolbox. For example, the **StatusBarPanel** control is not visible on the Toolbox by default.

You can customize the Toolbox by adding and removing items from it. The **Customize Toolbox** dialog box displays tabbed lists of components that are recognized on your machine. Use the **Customize Toolbox** dialog box to add controls to the Toolbox or remove controls from it.

Note The **Customize Toolbox** dialog box replaces the **Components** dialog box in previous versions of Visual Basic.

Procedure: Customizing the Controls Toolbox

To customize the Controls Toolbox:

1. Right-click the Toolbox.
2. Click **Customize Toolbox**.
3. Click the **.NET Framework Components** tab or the **COM Components** tab, and select the required controls.

Note You can add code fragments to the Toolbox by selecting the code fragment or text and dragging it to the Toolbox. A new entry beginning with **text** will appear in the Controls Toolbox.

Practice: Creating a Form and Adding Controls

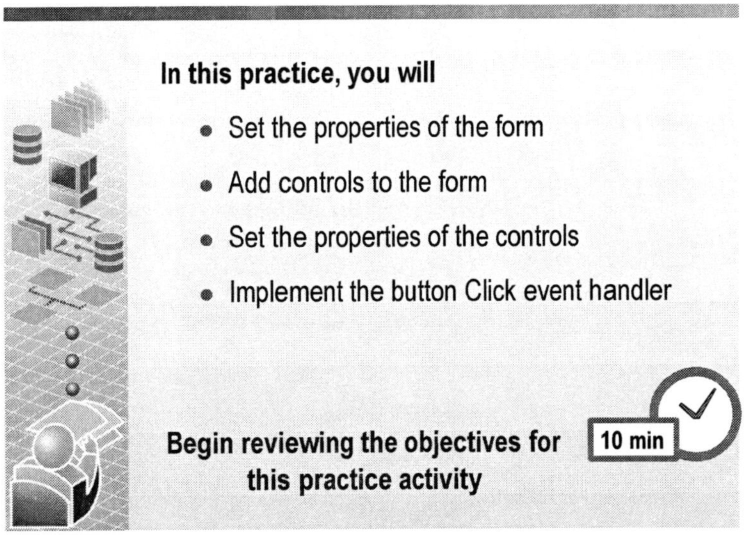

Introduction

In this practice, you will open an existing project and modify the properties on the default form. You will also add controls to the form and implement the **Click** event for two buttons.

Instructions

► Open the project file for this practice activity

1. Use Windows Explorer and browse to *install_folder*\Practices\Mod01\Mod01_01\Starter.

Note If you performed a default installation of the course files, *install_folder* corresponds to C:\Program Files\Msdntrain\2565.

---

2. Double-click the CreatingForms.sln solution file to open the project.

► Set the properties of a form

1. Open the CreatingForms.vb file in Design view.
2. If the Properties window is not visible, on the **View** menu, click **Properties Window**.
3. Set the remaining form properties to the indicated values.

Property	Value
ControlBox	**false**
Font	**Trebuchet MS, 10pt**
FormBorderStyle	**Fixed3D**
Size	**300, 175**
Text	**Hello World**

▶ Add controls to the form

1. If the Toolbox is not visible, on the **View** menu, click **Toolbox**.
2. In the Toolbox, double-click the **Label** control to add it to the form.
3. Double-click the **Button** control to add it to the form.
4. Double-click the **Button** control again to add a second button to the form.
5. Position the **Label** control near the top center of the form.
6. Position the buttons next to each other near the bottom of the form—with **button1** on the left and **button2** on the right.

▶ Set the properties of the controls

1. Click the **Label1** control.
2. Set the following properties for the **Label1** control to the values provided.

Property	Value
(Name)	**OutputLabel**
BorderStyle	**Fixed3D**
Font	**Trebuchet MS, 10pt, Bold**
ForeColor	**ActiveCaption**
Location	**14,30**
Size	**264, 23**
Text	**(Delete existing text and leave it blank)**
TextAlign	**MiddleCenter**

3. Click **Button1**.
4. Set the following properties for the **Button1** control to the values provided in the following table.

Property	Value
(Name)	**HelloButton**
Location	**57, 87**
Size	**75, 25**
Text	**&Say Hello**

5. Click **Button2**.
6. Set the following properties for the **Button2** control to the values provided in the following table.

Property	Value
(Name)	**ExitButton**
Location	**161, 87**
Size	**75, 25**
Text	**E&xit**

7. Double-click the **Say Hello** button to create the **Click** event handler.

8. In the **Click** event handler for **HelloButton**, add the following line of code:

```
OutputLabel.Text = "Hello, World!"
```

9. Switch back to Design view of the form.

10. Double click the **Exit** button to create the **Click** event handler.

11. In the **Click** event handler for **ExitButton**, add the following line of code:

```
Me.Close()
```

12. Switch back to Design view of the form.

13. Set the **AcceptButton** property to **HelloButton** and the **CancelButton** property to **ExitButton**.

► **Build and run the application**

1. To build the application, click the **Build** menu, and then click **Build Solution**.

2. Run the application by pressing F5.

Lesson: Creating an Inherited Form

- Access Modifiers
- How to Create an Inherited Form
- Practice: Creating an Inherited Form

Introduction

Creating new Windows Forms by inheriting from base forms is an efficient way to duplicate your best efforts without going through the process of entirely recreating a form every time you require it. The process of inheriting a form from an existing one is called *Visual Inheritance*. This lesson covers how to inherit from an existing form by using Visual Inheritance.

Lesson objective

After completing this lesson, you will be able to create an inherited form.

Access Modifiers

Access Modifier	Description
Private	Read-only to a child form, all of its property values in the property browser are disabled
Protected	Accessible within the class and from any class that inherits from the class that declared this member
Public	Most permissive level. Public controls have full accessibility

Introduction

Not only can you inherit controls and properties from a base form, you can also inherit code. This means that a code library can be built to enhance code reuse. The major advantage of using Inheritance is that you can override the code if it is not applicable in a particular circumstance.

To be able to override an event in the child form, you must make it visible to the child. This means that it must be defined as **Public** or **Protected** (protected is the default for events), and its **Modifiers** keyword cannot be private.

Access modifiers

The **Modifiers** property determines the accessibility level of a control; such as how a control behaves and what functionality it has when its form is used as a base form. An inherited form displays the controls in a different shade of grey depending upon the value of this property. Some of the values of the **Modifiers** property include **Public**, **Private**, and **Protected**.

Friend By Default

Protected Friend
union of Protected & friend

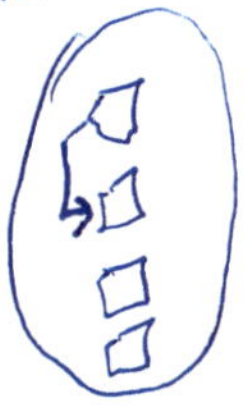

The values of the control's properties are the same as those on the parent object, and when they are altered on the child form that property becomes bold in the Properties window. To reset all values to those held by the parent, right-click the Properties window, and then click **Reset**.

- **Private**

  A **Private** control is read-only to a child form. Because a **Private** control cannot be modified, all of its property values in the Properties window are disabled. Copying this control elsewhere on the form or project produces a fully editable version.

- **Protected**

  A protected member is accessible within the class and from any class that inherits from the class that declared this member. If a change is made to a **Protected** control on a child form, then those changes will remain even if a change is made to the parent form. For the other types of controls, changes to the parent form will override those made to the child.

- **Public**

  Public is the most permissive level. **Public** controls have full accessibility.

Note The **Public**, **Protected**, and **Private** property values are the three property values that are common across all the .NET Language projects. Visual Basic .NET supports two other values, **Friend** and **Protected Friend**.

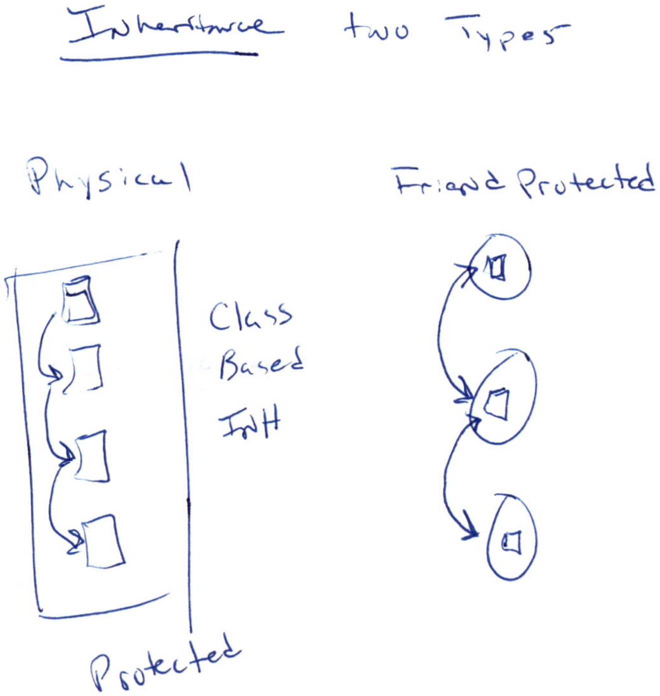

How to Create an Inherited Form

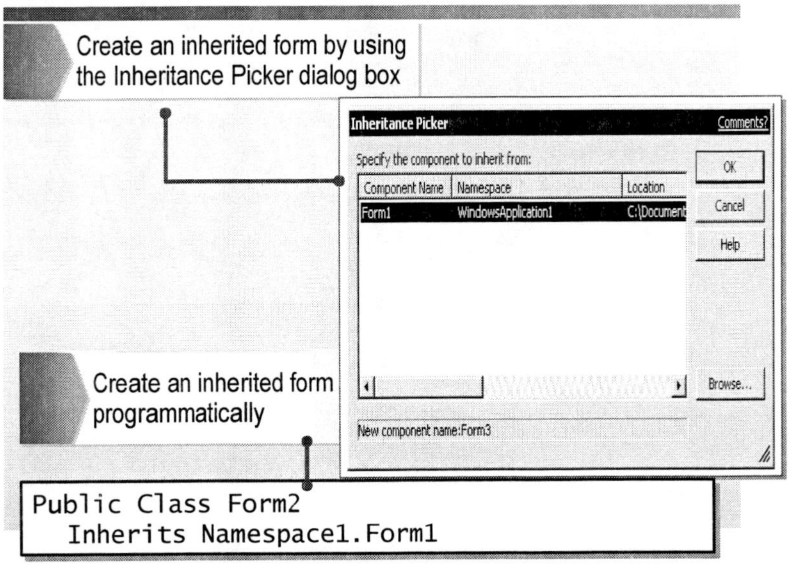

Introduction

Visual Inheritance offers many advantages to developers. If you already have designed a form for a different project that is similar to the one you need in the current project, you can inherit from the earlier form. It also means that you can create a base form as a template to use later. It is a useful way of duplicating the main functionality of particular forms without having to recreate them from the beginning. Changes to the base form will be reflected in those forms that are inherited from it; so changes to the underlying template form will change all forms based on it.

Procedure: Inheriting from an existing form

There are two ways of implementing Visual Inheritance in a Visual Studio .NET project.

To create an inherited form programmatically:

1. Create a new project in Visual Studio .NET.
2. Add another form, or view the code of Form1, which is created by default.
3. In the class definition, add a reference to the form to inherit from. The reference should include the namespace that contains the form, followed by a period, and then the name of the base form itself.

   ```
   Public Class Form2
       Inherits Namespace1.Form1
   ```

   The form now takes on the characteristics of the inherited form. It contains the controls that were on the inherited form, the code, and the properties.

To create an inherited form by using the **Inheritance Picker** dialog box:

Note Make sure that you build the solution before you inherit from an existing form in the project.

---

1. On the **Project** menu, click **Add Inherited Form**. The dialog box is identical for C# and for Visual Basic.

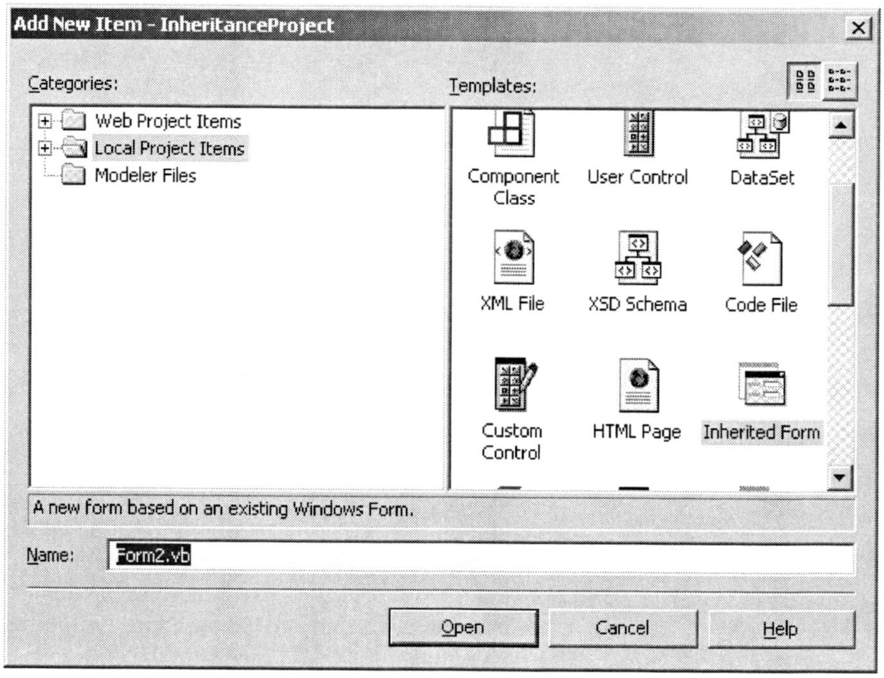

2. In the Categories pane, click **Local Project Items**, and in the Templates pane, click **Inherited Form**. In the **Name** box, type a name, and then click **Open**. This will open the **Inheritance Picker** dialog box.

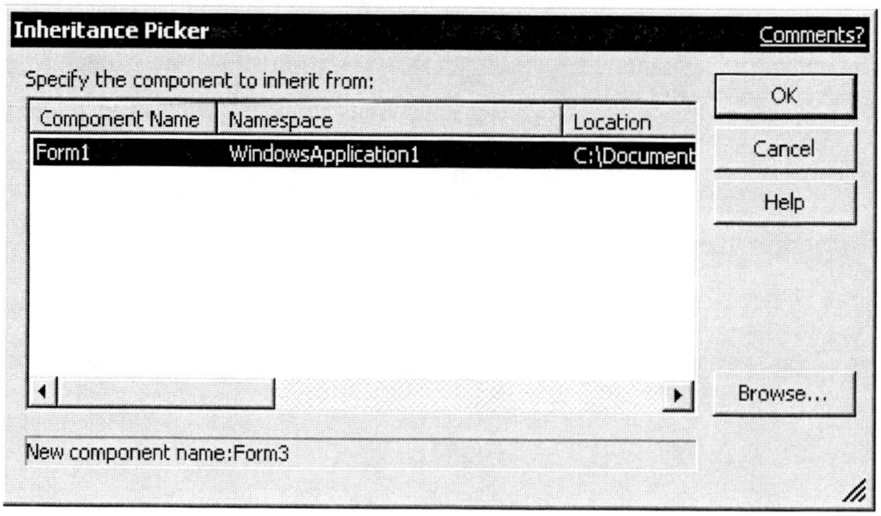

3. Click **Browse**, and locate the compiled executable of the project that contains your form. Click **OK**.

   The new form should now be added into the project and be based on your inherited form. It contains the controls on the base form.

Important After the new form has been added and has been inherited from the base form, the project must be rebuilt to complete the inheritance relationship. The new form can then be displayed in Design view.

Practice: Creating an Inherited Form

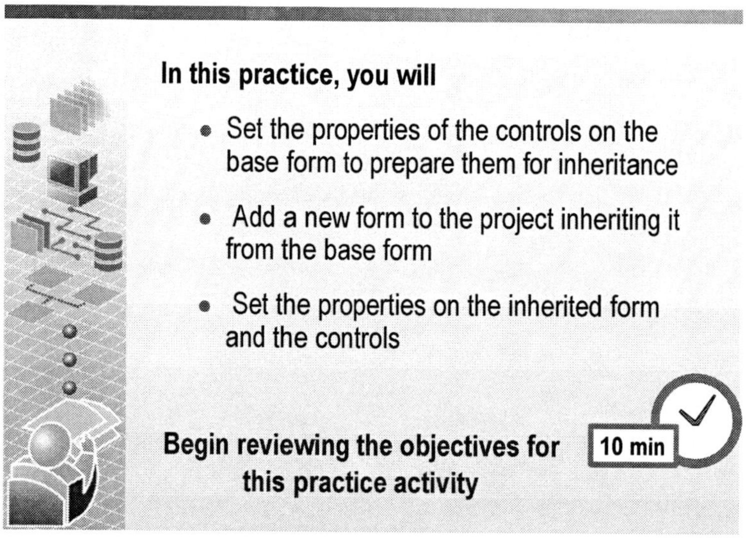

Introduction

In this practice, you will modify an existing form to allow it to be inherited by other forms. You will create a new form and inherit it from the base form. You will then modify the inherited form to customize it for a particular application.

Instructions

► **Open the practice project**

1. Use Windows Explorer and browse to *install_folder*\Practices\Mod01\Mod01_02\Starter.
2. Double-click the WindowsCalculator.sln solution file to open the project.

► **Modify a form's properties**

1. If Solution Explorer is not visible, on the **View** menu, click **Solution Explorer**.
2. If the Properties window is not visible, on the **View** menu, click **Properties Window**.
3. Open BaseAboutForm.vb in Design view.
4. Click the **Product Name** label, and ensure that the **Modifiers** property is set to **Protected**.
5. Ensure that the **Modifiers** property is set to the given values for the following controls.

Control	Modifiers Property
Version <1.0.0000> Label	**Protected**
Copyright © yyyy Contoso, Ltd. Label	**Protected**
All Rights Reserved Label	**Protected**
OK button	**Protected**

6. Save the project.

▶ **Add an inherited form**

1. From the **Project** menu, click **Add New Item**.
2. In the Categories pane, click **Local Project Items**.
3. In the Templates pane, click **Inherited Form**.
4. In the **Name** field, type **AboutForm.vb** and then click **Open** to open the form.
5. In the **Inheritance Picker** dialog box, select **BaseAboutForm**.
6. Build the project.

   This creates the inheritance relationship between the two forms, including the access modifiers for the forms and controls.
7. Open **AboutForm.vb** and switch to Design view.
8. Set the form's **Size** property to **504,216**.
9. Set the **BackColor** property of the form to **Control**.
10. Set the **Text** property to **About Simple Windows Calculator**.
11. Click the **Product Name** label. Set the **Text** property to **Simple Windows Calculator**.
12. Set the properties for the following controls.

Control	Properties
Version <1.0.0000> Label	Text: **Version 2.53.1892**
Copyright © yyyy Contoso, Ltd. Label	Text: **Copyright © 2002 Contoso, Ltd.**

► Implement the About menu item and test the application

1. Open the source code for CalcUI.vb.
2. On the **View** menu, click **Show Tasks**, and then click **Comment**.
3. In the Task List window, locate the TODO comment. Add code to show the About window when the menu item is clicked:

```
Dim aboutForm As New AboutForm()
aboutForm.ShowDialog()
```

4. Build and run the application.
5. When the Simple Calculator window appears, on the **Help** menu, click **About**. The inherited **About** box will appear. Notice that the background of the **System Info** button is still the background set on the base form, but the other controls have the background color set in the inherited form.

Lesson: Organizing Controls on a Form

- How to Arrange Controls on a Form by Using the Format Menu
- How to Set the Tab Order for Controls
- How to Anchor a Control in Windows Forms
- How to Dock a Control in Windows Forms
- Demonstration: Organizing Controls on a Form

Introduction

Often you want to change the position and dimensions of controls at run time. Currently, you handle the **resize** event (WM_SIZE for Application Programming Interface [API] programmers), calculate the new position, width, and height, and call some methods like **Move** or **SetWindowPos**. The Windows Forms library offers two very helpful concepts to simplify these proceedings: anchoring and docking. In addition, Visual Studio .NET provides the **Format** menu, which allows you to arrange controls on a form.

This lesson covers the **Format** menu and how to anchor and dock controls on a form. The lesson also covers setting the tab order for controls.

Lesson objectives

After completing this lesson, you will be able to:

- Arrange controls on a form by using the **Format** menu.
- Set the tab order for the controls on a form.
- Anchor controls to a form.
- Dock controls on a form.

How to Arrange Controls on a Form by Using the Format Menu

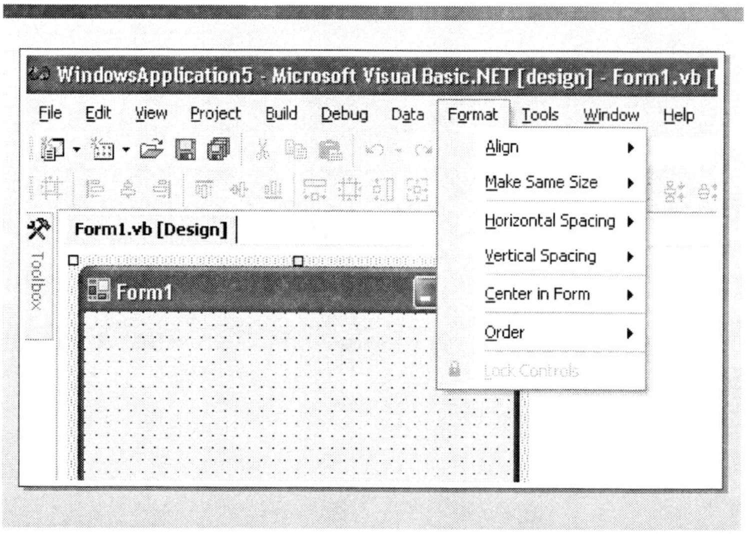

Introduction

You can use the **Format** menu or the Layout Toolbar in the Visual Studio Integrated Development Environment (IDE) to align, layer, and lock controls on a form.

Format menu options

The **Format** menu provides many options for organizing controls. When you use the **Format** menu options for organizing controls, select controls so that the last control that you select is the primary control to which the others are aligned. The primary control has dark sizing handles whereas other controls have light sizing handles around them.

The choices and their functions are listed in the following table.

Choice	Description
Align	Aligns all the controls with respect to the primary control
Make Same Size	Resizes multiple controls on a form
Horizontal Spacing	Increases horizontal spacing between controls
Vertical Spacing	Increases vertical spacing between controls
Center in Form	Centers the controls on a form
Order	Layers controls on a form
Lock Controls	Locks all controls on a form

Procedure: Arranging controls on a form

To align multiple controls:

1. In the Windows Forms Designer, open the form that contains the controls that you want to position.
2. Select the controls that you want to align so that the last control that you select is the primary control to which the others are aligned.
   - On the **Format** menu, point to **Align**, and then click any of the seven choices available.

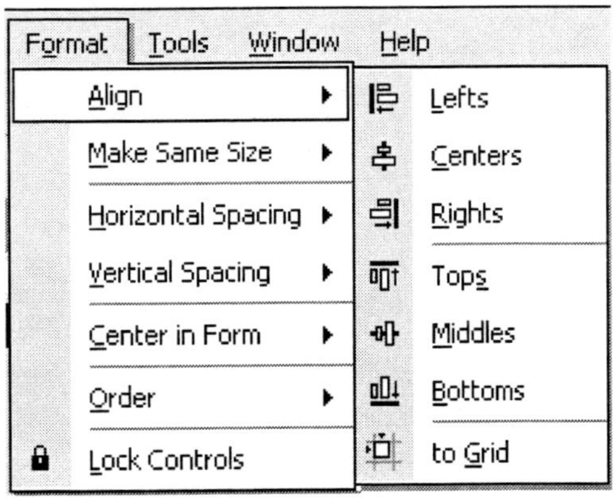

When creating complex user interfaces, you may want to layer controls on a form. To layer controls on a form:

1. Select a control.
2. On the **Format** menu, point to **Order**, and then click **Bring To Front** or **Send To Back**.

You can lock all controls on a form. This prevents any accidental moving or resizing of controls if you are setting other properties for controls. To lock all controls on a form, on the **Format** menu, click **Lock Controls**.

How to Set the Tab Order for Controls

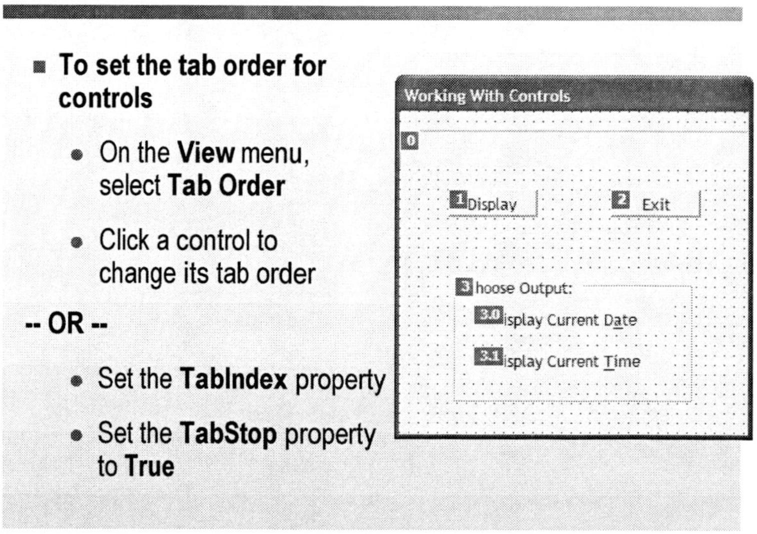

Introduction

The tab order is the order in which a user moves focus from one control to another by pressing the TAB key. Each form has its own tab order. By default, the tab order is the same as the order in which you created the controls. Tab order numbering begins with zero.

Procedure: Setting the tab order

You can set tab order in the Properties window by using the **TabIndex** property. The **TabIndex** property of a control determines where it is positioned in the tab order. By default, the first control drawn has a TabIndex value of **0**, the second has a TabIndex of **1**, and so on.

To set the tab order by using the **View** menu:

1. On the **View** menu, click **Tab Order**.
2. Click the controls sequentially to establish the tab order that you want.
3. When you are finished, on the **View** menu, click **Tab Order**.

To set the tab order by using the **TabIndex** property:

1. Select the control.
2. Set the **TabIndex** property to the required value.
3. Set the **TabStop** property to **True**.

   By turning off the **TabStop** property, you enable a control be passed over in the tab order of the form. A control in which the **TabStop** property has been set to **False** still maintains its position in the tab order, even though the control is skipped when you cycle through the controls with the TAB key.

How to Anchor a Control in Windows Forms

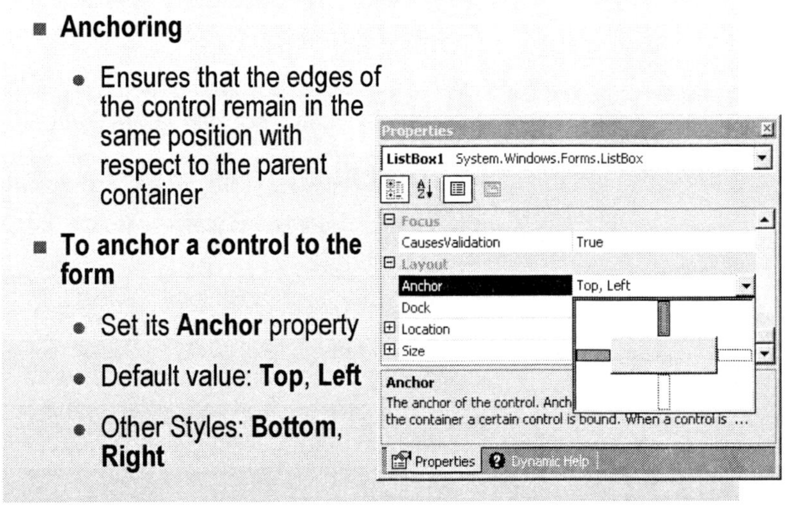

Introduction

If you are designing a form that the user can resize at run time, the controls on the form should resize and reposition properly. When a control is anchored to a form (or another container) and the form is resized, the control maintains the distance between the control and the anchor positions (which is the initial position). You use the **Anchor** property editor to anchor.

Procedure: Anchoring a control on a form

To anchor a control on a form:

1. Select the control that you want to anchor.
2. In the **Properties** window, click the **Anchor** property, and then click the **Anchor** arrow.

   The **Anchor** property editor is displayed; it contains a top bar, left bar, right bar, and bottom bar.
3. To set an anchor, click the top, left, right, or bottom bars in the **Anchor** property editor. Controls are anchored to the top and left by default. To clear a side of the control that has been anchored, click the bar on that side.

How to Dock a Control in Windows Forms

- **Docking**
  - Enables you to glue the edges of a control to the edges of its parent control
- **To dock a control**
  - Set the **Dock** property

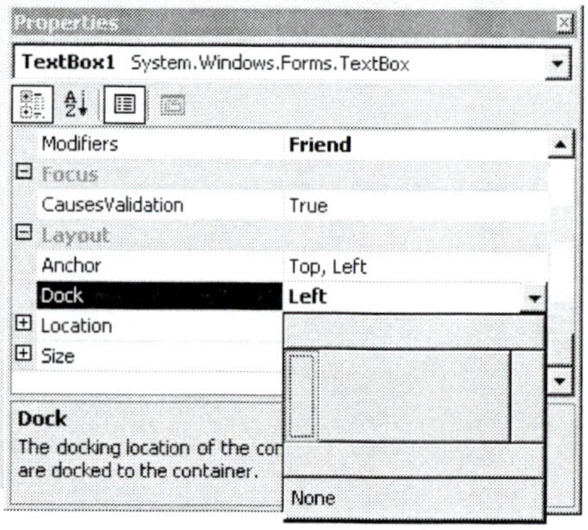

Introduction

You can dock controls to the edges of your form. For example, Windows Explorer docks the **TreeView** control to the left side of the window and the **ListView** control to the right side of the window. Use the **Dock** property for all visible Windows Forms controls to define the docking mode.

If you use the **Dock** property, a control is coupled with two edges of the container. Then, the control is horizontally or vertically resized when the container is resized. In real life, you do not indicate the edges, you indicate a border. If you dock a control to the left border, it is connected with the top left and bottom left edge. The value of the **Dock** property is one of the **DockStyle** values.

A special case is **DockStyle.Fill**. This value docks the control to all edges. The control fills in the complete client area of the container.

Procedure: Docking a control on a form

To dock a control on a form:

1. Select the control that you want to dock.
2. In the Properties window, click the arrow to the right of the **Dock** property.

   The **Dock** property editor is displayed; it contains a series of buttons that represent the edges and the center of the form.
3. Click the button that represents the edge of the form where you want to dock the control. To fill the contents of the control's form or container control, click the **Fill** (center) button. Click **None** to disable docking.

   The control is automatically resized to fit the boundaries of the docked edge.

Demonstration: Organizing Controls on a Form

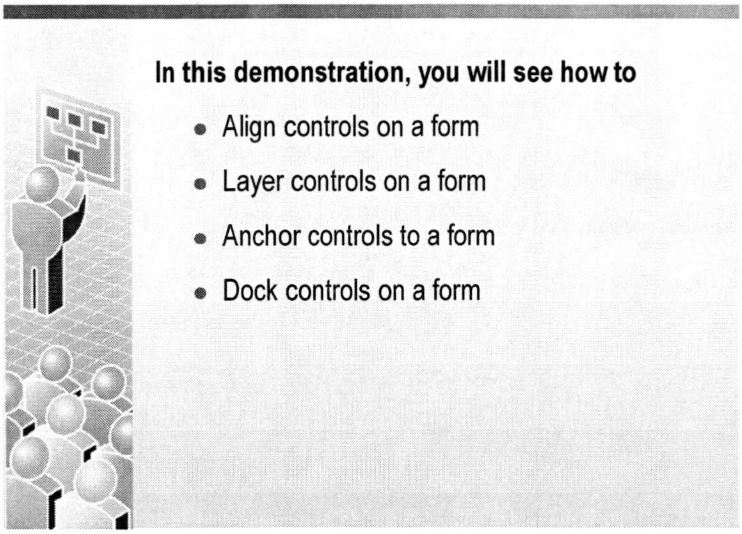

Introduction

In this demonstration, you will see how to organize controls on a form.

Instructions

► **Organize controls by using the Format menu**

1. Open the WorkingWithControls project in Visual Studio .NET from *install_folder*\Democode\ Mod01\Mod01_01\Starter.
2. If the WorkingWithControls.vb form is not visible, display it in Design view. You will notice that the controls on the forms are not organized very well.
3. Organize the buttons on the form so that the **Display** button is positioned to the left of the **Exit** button.
4. Click the **Exit** button, hold down CTRL, and click the **Display** button. Both buttons are selected.
5. On the **Format** menu, click **Align**, and then click **Tops**. The **Exit** button aligns with the top of the **Display** button.
6. While the two buttons are selected, on the **Format** menu, click **Center in Form**, and then click **Horizontally**.
7. Select the **Choose Output** group box.
8. On the **Format** menu, click **Center in Form**, and then click **Horizontally**.
9. While the group box is selected, press the **up arrow** key twice to move the group box up.
10. Select the **Display Current Time** option button, hold down CTRL, and then click the **Display Current Date** option button.
11. On the **Format** menu, click **Align**, and then click **Lefts**.

12. While the two option buttons are selected, on the **Format** menu, click **Vertical** spacing, and then click **Increase**. Perform this step a second time further to increase the space between the two controls.
13. While the option buttons are selected, on the **Format** menu, click **Center in Form**, and then click **Horizontally**.
14. While the option buttons are selected, on the **Format** menu, click **Center in Form**, and then click **Vertically**.

► **Set the tab order**

1. On the **View** menu, click **Tab Order**.
2. Change the tab order by clicking each of the controls. Click the controls in the following order: **Label**, **Display** button, **Exit** button, **Choose Output** group box, **Display Current Date** option button, and **Display Current Time** option button. The resulting tab order will look like this.

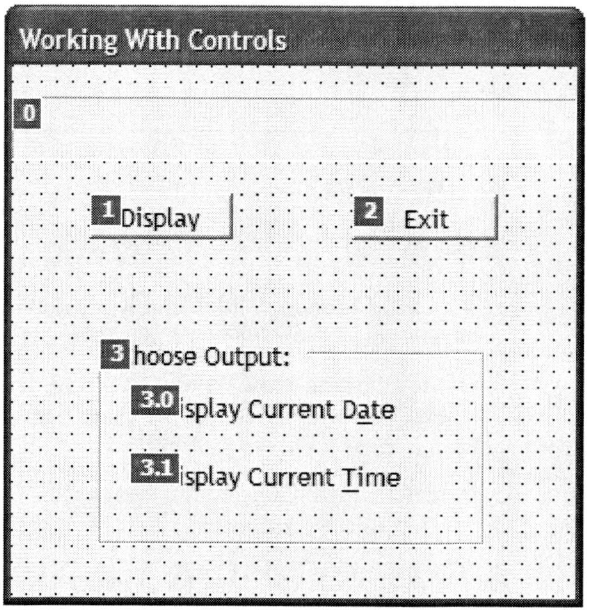

3. On the **View** menu, click **Tab Order**.

► **Anchor and dock the controls**

1. Click the **Label** control, and then set the **Dock** property to **Top**.
2. Click the **Exit** button, and then set the **Anchor** property to **Top, Right**.
3. Click the **Groupbox** control, and then set the **Anchor** property to **Bottom, Left, Right**.
4. Click the **Display Current Date** option button, and then set the **Anchor** property to **Top**.
5. Click the **Display Current Time** button, and then set the **Anchor** property to **Bottom**.
6. Build and run the application.
7. When the form appears, resize it to see how the controls behave with regard to their positioning.

Lesson: Creating MDI Applications

- SDI vs. MDI Applications
- How to Create MDI Applications
- How Parent and Child Forms Interact
- Practice: Creating an MDI Application

Introduction

When creating Windows-based applications, you can use different styles for the user interface. Your application can have a single-document interface (SDI) or a multiple-document interface (MDI), or you can create an explorer-style interface. For more information about the different types of application interface, see the .NET Framework software development kit (SDK).

This lesson covers how to create and use MDI applications.

Lesson objectives

After completing this lesson, you will be able to:

- List the differences between SDI and MDI applications.
- Create MDI applications.
- Explain how parent and child forms interact.

SDI vs. MDI Applications

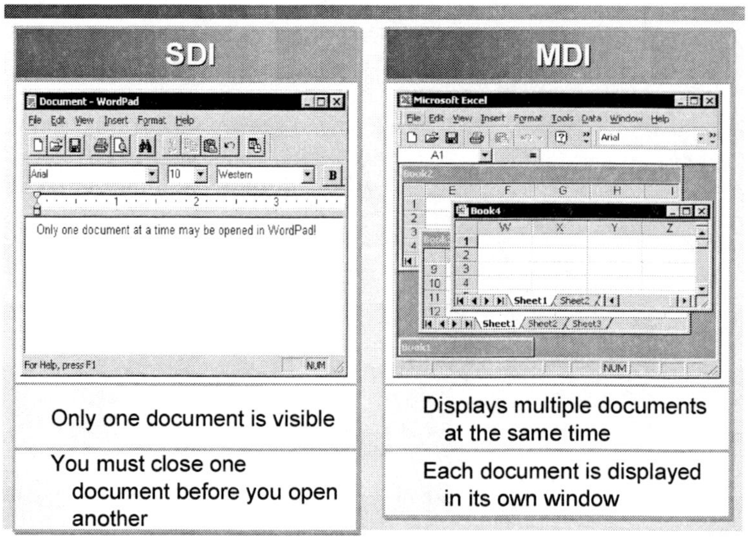

Introduction

Before you create a Windows-based application, you must determine the style of user interface for the application.

SDI vs. MDI

As the name suggests, single-document interface (SDI) applications can support only one document at a time, whereas a multiple-document interface (MDI) application can support several documents simultaneously. The following table lists the differences between SDI and MDI applications and also provides examples of which interface style to use for which scenario.

SDI	MDI
Only one document is visible at a time.	Several documents are visible at the same time.
Must close one document before opening another.	Each document is displayed in its own window.
Example: Microsoft WordPad	**Example**: Microsoft Excel
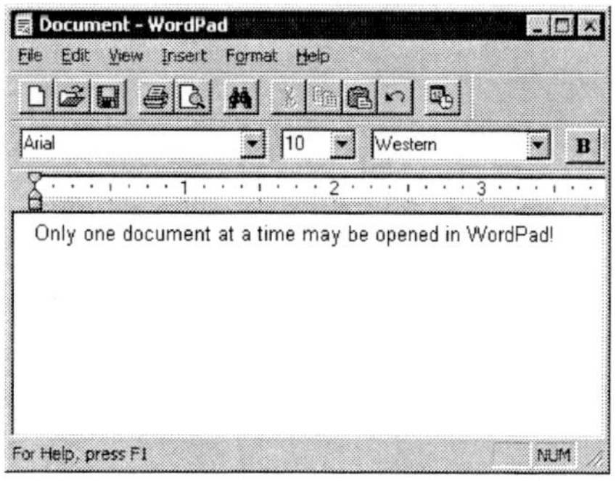	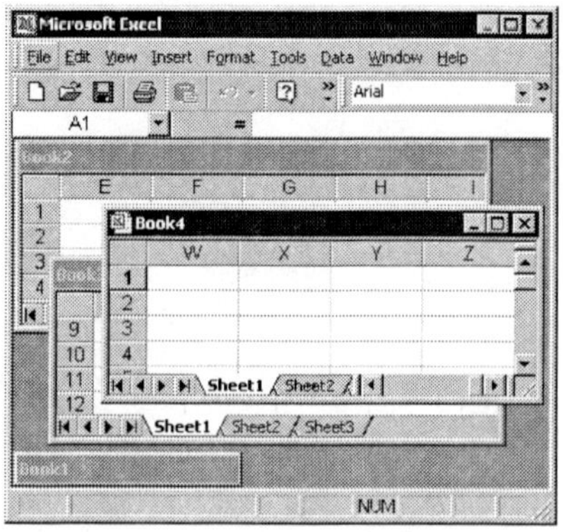
Scenario: A calendar application (because you may not need more than one instance of a calendar open at a time).	**Scenario**: An insurance application in which the user needs to work with multiple application forms.

How to Create MDI Applications

- **To create a parent form**
  - Create a new project
  - Set the **IsMdiContainer** property to **True**
  - Add a menu item to invoke the child form
- **To create a child form**
  - Add a new form to the project
- **To call a child form from a parent form**

```
Protected Sub MenuItem2_OnClick(ByVal sender As System.Object, ByVal
   e As System.EventArgs) Handles MenuItem2.Click
   Dim NewMdiChild As New Form2()
   'Set the Parent Form of the Child window.
   NewMdiChild.MdiParent = Me
   'Display the new form.
   NewMdiChild.Show()
End Sub
```

Introduction

There are three main steps involved in creating an MDI application: creating a parent form, creating a child form, and calling the child form from a parent form.

Procedure: Creating MDI applications

To create the parent form at design time:

The Parent form in an MDI application is the form that contains the MDI child windows. Child windows are used for interacting with users in an MDI application.

1. Create a new project.
2. In the Properties window, set the **IsMdiContainer** property to **True**.

   This designates the form as an MDI container for child windows.

   Note When you are setting properties in the Properties window, you can also set the **WindowState** property to **Maximized**. This allows you to easily manipulate MDI child windows when the parent form is maximized.

3. From the Toolbox, drag a **MainMenu** component to the form.

   You need a menu to invoke the child forms from the parent form. As an example, create a top-level menu item with the **Text** property set to **&File** with submenu items called **&New** and **&Close**. Also create a top-level menu item called **&Window**.

4. Set the **MdiList** property of the **Windows** menu item to **True**.

MDI child forms are critical for MDI applications because users interact with the application through child forms.

To create the child form at design time:

- In the same project that contains the parent form, create a new form.

To call the child form from the parent form:

1. Create a **Click** event handler for the **New** menu item on the parent form.
2. Insert code similar to the following code to create a new MDI child form when the user clicks the **New** menu item.

```
Protected Sub MenuItem2_OnClick(ByVal sender As
System.Object, ByVal e As System.EventArgs) Handles
MenuItem2.Click
   Dim NewMdiChild As New Form2()
   'Set the Parent Form of the Child window.
   NewMdiChild.MdiParent = Me
   'Display the new form.
   NewMdiChild.Show()
End Sub
```

How Parent and Child Forms Interact

- **To list the available child windows that are owned by the parent**
  - Create a menu item (Windows) and set its **MdiList** property to **True**
- **To determine the active MDI child**
  - Use the **ActiveMdiChild** property

```
Dim activeChild As Form = Me.ActiveMdiChild
```

- **To arrange child windows on the parent form**
  - Call the **LayoutMdi** method

Introduction

In an MDI application, a parent form has several child forms, and each of the child forms interacts with the parent form. Visual Studio .NET includes several properties that allow parent and child forms in an MDI application to interact.

Procedure: Listing the child windows of a parent form

An easy way to keep track of the different MDI child windows an application has open is to use a **Window** list. The functionality to keep track of all the open MDI child forms as well as which child form has focus is part of the Visual Studio .NET and is set with the **MdiList** property of a menu item.

To list the child windows of a parent form by using the Window list:

1. Add a **MainMenu** component to the parent form.
2. Add the following top-level menu items to the **MainMenu** component by using the Menu Designer.

Menu item	Text
MenuItem1	&File
MenuItem2	&Window

3. Set the **MdiList** property of the **Windows** menu item to **True**.

Procedure: Determining the active child form

When you are completing certain procedures in an application, it is important to determine the active form.

Because an MDI application can have many instances of the same child form, the procedure must know which form to use. To specify the correct form, use the **ActiveMdiChild** property, which returns the child form that has the focus or that was most recently active.

Use the following code to determine the active child form.

```
Dim activeChild As Form = Me.ActiveMDIChild
```

Procedure: Arranging child windows on the parent form

To arrange child windows on a parent form, you can use the **LayoutMdi** method with the **MdiLayout** enumeration to rearrange the child forms in an MDI parent form.

There are four different **MdiLayout** enumeration values that can be used by the **LayoutMdi** method. These values help you display the form as cascading, horizontally or vertically tiled, or as child form icons arranged along the lower portion of the MDI form.

To arrange child forms, in an event, use the **LayoutMdi** method to set the **MdiLayout** enumeration for the MDI parent form.

You can use the following members of the **MdiLayout** enumeration when calling the **LayoutMdi** method of the **Form** class.

Member	Description
ArrangeIcons	All MDI child icons are arranged in the client region of the MDI parent form.
Cascade	All MDI child windows are cascaded in the client region of the MDI parent form.
TileHorizontal	All MDI child windows are tiled horizontally in the client region of the MDI parent form.
TileVertical	All MDI child windows are tiled vertically in the client region of the MDI parent form.

The following example uses the Cascade setting of the **MdiLayout** enumeration for the child windows of the MDI parent form (Form1).

```
Protected Sub CascadeWindows_Click(ByVal sender As
System.Object, ByVal e As System.EventArgs)
   Me.LayoutMdi(System.Windows.Forms.MdiLayout.Cascade)
End Sub
```

Practice: Creating an MDI Application

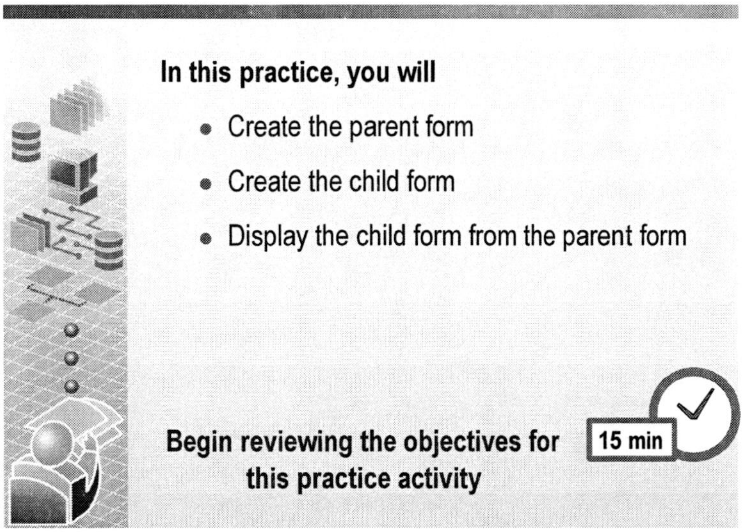

Introduction

In this practice, you will create an MDI application.

Instructions

► **Open the practice project**

1. Use Windows Explorer, and browse to *install_folder*\Practices\Mod01\Mod01_03\Starter.
2. Double-click the MdiApplication.sln solution file to open the project.

► **Create the parent form**

1. Open ParentForm.vb in Design view.
2. Set the **IsMdiContainer** property to **True**.

► **Create the File menu**

1. Open the Toolbox, add the **MainMenu** control to the form, and set its **Name** property to **MdiMenu**.
2. Click the menu at the top of the form and set the **Text** property of the first menu item to **&File**.
3. Set the **Name** property of the **File** menu to **FileMenuItem** and the **MergeOrder** property to **0**.
4. Open the **File** menu.
5. Click the menu item that appears under **File**, and set its **Text** property to **&New**.
6. Set the **Name** property of the **New** menu to **NewMenuItem**.
7. Click the menu item that appears under **New**, and set its **Text** property to **&Exit**.

8. Set the **Name** property of the **Exit** menu to **ExitMenuItem**.
9. Double-click the **Exit** menu item to create the **Click** event handler.
10. In the **exit** event handler, add the following code:

```
Me.Close()
```

► **Create the Window menu**

1. Switch to Design view.
2. Click the second menu item to the right of **File**, and set the **Text** property to **&Window**.
3. Set the **Name** property of the **Window** menu to **WindowMenuItem** and the **MergeOrder** property to **2**.
4. Set the **MdiList** property of the **Window** menu item to **True**.
5. Open the **Window** menu.
6. Click the menu item that appears under **Window**, and set its **Text** property to **&Cascade**.
7. Set the **Name** property of the **Cascade** menu to **WindowCascadeMenuItem**.
8. Click the menu item that appears under **Cascade**, and set its **Text** property to **&Tile**.
9. Set the **Name** property of the **Tile** menu to **WindowTileMenuItem**.
10. Double-click the **Cascade** menu, and add the following code to the **Click** event handler:

```
Me.LayoutMdi (System.Windows.Forms.MdiLayout.Cascade)
```

11. Return to Design view and double-click the **Tile** menu item.
12. Add the following code to the **Click** event handler for the **Tile** menu item:

```
Me.LayoutMdi _
    (System.Windows.Forms.MdiLayout.TileHorizontal)
```

► **Create the child form**

1. Open the **Project** menu, and click **Add Windows Form**.
2. Set the name of the form to **ChildForm.vb**.
3. Set the **Text** property of the form to **Child Form**.
4. From the Toolbox, drag a **RichTextBox** control to the form, and set its **Name** property to **ChildTextBox**.
5. Set the **Dock** property of the **RichTextBox** to **Fill**.
6. Delete the existing value of the **Text** property of the **RichTextBox** and leave it blank.
7. From the Toolbox, drag a **MainMenu** control to the form.
8. Set the **Name** property of the **MainMenu** control to **ChildWindowMenu**.
9. Click the menu at the top of the form and set the text to F&ormat.
10. Set the **Name** property of the **Format** menu to **FormatMenuItem**, and set the **MergeOrder** property to **1**.
11. Click the entry below the **Format** menu, and set the text to **&Toggle Foreground**.

12. Set the **Name** property of the **Toggle Foreground** menu item to **ToggleMenuItem**.

13. Double-click the **Toggle Foreground** menu, and add the following code to the **Click** event handler:

```
If ToggleMenuItem.Checked Then
   ToggleMenuItem.Checked = False
   ChildTextBox.ForeColor = System.Drawing.Color.Black
Else
   ToggleMenuItem.Checked = True
   ChildTextBox.ForeColor = System.Drawing.Color.Blue
End If
```

► **Display the child form from the parent form**

1. View ParentForm in Design view.
2. Double-click the **New** menu item on the **File** menu to create the **Click** event handler.
3. Add the following code to the **Click** event for the **New** menu item:

```
Dim newChild As New ChildForm()
newChild.MdiParent = Me
newChild.Show()
```

► **Build and run the application**

1. Build the application and run it.
2. When the parent form appears, on the **File** menu, click **New**.

   A new child window appears inside the parent window. Notice how the menu from the child window merges with the menu of the parent window and orders the menu according to the **MergeOrder** properties set in the **Display the child form from the parent form** procedure.

3. Type some text in the child form and use the Format menu to change the color of the text.
4. Open a few more child windows.
5. Click the **Window** menu and select **Tile**. Notice how the child windows are reorganized in a tiled manner.
6. Close all the child windows. Notice that when the last child window is closed, the menu in the parent form changes by removing the **Format** menu.
7. On the **File** menu, click **Exit** to end the application.

Review

- Creating a Form
- Adding Controls to a Form
- Creating an Inherited Form
- Organizing Controls on a Form
- Creating MDI Applications

1. List some reasons why you would use Windows Forms as opposed to Web forms.

   stand a lone application – offline
   faster – response time
   Graphics – user interface

2. What is Visual Inheritance?

   reusability

3. What is the difference between anchoring and docking a control to a form?

   Docking = fixed (corner)
   Anchoring – resizable

4. What are the differences between SDI and MDI applications?

   Single / open
   Multipal / open   relationship (o/d)

5. When creating a form, what class must the form inherit from to make it a Windows Form?

   System windows form

6. You want to perform some totaling of numbers as a form is being dismissed. Into which event handler should you add the code?

   Activate

7. When creating a form that inherits from a base form, what must be available to override the base version of the methods of a control on the base form?

   Public Protected

Lab 1.1: Creating Windows Forms

- Exercise 1: Creating a New Windows Form
- Exercise 2: Inheriting a New Form from an Existing Windows Form

Objectives

After completing this lab, you will have demonstrated your ability to:

- Create a new form.
- Inherit a new form from an existing form.
- Add controls to a form.
- Set form and control properties.

Note This lab focuses on the concepts in Module 1, "Introducing Windows Forms," in Course 2565A, *Developing Microsoft .NET Applications for Windows (Visual Basic .NET)*. As a result, this lab may not comply with Microsoft security recommendations.

Prerequisites

Before working on this lab, you must have: the knowledge and skills to develop a simple Windows Forms application by using a Visual Studio .NET–compatible programming language.

Scenario

The Internal Business Application shell provides a common access point to various internal business applications. To ensure that the information provided by the application is viewed by the appropriate user, the application requires a logon form.

The logon form will prompt the user for his or her user name and password. The logon form will then attempt to authenticate the user's credentials to determine if the user is permitted to access various internal applications.

In this lab, you will add a new form to the Internal Business Application shell and populate it with controls. You will also implement the **Click** event handler for the buttons on the logon form. In addition, you will create the **About** dialog box by inheriting a new form from an existing form.

Estimated time to complete this lab: 45 minutes

Exercise 1
Creating a New Windows Form

In this exercise, you will update the Internal Business Application shell by adding a logon form and populating it with controls. You will also set form and control properties and implement the **Click** event handlers for the buttons on the logon form.

There are starter and solution files associated with this exercise. Browse to *install_folder*\Labfiles\Lab01_1\Ex01\Starter to find the starter files, and browse to *install_folder*\Labfiles\Lab01_1\Ex01\Solution to find the solution files. If you performed a default installation of the course files, *install_folder* corresponds to C:\Program Files\Msdntrain\2565.

Tasks	Additional information
1. Open the InternalBusinessApp project in Visual Studio .NET. Browse to the *install_folder*\Labfiles\Lab01_1\Ex01\Starter to find this project. **Note:** The project will not build until you complete this exercise.	**a.** For more information about opening a project file and starting an application, see the following resource: • The Visual Studio .NET Help documentation. For additional information about opening a project file, in Search, select the **Search in titles only** check box, then search by using the phrase **Open Project Dialog Box**. For additional information about starting an application from within Designer, in Index, search by using the phrase **Debugging Windows Applications**.
2. Add a new form to the project. Use the form name LoginForm, and use the file name LoginForm.vb.	**a.** For more information about Windows Forms, see the following resources: • Practice: Creating a Form in Module 1, “Introducing Windows Forms,” in Course 2565A, *Developing Microsoft .NET Applications for Windows (Visual Basic .NET)*. This practice contains information about how to add a new form to a project. • Lesson: Creating a Form in Module 1, “Introducing Windows Forms,” in Course 2565A, *Developing Microsoft .NET Applications for Windows (Visual Basic .NET)*. This lesson contains information about how to create a form. • The Windows Forms section of the .NET Framework SDK documentation.

<table>
<tr><th>Tasks</th><th>Additional information</th></tr>
<tr><td>

3. Set form properties. Use the following table to set the properties of the form.

Property	Value
(Name)	LoginForm
ControlBox	False
FormBorderStyle	Fixed3D
MaximizeBox	False
MinimizeBox	False
Size	322, 210
Text	Internal Business Application Logon

</td><td>

a. For more information about form properties and Windows Forms, see the following resources:

- Practice: Creating a Form in Module 1, "Introducing Windows Forms," in Course 2565A, *Developing Microsoft .NET Applications for Windows (Visual Basic .NET)*. This practice contains information about how to set form properties.
- Lesson: Creating a Form in Module 1, "Introducing Windows Forms," in Course 2565A, *Developing Microsoft .NET Applications for Windows (Visual Basic .NET)*.
- The Windows Forms section of the .NET Framework SDK.

</td></tr>
<tr><td>

4. Add controls to the form. Add two labels, two text boxes, and two buttons to the form.

</td><td>

a. For more information about adding controls to a form and Windows Forms, see the following resources:

- Practice: Creating a Form, in Module 1, "Introducing Windows Forms," in Course 2565A, *Developing Microsoft .NET Applications for Windows (Visual Basic .NET)*.
- Lesson: Creating a Form, in Module 1, "Introducing Windows Forms," in Course 2565A, *Developing Microsoft .NET Applications for Windows (Visual Basic .NET)*.
- The Windows Forms section of the .NET Framework SDK.

</td></tr>
</table>

Tasks

5. Set the control properties. Use the following tables to set the properties of the controls.

Label1 Property	Value
(Name)	UserNameLabel
Location	64, 31
Size	63, 14
Text	Username

Label2 Property	Value
(Name)	PasswordLabel
Location	64, 71
Size	64, 14
Text	Password

Textbox1 Property	Value
(Name)	UserNameTextBox
Location	128, 29
Size	120, 20
Text	(Delete existing text and leave it blank)

Textbox2 Property	Value
(Name)	PasswordTextBox
Location	128, 64
PasswordChart	*
Size	120, 20
Text	

Button1 Property	Value
(Name)	LogonButton
Location	67, 116
Size	75, 30
Text	&Log On

Button2 Property	Value
(Name)	CancelAppButton
Location	171, 116
Size	75, 30
Text	&Cancel

Additional information

a. For more information about control properties and Windows Forms, see the following resources:

- Practice: Creating a Form, in Module 1, "Introducing Windows Forms," in Course 2565A, Developing *Microsoft .NET Applications for Windows (Visual Basic .NET)*. This practice contains information about how to set control properties.
- Lesson: Creating a Form, in Module 1, "Introducing Windows Forms," in Course 2565A, Developing *Microsoft .NET Applications for Windows (Visual Basic .NET)*.
- The Windows Forms section of the .NET Framework SDK.

Tasks	Additional information
6. Set the tab order for the controls on the form. The tab order should resemble the following diagram. 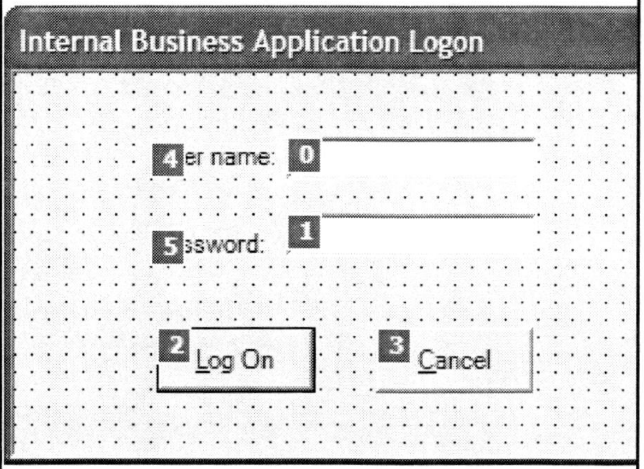	**a.** For more information about setting tab order on a form and Windows Forms, see the following resources: • Lesson: Organizing Controls on a Form, in Module 1, "Introducing Windows Forms," in Course 2565A, *Developing Microsoft .NET Applications for Windows (Visual Basic .NET)*. • The Windows Forms section in the .NET Framework SDK.
7. Complete the form properties. Use the following table to set the remaining properties of the form. **Property** — **Value** AcceptButton — LogonButton CancelButton — CancelAppButton	**a.** For more information about setting form properties and Windows Forms, see the following resources: • Practice: Creating a Form, in Module 1, "Introducing Windows Forms," in Course 2565A, *Developing Microsoft .NET Applications for Windows (Visual Basic .NET)*. • Lesson: Creating a Form, in Module 1, "Introducing Windows Forms," in Course 2565A, *Developing Microsoft .NET Applications for Windows (Visual Basic .NET)*. • The Windows Forms section of the .NET Framework SDK.
The following four steps (Steps 8, 9, 10, and 11) are not required to meet the objectives of the labs but are required to run the application and view results.	
8. Declare class member fields in the **LoginForm** class. Open the LoginFormCode.txt file, and copy the code under the heading *Declare these class members in the LoginForm class.*	Additional information is not necessary for this task.
9. Implement properties for the class. Open the LoginFormCode.txt file, and copy the code under the heading *Add these properties to the LoginForm class.*	Additional information is not necessary for this task.
10. Implement the **Click** event handler for the **Cancel** button. Open the LoginFormCode.txt file, and copy the required code under the heading *Create a Click event handler for the Cancel button and add the following code to the event handler.*	Additional information is not necessary for this task.

Tasks	Additional information
11. Implement the **Click** event handler for the **Log On** button. Open the LoginFormCode.txt file, and copy the required code under the heading *Create a Click event handler for the Log On button and add the following code to the event handler.*	Additional information is not necessary for this task.
12. Build and run the application. Specify **mario** for the user name and **P@ssw0rd** for the password.	**a.** For more information about working with forms and Windows Forms, see the following resources: • Practice: Creating a Form, in Module 1, "Introducing Windows Forms," in Course 2565A, *Developing Microsoft .NET Applications for Windows (Visual Basic .NET).* • Lesson: Creating a Form, in Module 1, "Introducing Windows Forms," in Course 2565A, *Developing Microsoft .NET Applications for Windows (Visual Basic .NET).* • The Windows Forms section of the .NET Framework SDK.

Exercise 2
Inheriting a New Form from an Existing Windows Form

In this exercise, you will update the Internal Business Application shell by adding an About dialog by inheriting from a generic Windows Form.

There are starter and solution files associated with this exercise. Browse to *install_folder*\Labfiles\Lab01_1\Ex02\Starter to find the starter files, and browse to *install_folder*\Labfiles\Lab01_1\Ex02\Solution to find the solution files. If you performed a default installation of the course files, *install_folder* corresponds to C:\Program Files\Msdntrain\2565.

Important In the InternalBusinessApp.sln project in *install_folder*\Labfiles\Lab01_1\Ex02\Solution, because the About Internal Business Application dialog box for the project is an inherited form, you must build the solution before you can view the AppControlAboutForm form in Windows Forms Designer.

Tasks	Additional information
1. Open the InternalBusinessApp project in Visual Studio .NET. Browse to *install_folder*\Labfiles\Lab01_1\Ex02\Starter to find this project.	**a.** For more information about opening a project file and starting an application, see the following resource: • The Visual Studio .NET Help documentation. For additional information about opening a project file, in Search, select the **Search in titles only** check box, then search by using the phrase **Open Project Dialog Box.** For additional information about starting an application from within Designer, in Index, search by using the phrase **Debugging Windows Applications**.
2. Open the BaseAboutForm form in Design view.	**a.** For more information about adding new forms to a project and Windows Forms, see the following resources: • Practice: Creating an Inherited Form, in Module 1, "Introducing Windows Forms," in Course 2565A, *Developing Microsoft .NET Applications for Windows (Visual Basic .NET).* • Lesson: Creating an Inherited Form, in Module 1, "Introducing Windows Forms," in Course 2565A, *Developing Microsoft .NET Applications for Windows (Visual Basic .NET).* • The Windows Forms section of the .NET Framework SDK.

<table>
<tr><th>Tasks</th><th>Additional information</th></tr>
<tr><td>3. Use the following table to set the Modifier property of each control. To set a property for multiple controls simultaneously, use the CTRL key to select the controls.

<table><tr><th>Control</th><th>Modifier Property Value</th></tr><tr><td>ProductNameLabel</td><td>protected</td></tr><tr><td>VersionNumber</td><td>protected</td></tr><tr><td>CopyrightLabel</td><td>protected</td></tr><tr><td>AllRightsReservedLabel</td><td>protected</td></tr><tr><td>AboutOkButton</td><td>protected</td></tr></table></td><td>a. For more information about adding new forms to a project and Windows Forms, see the following resources:
• Practice: Creating an Inherited Form, in Module 1, “Introducing Windows Forms,” in Course 2565A, Developing Microsoft .NET Applications for Windows (Visual Basic .NET).
• Lesson: Creating an Inherited Form, in Module 1, “Introducing Windows Forms,” in Course 2565A, Developing Microsoft .NET Applications for Windows (Visual Basic .NET).
• The Windows Forms section of the .NET Framework SDK.</td></tr>
<tr><td>4. Save the BaseAboutForm, and build the project.</td><td>Additional information is not necessary for this task.</td></tr>
<tr><td>5. Add a new form to the project by using the Inheritance Picker dialog box. Use the form name AppControlAboutForm. Inherit the form from the BaseAboutForm form. Save the new form and build the project.</td><td>a. For more information about adding new forms to a project and Windows Forms, see the following resources:
• Practice: Creating an Inherited Form, in Module 1, “Introducing Windows Forms,” in Course 2565A, Developing Microsoft .NET Applications for Windows (Visual Basic .NET).
• Lesson: Creating an Inherited Form, in Module 1, “Introducing Windows Forms,” in Course 2565A, Developing Microsoft .NET Applications for Windows (Visual Basic .NET).
• The Windows Forms section of the .NET Framework SDK.</td></tr>
</table>

<table>
<tr><th>Tasks</th><th>Additional information</th></tr>
<tr><td>

6. Complete the properties on the AppControlAboutForm form. Use the following table to set the properties of the form.

<table>
<tr><th>Form</th><th>Value</th></tr>
<tr><td>BackColor</td><td>Control</td></tr>
<tr><td>Size</td><td>500, 212</td></tr>
<tr><td>Text</td><td>About Internal Business Application</td></tr>
</table>

Use the following table to set the properties of the controls.

<table>
<tr><th>Control Property</th><th>Value</th></tr>
<tr><td>ProductNameLabel.Text</td><td>Internal Business Application</td></tr>
<tr><td>VersionNumber.Text</td><td>Version 1.0.3153</td></tr>
<tr><td>CopyrightLabel.Text</td><td>Copyright © 2002 Contoso, Ltd.</td></tr>
</table>

</td><td>

a. For more information about working with inherited forms and Windows Forms, see the following resources:

- Practice: Creating an Inherited Form, in Module 1, "Introducing Windows Forms," in Course 2565A, *Developing* Microsoft *.NET Applications for Windows (Visual Basic .NET)*. This practice contains information about how to set inherited form and control properties.
- Lesson: Creating and Inherited Form, in Module 1, "Introducing Windows Forms," in Course 2565A, *Developing Microsoft .NET Applications for Windows (Visual Basic .NET)*. This lesson contains information about how to work with inherited forms.
- The Windows Forms section of the .NET Framework SDK.

</td></tr>
<tr><td>

7. In AppControlForm, implement click event handler for the **About** menu item.

</td><td>

a. For more detailed information about the tasks that you must perform, see the TODO comments in the code.

b. For more information about Windows Forms, see the following resource:

- The Windows Forms section of the .NET Framework SDK.

</td></tr>
<tr><td>

8. Run the application to test the inherited **About** dialog box.

</td><td>

a. For more information about Windows Forms, see the following resource:

- The Windows Forms section of the .NET Framework SDK.

</td></tr>
</table>

msdn training

Colections in .Net is actually an Array List

Module 2: Working with Controls

Contents

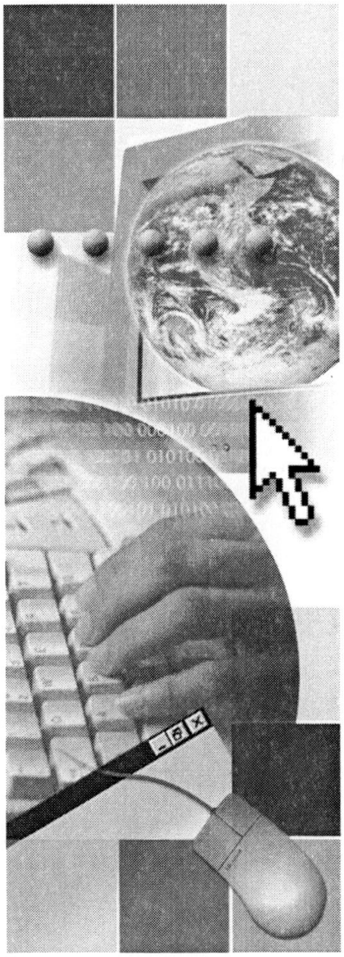

Microsoft

enumeration / fixed Array

Overview

- Creating an Event Handler for a Control
- Using Windows Forms Controls
- Using Dialog Boxes in a Windows Forms Application
- Adding Controls at Run Time
- Creating Menus
- Validating User Input

Introduction

When you design the user interface (UI) and develop the code that operates behind the UI of an application, you will need to work with controls and their events, properties, and methods to meet the design requirements that you have been given.

This module covers how to create event *procedures* (or handlers) in your application that will run in response to user actions. You will learn how to add programming logic to the event procedures of a control, how to use the Microsoft® .NET Framework Windows Forms intrinsic controls, dialog boxes, and menus, and how to validate the data entered by users of your application.

Objectives

After completing this module, you will be able to:

- Create an event handler for a control.
- Select and use the appropriate controls in a Windows Forms application.
- Use dialog boxes in a Windows Forms application.
- Add controls to a form at run time.
- Create and use menus in a Windows Forms application.
- Validate user input in a Windows Forms application.

Lesson: Creating an Event Handler for a Control

- **Event Model in the .NET Framework**
- **What Is an Event Handler?**
- **Handles Keyword**
- **How to Create Event Handlers for Control Events**
- **How to Add and Remove Event Handlers at Run Time**
- **Practice: Creating an Event Handler for a Control**

Introduction

In the Microsoft .NET Framework, an event is a message sent by an object to signal the occurrence of an action that is either invoked by a user or programmatically. Each event has a sender that raises the event and a receiver that handles the event.

In this lesson, you will learn about events and the ways in which events can be handled in your application. You will then learn how to create procedures that handle events and how to add and remove event handlers at run time.

Lesson objectives

After completing this lesson, you will be able to:

- Describe the event model in the .NET Framework.
- Create and use event handlers.
- Create event procedures by using the **Handles** and **WithEvents** keywords.
- Add and remove event handlers from event procedures at run time.

Event Model in the .NET Framework

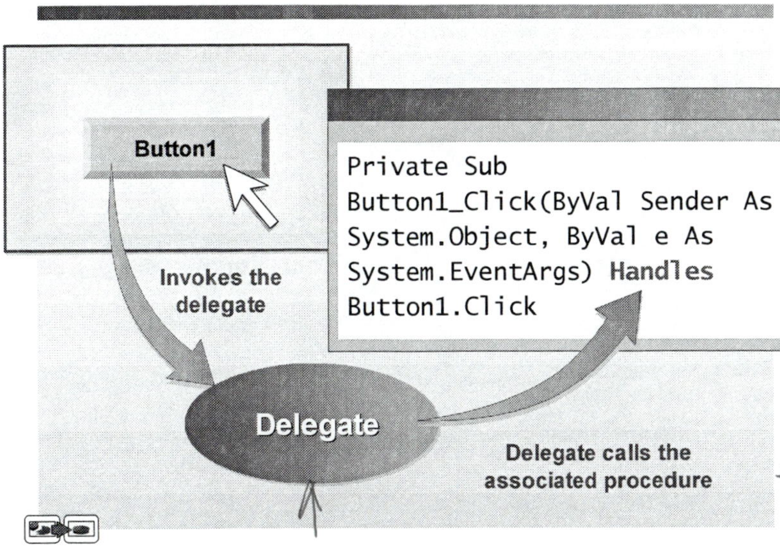

Introduction

In the .NET Framework, an event is used to signal the occurrence of an action. For example, this action could be user invoked, such as the **Click** event of a **Button** control, or the event could be raised programmatically to signal the end of a long computation.

Events and delegates

The object that raises (triggers) the event is referred to as the *event sender*. The procedure that handles the event is referred to as the *event receiver*. In either case, the sender does not know which object or method will respond to the events that it raises. Therefore, it is necessary to have a component that links the event sender with the event receiver. The .NET Framework uses a delegate type to work as a function pointer between the sender and the event receiver. In most cases, the .NET Framework creates the delegate and takes care of the details for you. However, you can create your own delegates for cases when you want an event to use different event handlers under different circumstances.

Creating delegates

Delegates are objects that you can use to call the methods of other objects. You can use the **Delegate** keyword in a declaration statement to create your own delegate that derives from the **MulticastDelegate** class. Creating your own delegates can be useful in situations where you need an intermediary object between a calling procedure and the procedure being called. For more information about creating and using delegates, search by using the phrase **Delegate Class** in the Microsoft Visual Studio® .NET Help documentation.

Handles keyword

The .NET Framework also provides the **Handles** keyword as an easy way to associate an event procedure, or a handler, with an event. The **Handles** keyword associates a procedure with an event that was raised by an object declared by using the **WithEvents** keyword. Because every control that you add to a form is automatically declared by using the **WithEvents** keyword, using **Handles** is the way that you will normally associate a control event with an event procedure.

What Is an Event Handler?

- **Event Handlers**
  - Methods bound to an event
  - When the event is raised, the code within the event handler is executed
- **Two Event Arguments with Event Handlers**
  - An object representing the object that raised the event
  - An event object containing any event-specific information

```
Private Sub Button1_Click (ByVal Sender As
  System.Object, ByVal e As System.EventArgs)
```

Introduction

Functionality is added to controls by raising and consuming events. Before your application can respond to an event, you must create an event handler. The event handler (event procedure) contains the program logic that runs when the event is raised.

Definition

An event handler is a method (generally a Sub procedure) that is bound to an event. When the event is raised, the code in the event handler runs. You can use the same event handler to handle more than one event. For example, you can create a single event handler to handle events of a button and a menu item that are used for the same purpose. Similarly, if you have a group of **RadioButton** controls on a form, you could create a single event handler and have each control's **Click** event bound to the single event handler.

Important Microsoft Visual Basic® .NET no longer supports control arrays. Changes to the event model make control arrays unnecessary. Just as control arrays in Visual Basic version 6.0 could share events, the event model in Visual Basic .NET allows any event handler to handle events from multiple controls. In effect, this allows you to create groups of controls of disparate types that share the same events.

Example of event handler

The following code example is an event handler for the **Click** event of a button.

```
Private Sub Button1_Click(ByVal Sender As System.Object, ByVal
e As System.EventArgs) Handles Button1.Click
```

The following code example shows how you can use a single event handler to handle events for multiple controls.

```
Private Sub MyHandler(ByVal sender As System.Object, ByVal e
As System.EventArgs) Handles RadioButton1.Click,
RadioButton2.Click, RadioButton3.Click
```

Event handler parameters

Each event handler provides two parameters that allow you to handle the event properly:

- The first parameter (*Sender* in the previous code example) provides a reference to the object that raised the event. It specifies the source that raised the event.
- The second parameter (*e* in the previous code example) passes an object specific to the event being handled. This parameter contains all of the data that is required to handle the event.

Handles Keyword

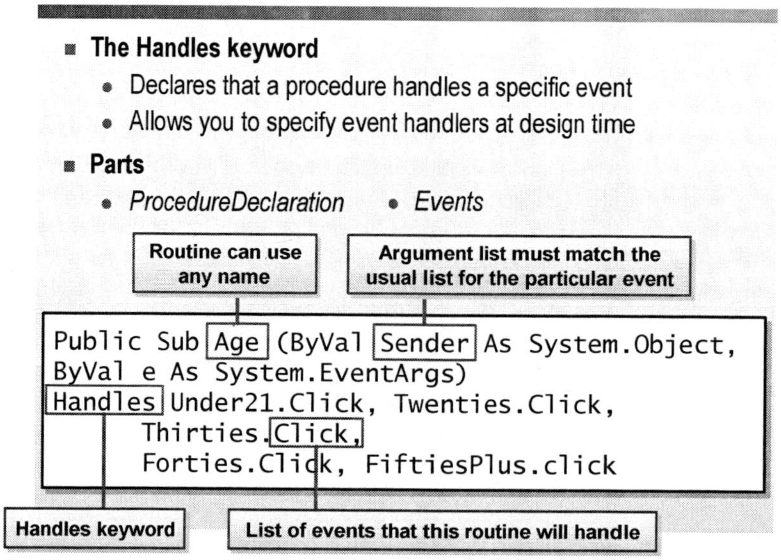

Introduction

The way you construct an event handler depends on the way you want to associate it with events. The standard way to create event handlers is to use the **Handles** keyword for objects that were declared by using the **WithEvents** keyword.

Handles keyword

The **Handles** keyword allows you to declare event handlers at design time. It is used to declare that a procedure handles a specific event. Use the **Handles** keyword at the end of a procedure declaration to cause it to handle events raised by an object variable declared by using the **WithEvents** keyword. The **Handles** keyword can also be used in a derived class to handle events from a base class.

Parts of the Handles keyword

The **Handles** keyword uses the following declaration.

```
Proceduredeclaration Handles event
```

- *Proceduredeclaration*

  Proceduredeclaration is the Sub procedure declaration for the procedure that will handle the event.

- *Event*

  Event is the name of the event being handled. This event must be raised by either the base class for the current class or by an object declared by using the **WithEvents** keyword.

Programming to D.Net framework

How to Create Event Handlers for Control Events

- **Use WithEvents keyword to declare object variables that will be used with the Handles statement**
- **Use the Handles keyword at the end of the procedure declaration**

```
Friend WithEvents Button1 As System.Windows.Forms.Button

Private Sub Button1_Click(ByVal sender As System.Object,
  ByVal e As System.EventArgs) Handles Button1.Click

      MessageBox.Show("MyHandler captured the event")

End Sub
```

Introduction

The standard way to create handlers (event procedures) in Visual Basic .NET is to use the **Handles** keyword. The **Handles** keyword works with objects that were declared by using the **WithEvents** keyword. Because the controls that you add to a form are automatically declared by using the **WithEvents** keyword, the following procedure applies to the events raised by controls.

Procedure

To create an event procedure that uses the **Handles** keyword:

1. In the Declarations section of the module that will handle the event, use the **WithEvents** keyword to declare an object variable for the source of your events. For a control that is added to a form, this is done for you, as in the following code example:

```
Friend WithEvents Button1 As System.Windows.Forms.Button
```

2. In the Code Editor, in the **Class Name** list, click the object variable you just declared. This is the object that was declared by using the **WithEvents** keyword.
3. In the **Method Name** list, click the event you want to handle. The Code Editor creates the empty event handler procedure with a Handles clause.
4. Add event-handling code to the event handler procedure by using the supplied arguments. The following code provides an example:

```
Sub Button_Click(ByVal sender As Object, ByVal e As
System.EventArgs) Handles Button1.Click

      MessageBox.Show("MyHandler received the event")

End Sub
```

How to Add and Remove Event Handlers at Run Time

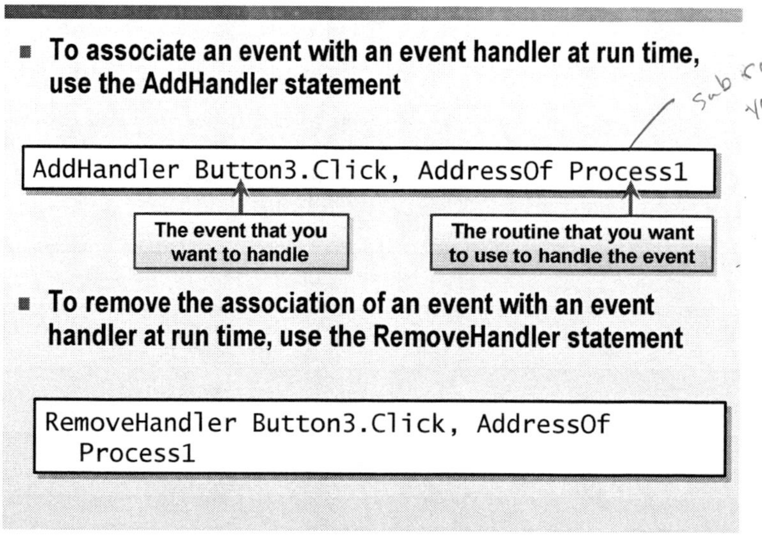

Introduction

In Visual Basic .NET, you can add and remove event handlers at run time by using the **AddHandler** and **RemoveHandler** statements. The **AddHandler** statement is similar to the Handles clause; both allow you to specify an event handler that will handle an event. However, **AddHandler** along with **RemoveHandler** provide greater flexibility than the Handles clause and allow you to dynamically add, remove, and change the event handler associated with an event. Unlike the **Handles** keyword, **AddHandler** allows you to associate multiple event handlers with a single event.

Procedure: Adding event handlers by using AddHandler

To add event handlers by using **AddHandler**:

1. Declare an object variable of the class that is the source of the events you want to handle. For example:

```
Dim Button1 As System.Windows.Forms.Button
```

2. Use the **AddHandler** statement to specify the name of the event sender, and the **AddressOf** statement to provide the name of your event handler, as shown in the following code example:

```
AddHandler Button3.Click, AddressOf Process1
```

3. Add code to the event handler, as in the following code example:

```
Private Sub Process1(ByVal sender As System.Object, _
                     ByVal e As System.EventArgs)
    MessageBox.Show("Use Process 1 to Perform the Task")
End Sub
```

Procedure: Removing event handlers by using RemoveHandler

To remove event handlers by using **RemoveHandler**:

- Use the **RemoveHandler** statement to specify the name of the event sender, and the **AddressOf** statement to provide the name of your event handler.

```
RemoveHandler Button3.Click, AddressOf Process1
```

Practice: Creating an Event Handler for a Control

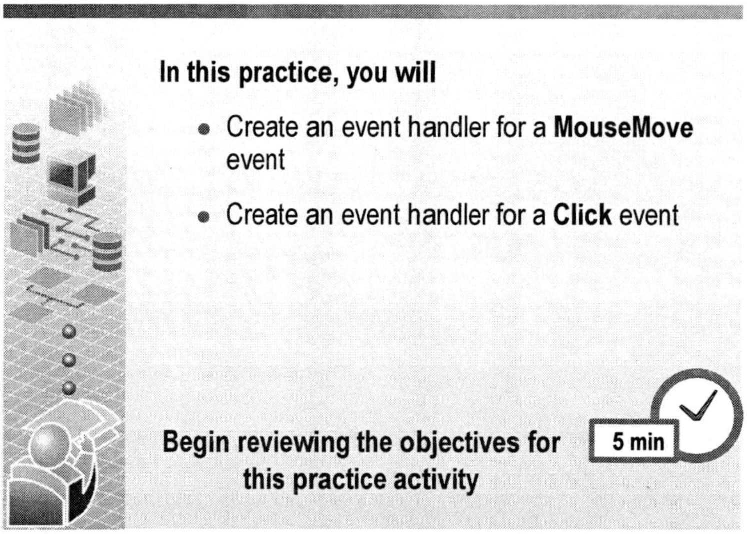

Introduction

In this practice, you will create an event handler for a control.

Instructions

► **Open the practice project**

1. Using Windows Explorer, navigate to *install_folder*\Practices\Mod02\Mod02_01\Starter.

> **Note** If you performed a default installation of the course files, *install_folder* corresponds to C:\Program Files\Msdntrain\2565.

2. Double-click the EventHandlers.sln solution file to open the project.

► **Create an event handler for a MouseMove event**

1. Open Form1.vb in the Code Editor.
2. In the **Class Name** list, click **csButton**.
3. In the **Method Name** list, click **MouseMove**.
4. Add the following code statements to the **csButton_MouseMove** subroutine:

```
csButton.Top -= e.Y
csButton.Left += e.X
If csButton.Top < -16 Or csButton.Top > 160 Then _
csButton.Top = 73
If csButton.Left < -64 Or csButton.Left > 384 Then _
csButton.Top = 160
```

5. What is the purpose of the second parameter (e) that is passed to this event handler?

____

____

____

____

6. Run the application and click each button on the form.
7. Close the application.

► **Create an event handler for a Click event**

1. Open Form1.vb in Design view.
2. Double-click the **Close** button control.
3. Why is a **Click** event handler created for you?

____

____

4. Add the following code statement to the **closeButton_Click** subroutine:

```
End
```

5. Run the application, and then click the **Close** button.
6. Save your project, and then close Visual Studio.

Lesson: Using Windows Forms Controls

- **Selecting a Windows Forms Control Based on Function**
- **How to Use the StatusBar Control**
- **How to Use the ListBox Control**
- **How to Use the GroupBox and Panel Controls**
- **How to Use the ToolBar and ImageList Controls**
- **Practice: Creating and Using a ToolBar Control**
- **Demonstration: Implementing Drag-and-Drop Operations Between Controls**

Introduction

The **Windows Forms** tab in the Visual Studio .NET Toolbox offers a variety of very useful controls, such as the **ToolBar**, **StatusBar**, **ListBox**, **GroupBox**, **ImageList**, **OpenFileDialog**, and **MainMenu** controls. The controls listed in the Toolbox can be categorized based on the functionality that they add to your applications. In this lesson, you will learn about the different categories of Windows Forms controls and you will then learn how to use controls from the categories. This lesson focuses on the controls that are used in the sample applications for Course 2565A, *Developing Microsoft .NET Applications for Windows (Visual Basic .NET)*. Some of the controls will be covered in greater detail in the Using Dialog Boxes in a Windows Forms Application and the Creating Menus lessons in this module.

Lesson objectives

After completing this lesson, you will be able to:

- Select appropriate Windows Forms controls for adding the desired functionality to a user interface.
- Use the **StatusBar** control in a Windows Forms application to display text information.
- Use the **ListBox** control in a Windows Forms application to provide the user with a predefined list of items.
- Use **GroupBox** and **Panel** controls in a Windows Forms application as containers for other controls.
- Use the **ToolBar** and **ImageList** controls in a Windows Forms application to display command buttons as an array of graphic images.
- Implement drag-and-drop operations between controls.

Selecting a Windows Forms Control Based on Function

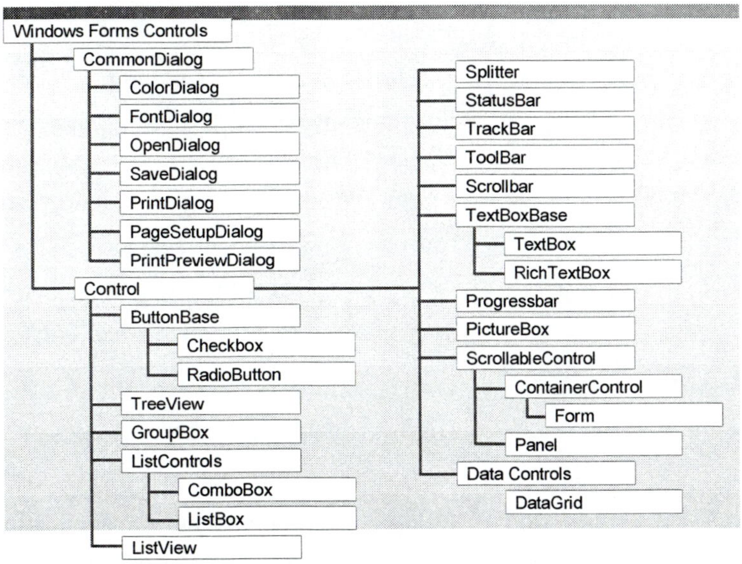

Introduction

Windows Forms controls are reusable components that encapsulate user interface functionality and are used in a Windows Forms application. Not only does the .NET Framework Class Library provide many ready-to-use controls, it also provides the infrastructure for developing your own controls.

The controls that appear on the Windows Forms tab of the Toolbox can be categorized based on their functions. Depending on the functionality that you want to provide in the user interface of your application, you will select a control from one of the following categories: Commands, Text, Options, Containers, Graphics, Menus, or Dialog boxes. Notice that the class hierarchy and the functional category for a control do not always match one another.

Commands category controls

The following are the categories of command controls:

- **Button**

  Used to start, stop, or interrupt a process.

- **LinkLabel**

  Displays text as a Web-style link and triggers an event when the user clicks the special text. Usually the text is a link to another window or a Web site.

- **NotifyIcon**

  Displays an icon in the status notification area of the taskbar that represents an application running in the background.

- **ToolBar**

  Contains a collection of button controls.

Text category controls

The following text controls are used to enable users to enter text and edit the text contained in these controls at run time:

- **Textbox**

  Displays text entered at design time that can be edited by users at run time, or changed programmatically.

- **RichTextBox**

  Enables text to be displayed with formatting in plain text or rich-text format (RTF).

The following additional text controls can be used to display text but do not allow application users to directly edit the text content that they display:

- **Label**

  Displays text that users cannot directly edit.

- **StatusBar**

  Displays information about the application's current state by using a framed window. A status bar is usually located at the bottom of a parent form.

Options category controls

The following selection controls allow users to select a value from a list:

- **CheckedListBox**

  Displays a scrollable list of items, each accompanied by a check box.

- **ComboBox**

  Displays a drop-down list of items.

- **DomainUpDown**

  Displays a list of text items that users can scroll through by using up and down buttons.

- **ListBox**

  Displays a list of text and graphical items (icons).

- **ListView**

  Displays items in one of four different views. Views include text only, text with small icons, text with large icons, and a report view.

- **NumericUpDown**

  Displays a list of numerals that users can scroll through by using up and down buttons.

- **TreeView**

  Displays a hierarchical collection of node objects that can consist of text with optional check boxes or icons.

Containers category controls

Container controls can be used to group other controls on a form. Some examples of container controls are:

- **Panel**

  Groups a set of controls on an unlabeled, scrollable frame.

- **GroupBox**

  Groups a set of controls (such as radio buttons) on a labeled, nonscrollable frame.

- **TabControl**

  Provides a tabbed page for organizing and accessing grouped objects efficiently.

Graphics category controls

The following are the categories of graphic controls:

- **ImageList**

  Serves as a repository for images. ImageList controls and the images they contain can be reused from one application to the next.

- **PictureBox**

  Displays graphical files, such as bitmaps and icons, in a frame.

Dialog boxes category controls

Visual Studio .NET provides a set of common dialog boxes. These include **ColorDialog**, **FontDialog**, **PageSetupDialog**, **PrintDialog**, **OpenFileDialog**, and so on. You will learn more about dialog boxes in the lesson, Using Dialog Boxes in a Windows Forms Application, in this module.

Menus category controls

The following are the categories of menu controls:

- **MainMenu**

  Provides a design-time interface for creating menus.

- **ContextMenu**

  Implements a menu that appears when the user right-clicks an object.

How to Use the StatusBar Control

1. Add a **StatusBar** control to the form
2. Click the **Panels** property and open the StatusBarPanel Collection Editor
3. Use the Add and Remove buttons to add and remove panels from the **StatusBar** control
4. Configure the properties of the individual panels
5. Click OK to close the dialog box and create the panels you specified
6. In the Properties window, set the **ShowPanels** property to true

Introduction

The **StatusBar** control is an interesting example of a control that is used to display text information. A status bar is a horizontal window at the bottom of a parent window in which an application can display various kinds of status information. The status bar can be divided into parts to display more than one type of information. **StatusBar** controls can have status bar panels on them that display text or icons to indicate state, or a series of icons in an animation that indicate a process is working, such as the status bar in Microsoft Word indicating that the document is being saved.

Procedure: Using the StatusBar control

The .NET Framework offers the **StatusBar** control for the status bar. You can create panels in the status bar by using the **Add** method of the **Panels** collection. To display the panels, you must set the **ShowPanels** property to **True**. You can indicate the size and alignment of each panel by setting additional properties.

To create a status bar with panels:

1. Add a **StatusBar** control to the form.
2. In the Properties window, click the **Panels** property to select it. Then click the ellipsis (…) button to open the StatusBarPanel Collection Editor.
3. Use the **Add** and **Remove** buttons to add and remove panels from the **StatusBar** control at design time. You can use the **Add** and **Remove** methods of the **StatusBarPanels** object to add and remove panels at run time.
4. Configure the properties of the individual panels in the Properties window. The following table lists the important properties and their descriptions.

Property	Description
AutoSize	Determines the resize behavior of the panel.
Alignment	Sets the alignment of the panel in the **StatusBar** control.
BorderStyle	The type of border displayed at the edges of the panel.
Icon	The icon (.ico file) displayed in the panel.
Style	Sets the style of the panel. It must be one of the values of the **StatusBarPanelStyle** enumeration.
Text	The text string displayed in the panel.
MinWidth	The minimum width of the panel in the status bar.

5. Click **OK** to close the dialog box and create the panels you specified.
6. In the Properties window, set the **ShowPanels** property to **True**.

How to Use the ListBox Control

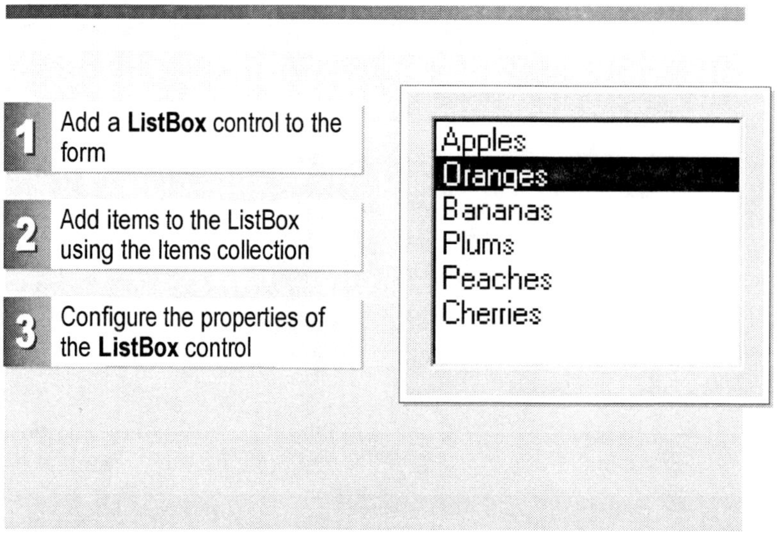

Introduction

The **ListBox** control is a good example of a control from the options category of controls. A Windows Forms **ListBox** control displays a list of items from which the user can select one or more. If the total number of items exceeds the number that can be displayed, a scroll bar is automatically added to the **ListBox** control.

ListBox properties

The following table lists the important properties of the **ListBox** control.

Property	Description
MultiColumn	When set to **True**, the list box displays items in multiple columns and a horizontal scroll bar appears. When set to **False**, the list box displays items in a single column and a vertical scroll bar appears.
ScrollAlwaysVisible	When set to **True**, the scroll bar appears regardless of the number of items.
SelectionMode	Determines how many list items can be selected at a time.
SelectedIndex	Returns an integer value that corresponds to the first selected item in the list box. If no item is selected, the **SelectedIndex** value is **-1**. If the first item in the list is selected, then the **SelectedIndex** value is **0**.
Items.Count	Reflects the number of items in the list.
Items.Add/Items.Insert	Adds items to the **ListBox** control.
Items.Remove/Items.Clear	Removes items from the **ListBox** control.
DataSource	Binds the **ListBox** to a data source.
DisplayMember	Binds the **ListBox** to a name of the column in the Data source.

Procedure: Using the ListBox control

To use a **ListBox** control:

1. Add a **ListBox** control to the form.
2. Add items to the **ListBox** by using the **Items** collection.

   You can add multiple items to the **ListBox** at the same time by using the **AddRange** method.

   ```
   ListBox1.Items.Addrange(NewObject() {"Apples", "Oranges",
   "Bananas"})
   ```
3. Configure the properties of the **ListBox** control.

How to Use the GroupBox and Panel Controls

1. Drag a container (Panel or GroupBox) control from the Toolbox onto a form
2. Add other controls to the container control, drawing each inside the panel
3. If you have existing controls that you want to enclose in the container, drag them into the container
4. To display scroll bars for the **Panel** control, set its **AutoScrollbar** property to **True**
5. To display a caption on the GroupBox, set its **Text** property to an appropriate caption

Introduction

When you want the user to select one or more options from a group of available options, you typically use check boxes (more than one selection) or radio buttons (single selection) grouped inside a container control. All controls in a container control function as a group. The following are three main reasons to group controls:

- Visual grouping of related form elements for a clear user interface
- Moving the controls as a unit at design time
- Programmatic grouping of controls

Visual Studio .NET includes container controls such as **GroupBox** and **Panel** that allow you to group radio buttons, check boxes, or any other controls that you want to treat as part of a control collection. The **Panel** control is similar to the **GroupBox** control, however the **Panel** control can have scroll bars, and only the **GroupBox** control displays a caption.

Procedure: Creating and populating container controls

To create and populate a container control:

1. Drag a container (**Panel** or **GroupBox**) control from the Windows Forms tab of the Toolbox onto a form.
2. Add other controls to the container control, drawing each inside the panel.
3. If you have existing controls that you want to enclose in the container, drag them into the container.
4. To display scroll bars for the **Panel** control, set its **AutoScrollbar** property to **True**.
5. To display a caption on the **GroupBox**, set its **Text** property to an appropriate caption.

The controls grouped in a container control can be accessed by using the **Controls** property. Each control that is grouped inside a **Panel** or a **GroupBox** is a member of the **Control.ControlCollection** object, which is assigned to the **Control** property of the container. You will learn more about the ControlCollection in the lesson, Adding Controls at Run Time, in this module.

How to Use the ToolBar and ImageList Controls

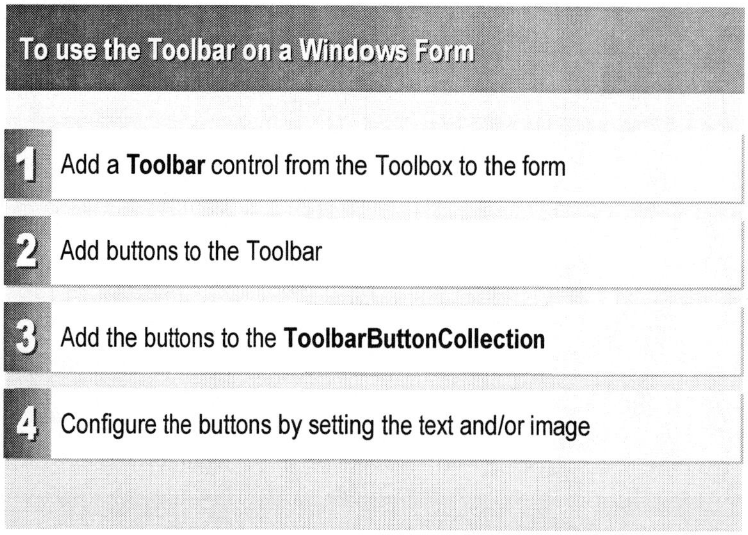

Introduction

The **ToolBar** control is a good example of a control that is used to accept user commands. Toolbars are an alternative graphical user interface (GUI) element to menus. A toolbar contains a set of buttons, which are represented by the **ToolBarButton** class in the .NET Framework.

Procedure: Using the ToolBar

To use a **ToolBar** in a Windows Forms application:

1. Add a **Toolbar** from the Toolbox to the form.
2. Add buttons to the **Toolbar**.

   You can use the **Buttons** property to add buttons to the **Toolbar**.
3. Add the buttons to the **ToolbarButtonCollection** by using the **Buttons** property.

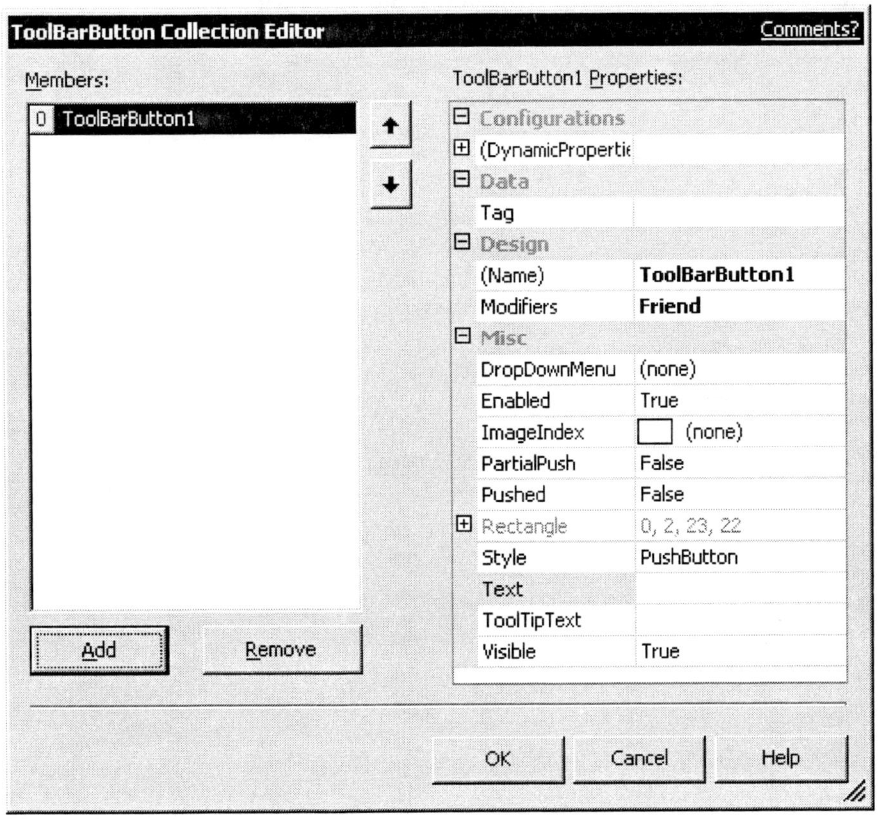

4. Configure the buttons by setting the text, image, and so on.

   Each button on the **Toolbar** can have its own look. The caption and the image are optional. Similar to the **ListView** and **TreeView** control, toolbar images are stored in an image list. The **ToolBarButton** class has an **Index** property which refers to the image in this list.

   Toolbar buttons can appear in different types. The **Style** property can be set to one of the **ToolBarButtonStyle** values shown in the following table.

Value	Description
DropDownButton	A drop-down control that displays a menu or other window when clicked.
PushButton	A standard, three-dimensional button.
Separator	A space or line between toolbar buttons. The appearance depends on the value of the **Appearance** property.
ToggleButton	A toggle button that appears sunken when clicked and retains the sunken appearance until clicked again.

Note To display a tooltip for a button, set the **ShowToolTips** property to **True**. You can define the content of a tooltip by setting the **ToolTipText** property of the button.

Procedure: Using the ImageList

The Windows Forms **ImageList** control is used to store images, which can then be displayed by controls. For example, you can enable the button to display different images by changing the **ImageIndex** property. You can also associate the same image list with multiple controls. You can use an image list with any control that has an **ImageList** property—or, in the case of the **ListView** control, the **SmallImageList** and **LargeImageList** properties. The controls that can be associated with an image list include the **ListView**, **TreeView**, **ToolBar**, **TabControl**, **Button**, **CheckBox**, **RadioButton**, and **Label** controls.

To associate the image list with a control, set the control's **ImageList** property to the name of the **ImageList** control. The key property of the **ImageList** control is **Images**, which contains the pictures to be used by the associated control. Each individual image can be accessed by its index value. The **ColorDepth** property determines the number of colors that the images are rendered with. The images are all displayed at the same size; this is determined by the **ImageSize** property. Images that are larger will be scaled to fit.

Procedure: Triggering events for toolbar buttons

If your Windows Forms application features a **ToolBar** control with buttons, you will want to know which button the user clicks. To determine which button is clicked, add an event handler to the **ButtonClick** event of **ToolBar** control. Use a **Select Case** statement and the **ToolBarButtonClickEventArgs** class to determine the toolbar button that is clicked. The following example shows how to use the **Button** property of the **ToolBarButtonClickEventArgs** object to determine which button is clicked.

Note The following code example uses the **Tag** property to determine the control that is clicked, but you can also do this by using the index value of a control. However, using the index value of controls makes it difficult to keep track of controls and their corresponding index values. For example, if you have a separator in your form, the separator will also use an index value, and you need to take the separator into account when referencing the index value.

```
Private Sub ToolBar1_ButtonClick(ByVal sender As _
System.Object, ByVal e As _
System.Windows.Forms.ToolBarButtonClickEventArgs) Handles _
ToolBar1.ButtonClick
      Select Case e.Button.Tag
          Case "Cut"
              Me.cutRadioButton.Checked = True
              Me.StatusBar1.Panels(0).Text = _
              Me.cutRadioButton.Text & _
              " Radio Button is checked"

          Case "Copy"
              Me.copyRadioButton.Checked = True
              Me.StatusBar1.Panels(0).Text = _
              Me.copyRadioButton.Text & _
              " Radio Button is checked"

      End Select

      MessageBox.Show("The " & e.Button.Tag & _
      " button is index number " & _
      ToolBar1.Buttons.IndexOf(e.Button) & " on the toolbar")

End Sub
```

Practice: Creating and Using a ToolBar Control

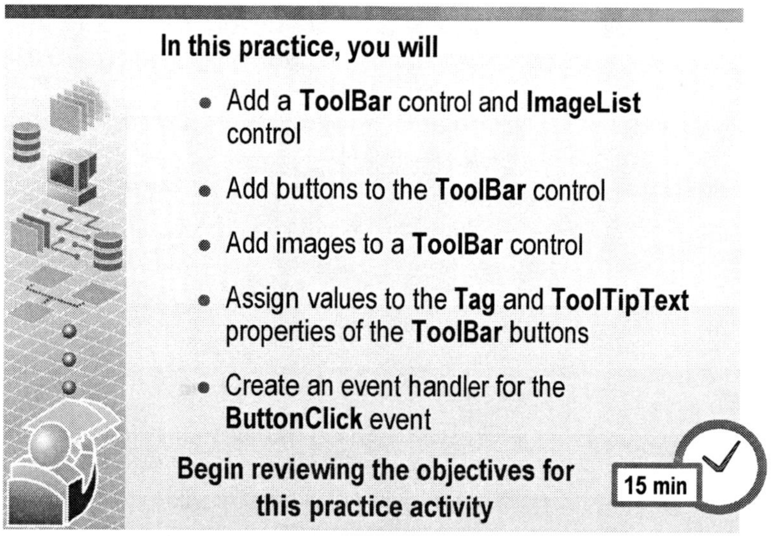

Introduction

In this practice, you will create and use a **ToolBar** control.

Instructions

► **Open the practice project**

1. Using Windows Explorer, navigate to *install_folder*\Practices\Mod02\Mod02_02\Starter.
2. Double-click the **ToolBar.sln** solution file to open the project.

► **Add a ToolBar control and ImageList control to your project**

1. Open Form1.vb in Design view.
2. In the Toolbox, double-click **ImageList**.
3. In the Toolbox, double-click **ToolBar**.

► **Add buttons to the ToolBar control**

1. On the form, click **ToolBar1**.
2. In the ToolBar1 Properties window, click **Buttons**.
3. In the value column for the **Buttons** property, click the **ellipsis** (…) button.
4. On the ToolBarButton Collection Editor window, click **Add**.
5. Use the **Add** button to add six more buttons to the **ToolBar** control.
6. Click **ToolBarButton5**, and then, in the properties table, click **Style**.
7. In the **Style** property value list, click **Separator**.

8. Why can't you add images to the **ToolBar** buttons yet?

____

____

____

9. Click **OK**.

▶ **Add images to a ToolBar control by using an ImageList control**

1. In the **ToolBar1** Properties window, scroll down until you see the **ImageList** property, and then click **ImageList**.
2. Open the list for the **ImageList** property, and then click **ImageList1**.
3. In the component tray at the bottom of Design view, click **ImageList1**.
4. In the **ImageList1** Properties window, click **Images**.
5. In the value column for the **Images** property, click the **ellipsis** (…) button.
6. In the **Image Collection Editor** dialog box, click **Add**.
7. In the **Look in** list, navigate to *install_folder*\Practices\Mod02\Mod02_02\Starter\bin, click **CUT.BMP**, and then click **Open**.
8. Repeat steps 6 and 7 to add the Copy.bmp, Paste.bmp, Delete.bmp, New.bmp, and Open.bmp images to **ImageList1**, and then click **OK**.
9. Open the ToolBarButton Collection Editor, and then click **ToolBarButton1**.
10. In the ToolBarButton1 Properties window, click **ImageIndex**, and then, in the **ImageIndex property** value list, click **image index 0** (the scissors icon).
11. Use the properties table for ToolBar buttons 2-4 and 6-7 to assign a value to the **ImageIndex** property. When you have finished adding images to **ToolBar1**, it should appear as follows:

12. Click **OK**, and then save the changes to your application.
13. Run the application. Does anything happen when you click a ToolBar button? What event must be handled to respond to **ToolBar** button clicks?

____

____

14. Close the application.

► **Assign values to the Tag and ToolTipText properties of the ToolBar buttons**

1. Open the ToolBarButton Collection Editor, and then click **ToolBarButton1**.
2. In the ToolBarButton1 Properties table, double-click **Tag**, type **Cut** and then press ENTER.
3. Use the properties table for **ToolBarButton2**, **ToolBarButton3**, **ToolBarButton4**, **ToolBarButton6**, and **ToolBarButton7** to assign **Tag** property values to the buttons in the following order: **Copy**, **Paste**, **Delete**, **New**, and **Open**.
4. In the **ToolBarButton1** Properties table, double-click **ToolTipText**, type **Cut item** and then press ENTER.
5. Optional: Use the Properties table for **ToolBarButton2**, **ToolBarButton3**, **ToolBarButton4**, **ToolBarButton6**, and **ToolBarButton7** to assign **ToolTipText** property values to the buttons in the following order: **Copy item**, **Paste item**, **Delete an existing item**, **Create a New item**, and **Open an existing item**.
6. Click **OK**, and then save the changes to your application.

► **Create an event handler for the ButtonClick event**

1. Open Form1.vb in the Code Editor.
2. In the **Class Name** list, click **ToolBar1**.
3. In the **Method Name** list, click **ButtonClick**.
4. Add the following code statements to the **ToolBar1_ButtonClick** subroutine:

```
Select Case e.Button.Tag
   Case "Cut"
       Me.cutRadioButton.Checked = True
       panelText = Me.cutRadioButton.Text & _
       " Radio Button is checked"

End Select
Me.StatusBar1.Panels(0).Text = panelText
MessageBox.Show("The " & e.Button.Tag & _
" button is index number " & _
ToolBar1.Buttons.IndexOf(e.Button))
```

5. On the **View** menu, point to **Show Tasks**, and then click **Comment**.
6. In the Task List, double-click **TODO: paste inside Select Case**.
7. Use a cut-and-paste operation to move the commented code inside the Select Case structure that you just created, and then uncomment the code statements.

8. What are some of the reasons for using the **Tag** property to determine which **ToolBar** button was clicked?

   ____

   ____

9. Run the application. Test the ToolTips for the **ToolBar** buttons by positioning the mouse pointer over a button. Test the **ButtonClick** event handler by clicking the **ToolBar** buttons.

10. If time permits, examine the code used to construct the **StatusBar** control.

11. Save your project, and then close Visual Studio.

Demonstration: Implementing Drag-and-Drop Operations Between Controls

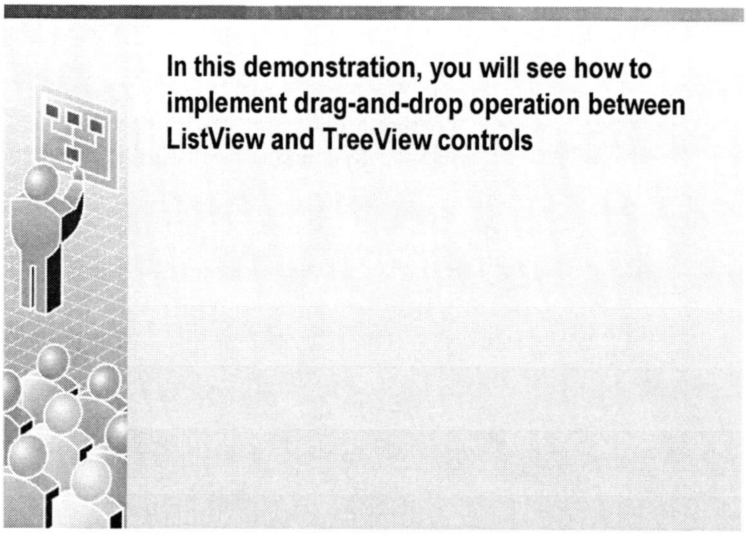

Introduction

Another way in which you can enhance the usefulness of the controls you add to your application is to enable drag-and-drop operations. The concept of drag-and-drop functionality is familiar to users, and in some cases, it is even expected. The manner in which you implement drag-and-drop functionality depends on the controls being used. The following demonstration walks you through the code that must be added to an application to use drag-and-drop operations to move data between two **TextBox** controls, and between two **TreeView** controls.

Instructions

► **Open the SimpleDragDrop solution file**

- Open the SimpleDragDrop.sln solution in Visual Studio .NET from *install_folder*\Democode\Mod02\Mod02_04\SimpleDragDrop.

► **Run the application and demonstrate a drag-and-drop operation between the TextBox controls**

1. Run the application.
2. Position the mouse over the **TextBox** control on the left side of the form.
3. Use a left-click and drag operation to drag the contents of the left **TextBox** control and position it over the upper-right TextBox.
4. Notice that the mouse pointer changes to indicate when a control has been configured to accept dropped data. This control will not accept dropped data.
5. With the mouse positioned over the upper-right TextBox, release the left mouse button.
6. Use a left-click and drag operation to drag the contents of the left **TextBox** control to a position over the lower-right **TextBox** control.

7. Notice that the mouse pointer changes to indicate that this control will accept dropped data.
8. With the mouse positioned over the lower-right **TextBox** control, release the left mouse button.
9. Close the application.

► **Walk through the code that is used to support drag-and-drop operations between two TextBox controls**

1. Open Form1.vb in Design view.
2. Click the upper-right **TextBox** control. Notice that the **AllowDrop** property is set to False.
3. Click the lower-right **TextBox** control. Notice that the **AllowDrop** property is set to True.
4. Open Form1.vb in the Code Editor.
5. Examine the TextBox1_MouseDown handler that is used to initiate this drag-and-drop operation.

   Notice that the **DoDragDrop** method is used to specify the data that will be used in the drag-and-drop operation. The **DoDragDrop** method is also used to specify the type, or types, of operations allowed. The information associated with this operation is stored in the event arguments variable.
6. Examine the TextBox2_DragEnter handler.

   Notice that the data type of the data being dragged is checked to ensure that the data can be used as intended. The *DragEventArgs* parameter is used to access the data, and, if the data is of an inappropriate type, the **DragEventArgs.Effect** property is set to **DragDropEffects.None**.
7. Examine the TextBox2_DragDrop handler.

   Notice that data contained in the **GetData** method of the **DragEventArgs.Data** property is used to extract the data that will be placed in the control.

► **Run the application and demonstrate a drag-and-drop operation between TreeView controls**

1. Run the application.
2. Position the mouse over the Mustard node displayed on the left **TreeView** control.
3. Use a left-click and drag operation to drag the Mustard node to a position over the Garnishes node of the right **TreeView** control.
4. With the mouse positioned over the Garnishes node, release the left mouse button.
5. Close the application.

► Walk through the code that is used to support drag-and-drop operations between two TreeView controls

1. Open Form1.vb in the Code Editor.
2. Examine the **TreeView_ItemDrag** handler that is used to initiate this drag-and-drop operation.

   Notice the **TreeView** control includes a special event designed for initiating a drag-and-drop operation. The **DoDragDrop** method is used again to specify the data (in this case the currently selected item) that will be used in the drag-and-drop operation if the type of operation is allowed.
3. Examine the **TreeView_DragEnter** handler.

   Notice that the **DragEnter** event handler is used in the same way it was used when performing a drag-and-drop operation between **TextBox** controls.
4. Examine the **TreeView_DragDrop** handler.

   Notice how **TreeNodes** are handled in this procedure.
5. Close Visual Studio .NET.

Lesson: Using Dialog Boxes in a Windows Forms Application

- Selecting Dialog Boxes in Visual Studio .NET
- How to Display Dialog Boxes in an Application
- DialogResult Property
- How to Use Input from Dialog Boxes
- Demonstration: Using the OpenFileDialog Control

Introduction

Dialog boxes are used to interact with the user and retrieve user input. Visual Studio .NET provides some preconfigured dialogs that can be used in Windows Forms applications to interact with users. This lesson introduces the standard dialogs provided by Visual Studio .NET and also covers how to use these dialog boxes to retrieve user input.

Lesson objectives

After completing this lesson, you will be able to:

- Select appropriate Visual Studio .NET dialog boxes for a Windows Forms application.
- Use the dialog boxes available in Visual Studio .NET in a Windows Forms application.
- Retrieve user input by using the **DialogResult** property.

Selecting Dialog Boxes in Visual Studio .NET

OpenFileDialog	Allows users to open files through a preconfigured dialog box
SaveFileDialog	Selects files to save and the location where they are saved
ColorDialog	Allows users to select a color from the palette and add colors to it
FontDialog	Exposes the fonts that are currently installed on the system
PrintDialog	Selects a printer and other printer-related settings
PageSetupDialog	Sets up page details for printing
PrintPreviewDialog	Displays a document as it would appear when it is printed

Introduction

Visual Studio .NET includes a set of preconfigured dialogs boxes, which you can adapt for your own applications. Depending on the requirement of the application, you can select an appropriate dialog box from any of the preconfigured dialog boxes.

OpenFileDialog

Use the **OpenFileDialog** control in a Windows Forms application as a simple solution for file selection instead of configuring your own dialog box. When using the **OpenFileDialog** control, you must write your own file-opening logic. **OpenFileDialog** is the same **File Open** dialog box used in the Microsoft Windows® operating system. When it is added to a form, the **OpenFileDialog** control appears in the tray at the bottom of the Windows Forms Designer. It inherits from the **CommonDialog** class.

SaveFileDialog

The **SaveFileDialog** control enables users to save files in an application. As with the other dialog boxes, when using the **SaveFileDialog** control, you must write your own file-saving logic. **SaveFileDialog** is the same as the standard **Save File** dialog box used by Windows. It inherits from the **CommonDialog** class.

ColorDialog

The Windows Forms **ColorDialog** control is a preconfigured dialog box that allows the user to select a color from a palette and to add custom colors to that palette. It is the same dialog box that you see in other Windows applications to select colors.

The color selected in the dialog box is returned in the **Color** property. If the **AllowFullOpen** property is set to **False**, the **Define Custom Colors** button is disabled and the user is restricted to the predefined colors in the palette. If the **SolidColorOnly** property is set to **True**, the user cannot select dithered colors.

FontDialog

The Windows Forms **FontDialog** control is the standard Windows **Font** dialog box used to expose the fonts that are currently installed on the system. By default, the dialog box includes options for Font, Font style, and Size. It also includes check boxes for effects like Strikeout and Underline, and a drop-down list for Script.

PrintDialog

The **PrintDialog** control is used to select a printer, choose the pages to print, and determine other print-related settings in Windows applications. You can provide users with options such as print all, print a specified page range, or print a selection.

PageSetupDialog

The **PageSetupDialog** control is used to set page details for printing in Windows applications. You can enable users to set border and margin adjustments, headers and footers, and portrait or landscape orientation.

The **PageSetupDialog** allows users to set properties that relate to either a single page (**PrintDocument** class) or any document (**PageSettings** class). Additionally, the **PageSetupDialog** control can be used to determine specific printer settings, which are stored in the **PrinterSettings** class.

PrintPreviewDialog

The **PrintPreviewDialog** control is used to display how a document will appear when printed. The control contains buttons for printing, zooming in, displaying one or multiple pages, and closing the dialog box.

How to Display Dialog Boxes in an Application

- **To display a preconfigured Visual Studio .NET dialog box**

```
Private Sub Button1_Click(ByVal sender as
  System.Object,ByVal e as System.EventsArgs)
  OpenFileDialog1.ShowDialog()
End Sub
```

- **To display a message dialog box**

```
Private Sub PerformSearch()
MessageBox.Show("The search is now complete", _
  "My Application", MessageBoxButtons.OKCancel, _
  MessageBoxIcon.Asterisk)
End Sub
```

Introduction

You display dialog boxes in an application the same way you display a form. To display any of the Visual Studio .NET dialog boxes in an application, you need to write the code to load and display it, just the way you would display a second form in the main form.

Procedure: Displaying a preconfigured dialog box

To display a preconfigured dialog box:

1. In the Code Editor, navigate to the event handler with which you want to open the dialog box.

   The first step is to locate the event handler that will be used to display the dialog box. In an application, a dialog box is typically opened in response to a button click or a menu command, but any event can be used.

2. Add the code to show the dialog box.

   You use the **ShowDialog** method to display a dialog box in Windows Forms applications.

```
Private Sub Button1_Click(ByVal sender as
System.Object,ByVal e as System.EventsArgs)
  OpenFileDialog1.ShowDialog()
End Sub
```

Procedure: Displaying a message box

You can display a message box by using the **Show** method of the **MessageBox** class. The **Show** method requires that you supply the text of the message and you can optionally specify the following: the dialog box caption, the buttons, the icon, the default button, and options relating to how the message box and the text that it contains will display.

```
Private Sub PerformSearch()
MessageBox.Show("The search is now complete", _ "My
Application", MessageBoxButtons.OKCancel, _
MessageBoxIcon.Asterisk)
End Sub
```

DialogResult Property

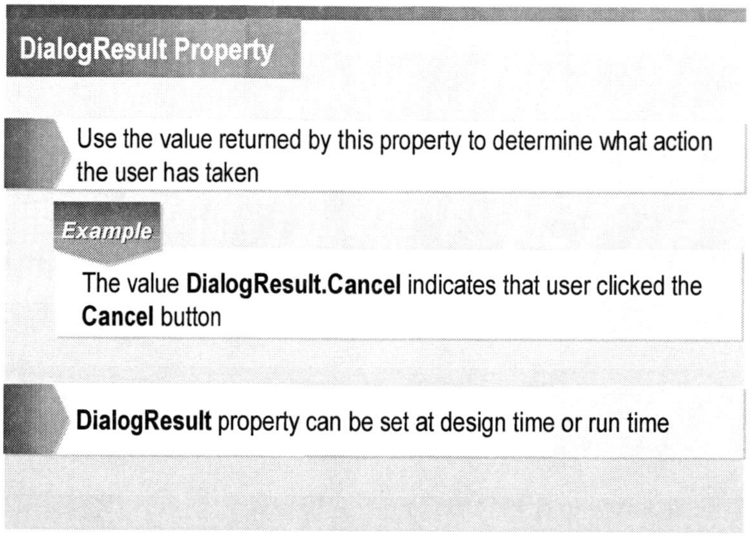

Introduction

When you display a dialog box in an application, it is very important to know the result input. For example, if you display a dialog box that prompts the user to **OK** or **Cancel** an action, you need to know whether the user clicked the **OK** or the **Cancel** button.

DialogResult property

The user input in any dialog box is processed by the form that displays the dialog box. You can use the **DialogResult** property of the form to determine the result of the user input. Based on the value returned by the **DialogResult** property, you can decide whether to discard or use the information returned by the dialog box.

Example

If a user clicks the **Cancel** button in a dialog box, the value of the **DialogResult** property is set to **DialogResult.Cancel**. The parent form then retrieves this value and discards the information in the dialog box.

Set DialogResult property at design time or run time

You can set the **DialogResult** property at design time or run time. At design time, you can set the **DialogResult** property for all the button controls in the dialog box. Setting the **DialogResult** property at run time allows you to dynamically handle user responses.

How to Use Input from Dialog Boxes

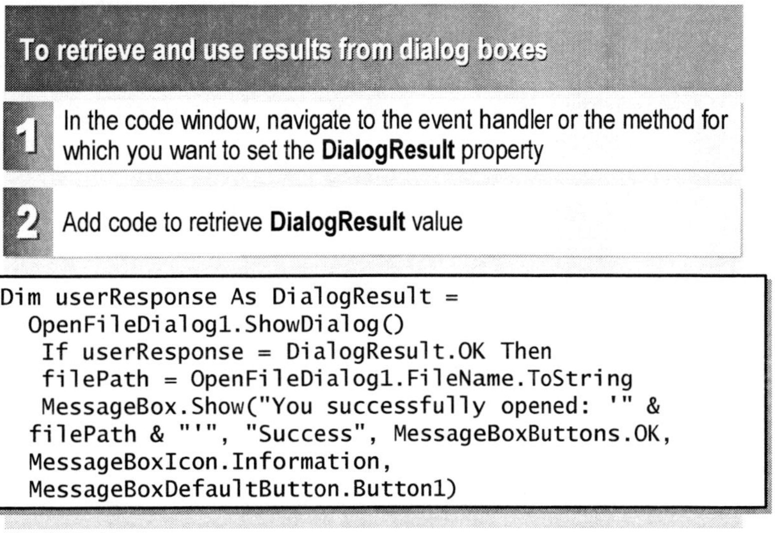

Introduction

After the dialog box is closed, the form that displayed the dialog box can reference the values from the **DialogResult** property.

Procedure

To retrieve and use input from a dialog box:

1. In the Code Editor, navigate to the event handler or the method for which you want to set the **DialogResult** property.
2. Add code to retrieve the **DialogResult** value.

   The following code shows how user input is retrieved from an **Open File** dialog box.

```
Dim userResponse As DialogResult =
OpenFileDialog1.ShowDialog()
If userResponse = DialogResult.OK Then
   filePath = OpenFileDialog1.FileName.ToString
   MessageBox.Show("You successfully opened: '" _
   & filePath & "'", "Success", _
   MessageBoxButtons.OK, _
   MessageBoxIcon.Information, _
   MessageBoxDefaultButton.Button1)
  Else
   MessageBox.Show("You canceled the open _
   file operation.", "Warning", _
   MessageBoxButtons.OK, _
   MessageBoxIcon.Warning, _
   MessageBoxDefaultButton.Button1, _
   MessageBoxOptions.RightAlign)
End If
```

Demonstration: Using the OpenFileDialog Control

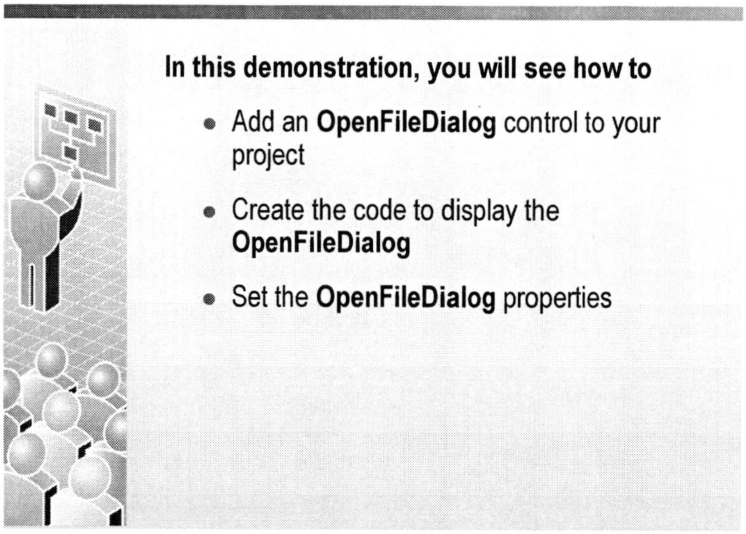

Introduction

In this demonstration, you will see how to use the **OpenFileDialog** control in a Windows Forms application.

Instructions

► **Open the OpenFileDialog.sln file**

- Open the OpenFileDialog.sln solution in Visual Studio .NET from *install_folder*\Democode\Mod02\Mod02_05\Starter.

► **Add an OpenFileDialog control to your project**

1. Open Form1.vb in Design view.
2. In the Toolbox, double-click **OpenFileDialog**.

► **Create the code to display the OpenFileDialog**

1. Open Form1.vb in the Code Editor.
2. On the **View** menu, point to **Show Tasks**, and then click **Comment**.
3. In the Task List, double-click **TODO: show the OpenFileDialog and check DialogResult**.
4. Add the following code statement below the TODO line:
   ```
   OpenFileDialog1.ShowDialog
   ```
5. Run the application, and then click **Use the OpenFileDialog Control**.
6. Click **Cancel**, and then close the application.
7. What can you do to determine if the dialog box was closed by clicking **Open** or by clicking **Cancel**?

   ____

   ____

8. Replace the 'OpenFileDialog1.ShowDialog' code statement with the following code statements:

```
If OpenFileDialog1.ShowDialog = DialogResult.OK Then
   filePath = OpenFileDialog1.FileName.ToString
   MessageBox.Show("You successfully opened: '" & _
       filePath & "'", _
       "Success", _
       MessageBoxButtons.OK, _
       MessageBoxIcon.Information, _
       MessageBoxDefaultButton.Button1)

Else
   MessageBox.Show("You canceled the operation.", _
       "Warning", _
       MessageBoxButtons.OK, _
       MessageBoxIcon.Warning, _
       MessageBoxDefaultButton.Button1, _
       MessageBoxOptions.RightAlign)

End If
```

9. Run the application, and then click **Use the OpenFileDialog Control**.
10. Click **Cancel**, and then close the application.

► **Set the OpenFileDialog properties**

1. In the Task List, double-click **TODO: set the initial directory and filter properties**.
2. Add the following code statement below the TODO line:

```
OpenFileDialog1.InitialDirectory = Application.StartupPath
OpenFileDialog1.Filter = "Text Files (*.txt)|*.txt"
```

3. Run the application, and then click **Use the OpenFileDialog Control**.
4. Use both **Open** and **Cancel** to close the dialog box, and then close the application.
5. What happens when you select a file and click **Open**?

____

____

____

6. If time permits, experiment with additional **OpenFileDialog** properties, such as **Multiselect** and **CheckPathExists**, and modify the appearance of the message dialog boxes.
7. Save your project, and then close Visual Studio .NET.

Lesson: Adding Controls at Run Time

- Controls Collection
- How to Add Controls at Run Time
- Practice: Adding and Removing Controls at Run Time

Introduction

Visual Studio .NET provides you with the flexibility of adding controls at run time. This lesson introduces the controls collection and how controls can be added at run time.

Lesson objectives

After completing this lesson, you will be able to:

- Use the **Controls** property to access the **ControlCollection** object of a container.
- Add and remove controls from a container at run time.

Controls Collection

- **Controls Collection**
  - Represents a collection of Control objects
  - Use the **Add**, **Remove**, and **RemoveAt** methods to add and remove controls from the collection

```
Form1.Controls.Add(textbox1)
```

```
Form1.Controls.Remove(textbox1)
```

  - Use the **Contains** method to determine whether or not a control is a part of the collection

```
Form1.Controls.Contains(textbox1)
```

Introduction

Visual Studio .NET provides a collection object that contains all the controls on a form or on a container control. This object is known as the **ControlCollection** object and is accessed by using the **Controls** property of the form or control. The controls collection represents a collection of Control objects. You can add and remove controls from a container at run time by using the **Controls** property. The **ControlCollection Count** property returns the number of controls on the container and can be used to loop through the controls collection.

ControlCollection Methods

The following table lists some of the methods of **ControlCollection**.

Method	**Description**
Add	Adds the specified control to the control collection.
AddRange	Adds an array of control objects to the collection.
Clear	Removes all controls from the collection.
Contains	Determines whether the specified control is a member of the collection.
Remove	Removes the specified control from the control collection.
RemoveAt	Removes a control from the control collection at the specified indexed location.
ToString (inherited from Object)	Returns a String that represents the current Object.
IndexOf	Retrieves the index of the specified control in the control collection.
GetEnumerator	Returns an enumerator that can be used to iterate through the control collection.

How to Add Controls at Run Time

To add controls at run time

1 Create the control that will be added to your container

```
Dim signatureCheckBox As New CheckBox()
' set properties
signatureCheckBox.Left = 24
signatureCheckBox.Top = 80
signatureCheckBox.Text = "Signature required"
```

2 Add the control to the container using the **Add** method of the **Controls** property

```
' add the new control to the collection
GroupBox1.Controls.Add(signatureCheckBox)
```

Introduction

You can add and remove controls at run time by using the **Controls** property. The ability to add controls at run time allows you to customize your application based on user input. For example, you may want the application to display additional menu items depending on the user input.

Procedure

To add controls at run time:

1. Create a control that will be added to the form at run time.

   The following code shows an example of how to create a CheckBox control.

   ```
   Dim signatureCheckBox As New CheckBox()
   ```
2. Add the control to the form or container control by using the **Add** method of the **Controls** property.

   The following code adds the button control at a specific location in the form.

   ```
   signatureCheckBox.Name = "myCheckBox"
   signatureCheckBox.Text = "Signature required"
   signatureCheckBox.Width = 224
   signatureCheckBox.Left = 24
   signatureCheckBox.Top = 80

   GroupBox1.Controls.Add(signatureCheckBox)
   ```

Note When adding several controls to a parent control, it is recommended that you call the **SuspendLayout** method before initializing the controls to be added. After adding the controls to the parent control, call the **ResumeLayout** method. This will increase the performance of applications with many controls.

Practice: Adding and Removing Controls at Run Time

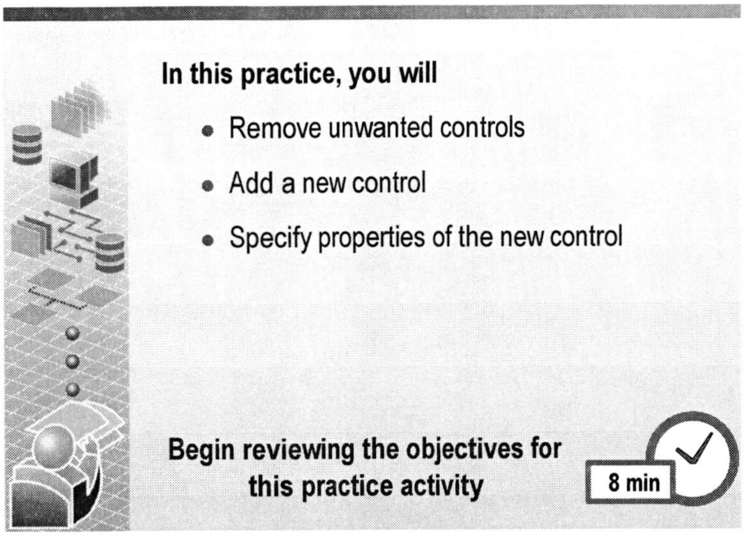

Introduction

In this practice, you will add and remove controls at run time.

Instructions

► **Open the practice project**

1. Using Windows Explorer, navigate to *install_folder*\Practices\Mod02\Mod02_03\Starter.
2. Double-click the **AddingAndRemovingControls.sln** solution file to open the project.

► **Remove unwanted controls**

1. Open Form1.vb in the Code Editor.
2. On the **View** menu, point to **Show Tasks**, and then click **Comment**.
3. In the Task List, double-click **TODO: remove controls from GroupBox1**.
4. Add the following code statements below the TODO line:

```
lcv = GroupBox1.Controls.Count
Do While lcv > 2
   GroupBox1.Controls.Remove(GroupBox1.Controls(lcv - 1))
   lcv -= 1

Loop
```

5. Run the application, click **Use International Policies**, and then click **Use Domestic Policies**.
6. Close the application.

► Add a new control

1. In the Task List, double-click **TODO: create an instance of a CheckBox**.
2. Add the following code statement below the TODO line:

```
Dim decimalCheckBox As New CheckBox()
```

3. In the Task List, double-click **TODO: add a control to GroupBox1**.
4. Add the following code statement below the TODO line:

```
GroupBox1.Controls.Add(decimalCheckBox)
```

5. Run the application, click **Use International Policies**, and then click **Use Domestic Policies**.
6. Why does the **decimalCheckBox** appear in the upper-left corner of **GroupBox1**?

   ____

   ____

7. Close the application.

► Specify properties of the new control

1. In the Task List, double-click **TODO: specify the control properties**.
2. Add the following code statement below the TODO line:

```
decimalCheckBox.Left = 24
decimalCheckBox.Top = _
  GroupBox1.Controls(GroupBox1.Controls.Count - 1).Top _
   + 32
decimalCheckBox.Text = "Use comma separated decimals"
decimalCheckBox.Name = "commaSeparatedDecimalsCheckBox"
```

3. Run the application, click **Use International Policies**, and then click **Use Domestic Policies**.
4. Close the application.
5. In the Task List, double-click **TODO: specify the control properties**.
6. Add the following code statement below the TODO line:

```
decimalCheckBox.Width = 224
```

7. Run the application, click **Use International Policies**, and then click **Use Domestic Policies**.
8. Close the application.

9. If time permits, open Form1.vb in Design view and perform the following steps:

   a. Drag the **Use local dataset when available CheckBox** from **GroupBox1** to **GroupBox2** and then drag it back to its original position on **GroupBox1**.

      This is now the last control added to **GroupBox1**.

   b. Run the application and test your code by clicking the radio buttons.

   c. Remove **Print report automatically** from **GroupBox1** and then replace it.

      Print report automatically is now the last control in the **ControlCollection** of **GroupBox1**.

   d. Test your application again to see that your code now adds controls to **GroupBox1** in the desired locations.

10. Save your project, and then close Visual Studio .NET.

Lesson: Creating Menus

- How to Add a Context Menu to a Form
- How to Add Menu Items at Run Time
- How to Create Event Handlers for Menu Items
- How to Use Menu Properties
- Practice: Updating Menus at Run Time

Introduction

Menus and context menus are ways of exposing functionality to your users or alerting them to important information in your application. Menus hold commands, grouped by a common theme. Context menus pop up in response to a right-click of the mouse and hold commonly used commands for a particular area of an application.

Note You can have multiple main menus for an application. If your application is large, then you could use different menus for different parts of an application.

Lesson objectives

After completing this lesson, you will be able to:

- Create context menus.
- Add menu items at run time.
- Create shortcuts for menus.
- Enable the checked property for menu items.

How to Add a Context Menu to a Form

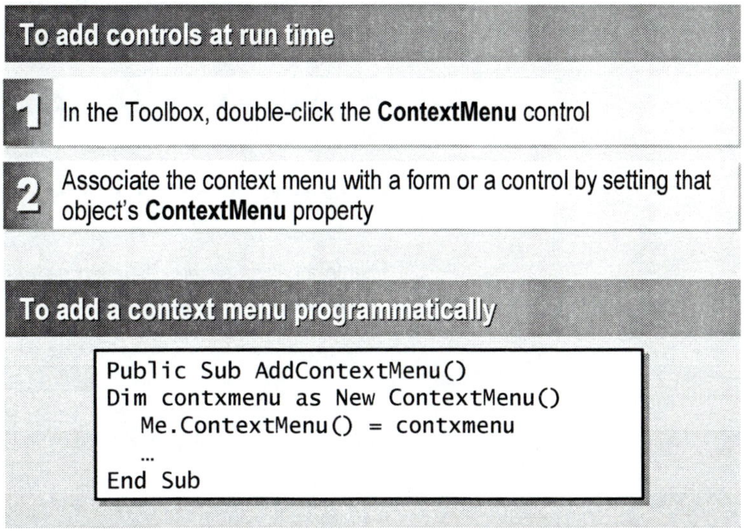

Introduction

The Windows Forms **ContextMenu** control is used to provide users with an easily accessible menu of frequently used commands that are associated with the selected object. The items in a context menu are frequently a subset of the items from main menus that appear elsewhere in the application. Context menus are usually available by right-clicking the mouse. On Windows Forms they are associated with controls.

Procedure: Adding a context menu at design time

To add a context menu at design time:

1. Add the context menu from the Toolbar to the form.

   In the Toolbox, double-click the **ContextMenu** control.

2. Associate the context menu with a form or a control by setting that object's **ContextMenu** property.

   You can associate a context menu with a control by setting the control's **ContextMenu** property to the **ContextMenu** control. You can associate a single context menu with multiple controls, but each control can have only one context menu.

Procedure: Adding a context menu at design time

To add a context menu at design time:

1. Create a new method that will include the code required to create a menu item.

```
Public Sub AddContextMenu()
   ...
End Sub
```

2. Create an instance of the context menu.

   Add the code as shown to create an instance of the context menu.

```
Dim contxmenu as New ContextMenu()
Me.ContextMenu() = contxmenu
```

How to Add Menu Items at Run Time

To add menu items to a context menu at run time

1. Within the method, create **MenuItem** objects to add to the Context Menu Object collection

```
Dim menuItemNew as New MenuItem()
```

2. Within the method, set the Text property for each menu item

```
MenuItemNew.Text = "New"
```

3. Within the method, add menu items to the MenuItems collection of the ContextMenu object

```
contxMenu.MenuItems.Add(menuItemNew)
```

Introduction

After you add a **ContextMenu** control to your form, you add menu items to it. Menu contents are stored in a collection. You can add menu items to a context menu at run time by adding **MenuItem** objects to this collection.

Procedure

The key property of the **ContextMenu** control is the **MenuItems** property. You can add menu items by programmatically creating **MenuItem** objects and adding them to the **MenuItems** collection of the context menu. Because the items in a context menu are usually drawn from other menus, you will most frequently add items to a context menu by copying them. You can also disable, hide, or delete menu items.

To add items to a context menu at run time:

1. In the method to create a context menu, create **MenuItem** objects which are added to the **Controls** collection.

   ```
   Dim menuItemNew as New MenuItem()
   ```
2. Set the **Text** property for each menu item.

   ```
   MenuItemNew.Text ="New"
   ```
3. Add menu items to the **MenuItems** collection of the **ContextMenu** object.

   ```
   contxMenu.MenuItems.Add(menuItemNew)
   ```

Note You can also add images to menu items. To add images to menu items, create an instance of the **MenuItem** class, override the **OnPaint()** method, and draw the image next to the menu item text.

How to Create Event Handlers for Menu Items

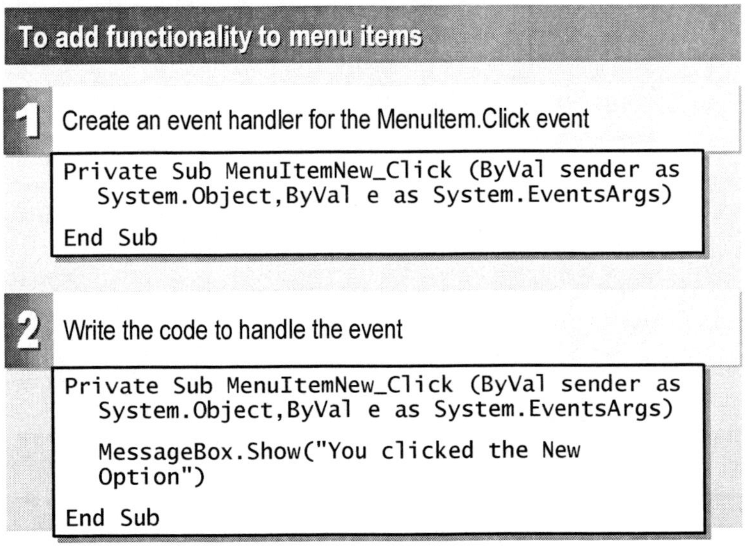

Introduction

After a menu structure is established, you provide functionality to it. You provide functionality to a menu by creating an event handler for the **MenuItem.Click** event and writing code to handle the event.

Procedure

To add functionality to menu items:

1. Create an event handler for **the MenuItem.Click** event.

```
Private Sub MenuItemNew_Click (ByVal sender As
System.Object,ByVal e as System.EventsArgs)
End Sub
```

2. Write the code to handle the **MenuItem.Click** event.

```
Private Sub MenuItemNew_Click (ByVal sender As
System.Object,ByVal e as System.EventsArgs)
   MessageBox.Show("You clicked the New Option")
End Sub
```

How to Use Menu Properties

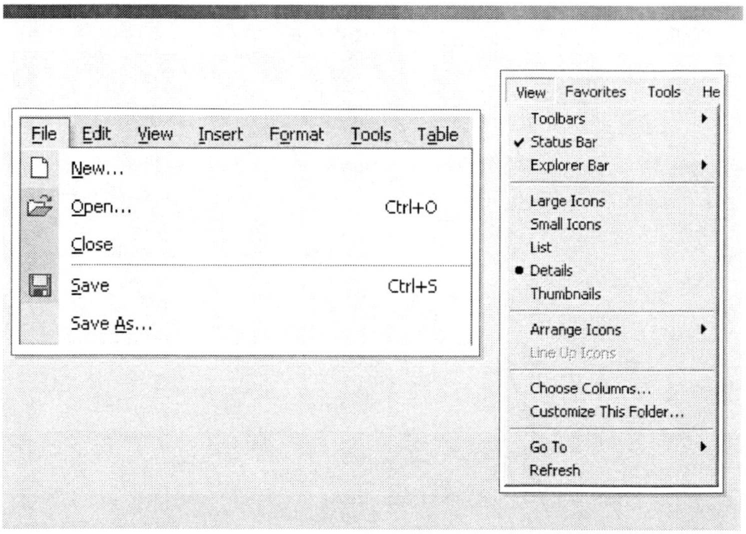

Introduction

Menu items include several properties that enable you to enhance the user experience. These properties include properties for creating shortcut keys and enabling and disabling menu items by using check marks, radio buttons, and so on.

Procedure: Creating shortcut keys

Shortcut keys provide a method for users to activate frequently used menu items in the menu system and to provide keyboard access to the application.

For example, in Microsoft Word, you can open a file by using the Ctrl+O shortcut or save a file by pressing Ctrl+S.

To create a shortcut for menu items:

1. Select the menu item for which you need to create a shortcut.
2. In the **Properties** dialog box, select the **Shortcut** property.

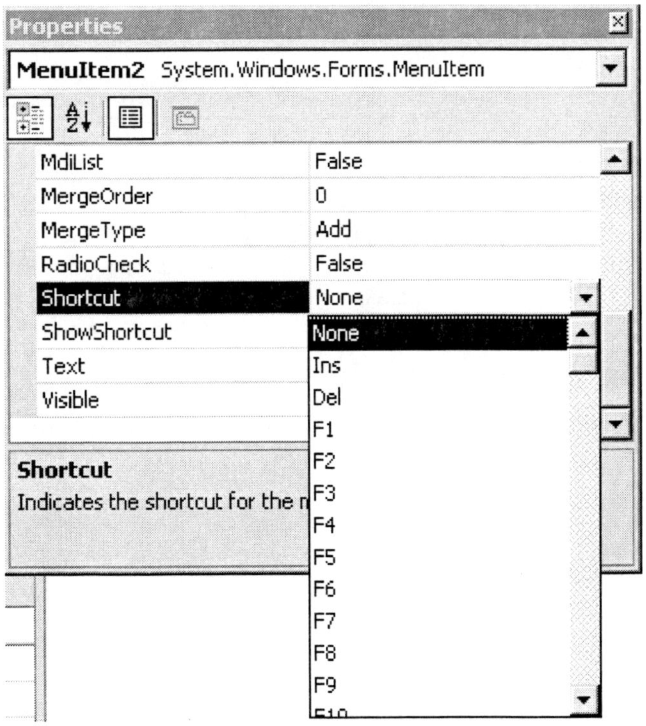

3. Select the required shortcut in the shortcut list.
4. In the **Properties** dialog box, set the **ShowShortcut** property to **True**.

Procedure: Displaying checked menu items

You can use the **Checked** and **RadioCheck** property to identify the selected menu item in a group of mutually exclusive menu items. You can also place a check mark on a menu item in a group of items to identify the size of the font to be displayed for the text in an application.

For example, mutually exclusive items on the **View** menu in Windows Explorer use a check or a radio button to show the selected option.

To display checked menu items:

1. Select the menu item.
2. In the **Properties** dialog box, set the **Checked** property to **True**.

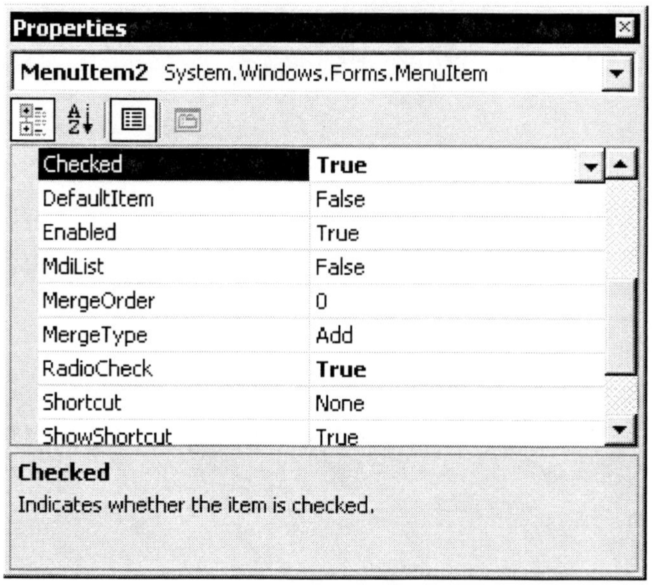

To display the radio check for menu items:

1. Select the menu item.
2. In the **Properties** dialog box, set the **Checked** property to **True**.
3. Set the **RadioCheck** property to **True**.

Procedure: Enabling and disabling menu items

You may want to disable certain menu items for users depending on their roles, permission, or their input. You can use the **Enable** property to enable or disable menu item. If the value of the **Enable** property is set to **True**, the menu item is enabled. However, if the value is set to **False**, the menu item is disabled.

To enable or disable menu items:

1. Select the menu item.
2. Set the **Enabled** property to **True** or **False**.

Practice: Updating Menus at Run Time

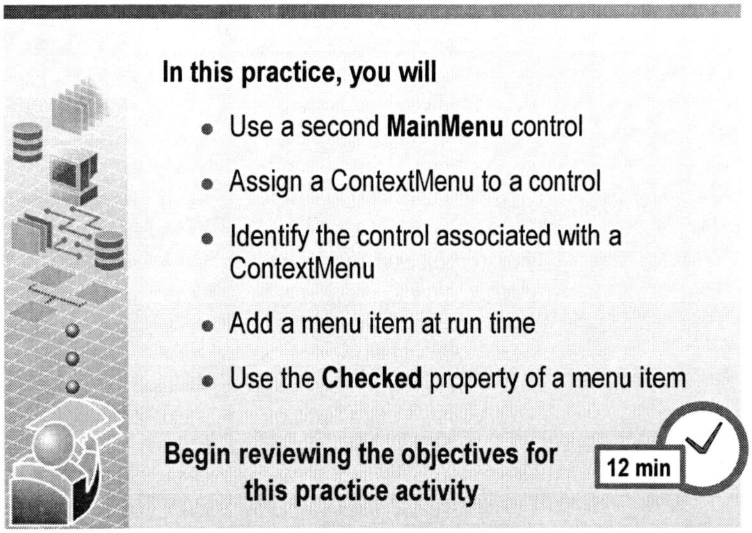

Introduction

In this practice, you will update the menus in an application at run time.

Instructions

► **Open the practice project**

1. Using Windows Explorer, navigate to *install_folder*\Practices\Mod02\Mod02_04\Starter.
2. Double-click the **RuntimeMenus.sln** solution file to open the project.

► **Use a second MainMenu**

1. Run the application, open the **File** menu, and then open the **View** menu.
2. On the **Reports** tab, open the **File** menu, open the **View** menu, and then close the application.

   Notice that the menu items do not really match the requirements of the **Reports** tab.
3. In Solution Explorer, click **Form1**, and then click **View Code**.
4. On the **View** menu, point to **Show Tasks**, and then click **Comment**.
5. In the Task List, double-click **TODO: assign a different MainMenu to a form**.
6. Add the following code statement below the TODO line:

```
Me.Menu = MainMenu2
```

7. Run the application, open the **File** menu, and then open the **View** menu.
8. Click the **Reports** tab, open the **File** menu, and then open the **View** menu again.

9. When would you use more than one **MainMenu** control in an application?

    ____

    ____

10. Close the **View** menu, and then close the application.

► Assign a ContextMenu to a control

1. In the Task List, double-click **TODO: create a control and assign a context menu to it**.
2. Add the following code statements below the TODO line:

```
Dim fileLabel1 As New Label()
fileLabel1.Dock = DockStyle.Top
fileLabel1.Text = Application.StartupPath & "\Chai.txt"
fileLabel1.ContextMenu = ContextMenu1
Me.Panel1.Controls.Add(fileLabel1)
```

3. Run the application, right-click the **Label** control displaying the Chai.txt file path, and then click **Open**.
4. Click **OK**, and then close the application.
5. How can you identify which control is associated with a **ContextMenu**?

    ____

    ____

► Identify the control associated with a ContextMenu

1. In the Task List, double-click **TODO: use the SourceControl property**.
2. Add the following code statements below the TODO line:

```
Panel1.Controls.Remove(ContextMenu1.SourceControl)
```

3. Run the application, right-click the **Label** control displaying the Chai.txt file path, and then click **Remove from list**.
4. On the **View** menu, click **Show Previously Opened Files**, and then open the **File** menu.
5. Close the **File** menu, and then close the application.
6. What method of a **MenuItem** object is used to add a menu item at run time?

    ____

▶ Add a menu item at run time

1. In the Task List, double-click **TODO: add a menu item to a menu.**
2. Add the following code statements below the TODO line:

```
fileMenuItem.MenuItems.Add(previousFile1)
```

3. Run the application, and then, on the **View** menu, click **Show Previously Opened Files.**
4. Open the **File** menu, and then open the **View** menu.

   Notice that the item has been added to the **File** menu.
5. Close the application.
6. Is there any way to show the user that you are currently displaying the previously opened file on the **File** menu?

   ____

   ____

   ____

▶ Use the Checked property of a menu item to signal the user

1. In the Task List, double-click **TODO: display a menu item as checked.**
2. Add the following code statements below the TODO line:

```
viewShowPreviousMenuItem.Checked = True
```

3. Run the application, and then, on the **View** menu, click **Show Previously Opened Files.**
4. Open the **File** menu, and then open the **View** menu.
5. On the **View** menu, click **Show Previously Opened Files.**
6. Open the **File** menu, and then open the **View** menu.
7. If time permits, examine the code used to remove the menu item from the **File** menu and the code used to respond to the click events of the second context menu.
8. Close the application, save your project files, and then close Visual Studio .NET.

Lesson: Validating User Input

- How to Validate Controls by Using the Validating Event
- ErrorProvider Control
- How to Use the ErrorProvider Control
- Demonstration: Validating Data in a Windows Forms Application

Introduction

Whether you are writing a simple calculator application or an interface for a complex database, you will need to validate information entered by a user. This lesson describes how to validate user input in a Windows Forms application. It also describes how to display an error message if the user input is invalid.

Lesson objectives

After completing this lesson, you will be able to:

- Validate user input by using the **Validating** event of a control.
- Use the **ErrorProvider** control to notify the user when an entered value does not meet acceptance criteria.
- Display appropriate error messages when users enter invalid data.

How to Validate Controls by Using the Validating Event

- **Use the Validating event of a control to validate user input**

  CodeExample

- **The Validated event fires after the validation of the controls finishes running the validating events**
- **The CausesValidation property determines whether the previous control will participate in validation. If set to False for a control, the previous control does not fire the validation event**

Introduction

In most applications, a user enters information for the application to process. Data validation ensures that every data value entered into your application is accurate and of a valid data type.

Visual Studio .NET includes the **Validating** event for controls, which occurs before a control loses focus. This event occurs only when the **CausesValidation** property of the control that is about to receive the focus is set to **True** (which is the default). Use both the **Validating** event and **CausesValidation** property for a control to evaluate input before allowing the user to move focus away from that control.

Validating event

The simplest way to validate data in a Windows Forms application is to use the **Validating** event. The **Validating** event also allows you to control when focus can be moved to other controls. By using the **Validating** event, you can prevent the focus from shifting to another control until all validation rules have been met. Possible uses for the **Validating** event include:

- A data entry application must perform more sophisticated validation than is provided by the **Masked Edit** control.
- A form must prevent users from moving off a control, by pressing TAB or a shortcut key, until data has been entered in a field.

CausesValidation property

The **CausesValidation** property works with the **Validating** event to limit when a control can lose focus. You can set the **CausesValidation** property to determine whether the **Validating** event will occur on a second control from which the focus is being shifted. If the **Validating** event is being handled for a **TextBox**, and the user clicks a button that has its **CausesValidation** property set to **True**, the **Validating** event for the text box will fire. However, if the **CausesValidation** property for the button is set to **False**, the **Validating** event will not fire. By default, the **CausesValidation** property is set to **True** for all controls.

Procedure: Validating a control

To use the **Validating** event of a **TextBox** control:

1. Add a **TextBox** control to a form.
2. In the Code Editor, in the procedure list, click the **Validating** event.
3. Type a validation code in the **Validating** event for the **TextBox**.

```
Private Sub minValueTextBox_Validating(ByVal sender As
Object, ByVal e As System.ComponentModel.CancelEventArgs)
Handles minValueTextBox.Validating
   If CInt(minValueTextBox.Text) >= _
   CInt(maxValueTextBox.Text) Then
       e.Cancel = True
           MessageBox.Show("You must enter a minimum" & _
           "value that is less than the maximum value")
End If
```

4. Set the **CausesValidation** property to **False** for any controls for which you do not want the **Validating** event to fire, such as a **Help** button.

ErrorProvider Control

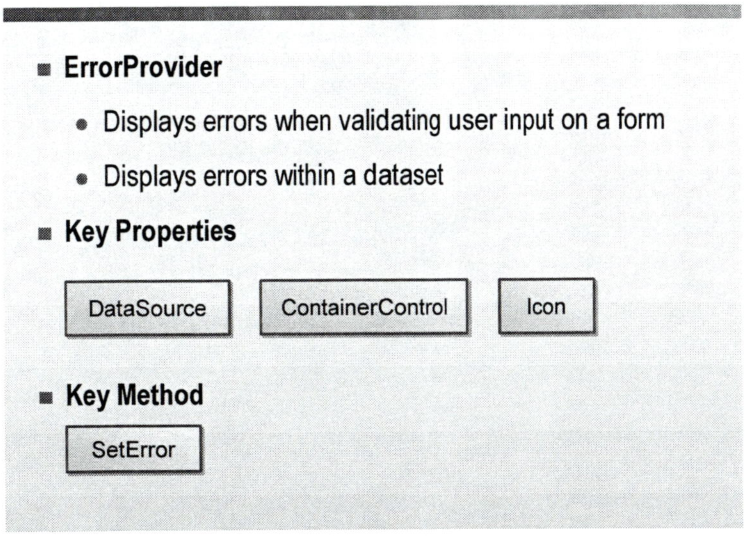

Introduction

The Windows Forms **ErrorProvider** control allows you to display an error message if the data entered by the user is invalid. It is used with validating user input on a form or displaying errors in a dataset.

Advantage of using ErrorProvider

An error provider is a better alternative than displaying an error message in a message box. If you display the error message in a message box, the error message is no longer visible if the user dismisses the message box. In the case of the **ErrorProvider** control, it displays an error icon next to the relevant control. When the user positions the mouse pointer over the error icon, a ToolTip appears, showing the error message string.

ErrorProvider properties

The key properties of the **ErrorProvider** control are:

- **ContainerControl**

  You must set the **ContainerControl** property to the appropriate container for the **ErrorProvider** control to display an error icon on the form. When you add the control in the designer, the **ContainerControl** property is automatically set to the containing form. If you add the control in code, you must set it manually.

- **DataSource**

  When the **DataSource** property is set, the **ErrorProvider** control displays error messages for a dataset.

- **Icon**

  The **Icon** property can be set to a custom error icon instead of the default.

ErrorProvider methods

The key method of the **ErrorProvider** control is the **SetError** method, which specifies the control that the error icon should appear next to, and the value of the error message string.

How to Use the ErrorProvider Control

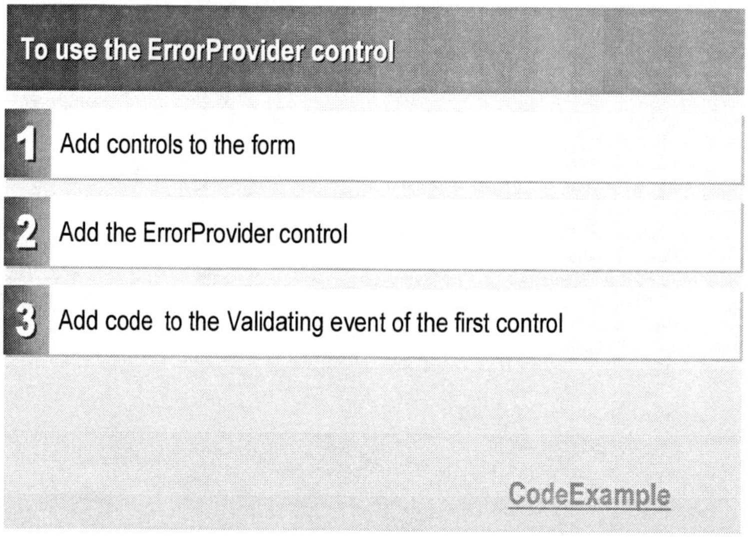

Introduction

You can use a Windows Forms **ErrorProvider** control to display an error icon when the user enters invalid data.

Procedure

To display an error icon by using the **ErrorProvider** control:

1. Add the controls to be validated to the form.
2. Add the **ErrorProvider** control.
3. Select the first control and add code to its **Validating** event handler.

   The following code tests for numeric values in a text box. If the data is invalid, an error icon displays next to the text box.

```
Private Sub TextBox1_Validating(ByVal sender As Object,
ByVal e As System.ComponentModel.CancelEventArgs) Handles
TextBox1.Validating
   'If the value in Textbox1 is not numeric
   If Not IsNumeric(TextBox1.Text) Then
       'Use the SetError method of the ErrorProvider
       ErrorProvider1.SetError(TextBox1, _
                      "Not a numeric value.")
       'make sure the focus does not shift
       e.Cancel = True
   Else
       'If the value is numeric, set the error value to ""
       ErrorProvider1.SetError(TextBox1, "")
   End If
End Sub
```

Demonstration: Validating Data in a Windows Forms Application

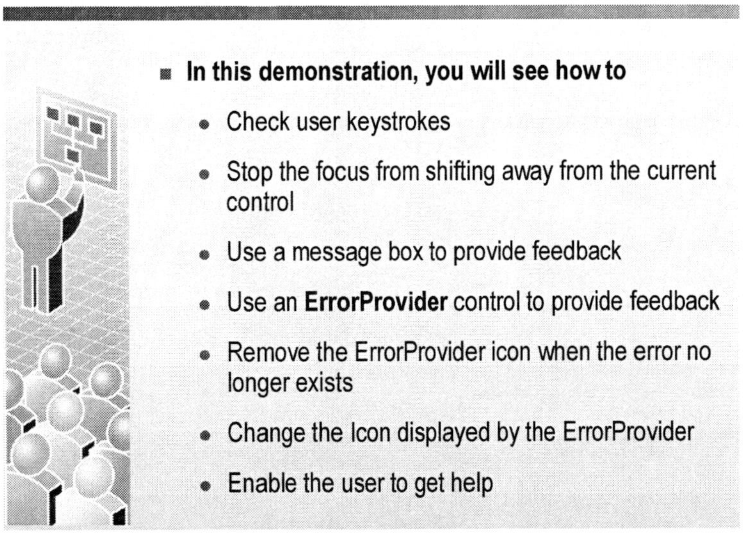

Introduction

In this demonstration, you will see how to validate user input in a Windows Forms application.

Instructions

► **Open the ValidatingInput.sln file**

1. Open the ValidatingInput.sln solution in Visual Studio .NET from *install_folder*\Democode\Mod02\Mod02_06\Starter.
2. Open Form1.vb in Design view.
3. In the Toolbox, double-click **ErrorProvider**.

► **Check user keystrokes**

1. Open the Form1.vb in the Code Editor.
2. On the **View** menu, point to **Show Tasks**, and then click **Comment**.
3. In the Task List, double-click **TODO: check for valid characters**.
4. Add the following code statements below the TODO line:

```
If e.KeyChar.IsDigit(e.KeyChar) = False Then
   e.Handled = True
   MessageBox.Show("Integer numbers only")

End If
```

5. Run the application, press a letter key on the keyboard, and then click **OK**.
6. Close the application.
7. What happens if you don't include the code statement that sets the value of the **Handled** property to **True**?

____

____

► Stop the focus from shifting away from the current control

1. In the Task List, double-click **TODO: don't let the focus shift**.
2. Add the following code statement below the TODO line:

```
e.Cancel = True
```

3. Run the application, type **15** and then click **Submit Data and Exit**.
4. Type **5** and then click **Submit Data and Exit**.
5. Close the application.

► Use a message box to provide feedback

1. In Task List, double-click **TODO: give the user feedback using a messagebox**.
2. Add the following code statement below the TODO line:

```
MessageBox.Show("You must enter a minimum value that " & _
   "is less than the maximum value")
```

3. Run the application, type **15** and then click **Submit Data and Exit**.
4. Type **5** and then click **Submit Data and Exit**.
5. Close the application.

► Use an ErrorProvider control to provide feedback

1. Open Form1.vb in the Code Editor.
2. In Task List, double-click **TODO: use the error provider to provide a message**.
3. Add the following code statement below the TODO line:

```
ErrorProvider1.SetError(epMinTextBox, _
   "The minimum value must be smaller " & _
   "than the maximum value")
```

4. Run the application, press TAB, press TAB again, type **15** and then click **Submit Data and Exit**.
5. Position the mouse over the **ErrorProvider** icon that is displayed to the right of the text box.
6. Type **5** and then click inside one of the other text boxes on the form.
7. What can you do to remove the ErrorProvider message?

   ____

   ____

8. Close the application.

▶ Remove the ErrorProvider icon when the error no longer exists

1. In Task List, double-click **TODO: reset the error provider**.
2. Add the following code statement below the TODO line:

```
ErrorProvider1.SetError(epMinTextBox, "")
```

3. Run the application, press TAB, press TAB again, type **15** and then click **Submit Data and Exit**.
4. Type **5** and then click inside one of the other text boxes on the form.
5. Close the application.

▶ Change the icon displayed by the ErrorProvider

1. In Task List, double-click **TODO: change the icon displayed by the error provider**.
2. Add the following code statements below the TODO line:

```
Dim ico As New Icon(Application.StartupPath & _
    "\msgbox01.ico")
ErrorProvider1.Icon = ico
```

3. Run the application, press TAB, press TAB again, type **6** and then press TAB.
4. Type **4** and then click **Submit Data and Exit**.
5. Type **8** and then click **Submit Data and Exit**.

▶ Enable the user to get help

1. Run the application, press TAB, press TAB again, type **15** and then click **Help**.
2. Type **4** and then click **Submit Data and Exit**.
3. Open Form1.vb in Design view.
4. Click **Help**, and then, in the Properties window, set the value of **CausesValidation** to False.
5. Run the application, press TAB, press TAB again, type **15** and then click **Help**.
6. Close the application.
7. Save your project, and then close Visual Studio .NET.

Review

- Creating an Event Handler for a Control
- Using Windows Forms Controls
- Using Dialog Boxes in a Windows Forms Application
- Creating Controls at Run Time
- Creating Menus
- Validating User Input

1. How are events raised and handled in the .NET Framework?

2. What methods do you use to add and remove event handlers at run time?

3. In the user interface of a hotel room reservation application, you want to let users choose a mode of payment (credit, cash, or check). What controls could you use to create this feature in your application?

4. How do you display tooltips for the Toolbar buttons?

5. How can you determine the action taken by a user when the user closes a dialog box?

6. How is an **ErrorProvider** control used?

7. What property of a container control is used to access the **ControlCollection** and what are the primary properties and methods of the **ControlCollection** class that can be accessed using this property?

8. How can you identify which displayed a shortcut menu (**ContextMenu**)?

Lab 2.1: Working with Controls

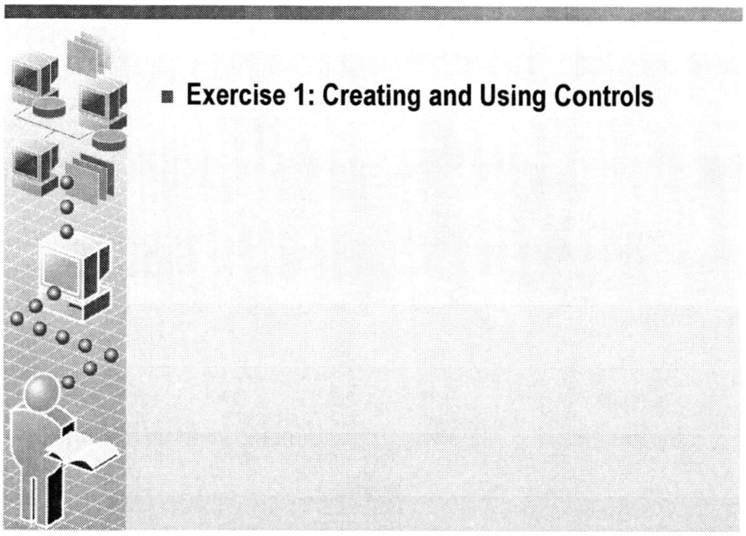

Objectives

After completing this lab, you will have demonstrated your ability to:

- Create an event handler for a control.
- Create and use a **ToolBar** control.
- Add and remove a control from **ControlCollection** at run time.
- Assign a context menu to a control at run time.

Note This lab focuses on the concepts in Module 2, "Working with Controls," in Course 2565A, *Developing Microsoft .NET Applications for Windows (Visual Basic .NET)*. As a result, this lab may not comply with Microsoft security recommendations.

Prerequisites

Before working on this lab, you must have:

- The knowledge and skills to develop a simple Windows Forms application by using a Visual Studio .NET–compatible programming language.
- The knowledge and skills to create and use a **ToolBar** control.
- The knowledge and skills to add and remove controls from **ControlCollection** at run time.
- The knowledge and skills to use a context menu as a short cut menu for a control.

Scenario

You are an application developer at a trading company called Northwind Traders. The department that you work in is developing a Purchase Order application that will be used by the Northwind Traders sales force. You have been assigned the task of completing the user interface and generating some of the underlying code for the Purchase Order application.

To complete this task, you must add a toolbar to the project and assign properties to the buttons of the toolbar, create an event handler that specifies which toolbar button was clicked by a user, and call the appropriate procedure for each button. You must also develop code that creates an instance of a composite control at run time, assigns a context menu to the new control, and adds the new control to the control collection of a **Panel** control that already exists on the main form of the application. To finish this task, you will develop code that handles the click event for a **ContextMenu** control, determines the control that raised the event, and removes that control from a control collection.

Estimated time to complete this lab: 60 minutes

Exercise 1
Creating and Using Controls

In this exercise, you will begin by opening an existing Windows Forms application. You will add a **ToolBar** control to the main form of the application, add the appropriate number of buttons to the **ToolBar** control, and set values for each of the buttons. After the design for the toolbar is complete, you will develop the code that handles the **ButtonClick** event of the toolbar and responds appropriately for each of the different buttons. You will then develop the code statements required to create an instance of a composite control, associate a context menu with the control, and then add the control to the control collection of a **Panel** control that already exists on the form. You will finish this exercise by creating the event handler for a **ContextMenu** control, developing the code that determines which control raised the event, and removing that control from the controls collection of the **Panel** control to which it belongs. This exercise assesses your knowledge of events and event handlers as well as your ability to use Windows Forms controls and **ContextMenus** at run time.

There are starter and solution files associated with this exercise. Browse to *install_folder*\Labfiles\Lab02_1\Ex01\Starter to find the starter files, and browse to *install_folder*\Labfiles\Lab02_1\Ex01\Solution to find the solution files. If you performed a default installation of the course files, *install_folder* corresponds to C:\Program Files\Msdntrain\2565.

Scenario

You have been given the task of adding a toolbar to the Purchase Order application and completing some code sections that are used to display purchase item data. You have been given the following table that contains design specification data for the toolbar. You will use this design information to construct the toolbar and the buttons that it contains.

Item	Item property	Property value
ToolBar	**Name**	POToolBar
POToolBar	**ImageList**	POImageList
POToolBar Member 0	**Name**	RefreshToolBarButton
POToolBar Member 1	**Name**	AddOrderItemToolBarButton
POToolBar Member 2	**Name**	SaveOrderToolBarButton
POToolBar Member 3	**Name**	PrintPreviewToolBarButton
POToolBar Member 4	**Name**	SubmitToolBarButton
POToolBar Member 5	**Name**	ViewUnsubmittedToolBarButton
POToolBar Member 6	**Name**	ViewSubmittedToolBarButton
RefreshToolBarButton	**Tag**	Refresh
RefreshToolBarButton	**ImageIndex**	0
RefreshToolBarButton	**ToolTipText**	Refresh product and customer data
AddOrderItemToolBarButton	**Tag**	Add
AddOrderItemToolBarButton	**ImageIndex**	1
AddOrderItemToolBarButton	**ToolTipText**	Add a new order item to the purchase order
SaveOrderToolBarButton	**Tag**	Save
SaveOrderToolBarButton	**ImageIndex**	2
SaveOrderToolBarButton	**ToolTipText**	Save the current purchase order

(continued)

Item	Item property	Property value
PrintPreviewToolBarButton	**Tag**	PrintPreview
PrintPreviewToolBarButton	**ImageIndex**	3
PrintPreviewToolBarButton	**ToolTipText**	Print preview
SubmitToolBarButton	**Tag**	Submit
SubmitToolBarButton	**ImageIndex**	4
SubmitToolBarButton	**ToolTipText**	Submit purchase order data to the NWTraders database
ViewUnsubmittedToolBarButton	**Tag**	Unsubmitted
ViewUnsubmittedToolBarButton	**ImageIndex**	5
ViewUnsubmittedToolBarButton	**ToolTipText**	View the unsubmitted orders
ViewSubmittedToolBarButton	**Tag**	Submitted
ViewSubmittedToolBarButton	**ImageIndex**	6
ViewSubmittedToolBarButton	**ToolTipText**	View report of submitted orders

After you have created the toolbar, you will develop code for the **ToolBar.ButtonClick** event. The following table identifies the actions that should be taken when each button is clicked.

Toolbar button name	Action taken when this button is clicked
RefreshToolBarButton	DataRefreshMenuItem.PerformClick()
AddOrderItemToolBarButton	NewOrderItemButton.PerformClick()
SaveOrderToolBarButton	SaveOrderButton.PerformClick()
PrintPreviewToolBarButton	PrintPreview()
SubmitToolBarButton	DataSubmitMenuItem.PerformClick()
ViewUnsubmittedToolBarButton	ViewUnsubmittedOrdersMenuItem.PerformClick()
ViewSubmittedToolBarButton	ViewSubmittedOrdersMenuItem.PerformClick()

After the toolbar is complete, you will develop the code to add and remove an instance of a composite control from the controls collection of a container control (the **Panel** control, **ProductOrderPanel**, has already been added to the main form of the Purchase Order application). Each composite control represents a single purchase item; together, these purchase items make up a purchase order. Although users can add a new purchase item by using either **NewOrderItemButton** or **AddOrderItemToolBarButton**, you will add your code to the event handler for the **NewOrderItemButton.Click** event. You will add code to this event handler that creates an instance of the composite control (**PurchaseOrder.OrderItemControl**), sets the **ContextMenu** property of the new control (the context menu is used by the application user to remove a purchase item from the **Panel** control), and adds the control to the controls collection. To finish up this task, you will create an event handler that responds to a context menu click event, and you will develop the code that removes a purchase item (the purchase item that raised the context menu click event) from the controls collection of **ProductOrderPanel**.

Tasks	Additional information
1. Open the Lab02Application.sln file in Visual Studio .NET. The solution file is located in *install_folder*\Labfiles\Lab02_1\Ex01\Starter\Lab02Application.	**a.** For more information about opening a project file and starting an application, see the following resource: • The Visual Studio .NET Help documentation. For additional information about opening a project file, in Search, select the **Search in titles only** check box, then search by using the phrase **Open Project Dialog Box**. For additional information about starting an application from in Designer, search the Index by using the phrase **Debugging Windows Applications.**
2. In the Design view, add a **ToolBar** control to MainForm.vb. Configure the Toolbar as specified in the scenario.	**a.** For more information about the **ToolBar** control, see the following resources: • Lesson, Using Windows Forms Controls, in Module 2, "Working with Controls," in Course 2565A, Developing Microsoft .NET Applications for Windows (Visual Basic .NET). • Practice, Creating and Using a ToolBar Control, in Module 2, "Working with Controls," in Course 2565A, Developing Microsoft .NET Applications for Windows (Visual Basic .NET). • The Visual Studio .NET Help documentation. Search by using the phrase **Introduction to the Windows Forms ToolBar Control.**
3. Use the Task List to locate the code section 'TODO: create an event handler for the POToolBar.ButtonClick event', and then create an event handler for the **POToolBar.ButtonClick** event. Develop the code that will invoke the appropriate action when a **ToolBar** button is clicked.	**a.** For more information about the **ToolBar.ButtonClick** event and determining which button on a toolbar caused the **ButtonClick** event to be raised, see the following resources: • Lesson, Using Windows Forms Controls, in Module 2, "Working with Controls," in Course 2565A, Developing Microsoft .NET Applications for Windows (Visual Basic .NET). • Practice, Creating and Using a ToolBar Control, in Module 2, "Working with Controls," in Course 2565A, Developing Microsoft .NET Applications for Windows (Visual Basic .NET). • The Visual Studio .NET Help documentation. For additional information about handling the **ButtonClick** event of a **ToolBar** control and to see an example demonstrating a method for determining which button of a toolbar raised the **ButtonClick** event, search by using the phrase **ToolBar.ButtonClick Event.**
4. Run your application to test the toolbar and the **ButtonClick** event handler. You can position the mouse over the **ToolBar** buttons to display ToolTips and click the buttons to make sure that your **ButtonClick** event handler is working correctly.	**a.** For more information about the purchase order sample application, see the following resources: • Demonstration, Purchase Order Application, in Module 0, "Introduction," in Course 2565A, *Developing Microsoft .NET Applications for Windows (Visual Basic .NET).*

Tasks	Additional information
5. Use the Task List to locate the code section 'TODO: create a purchase item', and then create an instance of the **PurchaseOrder.OrderItem Control** control named **tempProductOrder** that uses **ProductContextMenu** as a context menu.	**a.** For more information about using a **ContextMenu** control at run time, see the following resources: • Lesson, Creating Menus, in Module 2, "Working with Controls," in Course 2565A, *Developing Microsoft .NET Applications for Windows (Visual Basic .NET)*. • Practice, Updating Menus at Run Time, in Module 2, "Working with Controls," in Course 2565A, *Developing Microsoft .NET Applications for Windows (Visual Basic .NET)*. • The Visual Studio .NET Help documentation. Search by using the phrase **Adding Context Menus to Windows Forms**.
6. Use the Task List to locate the code section 'TODO: add a purchase item to ProductOrderPanel', and then add the new purchase item to the controls collection of the **ProductOrderPanel** control.	**a.** For more information about adding controls to a control collection, see the following resources: • Lesson, Adding Controls at Run Time, in Module 2, "Working with Controls," in Course 2565A, *Developing Microsoft .NET Applications for Windows (Visual Basic .NET)*. • Practice, Adding and Removing Controls at Run Time, in Module 2, "Working with Controls," in Course 2565A, *Developing Microsoft .NET Applications for Windows (Visual Basic .NET)*. • The Visual Studio .NET Help documentation. Search by using the phrase **Control.Controls Property**.
7. Use the Task List to locate the code section 'TODO: handle the click event for the DeleteOrderItemMenuItem', and then create an event handler for the **Click** event of the **DeleteOrderItemMenuItem** menu item that calls the **DeleteOrderItem()** procedure.	**a.** For more information about creating event handlers, see the following resources: • Lesson, Creating an Event Handler for a Control, in Module 2, "Working With Controls," in Course 2565A, *Developing Microsoft .NET Applications for Windows (Visual Basic .NET)*. • Practice, Creating and Event Handler for a Control, in Module 2, "Working With Controls," in Course 2565A, *Developing Microsoft .NET Applications for Windows (Visual Basic .NET)*. • The Visual Studio .NET Help documentation. Search by using the phrase **Consuming Events**.
8. Use the Task List to locate the code section 'TODO: determine the index number of the control that will be deleted', and then assign the index number of the control that displayed the context menu to a variable named *currentControlIndex*.	**a.** For more information about determining which control displayed a context menu, see the following resources: • Lesson, Creating Menus, in Module 2, "Working with Controls," in Course 2565A, *Developing Microsoft .NET Applications for Windows (Visual Basic .NET)*. • Practice, Updating Menus at Run Time, in Module 2, "Working with Controls," in Course 2565A, *Developing Microsoft .NET Applications for Windows (Visual Basic .NET)*. • The Visual Studio .NET Help documentation. Search by using the phrase **ContextMenu.SourceControl**.

Tasks	Additional information
9. Use the Task List to locate the code sections 'TODO: remove a control from the middle of the ProductOrderPanel control collection' and 'TODO: remove a control from the end of the ProductOrderPanel control collection' and then, in each case, create a code statement that will remove the control that displayed the context menu from the controls collection of **ProductOrderPanel**.	**a.** For more information about removing controls from **ControlCollection**, see the following resources: • Lesson, Adding Controls at Run Time, in Module 2, "Working with Controls," in Course 2565A, *Developing Microsoft .NET Applications for Windows (Visual Basic .NET)*. • Practice, Adding and Removing Controls at Run Time, in Module 2, "Working with Controls," in Course 2565A, *Developing Microsoft .NET Applications for Windows (Visual Basic .NET)*. • The Visual Studio .NET Help documentation. Search by using the phrase **Control.ControlCollection.Remove Method**.
10. Run your application to test the code that you just created. You should now be able to add and remove purchase items from the controls collection of **ProductOrderPanel**.	Additional information is not necessary for this task.
11. Save your changes, and then close Visual Studio .NET.	Additional information is not necessary for this task.

msdn training

Module 3: Building Controls

Contents

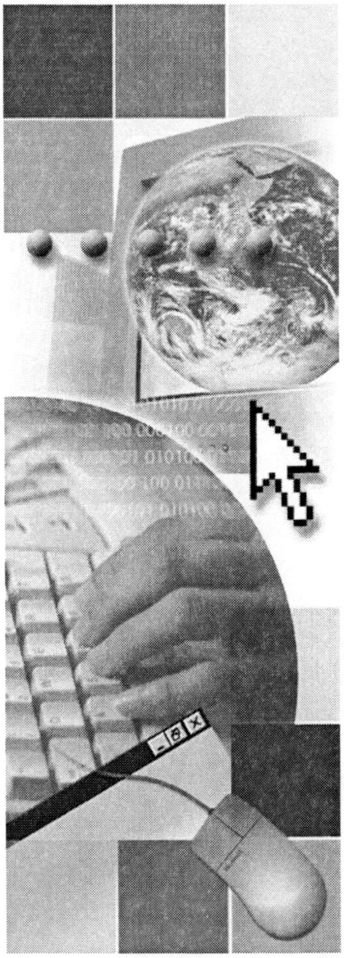

Microsoft

Overview

- Extending and Creating Controls
- Adding Design-Time Support for Controls
- Licensing a Control

Introduction

Microsoft® .NET Framework Windows Forms controls are reusable components that encapsulate user interface functionality and are used in client-side Microsoft Windows® applications. Windows Forms provide many ready-to-use controls, but they also provide the infrastructure for developing your own controls.

Objectives

After completing this module, you will be able to:

- Extend an existing control.
- Create a composite control by combining functionality of several existing Windows Forms controls.
- Describe the design-time support options for components provided by Microsoft Visual Studio® .NET.
- Add attributes that provide information to the Visual Designer.
- Create and validate licenses for controls.

Lesson: Extending and Creating Controls

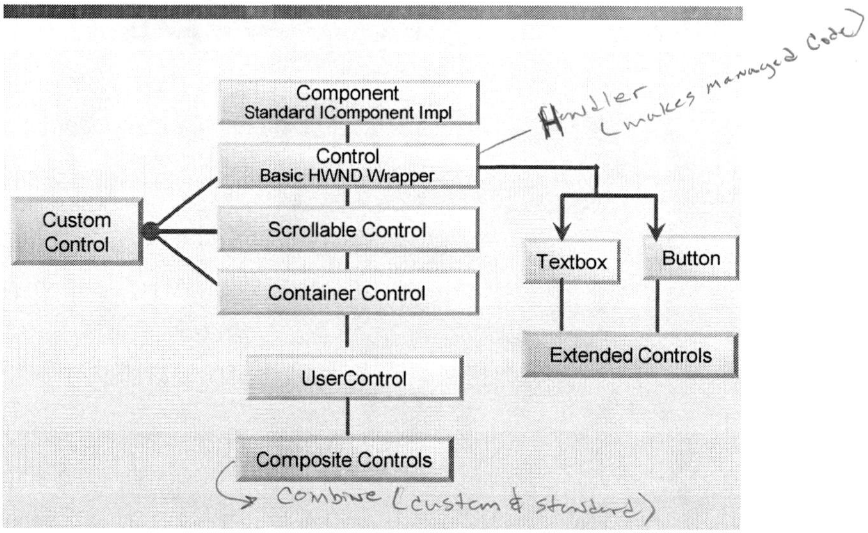

Introduction

Windows Forms provides several options for authoring controls. You can combine existing controls, extend existing controls, or author your own custom controls. This lesson provides background information about the various options that are available for creating Windows Forms controls.

Lesson objectives

After completing this lesson, you will be able to:

- Determine the various options for authoring controls.
- Expose and override properties for controls.
- Raise and override events for controls.
- Test a control.

Options for Building Controls

- **Extended controls**

```
Public Class NumericTextBox
   Inherits System.Windows.Forms.TextBox

   End Sub
End Class
```

- **Composite controls**
  - Controls that are composed of other controls
  - Designed to act as containers for other controls
- **Custom controls**

CodeExample

Introduction

One of the options for creating a Windows Forms control is to extend an existing control. You can extend an existing control to customize it or add additional functionality to it. Extend an existing control if the control that you want to create is quite similar in functionality to an existing control.

Another way of creating your own controls is to combine existing controls to create composite controls. Create composite controls when you need complex functionality that requires the use of more than one control.

If you do not want to combine or extend existing controls, you have the option of creating your own custom controls.

Extended controls

You can customize any Windows Forms control by deriving from it and overriding its properties, methods, and events. This entire procedure of creating a customized control from an existing control is referred to as extending a control. When you inherit from an existing a control, you have the options of using the members of the inherited class, overriding the members of the inherited class, or creating your own custom members.

When inheriting from an existing control, you use the **MyBase** keyword to implement the constructor of the inherited object. This is required because constructors are not inherited. The following example shows how to implement the functionality provided by the default constructor in an extended class.

```
Public Sub New()
  MyBase.New()
End Sub
```

Example of extending a control

Some examples of extended controls include a text box that can accept only numeric values or a button that has some additional properties, such as a property that can record how many times the button has been clicked.

The following code shows a numeric text box that is inherited from the Windows **TextBox** control. It also shows how the **OnKeyPress** event of the base **TextBox** class is overridden to provide custom functionality.

```
Public Class NumericTextBox
  Inherits System.Windows.Forms.TextBox

  Protected Overrides Sub OnKeyPress(ByVal e As
System.Windows.Forms.KeyPressEventArgs)

  End Sub
End Class
```

Because this control inherits from **TextBox**, all the members associated with the **TextBox** control are exposed in the extended control. For example, you can use the functionality of the **Clear()** method of the of **TextBox** control from the extended control.

```
Private MyNumericControl as New NumericTextBox()
MyNumericControl.Clear()
```

Composite controls

You can create new controls by using class composition to combine existing controls. A composite control renders a user interface that reuses the functionality of existing controls. A composite control can synthesize properties from the properties of its child controls and handle events raised by its child controls. It can also expose custom properties and events. All composite controls derive from **System.Windows.Forms.UserControl**. There is full design-time support for creating composite controls with the Visual Studio .NET Windows Forms Designer.

Composite controls can act as containers for other controls because they extend the **ContainerControl** class.

The **ContainerControl** class defines a logical boundary for controls that it contains. This class provides focus management, which means that it is aware of active controls and can change focus from one control to another. It also supports methods for adding, removing, and retrieving child controls. The **Form** class also inherits from the **ContainerControl** class.

For more information about the **ContainerControl** class, see "ContainerControl Class" in the Visual Studio .NET Help documentation.

Custom controls

Custom controls display user interface (UI) elements by making calls to a GDI+ **Graphics** object in the **OnPaint** event. Custom controls are generally derived from the base class **System.Windows.Forms.Control**.

```
Public Class NewControl
  Inherits Control
  ...
End Class
```

To create a custom control, you generally inherit from the **Control** class, which draws a blank square on your form, override the **OnPaint** event of the **Control** class, and use GDI+ to draw your own UI. For more information about using GDI+ in greater detail, see Module 6, "Printing and Reporting in Windows Forms Applications," in Course 2565A, *Developing Microsoft .NET Applications for Windows (Visual Basic® .NET)*.

You can add as well as override properties, methods, and events of the base class (**Control**). The base class provides the plumbing required for visual display in client-side Windows applications. The **Control** class provides a window handle, manages message routing, and provides mouse and keyboard events as well as many other user interface events. It provides advanced layout and has properties specific to visual display, such as **ForeColor**, **BackColor**, **Height**, **Width**, and many others.

Example of a Custom control

```
Imports System
Imports System.ComponentModel
Imports System.Windows.Forms
Imports System.Drawing

Public Class CustomControl
    Inherits System.Windows.Forms.Control

Protected Overrides Sub OnPaint(ByVal e As _
System.Windows.Forms.PaintEventArgs)
e.Graphics.DrawString("Written with GDI+ on OnPaint event",
New Font("Arial", 12), New SolidBrush(Color.Red), 0, 0)
    End Sub

End Class
```

How to Expose and Override Properties for Controls

- **Exposing properties of a control within a container**

```
Public Property QuantityTextBoxContextMenu() As
   ContextMenu
        Get
                Return txtQuantity.ContextMenu
        End Get
        Set(ByVal Value As ContextMenu)
                txtQuantity.ContextMenu = Value
        End Set
End Property
```

- **Overriding properties**

CodeExample

Introduction

A Windows Forms control inherits many properties form the base class **System.Windows.Forms.Control**. These include properties such as **Font**, **ForeColor**, **BackColor**, **Bounds**, **ClientRectangle**, **DisplayRectangle**, **Enabled**, **Focused**, **Height**, **Width**, **Visible**, as well as many others. You can override inherited properties in your control as well as define new properties.

A component should define properties instead of public fields because visual designers such as Visual Studio .NET display properties, but not fields, in the Properties window.

Property definitions

Property definitions include two parts: a private variable to hold the value of a property for an instance of a control, and a property definition that exposes the private variable.

Although a property definition generally includes a private data member, this is not required. The Get accessor can return a value without accessing a private data member. An example is a property whose get method returns the system time. Properties enable data hiding, in which the accessor methods hide the implementation of the property.

Procedure: Exposing properties of control in a container

The properties for controls contained by composite controls are not directly exposed to developers. For example, to access the **Text** property of a text box in a composite control, you may have to iterate through the **Controls** collection of the composite control to access the property. A common practice with composite controls is to expose properties of child controls as properties of the composite control.

The following code example shows how to expose the **ContextMenu** property of a control contained in a composite control.

```
Public Property QuantityTextBoxContextMenu() As ContextMenu
     Get
            Return txtQuantity.ContextMenu
     End Get
     Set(ByVal Value As ContextMenu)
            txtQuantity.ContextMenu = Value
     End Set
End Property
```

The **Get** and **Set** methods are generally not different from other methods. They can perform any program logic, throw exceptions, be overridden, and can be declared with any modifiers allowed by the programming language. You can make a property read-only or write-only by using the **ReadOnly** and **WriteOnly** key words and only using a Get or Set accessor respectively. The following code is an example of a **ReadOnly** property.

```
Public ReadOnly Property MyProperty() As String
     Get
     ...
     End Get
End Property
```

Procedure: Overriding properties

When you extend an existing control, you can override the properties of the base class to provide custom functionality. The following code overrides the **Text** property of the **TextBox** control and allows only numeric characters to be set on the property.

```
Public Class NumericTextBox
  Inherits System.Windows.Forms.TextBox

  Public Overrides Property Text() As String
     Get
            Return MyBase.Text
     End Get
     Set(ByVal Value As String)
            Select Case Value
               Case IsNumeric(Value)
                  MyBase.Text = Value
               Case Nothing
                  MyBase.Text = Value
               Case Else
                  Exit Property
               End Select
     End Set
  End Property
End Class
```

When overriding members of an extended class, use the **MyBase** keyword to implement the functionality of the base member. The previous example uses **MyBase.Text** to refer to the property in the derived class.

How to Raise and Override Events for Controls

- **To raise events for a composite control**

```
Public Event AddUserControl()
...
If e.KeyCode = Keys.Enter Then
   RaiseEvent AddUserControl()
End If
```

- **To override events**

```
Public Class FirstControl
   Inherits Control
   ...
   Protected Overrides Sub OnPaint(e As
   PaintEventArgs)
```

Introduction

When authoring controls, you can raise your own custom events or override the events of the base class.

Procedure: Raising events

When creating controls, you use events to notify host applications when something occurs in a control. To create an event, declare it by using the **Event** keyword and define any parameters to be passed to the host when the event is invoked. To invoke the event in the control, use the **RaiseEvent** keyword.

The following code defines an event called **MyEvent** that passes a string data type when invoked.

```
Public Event MyEvent(ByVal stringPassed as String)
'to invoke the event use RaiseEvent
RaiseEvent("Pass this string to host")
```

You can then make the host application aware of the control event by delegating a procedure to the event. You use the same **Handles** or **AddHandler** keywords to handle a custom event that you use with the intrinsic controls.

Procedure: Overriding an event

The **Control** class provides a base set of events that allow you to monitor activities such as property modifications and user actions. When you create controls, you can access events exposed by the **Control** class and other base classes and override them. Each base event provides event-specific information with the *EventArgs* parameter. This parameter (and parameters that derive from it such as *KeyEventArgs* and *MouseEvtsArgs*) provides event specific information, such as which key was pressed or the X,Y position of the mouse pointer.

The following code shows how to override an event. The example overrides the **OnKeyPress** event of a **TextBox** control. The event contains a *KeyPressEventArgs* parameter that contains data about the keys that were pressed (e.KeyChar) and a Boolean value (e.Handled) that allows you to indicate if the event was handled (**True**) or if the event should be passed to Windows for processing (**False**). If the event is handled in the procedure, then it raises a custom event and passes an instance of the object (**Me**) along with the *KeyPressEventArgs* passed to the event.

```
Protected Overrides Sub OnKeyPress(ByVal e As _
System.Windows.Forms.KeyPressEventArgs)
        Dim asciiInteger As Integer = Asc(e.KeyChar)
        Select Case asciiInteger
                             Case 47 To 57
               e.Handled = False
            'If the value represents BACKSPACE
               Case 8
               e.Handled = False
              'If the value is anything else
               Case Else
               e.Handled = True
              RaiseEvent InvalidUserEntry(Me, e)
       End Select
End Sub
```

How to Test a Control

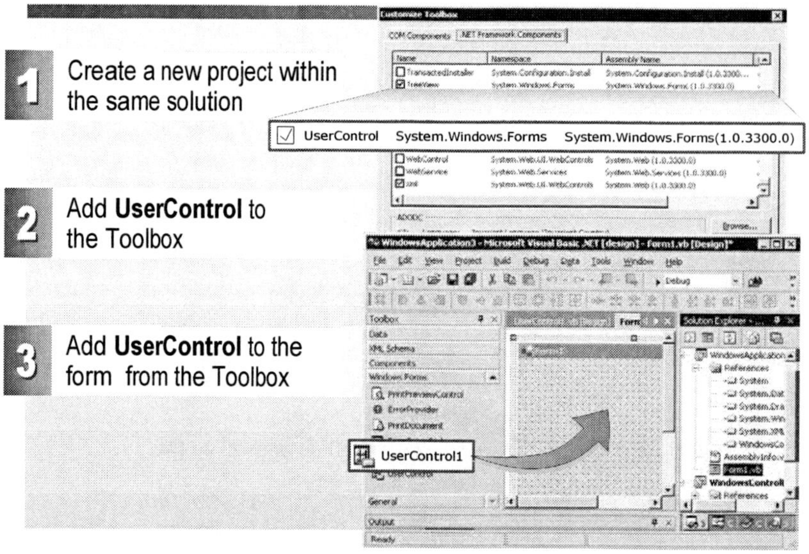

Introduction

The Microsoft .Net Framework eliminates many of the original problems with versioning that existed with COM. For example, you can have more than one version of a component supporting different applications without having to be concerned with backwards compatibility.

When you create and compile a Windows Forms application by using the Visual Studio .NET integrated development environment (IDE), any external assemblies referenced in the application are built into the /Bin folder of the application. Because the application has its own copy of the component, any modification to the original component will not affect it. However, if you are testing a component in an application, you must remove the previous component and add the newer one every time you modify the component.

If you want to test a component without adding a new reference to the control every time you modify the control, you can add a forms application to the component solution. The Visual Studio .NET IDE is aware of the component project and adds an implicit reference to the component. This reference is automatically updated whenever you rebuild the component.

Procedure

1. Create a new form in the same project.
2. Add **UserControl** to the Toolbox.
3. Add the **UserControl** to the form from the Toolbox.

   After you add the **User** control to the toolbox, it is visible on theToolbox. To add the **User** control to the project, drag the control to the form, just as you do with other controls.

Code Walkthrough: Creating Controls

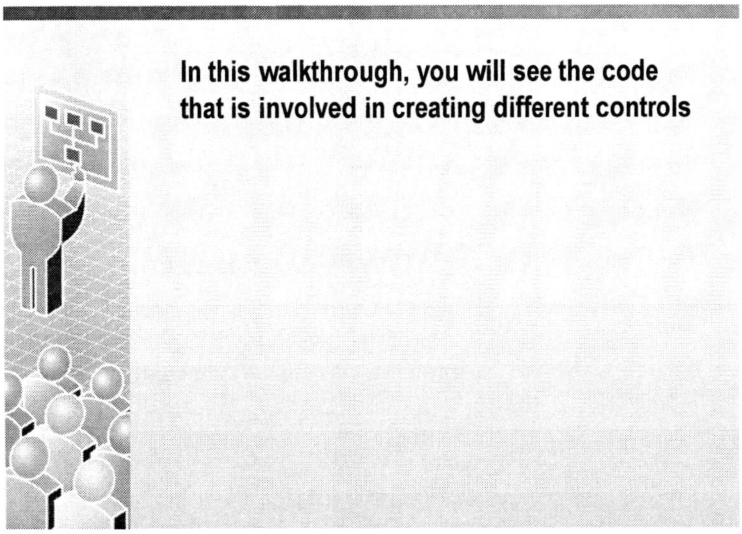

Introduction

In this walkthrough, you will see examples of extended, composite, and custom controls. The instructor will walk you through the code required to extend a control, create a composite control, and build a custom control.

Instructions

► **Open the Controls.sln solution file**

- Open the Controls.sln solution in Visual Studio .NET from *install_folder*\Democode\Mod03\Mod03_01\Starter\Controls.

Note If you performed a default installation of the course files, *install_folder* corresponds to C:\Program Files\Msdntrain\2565.

► **Walkthrough the NumericTextBox control**

1. Open NumericTextBox.vb in the Code Editor.
2. Point out the following line of code. Explain that to create an extended control, you inherit directly from an existing control.

```
Inherits System.Windows.Forms.TextBox
```

3. Scroll to the following line of code. You can override the events of the base control.

```
Protected Overrides Sub OnKeyPress(ByVal e As _
System.Windows.Forms.KeyPressEventArgs)
```

4. Scroll to the following line of code to explain that you can also override the properties of the base control.

```
Public Overrides Property Text() As String
```

► **Walkthrough the OrderItemControl**

1. Open the Design view of OrderItemControl.vb.
2. Composite controls are composed of a **UserControl** and one or more controls. Explain the significance of the controls contained in the **UserControl**.
3. Open OrderItemControl.vb in the Code Editor.
4. A composite control inherits from the **UserControl** class. Point out the following line of code.

```
Inherits System.Windows.Forms.UserControl
```

5. To access the properties of constituent controls, you must expose them explicitly. Scroll down to the following lines of code to show how the properties of constituent controls are exposed.

```
Public Property OrderQuantity() As String
Get
            Return QuantityTextBox.Text
        End Get
        Set(ByVal Value As String)
            QuantityTextBox.Text = Value
        End Set
End Property
```

6. The **OrderItemControl** exposes a method that binds data to constituent controls. Explain the significance of the following procedure.

```
Public Sub GetProductData(ByVal dsproducts As _
System.Data.DataTable)
```

► **Walkthrough the VerticalLabel control**

1. Open VerticalLabel.vb in the Code Editor.
2. Custom controls generally inherit from the **Control** class. Explain the significance of the following line of code.

```
Inherits System.Windows.Forms.Control
```

3. To implement a custom control you must override the **OnPaint** event and use GDI+ to draw the control. Explain the following procedure to show how to override the **OnPaint** event of the **Control** class.

```
Protected Overrides Sub OnPaint(ByVal e As _
System.Windows.Forms.PaintEventArgs)
```

4. The **Control** class exposes many properties, methods, and events that can be overridden. These properties, methods, and events are shared by all controls. Explain the significance of the following line of procedure.

```
Public Overrides Property Text() As String
```

► **Display the controls at design time in the Controls_Host project**

1. In Solution Explorer, right-click the **Controls** project, and then click **Build**.
2. In the Controls_Host project, open the Design view of Form1.vb.
3. On the **Tools** menu, click **Customize Toolbox**.
4. In the **Customize Toolbox** dialog box, click the **.NET FrameworksComponents** tab, and then click **Browse**.
5. In the **Open** dialog box, select **Controls.dll** from *install_folder*\Democode\Mod03\Mod03_01\Starter\Controls\obj\Debug\, click **Open**, and then click **OK**.
6. Add a **NumericTextBox** to Form1 under the designated label. Attempt to set the **Text** property to a non-numeric value.

   The control enforces the property logic at design time.
7. Add an **OrderItemControl** to Form1 under the designated label. Either instance in the Toolbox will work.
8. In the Properties window, display the **OrderQuantity** property.

   The **OrderItemControl** property exposes the property of a constituent control.
9. Add a **VerticalLabel** to Form1 under the designated label.
10. Set the **ForeColor** property to **ActiveCaption** and the **Font** property to **Italic**.

    The **OnPaint** event fires at design time as it will at run time.

► **Display the controls at run time in the Controls_Host project**

1. In Solution Explorer, right-click the **Controls_Host** project, and then click **Set as Startup Project**.
2. Press F5 to run the application.
3. Attempt to enter non-numeric characters into the **NumericTextBox** control.

   The control enforces property logic at run time.
4. Navigate through the products in the **OrderItemControl**.

   The constituent controls are data bound.

Practice: Creating a Composite Control

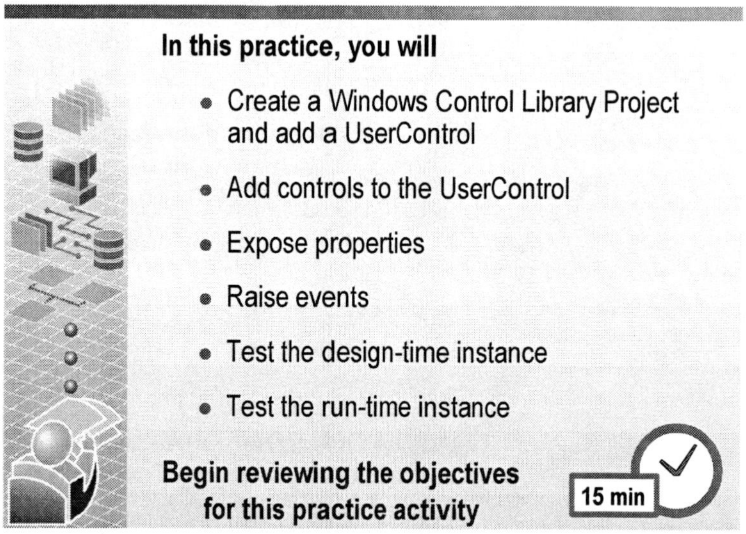

Introduction

In this practice, you will build a composite control that displays the current time. The composite control includes a **Label** to display the time and a **Timer** control. The **Timer** control has a **Tick** event that fires repeatedly with a period based on the **Interval** property. The default value of the **Interval** property is 100 milliseconds, meaning that the **Tick** event will fire every second.

You will create a composite control that exposes properties of the **Label** and **Timer** controls and raises the **Tick** event to host applications.

► **Create a Windows Control Library project and add a UserControl**

1. Open Visual Studio .NET.
2. On the **File** menu, point to **New**, and then click **Project**.
3. In the **New Project** dialog box, click **Windows Control Library**, name it **DigitalClock**, and then click **OK**.
4. Delete **UserControl1** from the project.

   You can also rename **UserControl1** to **DigitalClock** and skip step 5, however you must remember to change the file name and the class name to **DigitalClock**.
5. On the **Project** menu, click **Add UserControl**, name it **DigitalClock.vb**, and then click **Open**.

▶ Add controls to the UserControl

1. Add the following controls to the **UserControl**.

Control	Name	Text
Label	LocalTimeLabel	“”
Timer	Timer1	*N/A*

2. Set **BackColor** of **LocalTimeLabel** to **ControlDark**.
3. Center **LocalTimeLabel** in the **UserControl**. Your **UserControl** should look like the following.

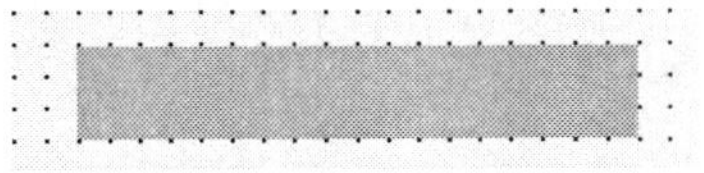

▶ Add code to expose the properties of LocalTimeLabel and Timer1 to the host application

1. Create a **Public** property named **Timer1_Enabled** that exposes the Boolean **Enabled** property of **Timer1**. Your code should look like the following.

```
Public Property Timer1_Enabled() As Boolean
        Get
            Return Timer1.Enabled
        End Get
        Set(ByVal Value As Boolean)
            Timer1.Enabled = Value
        End Set
End Property
```

2. Create a **Public** property named **LocalTimeLabel_BackColor** that exposes the **BackColor** property of **LocalTimeLabel**. Your code should look like the following.

```
Public Property LocalTimeLabel_BackColor() As Color
        Get
            Return LocalTimeLabel.BackColor
        End Get
        Set(ByVal Value As Color)
            LocalTimeLabel.BackColor = Value
        End Set
End Property
```

► Add code that raises the Timer1.Tick event to host applications

1. Declare a **Public** event named **RaiseTimer1_Tick** that passes an **Object** and **EventArgs** to the host application.
2. Create the **Timer1_Tick** event procedure and update the **Text** property of **LocalTimeLabel** to reflect the current time (use the **Now.ToString** function).
3. In the **Timer1_Tick** event procedure, raise the **RaiseTimer1_Tick** event and pass the **sender** and **e** event arguments.

   Your code should look like the following.

```
Public Event RaiseTimer1_Tick(ByVal sender As Object, _
ByVal e As EventArgs)

Private Sub Timer1_Tick(ByVal sender As Object, _
ByVal e As System.EventArgs) Handles Timer1.Tick
        LocalTimeLabel.Text = Now.ToString
        RaiseEvent RaiseTimer1_Tick(sender, e)
End Sub
```

► Test the design-time instance of your Composite Control in a host application

1. On the **Build** menu, click **Build Solution** to compile the **DigitalClock** control.
2. On the **File** menu, click **Add Project**, and then click **New Project**.
3. Create a new Windows Application and name it **TestClock**.
4. Add the **DigitalClock** control from the Toolbox to **Form1** in **TestClock**.

Note Notice that two new controls are added to the Toolbox: **UserControl1**, which was added with the new Windows Control Library project, and **DigitalClock**.

5. In the Properties window, set the **Timer1_Enabled** property to **True**.

   The **DigitalClock** control is running while the host application is in Design view.
6. In the Properties window set the **LocalTimeLabel_Color** property to **ControlLight**.

   This property would not be available to developers in the IDE if you did not explicitly expose it by using a property procedure.
7. Add a **Label** to Form1 and name it **UniversalTimeLabel**.
8. Create the **DigitalClock1_RaiseTimer1_Tick** event procedure and update the **Text** property of **UniversalTimeLabel** to reflect the coordinated universal time (use the **Now.UtcNow** function). Your code should look like the following.

```
Private Sub DigitalClock1_RaiseTimer1_Tick _
(ByVal sender As Object, ByVal e As System.EventArgs) _
Handles DigitalClock1.RaiseTimer1_Tick
        UniversalTimeLabel.Text = Now.UtcNow
End Sub
```

9. Add a **Button** to Form1 and name it **StartStopButton**.

10. Create the **StartStopButton_Click** event procedure and write the code to switch the **Timer1_Enabled** property of **DigitalClock1** in the procedure (If the Timer1_Enabled property is **True** make it **False** and if it is **False** make it **True**). Your code should look like the following:

```
Private Sub StartStopButton_Click _
(ByVal sender As System.Object, ByVal e As
System.EventArgs) Handles StartStopButton.Click
        DigitalClock1.Timer1_Enabled = _
        Not (DigitalClock1.Timer1_Enabled)
End Sub
```

► **Test the run-time instance of your control in a host application**

1. Place a breakpoint on the **Get** and **Set** statements of the **Timer1_Enabled** event procedure in the **DigitalClock** composite control.
2. In Project Explorer, right-click **TestClock** project, and then click **Set as Startup Project**.
3. Press F5 to compile and run the application.
4. Step through each line of the code in the debug mode by pressing F11.
5. Click **StartStopButton** and step through each line of code in debug mode by pressing F11.

   By adding a test host project to the control project, you can easily debug the control. In addition, you will not be required to refresh the reference to the control every time you rebuild it.

If time permits

► **Test the DigitalClock in separate instances of Visual Studio .NET**

1. Open a new instance of Visual Studio .NET
2. On the **File** menu, click **Add Project**, and then click **New Project**.
3. Create a new Windows application and name it **TestClock2**.
4. On the **Tools** menu, click **Customize Toolbox**.
5. Click the **.NET Framework Components** tab, and then click **Browse**.
6. In the **Open** dialog box, navigate to the **DigitalClock.dll** located in the \bin directory of the DigitalClock project, click **Open**, and then click **OK**.
7. Add a **DigitalClock** control to **Form1**.
8. Switch back to the Visual Studio .NET instance that includes the DigitalClock source code and set the **BackColor** property of **LocalTimeLabel** to **ControlLightLight**.
9. On the **Build** menu, click **Rebuild Solution**.
10. Switch back to the Visual Studio instance that includes the TestClock2 project and run it by pressing F5.

    The control displays the original value (**ControlDark**) and not the most recent one (**ControlLightLight**). To update the TestClock2 project to use the most recent **DigitalClock** control, you must refresh the reference to the control.

Lesson: Adding Design-Time Support for Controls

- Property Attributes
- How to Add Attributes That Provide Information to the Visual Designer
- Design-Time Support Options Built into the .NET Framework
- Practice: Adding Design-Time Support for Controls

Introduction

Design-time attributes are essential to display a control and its members correctly at design time because they provide valuable information to a visual design tool. This lesson describes some of the design-time options that are built into the .NET Framework. The lesson also describes how to add the attributes that provide information to the visual design tool.

Lesson objectives

After completing this lesson, you will be able to:

- Describe property attributes.
- Add attributes that provide information to the Visual Designer.
- Describe the built-in design-time options for components in Visual Studio .NET.

Property Attributes

- **Property Attributes**
  - Allow you to specify the behavior of properties at design time
- **Property attributes allow you to specify**
  - Grouping options for custom properties in the Properties window of the Visual Studio .NET environment
  - Default values
  - Custom editors for custom properties
- **Examples of Property Attributes**
  - Browsable
  - Category
  - TypeConverter
  - Description
  - DefaultProperty
  - Editor

Introduction

Attributes associate design-time functionality with a component. Design-time attributes can be applied to properties, events, classes, and even assemblies.

Definition

Attributes are the glue that binds design-time functionality to a component. Property attributes allow you to specify the behavior of properties at design time. Attributes can also be applied at the control level and to events as well. In the .NET Framework, design-time functionality is implemented not in a component but outside the component, and it is associated with the component through metadata supplied by custom attributes.

Property attributes allow you to specify:

- Grouping options for custom properties in the Properties window of Visual Studio .NET.
- Default values.
- Custom editors for custom properties.

List of property attributes

The following table lists some of the property attributes and their descriptions.

Property Attributes	Description
Browsable	Specifies whether a property or an event should be displayed in the Property browser.
Category	Specifies the name of the category in which to group a property or event. When categories are used, component properties and events can be displayed in logical groupings in the Properties window.
Description	Defines a small block of text to be displayed at the bottom of the Properties window when the user selects a property or event.
DefaultProperty	Specifies the default property for the component. This property is selected in the Properties window when a user clicks the control.
DefaultValue	Sets a default value for a property.
TypeConverter	Specifies the type converter to use for converting the type of the property to another data type.
Editor	Specifies the editor to use for editing (changing) a property in the Visual Designer.
RefreshProperties	Indicates how a designer refreshes when the associated property value changes. This class cannot be inherited.

In addition to property attributes, there are some control attributes, such as the **ToolBoxBitMap** attribute, that allow you to specify control behavior. The **ToolBoxBitMap** allows you to specify a bitmap or icon image to represent a control in the Toolbox of the Visual Studio .NET IDE.

How to Add Attributes That Provide Information to the Visual Designer

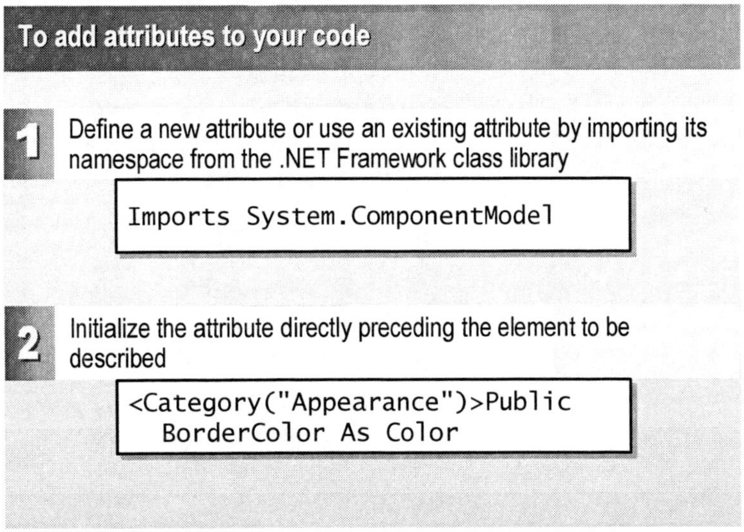

Introduction

Attributes associate design-time functionality with a component. Design-time attributes can be applied to properties, events, classes, and even assemblies.

Procedure

To add attributes:

1. Define a new attribute or use an existing attribute by importing its namespace from the .NET Framework class library.

   ```
   Imports System.ComponentModel
   ```

   When you derive a component or control from a base component that has design-time attributes, your component inherits the design-time functionality of the base class. If the base functionality is adequate for your purposes, you do not have to reapply the attributes. However, you can always override attributes or apply additional attributes to the derived component. Only classes that directly or indirectly implement **System.ComponentModel.IComponent** have design-time support in the Visual Designer.

2. Initialize the attribute directly preceding the element to be described.

   In the following code fragment, the **Category** attribute enables the Properties window to display the **Color** property in the Appearance category.

   ```
   <Category("Appearance")>Public BorderColor As Color
   ```

Design-Time Support Options Built into the .NET Framework

- **Property Browser**
  - Associates property editors for different data types
- **Type Converter**
  - Converts the value entered into the Properties window to the correct data type within a control
- **Custom UI Editors**
  - Chooses the correct UI editor for the Properties window based on the type of property
- **Custom Designers**
  - Allows you to modify the design-time appearance and behavior of controls and objects
- **Extenders**
  - Provide the ability to add or filter properties for controls

Introduction

Design-time functionality refers to the display and behavior of a component or control in a visual designer. The .NET Framework includes several features that support the development of design-time behavior for controls.

Design-time support options

- Property browser

  When a control exposes properties, the Visual Studio .NET IDE displays them at design time in the Properties window. Most properties are modified by typing string values into the property browser. The property browser then converts the string values to the correct type. So, for example, if you expose a property of type integer and attempt to enter a non-numeric value for it in the property browser, it will raise an error.

  The property browser is also capable of associating more advanced property editors for different data types. For example, the property editor exposes a color palette for **Color** types and a **DateTimePicker** control for **Date** types.

- Type converter

  A type converter is used to convert the value entered into the Properties window. A simple example is the conversion from a string to an integer and back. Type converters are primarily used for string-to-value conversions and for validation at design time and at run time. Most native data types (Int32, String, enumeration types, and others) have default type converters. You can create a custom type converter, by inheriting from the **System.ComponentModel.TypeConverter** class, if a custom property does not have an associated type converter.

  After you create a type converter, you can apply the **TypeConverter** attribute to a property to associate the property with the type converter. For example, you can use a **TypeConverter** to convert two strings entered in the Properties window to a **Point** type.

- Custom UI editors

  In some situations, a simple value-to-string conversion that allows a property to be displayed as text in the Properties window might not be adequate. For instance, in the case of a color property, a visual representation is more desirable. A UI type editor allows such a representation and is intended for use with property browsers and other advanced design-time hosts.

  To implement a custom UI type editor for Windows Forms, you define a class that is derived from **System.Drawing.Design.UITypeEditor**. You then apply the **Editor** attribute to a property to associate the property with the UI editor.

- Custom Designers

  Designers are classes that allow you to modify the design-time appearance and behavior of components and controls. Although the usual goal of any WYSIWYG form designer is to minimize differences between design-time and run-time appearance, some special design-time cues are necessary. For example, a **System.Windows.Forms.Panel** object might not have a visible border at run time. However, without a border the panel is invisible to the developer designing a form that contains the panel. Therefore, the designer for the **System.Windows.Forms.Panel** object draws a dotted line border around the panel.

  To create a custom designer, create a class that implements the **IDesigner** interface and apply the **Designer** attribute to the control.

- Extenders

  Extender providers add properties to other controls. In the .NET Framework, extender providers require no special support. At design time, extender properties appear in the Properties window as properties on the objects that they extend, rather than on the actual extender object.

  An example of an extender is the **ToolTip** control. The **ToolTip** property is not available to controls on a form until you add the **ToolTip** control to the form.

  To create an extender control, create a class that implements the **System.ComponentModel.IExtenderProvider** interface.

Note Controls support two modes of behavior: design-time and run-time. You can use the **DesignMode** property to determine the behavior mode of a control.

Practice: Adding Design-Time Support for Controls

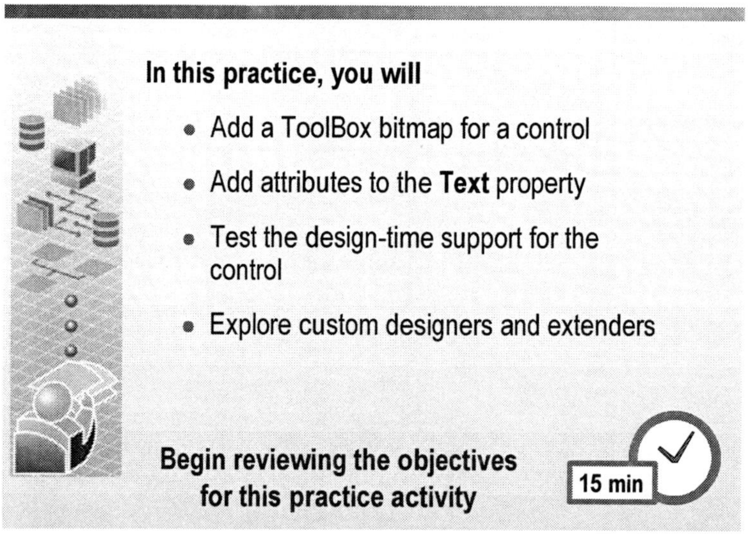

Introduction

In this practice, you will learn how to add design-time support for controls. The exercises involve adding a special icon for a vertical label control on the Toolbox. In addition, you will add an attribute to the **Text** property of the vertical label.

Instructions

► **Open the practice project**

1. Use Windows Explorer to browse to *install_folder*\Practices\Mod03\Mod03_02\Starter\VerticalLabel.

Note If you performed a default installation of the course files, *install_folder* corresponds to C:\Program Files\Msdntrain\2565.

---

2. Double-click the **VerticalLabel.sln** solution file to open the project.
3. On the **Build** menu, click **Build Solution**.

► **Add a ToolBox bitmap for a control**

1. On the **Project** menu, click **Add Existing Item**, change the File Type filter to **All Files**, select the **VerticalLabel.ico** file located in *install_folder*\Practices\Mod03\Mod03_02\Starter\VerticalLabel, and then click **Open**.
2. In Solution Explorer, click **VerticalLabel.ico**. In the Properties window, set the **Build Action** property to **Embedded Resource**.

   There are various options for associating an image with a control's ToolBox bitmap. In this exercise, you will embed the image in the compiled project. In this case, the **ToolBoxBitmap** attribute requires two arguments: the **Type** where the image is located and a **String** that represents the name of the image.

3. Open VerticalLabel.vb in the Code Editor.
4. Add a **ToolBoxBitmap** attribute to the **VerticalLabel** class. Use the **GetType** function to return a **VerticalLabel** type for the first argument and **VerticalLabel.ico** as a string for the second argument. Your code should look like the following.

```
<ToolBoxBitmap (GetType(VerticalLabel),
"VerticalLabel.ico")> _
 Public Class VerticalLabel
```

► **Add attributes to the Text property**

1. Import the **System.ComponentModel** namespace.
2. Add a **Category** attribute to the **Text** property and set it to **VerticalLabel**.
3. Add a **Description** attribute to the **Text** property and set it to **Text is displayed vertically in container**. Your code should look like the following.

```
Imports System.ComponentModel
...
<Category("VerticalLabel"), _
Description("Text is displayed vertically in container")> _
Public Overrides Property Text() As String
...
```

4. On the **Build** menu, click **Build Solution**.

► **Test the design-time support for the control**

1. On the **File** menu, click **Add Project**, and then click **New Project**.
2. Click the **Windows Application** template, name it **Test**, and then click **OK**.
3. On the **Tools** menu, click **Customize Toolbox**.
4. In the **Customize Toolbox** dialog box, click the **.NET Frameworks Components** tab, and then click **Browse**.
5. In the **Open** dialog box, click *install_folder*\Practices\Mod03\Mod03_02\Starter\VerticalLabel\obj\Debug\ VerticalLabel.dll, click **Open**, and then click **OK**.
6. Ensure that the control is correctly represented by the VerticalLabel.ico in the Toolbox.
7. Add a **VerticalLabel** control to Form1 from the Toolbox. View the **Text** property in the Properties window to ensure that **Category** and **Description** are displayed.

► **Explore custom designers and extenders**

1. Add a **Panel** control to **Form1**.

   The **Panel** control displays an outline of its borders at design time. At run time the outline is not displayed. This is an example of a custom designer.

2. Add a **ToolTip** control to **Form1** and view the **ToolTip on ToolTip1** property that is exposed on both the **Panel** control and the **VerticalLabel** control.

   The **ToolTip** control extends the **ToolTip** property to other controls. This is an example of an extender control.

Lesson: Licensing a Control

- Files in Licensing
- How to Enable Licensing for a Control
- Demonstration: Creating and Validating a License for a Control
- How LicFileLicenseProvider Works in .NET

Introduction

The .NET Framework provides a licensing model that is identical for all components including Windows Forms controls and ASP.NET server controls, although the implementation is different.

Licensing allows control authors to protect their property by checking that a user is authorized to use the control. This check is more important at design time, when the control is incorporated into an application, than at run time. When a licensed control is used legally at design time, the application gets a run-time license that can be freely distributed.

Licensing provides a model that allows component and control vendors to create and distribute classes that have varying degrees of functionality depending on the presence or absence of a license on the developer's or end user's computer.

Components of the licensing model

Licensing is built into the .NET Framework, and developers use classes built into the **System.ComponentModel** namespace to provide custom licensing solutions. There are two components of the licensing model the **LicenseManager** and the **LicenseProvider**.

- The **LicenseManager** class is responsible for validating licensed controls at both run time and design time. The **LicenseManager** class is part of the runtime, and when a class is instantiated, **LicenseManager** uses the proper validation mechanism for the control or component.
- The **LicenseProvider** class is the place to put custom validation code. You can create unique licensing by extending the **System.ComponentModel.LicenseProvider** class. By extending this class, you can create unique licensing models. For example, you can create the license for a control once and allow it to be reused as many times as necessary, or you could create a licensing mechanism that expires after a certain period of time.

  Visual Studio .NET ships with the **LicFileLicenseProvider**, which is derived from the **System.ComponentModel.LicenseProvider** object. The **LicFileLicenseProvider** is built for demonstration purposes and is not intended for production licensing behavior. You can build more advanced licensing scenarios by building additional classes that derive from **System.ComponentModel.LicenseProvider**.

Note There are two modes of consumption for licensed controls, design-time and run-time. At design time, a license provider can obtain a valid license from anywhere, such as a .LIC file from a hard disk or from an XML Web service. Then at run time for client apps, this license is converted into a license key and embedded into the executing assembly.

Lesson objectives

After completing this lesson, you will be able to:

- Describe the files needed for licensing a control.
- Enable licensing for a control.
- Explain how licensing works in the .NET Framework.

Files in Licensing

- **LIC file**
  - Design-time license file that exists anywhere that the LicenseProvider class specifies

```
"Namespace.ClassName is a licensed component"
```

- **LICX file**
  - Design-time license that resides with the assembly that consumes a licensed component

```
"Namespace.ClassName, ClassName, Version,
  Culture, PublicKeyToken"
```

- **.Licenses file**
  - Binary run-time license file used at run time

Introduction

Most controls should support design-time licensing and run-time licensing. Design-time licensing ensures that a developer is building an application with a legally purchased control; run-time licensing ensures that a user is running an application that contains a legally purchased control. There are several licensing options available, such as time-based expiration licensing, per-processor licensing, or per-use licensing.

Files involved in licensing with the LicFileLicenseProvider

Visual Studio .NET uses several files that are required for design-time and run-time licensing.

- .LIC file

  This is the design-time license file. It can exist anywhere that the **LicenseProvider** class specifies. So, for example, the .LIC file can exist with the assembly, somewhere on the hard drive, or it can be retrieved by using a Web service.

  If you use the **LicLicenseFileProvider** file, the .LIC file is a text file that resides in the same folder as the built assembly and has a specific format as shown below.

```
"Namespace.ClassName is a licensed component"
```

  Currently you have to manually add this text file to the assembly folder with this correct format and the .LIC extension.

Note If the control is in the same solution project (like when you are testing it) as the project that is using it, the .LIC file must reside in the \obj\Debug folder.

- .LICX file

  This is a design-time file that resides with the assembly that consumes a licensed component. It is a text file that resides in the Project folder of an application. It lists all the licensed components used in an application. The .LICX file has a specific format as shown below.

  ```
  "Namespace.ClassName, ClassName, Version, Culture,
  PublicKeyToken"
  ```

  This file is created automatically when you add a licensed component to an application.

- .Licenses file

  This is the binary run-time license file used at run time. This file is created automatically in Visual Studio .NET. It can be generated manually by using the LC.exe utility. This file resides in the same folder as the built assembly.

How to Enable Licensing for a Control

To enable licensing for a control

1. Import the **System.ComponentModel** namespace
2. Append the **LicenseProvider** attribute to the declaration of the class you want to license
3. Declare a **License** object
4. Call the **Validate** or **IsValid** methods of the **LicenseManager** to fill the License object with a valid license
5. Override the **Dispose** method of the licensed class and explicitly call the **Dispose** method on the **License** object
6. Create a text file with a .LIC extension and the correct format and save it to the assembly folder

---

Introduction

To enable licensing for a control, you need the licensing files as well as some licensing objects and attributes such as **LicenseProvider** attribute, a class that derives from **System.ComponentModel.LicenseProvider**, **License** object, and **LicenseManager** object.

Procedure

To enable licensing for a control:

1. Include the **System.ComponentModel** namespace.

   All of the licensing mechanisms reside in the **System.ComponentModel** namespace.

   ```
   Imports System.ComponentModel
   ```

2. Apply a **LicenseProviderAttribute** to the class.

   The granting of licenses and the validation logic is performed by a license provider, which is a class that derives from **System.ComponentModel.LicenseProvider**. When you create a component that you want to license, you must specify the type of **LicenseProvider** by marking the component with a **LicenseProviderAttribute**. Visual Studio .NET supplies the default **LicFileLicenseProvider LicenseProvider** class. This **LicFileLicenseProvider** is easy to use because it is built into the .NET Framework, but its validation logic is not very secure. You can extend this class to provide more robust licensing scenarios.

   ```
   <LicenseProvider(GetType(LicFileLicenseProvider))> Public
   Class MyControl
   ```

3. Declare a license object.

   The **License** object is used at run time to hold the validated license. You use the **LicenseManager** object to fill the **License** object with a validated license.

   ```
   Private License As License
   ```

4. Validate the license by using **LicenseManager.Validate** or **LicenseManager.IsValid** in the constructor of the control.

   LicenseManager provides properties and methods to add a license to a component and to manage a **LicenseProvider**. Call **Validate** or **IsValid** in the constructor of the component to validate a license. **Validate** throws a **LicenseException** when it tries to create an instance without a valid license and makes the control unavailable. The **IsValid** method returns a Boolean value that identifies if a valid license was available. **IsValid** does not throw an exception and the control can still be used. You could use this method to modify the behavior of the control based on whether or not a license was available. For example, you could limit features of the control if no license is available.

   ```
   'Using the Validate method of LicenseManager
   Private myLicense as System.ComponentModel.License
   myLicense=LicenseManager.Validate(GetType(LicensedControl),
   Me)

   'Using the IsValidate method of LicenseManager
   Private validLicense as Boolean
   validLicense =
   LicenseManager.IsValid(GetType(LicensedControl))
   ```

5. Dispose of any license that is granted when the component is disposed or finalized.

   Call the **Dispose** method when you are finished by using the license. The **Dispose** method leaves the license in an unusable state. After calling **Dispose**, you must release all references to the license so that the memory it was occupying can be reclaimed by garbage collection. This is an important step to take so that your control does not leak licenses. Not doing this might allow malicious code to get the license before the garbage collector does.

6. Create a text file with the .LIC extension and the correct format, and then save it to the assembly folder.

Example

```
'Import the System.ComponentModel namespace to access the
'licensing features built into the framework
Imports System.ComponentModel
'We are using the LicenseProvider shipped with Visual Studio
'.NET
<LicenseProvider(GetType(LicFileLicenseProvider))> Public
Class LicensedControl
    Inherits System.Windows.Forms.UserControl

    Private myLicense As System.ComponentModel.License
    Private IsValid As Boolean

    Public Sub New()
        MyBase.New()

        InitializeComponent()
        'Call the Validate method to validate
        'the current instance of the LicensedClass
               myLicense = LicenseManager.Validate_
               (GetType(LicensedControl), Me)
        'or call the IsValid method of the _
        LicensedClass control
        'to determine if a valid license exists
               IsValid = LicenseManager.IsValid_
               (GetType(LicensedControl))
    End Sub

     Protected Overloads Overrides Sub _
     Dispose(ByVal disposing As Boolean)
        If disposing Then
            If Not (components Is Nothing) Then
                components.Dispose()
            End If
        End If
        'Explicity destroy the license object to _
        prevent 'security issues
            If Not (myLicense Is Nothing) Then
                myLicense.Dispose()
                myLicense = Nothing
            End If

        MyBase.Dispose(disposing)
    End Sub
```

Demonstration: Creating and Validating a License for a Control

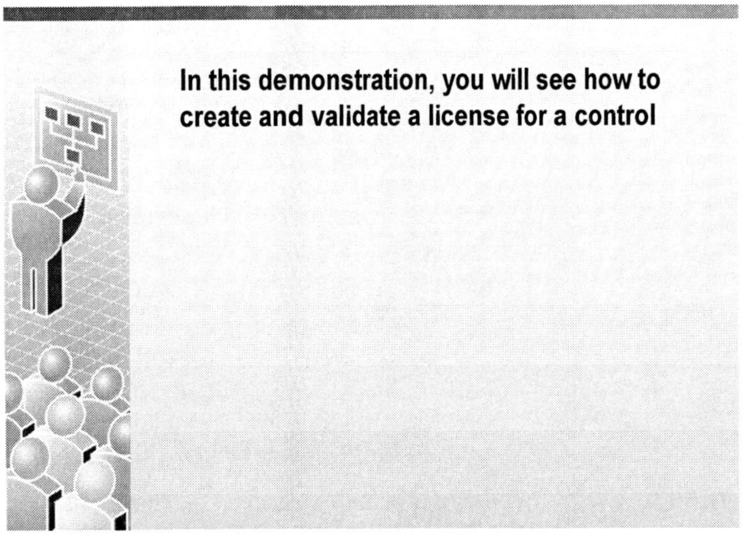

Introduction

In this demonstration, you will see how to enable licensing for a control. The demonstration uses the example of a **NumericTextBox** control, which is a **TextBox** that accepts only numeric characters in the **Text** property.

Instructions

► **Open the NumericTextBox.sln solution file**

- Open the NumericTextBox.sln solution in Visual Studio .NET from *install_folder*\Democode\Mod03\Mod03_02\Starter.

► **Apply a LicenseProviderAttribute to the NumericTextBox class**

1. Open the NumericTextBox.vb file in the Code Editor and import the **System.ComponentModel** namespace.
2. Append the **LicenseFileProviderAttribute** to the class and use the **LicFileLicenseProvider LicenseProvider**. Your code should look like the following.

```
Imports System.ComponentModel

<ToolBoxBitmap(GetType(NumericTextBox), _
"NumericTextBox.ico"), _
LicenseProvider(GetType(LicFileLicenseProvider))> _
Public Class NumericTextBox
```

► Write the code to create and destroy a license

1. Declare a class level **License** called **validatedLicense**.
2. In the control constructor, use the **Validate** method of the **LicenseManager** to generate a **License** and return it to the *validatedLicense* variable. Your code should look like the following.

```
validatedLicense = _
LicenseManager.Validate(GetType(NumericTextBox), Me)
```

3. In the control destructor, explicitly destroy the **License** object. Your code should look like the following.

```
If Not (validatedLicense Is Nothing) Then
   validatedLicense.Dispose()
   validatedLicense = Nothing
End If
```

► Add the NumericTextBox to the Toolbox and test it

1. On the **Build** menu, click **Build Solution**.
2. On the **File** menu, click **Add Project**, and then click **New Project**.
3. Create a new Windows application and name it **Test**.
4. On the **Tools** menu, click **Customize Toolbox**.
5. Click the **.NET Framework Components** tab, and then click **Browse**.
6. Open the NumericTextBox.dll file from *install_folder*\Democode\Mod03\Mod03_02\Starter\bin, and then click **OK**.
7. Attempt to add a **NumericTextBox** to the form. You will get an error stating that a valid license could not be granted.

► Add a .LIC license file to the NumericTextBox

1. Expand the **References** folder in the Test Windows application and display the **Path** property of the **NumericTextBox** reference. This is where you will need to create the .lic license file.
2. Open Microsoft Notepad.
3. Type the following code.

```
NorthwindControls.NumericTextBox is a licensed component.
```

4. Save the file in *install_folder*\Democode\Mod03\Mod3_02\Starter\obj\Debug, and name it **NorthwindControls.NumericTextBox.lic**.
5. Close Notepad.

► Test the licensed NumericTextBox and examine the supporting files

1. Add a licensed **NumericTextBox** to the form in the Windows application.
2. In Solution Explorer, click **Show All Files**.
3. Open the **Licenses.licx** file and review the syntax.
4. Expand the \bin folder and observe that there is no run-time .license file for the application.
5. Set the Test Windows application as the startup project, and run the application.
6. Close the application.
7. In Solution Explorer, click **Refresh**, and then display the run-time **Text.exe.licenses** file in *install_folder*\Democode\Mod03\Mod3_02\Starter\obj\Debug.

How LicFileLicenseProvider Works in .NET

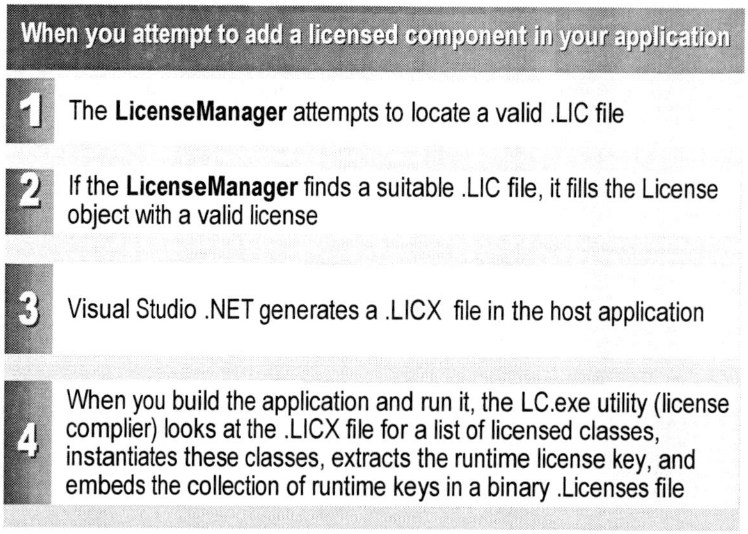

Introduction

When you attempt to add a licensed component to your application, a series of steps take place in Visual Studio .NET to find a licensed file.

Procedure

When you attempt to add a licensed component in your application, the following steps take place in Visual Studio .NET.

1. The **LicenseManager** attempts to locate a valid .LIC file in the same folder as the referenced licensed assembly.
2. If the **LicenseManager** finds a suitable .LIC file, it fills the **License** object with a valid license.
3. Visual Studio .NET generates a .LICX file in the host application that lists attributes of all the licensed controls used by the host application.
4. When you build the application and run it, the LC.exe utility (license complier) looks at the .LICX file for a list of licensed classes, instantiates these classes, extracts the run-time license key, and embeds the collection of run-time keys in a binary .Licenses file.

Review

- Extending and Creating Controls
- Adding Design-Time Support for Controls
- Licensing a Control

1. What is the difference between a composite control and a custom control?

2. How do you test a (custom) control? add control to tool Box

3. What are property attributes?

   Meta data

   Property Box & tool Box

Property atribute

get & set

Behavior

4. List some property attributes built into Visual Studio .NET.

5. What are extenders?

add property to control

6. What is the purpose of LicenseManager and LicenseProvider in licensing controls?

Lab 3.1: Building Controls

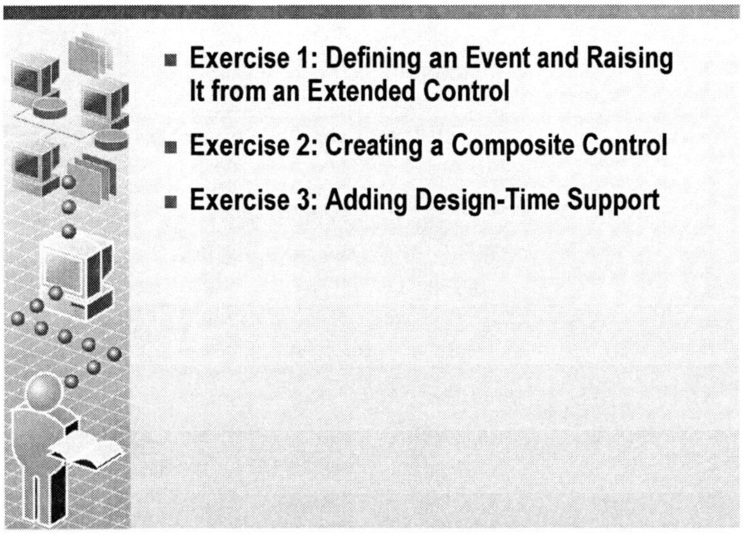

Objectives

After completing this lab, you will have demonstrated your ability to:

- Declare and raise an event in a custom control to a host application.
- Create a composite control.
- Define property procedures in a composite control to read, write, and format properties of constituent controls.
- Add design-time support to custom controls.
- Test custom controls.

Note This lab focuses on the concepts in Module 3, "Building Controls," in Course 2565A, *Developing Microsoft .NET Applications for Windows (Visual Basic .NET)*. As a result, this lab may not comply with Microsoft security recommendations.

Prerequisites

Before working on this lab, you must have:

- The knowledge and skills to develop a simple Windows Forms application by using a Visual Studio .NET–compatible programming language.
- The knowledge and skills to use intrinsic controls in a Visual Studio .NET–based application.
- The knowledge and skills to create custom controls in a Visual Studio .NET–based application.
- The knowledge and skills to add design-time support custom controls in a Visual Studio .NET–based application.
- The knowledge and skills to debug a custom control project in a Visual Studio .NET–based application.

Scenario

You are a developer in a trading company called Northwind Traders. The department you work in is developing a purchase order application that will be used by the Northwind Traders sales force. When developing purchase order applications that cater to different people, you often write the same code (code that has the same functionality) for different applications. Instead of writing the same code repeatedly, you decide to take advantage of component-based development and develop classes and controls that can be reused in other applications.

A common task that you perform in applications is writing code that prevents users from entering non-numeric values in text boxes that display information such as account balances and telephone numbers. You decide to create a group of extended controls that inherit from the **TextBox** class and enforce the required logic. Some may enforce numeric constraints; others may enforce string formatting.

In addition, to increase the efficiency of your development time and provide a consistent interface for the purchase order applications, you decide to create a custom composite control that includes all the constituent controls required to display order information.

Estimated time to complete this lab: 60 minutes

Exercise 1
Defining an Event and Raising It from an Extended Control

In this exercise, you will define an event for the **NumericTextBox** control, raise it from the control, pass event information, and respond to it from a host application.

There are starter and solution files associated with this exercise. Browse to *install_folder*\Labfiles\Lab03_1\Ex01\Starter to find the starter files, and browse to *install_folder*\Labfiles\Lab03_1\Ex01\Solution to find the solution files. If you performed a default installation of the course files, *install_folder* corresponds to C:\Program Files\Msdntrain\2565.

Scenario

The **NumericTextBox** control is an extended control that inherits from the **TextBox** class. The control accepts only numeric characters and allows the use of the BACKSPACE key. Your users are complaining because the current version of the control does not provide feedback when an invalid character is entered. You have been asked to expose an event on the **NumericTextBox** control that passes event arguments to host applications when an invalid key is pressed. The host applications can then display the source and details of the error in the control to the user.

Tasks	Additional information
1. Open Visual Studio .NET, and open the NumericTextBox.sln file. To open the solution file, browse to *install_folder*\Labfiles\Lab03_1\Ex01\Starter\NumerictextBox.	**a.** For more information about opening a project file, see the following resources: • The Visual Studio .NET Help documentation. For additional information about opening a project file, in Search, select the **Search in titles only** check box, then search by using the phrase **Open Project Dialog Box**.
2. Use the Task List in the NumericTextBox.vb file to locate the code section 'TODO: 1. Modify the Inherits statement so that the NumericTextBox class inherits from the System.Windows.Forms.TextBox class.	**a.** For more information about creating extended controls and why you should use them, see the following resources: • Lesson: Extending and Creating Controls in Module 3, "Building Controls," in Course 2565A, *Developing Microsoft .NET Applications for Windows (Visual Basic .NET).* • The .NET Framework SDK documentation. For additional information about creating extended controls, search by using the phrase **Windows Forms Control Development Basics.**
3. Use the Task List in the NumericTextBox.vb file to locate the code section 'TODO: 2. Declare the **InvalidUserEntry** event that passes an Object type and **KeyPressEventArgs** event arguments.	**a.** For more information declaring an event, see the following resources: • Lesson: Extending and Creating Controls in Module 3, "Building Controls," in Course 2565A, *Developing Microsoft .NET Applications for Windows (Visual Basic .NET).* • Practice: Creating a Composite Control in Module 3, "Building Controls," in Course 2565A, *Developing Microsoft .NET Applications for Windows (Visual Basic .NET).* • The .NET Framework SDK documentation. For additional information about raising events from custom controls, search by using the phrase **Defining an Event.**

Tasks	Additional information
4. Use the Task List in the NumericTextBox.vb file to locate the code section 'TODO: 3. Raise the **InvalidUserEntry** event, passing the current instance of the NumericTextBox control and the instance of the KeyPressEventArgs event. The **InvalidUserEntry** event will fire every time a user enters an invalid character.	**a.** For more information about how to raise an event, see the following resources: • Lesson: Extending and Creating Controls in Module 3, "Building Controls," in Course 2565A, *Developing Microsoft .NET Applications for Windows (Visual Basic .NET).* • Practice: Creating a Composite Control in Module 3, "Building Controls," in Course 2565A, *Developing Microsoft .NET Applications for Windows (Visual Basic .NET).* • The .NET Framework SDK documentation. For additional information about raising events from custom controls, search by using the phrase **Defining an Event**.
5. Rebuild the NumericTextBox project.	**a.** For more information about building your application, see the following resource: • The Visual Studio .NET Help documentation. Search by using the phrase **Default and Custom Builds**.
6. Add a Windows Application project to the NumericTextBox solution, and name it **Test**.	**a.** For more information about adding a project to an existing solution for testing, see the following resources: • Lesson: Extending and Creating Controls in Module 3, "Building Controls," in Course 2565A, *Developing Microsoft .NET Applications for Windows (Visual Basic .NET).* • Practice: Creating a Composite Control in Module 3, "Building Controls," in Course 2565A, *Developing Microsoft .NET Applications for Windows (Visual Basic .NET).* • The .NET Framework SDK documentation. For help with the code editor, search by using the phrase **Debugging Preparation: Windows Control Libraries**.
7. Open Design view of Form1 in the Test project, and add the **NumericTextBox** control to the Toolbox. Then, add a **NumericTextBox** control from the Toolbox to Form1. Make sure to reference the version of the control in the Debug folder.	**a.** For more information about customizing the Toolbox, see the following resources: • Code Walkthrough: Creating Controls in Module 3, "Building Controls," in Course 2565A, *Developing Microsoft .NET Applications for Windows (Visual Basic .NET).* • The Visual Studio .NET Help documentation. Search by using the phrase **Using** the **Toolbox**.

Tasks	Additional information
8. Add an event handler to Form1 for the NumericTextBox **InvalidUserEntry** event. In the event handler, use the **KeyPressEventArgs** event arguments to display the value of the invalid key that is pressed in a message box.	**a.** For more information about creating event handlers, see the following resources: • Lesson: Creating an Event Handler for a Control in Module 2, "Working with Controls," in Course 2565A, *Developing Microsoft .NET Applications for Windows (Visual Basic .NET).* • Practice: Creating an Event Handler for a Control in Module 2, "Working with Controls," in Course 2565A, *Developing Microsoft .NET Applications for Windows (Visual Basic .NET).* • The .NET Framework SDK documentation. Search by using the phrase **Consuming Events**.
9. Set the Test project as the **Startup Project**, rebuild the project, and then start the NumericTextBox solution. Enter a non-numeric character in the **NumericTextBox** control. The **InvalidUserEntry** event procedure should run and display a message box that includes the value of the invalid key that was pressed.	**a.** For more information about building and debugging your applications, see the following resource: • The Visual Studio .NET Help documentation. Search by using the phrases **Default and Custom Builds** and **Using the Debugger**.

Exercise 2
Creating a Composite Control

In this exercise, you will create a composite control by using the Windows Control Library template and define properties procedures that read, write, and format the properties of constituent controls. You will then test the composite control in a host application.

Scenario

As a developer at Northwind Traders, you realize that many applications are being built to enable the sales force to create purchase orders. Rather than create individual controls that offer this functionality in each application, you decide to create a single composite control that contains all the controls required to accomplish this task. You decide to first create the composite control and define all the properties. You will add the data binding code to the control afterward.

The composite control will be called **OrderItemControl**. The **OrderItemControl** control includes four **TextBox** controls and a **ComboBox** control that will be used to display the quantity, product name, price, discount, and quantity/unit of orders.

The following image shows what the **OrderItemControl** control looks like.

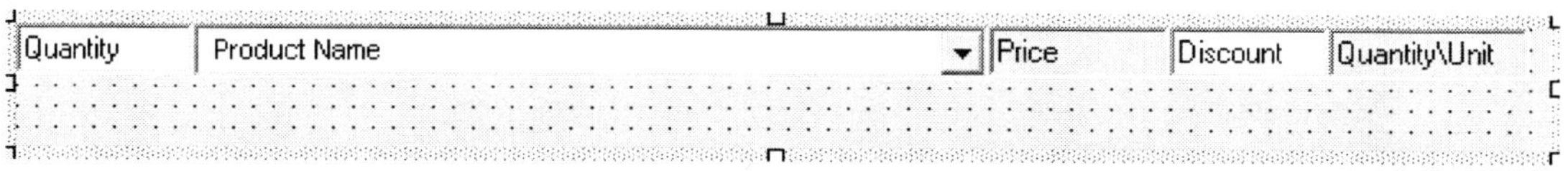

There are solution files associated with this exercise. Browse to *install_folder*\Labfiles\Lab03_1\Ex02\Solution to find the solution files. If you performed a default installation of the course files, *install_folder* corresponds to C:\Program Files\Msdntrain\2565.

Tasks	Additional information
1. Open Visual Studio .NET, create a new Windows Control Library project, and name it **OrderItemControl.** Save the project in *install_folder*\Labfiles\Lab03_1\Ex02.	**a.** For more information about creating a project, see the following resources: • Practice: Creating a Composite Control in Module 3, "Building Controls," in Course 2565A, *Developing Microsoft .NET Applications for Windows (Visual Basic .NET).* • The Visual Studio .NET Help documentation. Search by using the phrase **Adding Projects and Items to the New Application**.
2. Add a new UserControl component to the OrderItemControl project, and name it **OrderItemControl.vb.** Delete **UserControl1** from the project. You need to delete the existing **UserControl** from the project or else it will generate errors.	**a.** For more information about adding new items to a project, see the following resources: • Practice: Creating a Composite Control in Module 3, "Building Controls," in Course 2565A, *Developing Microsoft .NET Applications for Windows (Visual Basic .NET).* • The Visual Studio .NET Help documentation. Search by using the phrase **Adding Projects and Items to the New Application**.

Tasks	Additional information
3. Add a **TextBox** control to OrderItemControl. Set the **Name** property to **QuantityTextBox**. Use the image of the OrderItemControl shown in the illustration to determine where to place the **QuantityTextBox** control.	**a.** For more information about adding controls to a User Control and configuring properties, see the following resource: • The Visual Studio .NET Help documentation. Search by using the phrases **User Control Designer** and **Setting Properties for Controls, Documents, and Forms**.
4. Add a ComboBox to OrderItemControl. Set the **Name** to **ProductNameComboBox**. Set the **Items** property to **A**, **B**, **C**—placing each value on a separate line. Use the image of the OrderItemControl shown in the illustration to determine where to place **ProductNameComboBox**.	**a.** For more information about adding controls to a User Control, configuring properties, and setting the Items collection of a ComboBox, see the following resources: • Lesson: Extending and Creating Controls in Module 3, "Building Controls," in Course 2565A, *Developing Microsoft .NET Applications for Windows (Visual Basic .NET)*. • Practice: Creating a Composite Control in Module 3, "Building Controls," in Course 2565A, *Developing Microsoft .NET Applications for Windows (Visual Basic .NET)*. • The Visual Studio .NET Help documentation. Search by using the phrases **User Control Designer**, **Setting Properties for Controls, Documents, and Forms** and **String Collection Editor**.
5. Add a TextBox to OrderItemControl. Set the **Name** to **PriceTextBox**. Set the **Enabled** property to **False**. Use the image of the OrderItemControl shown in the illustration to determine where to place **PriceTextBox**.	Additional information is not necessary for this task.
6. Add a TextBox to OrderItemControl. Set the **Name** to **DiscountTextBox**. Use the image of the OrderItemControl shown in the illustration to determine where to place **DiscountTextBox**.	Additional information is not necessary for this task.
7. Add a TextBox to OrderItemControl. Set the **Name** to **QuantityPerUnitTextBox**. Set the **Enabled** property to **False**. Use the image of the OrderItemControl shown in the illustration to determine where to place QuantityPerUnitTextBox.	Additional information is not necessary for this task.

Tasks	Additional information
8. In **OrderItemControl**, create a **Public** property named **OrderQuantity** that returns a **String** and gets and sets the **Text** property of **QuantityTextBox**.	**a.** For more information about creating property procedures, see the following resources: • Lesson: Extending and Creating Controls in Module 3, "Building Controls," in Course 2565A, *Developing Microsoft .NET Applications for Windows (Visual Basic .NET).* • Practice: Creating a Composite Control in Module 3, "Building Controls," in Course 2565A, *Developing Microsoft .NET Applications for Windows (Visual Basic .NET).* • The .NET Framework SDK documentation. Search by using the phrase **Properties Overview**.
9. In **OrderItemControl**, create a **Public** property named **OrderProductName** that returns a **String** and gets and sets the **Text** property of **ProductNameComboBox**.	**a.** For more information about creating property procedures, see the following resources: • Lesson: Extending and Creating Controls in Module 3, "Building Controls," in Course 2565A, *Developing Microsoft .NET Applications for Windows (Visual Basic .NET).* • Practice: Creating a Composite Control in Module 3, "Building Controls," in Course 2565A, *Developing Microsoft .NET Applications for Windows (Visual Basic .NET).* • The .NET Framework SDK documentation. Search by using the phrase **Properties Overview**.
10. In **OrderItemControl**, create a **Public** property named **OrderPrice** that returns a **String** and gets and sets the **Text** property of **PriceTextBox.** In the **Set** block, use the **Format** function to convert **Value** to **Currency**. Using property procedures gives you greater control over how properties are set and retrieved.	**a.** For more information about creating property procedures and using the Format function, see the following resources: • Lesson: Extending and Creating Controls in Module 3, "Building Controls," in Course 2565A, *Developing Microsoft .NET Applications for Windows (Visual Basic .NET).* • Practice: Creating a Composite Control in Module 3, "Building Controls," in Course 2565A, *Developing Microsoft .NET Applications for Windows (Visual Basic .NET).* • The .NET Framework SDK documentation. Search by using the phrases **Properties** Overview and **Format Function.**
11. In **OrderItemControl**, create a **Public** property named **OrderDiscount** that returns a **String** and gets and sets the **Text** property of **DiscountTextBox.**	**a.** For more information about creating property procedures, see the following resources: • Lesson: Extending and Creating Controls in Module 3, "Building Controls," in Course 2565A, *Developing Microsoft .NET Applications for Windows (Visual Basic .NET).* • Practice: Creating a Composite Control in Module 3, "Building Controls," in Course 2565A, *Developing Microsoft .NET Applications for Windows (Visual Basic .NET).* • The .NET Framework SDK documentation. Search by using the phrase **Properties Overview**.

Tasks	Additional information
12. In **OrderItemControl**, create a **Public** property named **OrderQuantityPerUnit** that returns a **String** and gets and sets the **Text** property of **QuantityPerUnitTextBox**.	**a.** For more information about creating property procedures, see the following resources: • Lesson: Extending and Creating Controls in Module 3, "Building Controls," in Course 2565A, *Developing Microsoft .NET Applications for Windows (Visual Basic .NET)*. • Practice: Creating a Composite Control in Module 3, "Building Controls," in Course 2565A, *Developing Microsoft .NET Applications for Windows (Visual Basic .NET)*. • The Visual Studio .NET Help documentation. Search by using the phrase Properties **Overview**.
13. Add a Windows Application project to the OrderItemControl solution, and name it **Test**.	**a.** For more information about adding a project to an existing solution for testing, see the following resources: • Lesson: Extending and Creating Controls in Module 3, "Building Controls," in Course 2565A, *Developing Microsoft .NET Applications for Windows (Visual Basic .NET)*. • Practice: Creating a Composite Control in Module 3, "Building Controls," in Course 2565A, *Developing Microsoft .NET Applications for Windows (Visual Basic .NET)*. • The .NET Framework SDK documentation. For help with the code editor, search by using the phrase **Debugging Preparation: Windows Control Libraries.Control Libraries**.
14. Open Design view of Form1 in the Test project, and add an **OrderItemControl** control from the Toolbox. Resize Form1 to make the control fit. When you use User Controls to create composite controls, they are automatically added to the Toolbox in the design time environment of the solution. When you develop extended controls and custom controls, you must manually add them to the ToolBox.	**a.** For more information about adding user controls from the Toolbox, see the following resources: • Lesson: Extending and Creating Controls in Module 3, "Building Controls," in Course 2565A, *Developing Microsoft .NET Applications for Windows (Visual Basic .NET)*. • Practice: Creating a Composite Control in Module 3, "Building Controls," in Course 2565A, *Developing Microsoft .NET Applications for Windows (Visual Basic .NET)*. • The Visual Studio .NET Help documentation. Search by using the phrase **Using the Toolbox**.

Tasks	Additional information
15. Add a **Button** control to Form1, accept the default name, and in the **Click** event procedure, perform the following steps: • Assign the **OrderItemProductName** property of the **OrderItemControl** control to the **OrderItemQuantity** property. • Assign the **OrderDiscount** property of the **OrderItemControl** control to the **OrderPrice** property. • Assign the **OrderDiscount** property of the **OrderItemControl** control to the **OrderQuantityPerUnit** property. This is only to test the **Get** and **Set** statements of the property procedures that you created.	**a.** For more information about creating event handlers, see the following resources: • Lesson: Creating an Event Handler for a Control in Module 2, "Working with Controls," in Course 2565A, *Developing Microsoft .NET Applications for Windows (Visual Basic .NET).* • Practice: Creating an Event Handler for a Control in Module 2, "Working with Controls," in Course 2565A, *Developing Microsoft .NET Applications for Windows (Visual Basic .NET).* • The .NET Framework SDK documentation. Search by using the phrase **Consuming Events**.
16. Set a breakpoint on the first line in the **Button1** click event procedure created in the step 15. Set the Test project as **Startup Project**, rebuild the solution, and then run the OrderItemControl solution. Select **B** in the **ProductNameComboBox** control, and type **12** in the **DiscountTextBox** control. Click **Button1**, and view the results.	**a.** For more information about building and debugging your applications, see the following resource: • The Visual Studio .NET Help documentation. Search by using the phrases **Default and Custom Builds** and **Using the Debugger**.

Exercise 3
Adding Design-Time Support

In this exercise, you will add attributes to properties of the **OrderItemControl** control. You will then test the design-time support features that you added.

Scenario

As the developer of the OrderItemControl, you do not know how developers will use it and the kind of support that they will require to be able to use the control. You decide to add some design-time support to the control to enable other developers to use the control easily. You will add description and category information to the properties that you created in the previous exercise so that it is easy for other developers to understand the function of each property.

There are starter and solution files associated with this exercise. Browse to *install_folder*\Labfiles\Lab03_1\Ex03\Starter to find the starter files, and browse to *install_folder*\Labfiles\Lab03_1\Ex03\Solution to find the solution files. If you performed a default installation of the course files, *install_folder* corresponds to C:\Program Files\Msdntrain\2565.

Tasks	Additional information
1. Open Visual Studio .NET, and open the OrderItemControl.sln file. To open the solution files, browse to *install_folder*\Labfiles\Lab03_1\Ex03\Starter\OrderItemControl.	**a.** For more information about opening a project file and starting an application, see the following resource: • The Visual Studio .NET Help documentation. For additional information about opening a project file, in Search, select the **Search in titles only** check box, then search by using the phrase **Open Project Dialog Box**.
2. Add **Category** and **Description** attributes to each property of the OrderItemControl. Use **OrderItemControl** as the **Category**.	**a.** For more information about adding design-time support to control properties, see the following resources: • Lesson: Adding Design-Time Support for Controls in Module 3, "Building Controls," in Course 2565A, *Developing Microsoft .NET Applications for Windows (Visual Basic .NET)*. • Practice: Adding Design-Time Support for Controls in Module 3, "Building Controls," in Course 2565A, *Developing Microsoft .NET Applications for Windows (Visual Basic .NET)*. • The Visual Studio .NET Help documentation. Search by using the phrase **Attributes and Design-Time Support**.
3. Build the OrderItemControl project. Add a Windows Application project to the OrderItemControl solution, and name it **Test**. Add an OrderItemControl from the ToolBox, and view the custom properties in the Properties window. Make sure to enable the **Categorized** button so that you can see how your control properties are sorted.	**a.** For more information about building and debugging your applications, see the following resource: • The Visual Studio .NET Help documentation. Search by using the phrases **Default and Custom Builds** and **Using the Debugger**.

msdn® training

Module 4: Using Data in Windows Forms Applications

Contents

Microsoft®

Overview

- **Adding ADO.NET Objects to and Configuring ADO.NET Objects in a Windows Forms Application**
- **Accessing and Modifying Data by Using DataSets**
- **Binding Data to Controls**
- **Overview of XML Web Services**
- **Creating a Simple XML Web Services Client**
- **Persisting Data**

Introduction

Data binding provides a simple, convenient, powerful, and transparent way for developers to create a read/write link between the controls on a form and the data in their applications.

Windows Forms, which are part of the new Microsoft® .NET Framework, support binding data to Microsoft ADO.NET DataSets, arrays, collections, and other controls. A control can be bound to any collection that supports indexed access to the elements in that collection.

XML Web services enable the exchange of data and the remote invocation of application logic by using XML messaging to move data through firewalls and among many heterogeneous systems.

Developers can create applications that weave together XML Web services from a variety of sources in much the same way that developers traditionally use components when creating a distributed application.

Objectives

After completing this module, you will be able to:

- Describe the objects in the ADO.NET object model.
- Add and configure ADO.NET objects in a Windows Forms application.
- Access and modify data from a database by using DataSets.
- Bind data to controls.
- Describe the XML Web services model and the roles of HTML, SOAP, and XML in the XML Web services model.
- Create and test a simple XML Web service client application.
- Persist data to files, serialize objects, use isolated storage, and persist application settings.

Lesson: Adding ADO.NET Objects to and Configuring ADO.NET Objects in a Windows Forms Application

- ADO.NET Objects
- What Is a DataSet?
- What Is a Typed DataSet?
- How to Add ADO.NET Objects to and Configuring ADO.NET Objects in a Windows Forms Application
- Practice: Adding ADO.NET Objects to and Configuring ADO.NET Objects in a Windows Forms Application

Introduction

As application development has evolved, a lot of new applications are based on the Web application model. An increasing number of applications use XML to encode data to be passed over network connections. ADO.NET provides a programming model that incorporates features of both XML and ADO.NET in the .NET Framework.

ADO.NET is a set of classes that allow .NET-based applications to read and update information in databases and other data stores. You can access these classes through the .NET Framework **System.Data** namespace.

ADO.NET provides consistent access to a wide variety of data sources, including Microsoft SQL Server™ databases, OLE DB–compliant databases, non-relational sources such as Microsoft Exchange Server, and XML documents.

ADO.NET is designed for working with disconnected data in a multi-tier environment. ADO.NET uses XML as the format for transmitting disconnected data, which makes it easier to communicate with client applications that are not based on Windows Forms.

Lesson objectives

After completing this lesson, you will be able to:

- Describe the objects in the ADO.NET object model.
- Describe datasets.
- Describe typed datasets.
- Add to ADO.NET objects and configure ADO.NET objects in a Windows Forms application.

ADO.NET Objects

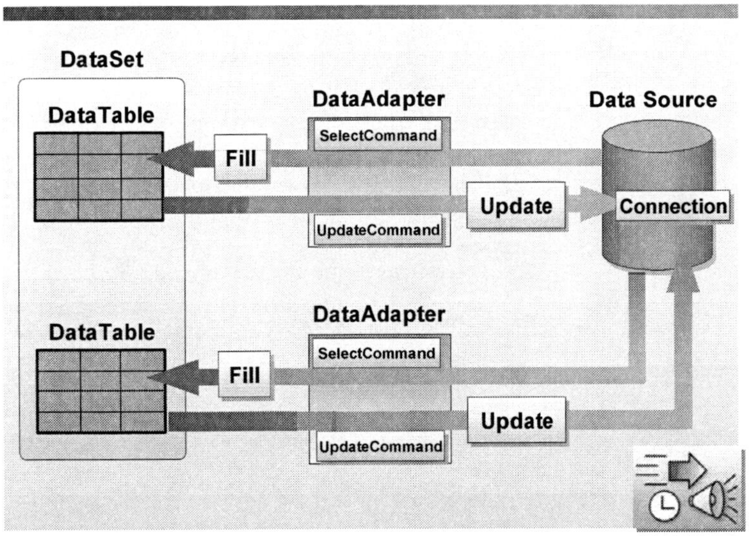

Introduction

ADO.NET evolved from the ADO data access model. By using ADO.NET, you can develop applications that are robust and scalable and that can use XML.

ADO.NET has some of the same objects as ADO (like the **Connection** and **Command** objects), and introduces new objects, such as **Dataset**, **DataReader**, and **DataAdapter**.

Connection object

To move data between a data store and your application, you must first have a connection to the data store. In ADO.NET you can create and manage a connection by using a **Connection** object. Applications use **Connection** objects to communicate with databases. The **ConnectionString** property determines connection settings. These connection settings access a particular **DataSource**. A typical **ConnectionString** property might look like the following code:

```
Provider=SQLOLEDB.1;Data Source=MySQLServer;Initial
Catalog=NORTHWIND;Integrated Security=SSPI
```

There are two kinds of connection objects in ADO.NET: **SqlConnection** and **OleDbConnection**.The **SqlConnection** object manages a connection to Microsoft SQL Server version 7.0 or later. The **SqlConnection** object is optimized for use with SQL Server 7.0 or later by bypassing the OLE DB layer. The **OleDbConnection** object manages a connection to any data store accessible through OLE DB. The **OleDbConnection** object interacts with OLE DB to expose a consistent API for a variety of data sources—everything from simple text files to spreadsheets and full-featured databases.

Note The **Connection** object is one component of a .NET Framework data provider. A data provider in the .NET Framework serves as a bridge between an application and a data source and is used to retrieve data from a data source and to reconcile changes to that data back to the data source.

Command object

You can use **Command** objects to access data directly in the database in a connected environment. **Command** objects use SQL statements or stored procedures to retrieve data. Commands travel across connections, and result sets are returned in the form of streams that can be read by **DataReaders** or pushed into **DataSet** objects. **Command** objects contain a **Parameters** collection that populates the input and output arguments of SQL statements or stored procedures. For example, if you have a SQL statement that returns all of the rows in the **Orders** table where the **EmployeeID** is equal to a value determined at run time, you add the value of **EmployeeID** to the **Parameters** collection of the **Command** object.

A **Command** object contains a reference to a SQL statement or stored procedure that you can execute directly. The two **Command** classes are described in the following table.

Command class	Description
System.Data.SqlClient.SqlCommand	SQL Server .NET Data Provider command
System.Data.OleDb.OleDbCommand	OLE DB .NET Data Provider command

DataReader object

The **DataReader** is a fast, forward-only cursor that loops through a stream of rows. When you execute a **Command** object that returns a set of rows, you use a **DataReader** to loop through the set of rows. You can use a **Command** object and the **ExecuteReader** method to return a **DataReader**. You can execute any **SELECT** statement or a stored procedure that contains a **SELECT** statement.

The **DataReader** provides strongly typed methods to get the value of a specific column in the current row. You can also obtain metadata about the rows, such as the column name and the column data type.

When you process a result set with a **DataReader**, the associated connection is kept busy until you close the **DataReader**. For this reason, you should close the **DataReader** as soon as you finish processing the result set.

DataSet object

Datasets store data in a disconnected cache. The structure of a dataset is similar to that of a relational database; it exposes a hierarchical object model of tables, rows, and columns. In addition, it contains constraints and relationships defined for the dataset.

DataAdapter object

The **DataSet** object represents a local copy of data from a data source and is one of the key innovations of the Microsoft .NET Framework. By itself, the **DataSet** object is useful for reference. However, to serve as a true data-management tool, a **DataSet** must be able to interact with a data source. To accomplish this, the .NET Framework provides the **DataAdapter** class. A **DataAdapter** object serves as a bridge between a **DataSet** and a data source for retrieving and saving data. The **DataAdapter** class represents a set of database commands and a database connection that you use to fill a **DataSet** and update the data source. **DataAdapter** objects are part of the Microsoft ADO.NET data providers, which also include connection objects, data-reader objects, and command objects. Microsoft Visual Studio® .NET makes two primary **DataAdapters** available for use with databases. In addition, other **DataAdapters** can be integrated with Visual Studio. The primary **DataDdapters** are:

- **OleDbDataAdapter**, which is suitable for use with any data source that is exposed by an OLE DB provider.
- **SqlDataAdapter**, which is specific to a SQL Server version 7.0 or later database. The **SqlDataAdapter** is faster than the **OleDbDataAdapter** because it works directly with SQL Server and does not go through an OLE DB layer.

What Is a DataSet?

- **Datasets can include multiple DataTables**
- **Relationships between tables are represented using DataRelations**
- **Constraints enforce primary and foreign keys**
- **Use the DataRow and DataColumn to access values in Tables**

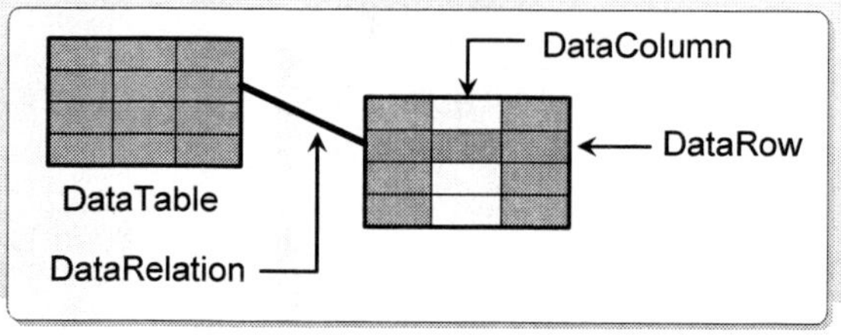

Introduction

In ADO.NET, by using datasets you can represent data in a local cache and provide a relational programming model for the data regardless of its source.

Definition

The ADO.NET DataSet is an in-memory cache of data that functions as a disconnected relational view of the data. The connection to the data source does not need to be active for an application to view and manipulate data in a DataSet. This disconnected architecture enables greater scalability by using database server resources only when reading from, or writing to, the data source.

DataSets store data similarly to the way data is stored in a relational database, with a hierarchical object model of tables, rows, and columns. Additionally, you can define constraints and relationships for the data in the DataSet.

DataTables in DataSets

DataTable objects represent the tables in a DataSet. A **DataTable** represents onc tablc of in-memory relational data. The data is local to the .NET-based application in which it resides, but it can be populated from an existing data source. A **DataTable** is composed of **DataColumns**.

DataColumns in DataTables

A DataColumn is the building block for creating the schema of a **DataTable**. Each **DataColumn** has a **DataType** property that determines the kind of data that each **DataColumn** contains. For example, you can restrict the data type to integers, strings, or decimals. Because data contained in the **DataTable** is typically merged back into the original data source, you must match the data types to those in the data source.

Tables in a DataSet

The **DataSet** class has a **Tables** property that gets a collection of **DataTable** objects in the DataSet, and a **Relations** property that gets a collection of the **DataRelation** objects in the DataSet.

A **DataTable** object contains several collections that describe the data in the table and cache the data in memory. The following table describes the most important collections.

Collection name	Type of object in collection	Description of object in collection
Columns	DataColumn	Contains metadata about a column in the table, such as the column name, data type, and whether rows can contain a NULL value in this column.
Rows	DataRow	Contains a row of data in the table. A **DataRow** object also maintains the original data in the row, before any changes were made by the application.
Constraints	Constraint	Represents a constraint on one or more **DataColumn** objects. **Constraint** is an abstract class. There are two concrete subclasses: **UniqueConstraint** and **ForeignKeyConstraint**.
ChildRelations	DataRelation	Represents a relationship to a column in another table in the DataSet. You use **DataRelation** objects to create links between primary keys and foreign keys in your tables.

What Is a Typed DataSet?

- **Typed datasets**
  - Derive from the base **DataSet** class
  - Provide type checking at compile time
  - Provide faster access to tables and columns in the dataset
  - Generated from XML Schema (.xsd) files by using the XSD.exe tool
- **To access tables and columns**
  - Untyped dataset

```
pubsDataSet.Tables("Titles")
```

  - Typed dataset

```
pubsDataSet.Titles
```

Introduction

Datasets can be typed or untyped. Typed datasets are classes that are generated from XML Schema (.xsd) files. An untyped dataset, in contrast, has no corresponding built-in schema.

Definition

A typed dataset is a class that derives from the base **DataSet** class. It inherits all the methods, events, and properties of a dataset. In addition, a typed dataset provides strongly typed methods, events, and properties. This means that you can access tables and columns by name, instead of by using collection-based methods. For example, to access the Titles table from a dataset named pubsDataSet1, you use the following code:

```
pubsDataSet.Tables("Titles")
```

However, with a typed dataset, you can directly access the Titles table by using the following code:

```
pubsDataSet.Titles
```

Advantages of typed datasets

Typed datasets are not only easier to read, but they are also fully supported by the Microsoft IntelliSense® technology in the Code Editor in Visual Studio .NET. In addition to being easier to work with, the syntax for the typed dataset provides type checking at compile time; this greatly reduces the possibility of errors in assigning values to dataset members. Access to tables and columns in a typed dataset is also slightly faster at run time because access is determined at compile time—not through collections at run time.

You can generate a strongly typed dataset from within the Visual Studio .NET integrated development environment (IDE) by selecting tables from an existing database or by creating one using the XML Designer.

How to Add ADO.NET Objects to and Configure ADO.NET Objects in a Windows Forms Application

1. Drag an **OleDbDataAdapter** or **SqlDataAdapter** object from the Toolbox to a form
2. Specify connection and SQL command information
3. Select the adapter or adapters that will be used to transfer data between the data source and the dataset
4. On the **Data** menu, choose **Generate Dataset**
5. Select **New** and then specify a name for the new dataset

Introduction

The data design tools in Visual Studio .NET provide a simple way to connect to a database, retrieve data from it, and generate a typed dataset.

You can use either of the following data design tools to connect to a data source:

- DataAdapter Configuration Wizard

  This wizard prompts you for information to create a connection that is in turn linked to a data adapter.

- Data Form Wizard

  This wizard creates the connection object as part of the form that it is configuring.

This topic explains how to connect to a data source by using DataAdapter Configuration Wizard.

Note When you use data design tools, you need not create explicit connections to a data source; however, there are times when you need to create just a connection. For more information about how to create a connection, in the Visual Studio .NET documentation, search by using the phrase **Creating ADO.NET Connection Objects**.

Procedure: Adding ADO.NET objects

Data Adapter Configuration Wizard helps you set the properties of a new or existing data adapter. A data adapter contains SQL commands or stored procedures that your application can use to read data into a dataset from a database and write it back again. The wizard can also create a data connection that allows the adapter to communicate with a database.

To use the DataAdapter Configuration Wizard:

1. Drag an **OleDbDataAdapter** or **SqlDataAdapter** object from the Toolbox onto a form or component.
2. Specify connection and SQL command information.

   The wizard displays several dialog boxes:

   - If you ask to create a connection, the wizard displays the **Connection** tab of the **Data Link Properties** dialog box, which allows you to specify a provider, server name, database name, user name, and password for the connection.
   - To help you create SQL statements, the wizard provides the Query Builder, a utility that allows you to create and test a **Select** statement by using visual tools. To launch it, click the **Query Builder** button when asked for a SQL statement.
3. In Component Designer, select the adapter or adapters that will transfer data between the data source and the dataset.

   Typically, each data adapter accesses data in a single table. Therefore, to create a dataset that contains multiple data tables, select all the adapters for the tables that you want to work with.
4. On the **Data** menu, choose **Generate Dataset**.

   The **Generate DataSet** dialog box appears.

   Click **New**, and then specify a name for the new dataset. If you want to add the dataset to your form or component, click **Add an instance of this DataSet to the designer**.

   This generates a typed dataset.

Practice: Adding ADO.NET Objects to and Configuring ADO.NET Objects in a Windows Forms Application

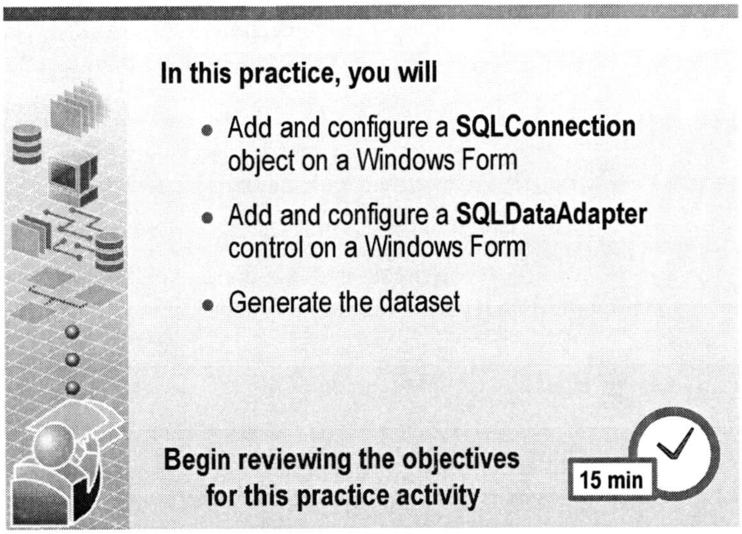

Introduction

In this practice, you will add ADO.NET objects to and configure ADO.NET objects on a form by using Data Adapter Configuration Wizard.

Instructions

► **Create a Windows application project**

1. Open Visual Studio .NET.
2. On the **File** menu, point to **New**, and then click **Project**.
3. In the **New Project** dialog box, select **Windows Application**, name it **BuildingDataSets**, and then click **OK**.

► **Add a SQLConnection control to the form and configure it**

1. Drag a **SQLConnection** control from the ToolBox to Form1.

   The SQLConnection control is on the **Data** tab of the Toolbox.
2. In the Properties window, click the **ConnectionString** property, click the arrow, and then click **New Connection.**
3. In the **Data Link Properties** dialog box, type *<computername>***MOC**, where *<computername>* is the name of your computer.
4. Select the **Use Windows NT Integrated Security** option.
5. Select the **pubs** database from the drop-down list, click **Test Connection** to ensure that you can access the **pubs** database, and then click **OK**.
6. Click **OK** to close the **Data Link Properties** dialog box.
7. Review the **ConnectionString** text that is generated.

► **Add a SQLDataAdapter control to the form and configure it**

1. Drag a **SQLDataAdapter** control from the ToolBox to Form1.
2. In opening page of the Data Adapter Configuration Wizard, click **Next**.
3. In the data connection drop-down list, click *<computername>***\moc\pubs.dbo**, and then click **Next**.
4. In the **Choose a Query Type** dialog box, click **Next**.

   You can use this wizard create SQL statements and stored procedures or modify existing stored procedures.
5. On the Toolbar, click the **Query Builder** button.
6. In the **Add Table** dialog box, select the **Titles** tables, click **Add**, and then click **Close**.
7. In the **Query Builder** dialog box, in the Titles table, select **All Columns**, and then click **OK**.
8. Click Next to open the **View Wizard Results** dialog box.
9. Review the information in the **View Wizard Results** dialog box, and then click **Finish**.

► **Review the code generated**

1. Review the **SelectCommand**, **DeleteCommand**, **InsertCommand** and **UpdateCommand** properties of the **SQLDataAdapter1** control in the Properties window.

   Each of these properties is associated with a **SQLCommand** object that was generated by the wizard. Each operation (SELECT, INSERT, UPDATE, DELETE) uses a specific **SQLCommand** to perform its task.
2. Expand the **DeleteCommand** property and review the **CommandText** property.

   Each **SQLCommand** object has a unique **CommandText** property that is generated by the wizard and enables the object to perform its task.

► Generate a typed DataSet

1. Right-click the **SQLDataAdapter1** control, and click **Generate DataSet.**

   Note If the **Generate DataSet** option is disabled, then click anywhere outside the Properties window before generating the DataSet.

2. Click **OK** in the **Generate Dataset** dialog box.

   A dataset control named **DataSet11** is added to Form1. **DataSet11** is an instance of the typed dataset **DataSet1**.

3. In Solution Explorer, double-click **DatSet1.xsd**.

   This is the visual representation of your dataset. In this view you can add new or existing tables to your dataset and create relationships between them.

4. Click **XML** in the lower left of the designer.

   This is the XML representation of your dataset.

5. In Solution Explorer, click **Show All Files**.
6. In Solution Explorer, expand **DataSet1.xsd**, and then double-click **DataSet1.vb**.
7. Review the code.

   The object created is a typed dataset that inherits from the **DataSet** class. The data information in the .xsd file is used to create the typed dataset.

Lesson: Accessing and Modifying Data by Using DataSets

- How to Populate a Dataset
- How to Update Data in a Dataset
- How to Update Data to a Data Source
- Practice: Populating and Updating DataSets
- How to Create Database Schema on the Client
- Demonstration: Creating Database Schema by Using the XML Schema Designer
- How to Read and Write XML Data into a DataSet

Introduction

ADO.NET provides you with the **DataSet** object for the caching of data on the client computer. This **DataSet** is automatically disconnected from the data source but maintains the ability to later update the source based on changes made at the client.

This lesson shows how to create **DataSets** and populate tables in them. This lesson also shows how to edit these tables and propagate those changes to the data source.

Lesson objectives

After completing this lesson, you will be able to:

- Populate a **DataSet** with data from a data source.
- Update the data in a **DataSet**.
- Update the data source by using a dataset.
- Create relationships between tables in a dataset.
- Create database schema on the client.
- Read and write XML data from a dataset.

How to Populate a Dataset

- **Use the DataAdapter object to fill the dataset**

```
Dim storesSQLDataAdapter As New SqlClient.SqlDataAdapter()
Dim storesSelectSQLCommand As New SqlClient.SqlCommand()
storesSelectSQLCommand.CommandText = "SELECT * FROM stores"
storesSelectSQLCommand.Connection = SqlConnection1
storesSQLDataAdapter.SelectCommand = storesSelectSQLCommand

storesSQLDataAdapter.Fill(storesDataSet.Tables("Stores")
```

Introduction

A **DataSet** is an in-memory representation of data and does not actually contain any data until you fill it by using a **DataAdapter** object. After you create the **DataAdapter** object, you use the **Fill** method, passing a **DataSet** and, optionally, the **DataTable** name as parameters.

Populating a dataset

The **DataAdapter** uses the **SelectCommand** object to execute the query and returns the results to the **DataSet** or to the **DataTable** referenced as parameters. The following code programmatically creates and configures a **SQLDataAdapter** and a **SQLCommand** and then uses the **Fill** method to populate a table in a dataset:

```
Dim storesSQLDataAdapter As New SqlClient.SqlDataAdapter()
Dim storesSelectSQLCommand As New SqlClient.SqlCommand()
storesSelectSQLCommand.CommandText = "SELECT * FROM stores"
storesSelectSQLCommand.Connection = SqlConnection1
storesSQLDataAdapter.SelectCommand = storesSelectSQLCommand

storesSQLDataAdapter.Fill(storesDataSet.Tables("Stores")
```

Passing parameters to SELECT statements

It is often necessary to pass parameters to a SQL statement. For example, when accessing rows from a data source, you use the **SELECT** statement, which uses a unique identifier to identify the rows to be accessed. The unique identifier is commonly the value of a primary key field. The **SELECT** statement uses parameters that contain the unique identifier, and the columns and values to be updated, as shown in the following SQL statement:

```
SELECT stor_id, ord_num, qty, ord_date, payterms, title_id
FROM sales WHERE (stor_id = @stor_id)
```

In the previous example, the **stor_id** field must be populated with a value from the **@stor_id** parameter for the SQL statement to return results.

A **Parameter** object holds the input and output parameters of SQL statement and stored procedures. The **Parameters** collection of a **Command** object is where you add the required arguments of SQL statements or stored procedures. There are a variety of ways to add **Parameter** objects to the **Parameters** collection. The following code uses the **SelectCommand** property to access a **Command** object and then assigns the value of *stor_id* to the **Value** property of the **Parameter** object in the **Parameters** collection that is identified by *@stor_id*:

```
storesSQLDataAdapter.SelectCommand.Parameters _
("@stor_id").Value = 6380
```

After all the arguments for a SQL statement or stored procedure are defined in **Parameter** objects, you can call the **Fill** method of the **DataAdapter** to get the results.

```
storesSQLDataAdapter.Fill(StoreSalesDataSet1.Tables("sales")
```

How to Update Data in a DataSet

- **Adding rows**

```
Dim newDataRow As DataRow = _
   pubsDataSet.Tables("Titles").NewRow
newDataRow ("title") = "New Book"
newDataRow ("type") = "business"
pubsDataSet.Tables("Titles").Rows.Add(newDataRow)
```

- **Editing rows**

```
changeDataRow.BeginEdit()
changeDataRow("Title") = changeDataRow("Title").ToString & _
" 1"
changeDataRow.EndEdit()
```

- **Deleting data**

```
Dim deleteDataRow As DataRow = _
   pubsDataSet.Tables("Titles").Rows(0)
   pubsDataSet.Tables("Titles").Rows.Remove(deleteDataRow)
```

Introduction

After you have created a **DataSet** of **DataTables**, you might want to add, update, and delete data. Any changes that you make to the data are stored in memory and later used to apply the changes to the data source.

Procedure: Adding rows to a DataSet

To add new rows to a **DataSet** table:

1. Instantiate a **DataRow** object by using the **NewRow** method of the **DataTable**.
2. Populate the columns with data.
3. Call the **Add** method of the **DataRows** collection, passing the **DataRow** object.

The following code shows how to add rows to a **DataSet**:

```
Dim newDataRow As DataRow = _
pubsDataSet.Tables("Titles").NewRow
newDataRow ("title") = "New Book"
newDataRow ("type") = "business"
pubsDataSet.Tables("Titles").Rows.Add(newDataRow)
```

Procedure: Editing rows in a DataSet

To edit existing rows in a **DataSet** table:

1. Call the **BeginEdit** method of the row.
2. Change the data in the columns.
3. Call **EndEdit** or **CancelEdit** to accept or reject the changes.

The following code shows how to edit data in an existing column:

```
Dim changeDataRow As DataRow = _
pubsDataSet.Tables("Titles").Rows(0)
changeDataRow.BeginEdit()
changeDataRow("Title")=changeDataRow("Title").ToString & _
"1"
changeDataRow.EndEdit()
```

Procedure: Deleting data in a DataSet

Use either of the following methods to delete a row:

- **Remove** method

  Call the **Remove** method of the **DataRows** collection. This permanently removes the row from the **DataSet**.

- **Delete** method

  Call the **Delete** method of the **DataRow** object. This only marks the row for deletion in the **DataSet**, and calling **RejectChanges** will undo the deletion.

  The following code shows how to delete an existing row from a **DataSet**:

```
Dim deleteDataRow As DataRow = _
pubsDataSet.Tables("Titles").Rows(0)
pubsDataSet.Tables("Titles").Rows.Remove(deleteDataRow)
```

How to Update Data to a Data Source

- **Explicitly specifying the updates**

```
Dim insertTitlesCommand As New SqlClient.SqlCommand _
("Insert titles (title_id, title, type) values " & _
"(@title_id,@title,@type)")

insertTitlesCommand.Parameters.Add("@title_id", _
SqlDbType.VarChar, 6, "title_id")

insertTitlesCommand.Parameters.Add("@title", _
SqlDbType.VarChar, 80, "title")

insertTitlesCommand.Parameters.Add("@type", _
SqlDbType.Char, 12, "type")

titlesSQLDataAdapter.InsertCommand = insertTitlesCommand
titlesSQLDataAdapter.Update(pubsDataSet, "titles")
```

Introduction

After you have updated the tables in your **DataSet**, you will want to replicate those changes to the underlying data source. To do this, use the **Update** method of the **DataAdapter** object, which is the link between dataset and data source.

The **Update** method, like the **Fill** method, takes two parameters: the **DataSet** and the name of the **DataTable** in which the changes have been made. (You can also pass table and row objects.) The **Update** method determines the changes to the data and executes the appropriate SQL command (Insert, Update, or Delete) against the source data.

Explicitly specifying the updates

You use the **InsertCommand**, **UpdateCommand**, and **DeleteCommand** properties of the **DataAdapter** to identify the changes occurring in your dataset. You specify each of these as an existing command object for an Insert, Update, or Delete SQL statement. For any variable columns in the statements, you use **SqlParameter** objects to identify the column, data type, size, and data to be inserted.

The following code shows how to use the **InsertCommand** property to add a row to the Titles table in the **pubs** database:

```
Dim insertTitlesCommand As New SqlClient.SqlCommand _
("Insert titles (title_id, title, type) values " & _
"(@title_id,@title,@type)")

insertTitlesCommand.Parameters.Add("@title_id", _
SqlDbType.VarChar, 6, "title_id")

insertTitlesCommand.Parameters.Add("@title", _
SqlDbType.VarChar, 80, "title")

insertTitlesCommand.Parameters.Add("@type", _
SqlDbType.Char, 12, "type")

titlesSQLDataAdapter.InsertCommand = insertTitlesCommand
titlesSQLDataAdapter.Update(pubsDataSet, "titles")
```

Practice: Populating and Updating DataSets

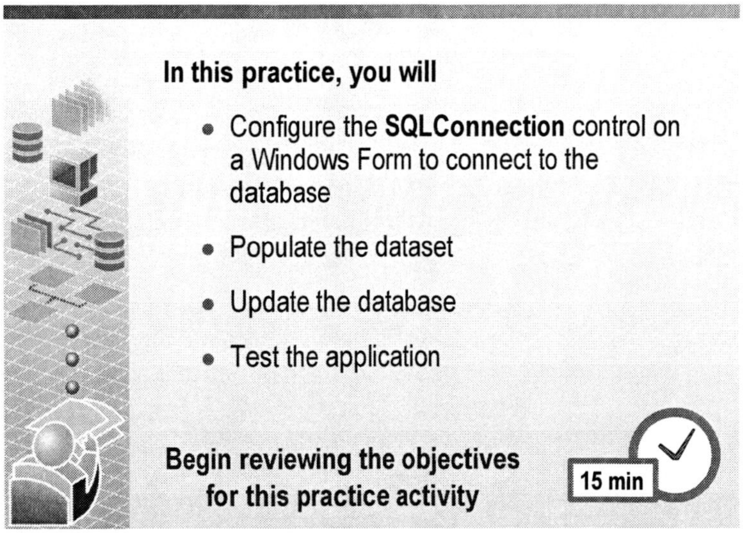

Introduction

In this practice, you will populate a dataset and update a database with the changes made to the dataset. You will fill the dataset with the Stores and Sales tables of the pubs database. For the Stores table, you will write all of the code required to populate the dataset. For the Sales table, you will use the code generated by Data Adapter Configuration Wizard and a typed dataset. You will also update the database with any changes to the Sales table.

Instructions

► **Open the practice project**

1. Use Microsoft Windows® Explorer to browse to *install_folder*\Practices\Mod04\Mod04_02\Starter.

Note If you performed a default installation of the course files, *install_folder* corresponds to C:\Program Files\Msdntrain\2565.

2. Double-click the PopulatingAndUpdatingDataSets.sln solution file to open the project.

► **Populate StoreSalesDataSet1 with data from the Stores table**

1. Show TODO comments in the Task List.

   To show TODO comments, click the **View** menu, point to **Show Tasks**, and then click **All**.

2. Locate TODO: 1 in the Code Editor of Form1.
3. Under TODO: 1, declare and instantiate a **SqlDataAdapter** named **storesSQLDataAdapter**.
4. Declare and instantiate a **SqlCommand** named **storesSelectSQLCommand**.
5. Declare a **DataTable** named **storesTable** and initialize it with the String **Stores**. Your code should look like this:

```
Dim storesSQLDataAdapter As New SqlClient.SqlDataAdapter()
Dim storesSelectSQLCommand As New SqlClient.SqlCommand()
Dim storesTable As New Data.DataTable("Stores")
```

6. Locate TODO: 2 in the Code Editor of Form1.
7. Under TODO: 2, set the **CommandType** property of **storesSelectSQLCommand** to **CommandType.Text**.
8. Set the **CommandText** property of **storesSelectSQLCommand** to, "SELECT stor_id, stor_name FROM stores".
9. Set the **Connection** property of **storesSelectSQLCommand** to **SQLConnection1**.
10. Set the **SelectCommand** property of **storesSQLDataAdapter** to **storesSelectSQLCommand**. Your code should look like this:

```
storesSelectSQLCommand.CommandType = CommandType.Text
storesSelectSQLCommand.CommandText = _
"SELECT stor_id, stor_name FROM stores"
storesSelectSQLCommand.Connection = SqlConnection1
storesSQLDataAdapter.SelectCommand = storesSelectSQLCommand
```

11. Locate TODO: 3 in the Code Editor of Form1.
12. Under TODO: 3, use the **Fill** method of **storesSQLDataAdapter** to populate **storesTable**.
13. Use the **Add** method to add **storesTable** to the **Tables** collection of the existing **StoreSalesDataSet** dataset. Your code should look like this:

```
storesSQLDataAdapter.Fill(storesTable)
storeSalesDataSet1.Tables.Add(storesTable)
```

► **Use existing code generated by Data Adapter Configuration Wizard and a typed dataset to populate StoreSalesDataSet1 with data from the Sales table**

The **CommandText** property of **SalesSQLSelectCommand** is set to the following:

```
"SELECT stor_id, ord_num, qty, ord_date, payterms, title_id
FROM sales WHERE (stor_id = @stor_id)"
```

You must assign the **@stor_ID** parameter a value to get the required results. You use the **Parameters** collection of the **SQLCommand** object to assign this value.

1. Locate TODO: 4 in the Code Editor of Form1.
2. Under TODO: 4, use the **SelectCommand** property of **SalesSqlDataAdapter** to access **SalesSQLSelectCommand** and set the **Value** property of the **@storeid** parameter in the **Parameters** collection to **storeID**. Your code should look like this:

   ```
   SalesSqlDataAdapter.SelectCommand.Parameters _
   ("@stor_id").Value = storeID
   ```
3. Locate TODO: 5 in the Code Editor of Form1.
4. Under TODO: 5 use the **Clear** method of **Sales** DataTable in **StoreSalesDataSet1** to clear the **Sales** table of any existing data. Your code should look like this:

   ```
   StoreSalesDataSet1.sales.Clear()
   ```
5. Locate TODO: 6 in the Code Editor of Form1.
6. Under TODO: 6, use the **Fill** method of **SalesSQLDataAdapter** to populate the **sales** property of **StoreSalesDataSet1**. Your code should look like this:

   ```
   SalesSqlDataAdapter.Fill(StoreSalesDataSet1.sales)
   ```

► **Update the pubs database with the changes in StoreSalesDataSet1**

1. Locate TODO: 7 in the Code Editor of Form1.
2. Under TODO: 7, use the **Update** method of **SalesSqlDataAdapter** and pass **StoreSalesDataSet1** as an argument. Your code should look like this:

   ```
   SalesSqlDataAdapter.Update(StoreSalesDataSet1)
   ```

► Test the application

1. Press F5 to compile and run the application.
2. In the **Stores** list, click **News and Brews**.

Tip You may want to set breakpoints in your code to follow the execution path.

---

3. Click the bottom row of the DataGrid to create a new row and enter the following fields.

Note The date in the following table is in the mm/dd/yy format for the purposes of practicing the concepts learned in the lesson. However, when you create an application for an international audience, you should use a different method of capturing the date - like a pop-up calendar to select the date, or three individual list boxes: for the month, day, and year.

Field	Value
stor_id	7067
ord_num	P2122
qty	12
ord_date	6/13/2002
payterms	Net 60
title_id	PC9999

4. Click **Update**.
5. Switch to the Visual Studio .NET IDE, and use Server Explorer to verify that the database was updated.
6. Switch back to the Store Orders application, set the **qty** field of the new row to **24**, and then click **Update**.
7. Switch to the Visual Studio .NET IDE, and use Server Explorer to verify that the database was updated.

   To refresh the view, right-click the results, and then click **Run**.
8. Switch back to the Store Orders application, delete the new row, and then click **Update**.
9. Switch to the Visual Studio .NET IDE, and use Server Explorer to verify that the database was updated.

How to Create Database Schema on the Client

- **XML Schema files (.xsd) enforce data integrity on the client**
- **Use the XML Designer to create and modify XML Schema files**
  1. Determine the schema design
  2. On the **Project** menu, click **Add New Item**
  3. Add the schema
  4. Create the schema

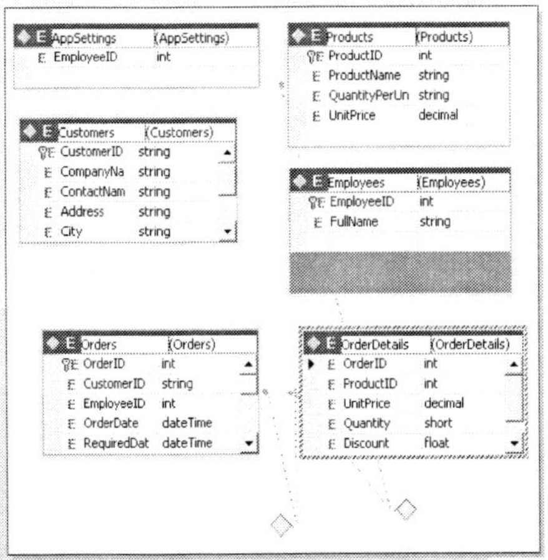

Introduction

When a typed dataset is generated at design time, a dataset class and an associated XML Schema file is created in your project. XML Schema files define and validate the data being imported from XML streams or documents into typed datasets. The XML Schema file associated with the dataset can be loaded into the XML Designer providing a visual representation of the dataset structure that can be edited and viewed. You can create and edit table structures and create relations between tables by using the XML Designer.

In typed datasets, XML Schema (.xsd) files establish the relational structure of the dataset's tables and columns, the key columns, constraints, and relationships between tables. The relational structure information is used when generating a **DataSet** class. The table relation information is available within a dataset, and referential integrity can be maintained within the dataset.

Procedure: Creating an XML schema

To create an XML schema:

1. Determine the design needed for your schema.
2. On the **Project** menu, click **Add New Item**.
3. Do one of the following:
   - Add a schema. To add a schema, open the appropriate folder, and then double-click **XML Schema**.

     An XML Schema (.xsd) file is added to your project.

     \- Or -
   - Add a dataset. To add a dataset, open the appropriate folder, and then double-click **DataSet**.

     An XML Schema file and typed DataSet class file (.vb or .cs file) are added to your project.
4. To create the schema, add elements and attributes.

Demonstration: Creating Database Schema by Using the XML Schema Designer

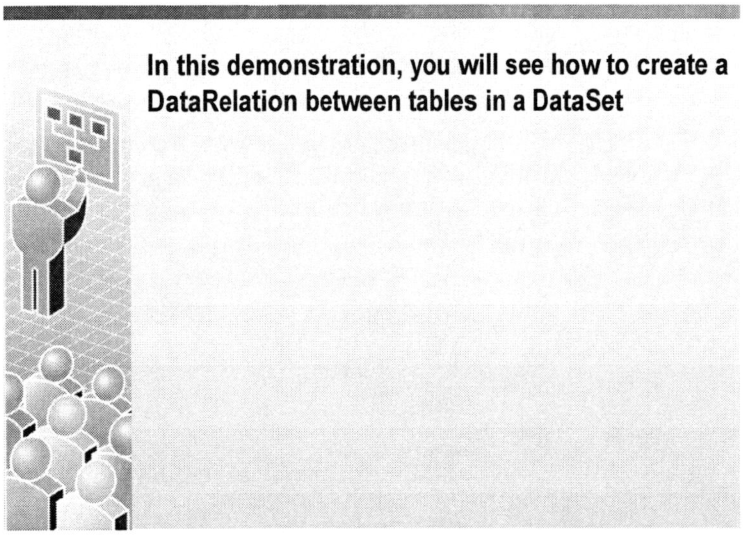

Introduction

In this demonstration, you will see the creation of a DataRelation in a **DataSet** between the Suppliers and Products tables of the **Northwind** database. After the DataRelation is created, you will see how referential integrity is maintained on the client in the **DataSet**.

Instructions

► **Open the CreatingRelations.sln solution file**

- Open the CreatingRelations.sln solution file in Visual Studio .NET from *install_folder*\Democode\ Mod04\Mod04_01\Starter.

► **Test the behavior of the DataSet before the relation is created**

1. Press F5 to compile and run the application.

   On the **Load** event of Form1, the **SuppliersSqlDataAdapter** and the **ProductsSqlDataAdapter** fill the **SuppliersProductsDataSet1** dataset.

2. Select the first row in the **Suppliers** DataGrid, and press DELETE.

   Because there is no relationship between the tables on the client dataset, the dataset does not maintain referential integrity.

3. Click the **Submit Data** button.

   The database is aware of the relationship between the **Suppliers** and **Products** tables and prevents the changes from being persisted.

4. Close the application.

► Create a relationship between the Suppliers and Products tables in the SuppliersProductsDataSet DataSet

1. Open SuppliersProductsDataSet.xsd in Design view.
2. Drag a **Relation** control from the Toolbox to the Suppliers table.
3. In the **Edit Relation** dialog box, in the **Parent element** list, click **Suppliers**, and in the **Child element** list, click **Products**.

   Notice the **Update rule**, **Delete rule**, and **Accept/Reject rule** lists. You can control how a dataset manages DataRelations between tables when changes and updates occur. For example, if you set the **Delete rule** to **Cascading** (the default) the dataset will automatically delete all child elements when a parent is deleted to enforce referential integrity.
4. Click **OK**.
5. Close SuppliersProductsDataSet.xsd, and then click **Yes** to save the changes.

► Test the behavior of the DataSet and notice that a relation exists

1. Press F5 to compile and run the application.
2. Notice that the first row of the Products DataGrid displays the product Chai, which has a SupplierID of 1.
3. Select the first row in the Suppliers DataGrid (where SupplierID = 1), and press DELETE.

   Because the DataRelation exists, the dataset cascades the deletion of all the products that are associated with the Supplier parent and maintains referential integrity.

How to Read and Write XML Data into a DataSet

- **Use ReadXML to load data from a file or stream**

```
purchaseDataSet.ReadXml _
   ("C:\sampledata\PurchaseData.xml", _
      XmlReadMode.IgnoreSchema)
```

- **Write data and schema information from a DataSet to a file or stream by using the WriteXML method**

```
("C:\sampledata\CurrentOrders.xml", _
      XmlWriteMode.IgnoreSchema)
```

Introduction

You can use the **ReadXml** method of the **Dataset** object to load data from an XML file into a dataset. When you use this method, you can load data from XML files that contain only XML data or from files that contain XML data as well as an inline schema. You can write data and schema information from a dataset to a file or stream by using the **WriteXml** method of the **Dataset** object.

An *inline schema* is an XSD schema that appears at the beginning of the XML data file. This schema describes the XML information that appears after the schema in the XML file.

Simplified syntax for reading XML data

The **ReadXml** method is overloaded and can be used to read from a stream object, an XML file, a **TextReader** subclass object, or an **XmlReader** subclass object, as shown in the following code:

```
Dataset.ReadXml(Stream | FileName | TextReader | XmlReader, {
ByVal mode as XmlReadMode })
```

Use the *XmlReadMode* parameter to specify what the XML file contains and what information should be loaded from the file. This parameter is optional. If no **XmlReadMode** value is supplied, the default value **Auto** is used.

XmlReadMode parameter values

The following table shows the values for the *XmlReadMode* parameter of the **ReadXml** method of the **DataSet** object.

XmlReadMode value	Description
ReadSchema	Reads any inline schema and then loads the schema and data: • If the dataset already contains a schema, any new tables that are defined by an inline schema are added to the dataset. • If the inline schema defines a table that is already in the dataset, an exception is thrown. • If the dataset does not contain a schema, and there is no inline schema, no data is read.
IgnoreSchema	Ignores any inline schema and loads data into the existing dataset. Any data that does not match the existing schema is discarded.
InferSchema	Ignores any inline schema and infers a new schema based on the structure of the XML data. If the dataset already defines a schema, tables are added to this schema. The data is then loaded into the dataset.
DiffGram	Reads a DiffGram and adds the data to the current schema in the dataset. A DiffGram is an XML format that is used to identify current and original versions of data elements.
Fragment	Reads XML fragments and appends data to appropriate dataset tables. This setting is typically used to read XML data generated directly from SQL Server.
Auto	Examines the XML file and chooses the most appropriate option. • If the dataset contains a schema or the XML contains an inline schema, ReadSchema is used. • If the dataset does not contain a schema and the XML does not contain an inline schema, **InferSchema** is used. For best performance, specify an **XmlReadMode** rather than **Auto**.

Example of loading a schema and data into a dataset

The following example first loads a schema into a new dataset by using the **ReadXmlSchema** method and then loads the data from an XML file by using the **ReadXml** method with the **IgnoreSchema** option of the *XmlReadMode* parameter:

```
Private Sub ReadXmlDataOnly()
  Try
      purchaseDataSet = New DataSet()
      Console.WriteLine("Reading the Schema file")
      purchaseDataSet.ReadXmlSchema _
      ("C:\sampledata\Purchase.xsd")
      Console.WriteLine("Loading the XML data file")
      purchaseDataSet.ReadXml _
      ("C:\sampledata\PurchaseData.xml", _
      XmlReadMode.IgnoreSchema)

      DataGrid1.DataSource = purchaseDataSet.Tables(0)

  Catch e as Exception
      Console.WriteLine("Exception: " & e.ToString())
  End Try
End Sub
```

Partial syntax for writing XML data

The following code shows partial syntax for the **WriteXml** method of the **DataSet** object:

```
Overloads Public Sub WriteXml (ByVal filename As String |
stream As Stream | writer as TextWriter | writer as XmlWriter,
{ByVal mode As XmlWriteMode})
```

XmlWriteMode values

When you use the **WriteXml** method, you can specify an optional value for the *XmlWriteMode* parameter. This parameter specifies whether to generate a file that contains only XML data, XML data with an inline XSD schema, or a DiffGram.

The following table describes the different values for the *XmlWriteMode* parameter of the **WriteXml** method of the **Dataset** object.

XmlWriteMode value	What is generated
IgnoreSchema	An XML file containing the data from a dataset. No schema information is included. If the dataset is empty, no file is created.
WriteSchema	An XML file containing an inline schema and the data from a populated dataset. If the dataset contains only schema information, an inline schema is written to the output file. If the dataset does not include schema information, no file is created.
DiffGram	An XML file in the form of a DiffGram, containing both the original and current values for the data.

Example of writing XML data to a file

The following code saves the data stored in a **dataset** as an XML file but does not write any schema information:

```
Private Sub SaveXMLDataOnly()
  Try
      Dim StrPurchaseSchema as String
      purchaseDataSet = New DataSet()

      'Load an inline schema and data from an XML file
      purchaseDataSet.ReadXml _
      ("C:\sampledata\PurchaseOrder.xml", _
      XmlReadMode.ReadSchema)

      'Save the data portion of the DataSet to a file
      purchaseDataSet.WriteXml _
      ("C:\sampledata\CurrentOrders.xml", _
      XmlWriteMode.IgnoreSchema)

  Catch e as Exception
      Console.WriteLine("Exception: " & e.ToString())
  End Try
End Sub
```

Lesson: Binding Data to Controls

- **How to Perform Simple Binding by Using the DataBindings Property**
- **How to Perform Complex Data Binding by Using the DataBound Windows Forms Controls**
- **Practice: Binding Controls to Data**
- **How to Maintain the Currency of a Control by Using CurrencyManager**
- **Demonstration: Maintaining the Currency of a Control by Using CurrencyManager**
- **How to Format and Parse Data Bound Values**
- **Practice: Formatting Data Bound Controls**

Introduction

In Windows Forms, you can bind to not just traditional data sources but also to almost any structure that contains data. You can bind to an array of values that you calculate at run time, read from a file, or derive from the values of other controls. In addition, you can bind any property of any control to the data source. In traditional data binding, you typically bind the display property (for example, the **Text** property of a **TextBox** control) to the data source. With the .NET Framework, you also have the option of binding other properties.

Windows Forms can take advantage of two types of data binding: simple binding and complex binding. This lesson covers how to bind data to controls by using simple binding and complex binding.

Lesson objectives

After completing this lesson, you will be able to:

- Describe the **ControlBindings** collection.
- Perform simple binding by using the **DataBindings** property.
- Perform complex binding by using data bound Windows Forms controls.
- Describe the **CurrencyManager** object.
- Maintain the currency of an object by using the **BindingContext** object.
- Format data-bound values.

How to Perform Simple Binding by Using the DataBindings Property

To use the DataBindings Collection to bind a control to a data source, set the DataBinding property of the control to the data source

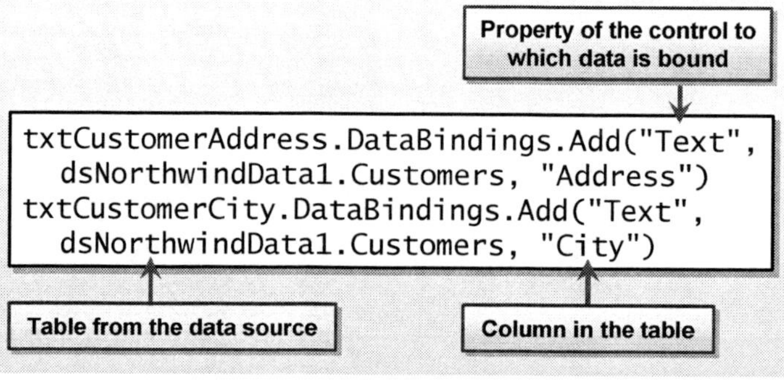

Introduction

In Windows Forms, you can bind to not just traditional data sources but also to almost any structure that contains data. For example, you can bind to arrays, collections, properties of other controls, and ADO.NET objects such as data views and table columns.

Simple data binding is accomplished by adding **Binding** objects to a **ControlBindingsCollection**. The **Binding** class is used to create and maintain a simple binding between the property of a control and the property of an object. Any object that inherits from the **Control** class maintains a list of the **Binding** objects in the **ControlBindingsCollection**. The **DataBindings** property exposes the **ControlBindingsCollection** and, like any collection, supports methods to Add, Remove, and Clear the objects (Bindings) in it.

Procedure: Performing simple binding at design time

To perform a simple bind of a control:

1. In the form, select the control and display the Properties window.
2. Expand the **(DataBindings)** property.

   The properties most often bound are displayed in the **(DataBindings)** property list. For example, in most controls, the **Text** property is most frequently bound.
3. If the property that you want to bind is not one of the commonly bound properties, click the **Ellipsis** button (…) in the **Advanced** box to display the **Advanced Data Binding** dialog box with a complete list of properties for that control.
4. Click the list arrow for the property that you want to bind.

   A list of available data sources is displayed.

5. Expand the data source that you want to bind to until you find the single data element that you want.

   For example, if you are binding to a column value in a dataset's table, expand the name of the dataset, and then expand the table name to display column names.

6. Click the name of an element to bind to it.

Procedure: Performing simple binding at run time

You can also create a **Binding** object programmatically at run time. To do so, use the **Add** method of the **DataBindings** collection. The method expects the following arguments:

- Name of the property of the control that will consume the data
- Data source
- Name of the field in the data source to bind to

The following code binds the **Text** property of the **txtCustomer** text box to the **Address** column of the **Customers** tables in the dsNorthwind1 typed dataset:

```
txtCustomerAddress.DataBindings.Add("Text",
dsNorthwindData1.Customers, "Address")
```

A period-delimited navigation path is required when the data source is set to an object that contains multiple **DataTable** objects (such as a **DataSet** or **DataViewManager**). For example, the previous code could also be written as shown.

```
txtCustomerAddress.DataBindings.Add("Text", dsNorthwindData1,
"Customers.Address")
```

How to Perform Complex Data Binding by Using the DataBound Windows Forms Controls

- **Complex data binding**
  - Bind a control property to a data table
  - Use with combo boxes, list boxes, data grids
  - Can bind controls to DataSets, Arrays, and ArrayLists
- **Complex databinding at design time**
  - Set the **DataSource** and **DataMember** properties
- **Complex databinding at run time**

```
DataGrid1.DataSource = productsDataSet
DataGrid1.DataMember = "Products"
```

Introduction

Instead of binding each data field to a separate control, you bind the complete data source to one control. This is called complex data binding. A very useful component for complex data binding is the **DataGrid** control.

Because a dataset can contain more than one DataTable, there are two relevant properties: **DataSource** and **DisplayMember**. **DataSource** refers to the dataset and **DisplayMember** refers to the contained DataTable. Alternatively, you can use the **SetDataBinding** method to set both values at once.

Procedure: Performing complex data binding at design time

To bind a combo box, list box, or data grid to a data source at design time:

1. Add the control to the form.
2. Select the control.
3. Set the **DataSource** property to the data source, such as a dataset.
4. Set the **DisplayMember** property to the name of a column in the data source.

Procedure: Performing complex data binding at run time

To bind a data-bound control to a data source at run time, add the following lines of code that set the **DataSource** and **DisplayMember** properties:

```
DataGrid1.DataSource = productsDataSet
DataGrid1.DataMember = "Products"
```

If the **DataSource** property is not ambiguous, you can use it without defining the **DataMember**. The following code accomplishes the same results as the previous line of code:

```
DataGrid1.DataSource = productsDataSet.Tables("Products")
```

Practice: Binding Controls to Data

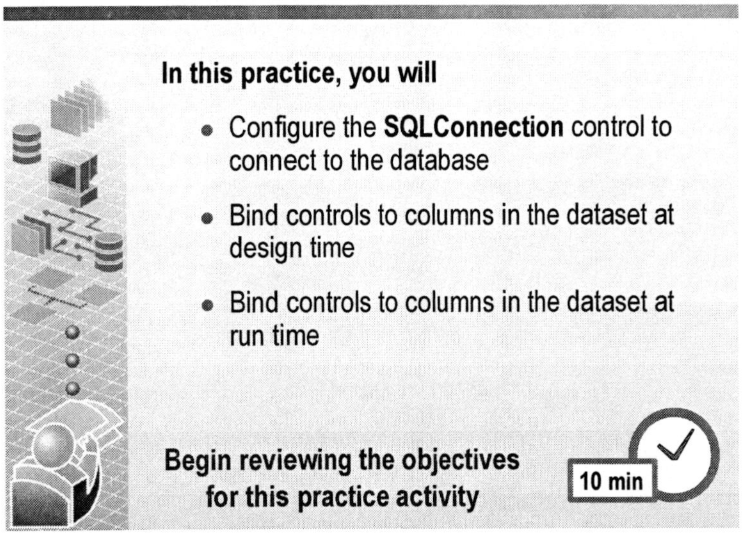

Introduction

In this practice, you will bind various controls to data in a dataset at design time and also programmatically at run time. You will begin by using simple binding to bind data to **Label** controls and then you will use complex data binding to bind data to a **ComboBox** and a DataGrid.

Instructions

► **Open the practice project**

1. Use Windows Explorer to browse to *install_folder*\Practices\Mod04\Mod04_03\Starter.
2. Double-click the DataBinding.sln solution file to open the project.

► **Bind StateLabel control to the State column by using the Properties window**

1. Open Form1 in Design view.
2. In the Properties window, select **StateLabel** on Form1, and then expand **DataBindings**.
3. Select the **Text** property, click the **Text Property** arrow, expand **StoresSalesDataSet1**, expand **Sales**, and then click **State**.

► **Bind CityLabel to the city column programmatically at run time**

1. Show TODO comments in the Task List.

   To show TODO comments, click the **View** menu, point to **Show Tasks**, and then click **All**.

2. Locate TODO: 1 in the Code Editor of Form1.
3. Under TODO: 1, call the **Add** method of the **DataBindings** collection of **CityLabel**, and pass **Text** as the name of the property, **StoreSalesDataSet1.sales** as the name of the data source, and **city** as the name of the column. Your code should look like this:

```
CityLabel.DataBindings.Add("Text", _
StoreSalesDataSet1.sales, "city")
```

► **Bind DataGrid1 to the sales table by using the Properties window**

1. Open Form1 in Design view.
2. Select **DataGrid1** on Form1 and use the Properties window to set the **DataSource** property to **StoreSalesDataSet1**.
3. Use the Properties window to set the **DataMember** to **sales**.

► **Bind StoresComboBox to the stores table programmatically at run time**

1. Locate TODO: 2 in the Code Editor of Form1.
2. Under TODO: 2, set the **DataSource** property of **StoresComboBox** to the **Stores** table in **StoreSalesDataSet1**.
3. Set the **DisplayMember** property of **StoresComboBox** to the **stor_name** column.
4. Set the **ValueMember** property of **StoresComboBox** to the **stor_id** column. Your code should look like this:

```
StoresComboBox.DataSource = _
StoreSalesDataSet1.Tables("Stores")

StoresComboBox.DisplayMember = "stor_name"

StoresComboBox.ValueMember = "stor_id"
```

Note The **ComboBox** control allows you to bind the **ValueMember** property to an alternate value that is not displayed in the **ComboBox**. This is often used when you want to display a user–friendly value to the user and bind to another field that is used programmatically, such as a primary key.

► **Test the application**

1. Press F5 to compile and run the application.
2. Select different stores in the **Stores** list to ensure the controls display the data bound values.

How to Maintain the Currency of a Control by Using CurrencyManager

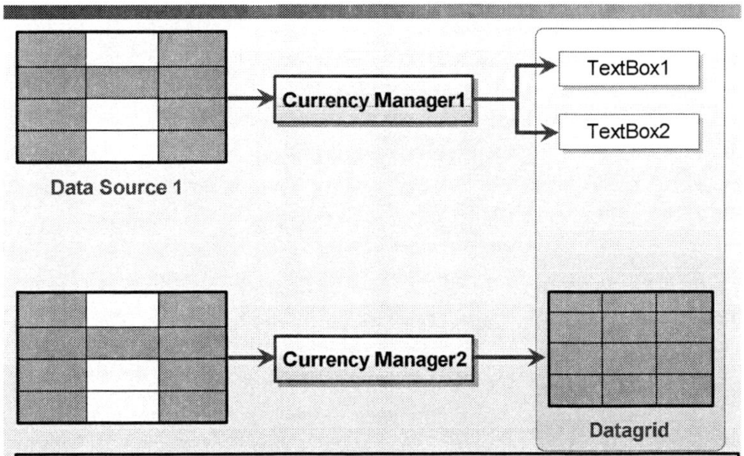


```
Dim cm As CurrencyManager
cm = Me.BindingContext(pubsDataSet, "Authors")
cm.Position += 1
```

Introduction

Any data source that you bind to a Windows Forms control to will have an associated **CurrencyManager** object. **CurrencyManager** is an object that is used to keep data-bound controls synchronized with a data source. The **CurrencyManger** object is important because data sources, such as Tables in DataSets, do not keep track of the currently selected row. You need an intermediary object that is aware of the currently selected position in a data source and can notify databound controls when the position changes. That intermediary object is **CurrencyManager**. The **CurrencyManager** object synchronizes data-bound controls with the data source by managing a collection of the bound data supplied by a data source.

For each data source associated with a Windows Form, the form maintains at least one **CurrencyManager**. There is a **CurrencyManager** object on the form for each discrete data source that you are binding to. If the controls on the form all bind to a single source (for example, if several **TextBox** controls are bound to the same data table), then they will share the same **CurrencyManager**. However, there are times when controls on the form will be bound to different sources. In that case, there are multiple **CurrencyManager** objects on the form, and each one tracks which record or data element is being used by the controls.

CurrencyManager properties

The following table lists some of the properties of the **CurrencyManager** object that helps it track data.

Property	Description
Bindings	Gets the collection of bindings being managed.
Count	Determines the last item in the list of rows.
Current	Contains the value of the current item in the data source.
List	Gets the data source (which implements IList) for this **CurrencyManager**.
Position	Specifies the position of the item in the underlying list.

Procedure: Maintaining the currency by using the CurrencyManager

Every Windows Form has a **BindingContext** object. The **BindingContext** object tracks all of the **CurrencyManager** objects on a form. Thus, any Windows Form with data-bound controls has at least one **BindingContext** object that tracks one (or more) **CurrencyManager** object or objects that track one data source (for each **CurrencyManager**).

For example, if you add a **TextBox** control to a form and bind it to a column of a table in a dataset, the control communicates with the **BindingContext** object for that form. The **BindingContext** object, in turn, communicates with the specific **CurrencyManager** object for that data association. If you query the **CurrencyManager's Position** property, it reports the current record for that **TextBox** control's binding.

You use the **BindingContext** of a form to access the various **CurrencyManagers**. To do so, you must specify the data source that the **CurrencyManager** is managing. For example, to access the **CurrencyManager** that manages the Authors table of **DataSet1** you would use the following code:

```
Dim cm As CurrencyManager
cm = Me.BindingContext(pubsDataSet, "Authors")
```

If you use a container control, such as a **GroupBox**, **Panel**, or **TabControl**, to contain data-bound controls, you can create a **BindingContext** for just that container control and its controls. This allows each part of your form to be managed by its own **CurrencyManager** object.

To determine the currency of a control, use the **Position** property of the **CurrencyManager** as shown.

```
cm.Position += 1
```

You can also use the following code to increment **CurrencyManager**.

```
Me.BindingContext(pubsDataSet, "Authors").Position += 1
```

Demonstration: Maintaining the Currency of a Control by Using CurrencyManager

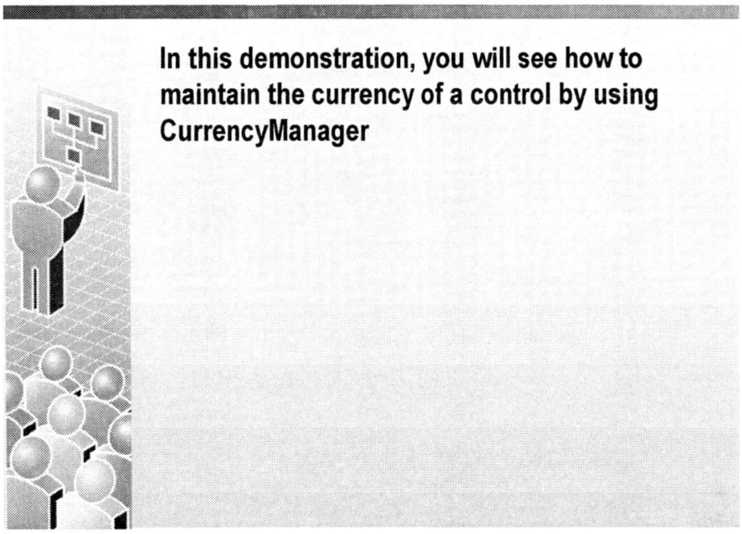

Introduction

In this demonstration, you will see how to maintain the currency of a control by using CurrencyManager.

Instructions

► **Create a Windows-based application project**

1. Open Visual Studio .NET.
2. On the **File** menu, point to **New**, and then click **Project**.
3. In the **New Project** dialog box, click **Windows Application**, name it **BindingContextNavigation**, and then click **OK**.

► **Use Data Form Wizard to create a data bound form**

1. On the **File** menu, click **Add New Item**.
2. In the **Add New Item** dialog box, in the **Templates** section, click **Data Form Wizard**, and then click **Open**.
3. In the opening page of Data Form Wizard, click **Next**.
4. Specify the name of the new dataset as **OrdersDataSet**, and click **Next**.
5. Select a connection to the **Northwind** database in the database connection drop-down list. If a connection does not exist, create a new connection. Click **Next**.
6. Add the **Orders** and **Order Details** tables by selecting them in the **Available Items** tree, click the **Add** (>) button, and then click **Next**.
7. In the **Name** box, type **OrderOrderDetailsRelation**

8. Set the following settings.

List	Setting
Parent table	Orders
Child table	Order Details
Keys (for both tables)	OrderID

9. Click the **Add (>)** button, and then click **Next**.
10. Ensure that the **Orders** table is set as the **Master or single table** and **Order Details** is set as the **Detail table**, and then click **Next**.
11. Select **Single record in individual controls**, and then click **Finish**.

▶ **Display and discuss the code generated for the navigation buttons**

1. Locate the **Click** event of the **btnNavNext** button in the Code Editor of DataForm1, and discuss the following line of code:

```
Me.BindingContext(objOrdersDataSet, "Orders").Position = _
(Me.BindingContext(objOrdersDataSet, "Orders").Position + _
1)
```

2. Locate the **objOrdersDataSet_PositionChanged()** procedure, and discuss the following line of code:

```
Me.lblNavLocation.Text = _
(((Me.BindingContext(objOrdersDataSet, _
"Orders").Position + 1).ToString + " of  ") _
+ Me.BindingContext(objOrdersDataSet, _
"Orders").Count.ToString)
```

3. Locate the **Click** event of the **btnLast** button in the Code Editor of DataForm1, and discuss the following line of code:

```
Me.BindingContext(objOrdersDataSet, "Orders").Position =
(Me.objOrdersDataSet.Tables("Orders").Rows.Count - 1)
```

4. In Solution Explorer, right-click the **BindingContextNavigation** project, and then click **Properties**.
5. Set **DataForm1** as the **Startup** object, and then click **OK**.
6. Press F5 to compile and run the application, and then demonstrate the use of the navigation buttons.
7. Close the application.

How to Format and Parse Data Bound Values

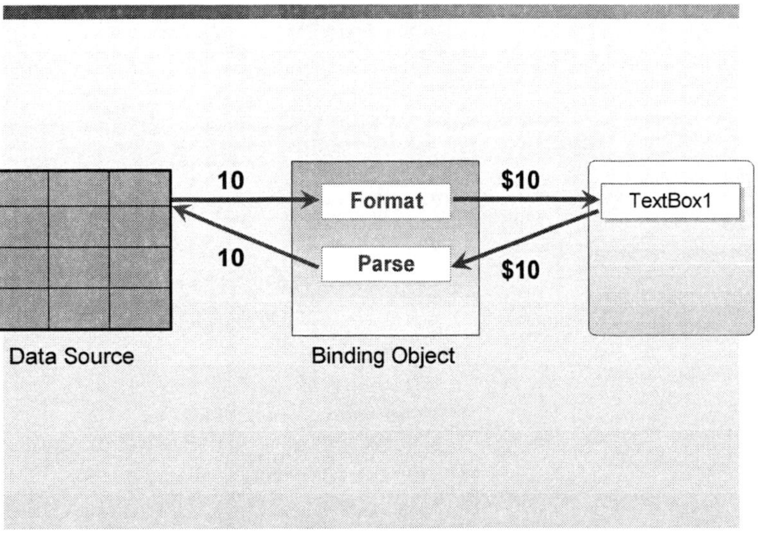

Introduction

Often the data retrieved from a data source may not match the data type accepted by a control in your application. The **Binding** object provides two methods—**Format** and **Parse**—to ensure that the data received and sent back to the data source is of the right data type.

Format and Parse events

The **Format** event occurs both when data is pushed from the data source into the control and when the data is pulled from the control into the data source. When the data is pushed from the data source into the control, the **Binding** object uses the **Format** event to put the formatted data into the control. When the data is pushed from the control into the data source, the **Binding** first parses the data by using the **Parse** event and then formats the data and sends it to the data source.

You can use the **Format** and **Parse** events to create custom formats for displaying data. For example, if the data in a table is of type **Decimal**, you can display the data in the local currency format by setting the **Value** property of the **ConvertEventArgs** object to the formatted value in the **Format** event. Consequently, you must remove the format from the displayed value in the **Parse** event.

The **Format** event occurs whenever the current value of the **BindingManagerBase** changes, which includes:

- The first time the property is bound.
- Any time the **Position** changes.
- Whenever the data-bound list is sorted or filtered, which is accomplished when a **DataView** supplies the list.

The **Parse** event occurs:

- After the **Validated** event of the **Control** object occurs.
- When the **EndCurrentEdit** method of the **BindingManagerBase** is called.
- When the current object of the **BindingManagerBase** changes (in other words, when the **Position** changes).

Procedure: Using the Format and Parse events

The following code creates event delegates for the **Parse** and **Format** events of a **Binding** object and then uses event procedures to format the data between a **String** and a **Decimal**:

```
Private Sub BindControl()
      Dim priceBinding As Binding = New Binding("Text", _
      TitlesDataSet1, "titles.price")
      AddHandler priceBinding.Parse, AddressOf _
      ParseStringToDecimal
      AddHandler priceBinding.Format, AddressOf _
      FormatDecimalToString
      PriceTextBox.DataBindings.Add(priceBinding)
End Sub

Private Sub FormatDecimalToString(ByVal sender As Object, _
ByVal convertArgs As ConvertEventArgs)
      Dim decimalValue As Decimal = convertArgs.Value
      convertArgs.Value = decimalValue.ToString("c")
  End Sub

Private Sub ParseStringToDecimal(ByVal sender As Object, -
ByVal convertArgs As ConvertEventArgs)
Dim stringValue As String = convertArgs.Value
convertArgs.Value = Decimal.Parse(stringValue,
NumberStyles.Currency)
End Sub
```

Practice: Formatting Data Bound Controls

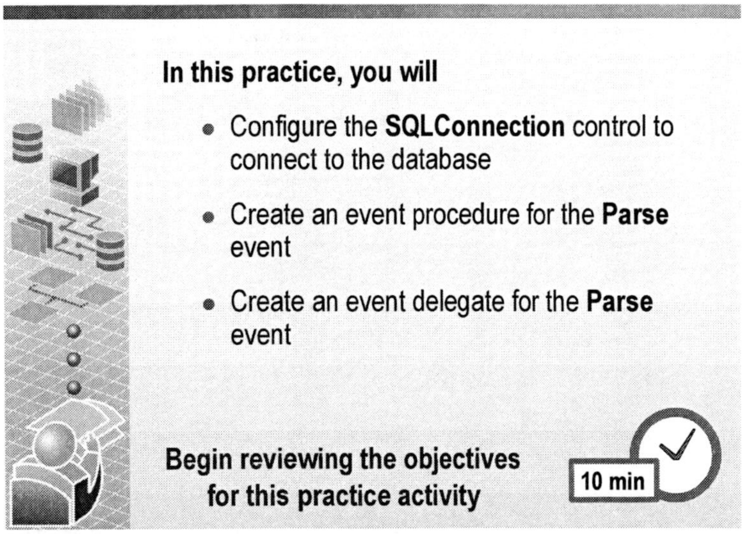

Introduction

In this practice, you will add event handlers to the **Format** and **Parse** events of a **Binding** object and then use the **ConvertEventArgs** class to apply appropriate formatting to the data bound value.

Instructions

► **Open the practice project**

1. Use Windows Explorer to browse to *install_folder*\Practices\Mod04\Mod04_04\Starter.
2. Double-click the FormatParse.sln solution file to open the project.

► **Create an event procedure invoked by the Parse event that converts the Value of ConvertEventArgs from a String to a Decimal**

1. Show TODO comments in the Task List.

   To show TODO comments, click the **View** menu, point to **Show Tasks**, and then click **All**.
2. Locate TODO: 1 in the Code Editor of Form1.
3. Under TODO: 1, create a procedure called *ParseStringToDecimal* that accepts two arguments: *sender* as an **Object** and *convertArgs* as a **ConvertEventArgs**.
4. Assign the **Value** of *convertArgs* to a String named *stringValue*.

5. Call the **Parse** method of the **Decimal** object and pass the two arguments: *stringValue* as the string to be formatted and **NumberStyles.Currency** as the NumberStyles constant.

6. Assign the results of the **Parse** method to **Value** property of *convertArgs*. Your code should look like this:

```
Private Sub ParseStringToDecimal(ByVal sender As Object, _
ByVal convertArgs As ConvertEventArgs)
    Dim stringValue As String = convertArgs.Value
    convertArgs.Value = Decimal.Parse(stringValue, _
    NumberStyles.Currency)
End Sub
```

The **Parse** method converts the String representation of a number in a specified style to its decimal equivalent by using the specified formatting style.

► Create an event delegate for the Parse event that references the FormatDecimalToString procedure

1. Locate TODO: 2 in the Code Editor of Form1.
2. Under TODO: 2, use **AddHandler** to create an event delegate for the **Parse** event of the **priceBinding** object that references the **ParseStringToDecimal** procedure. Your code should look like this:

```
AddHandler priceBinding.Parse, AddressOf
ParseStringToDecimal
```

3. The *priceBinding* object is a **Binding** object that is added to the **DataBindings** collection of **PriceTextBox**. Review the following code:

```
Dim priceBinding As Binding = New Binding("Text", _
TitlesDataSet1, "titles.price")
...
PriceTextBox.DataBindings.Add(priceBinding)
```

► Test the application

1. Press F5 to compile and run the application.
2. Select different titles in the **Book Titles** list, and review how the **Price** textbox is updated and formatted.
3. Use the **Price** text box to change the price of a book, and then click the **Debug.Write Value** button.
4. Display and review the results in the Output window of the Visual Stuio.NET IDE.

Lab 4.1: Accessing Data by Using ADO.NET

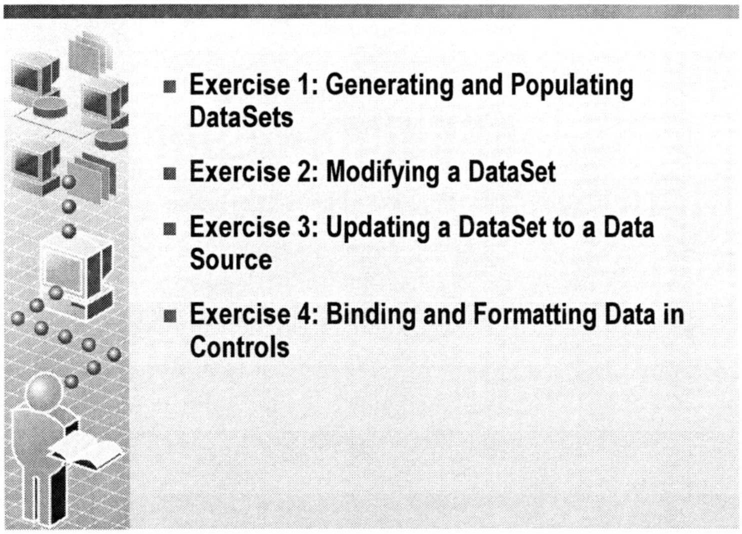

Objectives

After completing this lab, you will have demonstrated your ability to:

- Add and configure ADO.NET objects by using Component Designer.
- Configure DataAdapters by using Data Adapter Configuration Wizard.
- Generate typed datasets.
- Populate a dataset from data in a database.
- Create relationships between tables in a dataset.
- Update data to a data source by using typed datasets.
- Bind data to controls.
- Format the data bound to controls.

Note This lab focuses on the concepts in Module 4, "Using Data in Windows Forms Applications," in Course 2565A, *Developing Microsoft .NET Applications for Windows (Visual Basic® .NET).* As a result, this lab may not comply with Microsoft security recommendations.

Prerequisites

Before working on this lab, you must have:

- The knowledge and skills to develop a simple Windows Forms application by using a Microsoft Visual Studio® .NET–compatible programming language.
- The knowledge and skills to use Data Adapter Configuration Wizard in the Visual Studio .NET IDE.
- The knowledge and skills to access and update a database from a Visual Studio .NET–based application.
- The knowledge and skills to create Relations between tables in a dataset in a Visual Studio .NET–based application
- The knowledge and skills to bind data to controls in a Visual Studio .NET–based application
- The knowledge and skills to format data bound to controls in a Visual Studio .NET–based application

Scenario

You are an application developer at a trading company called Northwind Traders. The department that you work in is developing a Purchase Order application that will be used by the Northwind Traders sales force. You are responsible for completing data access code that will use ADO.NET objects to access the Northwind database. Much of the code was written by your colleagues, and you are responsible for creating the code that will populate and update the Order and Order Details tables. You are also responsible for writing the data binding code in the **OrderItemControl** control.

The Order and Order Details tables have a one-to-many relationship. To write the code that populates and updates these tables, you must understand the relationship between the tables and the fields involved. The following illustration represents the relations and fields in the Order and Order Details tables.

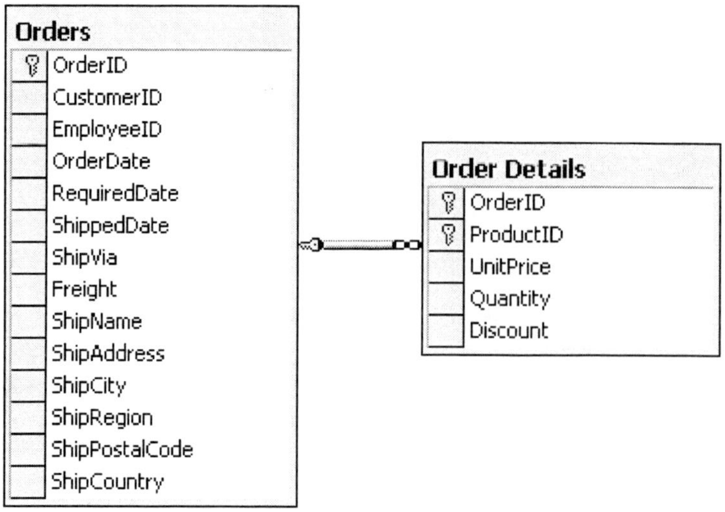

Estimated time to complete this lab: 75 minutes

Exercise 1
Generating and Populating DataSets

In this exercise, you will create a **SQLDataAdapter** by using Data Adapter Configuration Wizard and populate a dataset with data from a database at run time. You will use Component Designer to add and configure ADO.NET objects. You can use Component Designer to add subcomponents to a class, configure them, and code their events.

Scenario

You begin to build the data access features into the Purchase Order application. Your development team has built some of the preliminary data access code that you need to complete. Your responsibility is to create a **DataAdapter** that can access and update the Order table of the Northwind database.

The application uses employee information to load and create order entries. Each order is associated with a single employee. The Orders table includes an EmployeeID column that maps to the EmployeeID column in the Employees table. The **DataAdapter** that you create will use the value of the *employeeID* variable to determine which rows to return. You decide to use Data Adapter Configuration Wizard to configure the **SELECT** command of the **DataAdapter** and allow it to generate the **Update** command for you.

There are starter and solution files associated with this exercise. Browse to *install_folder*\Labfiles\Lab04_1\Ex01\Starter to find the starter files, and browse to *install_folder*\Labfiles\Lab04_1\Ex01\Solution to find the solution files. If you performed a default installation of the course files, *install_folder* corresponds to C:\Program Files\Msdntrain\2565.

<table>
<tr><th>Tasks</th><th>Additional information</th></tr>
<tr><td>1. Open Visual Studio .NET, and open the PurchaseOrderApplication .sln file. To open the solution file, browse to install_folder\Labfiles\ Lab04_1\Ex01\Starter\ OrderApplication.</td><td>For more information about opening a project file, see the following resource:
• The Visual Studio .NET Help documentation. For additional information about opening a project file, in Search, select the Search in titles only check box, then search by using the phrase Open Project Dialog Box.</td></tr>
<tr><td>2. Add a SQLDataAdapter control to OrderApplicationData Class. In Data Adapter Configuration Wizard, use the NorthwindConnection information, and create the following SQL Select statement:
SELECT * FROM Orders WHERE (EmployeeID = @EmployeeID)
• Ensure that the wizard created the Insert, Update, and Delete commands.
• Change the name of the new SQLDataAdapter to OrdersDataAdapter.</td><td>For more information about adding controls to Component Designer or by using Data Adapter Configuration Wizard, see the following resources:
• Lesson: Adding ADO.NET Objects to and Configuring ADO.NET Objects in a Windows Forms Application in Module 4, "Using Data in Windows Forms Applications," in Course 2565A, Developing Microsoft .NET Applications for Windows (Visual Basic .NET).
• Practice: Adding ADO.NET Objects to and Configuring ADO.NET Objects in a Windows Forms Application in Module 4, "Using Data in Windows Forms Applications," in Course 2565A, Developing Microsoft .NET Applications for Windows (Visual Basic .NET).
• The Visual Studio .NET Help documentation. Search by using the phrase Component Designer or the phrase Data Adapter Configuration Wizard.</td></tr>
<tr><td>3. Use the Task List to locate the code section 'TODO: 1', and create a local variable to hold an instance of NorthwindDataSet and name it tempDataSet.</td><td>Additional information is not necessary for this task.</td></tr>
<tr><td>4. Use the Task List to locate the code section 'TODO: 2', and add @employeeID (the global employee ID) to the Parameters collection of the SelectCommand property of OrdersDataAdapter and OrderDetailsDataAdapter.</td><td>For more information about assigning values to the Parameters collection of Command objects, see the following resources:
• Lesson: Accessing and Modifying Data by Using DataSets in Module 4, "Using Data in Windows Forms Applications," in Course 2565A, Developing Microsoft .NET Applications for Windows (Visual Basic .NET).
• Practice: Populating and Updating DataSets in Module 4, "Using Data in Windows Forms Applications," in Course 2565A, Developing Microsoft .NET Applications for Windows (Visual Basic .NET).
• The Visual Studio .NET SDK documentation. Search by using the phrase Using Parameters with a DataAdapter.</td></tr>
</table>

Tasks	Additional information
5. Use the Task List to locate the code section 'TODO: 3', and call the **Fill** method of **OrdersDataAdapter** and **OrderDetailsDataAdapter** to fill the **Orders** and **OrderDetails** tables of **tempDataSet**.	For more information about filling datasets with data by using a **DataAdapter**, see the following resources: • Lesson: Accessing and Modifying Data by Using DataSets in Module 4, "Using Data in Windows Forms Applications," in Course 2565A, *Developing Microsoft .NET Applications for Windows (Visual Basic .NET).* • Practice: Populating and Updating DataSets in Module 4, "Using Data in Windows Forms Applications," in Course 2565A, *Developing Microsoft .NET Applications for Windows (Visual Basic .NET).* • The.NET Framework SDK documentation. For additional information about assigning values to the **Parameters** collection of **Command** objects, search by using the phrase **Populating a DataSet from a DataAdapter**.
6. Place a breakpoint at the beginning of the **RefreshLocalData** procedure. Compile and run the application. From the **Data** menu, click **Refresh Data**, and step through each line of code. Locate and review the contents of the NorthwindData.XML file, which is in the most recent folder version folder of C:\Documents and Settings\ All Users\Application Data\ Northwind Traders\ PurchaseOrder\.	For more information about building and debugging your applications, see the following resource: • The Visual Studio .NET Help documentation. Search by using the phrases **Default and Custom Builds** and **Using the Debugger**.

Exercise 2
Modifying a DataSet

In this exercise, you will review the code that creates data tables objects, insert new data rows, and append the information to an existing dataset.

Scenario

The Orders table uses an auto incrementing column named **OrderID** to generate primary keys when new rows are created in the database. This value is also generated by datasets when a new row is inserted in the Orders table. The Purchase Order application uses a global dataset named **pendingOrdersData** to store all the orders until they are submitted to the database. Each order is associated with one or more order details. The Orders table includes an OrderID column that maps to the OrderID column of the Order Details table.

One of your colleagues has written a procedure called **SaveOrders** that creates new rows in the Orders table, captures the value of the OrderID generated by the dataset, and uses it to create rows in the Order Details table. After all of the rows in the Order Details table are created, the procedure persists the order information in an XML file named PendingOrders.XML. You decide to review the code more closely to understand how it works.

There are solution files associated with this exercise. Browse to *install_folder*\Labfiles\Lab04_1\Ex02\Solution to find the solution files. If you performed a default installation of the course files, *install_folder* corresponds to C:\Program Files\Msdntrain\2565.

Tasks	Additional information
1. Open Visual Studio .NET, and open the PurchaseOrderApplication.sln file. To open the solution file, browse to *install_folder*\Labfiles\Lab04_1\Ex02\Solution\OrderApplication.	For more information about opening a project file, see the following resource: • The Visual Studio .NET Help documentation. For additional information about opening a project file, in Search, select the **Search in titles only** check box, then search by using the phrase **Open Project Dialog Box**.
2. Place a breakpoint at the beginning of the **SaveOrders** procedure in MainForm. Compile and run the application. From the **Data** menu, click **Refresh Data**. To create different order items, click the **New Order Item** button and then click the **Save Order** button. Step over each line of code by pressing F10 and review the flow of the code. When reviewing the code, look for the following things: • The **SaveOrders** procedure creates a new row in the Orders table and assigns the columns to values from the controls of **MainForm**. When the row is added to the table, the auto incrementing OrderID generated by the dataset is stored in a variable named *clientOrderID*. • The **SaveOrders** procedure then creates rows in the Order Details table and uses the value of *clientOrderID* to populate the OrderID column for each row inserted into the Order Details table.	For more information about building and debugging your applications, see the following resource: • The Visual Studio .NET Help documentation. Search by using the phrases **Default and Custom Builds** and **Using the Debugger**.

Exercise 3
Updating a DataSet to a Data Source

In this exercise, you will create a relationship between two tables to create a typed dataset and then update the changes from the dataset to a DataSource.

Scenario

In the Northwind database, each order is associated with one or more order details. The Orders table includes an OrderID column that maps to the OrderID column of the Order Details table. When you create a new row in the Orders table, the **SaveOrders** procedure ensures that all child rows in the Order Details table have the same OrderID as the parent in the Orders table. When you update the dataset to a data source, you must first update the Orders table and then the Order Details table. When you update a row in the Orders table, however, a new OrderID will be generated by the database that might not match the child values in the Order Details table. This causes an error when you attempt to update the Order Details table.

One way to resolve this problem is to write code that uses dataset events to capture the new OrderID generated by the database and assign it to all child rows in the Order Details table. However, other options are available when you use typed datasets and DataAdapters for each table in a database. Instead of writing code for dataset events, you can use the **Refresh the DataSet** option in Data Adapter Configuration Wizard. With this option enabled, the wizard adds a **SELECT** statement after the **Insert** and **Update** statements to retrieve the Identity column generated by the database.

When you create a relation between tables by using XML Designer, you can choose how table relationships are handled when the parent table is modified. For example, if you set the **Delete Rule** to **Cascade** (the default), and you delete rows in a parent table, all the related rows in the child table are also deleted. When you create a relation between the Orders and Order Details tables, it is important that you set the value of the **Update Rule** option to **Cascade** (the default) so that any changes made to a parent table are cascaded to the child tables.

When you update a row in the Orders table, the DataAdapter returns the OrderID value generated by the database and changes the value in the Orders table of the dataset. With the cascading update rule, all the child rows in the Order Details table of the dataset will automatically be changed to the new OrderID of the parent. Now when you update the Order Details table to the database it will have the same OrderID as the parent.

There are starter and solution files associated with this exercise. Browse to *install_folder*\Labfiles\Lab04_1\Ex03\Starter to find the starter files, and browse to *install_folder*\Labfiles\Lab04_1\Ex03\Solution to find the solution files. If you performed a default installation of the course files, *install_folder* corresponds to C:\Program Files\Msdntrain\2565.

Tasks	Detailed steps
1. Open Visual Studio .NET, and open the PurchaseOrderApplication .sln file. To open the solution file, browse to *install_folder*\Labfiles\ Lab04_1\Ex03\Starter\ OrderApplication.	For more information about opening a project file, see the following resource: • The Visual Studio .NET Help documentation. For additional information about opening a project file, in Search, select the **Search in titles only** check box, then search by using the phrase **Open Project Dialog Box**.
2. Use XML Designer to create a relation between the Orders and Order Details tables in the NorthwindDataSet.xsd file.	For more information about using XML Designer, see the following resources: • Lesson: Accessing and Modifying Data by Using DataSets in Module 4, "Using Data in Windows Forms Applications," in Course 2565A, *Developing Microsoft .NET Applications for Windows (Visual C# .NET)*. • Demonstration: Creating Database Schema by Using the XML Schema Designer in Module 4, "Using Data in Windows Forms Applications," in Course 2565A, *Developing Microsoft .NET Applications for Windows (Visual C# .NET)*. • The Visual Studio .NET Help documentation. Search by using the phrase **XML Designer**.
3. Use the Task List to locate the code section 'TODO: 1' in the code view of OrderApplicationDataClass .vb and update the database by using the **Update** method of **OrdersDataAdapter** and **OrderDetailsDataAdapter**. The Cascading Update rule enforced by the relation between the two tables should automatically retrieve the OrderID generated by the server. When an Order row is created, it is assigned to related rows in the Order Details table on the client computer.	For more information about updating a data source, see the following resources: • Lesson: Accessing and Modifying Data by Using DataSets in Module 4, "Using Data in Windows Forms Applications," in Course 2565A, *Developing Microsoft .NET Applications for Windows (Visual Basic .NET)*. • Practice: Populating and Updating DataSets in Module 4, "Using Data in Windows Forms Applications," in Course 2565A, *Developing Microsoft .NET Applications for Windows (Visual Basic .NET)*. • The Visual Studio .NET Help documentation. Search by using the phrase **Updating the Database with a DataAdapter and the DataSet**.

Tasks	Additional information
4. Compile and run the application. On the toolbar, click the **Refresh** button, and choose an employee name. To create an order, click the **New Order Item** button. To save the order, click the **Save Order** button, and then click the **Submit** button on the Toolbar. Use Server Explorer to verify that the order was saved to the database.	For more information about building and debugging your applications and using Server Explorer, see the following resource: • The Visual Studio .NET Help documentation. Search by using the phrases **Default and Custom Builds**, **Using the Debugger**, and **Server Explorer Window**.

Exercise 4
Binding and Formatting Data in Controls

In this exercise, you will bind data to controls and format the data by using the events of the **Binding** class.

Scenario

The **OrderItemControl** control is under development and requires code to bind constituent controls to data from the Products table. A method in the control called **GetProductData** has been created, and it accepts a parameter named *productsTable* that contains data from the Products table. You need to bind data from this table to the constituent controls. You also need to convert the values in the Price column to currency when you bind them to UnitPriceTextBox control.

There are starter and solution files associated with this exercise. Browse to *install_folder*\Labfiles\Lab04_1\Ex04\Starter to find the starter files, and browse to *install_folder*\Labfiles\Lab04_1\Ex04\Solution to find the solution files. If you performed a default installation of the course files, *install_folder* corresponds to C:\Program Files\Msdntrain\2565.

Tasks	Detailed steps
1. Open Visual Studio .NET, and open the PurchaseOrderApplication.sln file. To open the solution file, browse to *install_folder*\Labfiles\Lab04_1\Ex04\Starter\OrderApplication.	For more information about opening a project file, see the following resources • The Visual Studio .NET Help documentation. For additional information about opening a project file, in Search, select the **Search in titles only** check box, then search by using the phrase **Open Project Dialog Box**.
2. Use the Task List to locate the code section 'TODO: 1' in the code view of OrderItemControl.vb, and assign the **DataSource** of **ProductNameComboBox** to the DataTable passed to the GetProductData procedure. Assign the **DisplayMember** and **ValueMember** of **ProductNameComboBox** to the ProductName and ProductID columns, respectively.	For more information about binding controls to data, see the following resources: • Lesson: Binding Data to Controls in Module 4, "Using Data in Windows Forms Applications," in Course 2565A, *Developing Microsoft .NET Applications for Windows (Visual Basic .NET).* • Practice: Binding Controls to Data in Module 4, "Using Data in Windows Forms Applications," in Course 2565A, *Developing Microsoft .NET Applications for Windows (Visual Basic .NET).* • The.NET Framework SDK documentation. For additional information about binding controls to data, search by using the phrase **Data Binding and Windows Forms**.

Tasks	Additional information
3. Use the Task List to locate the code section 'TODO: 2', and declare a **Binding** object, and use it to bind the **Text** property of **UnitPriceTextBox** to the UnitPrice column of the DataTable passed to the **GetProductData** procedure.	For more information about binding data to controls, see the following resources: • Lesson: Binding Data to Controls in Module 4, "Using Data in Windows Forms Applications," in Course 2565A, *Developing Microsoft .NET Applications for Windows (Visual Basic .NET).* • Practice: Binding Controls to Data in Module 4, "Using Data in Windows Forms Applications," in Course 2565A, *Developing Microsoft .NET Applications for Windows (Visual Basic .NET).* • The.NET Framework SDK documentation. For additional information about binding controls to data, search by using the phrase **Data Binding and Windows Forms**.
4. Use the Task List to locate the code section 'TODO: 3', and create an event procedure named **DecimalToCurrency** that converts the **ConvertEventArgs** event argument to a currency format.	For more information about creating event procedures for **Binding** objects, see the following resources: • Lesson: Binding Data to Controls in Module 4, "Using Data in Windows Forms Applications," in Course 2565A, *Developing Microsoft .NET Applications for Windows (Visual Basic .NET).* • Practice: Formatting Data Bound Controls in Module 4, "Using Data in Windows Forms Applications," in Course 2565A, *Developing Microsoft .NET Applications for Windows (Visual Basic .NET).* • The.NET Framework SDK documentation. For additional information about binding controls to data, search by using the phrase **Data Binding and Windows Forms**.
5. Use the Task List to locate the code section 'TODO: 4', and create an event handler for the **Format** event of the **Binding** object created in step 4.	For more information about creating event handlers, see the following resources: • Lesson: Creating an Event Handler for a Control in Module 2, "Working with Controls," in Course 2565A, *Developing Microsoft .NET Applications for Windows (Visual Basic .NET).* • Practice: Creating an Event Handler for a Control in Module 2, "Working with Controls," in Course 2565A, *Developing Microsoft .NET Applications for Windows (Visual Basic .NET).* • The Visual Studio .NET SDK documentation. For additional information about binding controls to data, search by using the phrase **Creating Event Handlers at Run Time for Windows Forms**.
6. Compile and run the application. On the toolbar, click the **Refresh** button, and choose an employee name. To populate the **OrderItemControl** control, click the **New Order Item** button. Navigate through the products by using the **ProductNameComboBox** control.	For more information about building and debugging your applications, see the following resource: • The Visual Studio .NET Help documentation. Search by using the phrases **Default and Custom Builds** and **Using the Debugger**.

Lesson: Overview of XML Web Services

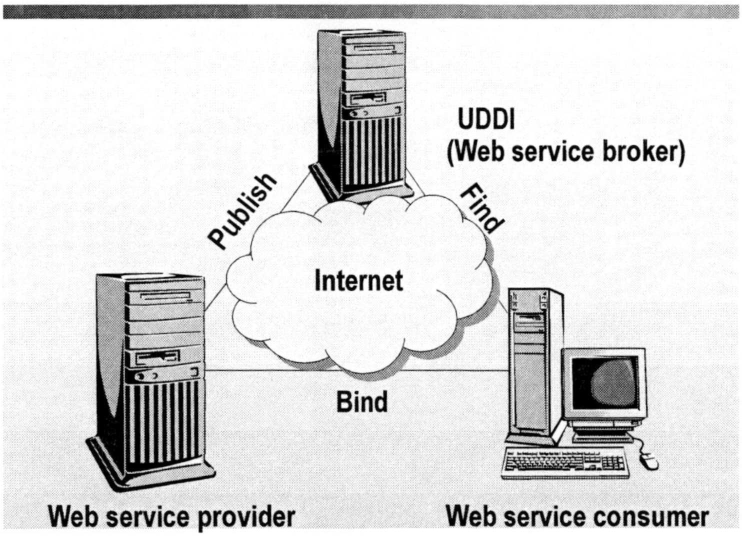

Introduction

XML Web services enable the exchange of data and the remote invocation of application logic by using XML messaging to move data through firewalls and between completely different systems.

XML Web services are accessible from just about any kind of application, including other XML Web services, Web applications, applications for the Windows operating system, and console applications. The only requirement is that the client must be able to send, receive, and process messages to and from the XML Web service.

An XML Web service can be used either internally by a single application or exposed externally over the Internet for use by any number of applications by using a service broker, which is a node that hosts a Universal Description, Discovery and Integration (UDDI) registry. Because it is accessible through a standard interface, an XML Web service allows completely different systems to work together as a single web of computation.

This lesson presents an overview of the XML Web services programming model and shows how to create applications that use XML Web services.

Lesson objectives

After completing this lesson, you will be able to:

- Describe the XML Web services model.
- Describe the roles of HTTP, Simple Object Access Protocol (SOAP), and XML in the Web services model.

What Are XML Web Services?

- **An XML Web service is a URL-addressable set of functions that is exposed over a network to serve as a building block for creating distributed applications**
  - Based on Internet technologies, such as HTTP, XML and SOAP
  - Building blocks
- **Basic elements**
  - XML Web service provider
  - XML Web service consumer
  - XML Web service broker

Introduction

In many cases, applications must access remote data or functionality. One way to make this happen is to call XML Web services.

Definition

An XML Web service is an URL-addressable set of functions that is exposed over a network to serve as a building block for creating distributed applications.

Example of an XML Web service

An example of an XML Web service is Microsoft Passport. Passport provides authentication services and all of its functionality is accessible through HTTP requests.

The foundations for XML Web services are HTTP, XML, and Simple Object Access Protocol (SOAP, a lightweight HTTP- and XML-based protocol used for information exchange). The development of these technologies is governed by the World Wide Web Consortium (W3C).

Like components, XML Web services are black boxes. They encapsulate the implementation and provide an interface for communicating with the Web service. Therefore, you can use XML Web services as building blocks for applications.

Basic elements of the XML Web service model

The basic elements of the XML Web service model are:

- The XML Web service broker, which is a network node hosting a global registry of available Web services, much like a telephone directory.
- The XML Web service provider, which is a network node hosting a Web service.
- The XML Web service consumer, which is a network node hosting any client that can communicate by using HTTP. The clients include browsers, console applications, and traditional graphical user interface (GUI) applications.

How Do XML Web Services Work?

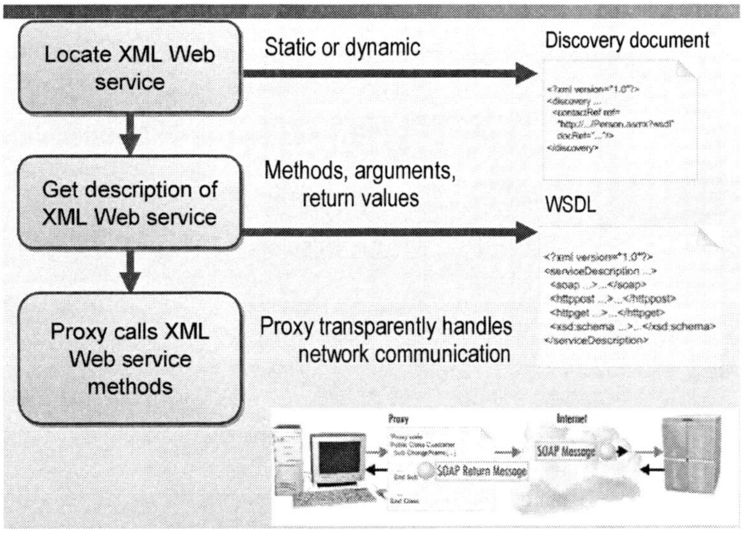

Introduction

One of the core characteristics of an XML Web service is the high degree of abstraction that exists between the implementation and consumption of a service. By using XML-based messaging as the mechanism by which the service is created and accessed, both the XML Web service client and the XML Web service provider are freed from needing any knowledge of each other beyond inputs, outputs, and locations.

Discovering the location of the XML Web service

You can discover the location of an XML Web service either statically or dynamically:

- If you know the location of the XML Web service you want to call, you explicitly provide it in your application. This is called *static discovery*.
- If you do not know the location of XML Web service you want to call, then you must use dynamic discovery methods.

For more information about static and dynamic discovery of XML Web services, see the lesson titled Creating a Simple XML Web Services Client in Module 4, "Using Data in Windows Forms Applications," in Course 2565A, *Developing Microsoft .NET Applications for Windows (Visual Basic .NET).*

XML Web service description

An XML Web service can be used either internally by a single application or exposed externally over the Internet for use by any number of applications. Because it is accessible through a standard interface, an XML Web service allows heterogeneous systems to work together as a single web of computation.

Proxy calls XML Web service methods

An XML Web service consumer must be able to construct the messages that are sent to a Web service and parse the messages that are received from a Web service. Manually writing the code to construct and parse the messages is time-consuming and prone to error. It is better to encapsulate this code in a class that can be reused. A class like this is called a *proxy class*.

When you reference an XML Web service from a consumer application, the .NET Framework generates a proxy for you.

What is SOAP?

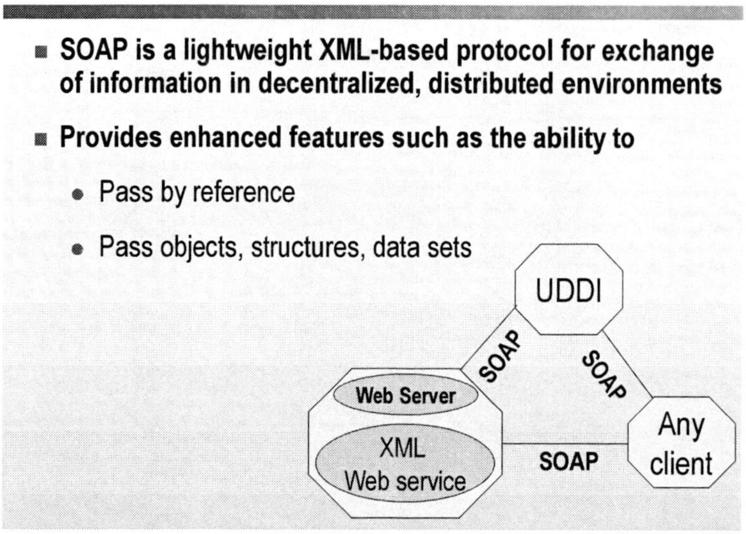

Introduction

XML Web services use SOAP as the protocol for network messages.

Definition

Simple Object Access Protocol (SOAP) is a lightweight XML-based protocol for exchange of information in decentralized, distributed environments.

Soap messages consist of two main parts:

- An envelope for handling extensibility and modularity.
- An encoding mechanism for representing types in an envelope.

The advantages of using SOAP

By using SOAP as an underlying protocol for XML, messages can pass data by reference and contain complex structures such as objects, structures, and data sets.

What is WSDL?

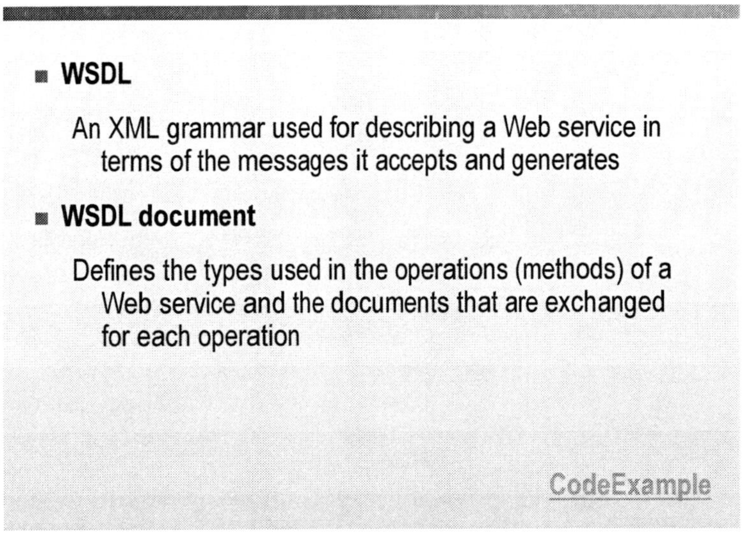

Introduction

To be able to use or consume a Web service, you must first know how to interact with it.

Definition

Web Services Description Language (WSDL) is an XML grammar that is used for describing a Web service in terms of the messages it accepts and generates. In other words, a WSDL file acts as a contract between a Web service consumer (client) and a Web service.

A WSDL document defines the types used in the operations (methods) of a Web service, and the documents that are exchanged for each operation. Then, these definitions are associated with a network protocol and grouped into messages to define an endpoint (the network location of a Web service). WSDL can describe endpoints and their operations without specifying the message formats or the network protocols to which an endpoint is bound.

Structure of a WSDL document

As a Web service consumer, it is important that you are familiar with WSDL to understand the contract defined in a WSDL document.

A WSDL document is just a list of definitions. In a WSDL file, the root element is named **definitions**. This element contains five primary child elements that define the Web service. The following table describes the five elements that appear in the **definitions** element in a WSDL file in the order specified.

Element	Description
types	Defines the various data types used to exchange messages.
message	Describes the messages to be communicated.
portType	Identifies a set of operations and the messages involved with each of those operations.
binding	Specifies the protocol details for various service operations and describes how to map the abstract content of these messages into a concrete format.
service	Groups a set of related ports together.

Example

The following code is an example of some of the contents of the WSDL document for the ExpenseReportWebService XML Web service that your client application will call in Lab 4.2: Calling an XML Web Service in Course 2565A, *Developing Microsoft .NET Applications for Windows (Visual Basic .NET)*:

```
<?xml version="1.0" encoding="utf-8" ?>
- <definitions
xmlns:http="http://schemas.xmlsoap.org/wsdl/http/"
xmlns:soap="http://schemas.xmlsoap.org/wsdl/soap/"
xmlns:s="http://www.w3.org/2001/XMLSchema"
xmlns:s0="http://localhost/ExpenseReportWebService"
xmlns:soapenc="http://schemas.xmlsoap.org/soap/encoding/"
xmlns:tm="http://microsoft.com/wsdl/mime/textMatching/"
xmlns:mime="http://schemas.xmlsoap.org/wsdl/mime/"
targetNamespace="http://localhost/ExpenseReportWebService"
xmlns="http://schemas.xmlsoap.org/wsdl/">
- <types>
- <s:schema elementFormDefault="qualified"
targetNamespace="http://localhost/ExpenseReportWebService">
<s:import namespace="http://www.w3.org/2001/XMLSchema" />
- <s:element name="AuthenticateUser">
- <s:complexType>
- <s:sequence>
<s:element minOccurs="0" maxOccurs="1" name="username"
type="s:string" />
<s:element minOccurs="0" maxOccurs="1" name="password"
type="s:string" />
<s:element minOccurs="0" maxOccurs="1" name="passwordToken"
type="s:string" />
</s:sequence>
</s:complexType>
</s:element>
 ...
```

Usually this information is transparent to the developer. The XML Web service description is just used by the .NET Framework when you add a reference to an XML Web service to your client application. You will see a more user-friendly display of the details of the methods, arguments, and return values associated with an XML Web service that you reference in the lesson titled Creating a Simple XML Web Services Client in Module 4, "Using Data in Windows Forms Applications," in Course 2565A, *Developing Microsoft .NET Applications for Windows (Visual Basic .NET)*.

Lesson: Creating a Simple XML Web Services Client

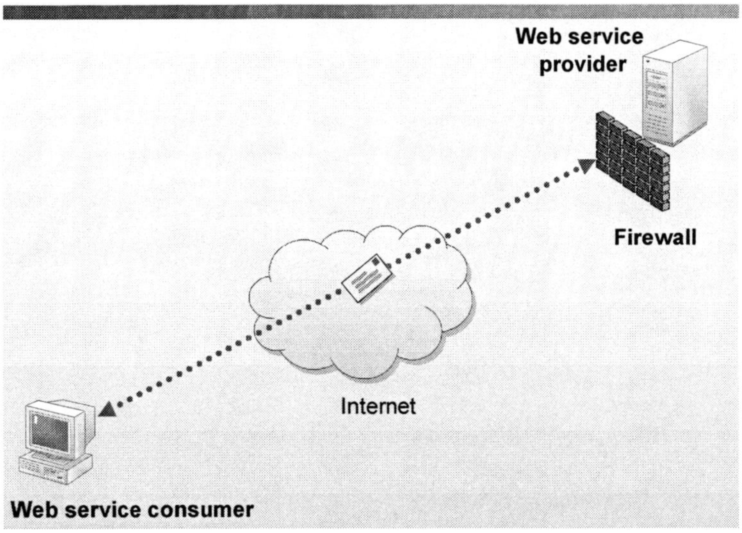

Introduction

This lesson shows how to create and test a client application that uses XML Web services.

Note For more information about how to make asynchronous calls to XML Web services to avoid blocking the user interface, see Module 7, "Asynchronous Programming," in Course 2565A, *Developing Microsoft .NET Applications for Windows (Visual Basic .NET).*

Lesson objective

After completing this lesson, you will be able to create and test a simple XML Web service client application.

How to Locate an XML Web Service

- **Static Discovery**
  - Provide explicit URL
  - Disco file
- **Dynamic Discovery**
  - UDDI
  - Vsdisco file

Introduction

The process by which you locate a Web service and its descriptions and learn how to interact with it is known as Web service discovery.

A Web service provider can make discovery information available to Web service consumer developers. It can do this by either statically or dynamically generating a document that contains a link to the WSDL document for all the Web services hosted by the provider.

Static discovery

Static discovery is possible when the location of a discovery document (usually with the extension .disco) is already known. Static discovery involves providing an explicit URL for an XML Web service or retrieving the discovery document by providing an explicit URL and interpreting its contents.

Dynamic discovery

Dynamic discovery takes place when all that is known to the consumer is the endpoint of the Web service provider. In this situation, there is no static list of .disco files at the endpoint. Instead, the list of available Web services and the associated service contracts must be dynamically retrieved from a UDDI directory by the consumer.

Note A static discovery document usually has the extension .disco and a dynamic discovery document has the extension .vsdisco.

How to Access an XML Web Service

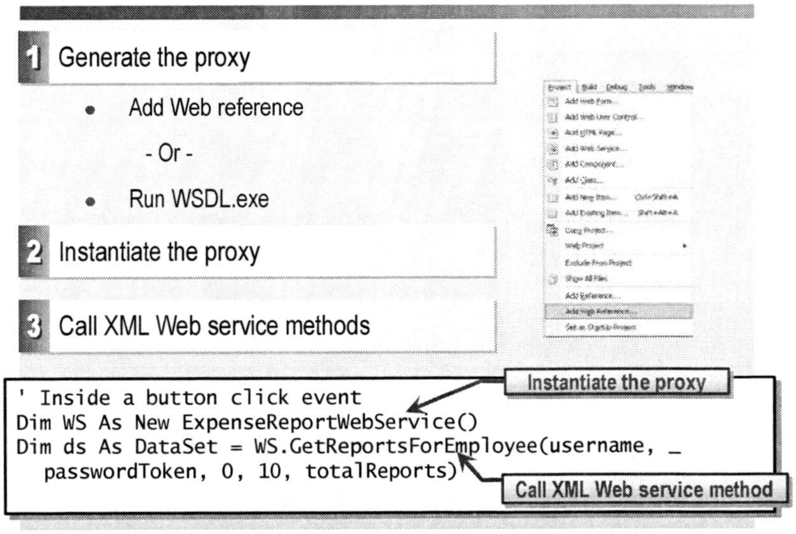

Introduction

Much of the work of calling an XML Web service is done for you by the .NET Framework, but you must add a few lines of code to your application to get the .NET Framework to do the work on your behalf. The following is an overview of the main steps that you must take in your application to call an XML Web service:

1. Generate the proxy that will call the XML Web service methods.

   You can either add a Web reference to your Visual Studio .NET project or call the command line utility WSDL.exe.

2. Instantiate the proxy.

   Based on the description of the XML Web service, instantiate the proxy object that you use to call the XML Web service methods.

3. Call the XML Web service methods that are required by your application.

   Based on the description of the XML Web service methods, call them appropriately.

Procedure: Generating the proxy

In Visual Studio .NET, you can generate a proxy by adding a Web Reference to your client application project.

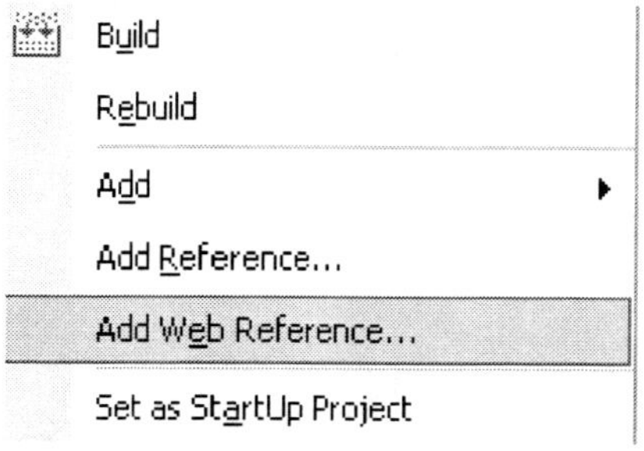

The following is the documentation for an XML Web service—a user-friendly summary of the WSDL document that contains a short description of the methods available. When you click the **Service Description** hyperlink, you will see the WSDL document.

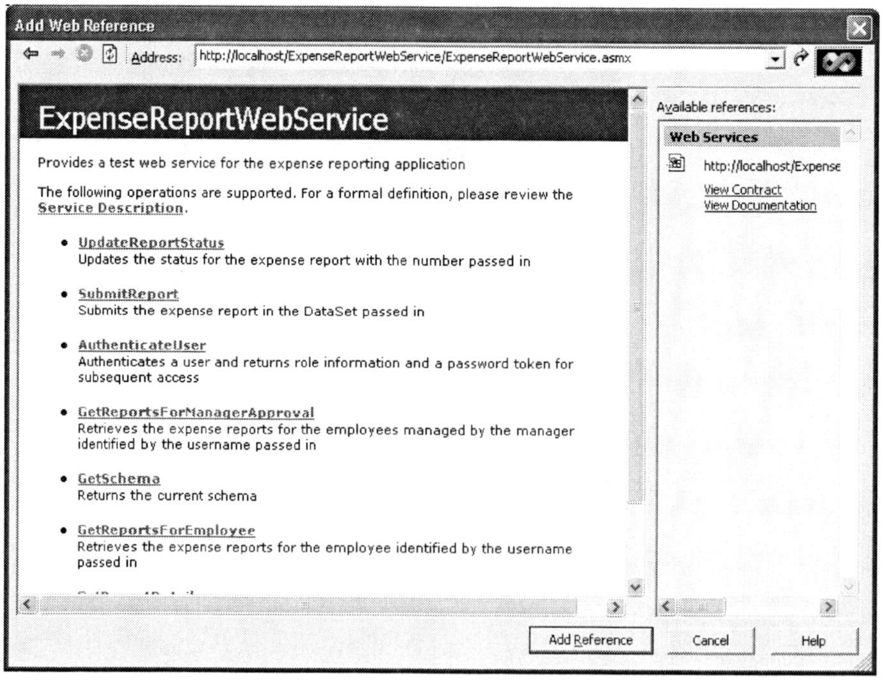

Alternatively, you can use WSDL to generate a proxy. The following code generates a proxy by using Visual Basic .NET and default protocol (SOAP).

```
wsdl http://www.contoso.com/ExpenseReportWebService/
ExpenseReportWebService.asmx?wsdl
```

Procedure: Instantiating the proxy

As shown in the code on the slide, the following statement generates the proxy to call the ExpenseReportWebService WS XML Web service:

```
Dim WS As New ExpenseReportWebService()
```

Procedure: Calling the XML Web service methods

As shown in the code on the slide, you can call the methods of the XML Web service, as appropriate, to get the data that your application needs:

```
Dim ds As DataSet = WS.GetReportsForEmployee(username, _
   passwordToken, 0, 10, totalReports)
```

How to Test an XML Web Services Client

1. Build the client application
2. Call the XML Web service installed on http://localhost
3. Handle exceptions thrown by the XML Web service

Introduction

After you have developed an XML Web services consumer application, you can test it on your own computer by using a URL that begins with \\localhost. To do this, the XML Web service that you are calling must be installed on your computer. For Course 2565A, *Developing Microsoft .NET Applications for Windows (Visual Basic .NET)*, you have ExpenseReportWebService installed to use in the practice called Calling an XML Web Service and in Lab 4.2: Calling an XML Web Service in Module 4, "Using Data in Windows Forms Applications."

Calling the XML Web service

If you experience an error when you try to call the XML Web service, you can place a breakpoint in your application at the point where you call a method of the XML Web service and then step through the code to get more details about the problems that are occurring.

Exceptions

Any exception thrown in the XML Web service call will be returned as a **SoapException**. The **Message** property of the exception contains a text representation of the exception. You can parse this property to provide customized error handling or display it to the user

Practice: Calling an XML Web Service

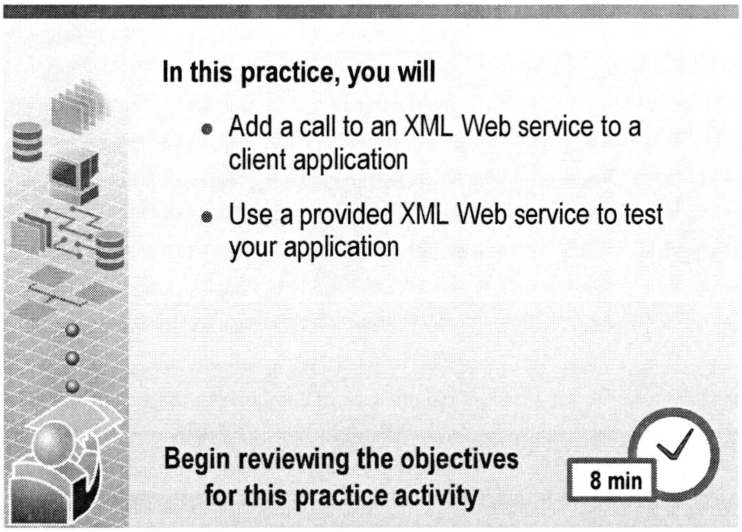

Introduction

In this practice, you will add a call to an XML Web service to a client application and then use a provided XML Web service to test your application.

Instructions

► **Add a call to the Web service**

1. Open the WebServiceClient project in *install_folder*\Practices\Mod04_05\Starter.
2. Open the MainForm form, and view its code.
3. To add a Web reference to the Expense Report Web service, in Solution Explorer, right-click **WebServiceClient**, and then click **Add Web Reference**.
4. In the **Add Web Reference** dialog box, in the **Address** box, type **http://localhost/ExpenseReportWebService/ExpenseReportWebService.asmx**, and then press ENTER.
5. After the Web reference information is loaded, click **Add Reference**.
6. Show TODO comments in the Task List.

   To show TODO comments, click the **View** menu, point to **Show Tasks**, and then click **All**.
7. In the **MainForm** source file, find the first TODO comment near the top of the file. Add the **Imports** statement for the **XML Web service** namespace.

   ```
   Imports WebServiceClient.localhost
   ```
8. Find the next TODO comment, which instructs you instantiate the XML Web service proxy class. Add the code to instantiate the proxy.

   ```
   WS = New ExpenseReportWebService()
   ```

9. Find the last TODO comment, which instructs you to add a call to the **GetReportsForEmployee** method of the Web service. Add the code to make the call to the method.

```
WS.GetReportsForEmployee(Nothing, Nothing, 0, 10, _
    TotalReports)
```

10. Build the project.

► **Test the call to the XML Web service**

1. Run the application.
2. Click **Call Web Service**.

   After the Web service call completes, a text message will appear in the application.

   If time permit, set a breakpoint in the **CallBtn_Click** method and step through the creation of the Web service proxy and the call to the XML Web service method.

Lesson: Persisting Data

- How to Persist Data in Files
- How to Serialize Objects
- How to Use Isolated Storage
- How to Persist Application Settings

Introduction

Many applications must persist, or store, data. This lesson presents techniques and locations for persisting data.

Lesson objectives

After completing this lesson, you will be able to:

- Persist data to and read data from files.
- Serialize objects.
- Use isolated storage.
- Persist application settings.

How to Persist Data in Files

- Use readers and writers for persisted data

Class	Description
BinaryReader and BinaryWriter	These classes read and write primitive types as binary values in a specific encoding to and from a stream.
StreamReader and StreamWriter	The implementations of these classes are designed for character input and output.
StringReader and StringWriter	The implementations of these classes are designed for string input and output.

Introduction

Many applications must persist, or store, data. Basic file input/output (I/O) functionality, found in the **System.IO** root, provides the ability to access, store, and manipulate data that is stored in hierarchical file systems that have files that are referenced by using unique paths.

When an application stores data in a file, you must carefully choose the file name and storage location to minimize the possibility that the storage location will be known to another application and, therefore, vulnerable to corruption. Isolated storage provides the means to manage downloaded Web application files to minimize storage conflicts.

Reading and writing files

The abstract **Stream** class is designed for byte input and output. You can use the reader and writer classes to input and output to streams and strings that use other types.

The following table describes some commonly used reader and writer classes.

Class	Description
BinaryReader and **BinaryWriter**	These classes read and write primitive types as binary values in a specific encoding to and from a stream.
StreamReader and **StreamWriter**	The implementations of these classes are designed for character input and output.
StringReader and **StringWriter**	The implementations of these classes are designed for string input and output.

A reader or writer is attached to a stream so that the required types can be read or written to easily.

The following code shows how to write data of type **Integer** to and read from a new, empty file stream that is named Test.data. After creating the data file in the current directory, the **BinaryWriter** class writes the integers 0 through 10 to Test.data. Then, the **BinaryReader** class reads the file and displays the file's content to the console.

```
Imports System
Imports System.IO

Class MyStream
   Private Const FILE_NAME As String = "Test.data"
   Public Shared Sub Main()
      ' Create the new, empty data file.
      If (File.Exists(FILE_NAME)) Then
         Console.WriteLine("{0} already exists!", FILE_NAME)
         Return
      End If
      Dim fs As New FileStream(FILE_NAME, FileMode.CreateNew)
      ' Create the writer for data.
      Dim w As New BinaryWriter(fs)
      ' Write data to Test.data.
      Dim i As Integer
      For i = 0 To 10
         w.Write(i)
      Next i
      w.Close()
      fs.Close()
      ' Create the reader for data.
      fs = New FileStream(FILE_NAME, FileMode.Open, _
         FileAccess.Read)
      Dim r As New BinaryReader(fs)
      ' Read data from Test.data.
      For i = 1 To 10
         Console.WriteLine(r.ReadInt32())
         w.Close()
      Next i
   End Sub
End Class
```

In the following example, the code defines a string and converts it to an array of characters, which can then be read as required by using the appropriate **StringReader.Read** method:

```
Imports System
Imports System.IO

Class CharsFromStr
    Public Shared Sub Main()
    ' Create a string to read characters from.
    Dim str As String = "Some number of characters"
    ' Size the array to hold all the characters of the
    ' string, so that they are all accessible.
    Dim b(24) As Char
    ' Create a StringReader and attach it to the string.
    Dim sr As New StringReader(str)
    ' Read 13 characters from the array that holds
    ' the string, starting from the first array member.
    sr.Read(b, 0, 13)
    ' Display the output.
    Console.WriteLine(b)
    ' Close the StringReader.
    sr.Close()
    End Sub
End Class
```

The preceding example produces the following output:

```
Some number o
```

System.Text.Encoding

Internally, the common language run time represents all characters as Unicode. However, Unicode can be inefficient when transferring characters over a network or when persisting in a file. To improve efficiency, the .NET Framework class library provides several types that are derived from the **System.Text.Encoding** abstract base class. These classes know how to encode and decode Unicode characters to ASCII, UTF-7, UTF-8, Unicode, and other arbitrary code pages. When you construct a **BinaryWriter** or **StreamWriter**, you can choose any of these encodings. The default encoding is UTF-8.

How to Serialize Objects

- **Binary serialization**

1. Add the **Serializable** attribute
2. Serialize the object to a file
3. Deserialize the file into an object

- **XML serialization**

1. Serialize the object to a file
2. Deserialize the file into an object

Introduction

Serialization is the process of converting the state of an object into a form that can be persisted or transported. The complement of serialization is *deserialization*, which converts a stream into an object. Together, these processes allow data to be easily stored and transferred. The .NET Framework features two serializing technologies: binary serialization and XML serialization.

Binary serialization

Binary serialization preserves type fidelity, which is useful for preserving the state of an object between different invocations of an application. For example, you can share an object between different applications by serializing it to the clipboard. You can serialize an object to a stream, disk, or memory; over the network; and so forth.

Procedure: Saving data by using binary serialization

There are three main steps to saving data by using binary serialization.

1. Add the **Serializable** attribute to the class to be serialized.

```
<Serializable>
Public Class My Object
  Public n1 As Integer = 0;
  Public n2 As Integer = 0;
  Public str As String = Nothing;
End Class
```

2. Serialize the object to a stream by using a **BinaryFormatter** object.

```
Dim obj As New MyObject()
obj.n1 = 1
obj.n2 = 24
obj.str = "Some String"
Dim formatter As IFormatter
formatter = New BinaryFormatter()
Dim stream As Stream
stream = New FileStream("MyFile.bin", FileMode.Create, _
   FileAccess.Write, FileShare.None)
formatter.Serialize(stream, obj)
stream.Close()
```

3. When your application needs the persisted data, deserialize the file to an object by using a **BinaryFormatter** object.

```
Dim formatter As IFormatter
formatter = New BinaryFormatter()
Dim stream As Stream
stream = New FileStream("MyFile.bin", FileMode.Open, _
   FileAccess.Read, FileShare.Read)
Dim obj As MyObject = CType( _
   formatter.Deserialize(stream), MyObject)
stream.Close()
```

For an object to be successfully serialized, every object it refers to must also be serializable. If the serialization engine encounters any object that is not serializable during serialization, it will throw a SerializationException.

By default, binary serialization stores all the members of an object, both public and private. The .NET Framework provides attributes to control which members are serialized; you can use these if you want to override the default behavior. In addition, you can implement the ISerializable interface if you need complete control of the binary serialization process.

Because binary serialization stores all the members of an object by default, versioning can be tricky. If you add or remove members from an object, serialized representations of that object may not deserialize correctly. Careful use of attributes to prevent the serialization of non-essential members may avoid this problem, but you may have to implement the ISerializable interface to allow backward compatibility if you make many changes to your objects.

For more information about binary serialization, see the Binary Serialization section in the .NET Framework software development kit (SDK) documentation.

XML serialization

XML serialization serializes only public properties and fields and does not preserve type fidelity. This is useful when you want to provide or consume data without restricting the application that uses the data. Because XML is an open standard, it is an attractive choice for sharing data across the Web.

Procedure: Saving data by using XML serialization

There are two main steps to saving data by using XML serialization.

1. Serialize the object to a file.

```
Public Class OrderForm
   Public OrderDate As DateTime
End Class

Dim myObject As New OrderForm()
' Insert code to set properties and fields of the object.
Dim mySerializer As XmlSerializer = New _
   XmlSerializer(GetType(OrderForm))
' To write to a file, create a StreamWriter object.
Dim myWriter As StreamWriter = New _
   StreamWriter("myFileName.xml")
mySerializer.Serialize(myWriter, myObject)
```

2. When your application needs the persisted data, deserialize the object from a file.

```
Dim myObject As OrderForm
Dim mySerializer As XmlSerializer = New _
   XmlSerializer(GetType(OrderForm))
' To read the file, create a FileStream object.
Dim myFileStream As FileStream = New _
   FileStream("myFileName.xml", FileMode.Open)
myObject = CType( _
   mySerializer.Deserialize(myFileStream), OrderForm)
```

The following items can be serialized using the **XmLSerializer** class.

- Public read/write properties and fields of public classes
- Classes that implement **ICollection** or **IEnumerable**

Note Only collections are serialized, not public properties.

- **XmlElement** objects
- **XmlNode** objects
- **DataSet** objects

As with binary serialization, the .NET Framework provides attributes and other techniques to control XML serialization more finely. In addition, XML serialization is used by the .NET Framework to create SOAP messages for XML Web service calls. For more information about XML serialization, see the XML Serialization section of the .NET Framework SDK documentation.

Comparison of binary and XML serialization

Generally speaking, binary serialization is best for storing private state and data used by one application or assembly. It produces compact files that are fast to save and load. XML serialization produces larger files and has more overhead, but is better for cases when data will be shared across systems, such as with XML Web services.

Binary serialization	XML serialization
Stores all members, both public and private, by default.	Only stores public members by default.
Usually produces very compact serialized representations of objects, with little overhead.	Usually produces larger serialized representations of objects, with more overhead.
Makes interoperation difficult, because object state is stored in a proprietary format.	Interoperation is easier, because it uses open standards such as XML and SOAP.

How to Use Isolated Storage

- **For scenarios that require higher security, such as the Internet, you should read and write data to isolated storage**
- **To access isolated storage**

1. Open the store
2. Create a stream for reading or writing files in the store
3. Close the stream and store

CodeExample

Introduction

For some applications, such as downloaded Web applications and code that may come from sources that are not trusted, the basic file system does not provide the necessary isolation and safety. *Isolated storage* is a data storage mechanism that provides isolation and safety by defining standardized ways of associating code with saved data.

Administrators can use tools that are designed to manipulate isolated storage to configure file storage space, set security policies, and delete unused data. With isolated storage, code no longer must invent unique paths to specify safe locations in the file system while data is protected from unauthorized access. There is no need for hard coding of information that indicates where an application's storage area is located. With isolated storage, partially trusted applications can store data in a manner that is controlled by the computer's security policy. Security policies rarely grant permission to access the file system by using standard I/O mechanisms. However, by default, code that runs from a local computer, a local network, or the Internet is granted the right to use isolated storage. Web applications can also use isolated storage with roaming user profiles, thereby allowing user's isolated stores to roam with their profile.

The namespace **System.IO.IsolatedStorage** contains the **IsolatedStorageFile** and **IsolatedStorageFileStream** classes, which applications can use to access the files and directories in their isolated storage area.

Procedure: Saving data by using XML serialization

There are three main steps to accessing isolated storage:

1. Open the store.

```
Dim isoStore As IsolatedStorageFile = Nothing
isoStore = IsolatedStorageFile.GetUserStoreForDomain()
```

2. Create a stream for reading or writing files in the store.

```
Dim dataFile As IsolatedStorageFileStream = Nothing
dataFile = New IsolatedStorageFileStream("myfile.txt", _
   FileMode.Open, isoStore);
' code to read from or write to file goes here
```

3. Close the stream and store.

```
dataFile.Close()
isoStore.Close()
```

How to Persist Application Settings

- **Choose a technique**
  - Use a DataSet object

    Good for tabular or relational data
  - Use reader/writer objects

    Complete control, but developer must write and maintain more code
  - Use serialization

    Good choice when application stores state in objects
- **Choose a storage location**
  - The file system
  - Isolated storage

Introduction

There are many techniques that you can use to save user data in Windows Forms applications. Your application may use one or all of the following techniques, depending on its particular requirements.

Storing user data in a DataSet object

If you have just a few properties to save, the **DataSet** object is a good candidate for saving user data. Data sets are easy to configure, access, and persist. Data sets are also obvious choices for user data in the form of rows and tables. For example, the expense report sample application stores saved reports and **DataSet** objects in isolated storage. Also, the order entry sample application uses a **DataSet** object to store some user setting, such as whether to play sounds when orders are entered.

Saving user data to a file manually

If you want complete control over saving user data, or if you need to save data to a specific file format, manually saving data in a file is the right choice. With this technique, you can use **StreamReader** and **StreamWriter** objects or **BinaryReader** and **BinaryWriter** objects to store data. The main disadvantage of this approach is that you must write and maintain all the code to save your data.

Saving user data by using serialization

Serialization is a good choice when your state is stored in a few objects, and you can use the serialization mechanisms in the .NET Framework to persist these objects. Depending on your particular needs, you can use binary serialization or XML serialization to persist your objects. Serialization provides very useful default behavior, but it also allows you a lot of flexibility if you need to customize its behavior.

Location of saved user data

In addition to the storage technique, you must also choose the location to which you will save user data. In addition to the file system, the .NET Framework provides isolated storage. Using isolated storage is a good choice when you want a simple virtual file system that is tied to the identity of your code and the user. You must use the file system when you need to write files that are used by other applications, or read files generated by other applications.

Lab 4.2: Calling an XML Web Service

Objectives

After completing this lab, you will have demonstrated your ability to:

- Add a Web reference.
- Create an XML Web service proxy object.
- Call methods in an XML Web service.

Note This lab focuses on the concepts in Module 4, "Using Data in Windows Forms Applications," in Course 2565A, *Developing Microsoft .NET Applications for Windows (Visual Basic .NET).* As a result, this lab may not comply with Microsoft security recommendations.

Prerequisites

Before working on this lab, you must have:

- The knowledge and skills to develop a simple Windows Forms application by using a Visual Studio .NET–compatible programming language.
- The knowledge and skills to debug an application by using Visual Studio .NET.
- The knowledge and skills to call XML Web services.

Scenario

Your organization, Contoso, Ltd., provides access to expense report information by using a private XML Web service. You are writing a Windows Forms client application that uses and updates expense report information. Your application will use your organization's XML Web service to accomplish this task.

Lab setup

There are starter and solution files associated with this lab. Browse to *install_folder*\Labfiles\Lab04_2\Ex01\Starter to find the starter files, and browse to *install_folder*\Labfiles\Lab04_2\Ex01\Solution to find the solution files. If you performed a default installation of the course files, *install_folder* corresponds to C:\Program Files\Msdntrain\2565.

Estimated time to complete this lab: 20 minutes

Exercise 1
Calling an XML Web Service

In this exercise, you will call some methods of an XML Web Service.

Tasks	Additional information
Open the ExpenseReport project in Visual Studio .NET. Browse to *install_folder*\Labfiles\Lab04_2\Ex01\Starter to find the project files.	For more information about opening a project file and starting an application, see the following resource: • The Visual Studio .NET Help documentation. For additional information about opening a project file, in Search, select the **Search in titles** only check box, then search by using the phrase **Open Project Dialog Box**. For additional information about starting an application from in the Designer, in Index, search by using the phrase **Debugging Windows Applications**.
Add a Web reference to the test XML Web service on your local computer. The URL for this XML Web service is: `http://localhost/ExpenseReportWebService/ExpenseReportWebService.asmx`	For more information about how to add a Web reference, see the following resources: • Practice: Calling an XML Web Service in Module 4, "Using Data in Windows Forms Applications," in Course 2565A, *Developing Microsoft .NET Applications for Windows (Visual Basic .NET)*. • Lesson: Creating a Simple XML Web Services Client in Module 4, "Using Data in Windows Forms Applications," in Course 2565A, *Developing Microsoft .NET Applications for Windows (Visual Basic .NET)*.
Open the ExpenseReportUtilities file. Find the TODO comment toward the bottom of the file. Add the code to create the XML Web service proxy object and store it in the **WSInternal** member of the class.	For more information about how to create an XML Web service proxy object, see the following resources: • Practice: Calling an XML Web Service in Module 4, "Using Data in Windows Forms Applications," in Course 2565A, *Developing Microsoft .NET Applications for Windows (Visual Basic .NET)*. • Lesson: Creating a Simple XML Web Services Client in Module 4, "Using Data in Windows Forms Applications," in Course 2565A, *Developing Microsoft .NET Applications for Windows (Visual Basic .NET)*.

<table>
<tr><th>Tasks</th><th>Additional information</th></tr>
<tr><td>Open the ExpenseReportList form, and view its code. Find the two TODO comments in the constructor. Add the code to make the XML Web service calls after the comments. In each case, you will retrieve the XML Web service proxy from the static (shared) Utilities object, by using the following syntax:

<code>Utilities.WS</code>

a. The first method call will be to the GetReportsForEmployee method. Store the return value from this call in the ExpRepDataSet data member, and pass the following parameters.

<table><tr><th>Parameter</th><th>Value</th></tr><tr><td>username</td><td>UCred.UserNameString</td></tr><tr><td>passwordToken</td><td>UCred.PasswordTokenString</td></tr><tr><td>reportIndex</td><td>RecordCursor</td></tr><tr><td>numberReports</td><td>10</td></tr><tr><td>totalNumberReports</td><td>TotalNumRecords</td></tr></table>
b. The second method call will be to the GetReportsForManagerApproval method. Again, store the return value from this call in the ExpRepDataSet data member, and pass the same parameters as in step 4a.</td><td>For more information about how to call a method of an XML Web service, see the following resources:

• Practice: Calling an XML Web Service in Module 4, “Using Data in Windows Forms Applications,” in Course 2565A, Developing Microsoft .NET Applications for Windows (Visual Basic .NET).

• Lesson: Creating a Simple XML Web Services Client in Module 4, “Using Data in Windows Forms Applications,” in Course 2565A, Developing Microsoft .NET Applications for Windows (Visual Basic .NET).</td></tr>
<tr><td>Build and run the application. Click the View Submitted Reports button and make sure the list of expense reports is populated.</td><td>Additional information is not necessary for this task.</td></tr>
</table>

Review

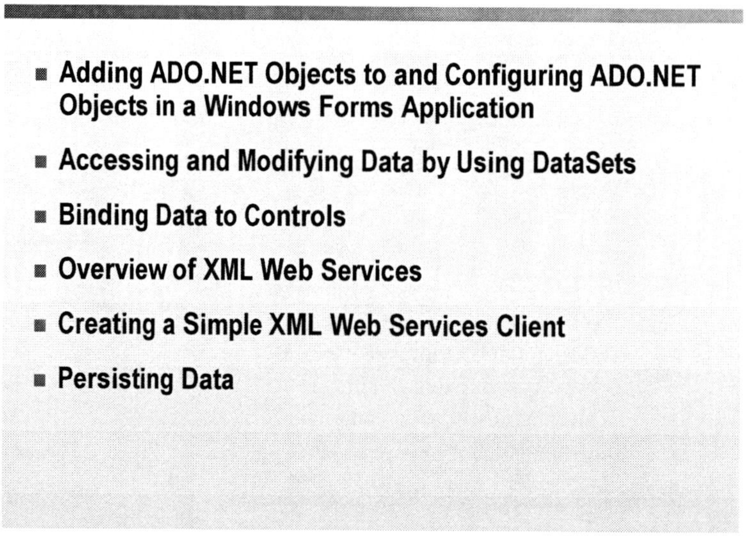

1. What is the difference between a connection object and a command object?

2. What is the difference between a dataSet and a DataAdapter?

3. How do you access tables and columns in a typed and untyped dataset?

4. How do you generate a new Database schema?

5. What are the functions of **ReadXML** and **WriteXML** methods?

6. What is **CurrencyManager**?

7. What are the main steps that you take in your application to call an XML Web service?

8. Describe the two ways to generate an XML Web service proxy.

9. List three techniques for persisting application settings.

msdn training

Module 5: Interoperating with Managed Objects

Contents

Microsoft

2557

Test going from com to .Net

Overview

- Using .NET and COM Components in a Windows Forms Application
- Calling Win32 APIs from Windows Forms Applications
- Upgrading Visual Basic 6.0 Applications to Visual Basic .NET

Introduction

With the advent of the Microsoft® .NET Framework there is need to upgrade existing software systems and for developers to adapt to the new platform. To provide a convenient and easy migration path for existing systems, the .NET Framework offers a broad interoperable functionality between managed code and existing COM components.

Two of the primary goals of .NET Interoperation are to ensure that:

1. Installation of the .NET Framework does not affect existing COM applications.

   Because .NET and COM can *coexist*, you can selectively upgrade COM components to .NET without affecting other COM or .NET-based applications. Therefore, you may or may not choose to upgrade COM components to .NET.

2. The .NET Framework and COM components can communicate with each other; they can cooperate.

   Because .NET and COM can *cooperate*, you can build .NET-based applications that implement functionality exposed by COM objects and COM applications that implement functionality exposed by .NET objects.

This module introduces you to the concepts and mechanics of the interoperation of .NET managed code with COM unmanaged code and platform services. The module also covers how to upgrade existing Microsoft Visual Basic® 6.0 applications to Visual Basic .NET.

Objectives

After completing this module, you will be able to:

- Use .NET and COM components in a Microsoft .NET Framework Windows Forms application.
- Call Microsoft Win32® APIs from a Windows Forms application.
- Upgrade Visual Basic 6.0 applications to Visual Basic .NET.

Lesson: Using .NET and COM Components in a Windows Forms Application

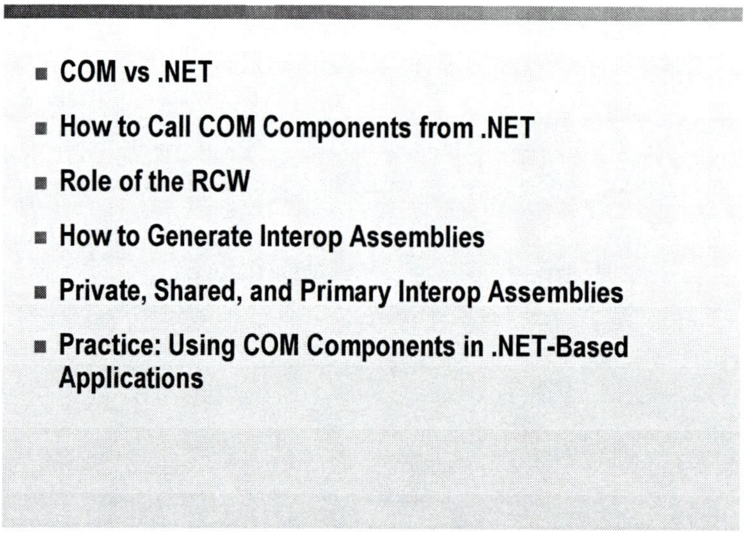

Introduction

The Microsoft .NET Framework provides interoperability services to use existing applications, smooth the migration path and simplify the interaction between managed and unmanaged code. Interop Services conceal from both clients and servers the differences between the managed world and the unmanaged world.

The common language runtime provides two mechanisms for interoperating with unmanaged code:

- Platform Invocation Services

  Platform invoke is a service that allows managed code to call unmanaged functions that are implemented in dynamic-link libraries (DLL). It locates and invokes an exported function and marshals its arguments (integers, strings, arrays, structures, and so on) across the interoperation boundary as needed.

- COM interop

  COM Interop is a bi-directional service that provides a bridge between the .NET Framework and COM. It allows .NET clients to call COM components and COM clients to call .NET Framework components.

  COM Interop maintains programming model consistency in both COM and .NET. It resolves the inconsistencies between the two models and makes the difference transparent to both clients and servers.

In this lesson, you will learn how to call COM components from the .NET Framework.

Lesson objectives

After completing this lesson, you will be able to:

- Identify the differences between COM and .NET programming models.
- Explain how to call COM components from the .NET Framework.
- Describe the role of the runtime callable wrapper (RCW) in interoperating.
- Generate interop assemblies.
- Describe private, shared, and primary interop assemblies.

Note This module does not cover using .NET objects from a COM client by using the COM callable wrapper (CCW). For more information about the CCW, see "COM Callable Wrapper" in the .NET Framework software development kit (SDK) documentation.

COM vs .NET

COM Model	.NET Framework Model
Interface based	Object based
GUIDs	Strong names
Binary standard	Type standard
Type library	Metadata
HResults	Exceptions
Reference counting	Garbage collection
Immutable	Resilient

Introduction

COM differs from the .NET Framework object model in several ways.

Differences between COM and .NET

The differences between COM and .NET are summarized in the following table.

Characteristic	COM	.NET Framework
Coding model	*Interface based.* COM objects always communicate through interfaces.	*Object based.* .NET Framework objects can pass data directly to each other, without implementing interfaces.
Identity	*Globally unique identifiers (GUIDs).* GUIDs identify a specific unmanaged type and provide no location information for that type.	*Strong names.* Strong names consist of a unique assembly name in addition to a type name. Because the assembly name uniquely identifies the type, you can reuse a type name across multiple assemblies. An assembly also introduces publisher key, version, and location information to a managed type.
Type compatibility	*Binary standard.* The internal binary layout of classes must comply with COM rules.	*Type standard.* The .NET common type system specification establishes a framework that enables cross-language integration, type safety, and so on.
Type definition	*Type library.* Type information is stored only for public types. Moreover, a type library is optional.	*Metadata.* Type information is stored as metadata and is mandatory for all types. Metadata is embedded inside assemblies.

(*continued*)

Characteristic	COM	.NET Framework
Error-handling mechanism	*HRESULTs*. A COM method returns an HRESULT to indicate whether the call succeeded or failed.	*Exceptions*. Managed code incorporates exceptions.
Object-lifetime management	*Reference counting*. Clients of COM objects manage object lifetime by means of reference counting.	*Garbage collection*. The common language runtime manages the lifetime of objects by means of garbage collection.
Versioning	*Immutable*. COM interfaces are immutable. In other words, if you change an interface, you must rename it with a new GUID.	*Resilient*. Managed types can evolve, retaining the same name.

How to Call COM Components from .NET

- **The CLR enables managed code to call COM objects through a proxy called the Runtime Callable Wrapper (RCW)**
- **The RCW is a managed object and subject to garbage collection**

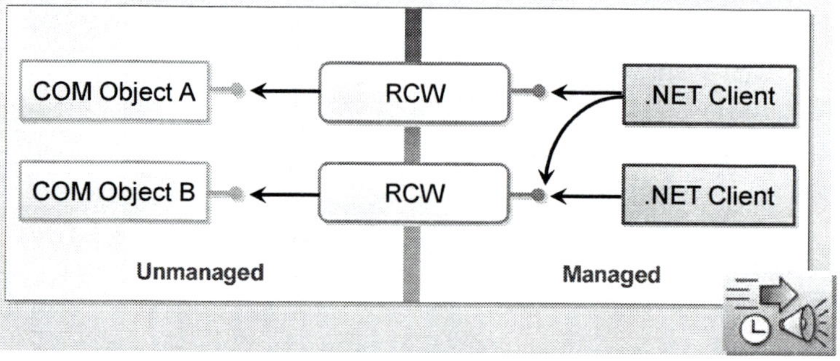

Introduction

Many organizations cannot afford to upgrade to .NET overnight. A lot of money has been invested in the existing systems and users need to preserve their investment. In addition, some critical business applications cannot be changed. Therefore, Interop Services enable developers to use existing code or migrate their existing systems to .NET in multiple stages.

Process

When a .NET client calls a COM component, a series of events take place.

1. When a .NET Client loads a COM object, a runtime callable wrapper (RCW) is created.

   The runtime creates exactly one RCW for each COM object, regardless of the number of references that exist on that object. This ensures that a single object identity is shared between the RCW and the COM object.

2. Using metadata derived from a type library, the runtime creates both the COM object being called and a wrapper for that object.
3. Each RCW maintains a cache of interface pointers on the COM object it wraps.
4. The runtime performs garbage collection on the RCW.

Role of the RCW

- **Maintains object lifetime**
- **Marshals method calls between managed and unmanaged code**
- **Consumes selected COM interfaces without exposing them to the .NET client**

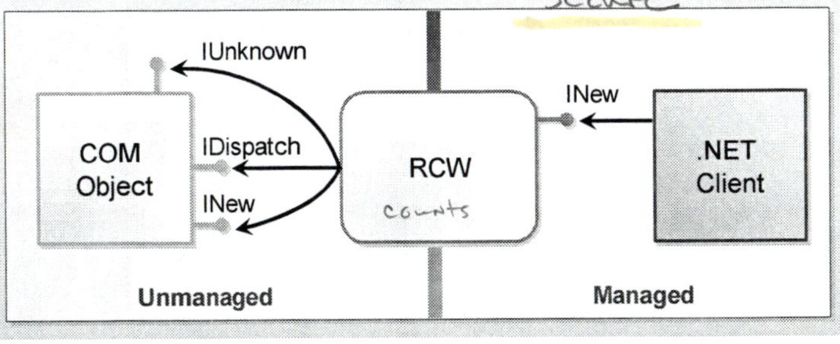

Introduction

The primary goal of the RCW is to hide the differences between the managed and unmanaged programming models.

Role of the RCW

The RCW is an important part of the interoperation model. It performs several roles.

1. Maintains object lifetime.

   The RCW is responsible for keeping the COM object alive as long as the RCW is being used. The runtime performs garbage collection on the RCW like any other managed object, but the RCW internally holds a reference to the COM object it wraps.

2. Marshals method calls between managed and unmanaged code.

   The RCW marshals method calls between managed and unmanaged code on behalf of the wrapped object. This involves several tasks, such as:

   a. Implicitly converting parameters passed between the two environments to the correct type.

      For example, when you pass a parameter of the type **System.String** to a COM function, the RCW automatically converts the parameter to the correct BSTR type expected by the COM component. If the COM function returns a BSTR parameter to the .NET client, the RCW automatically converts the parameter to **System.String**.

b. Translating HRESULT errors generated by COM objects to .NET exceptions.

   For example, RCW translates the **HRESULT** error **COR_E_UNAUTHORIZEDACCESS** to **UnauthorizedAccessException** exception in .NET.

Note There are some limitations to using the RCW. For example, Success HRESULTS are not returned from unmanaged code. Variable length arrays also pose challenges. For more information about these limitations and how to fix them, refer the "Interop Marshaling" section of the .NET Framework SDK.

---

3. Consumes selected COM interfaces without exposing them to the .NET client.

   An important role of the RCW is to make a .NET client act as if it is using a .NET object and to make a COM object act as if it is being used by a COM client. To accomplish this, the RCW consumes selected COM interfaces without exposing them to the managed client. For example, the COM IUnknown interface exposes methods for reference counting and querying interfaces on all COM objects. The RCW consumes this interface from the COM object but does not expose it to .NET clients. Instead, the RCW uses this interface internally to function as a COM object.

4. Allows developers to write code that treats COM objects wrapped by the RCW like any other object.

How to Generate Interop Assemblies

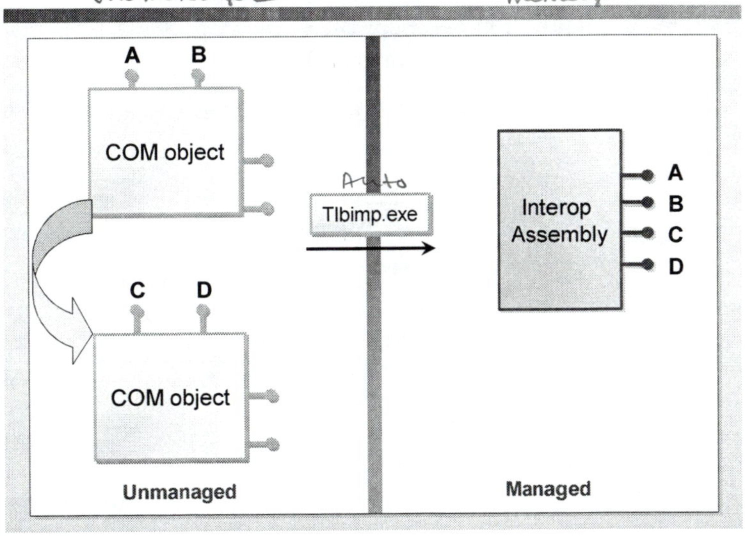

Introduction

.NET-based applications can bind to COM classes in an early or late bound fashion. Early binding requires complete type information for the COM class at compile-time and requires the underlying COM class to support early binding as well. COM type definitions usually reside in a type library. To use COM types in managed code, you must generate metadata from type libraries.

COM type libraries can be standalone .tlb files or they can be embedded in the resource section of a .dll or .exe file. Other sources of type-library information are .olb and .ocx files.

After locating the type library containing the implementation of your target COM type, you can generate an assembly containing type metadata. The metadata can be generated in various ways. Usually it is generated from an existing type library that describes the types with a tool called TLBIMP.exe (Type Library Importer).

After the metadata is generated, it is saved as a typical .NET assembly. The assemblies are commonly called *interop assemblies* because they contain metadata for COM types but no code.

Just like any other assembly, you can examine an interop assembly with tools like Ildasm.exe to browse the types defined in the assembly.

There are a variety of tools that allow you to generate interop assemblies. The most common include the Microsoft Visual Studio® .NET IDE and the Tlbimp.exe utility.

Procedure: Generate interop assemblies

To add a reference to a type library from the Visual Studio IDE:

1. On the **Project** menu, click **References**.
2. Click the **COM** tab.
3. In the **Available References** list, double-click the type library.
4. Click **OK** to run TLBIMP and add the assembly to the hidden Bin directory of the project.

Procedure: Add a reference to a type library by using the TLBIMP tool

You can build metadata by using the TLBIMP tool. The TLBIMP provides command-line switches to adjust metadata in the resulting interop file, imports types from an existing type library, and generates an interop assembly and a namespace. The TLBIMP provides a finer degree of control when creating interop assemblies.

Use the following syntax to generate an interop assembly by using the TLBIMP tool.

Tlbimp TlbFile [/out: *name*] **[/reference**: *file*] **[/silent] [/verbose] [/strictref] [/unsafe]**[**[/primary]**][**/publickey**: *file*] **[/keyfile**: *file*][**/keycontainer**: *name*]

TLBIMP uses the command line switches described in the following table.

Command Line Switch	Description
/out:*filename*	Specifies the name of the output file, assembly, and namespace in which to write the metadata definitions.
/keyfile:*filename* **/publickey:***filename* **/keycontainer:***containername*	Options for supplying information to generate a strongly named assembly.
/reference:*filename*	Specifies the assembly file to use to resolve references to types defined outside the current type library. If you do not specify the **/reference** option, TLBIMP.exe automatically recursively imports any external type library that the type library being imported references.
/primary	Produces a primary interop assembly for the specified type library. Information is added to the assembly indicating that the publisher of the type library produced the assembly.

Example

The following command line creates an interop assembly by using the Com1.tlb COM type library.

```
tlbimp COM1.tlb /keyfile:myPublicKeyFile.sn
/reference:COM2InteropAssembly.dll
/out:COM1InteropAssembly.dll
```

The example uses the myPublicKeyFile.sn file to assign a strong name to the assembly by using a public key. The COM1 component calls members of another COM class called COM2. However, if you have already created an interop assembly for COM2 called COM2InteropAssembly.dll, this will be a duplication of work. To prevent the TLBIMP tool from generating an interop assembly that contains information for both COM1 and COM2, add a reference to the existing COM2InteropAssembly.dll. This will ensure that metadata for COM2 will not be generated in the COM1InteropAssembly.

Private, Shared, and Primary Interop Assemblies

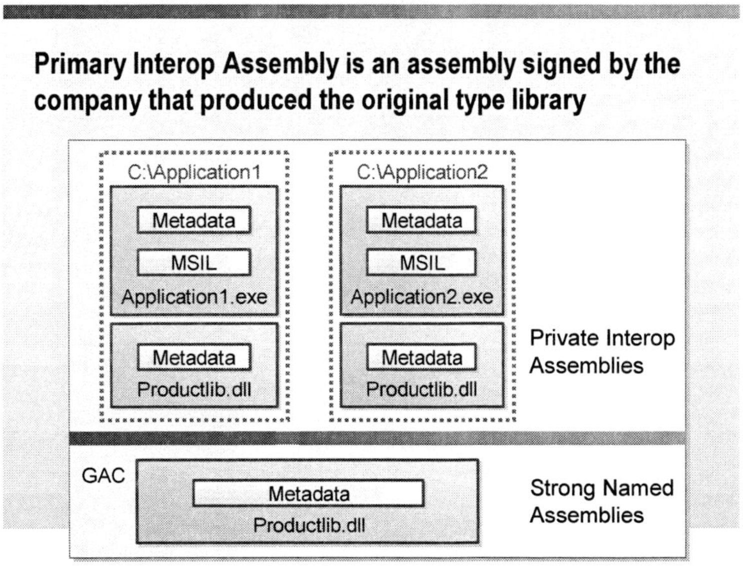

Introduction

When metadata is generated from a type library, the resulting assembly can be private and exposed only in the scope of an application or it can be shared by being placed in the global assembly cache.

Privateinterop assemblies

To install an assembly for private use, both the application EXE and the assembly containing imported COM types must be installed in the same directory structure. The illustration shows an unsigned assembly to be used privately by Application1.exe and Application2.exe, which reside in separate application directories. The interop assembly, which is called ProductLib.dll in this example, is installed twice.

Shared assemblies

Assemblies shared by multiple applications should be installed in a centralized repository called the global assembly cache. .NET clients can access the same copy of the interop assembly, which is signed and installed in the global assembly cache. A shared assembly has a strong name made up of the assembly name, version, culture, and the public key of the assembly publisher. TLBIMP includes the /keyfile, /publickey, and /keycontainer options for supplying information to generate strongly named assembly.

Primary interop assemblies

A shared interop assembly signed by the company that produced the original type library is called a primary interop assembly. An assembly signed by any other company or individual is called an alternate interop assembly.

Primary interop assemblies (PIA) are provided by the same publisher as the type library that they describe, and provide the official definitions of the types defined with that type library. Primary interop assemblies are always signed by their publisher to ensure uniqueness. A primary interop assembly is created from a type library by running TLBIMP with the **/primary** switch.

PIAs are important because they provide unique type identity. They distinguish the official type definitions from all other definitions provided by other interop assemblies, thereby ensuring type compatibility between applications that share the types defined in a PIA.

When available, always use the primary interop assembly published by the author of the COM component you intend to incorporate in your managed code. Types in the primary interop assembly are imported for you and are ready to activate and call from managed code. Avoid using interop assemblies that are not primary interop assemblies.

Practice: Using COM Components in .NET-Based Applications

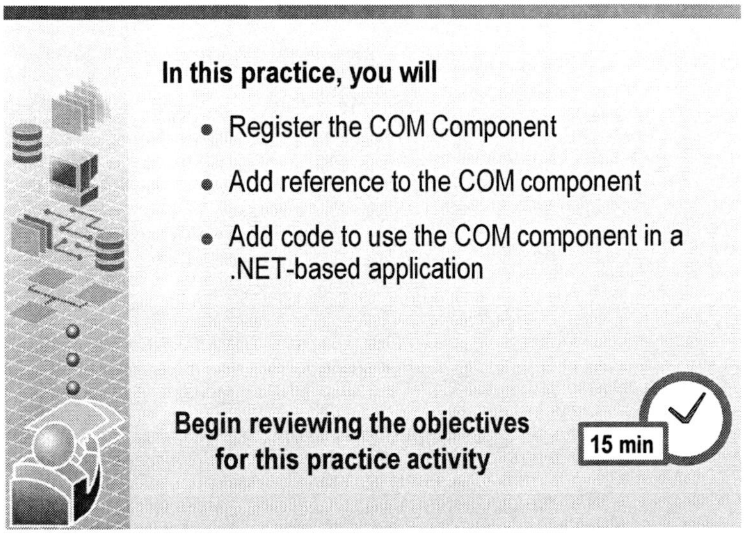

Introduction

In this practice, you will use two COM components in your .NET-based application, **Masked Edit ActiveX** and **NorthwindData_COM**.

The **Masked Edit ActiveX** control generally behaves as a standard text box control with enhancements for optional masked input and formatted output. The **Mask** property of the **Masked Edit** control allows developers to define the formatting of text in the control and the **ClipText** property provides access to the unformatted text.

The **NorthwindData_COM** component uses Microsoft ADO 2.6 to connect to the Northwind database. The component contains a class called **RemainingInventoryClass** that exposes the **ShowUnitsInStock** method. The **ShowUnitsInStock** method returns a live count of the number of units remaining in inventory for a product.

Instructions

► **Register the NorthwindData_COM component**

1. To open the Command Prompt window, click **Start**, point to **All Programs**, point to **Accessories**, and then click **Command Prompt**.
2. In the Command Prompt window, type the following and then press ENTER:

```
regsvr32 "C:\Program
Files\Msdntrain\2565\Practices\Mod05\Mod05_01\Starter\North
windData_COM.dll"
```

Note The path in step 2 will change if the starter files for the practices and demonstrations are installed in a different location on your computer.

Tip You can also drag the NorthwindData_COM.dll file from Windows Explorer to the **Run** dialog box or to the Command window, append **regsrv32** to the beginning of the file name, and then press ENTER.

A message box confirms a successful registration.

► Add a reference to the NorthwindData_COM component

1. Open Visual Studio .NET.
2. On the **File** menu, point to **New**, and then click **Project**.
3. In the **New Project** dialog box, click **Windows Application**, in the **Name** box, type **ComInterop** and then click **OK**.
4. On the **Project** menu, click **Add Reference**.
5. Click the **COM** tab, double-click the **NorthwindData_COM** component, and then click **OK**.

► Add the Masked Edit control to the Toolbox

1. On the **Tools** menu, click **Customize Toolbox**.
2. Select **Microsoft Masked Edit Control, version 6.0**, and then click **OK**.

   Confirm that the **MaskEdBox** control is added to the Toolbox in the Visual Studio IDE.

► Configure the controls on the form

1. Add the following controls to the form.

Control	Name	Text
Label	ProductIDLabel	ProductID
MaskEdBox	COMMaskEdBox	
Button	GetUnitsInStockButton	Get UnitsInStock
Label	UnitsInStockLabel	UnitsInStock

2. Set the **Mask** property of **COMMaskEdBox** to ##.

   Your form should look like the following illustration.

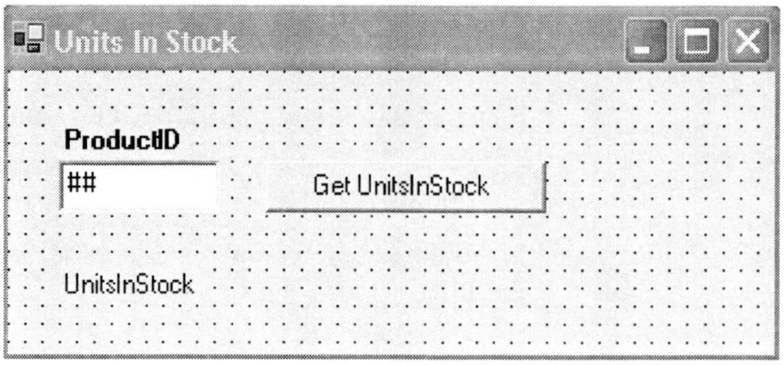

► Add code to use the COM objects in your .NET-based application

1. Create a procedure for the **Click** event of **GetUnitsInStockButton**.
2. Create a variable named *comObject* to hold an instance of the **NorhwindData_COM.RemainingInventoryClass** component.
3. Create an Integer variable called *productID* and assign it the value of the **ClipText** property of the **COMMaskedEdit** control. Convert the **ClipText** value to an Integer before assigning it to *productID.*
4. Call the **ShowUnitsInStock** method of *comObject* and pass *productID* as the first argument. Pass *(local)\MOC* as a string that identifies the local instance of Microsoft SQL Server™ with Northwind installed, as the second argument. Assign the string returned from the **ShowUnitsInStock** method to the **Text** property of **UnitsInStockLabel**. Your code should look like the following:

```
Private Sub GetUnitsInStockButton_Click(ByVal sender As
System.Object, ByVal e As System.EventArgs) Handles _
GetUnitsInStockButton.Click
   Dim comObject As New
NorthwindData_COM.RemainingInventoryClass()
   Dim prodID As Integer = CType(COMMaskEdBox.ClipText,
Integer)
   UnitsInStockLabel.Text =
comObject.ShowUnitsInStock(prodID, "(local)\MOC")
End Sub
```

► Test the application

1. Press F5 to compile and run the application.
2. Enter a number between **1** and **77**, and then click **GetUnitsInStock**.

   Confirm that the label reflects the number of items in stock.

Lesson: Calling Win32 APIs from Windows Forms Applications

- Platform Invocation Services
- How to Define Functions by Using the Declare Statement
- How to Define Functions by Using the DllImport Attribute
- How to Call Win32 APIs from a Windows Forms Application
- Practice: Calling Win32 APIs

Introduction

Windows APIs are DLLs that are part of the Microsoft Windows® operating system. You use them to perform tasks when it is difficult to write equivalent procedures of your own. The advantage of using Windows APIs in your code is that they can save development time because they contain hundreds of useful functions that are already written and waiting to be used. The disadvantage is that Windows APIs can be difficult to work with and unforgiving when things go wrong.

Windows DLLs represent a special category of interoperability. Windows APIs do not use managed code, do not have built-in type libraries, and use data types that are different than those used with Visual Studio .NET. Because of these differences, and because Windows APIs are not COM objects, interoperability with Windows APIs and the .NET Platform is performed by using platform invoke. Platform invoke is a service that enables managed code to call unmanaged functions implemented in DLLs. You can use platform invoke in Visual Basic .NET either by using the **Declare** statement or by applying the **DllImport** attribute to an empty procedure. This lesson covers how to call Win32 APIs from Windows Forms applications by using platform invoke.

After completing this lesson, you will be able to:

- Explain the role of the Platform Invocation Services in calling unmanaged code from managed code.
- Define functions in a DLL by using the **Declare** statement and the **DllImport** attribute.
- Call Win32 APIs from a Windows Forms application by using the **Declare** statement and the **DllImport** attribute.

Platform Invocation Services

The PInvoke Model

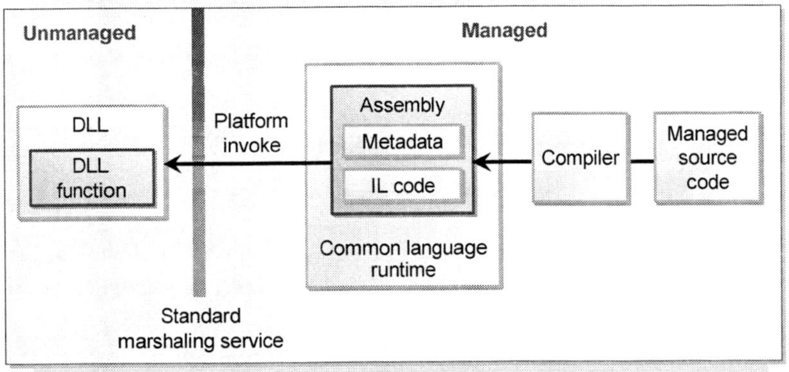

A platform invoke call to an unmanaged DLL function

Introduction

Platform Invocation Services is a mechanism by which managed code calls unmanaged code.

Definition

Platform invoke allows managed code to call unmanaged functions that are implemented in a DLL. Platform Invoke takes care of finding and invoking the correct function, as well as marshaling its managed arguments to and from their unmanaged counterparts (integers, strings, and so on). Platform invoke and COM Interop share much of the marshaling code inside the .NET Framework.

You can use the **DllImport** attribute or the **Declare** function to declare functions in DLLs.

Role of platform invoke in calling Win32 APIs

When platform invoke calls an unmanaged function, it performs the following set of actions.

1. Locates the DLL containing the function.

   To locate a function in a DLL, platform invoke must have the following information.

   a. The name of the DLL file, such as User32.dll, GDI32.dll, or Kernel32.dll.

   b. The name of the function or ordinal number, such as **MessageBox** or exported function number #**452**.

   c. The character set which will be used—ANSI or Unicode. .Net is unicode

      Win32 API contains two versions of each function: a single-Byte character ANSI version and a double-Byte character Unicode version. For instance, MessageBoxA is the ANSI entry point for the MessageBox function and MessageBoxW is the Unicode version.

      The character set is controlled by the value of the **CharSet** field of **DllImportAttribute**, which will be discussed later in more detail.

2. Loads the DLL into memory.
3. Locates the address of the function in memory and pushes its arguments onto the stack, marshaling data as required.
4. Transfers control to the unmanaged function.
5. Returns exceptions generated by the unmanaged function to the managed caller.

How to Define Functions by Using the Declare Statement

- **The Declare keyword can be used to create function definitions in Visual Basic .NET**
- **Can also use DllImport for more flexibility**

```
Public Class Win32PlaySound
Public Declare Auto Function PlaySound Lib
   "winmm.dll" Alias "PlaySound" _
(ByVal pszSound As String, ByVal hmod As Long,
   ByVal fdwSound As Long) As Boolean
End Class
```

Introduction

To call an unmanaged DLL function from managed code, you must first write the managed definition for the function in a managed class. Wrapping the definition of an unmanaged DLL function in a managed class effectively makes the function look and behave like a managed .NET Framework function. However, when the runtime encounters this function, platform invoke makes the transition from managed to unmanaged code and invokes the unmanaged function.

Procedure

The **Declare** statement in Visual Basic .NET uses the **Alias** keyword to specify the entry point of the function. It uses the **Ansi**, **Unicode**, and **Auto** keywords to specify character set behavior. The **Lib** keyword defines the name of the DLL that contains the function.

The following code shows how to define functions by using the **Declare** statement.

```
Public Class Win32PlaySound
Public Declare Auto Function PlaySound Lib "winmm.dll" Alias
"PlaySound" _
(ByVal pszSound As String, ByVal hmod As Long, ByVal fdwSound
As Long) As Boolean
End Class
```

Note The **Declare** statement has only a subset of the features provided by DllImport. So, in some cases, you may not be able to use the **Declare** statement. For example, the **Declare** statement does not allow you to alter the **ExactSpelling**, **CallingConvention**, or **SetLastError** default values. You must use **DllImport** to change these settings.

How to Define Functions by Using the DllImport Attribute

- DllImport attribute is used to define functions
- Parameters are used to specify specific behavior
  - CallingConvention
  - EntryPoint
  - CharSet
  - ExactSpelling

```
Imports System.Runtime.InteropServices
   <DllImport("KERNEL32.DLL",
   EntryPoint:="MoveFileW", SetLastError:=True, _
   CharSet:=CharSet.Unicode, ExactSpelling:=True, _
   CallingConvention:=CallingConvention.StdCall)> _
   Public Shared Function _
   MoveFile(ByVal src As String, ByVal dst As String)
   As Boolean
   End Function
```

Introduction

The **DllImport** attribute provides an alternative way of using functions in unmanaged code. The **DllImport** attribute is used to specify the DLL location that contains the implementation of an external method. **DllImport** is roughly equivalent to using a **Declare** statement but provides more control over how functions are called. However, **DllImport** can be placed only on method declarations.

DllImport parameters

DllImport has the following named parameters that specify the behavior of the attribute.

- *CallingConvention*

  The *CallingConvention* parameter indicates the calling convention for the entry point. If no *CallingConvention* is specified, a default of CallingConvention.Winapi is used.

- *CharSet*

  The *CharSet* parameter indicates the character set used in the entry point. If no *CharSet* is specified, a default of CharSet.Auto is used.

- *EntryPoint*

  The *EntryPoint* parameter gives the name of the entry point in the DLL. If no *EntryPoint* is specified, the name of the method is used.

- *ExactSpelling*

  The *ExactSpelling* parameter indicates whether *EntryPoint* must exactly match the spelling of the indicated entry point. If no *ExactSpelling* is specified, a default of **False** is used.

Procedure

Apply the **DllImport** attribute to the empty function. The first parameter is the name and location of the DLL containing the function that you are calling. You do not need to specify the path for files located in the Windows system directories. The second parameter is a named argument that specifies the name of the function in the Windows API.

```
<DllImport("KERNEL32.DLL", EntryPoint:="MoveFileW",
SetLastError:=True, _
CharSet:=CharSet.Unicode, ExactSpelling:=True, _
CallingConvention:=CallingConvention.StdCall)> _
Public Shared Function _
MoveFile(ByVal src As String, ByVal dst As String) As Boolean
End Function
```

How to Call Win32 APIs from a Windows Forms Application

- Determine the details of the function you want to call
- Create a new project in Visual Studio .NET
- Import the **System.Runtime.InteropServices** namespace

```
Imports System.Runtime.InteropServices
```

- Define a function using **Declare** or **DllImport**
- Add code to call the Win32 API from a Windows Form

```
Private myWin32Object As New Win32PlaySound ()
myWin32Object.PlaySound("C:\WINDOWS\Media\tada.wav", 0)
```

Introduction

So far, you have learned the components that are involved in calling a Win32 API from a .NET Framework-based application. Now you will look at the entire procedure of calling a Win32 API from a .NET Windows Forms application.

Procedure

To call a Win32 API:

1. Determine the name of the function that you want to call, its arguments, argument types, return value, and the name and location of the DLL that contains it.
2. Create a new class in Visual Studio .NET.
3. Import the **System.Runtime.InteropServices** namespace.

   ```
   Imports System.Runtime.InteropServices
   ```
4. Define a function by using **Declare** or **DllImport**.

   Add the following **Declare** function to either the declaration section of the startup form for your project or the declaration section of the class or module where you want to use the DLL.

   ```
   Public Class Win32PlaySound

      Public Declare Function PlaySound Lib "winmm.dll" _
      Alias "sndPlaySoundA" _
          (ByVal lpszSoundName As String, ByVal uFlags _
      As Long) As Long
   End Class
   ```

5. Add code to call the Win32 API from a Windows Form.

```
Private myWin32Object As New Win32PlaySound ()
myWin32Object.PlaySound("C:\WINDOWS\Media\tada.wav", 0)
```

Note Although calling an unmanaged DLL function from managed code is almost identical to calling a managed function, there are some differences when passing data structures and using callback functions. For more information about making advanced calls through platform invoke, see Course 2571A, *Application Upgrade and Interoperability Using Visual Studio .NET.*

Practice: Calling Win32 APIs

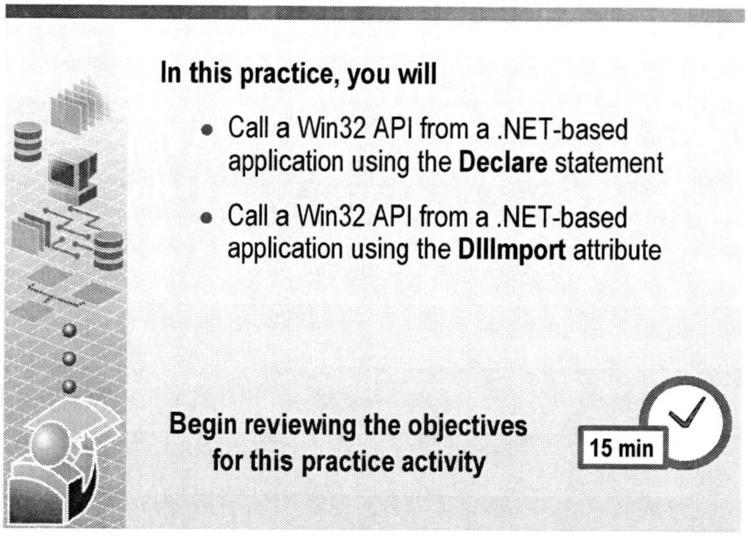

Introduction

In this practice, you will create and test a class that calls the Win32 PlaySound API.

The PlaySound API is used to play sound files such as .wav files and is located in the Winmm.dll file. It has the following signature:

```
BOOL PlaySound(
  LPCSTR pszSound,
  HMODULE hmod,
  DWORD fdwSound
);
```

Notice that the arguments of the API use unmanaged C++ variable types. You must understand these variables types to convert them to an equivalent .NET type.

For more information and a list of unmanaged data types and their managed equivalents, see the "Platform Invoke Data Types" section of the .NET Framework SDK.

The **PlaySound** function takes three arguments and returns a Boolean value indicating whether or not the function was able to play the sound file. The arguments include:

- **pszSound**

  A string that defines the name of the sound file.

- **hmod**

  Handle to the executable file that contains the resource to be loaded. This parameter must be **NULL** unless **SND_RESOURCE** is specified in **fdwSound**.

- **fdwSound**

  Flags that are used to determine how the sound is played. Examples of flags include whether the sound should play asynchronously or whether it should loop.

Instructions

► **Open the practice project**

1. Using Windows Explorer, navigate to *install_folder*\Practices\Mod05\Mod05_02\Starter.

> **Note** If you performed a default installation of the course files, *install_folder* corresponds to C:\Program Files\Msdntrain\2565.

2. Double-click the PInvoke.sln solution file to open the project.

► **Add a class to the PInvoke project and import the System.Runtime.InteropServices namespace**

1. On the **Project** menu, click **Add Class**.
2. Name the class **Win32PlaySoundClass.vb**, and then click **Open**.
3. Import the **System.Runtime.InteropServices** namespace by typing the following code above the **Win32PlaySoundClass**.

```
Imports System.Runtime.InteropServices
```

► **Use the Declare statement to expose the PlaySound Win32 API**

1. Inside the **Win32PlaySoundClass**, create a Public function named **PlaySound_Declare** that includes the **Declare** statement and uses the **Auto** alias to specify the character set behavior. Your code should look like the following.

```
Public Declare Auto Function PlaySound_Declare
```

2. Use the **Lib** clause to specify Winmm.dll, which contains the PlaySound function.
3. Use the **Alias** clause to indicate the name of the function as PlaySound. Your code should look like the following.

```
Public Declare Auto Function PlaySound_Declare Lib _
"winmm.dll" Alias "PlaySound"
```

4. Create the arguments required by the **PlaySound** function. The following table includes the argument names, the unmanaged type expected, and the .NET equivalent type.

Argument Name	Unmanaged Type	Managed Equivalent
pszSound	LPCSTR	System.String
hmod	HMODULE	System.Long
fdwSound	DWORD	System.Long

5. Use a Boolean value to hold the results of the function. Your code should look like the following.

```
Public Declare Auto Function PlaySound_Declare
Lib "winmm.dll" Alias "PlaySound" (ByVal pszSound As
String, _
ByVal hmod As Long, ByVal fdwSound As Long) As Boolean
```

► **Add code to test the PlaySound_Declare function**

1. Open PlaySoundForm in the Code Editor and locate the **PlayButton_Click** event procedure.
2. Declare a Boolean value named **result** to hold the results of the **PlaySound_Declare** function.
3. Declare a variable named **win32PlaySound** to hold an instance of **Win32PlaySoundClass** and instantiate it.
4. Call the **PlaySound_Declare** function of the **Win32PlaySound** class and assign the results to the result variable. Use the following table to fill the parameters.

Parameter	Value
pszSound	soundFileName
hmod	0
fdwSound	0

Your code should look like the following.

```
Dim result As Boolean
Dim win32PlaySound As New Win32PlaySoundClass()
result = win32PlaySound.PlaySound_Declare(soundFileName, 0,
0)
```

► **Test the PlaySound_Declare function**

1. Press F5 to build and run the application.
2. On the **File** menu, click **Open**.
3. Click the **Windows XP Startup.wav** file, and then click **Open**.
4. Click the **Play** button to test the sound.
5. Close the application.

Note If there are no speakers available to test the sound, test the value of the result variable in the debug mode.

▶ Resolve the errors in the PlaySound_Declare function of the Win32PlaySound_Error class

- Open the **Win32PlaySound_ErrorClass** file from *install_folder*\Practices\Mod05\Mod05_02\Starter, and review the **PlaySound_Declare** function. There is an error in the function. You can attempt to test it to confirm. What is the error?

____

____

____

____

▶ Use the DllImportAttribute to call the PlaySound Win32 API (optional)

1. Open the Win32PlaySoundClass file.
2. Inside the **Win32PlaySound** class, create a **DllImport** attribute that exposes the Winmm.dll and sets the **EntryPoint** parameter to **PlaySound**. Your code should look like the following.

```
<DllImport("winmm.dll", EntryPoint:="PlaySound")>
```

3. Append a Public Shared function to the **DllImport** attribute named **PlaySound_DllImport** and create the arguments required by the **PlaySound** function. The following table includes the argument names, the unmanaged type expected, and the .NET equivalent type.

Argument Name	Unmanaged Type	Managed Equivalent
pszSound	LPCSTR	System.String
hmod	HMODULE	System.Long
fdwSound	DWORD	System.Long

4. In the **PlaySound_DllImport** function, use a Boolean value to hold the results of the function and explicitly end the function.

   Your code should look like the following.

```
<DllImport("winmm.dll", EntryPoint:="PlaySound")> Public
Shared Function PlaySound_DllImport _
(ByVal pszSound As String, ByVal hmod As Long, _
 ByVal fdwSound As Long) As Boolean

End Function
```

► Add code to test the PlaySound_DllImport function (If time permits)

1. Open the PlaySoundForm, and then locate the **PlayButton_Click** event procedure.
2. Edit the code to call the **PlaySound_DllImport** function instead of the **PlaySound_Declare** function. Your code should look like the following.

```
result = win32PlaySound.PlaySound_DllImport _
(soundFileName, 0, 0)
```

► Test the PlaySound_DllImport function(If time permits)

1. Press F5 to build and run the application.
2. On the **File** menu, click **Open**.
3. Click the **Windows XP Startup.wav** file, and then click **Open**.
4. Click the **Play** button to test the sound.
5. Close the application.

Note If there are no speakers available to test the sound, test the value of the result variable in the debug mode.

► Resolve the errors in the PlaySound_DllImport function of the Win32PlaySound_Error class (If time permits)

- Open the **Win32PlaySound_ErrorClass** file and review the **PlaySound_DllImport** function. There is an error in the function. You can attempt to test it to confirm. What is the error?

____

____

____

____

Note You can also correct this error by setting the **EntryPoint** parameter to **PlaySoundA**; however, you must also set the **CharSet** parameter to **CharSet.Ansi**.

Lesson: Upgrading Visual Basic 6.0 Applications to Visual Basic .NET

- **Advantages of Upgrading**
- **Results of the Upgrade Wizard**
- **Demonstration: Upgrading Visual Basic 6.0 Applications to Visual Basic .NET**

Introduction

There are a significant number of changes in Visual Basic .NET, and to fully take advantage of the .NET Framework features, you must upgrade your applications to Visual Basic .NET.

Because of the significant number of changes, you will find that upgrading applications to Visual Basic .NET might take time and effort. The Visual Basic Upgrade Wizard is included to help you upgrade.

In this lesson, you will learn the factors you must consider when deciding whether to upgrade an existing application, the options you have for upgrading, and how to use the Upgrade Wizard.

Lesson objectives

After completing this lesson, you will be able to:

- Explain the advantages of upgrading applications to Visual Basic .NET.
- Explain the results of the Upgrade Wizard.
- Upgrade Visual Basic 6.0 applications to Visual Basic .NET.

Advantages of Upgrading

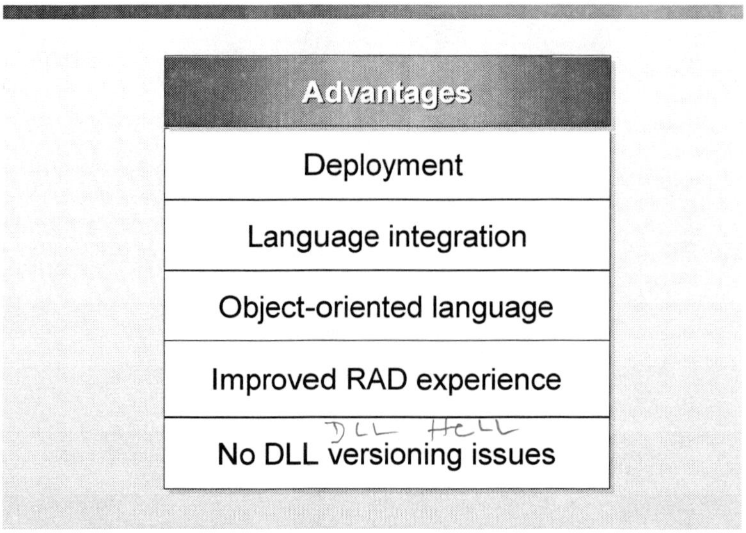

Introduction

The .NET Framework provides many features to the application developer that may enhance applications created in Visual Basic 6.0.

Advantages

The following are the major advantages that upgrading your application to Visual Basic .NET provides:

- Deployment

  Deployment is greatly simplified in the .NET Framework. Depending on the complexity of your application, deployment can consist of running an application directly from a server, using XCOPY to copy the application to a workstation or Web server, or installing by using Microsoft Windows Installer.

- Language integration

  Visual Basic .NET code fully integrates with code written in other .NET-compatible languages, such as C#. As a result, a Visual Basic developer can use the capabilities of the .NET Framework easily, without resorting to the programming that is traditionally required to make Windows APIs work. Visual Basic .NET has the same variable types, arrays, user-defined types, classes, and interfaces as C# and any other language that works with the runtime. To ensure language integration, some features, such as fixed-length strings and non-zero-based arrays, have been removed from Visual Basic.

- Object-oriented language

  Visual Basic .NET is truly object-oriented and supports implementation inheritance. In addition, some features that are not intuitive or consistent, such as **GoSub/Return**, have been removed from the language.

- Improved Rapid Application Development (RAD) experience

  With Visual Basic .NET, it is easy to visually develop Web applications, XML Web services, Windows-based applications, and server-side components. The Windows Forms Designer supports visual inheritance and contains new features, such as automatic form resizing, resource localization, and accessibility support. The data tools now inherently support XML data, and the design-time data binding works with disconnected data.

- No DLL versioning issues

  Visual Basic .NET enables XCOPY deployment of Windows-based applications, so you no longer need to worry about DLL versioning issues.

Results of the Upgrade Wizard

- **Language Changes**
  - Code upgraded to be syntactically correct in Visual Basic .NET
- **Form Changes**
  - Visual Basic Forms upgrade to Windows Forms
  - Most controls will upgrade
  - Controls that have no counterparts are upgraded as label controls
- **Other Changes**
  - Other functionality are upgraded to similar objects
  - ADO data environments are not upgraded

Introduction

After you have upgraded your application, the resulting project will still be very similar to the original.

Anything that can be upgraded is upgraded, and anything that cannot be upgraded or that is ambiguous is marked with comments and entered in the Upgrade Report. Links are created to relevant topics in the documentation files to help you resolve any outstanding issues.

Some Visual Basic 6.0 functions do not have equivalents in Visual Basic .NET, and these will be retained through use of compatibility functions.

Important There are a number of syntax changes between Visual Basic .NET and previous versions, and a few of the features that are supported in Visual Basic 6.0 have been removed from Visual Basic .NET. Therefore, it is important that you review your existing Visual Basic 6.0–based applications for incompatibility issues between the two languages and update those features before you upgrade the applications by using the Upgrade Wizard.

Language changes

The Upgrade Wizard modifies the code where possible to take into account the syntax changes in Visual Basic .NET. This includes:

- Resolving parameterless default properties.
- Adding the **ByRef** keyword to procedure parameters.
- Changing property procedures to the new syntax.
- Adding parentheses to all function calls.
- Changing all data types to their new equivalents.

Form changes

Visual Basic forms are upgraded to Windows Forms, although a few controls cannot be upgraded because they have no counterpart in Visual Basic .NET. These include the following, which all upgrade to Visual Studio .NET **Label** controls:

- **OLE Container** controls
- **Shape** controls
- **Line** controls

Other Changes

Other functionality in applications created in Visual Basic 6.0 may not have a direct counterpart in Visual Basic .NET but will be left as is or upgraded to similar objects. For example:

- Code that performs drag-and-drop operations will not upgrade.
- Code that uses GDI will not upgrade to GDI+.
- Resource files will upgrade to .resx files that can store any .NET data type.
- Web classes will not upgrade.
- ADO data environments will not upgrade.
- ADO code and ADO data binding will remain unchanged.
- Property pages are no longer used in Visual Basic .NET.
- 1 based arrays will not upgrade.

Demonstration: Upgrading Visual Basic 6.0 Applications to Visual Basic .NET

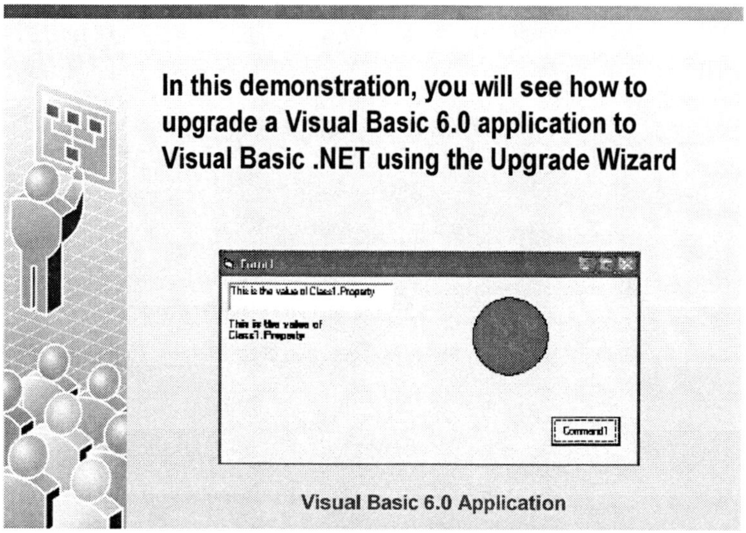

Do not use upgrade tool

Introduction

In this demonstration, you will see the conversion of a Visual Basic 6.0 application to Visual Basic.NET. The Visual Basic 6.0 application contains a form and a class module. The Visual Basic 6.0 form looks like the following.

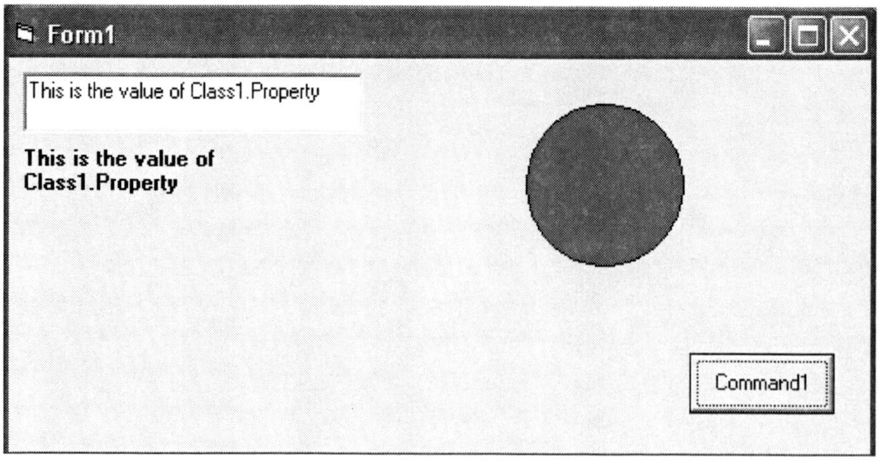

Instructions

► **Convert the VB6Application.vbp file to VB.NET**

1. Open Visual Studio .NET.
2. On the **File** menu, point to **Open**, and then click **Project**.
3. Open the **VB6Application.vbp** file from *install_folder*\Democode\Mod05\Mod05_03\VB6Application.
4. On the Welcome page of the Visual Basic Upgrade Wizard, click **Next**.
5. On the **Choose a Project Type** page, click **Next**.
6. Accept the default location for the new project and click **Next**.
7. Confirm that you want to create the new folder.
8. On the **Ready to Upgrade** page, click **Next**.

► **Review the modifications**

1. Review the visual modifications made to the form.
2. Review the syntax modification made to the form and class.
3. Review the _UpgradeReport.htm file.

Review

- Using .NET and COM Components in a Windows Forms Application
- Calling Win32 APIs from Windows Forms Applications
- Upgrading Visual Basic 6.0 Applications to Visual Basic .NET

1. List some of the differences between COM and .NET components.

2. How do you call COM components from a .NET-based application?

3. Describe the role of the RCW in interoperability.

4. What are the two most common methods used for generating interop assemblies?

5. List the functions of the platform invoke service.

① Identify what does DLL do

② function of DLL

③ Import ⇐ Transfer

④

handle exception

6. How do you call a Win32 API from a .NET-based application?

Key words
Declare or DLL Import

7. List some of the components of a Visual Basic 6.0 application that do not upgrade to .NET.

ADO
GDI change
Drag & Drop upgraded
Drag
ARRAY starts @ 1 Defaults starts
Now @ Ø

Lab 5.1: Interoperating with COM and Calling Win32 APIs

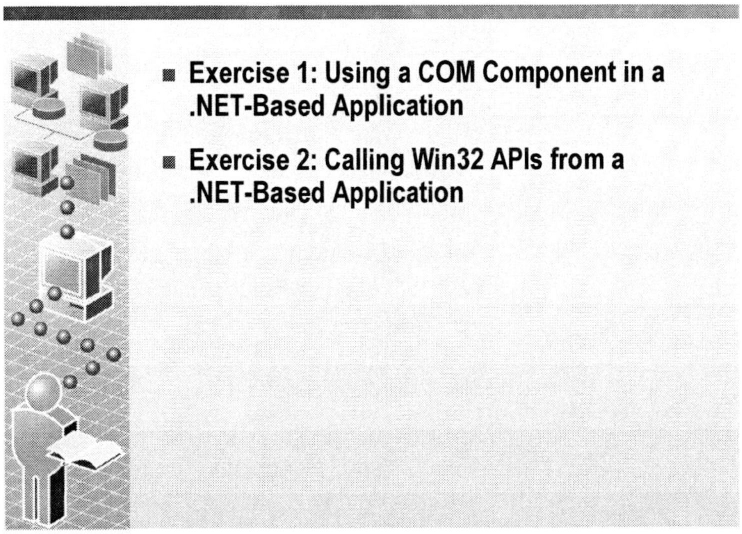

Objectives

After completing this lab, you will have demonstrated your ability to:

- Create an **Interop** assembly.
- View assembly information with ILDASM.
- Invoke functions on a COM component from managed code.
- Declare functions that expose Win32 DLLs.
- Invoke Win32 DLLs from managed code.

Note This lab focuses on the concepts in Module 5, "Interoperating with Managed Objects," in Course 2565A, *Developing Microsoft .NET Applications for Windows (Visual Basic .NET)*. As a result, this lab may not comply with Microsoft security recommendations.

Prerequisites

Before working on this lab, you must have:

- The knowledge and skills to develop a simple Windows Forms application by using a Visual Studio .NET–compatible programming language.
- The knowledge and skills to create an **Interop** assembly from the Visual Studio .NET IDE.
- The knowledge and skills to invoke COM functions from a Visual Studio .NET–based application.
- The knowledge and skills to expose Win32 DLLs in a Visual Studio .NET–based application.
- The knowledge and skills to invoke Win32 DLLs in a Visual Studio .NET–based application.

Scenario

You are a developer in a trading company called Northwind Traders. The department that you work in is developing a purchase order application that will be used by the Northwind Traders sales force. As you develop the Purchase Order application, you realize that there are some required functionalities that are either too difficult to include in the first version of the application or are inaccessible from the .NET Framework. One of these functionalities is the ability to do a live lookup on the database to determine how many units of a specified product remain in the inventory. The other functionality is to include sound files that play when a user successfully completes an operation.

You realize that you can re-use existing COM components in your application. A COM component called NorthwindData_COM already exists, and it performs the required lookup task. In addition, NorthwindData_COM was installed with a previous application on all the client computers on which the Purchase Order application will be installed.

You also realize that you can expose and invoke the Win32 APIs that play media files and use them in the Purchase Order application.

Estimated time to complete this lab: 60 minutes

Exercise 1
Using a COM Component in a .NET-Based Application

In this exercise, you will create a reference to a COM object, view the **Interop** assembly by using ILDASM, and invoke the COM component from a Windows Forms application.

Scenario

The sales staff of Northwind Traders has put in a request that the Purchase Order application be able to display the number of units in inventory for a specified product. Without knowing how much inventory is available, it is difficult for the sales staff to estimate the time it will take to deliver the order. By knowing the number of units in stock, they can anticipate late deliveries and warn the customer in advance.

You decide to use an existing COM component that was installed on the sales staff's laptops with a previous application. The existing COM component is called NorthwindData_COM, and it includes a class called **RemainingInventoryClass**. The **RemainingInventoryClass** class includes a method called **ShowUnitsInStock** that returns a string that identifies the product name and the number of units remaining in inventory.

All the functions that are available in NorthwindData_COM use ADO 2.6 and require a live connection to the database, so the salesperson must be connected to the database for the component to return the expected results. You intend to provide a disconnected feature that provides a similar function in the next version of the Purchase Order application.

There are starter and solution files associated with this exercise. Browse to *install_folder*\Labfiles\Lab05_1\Ex01\Starter to find the starter files, and browse to *install_folder*\Labfiles\Lab05_1\Ex01\Solution to find the solution files. If you performed a default installation of the course files, *install_folder* corresponds to C:\Program Files\Msdntrain\2565.

Tasks	Additional information
1. Open Visual Studio .NET, and open the PurchaseOrderApplication.sln file. To open the solution file, browse to *install_folder*\ Labfiles\ Lab05_1\Ex01\ Starter\OrderApplication.	**a.** For more information about opening a project file, see the following resource: • The Visual Studio .NET Help documentation. For additional information about opening a project file, in Search, select the **Search in titles only** check box, then search by using the phrase **Open Project Dialog Box**.
2. Register the NorthwindData_COM.dll located in *install_folder*\ Labfiles\Lab05_1\Ex01\ Starter\ using the **REGSVR32** utility and add a reference to the component. When you use the IDE to create a reference to a COM component, it uses TLBIMP to create an **Interop** assembly. If you have already registered this component in Practice: Using COM Components in .NET Applications in Module 5, "Interoperating with Managed Objects," in Course 2565A, *Developing Microsoft .NET Applications for Windows (Visual Basic .NET)*, then just add a reference to the NorthwindData_COM.dll component.	**a.** For more information about the adding a reference and creating an **Interop** assembly, see the following resources: • Lesson: Using .NET and COM Components in a Windows Forms Application in Module 5, "Interoperating with Managed Objects," in Course 2565A, *Developing Microsoft .NET Applications for Windows (Visual Basic .NET)*. • Practice: Using COM Components in .NET-Based Applications in Module 5, "Interoperating with Managed Objects," in Course 2565A, *Developing Microsoft .NET Applications for Windows (Visual Basic .NET)*. • The Visual Studio .NET Help documentation. For additional information about creating References, search by using the phrase **Adding and Removing References**. • The.NET Framework SDK documentation. For additional information about creating **Interop** assemblies, search by using the phrase **Importing a Type Library as an Assembly**.
3. Run ILDASM, and view the information for Interop.NorthwindData_COM .dll. This DLL is located in *install_folder*\Labfiles\ Lab05_1\Ex01\Starter\ OrderApplication\Bin. Interop.NorthwindData_COM .dll is the **Interop** assembly that was generated when you added a reference to the NorthwindData_COM.dll.	**a.** For more information about how to use ILDASM, see the following resource: • The .NET Framework SDK documentation. Search by using the phrase **MSIL Disassembler (Ildasm.exe)**.

Tasks	Additional information
4. Open MainForm in the Code Editor. Use the Task List to locate the code section 'TODO 1. Create an instance of the **NorthwindData_ COMRemainingInventory Class** COM component.	**a.** For more information about using COM components in managed code, see the following resources: • Lesson: Using .NET and COM Components in a Windows Forms Application in Module 5, "Interoperating with Managed Objects," in Course 2565A, *Developing Microsoft .NET Applications for Windows (Visual Basic .NET).* • Practice: Using COM Components in .NET-Based Applications in Module 5, "Interoperating with Managed Objects," in Course 2565A, *Developing Microsoft .NET Applications for Windows (Visual Basic .NET).* • The .NET Framework SDK documentation. For additional information about using COM components in .NET code, search by using the phrase **Using COM Types in Managed Code.**
5. Use the Task List to locate the code section 'TODO 2. Create an instance of the **OrderItemControl** control and assign it the **SourceControl** property of the **ProductContextMenu** control.	**a.** For more information about using the SourceControl method of the ContextMenu class, see the following resource: • The.NET Framework SDK documentation. Search by using the phrase **ContextMenu.SourceControl Property.**
6. Use the Task List to locate the 'TODO 3. Create a variable of the type **Short** and assign it the **OrderProductID** property of the **OrderItemControl.**	**a.** For more information about the **OrderItemControl**, see the following resource: • Lab 3.1: Building Controls in Module 3, "Building Controls," in Course 2565A, *Developing Microsoft .NET Applications for Windows (Visual Basic .NET).*
7. Use the Task List to locate the code section 'TODO 4. Create a **Try**, **Catch** block and call the **ShowUnitsInStock** method of the **RemainingInventoryClass** class, passing the Short variable containing the **ProductID** and the name of a SQL Server with the Northwind database installed. Display the results in a message box. The name of the SQL Server uses syntax similar to *LONDON\MOC.*	**a.** For more information about creating a Try Catch block and using COM components in managed code, see the following resource: • Lesson: Using .NET and COM Components in a Windows Forms Application in Module 5, "Interoperating with Managed Objects," in Course 2565A, *Developing Microsoft .NET Applications for Windows (Visual Basic .NET).* • Practice: Using COM Components in .NET-Based Applications in Module 5, "Interoperating with Managed Objects," in Course 2565A, *Developing Microsoft .NET Applications for Windows (Visual Basic .NET).* • The.NET Framework SDK documentation. For additional information about using Try Catch blocks, search by using the phrase **Using the Try/Catch Block to Catch Exceptions.** • The Visual Studio .NET SDK documentation. For help with using COM components in managed code, search by using the phrase **Using COM Types in Managed Code.**

Tasks	Additional information
8. Compile and run the application. Add an **OrderItemControl** control by clicking the **New Order Item** button. Right-click the ComboBox within the **OrderItemControl**, and click **Show Inventory**. Repeat this for other products. A message box appears that displays the current number of units in stock.	**a.** For more information about building and debugging your applications, see the following resource: • The Visual Studio .NET Help documentation. Search by using the phrases **Default and Custom Builds** and **Using the Debugger**.

Exercise 2
Calling Win32 APIs from a .NET-Based Application

In this exercise, you create a class that exposes a Win32 API. You will then invoke the Win32 API by using your class from a Windows Forms application. The **PlaySound** function takes three arguments and returns a Boolean value that indicates whether or not the function was able to play the sound file. The arguments include:

pszSound

A string that defines the name of the sound file.

Hmod

Handle to the executable file that contains the resource to be loaded. This parameter must be **NULL** unless **SND_RESOURCE** is specified in **fdwSound**.

fdwSound

Flags that are used to determine how the sound is played. Examples of flags include whether the sound should play asynchronously or whether it should loop.

Scenario

You decide to add sound effects to the Purchase Order application that will notify users when they successfully save an order and when they successfully update their orders to the database. However, the Win32 APIs that are responsible for playing media files are not exposed by the .NET Framework. You must create a class that exposes the winmm.dll and allows you to call the PlaySound API.

There are starter and solution files associated with this exercise. Browse to *install_folder*\Labfiles\Lab05_1\Ex02\Starter to find the starter files, and browse to *install_folder*\Labfiles\Lab05_1\Ex02\Solution to find the solution files. If you performed a default installation of the course files, *install_folder* corresponds to C:\Program Files\Msdntrain\2565.

Tasks	Additional information
1. Open Visual Studio .NET. Open the PurchaseOrderApplication.sln file. To open the solution file, browse to *install_folder*\Labfiles\Lab05_1\Ex02\Starter\OrderApplication.	**a.** For more information about opening a project file, see the following resource: • The Visual Studio .NET Help documentation. For additional information about opening a project file, in Search, select the **Search in titles only** check box, then search by using the phrase **Open Project Dialog Box**.
2. Add the Save.wav sound file located in *install_folder*\Labfiles\Lab05_1\Ex02\Starter to the Bin directory of the PurchaseOrderApplication project .	**a.** For more information about adding new items to a project, see the following resource: • The Visual Studio .NET Help documentation. Search by using the phrase **Adding Projects and Items to the New Application**.

Tasks	Additional information
3. Add a new class to the PurchaseOrderApplication project and name it **Win32PlaySound.vb**.	**a.** For more information about adding new items to a project, see the following resource: • The Visual Studio .NET Help documentation. Search by using the phrase **Adding Projects and Items to the New Application**.
4. Create a function that exposes the Win32 **PlaySound** function in the Winmm.dll.	**a.** For more information about creating functions that expose WIN32 DLLs, see the following resources: • Lesson: Calling Win32 APIs from Windows Forms Applications in Module 5, "Interoperating with Managed Objects," in Course 2565A, *Developing Microsoft .NET Applications for Windows (Visual Basic .NET).* • Practice: Calling Win32 APIs in Module 5, "Interoperating with Managed Objects," in Course 2565A, *Developing Microsoft .NET Applications for Windows (Visual Basic .NET).* • The .NET Framework SDK documentation. For help with using COM components in managed code, search by using the phrase **Consuming Unmanaged DLL Functions.**
5. Open MainForm in the Code Editor. Use the Task List to locate the code section 'TODO 1. Create a variable to hold an instance of the **Win32PlaySound** class. Call the **PlaySound** function with the variable. Pass **"Save.wav"** as the name of the media file, a **0** for the second argument, and a **0** for the third argument.	**a.** For more information about creating functions that expose WIN32 DLLs, see the following resources: • Lesson: Calling Win32 APIs from Windows Forms Applications in Module 5, "Interoperating with Managed Objects," in Course 2565A, *Developing Microsoft .NET Applications for Windows (Visual Basic .NET).* • Practice: Calling Win32 APIs in Module 5, "Interoperating with Managed Objects," in Course 2565A, *Developing Microsoft .NET Applications for Windows (Visual Basic .NET).* • The .NET Framework SDK documentation. For help with using COM components in managed code, search by using the phrase **Consuming Unmanaged DLL Functions.**
6. Compile and run the application. Click the **New Order Item** button, and then click the **Save Order** button to save an order. You should hear a sound play. If sound is not available with your computer, test the Boolean value returned by the **PlaySound** function; this value indicates success or failure.	**a.** For more information about building and debugging your applications, see the following resource: • The Visual Studio .NET Help documentation. Search by using the phrases **Default and** Custom **Builds** and **Using the Debugger**.

msdn® training

Module 6: Printing and Reporting in Windows Forms Applications

Contents

Microsoft®

Overview

- Printing from a Windows Forms Application
- Using the Print Preview, Page Setup, and Print Dialogs
- Constructing Print Document Content by Using GDI+
- Creating Reports by Using Crystal Reports

Introduction

Any application developed for the Microsoft® Windows® operating system that deals with data should include printing and reporting features for the users. This module explores how to implement printing in a Windows Forms application and how to create reports in a Windows Forms application by using Crystal Reports for Microsoft Visual Studio® .NET.

Objectives

After completing this module, you will be able to:

- Print documents in a Windows Forms application.
- Use the Visual Studio .NET printing dialog boxes in a Windows Forms application.
- Use GDI+ to construct print document content.
- Create and format reports by using Crystal Reports.

Lesson: Printing from a Windows Forms Application

- How Printing Works in a .NET Windows Forms Application
- PrintDocument Object
- PrintPage Event and PrintPageEventArgs
- How to Enable Printing in a Windows Forms Application
- Practice: Adding Print Support to a Windows Forms Application

Introduction

This lesson describes how to add basic print support to a Windows Forms application. Most applications developed for Windows include the ability to print some information. Visual Studio .NET provides components that simplify the print process in your Windows Forms application and provides you with control throughout the entire print process.

Lesson objectives

After completing this lesson, you will be able to:

- Add a **PrintDocument** control to a form and create a **PrintPage** event handler.
- Add programming logic to a **PrintPage** event procedure to construct page content.
- Add programming logic to a **PrintPage** event procedure that enables your application to print more than one page of content.

How Printing Works in a .NET Windows Forms Application

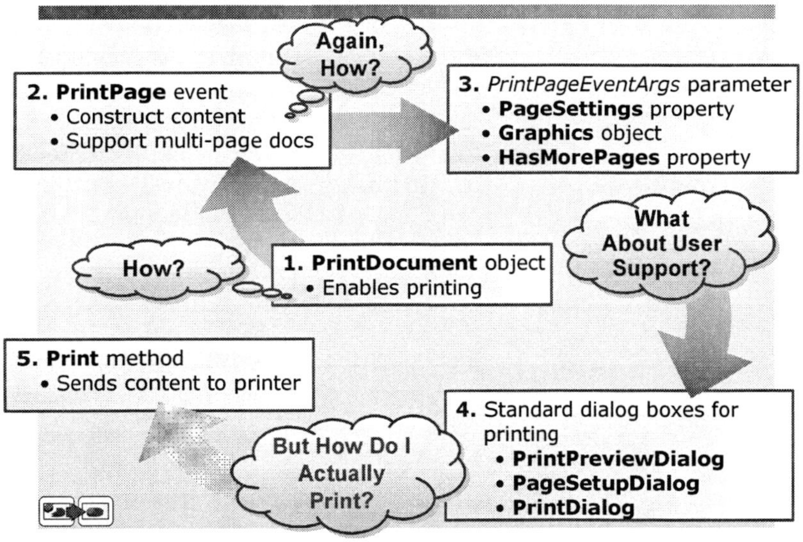

Introduction

Application developers who use Windows Forms will use the **PrintDocument** class to support printing in their .NET Windows Forms applications. However, the **PrintDocument** object is not the only component that you will be using when printing documents in Windows Forms applications.

Print procedure

1. Add the **PrintDocument** object.

   The **PrintDocument** object is central to printing in Windows Forms applications.

2. Create the **PrintPage** Event handler.

   The **PrintDocument** object uses the program logic that you create in the **PrintDocument.PrintPage** event to construct the content of the print document and indicate when additional pages must be generated.

3. Use the *PrintPageEventArgs* parameter.

   The **PrintPage** event uses the *PrintPageEventArgs* parameter that it receives to access and store information about the print document. Applications will generally use the **PageSettings** property to read information about document layout, construct page content by drawing text and graphics on the **Graphics** object, and then indicate when additional pages must be generated by setting the **HasMorePages** property.

Note More information about constructing print content by using the **Graphics** object supplied by the *PrintPageEventArgs* parameter is included in the lesson titled Constructing Print Document Content by Using GDI+ in Module 6, "Printing and Reporting in Windows Forms Applications," in Course 2565A, *Developing Microsoft .NET Applications for Windows (Visual Basic® .NET).*

---

4. Use the standard print dialog boxes available in Visual Studio .NET.

   User support can be added by using the three standard dialog boxes that are provided in the Design view Toolbox. The standard dialog boxes provide an easy way of adding powerful end user support in your applications with a familiar user interface (UI).

Note More information about **PrintPreviewDialog**, **PageSetupDialog**, and **PrintDialog** is included in the lesson titled Using the Print Preview, Page Setup, and Print Dialogs in Module 6, "Printing and Reporting in Windows Forms Applications," in Course 2565A, *Developing Microsoft .NET Applications for Windows (Visual Basic .NET)*.

---

5. Print the document by using the **Print** method.

   The **PrintDocument.Print** method is used to enable actual document printing.

PrintDocument Object

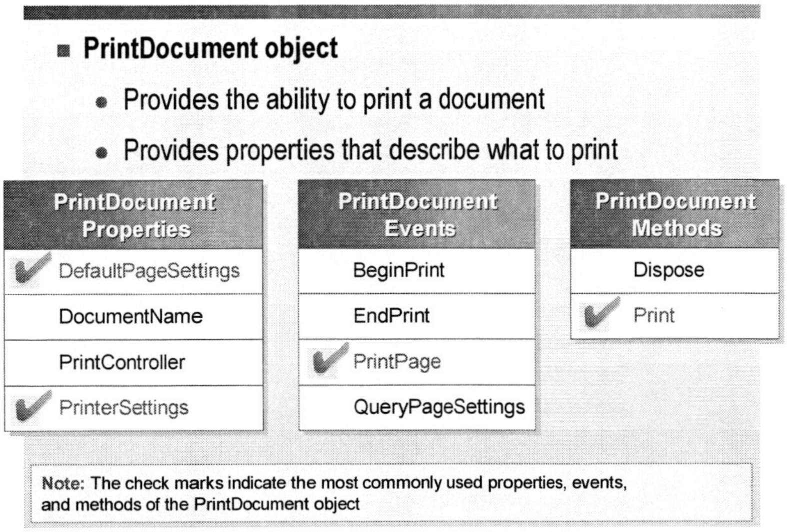

Introduction

The **PrintDocument** object is central to printing in Windows Forms applications. You use **PrintDocument** to set properties that specify what to print and to provide the properties, events, and methods that are required to print documents. The **PrintDocument** object is generally be added to a Form from the Toolbox at design time, but an instance of the **PrintDocument** class can be declared at run time as well.

PrintDocument properties

The **DefaultPageSettings** property gets or sets page settings that are used as defaults for all pages to be printed.

The **PrinterSettings** property can be used to get or set the printer that prints the document, modify the properties of the selected printer, and modify settings associated with the print job such as the number of copies that will be printed.

The following table describes some additional properties of the **PrintDocument** object that you can use to customize a print job.

Property	Description
DocumentName	Gets or sets the document name to display while printing the document.
PrintController	Gets or sets the print controller that guides the printing process.

For more information and a complete list of the properties of the **PrintDocument** object, in the Visual Studio .NET Help documentation, search by using the phrase **PrintDocument members**.

PrintDocument events

The **PrintPage** event is used to generate the content of the print document, and it is in the **PrintPage** event handler that you must include your own code to indicate when the document has additional pages of content to print.

The following table describes some additional events of the **PrintDocument** object that enable you to print output.

Event	Description
BeginPrint	Occurs when the **Print** method is called and before the first page of the document prints. One example of when to use **BeginPrint** is when you want to notify the user how many pages there are in a print job.
EndPrint	Occurs when the last page of the document has printed. One example of when **EndPrint** can be used is when you want to signal the user that the print job has completed.
QueryPageSettings	Occurs immediately before each **PrintPage** event. You can use **QueryPageSettings** when you want to use different **PageSettings** for one or more pages of a print document.

For more information and a complete list of the events of the **PrintDocument** object, in the Visual Studio .NET Help documentation, search by using the phrase **PrintDocument members**.

PrintDocument methods

After you have established the printer and default page settings and constructed the contents of the print document, you will use the **Print** method to start the print process. The **Print** method sends the contents of the print document to the printer by passing the print device a **Graphics** object that acts as a container for the content. The **Graphics** object is discussed in more detail in the PrintPage Event and PrintPageEventArgs topic in this module.

The **Dispose** method releases the resources used by the PrintDocument component.

For more information and a complete list of the methods of the **PrintDocument** object, in the Visual Studio .NET Help documentation, search by using the phrase **PrintDocument members**.

PrintPage Event and PrintPageEventArgs

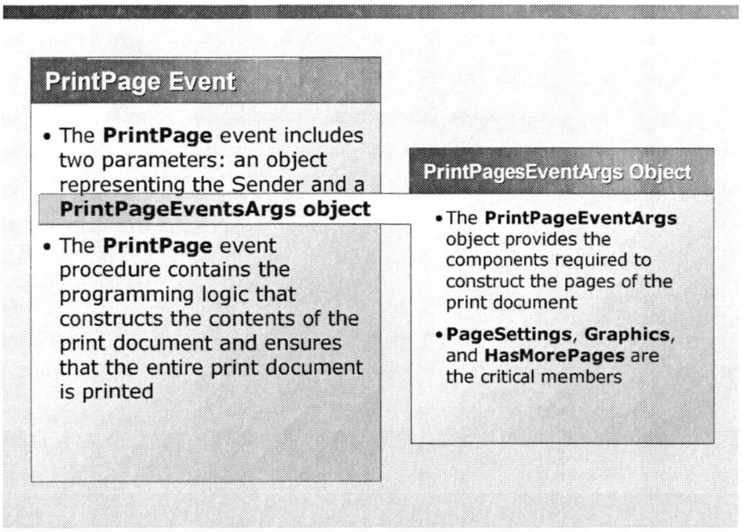

Introduction

A **PrintDocument.PrintPage** event occurs for every page of a print document that is displayed or printed. You create a subroutine to handle the **PrintPage** event and populate it with the code used to construct the content of the print document.

PrintPage event procedure

The event procedure that handles the **PrintDocument.PrintPage** event has two parameters: the object representing the sender that fired the event (**PrintDocument**) and the **PrintPageEventArgs** object. The subroutine that you create to handle the **PrintPage** event contains the programming logic required to construct the print document (using the components supplied by the **PrintPageEventArgs** object). The **PrintPage** event procedure also contains the programming logic that you develop to indicate when an additional page of content must be generated.

Members of the *PrintPageEventArgs* parameter

The *PrintPageEventArgs* parameter contains all the data required to construct a page of the print document. The **PrintPageEventArgs** object has six member components, including the **Graphics** object that is used as the "paper" on which the contents of a page are drawn. The other two most critical members are the **HasMorePages** property that you must set to **True** when there are more pages to print, and the **PageSettings** property that can be used to read the page setting values for the current page.

The other three properties of the *PrintPageEventArgs* parameter are **Cancel**, **MarginBounds** and **PrintBounds**. You can use the **Cancel** property to stop the construction of document pages before the end of the print document and the **PagesBounds** and **MarginBounds** properties to return the size of the current page and the size of the page inside the margins, respectively (both of which can be determined by using the **PageSettings** property).

PrintPageEventArgs. PageSettings

The **PageSettings** property supplied by the *PrintPageEventArgs* parameter is a read-only property that is used to get page settings for the current page. **PageSettings** includes **Bounds** and **Margins** members that supply the same information found in the **PageBounds** and **MarginBounds** properties.

Note To modify page settings, you must handle the **QueryPageSettings** event of the **PrintDocument** object.

The following example demonstrates how to use the **PageSettings** and **MarginBounds** properties inside a **PrintPage** event handler to determine the location of the left margin and the number of text lines that will fit on a page for a given font.

```
...
LeftMargin = e.PageSettings.Margins.Left
LinesPP = e.MarginBounds.Height/myFont.GetHeight(e.Graphics)
...
```

PrintPageEventArgs. Graphics

The **Graphics** object supplied by the *PrintPageEventArgs* parameter acts as a canvas for each page of a print document. You use the GDI+ drawing methods of the **Graphics** object to draw the text and graphics contents of the page. For example, to draw a text string inside a **PrintPage** event handler, you could use the **Graphics.DrawString** method as follows:

```
...
e.Graphics.DrawString(textString, myFont, myBrush, X, Y)
...
```

Note More information about constructing print content by using the **Graphics** object supplied by the *PrintPageEventArgs* parameter is included in the lesson titled Constructing Print Document Content by Using GDI+ in Module 6, "Printing and Reporting in Windows Forms Applications," in Course 2565A, *Developing Microsoft .NET Applications for Windows (Visual Basic .NET).*

PrintPageEventsArgs.HasMorePages

The **HasMorePages** property supplied by the *PrintPageEventArgs* parameter is a Boolean value that is **False** by default. You must manually set the value of the **HasMorePages** property to **True** to indicate that an additional page should be printed. The following example demonstrates how to set the **HasMorePages** property to **True** when the next line of text would occur below the bottom margin on the page.

```
...
  While CurrentLine < LinesPerPage
      textLine = StreamToPrint.ReadLine()
      If textLine Is Nothing Then Exit While
      <draw textLine and increment CurrentLine>
  End While

  If Not (textLine Is Nothing) Then
      e.HasMorePages = True
  Else
      e.HasMorePages = False
  End If
...
```

How to Enable Printing in a Windows Forms Application

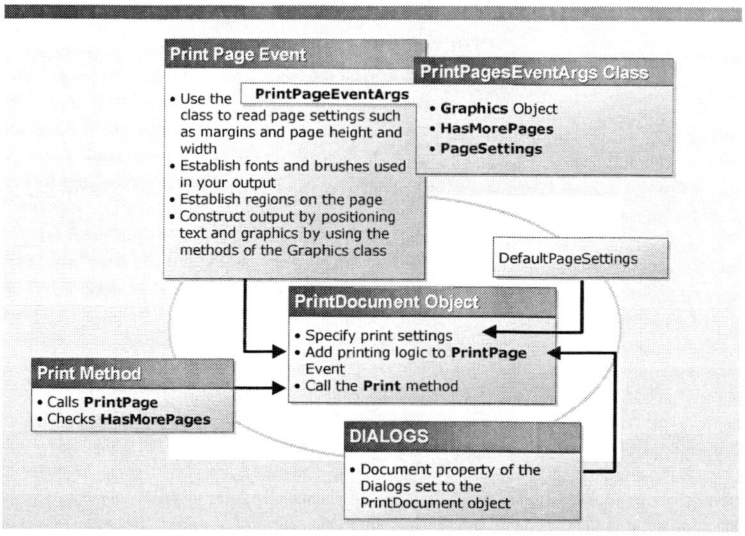

Introduction

To print from a Windows Form application, you will use a **PrintDocument** object to define the printer and characteristics of the print job, add programming logic to the **PrintPage** event, provide your users with run-time support (using the standard dialog boxes provided in Visual Studio .NET), and then call the **Print** method.

Procedure: Enabling printing in a Windows Forms application

To print a text document from a Windows Form application, you perform the following procedure:

1. Add an instance of the **PrintDocument** class to your application and create a **PrintPage** event procedure.

   To add a **PrintDocument** control to a Form, open the Toolbox, and then double-click **PrintDocument**. To create a **PrintPage** subroutine, open the Form in the Code Editor, click **PrintDocument1** in the **Class Name** list, and then click **PrintPage** in the **Method Name** list.

2. Begin adding programming logic to the **PrintDocument1_PrintPage** subroutine to construct the content of the print document.

   You can use the **PageSettings** property to define text and graphics regions on the page. A simple example is assigning the value of PageSettings.Margins.Left to a variable that will be used to position text on the left side of the page. You must use the GDI+ drawing methods of the **PrintPageEventArgs.Graphics** object to construct the contents of the print document page.

3. Add support for previewing your print document so that you can test the code that you developed up to this point. One simple way to preview your print document is to add a **PrintPreviewControl** to your Form from the Toolbox.

4. Add additional programming logic to the **PrintDocument1_PrintPage** subroutine that uses the **HasMorePages** property to indicate whether or not more pages must be printed. The manner in which you determine whether **HasMorePages** should be set to **True** depends on how your print document is being constructed.

Practice: Adding Print Support to a Windows Forms Application

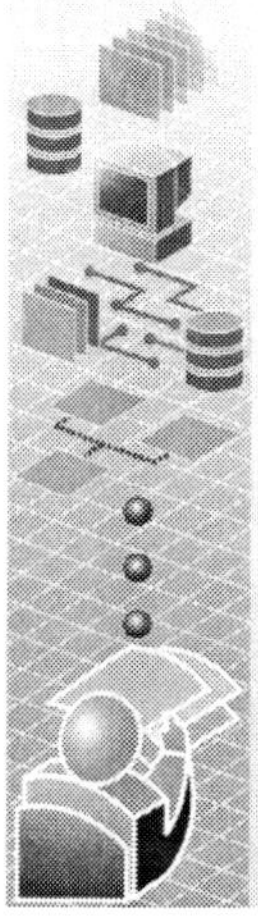

In this practice, you will

- Add a **PrintDocument** control to a project
- Create a **PrintPage** event procedure and develop code to construct the contents of a print document
- Set the value of the **HasMorePages** property to indicate when more pages should be printed

Begin reviewing the objectives for this practice activity

10 min

Introduction

In this practice, you will add print support to a Windows Forms application. The practice involves adding a **PrintDocument** control to a project, creating a subroutine to handle the **PrintPage** event, adding programming logic to the PrintPage subroutine, and using the **HasMorePages** property. You will see some questions in between some steps. Try and answer the question before you move to the next step.

Instructions

► **Open the practice project**

1. Use Windows Explorer to browse to *install_folder*\Practices\Mod06\Mod06_01\Starter.

Note If you performed a default installation of the course files, *install_folder* corresponds to C:\Program Files\Msdntrain\2565.

2. Double-click the PrintProcess.sln solution file to open the project.

► Add the PrintDocument control to your application

1. In Solution Explorer, click **Form1.vb**, and then click the **View Designer** icon.
2. In the **Toolbox**, scroll down until you see the **PrintDocument** control, and then double-click **PrintDocument**.
3. What functionality does the **PrintDocument** class provide to your application?

____

____

____

____

► Create a custom PrintPage subroutine

1. In Solution Explorer, click **Form1.vb**, and then click the **View Code** icon.
2. In the **Class Name** list, click **PrintDocument1**.
3. In the **Method Name** list, click **PrintPage**.
4. Change the name of the subroutine that handles the PrintDocument.PrintPage event from **PrintDocument1_PrintPage** to **MyPrintPage**.
5. What is the purpose of the **PrintDocument.PrintPage** event?

____

____

____

____

6. Add the following code statements to the **MyPrintPage** subroutine:

```
e.Graghics.Drawstring("Page " & currentPage.ToString & _
" text will go here.", myFont, myBrush, X, Y)

If currentPage < totalPages Then
   currentPage += 1
End If
```

7. Press F5, and then click **Print Preview**.
8. Close the **PrintPreviewDialog** dialog box.
9. Use the **NumericUpDown** control to add a second page to your print document, and then preview your document again.
10. Why doesn't your application display more than one page?

____

____

____

11. Close the PrintProcess application.

► Create a print loop to ensure that all of the document pages are printed

1. Modify the contents of the **If-Then-Else** statement near the bottom of your **MyPrintPage** subroutine so that it appears as follows:

```
If currentPage < totalPages Then
   currentPage += 1
   e.HasMorePages = True
Else
   e.HasMorePages = False
End If
```

2. Start the PrintProcess application.
3. Use the **NumericUpDown** control to add a second page to your document, and then preview your print document again. You should now be able to see both pages of your print document.

► Close your application and Visual Studio .NET

If time permits, use the two buttons at the bottom of Form1 to display some additional information that is available through the PrintDocument object, and then examine the underlying code.

1. Save the PrintProcess application.
2. Close the PrintProcess application.
3. Close Visual Studio .NET

Lesson: Using the Print Preview, Page Setup, and Print Dialogs

- How to Use the PrintPreviewDialog Control
- Practice: Using the PrintPreviewDialog Control
- How to Use the PageSetupDialog Control
- Practice: Using the PageSetupDialog Control
- How to Use the PrintDialog Control
- Practice: Using the PrintDialog Control

Introduction

Visual Studio .NET includes three preconfigured dialog boxes—**PrintPreviewDialog**, **PageSetupDialog**, and **PrintDialog**—that enable your application user to preview a print document, specify page settings, and establish the printer and print job settings from a Windows Forms application. Using these preconfigured dialog boxes in a Windows Forms application not only eases development, but also provides a clean, efficient, and familiar interface to the end users. This lesson explains how to use the three print dialog boxes in a Windows Forms application.

Lesson objectives

After completing this lesson, you will be able to:

- Display a print preview of the print document by using the **PrintPreviewDialog** and **PrintPreviewControl** controls.
- Use a **PrintPreviewControl** control to preview your print document.
- Specify page settings for a document by using the **PageSetupDialog** control.
- Select a printer and settings for the print job by using the **PrintDialog** control.

How to Use the PrintPreviewDialog Control

PrintPreviewDialog

- **Use PrintPreviewDialog to display how a document will appear when printed**
- **To display a print preview of a document**
  1. Create an instance of the PrintPreviewDialog component
  2. Set the Document property to the **PrintDocument** object
  3. Configure the desired display settings for the PrintPreviewDialog and the included **PrintPreviewControl**
  4. Display the dialog by using the **ShowDialog** method

CodeExample

Introduction

A common feature of applications is the ability to display a preview of the document to be printed. In Windows Forms applications, this feature is provided by using the **PrintPreviewDialog** control. The **PrintPreviewDialog** contains a **PrintPreviewControl** as well as controls for printing, zooming, displaying one or multiple pages, and closing the dialog box. The standard **PrintPreviewDialog** provides the user with a familiar tool for previewing documents, but you can develop your own custom preview form by using the same **PrintPreviewControl** used by the **PrintPreviewDialog** when your application or users require something different.

Procedure

To use the **PrintPreviewDialog** to display a print preview of a document:

1. Add a **PrintPreviewDialog** control to your project by using the Toolbox, or create a **PrintPreviewDialog** at run time by using code such as this:

```
Dim previewDialog As PrintPreviewDialog
previewDialog = New PrintPreviewDialog()
```

2. Set the **Document** property of the **PrintPreviewDialog** control to the PrintDocument component.

   After you have created a **PrintPreviewDialog** object, you must set its **Document** property to the **PrintDocument** object of your print document. You can set the **Document** property in the Properties window of the **PrintPreviewDialog** control at design-time or with the following code at run time:

```
previewDialog.Document = PrintDocument1
```

3. Properties of the **PrintPreviewDialog**, and the included **PrintPreviewControl**, can be used to establish display settings showing the dialog box:

```
previewDialog.WindowState = FormWindowState.Maximized
previewDialog.PrintPreviewControl.StartPage = 0
previewDialog.PrintPreviewControl.Zoom = 1.0
```

4. Display the **PrintPreviewDialog** by using the **ShowDialog** method.

   Like all other dialog boxes, you can use the **ShowDialog** method to display the **PrintPreview** dialog box at run time:

```
previewDialog.ShowDialog()
```

Example

The following code shows an example of how to use the **PrintPreviewDialog** control to display a print preview of a document. The example assumes that a **PrintPreviewDialog** control and a **PrintDocument** control were added to a Form and that the **PrintPreview** subroutine is called from an event handler.

```
Private Sub PrintPreview()
 ' ensure that the first page of the print document is shown
 PrintPreviewDialog1.PrintPreviewControl.StartPage = 0

 ' display the document two pages at a time
 PrintPreviewDialog1.PrintPreviewControl.Columns = 2

 ' maximize the size of the dialog box on the display screen
 PrintPreviewDialog1.WindowState = FormWindowState.Maximized

 ' display the contents of the appropriate print document
 PrintPreviewDialog1.Document = PrintDocument1
 PrintPreviewDialog1.ShowDialog

End Sub
```

PrintPreviewControl

The **PrintPreviewControl** is supplied in the Toolbox as a separate control that you can use to preview a print document. You use the **PrintPreviewControl** control when you want to define your own print-preview user interface. It has no buttons or other user interface elements.

Some of the properties of the **PrintPreviewControl** control include **Zoom**, **Columns**, **Rows**, and **StartPage**. These properties are available whether you are using the **PrintPreviewControl** separately or as part of the **PrintPreviewDialog**.

```
PrintPreviewControl.Columns = 2
PrintPreviewDialog.PrintPreviewControl.Columns = 2
```

For more information about **PrintPreviewControl**, in the Visual Studio .NET Help, search by using the phrase **PrintPreviewControl**.

Practice: Using the PrintPreviewDialog Control

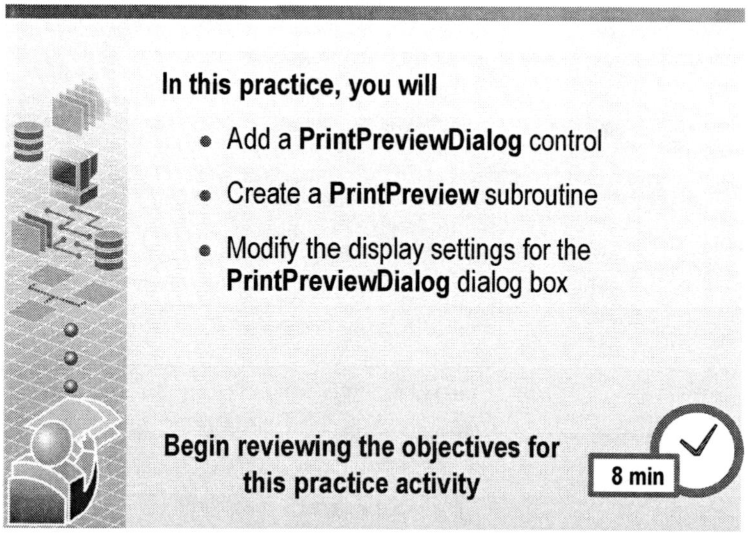

Introduction

In this practice, you will add a **PrintPreviewDialog** control and program logic to a project so that application users can preview a document before printing it.

Instructions

► **Open the practice project**

1. Use Windows Explorer to browse to *install_folder*\Practices\Mod06\Mod06_02\Starter.
2. Double-click the PrintPreviewDialog.sln solution file to open the project.

► **Add the PrintPreviewDialog control to your application**

1. In Solution Explorer, click **Form1.vb**, and then click **View Designer**.
2. In the Toolbox, scroll down until you see the **PrintPreviewDialog** control, and then double-click **PrintPreviewDialog**.
3. Where does the **PrintPreviewDialog** appear in the Design View window?

____

____

► **Create a PrintPreview subroutine that displays the print document**

1. In Solution Explorer, click **Form1.vb**, and then click **View Code**.
2. On the **View** menu, point to **Show Tasks**, and then click **Comment**.
3. In the Task List, double-click **TODO: create PrintPreview subroutine**.
4. Add the following code statement below the TODO line and press ENTER.

```
Private Sub PrintPreview
```

5. Add the following code statements to the **PrintPreview** subroutine.

```
PrintPreviewDialog1.Document = PrintDocument1
PrintPreviewDialog1.ShowDialog()
```

6. Run the PrintPreviewDialog application, and use the menu or button to display the print document.
7. Is there a way to make the dialog box larger by default?

____

____

8. Close the PrintPreviewDialog application.

► **Modify the display settings for the PrintPreviewDialog dialog box**

1. Add the following code line to the top of the **PrintPreview** subroutine.

```
PrintPreviewDialog1.WindowState = FormWindowState.Maximized
```

2. Run the PrintPreviewDialog application and use the menu or button to display the print document.
3. Change the displayed page number to **page 4**, and then close the dialog box.
4. Reopen the **PrintPreviewDialog**. Notice that the starting page is the page that was displayed when the dialog box was closed.
5. Click **Close**, close the application, and then add the following code lines to the top of the **PrintPreview** subroutine.

```
PrintPreviewDialog1.PrintPreviewControl.StartPage = 0
PrintPreviewDialog1.PrintPreviewControl.Zoom = 1.0
```

6. Run the PrintPreviewDialog application, and use the menu or button to display the print document. Verify that the **Print Preview Dialog** always shows page 1 at 100% when opened.
7. Optional: Open the PrintPreviewDialog, change the page that is being displayed to **page 2**, and then close and reopen the preview dialog box to verify that the initial page displayed is always page 1.
8. Close the dialog box, and then close the application.

If time permits

► **Examine some additional methods for displaying a print document**

1. In Design view, enable the two other buttons on Form1.
2. Start the application, and use each button to display the print document.
3. Close the application, and examine the code used to display the document.
4. When would you want to use a **PrintPreviewControl** rather than a **PrintPreviewDialog** to display a print document?

   ____

   ____

5. Close the solution.

How to Use the PageSetupDialog Control

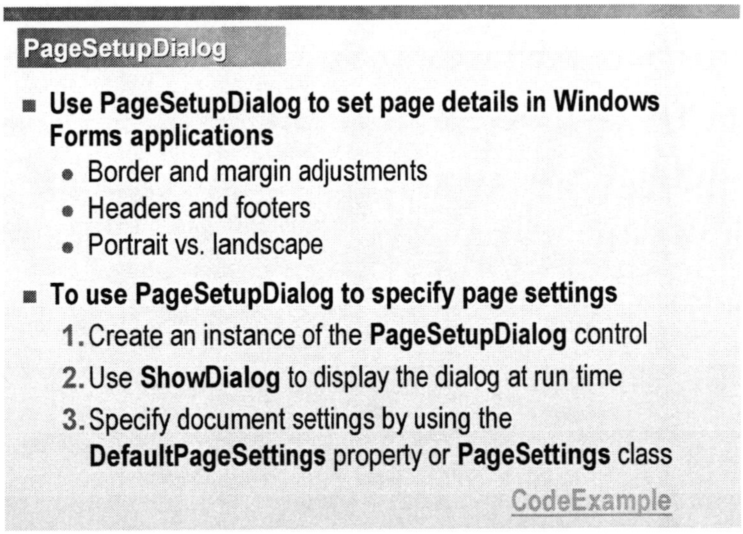

Introduction

The **PageSetupDialog** control is a pre-configured dialog box that you can use to set page layout details for printing in Windows Forms applications. The **PageSetupDialog** control provides an easy solution to specify page settings instead of configuring your own dialog box. With **PageSetupDialog**, you can allow users to set border and margin adjustments, headers and footers, and portrait versus landscape orientation by using a familiar tool.

Procedure: Using the PageSetupDialog

To use **PageSetupDialog** to specify page settings:

1. Create an instance of **PageSetupDialog**.

   The first step in using the **PageSetupDialog** in a Windows Forms application is to add a **PageSetupDialog** control to your form from the Toolbox or create a new instance of the **PageSetupDialog** control in code as shown below.

   ```
   Dim pageDlg As New PageSetupDialog()
   ```

2. Supply **PageSetupDialog** with a **PageSettings** object that can be used to store page settings and used for both the **PrintDocument** object and the **PageSetupDialog**.

   ```
   ...
   pageDlg.PageSettings = MyPageSettings
   ```

3. Use the **ShowDialog** method to display the dialog box at run time.

   To display the dialog box at run time, use the **ShowDialog** method as shown in the following code.

   ```
   pageDlg.ShowDialog
   ```

4. Apply the modified page settings to your **PrintDocument** object.

   To apply the new page settings to your document, use the **DefaultPageSettings** property of the **PrintDocument** object.

   ```
   PrintDocument1.DefaultPageSettings = myPageSettings
   ```

Example

The following code shows an example of how to use the **PageSetupDialog** control.

```
Private Sub PageSetup()

    Try
        Dim pageDialog As New PageSetupDialog()

        If (storedPageSettings Is Nothing) Then
            storedPageSettings = new PageSettings()
        End If

        pageDialog.PageSettings = storedPageSettings
        pageDialog.ShowDialog
    Catch ex As Exception
        MessageBox.Show(ex.Message)
    End Try
    PrintDocument1.DefaultPageSettings = storedPageSettings
End Sub
```

Customize sections of the PageSetup dialog box

The user can enable sections of the **PageSetup** dialog box to manipulate printing, margin, and paper orientation, and size.

Use the **Margins** and **MinMargins** properties to specify margins.

```
PageSetupDialog1.PageSettings.Margins.Top = 200
PageSetupDialog1.PageSettings.Margins.Left = 200
PageSetupDialog1.PageSettings.Margins.Bottom = 100
PageSetupDialog1.PageSettings.Margins.Right = 100

PageSetupDialog1.MinMargins.Top = 85
PageSetupDialog1.MinMargins.Left = 75
PageSetupDialog1.MinMargins.Bottom = 100
PageSetupDialog1.MinMargins.Right = 100
```

Set the **AllowPrinter**, **AllowOrientation**, and **AllowPaper** properties to **True** to allow users to specify these properties.

```
PageSetupDialog1.AllowOrientation = False
PageSetupDialog1.AllowPaper = False
PageSetupDialog1.AllowPrinter = False
```

Practice: Using the PageSetupDialog Control

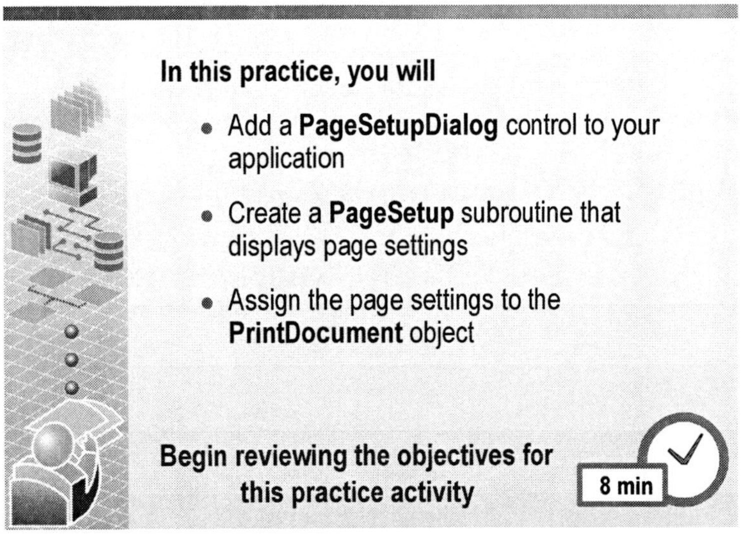

Introduction

In this practice, you will add a **PageSetupDialog** control and program logic to a project so that application users can specify page settings before printing a document.

Instructions

► **Open the practice project**

1. Use Windows Explorer to browse to *install_folder*\Practices\Mod06\Mod06_03\Starter.
2. Double-click the PageSetupDialog.sln solution file to open the project.

► **Add the PageSetupDialog control to your application**

1. In Solution Explorer, click **Form1.vb**, and then click **View Designer**.
2. In the Toolbox, scroll down until you see the **PageSetupDialog** control, and then double-click **PageSetupDialog**.
3. Where does the **PageSetupDialog** control appear in the Design View window?

____

____

► Create a PageSetup subroutine that displays page settings

1. On the **View** menu, point to **Show Tasks**, and then click **Comment**.
2. In the Task List, double-click **TODO: create PageSetup subroutine**.
3. Add the following code statement below the TODO line and then press ENTER.

   ```
   Private Sub PageSetup
   ```
4. Add the following code statement to the **PageSetup** subroutine.

   ```
   PageSetupDialog1.ShowDialog()
   ```
5. Run the PageSetupDialog application, and use the menu or button to display the **Page Setup** dialog box. Why does an error occur?

   ____

   ____

6. Close the application, and then add the following code lines to the top of the PageSetup subroutine.

   ```
   myPageSettings = New PageSettings
   PageSetupDialog1.PageSettings = myPageSettings
   ```
7. Run the PageSetupDialog application and display the **Page Setup** dialog box.
8. Change the Top and Left margins to 0.5 inches, and then click **OK**.
9. Display a preview of the print document. Why didn't the new settings take effect?

   ____

   ____

   ____

10. Close the **PrintPreviewDialog** and the application.

► **Assign the page settings to the PrintDocument object**

1. Add the following code lines to the bottom of the **PageSetup** subroutine.

```
If Not myPageSettings Is Nothing Then
   PrintDocument1.DefaultPageSettings = myPageSettings
End If
```

2. Run the PageSetupDialog application and use the menu or button to display the **PageSetup** dialog box.
3. Change the Top and Left margins to 0.5 inches and then preview the print document.
4. Reopen the **PageSetup** dialog box. Notice that the page settings have been lost.
5. Close the application and then, in the **PageSetup** subroutine, replace the "myPageSettings = New PageSettings()" code line with the following code lines.

```
If myPageSettings Is Nothing Then
   myPageSettings = New PageSettings()
End If
```

6. Run the PageSetupDialog application, and use the **PageSetup** dialog box to modify the document's page settings a couple of times.
7. Close the application.

If time permits

► **Examine some additional members of the PageSetupDialog control**

1. In the Code Editor, examine the code in the **pageSetupButton_Click** subroutine.
2. Remove the comment character from the front of the code lines one section at a time, and view the changes to the **PageSetup** dialog box and **Print Preview** by running the application and opening the two dialog boxes.
3. Close the application and Visual Studio .NET.
4. How could you use these additional members of the **PageSetupDialog** control?

____

____

____

How to Use the PrintDialog Control

PrintDialog

- **Use PrintDialog to specify printer-related settings**
  - Specify printer and print job properties
  - Specify print range and collate settings
- **To use a PrintDialog control for users to select a printer**
  1. Create an instance of the PrintDialog component
  2. Set the **Document** property to the **PrintDocument** object
  3. Capture user input by using the **DialogResult** property and display the Print dialog box

CodeExample

Introduction

Often, users will need to select a printer or set print properties before a particular print job. This can be done by using the **PrintDialog** control.

Procedure

To use the **PrintDialog** control to print a document:

1. Add a **PrintDialog** control to your project by using the Toolbox, or create an instance of the PrintDialog control at run time as follows:

```
Dim printDialog As New PrintDialog()
```

2. Set the **Document** property of the **PrintDialog** object to the PrintDocument component.

   You must set the **Document** property of the **PrintDialog** control to the **PrintDocument** object for document you are printing. Set the **Document** property of the **PrintDialog** control at design time in the Properties window, or at run time by using code as follows:

```
printDialog.Document = PrintDocument1
```

3. Capture the user's response to the **PrintDialog** by using a **DialogResult** object when constructing the code statement that displays the dialog box.

```
...
Dim userResponse As DialogResult = printDialog.ShowDialog
```

Example

The following code uses the **PrintDialog** control to provide the user with an opportunity to modify printer and print job settings before printing the document.

```
Private Sub PrintDoc()
  Dim userResponse As DialogResult

  PrintDialog1.Document = PrintDocument1

  userResponse = PrintDialog1.ShowDialog()

  If (userResponse = DialogResult.OK) Then
      PrintDocument1.Print()

  End If

End Sub
```

Practice: Using the PrintDialog Control

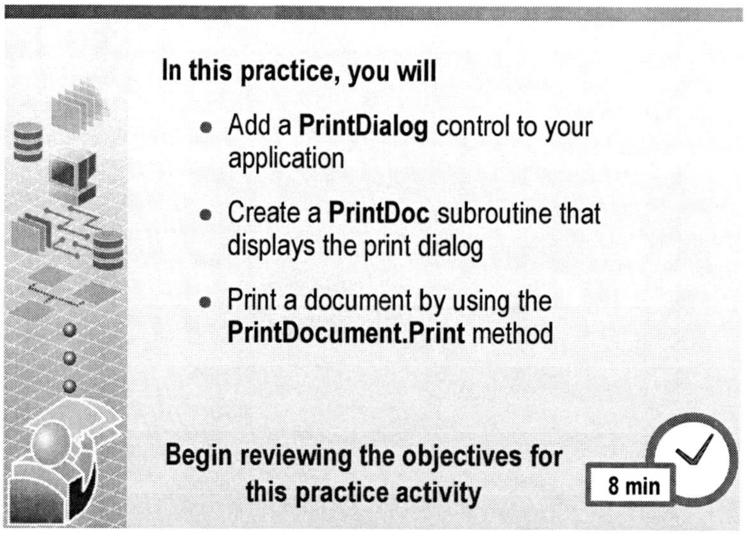

Introduction

In this practice, you will add a **PrintDialog** control and program logic to a project so that application users can specify printer and print job settings before printing a document.

Instructions

► **Open the practice project**

1. Use Windows Explorer to browse to *install_folder*\Practices\Mod06\Mod06_04\Starter.
2. Double-click the PrintDialog.sln solution file to open the project.

► **Add the PrintDialog control to your application**

1. In Solution Explorer, click **Form1.vb**, and then click the **View Designer** icon.
2. In the Toolbox, scroll down until you see the **PrintDialog** control, and then double-click **PrintDialog**.
3. Where does the **PrintDialog** control appear in the Design View window?

____

____

▶ Create a PrintDoc subroutine that displays the Print dialog box

1. Open Form1 in the Code Editor.
2. On the **View** menu, point to **Show Tasks**, and then click **Comment**.
3. In the Task List, double-click **TODO: create PrintDoc subroutine**.
4. Add the following code statement below the TODO line and press ENTER.

```
Private Sub PrintDoc
```

5. Add the following code statement to the **PrintDoc** subroutine.

```
PrintDialog1.ShowDialog()
```

6. Run the PrintDialog application, and click the menu item or button that is used display the **Print** dialog box. Why doesn't the **Print** dialog box open correctly?

   ____

   ____

7. Click **OK**, close the application, and then add the following code line to the top of the PrintDoc subroutine.

```
PrintDialog1.Document = PrintDocument1
```

▶ Print a document by using the PrintDocument.Print method

1. Run the PrintDialog application, and then display the **Print** dialog box.
2. Click **OK**.
3. Why didn't the document print?

   ____

   ____

   ____

   ____

Note For more information about the DialogResult object, see the Visual Studio .NET Help documentation.

---

4. Close the application, and then replace the "PrintDialog1.ShowDialog()" code line in the PrintDoc subroutine with the following lines of code.

```
Dim userResponse As DialogResult = PrintDialog1.ShowDialog
If userResponse = DialogResult.OK Then
   PrintDocument1.Print()
End If
```

5. Run the PrintDialog application, and display the print dialog box.
6. Click **OK**, and then, inside in the **Output File Name** box, type **C:\Text**
7. Click **OK**.

   Notice that a **Printing** dialog box opens automatically, providing the user with an opportunity to cancel the print job.
8. Close the application, and close Visual Studio .NET.

Lesson: Constructing Print Document Content by Using GDI+

- What Is GDI+?
- What Is the Graphics Object?
- How to Create and Use Pens, Brushes, and Fonts
- How to Draw and Measure Text in the PrintPage Event Procedure
- How to Generate Print Content by Using StreamReader
- Demonstration: Constructing Print Document Content by Using GDI+
- Practice: Constructing Print Document Content by Using GDI+

Introduction

In Windows Forms applications, you use GDI+ and the **PrintPage** event of the **PrintDocument** object to construct the contents of a print document. This lesson introduces GDI+ and covers how to use GDI+ methods to draw the text and graphics content of a print document from in a .NET Windows Forms application.

Lesson objectives

After completing this lesson, you will be able to:

- Identify the components of GDI+ and use GDI+ in your applications.
- Use a **Graphics** object as a canvas for creating the contents of a print document.
- Create and use the pens, brushes, and fonts that are required to draw text and graphics objects.
- Use the drawing methods of a **Graphics** object to draw text and two-dimensional (2-D) vector graphics.
- Generate print content by using StreamReader.

What Is GDI+?

- **GDI+ (the new graphics device interface)**
  - Enables applications to generate graphics and formatted text for the video display and the printer
  - Allows application developers to create device-independent applications
- **Three parts of GDI+**
  - 2-D vector graphics
  - Text
  - Images

Introduction

GDI+ is a graphics device interface that you can use to draw two-dimensional vector graphics, text, and bitmapped images. GDI+ expands on the features of GDI by providing new features such as gradient brushes and alpha blending. GDI+ makes graphic programming easier and more flexible. It enables applications to generate graphics and formatted text for the video display and the printer. It also allows application developers to create device-independent applications. For example, you can create a single **PrintPage** subroutine to construct graphical content that can be printed to most graphics printers or be shown as a print preview on a graphics display screen.

Three parts of GDI+

The services of GDI+ fall into three main categories:

- 2-D vector graphics

  Vector graphics involves drawing lines, curves, and figures that are defined by a set of points on a coordinate system. GDI+ provides classes and structures that store information about these objects. For example, the **Rectangle** object stores information about location and size of a rectangle and the **Graphics** class has methods for drawing lines, curves, and other shapes.

- Text

  GDI+ allows you to draw text in a variety of fonts, sizes, and styles.

- Images

  Certain graphics cannot be displayed as 2-D vector graphics and must be displayed as bitmaps. GDI+ provides the **Bitmap** class for displaying, manipulating, and saving bitmaps.

  For more information about bitmaps, see Appendix A, "Using Filled Shapes and Images," in the student workbook.

What Is the Graphics Object?

- **Graphics Object:**
  - Provides the drawing surface on which content is placed
  - Provides methods for drawing text and graphics at specified locations
  - Provides various tools for modifying its contents

```
Dim myGraphic as Graphics

' draw lines or outlined shapes using a Pen
myGraphic.DrawLine(myPen,X1,Y1,X2,Y2)

' draw filled shapes using a Brush
myGraphic.FillRectangle(myBrush,X1,Y1,X2,Y2)

' draw text using a Font and a Brush
myGraphic.DrawString(myText,myFont,myBrush,X1,Y1)
```

Introduction

To draw the text, lines, and shapes that make up the content of a print document, you must use a **Graphics** object.

Role of graphics object in GDI+

The **Graphics** object is central to GDI+ and the construction of print document content. It provides the drawing surface for the GDI+ drawing methods.

To construct print document content with GDI+:

- Set the properties of the **Graphics** object.
- Call the methods of the **Graphics** object to draw text, lines, and shapes.

Graphics object methods

The **Graphics** object provides an extensive assortment of methods that can be used to draw text, lines, and shapes. There are also methods for scaling, transforming, and measuring the contents that have or will be drawn on its surface. Some of the most common methods are listed in the following table.

Method	Description
Clear	Clears the entire drawing surface and fills it with the specified background color.
DrawLine	Draws a line connecting the two points specified by coordinate pairs.
DrawRectangle	Draws a rectangle specified by a coordinate pair, a width, and a height.
DrawString	Draws the specified text string at the specified location with the specified **Brush** and **Font** objects.
FillRectangle	Fills the interior of a rectangle.
MeasureString	Measures the specified string when drawn with the specified font and formatted with the specified format.

Example

The following code examples show how to draw objects by using the **Graphics** object provided by the *PrintPageEventArgs* parameter of the **PrintDocument.PrintPage** event.

```
'Create a graphics object
Dim myGraphic as Graphics

' draw lines or outlined shapes using a Pen
myGraphic.DrawLine(myPen,X1,Y1,X2,Y2)
myGraphic.DrawRectangle(myPen, X1, Y1, X2, Y2)

' draw filled shapes using a Brush
myGraphic.FillRectangle(myBrush,X1,Y1,X2,Y2)

' draw text using a Font and a Brush
myGraphic.DrawString(myText, myFont, myBrush, X1, Y1)

' measure text width on the Graphics object using a Font
textWidth = myGraphic.MeasureString(myText, myFont).Width
```

How to Create and Use Pens, Brushes, and Fonts

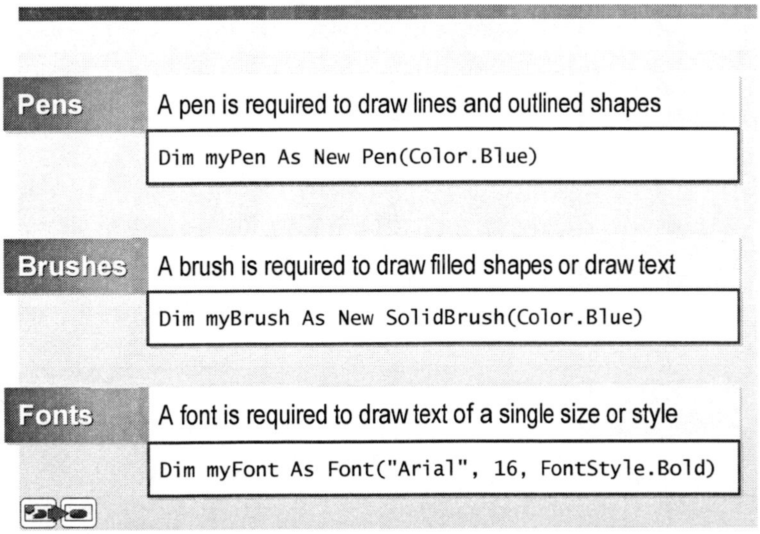

Introduction

You use **Pen**, **Brush**, and **Font** objects to construct 2-D vector graphics, text, and bitmap images with GDI+.

Procedure: Creating pens

A pen is required to draw lines, curves, and outlined shapes. To create a new pen, you must specify a color. You also have the option to specify values for the width and line style properties:

1. Create a new pen.

   The following code examples demonstrate creating pens by using different syntax.

   ```
   Dim myBluePen As New Pen(Color.Blue)
   Dim myRedPen as Pen = New Pen(Color.Red)
   Dim myBlackPen As Pen = Pens.Black
   ```

2. Apply width and style properties.

   The **Width** property for a **Pen** is of type **Integer** and has a default value of **1** (units are established by the **Graphics** object). The **DashStyle** property is also of type **Integer**, but your code will be easier to read if you use the **DashStyle** enumeration provided by the **Drawing2D** namespace. Although the **Width** property can be set when you instantiate a new **Pen**, the line style must be applied after the **Pen** has been created. The following code examples demonstrate creating pens with various width and style properties. Defaults are 1 for Width and Solid for Style.

   ```
   Dim myWideRedPen as Pen = New Pen(Color.Red, 4)
   Dim myDashedPen As New Pen(Color.Black)
   myDashedPen.DashStyle = Drawing2D.DashStyle.Dash
   myDashedPen.DashCap = Drawing2D.DashCap.Round
   ```

Procedure: Creating brushes

Brush objects are required for drawing text and filled shapes. You can create brushes that produce Solid, Hatched, Textured, and Gradient fills.

- Create a new **Brush**.

  The following code examples demonstrate creating a solid blue brush and a linear gradient brush by using white and light blue blended horizontally.

```
Dim myBrush As New SolidBrush(Color.Blue)
Dim myGradientBrush as New LinearGradientBrush( _
   myRectangle As New Rectangle(0,0,100,100), _
   Color.White, _
   Color.LightBlue, _
   LinearGradientMode.Horizontal)
```

For more information about Hatched, Textured, and Gradient see "Brushes and Filled Shapes" in the .NET Framework software development kit (SDK) and see Appendix A, "Using Filled Shapes and Images," in the student workbook.

Procedure: Creating fonts

Before you can draw text with GDI+, you must construct a **Font** object. The declaration statement for a **Font** object can include parameters for the **FontFamily** (such as Arial), **Size**, **Style**, and the **GraphicsUnits** used by the **Size** parameter. The **FontFamily** and **Size** properties are required when creating a new font.

- Create a new **Font** object.

  The following code example creates an Arial font of size 10 and a Lucida font with a style setting of bold and a size of 12 millimeters.

```
Dim fontSmall As Font = New Font("Arial", 10)
Dim fontLarge As Font
fontLarge = New Font("Lucida", 12, _
FontStyle.Bold, GraphicsUnit.Millimeters)
```

How to Draw and Measure Text in the PrintPage Event Procedure

- **To draw text**
  1. Calculate the location for the text
  2. Select the Font and Brush that you want to use for this text
  3. Call the **Graphics.DrawString** method

```
e.Graphics.DrawString(myText, myFont, myBrush, X1, Y1)
```

- **To measure text**

```
textWidth = e.Graphics.MeasureString(myText,
   myFont).Width
textHeight = e.Graphics.MeasureString(myText,
   myFont).Height
```

Introduction

GDI+ enables you to draw and measure text.

You can draw text by using the **DrawString** method of the **Graphics** object. To draw text, you must have a **Brush** object and a **Font** object.

If you need to determine the width or height of text as it will be drawn on the page of a print document or another **Graphics** object, you can use the **MeasureString** method of the **Graphics** object. For example, you must know the width and length of a string as it appears on the page to center the string in a region of the page. **MeasureString** can also be used to determine how many lines of text will fit on a page, whether a line of text will fit between the margins, and to right-align text.

Procedure: Drawing text

To construct text for your print document in the **PrintPage** event procedure:

1. Calculate the location on the page where the text will be placed.
2. Select the **Font** and **Brush** that you want to use for this text.

   You can either use **Fonts** and **Brushes** that you already created or create new ones. For more information about creating Fonts and Brushes, see the topic How to Create and Use Pens, Brushes, and Fonts in this lesson.
3. Call the **DrawString** method.

   To construct the text, call the **DrawString** method of the **Graphics** object.

```
e.Graphics.DrawString(myText, myFont, myBrush, X1, Y1)
```

Procedure: Measuring text

- To measure text, add the code as shown to the **PrintPage** event handler.

  The following code measures the width and height of the specified string.

```
textWidth = e.Graphics.MeasureString(myText, myFont).Width
textHeight = e.Graphics.MeasureString(myText,
myFont).Height
```

  Another option for getting the height of your text is to use the **GetHeight** method for **Font** and pass it the **Graphics** object as follows.

```
textHeight = myFont.GetHeight(e.Graphics)
```

How to Generate Print Content by Using StreamReader

Use StreamReader to read lines of information from a standard text file

```
Private Sub btnPrintPreviewControl_Click(ByVal
   sender As System.Object, ByVal e As _
   System.EventArgs) Handles _
   btnPrintPreviewControl.Click
         Try
             StreamToPrint = New
   StreamReader("PrintMe.Txt")
             Try
                 PrintPreviewControl()

             Finally
                 StreamToPrint.Close()

             End Try
```

Introduction

In addition to using GDI+ to generate print content, you can also use StreamReader as an input provider. You use StreamReader to read lines of information from a standard text file.

Example

The following example demonstrates how to use StreamReader with a **PrintPreviewControl**. When the **Print Preview** button is clicked, the stream of text is read from the file PrintMe.txt.

```
Private Sub btnPrintPreviewControl_Click(ByVal sender As _
System.Object, ByVal e As System.EventArgs) Handles _
btnPrintPreviewControl.Click
  Try
      streamToPrint = New StreamReader("PrintMe.Txt")
      Try
          PrintPreview()
      Finally
          streamToPrint.Close()
      End Try
  Catch Ex As Exception
      MessageBox.Show(Ex.Message)
  End Try
```

The following code shows that if no text is being read from StreamReader, the printing exits, or else it checks if there are more pages to print.

```
' inside the PrintPage event handler
While currentLine < linesPerPage
  ' read a line of text from the StreamReader object
  textLine = streamToPrint.ReadLine()

  If textLine Is Nothing Then Exit While

  ' position text, draw text, increment currentLine

End While

'If more lines exist in the file, print another page.
If Not (textLine Is Nothing) Then
  e.HasMorePages = True

Else
  e.HasMorePages = False

End If
```

Demonstration: Constructing Print Document Content by Using GDI+

Introduction

In this demonstration, you will see how to create print document content by using GDI+.

Instructions

► **Open the projects**

1. Start two instances of Visual Studio .NET.
2. Open the PurchaseOrderApplication solution file in one instance of Visual Studio .NET and the PrintingForm2565Class solution file in the other. The solution files can be found under *install_folder*\Sampapps, in the folders named OrderApplication and PrintingForm2565Class.

► **Examine and modify code in the PrintingForm2565Class project**

1. Open PrintingForm2565Class.vb in the Code Editor.
2. Mention that this class inherits from the **PrintDocument** class.
3. Describe the subroutines that are used to: define the regions of the form, draw the text, and 2-D vector objects that make up the blank form, receive text content from the host application, and fill in the content on the form.
4. Move down to the **PrintingEmptyForm2565** subroutine, and then show the code that is used to create the fonts and brushes for this document.
5. Scroll down and show some of the GDI+ code statements that draw the lines and filled shapes.
6. Scroll down further and show the process required to center the purchase item labels on the header row of the purchase item table.
7. Scroll back up to the top of this subroutine and change some of the pen and brush properties.
8. Rebuild the class.

► Examine and run the PurchaseOrderApplication project

1. Open MainForm.vb in the Code Editor.
2. Describe the subroutines that are used to: read content from the form, pass form content to the printing class, preview the print document, modify page settings, and print the document.
3. In Solution Explorer, remove the reference to the **PrintingForm2565Class** from the **PurchaseOrderApplication** project, and then add a reference to the newly built class by browsing to the bin folder of the PrintingForm2565Class folder and opening the PrintingFomr2565Class.dll file.
4. Rebuild the PurchaseOrderApplication solution, and then run the application.
5. Open the **Print Preview** dialog box to show your modifications.

Practice: Constructing Print Document Content by Using GDI+

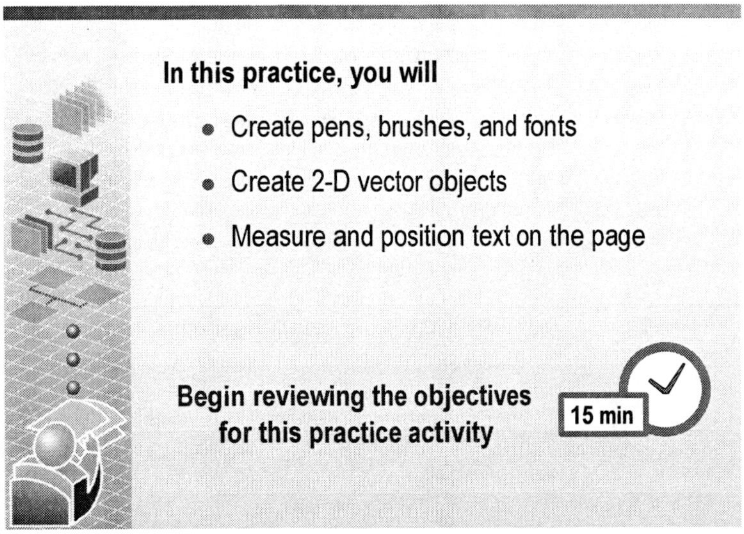

Introduction

In this practice, you will construct print document content by using 2-D vectors and text in GDI+.

Instructions

► **Open the practice project**

1. Use Windows Explorer to browse *install_folder*\Practices\Mod06\Mod06_05\Starter.
2. Double-click the PrintPageCode.sln solution file to open the project.

► **Create pens, brushes, and fonts**

1. Open Form1 in the Code Editor.
2. On the **View** menu, point to **Show Tasks**, and then click **Comment**.
3. In the Task List, double-click **TODO: create pens**.
4. Add the following code statements below the TODO line.

```
Dim penWideRed As Pen = New Pen(Color.Red, 10)
Dim penDashedBlack As Pen = New Pen(Color.Black, 6)
penDashedBlack.DashStyle = DashStyle.Dash
penDashedBlack.DashCap = DashCap.Round
```

5. In the Task List, double-click **TODO: create brushes**.
6. Add the following code statements below the TODO line.

```
Dim brushBlue As Brush = New SolidBrush(Color.Blue)
Dim brushBlack As Brush = Brushes.Black
```

7. In the Task List, double-click **TODO: create fonts**.

8. Add the following code statements below the TODO line.

```
Dim fontMedium As Font = New Font("Arial", 14)
Dim fontLargeBold As Font
fontLargeBold = New Font("Arial", 36, FontStyle.Bold)
```

9. Do any of the code statements that you entered require a reference to the **Drawing2D** namespace?

____

____

► Create 2-D vector objects

1. In the Task List, double-click **TODO: draw outline shapes**.
2. Add the following code statements below the TODO line.

```
e.Graphics.DrawLine(penWideRed, hPos1, yPos1, hPos2, yPos2)
e.Graphics.DrawRectangle(penDashedBlack, _
                  hPos1, _
                  vPos1, _
                  rectWidth, _
                  rectHeight)
```

3. In the Task List, double-click **TODO: draw filled shapes**.
4. Add the following code statements below the TODO line.

```
Dim fillRectangle As Rectangle
fillRectangle = New Rectangle( _
                   lgRectangle.Left, _
                   lgRectangle.Bottom, _
                   lgRectangle.Width, _
                   lgRectangle.Height)
e.Graphics.FillRectangle(brushBlue, fillRectangle)
```

▶ Measure and position text on the page

1. In the Task List, double-click **TODO: draw centered text**.
2. Add the following code statements below the TODO line.

```
textWidth = e.Graphics.MeasureString(centeredText, _
                        fontMedium).Width
textHeight = fontMedium.GetHeight(e.Graphics)
hPos = rectText.Left + (rectText.Width - textWidth) / 2
vPos = rectText.Top + (rectText.Height - textHeight) / 2
e.Graphics.DrawRectangle(Pens.Black, rectText)
e.Graphics.DrawString(stringMyText, _
                        fontLargeBold, _
                        brushBlack, _
                        poshorizontal, _
                        posVertical)
```

3. Run your application, and click **Print Preview** to view the GDI+ output.
4. Close the preview form, click **Draw gradient text**, and then click **Print Preview**.
5. How would you draw right-aligned text?

____

____

____

If time permits, examine the code used to create the gradient filled text.

6. Save your application, and then close Visual Studio .NET.

Lesson: Creating Reports by Using Crystal Reports

- Crystal Reports
- How to Create and Format a Report by Using Crystal Reports
- How to View a Report by Using Crystal Report Viewer
- How to Add DataSets to a Report
- Practice: Creating and Viewing Crystal Reports

Introduction

There are many ways to present data to users. For example, you could write code to loop through recordsets and print them inside your Windows-based application. However, by using such methods, any work beyond basic formatting can be complicated and difficult to program.

With Crystal Reports for Microsoft Visual Studio .NET, you can quickly create complex and professional-looking reports. Instead of writing code, you use the Crystal Report Designer interface to create and format the report that you need. The powerful Report Engine processes the formatting, grouping, and charting criteria you specify.

This lesson introduces Crystal Reports for Visual Studio .NET and also covers how to use Report Expert to create and format reports.

Lesson objectives

After completing this lesson, you will be able to:

- Explain how Crystal Reports helps in creating reports.
- Create and format a report by using Crystal Reports.
- View a report by using Crystal Report Viewer.
- Add datasets to a report.

Crystal Reports

Introduction

Crystal Reports is the standard reporting tool in Visual Studio .NET. It allows you to create a report from scratch or use one of the Report Expert Wizards. Before you learn how to use Crystal Reports for creating and formatting reports, you must understand the benefits of using Crystal Reports.

Benefits of using Crystal Reports

Crystal Reports:

- Allows you to choose the language and project.

  Use the programming language of your choice and access Crystal Report Designer from any project.

- Provides report viewers for Windows-based and Web applications.

  Crystal Reports provides two report viewers that you can use to view your report in your application: Web Forms Viewer for Web applications and Windows Forms Viewer for Windows-based applications.

- Allows run-time customization of reports.

  Crystal Reports enables the viewer to interact with other controls at run time. With run-time customization, users can view different reports or change the format, data selection, or export options of an existing report.

- Allows users to interact easily with reports.

  Because Crystal Reports can interact with other controls, users are able to filter report information by clicking a button or selecting from a combo box.

- Provides data-visualization and analysis capabilities.

  Crystal Reports provides developers with data visualization and analysis capabilities. It uses an open and flexible architecture—with standards like extensible markup language (XML)—to allow you to share reports and information over the Web. It also offers features such as details on charts, report navigation, and text search.

How to Create and Format a Report by Using Crystal Reports

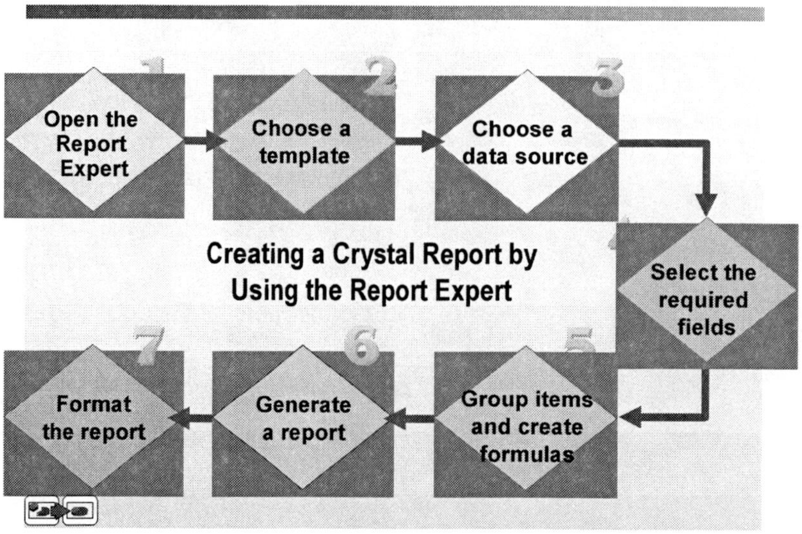

Introduction

You can use Crystal Reports to add reporting capabilities to your application. Crystal Reports allows you to create a report from the beginning or use the Report Expert, which helps you create a report by using a wizard.

Procedure: Create and format a report by using Report Expert

To create and format reports by using the Report Expert:

1. Open Report Expert.
   a. In Solution Explorer, right-click the project name, point to **Add**, and then select **Add New Item** from the shortcut menu.
   b. In the **Add New Item** dialog box, in the Templates pane, click **Crystal Report**.
   c. In the **Name** box, type a report name with an .rpt extension.
   d. Click **Open** to invoke Crystal Report Designer, which will help you create and design the new report.
   e. In Crystal Report Gallery, select the **Using the Report Expert** option.
2. Choose a template.

   Report Expert provides various templates for creating a report. Some of the templates are:

   - Standard
   - Form Letter
   - Form
   - Cross-Tab
   - Subreport
   - Mail Label
   - Drill Down

For more information about each of the templates, in the Visual Studio .NET Help documentation, search by using the phrase **Crystal Reports Experts**.

3. Choose a data source.

   Select the data source that your report will reference. You can use more than one data source in a report. You also choose the database tables that you want to use in the report. Crystal Reports can automatically link the tables, or you can specify how you want the tables linked. Database tables are linked so that records from one database match related records from another.

4. Select the required fields.

   After selecting the data source, select the fields that you want to display on the report.

5. Group items and create formulas.

   When you first insert a database field into your report, the data in the fields appears in the order in which it was originally entered into the database. Grouping, sorting, and totaling help turn disorganized data into useful information on a report.

   In most cases, the data needed for a report already exists in database table fields. Sometimes, you need to put additional data on the report that does not exist in any of the data fields. In cases such as this, you must create a formula. There are four different groups of formulas in Crystal Reports: report, conditional formatting, selection, and search. The majority of formulas in a report use the report and conditional formatting formulas.

   For more information about how to create and use these formulas, in the Visual Studio .NET Help documentation, search by using the phrase **Formula Overview**.

6. Generate the report.

   After you have added the required fields and formulas to the report, click **Finish** to generate the report.

7. Format the report.

   After a report is generated, you might want to make changes to the layout and design of the report, as well as the appearance of text, objects, or entire report sections. You can use various formatting options to change the layout of your reports.

   - To format an object, right-click the object, and then click **Format**.
   - To format a report section, right-click the report section, and then click **Format Section**.

How to View a Report by Using Crystal Report Viewer

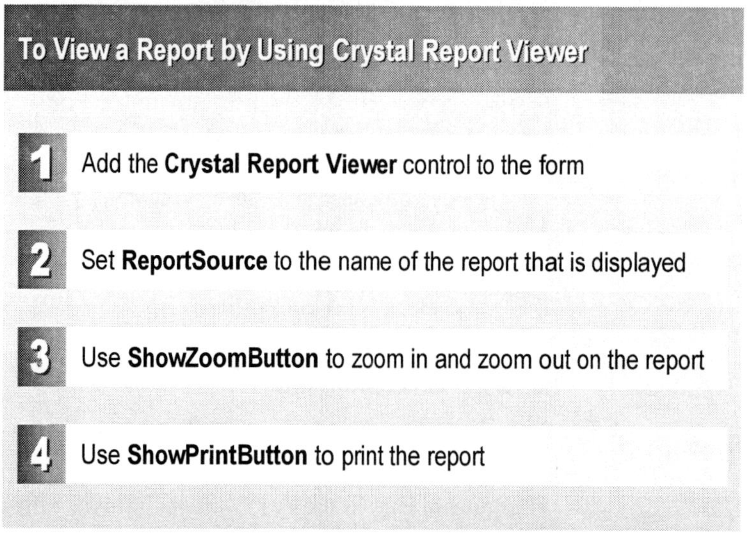

Introduction

Visual Studio .NET includes a **Crystal Report Viewer** control that enables you to view a report at run time. To specify the report that you want to view, you set the **ReportSource** property of the viewer.

Procedure: Viewing a report

To view a report by using the **Crystal Report Viewer** control:

1. Add a **Crystal Report Viewer** control to the form.

   The Controls Toolbox includes the **Crystal Report Viewer** control. To add the control to the form, drag the control from the Toolbox to the form.

2. Set the **ReportSource** property of the viewer.

   The next step is to set the **ReportSource** property of the Crystal Report viewer to the name of the report that is to be displayed. You can set the **ReportSource** property in the **Properties** window at design time or you can set it at run time.

3. Use the **ShowZoomButton** property to zoom in or zoom out on reports.

   The Crystal Report viewer includes the **ShowZoomButton** to zoom in or zoom out on reports. To enable this property, set the **ShowZoomButton** property to **True** in the Properties window.

4. Use the **ShowPrintButton** property to print the report.

   The **ShowPrintButton** property enables you to print the report. Set the **ShowPrintButton** property to **True** to enable the button on the viewer.

How to Add DataSets to a Report

- Adding datasets to reports allows you to create reports that are disconnected from the database
- To add datasets to a report, add the code to the Form_Load event

```
Private rpt As New OrderHistory()
Private dsReportInfo As New DataSet()
dsReportInfo.ReadXml("NorthwindData.xml")
rpt.SetDataSource(dsReportInfo)
CrystalReportViewer1.ReportSource = rpt
```

Introduction

Crystal Reports for Visual Studio .NET supports reports that access ADO.NET datasets.

Procedure: Adding an ADO.NET dataset to a report

To add an ADO.NET dataset to a report:

1. Create an instance of the report.

   To make the report display the data at run time, you must first create an instance of the report:

   ```
   Private rpt as New OrderHistory()
   ```
2. Generate a design time instance of a dataset.

   The design time instance of the dataset exposes the fields in the dataset to Report Expert. The design time dataset contains only the data description, and not the actual data. Therefore, when working with a report connected to a dataset object, you cannot browse field data in Crystal Report Designer at design time.

   ```
   Private dsReportInfo As New DataSet()
   ```
3. Populate the dataset.

   ```
   dsReportInfo.ReadXml("NorthwindData.xml")
   ```
4. Call the **SetDataSource** method of the report and pass an instance of the populated dataset.

   ```
   Rpt.SetDataSource(dsReportInfo)
   ```
5. Set the **ReportSource** property of the Crystal Report Viewer to the instance of the report.

   ```
   CrystalReportViewer1.ReportSource = rpt
   ```

Practice: Creating and Viewing Crystal Reports

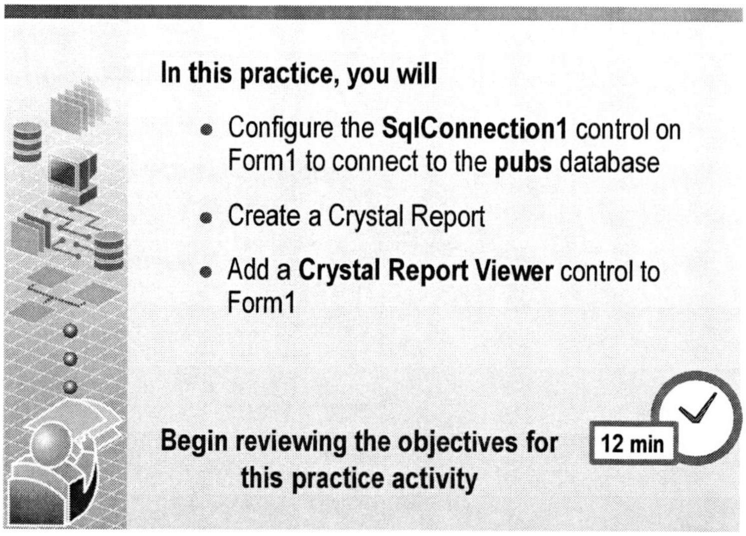

Introduction

In this practice, you will create and view crystal reports.

Instructions

► **Open the practice project**

1. Use Windows Explorer to browse to *install_folder*\Practices\Mod06\Mod06_06\Starter.
2. Double-click the CrystalReport.sln solution file to open the project.

► **Configure the SQLConnection1 control on Form1 to connect to the Pubs database**

1. Open Form1 in Design view.
2. Select **SQLConnection1**, and from the Properties window, click the **ConnectionString** property, click the arrow, and then click **New Connection**.

> **Note** Use the existing connection information for the **Pubs** database if it already exists and skip to the next procedure.

3. In the **Data Link Properties** dialog box, type *computername***MOC** where *computername* is the name of your computer.
4. Select the **Use Windows NT Integrated Security** option.
5. Select the **Pubs** database from the drop-down list, click **Test Connection** to ensure that you can access the **Pubs** database, click **OK**, and then click **OK** again.

► **Create a Crystal Report**

1. On the **File** menu, click **Add New Item**.
2. On the **Add New Item** dialog box, under **Template**, click **Crystal Report**.
3. Set the name of the report to **StoreSalesReport.rpt**, and then click **Open**.
4. Close the **Crystal Decisions Registration Wizard** dialog box.
5. On the **Crystal Report Gallery** dialog box, click **OK**.
6. On the **Data** tab, expand **Project Data**, expand **ADO.NET DataSets**, and then expand **CrystalReport.StoreSalesDataSet**.
7. Click **Insert Table**, and then click **Next**.
8. On the **Fields** tab, in **Available Fields** list, click **stor_id**, and then click **Add**.
9. Repeat step 8 to add all of the fields that are listed below **stores** table in the **Available Fields** list, and then click **Next**.
10. On the **Group** tab, in the **Available Fields** list, below **Report Fields**, click **stores.stor_name**, click **Add**, and then click **Next**.
11. On the **Total** tab, in the **Summarized Fields** list, click **stores.qty**, click **Remove**, and then click the **Style** tab.
12. Set the title to **Store Sales**, and then click **Finish**.

► **Add a Crystal Report Viewer control to Form1**

1. Open the Design view for **Form1**.
2. In the Toolbox, double-click **CrystalReportViewer**.
3. Set the **Dock** property of the CrystalReportViewer so that the control fills the entire form.
4. Open Form1 in the Code Editor.
5. On the **View** menu, point to **Show Tasks**, and then click **Comment**.
6. In Task List, double-click **TODO 1: create an instance of StoreSalesReport**.
7. Add the following code statement below the TODO line:
```
Private report As StoreSalesReport = New StoreSalesReport()
```
8. In Task List, double-click **TODO 2: Call the SetDataSource method of report and pass StoreSalesDataSet1**.
9. Add the following code statements below the TODO line:
```
report.SetDataSource(StoreSalesDataSet1)
CrystalReportViewer1.ReportSource = report
```
10. Build and run your application.
11. Use the CrystalReportViewer control to examine your report.

    Notice the features provided on the viewer's toolbar.
12. Save your project, and then close Visual Studio .NET.

Review

- Printing from a Windows Forms Application
- Using the Print Preview, Page Setup, and Print Dialogs
- Constructing Print Document Content by Using GDI+
- Creating Reports by Using Crystal Reports

1. List the tasks involved in printing simple text file output in Visual Studio .NET.

2. What property is used to capture user input from a dialog box?

3. What is the role of the **Graphics** object in printing by using GDI+?

4. What methods of GDI+ are used to draw text and graphics?

5. What kind of object does the following code create?

```
Dim g As Graphics = Me.CreateGraphics
Dim myBrush As New SolidBrush(Color.Red)
g.Fillrectangle(myBrush,ClientRectangle)
```

6. List some of the benefits of using Crystal Reports.

7. List the steps involved in creating a report by using Crystal Reports.

Lab 6.1: Printing Formatted Documents

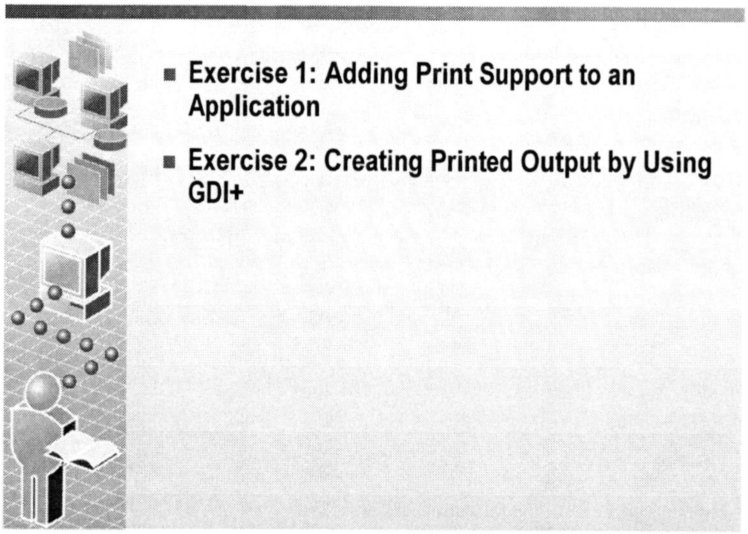

Objectives

After completing this lab, you will have demonstrated your ability to:

- Reference a namespace so that you don't have to fully qualify each namespace member in your code.
- Use the **PrintDocument** class and the **PrintPage** event to enable printing in a Windows Forms application.
- Use the **PageSetupDialog**, **PrintPreviewDialog**, and **PrintDialog** classes to provide user control over the print process.
- Create pens, brushes, and fonts for use with GDI+ drawing methods.
- Use GDI+ methods to draw outline and filled shapes on a print document.
- Measure and position text on a print document.

Note This lab focuses on the concepts in Module 6, "Printing and Reporting in Windows Forms Applications," in Course 2565A, *Developing Microsoft .NET Applications for Windows (Visual Basic .NET)*. As a result, this lab may not comply with Microsoft security recommendations.

Prerequisites

Before working on this lab, you must have:

- The knowledge and skills to develop a simple Windows Forms application by using a Visual Studio .NET–compatible programming language.
- The knowledge and skills to use elements of the **System.Drawing** namespace and the **PrintDocument** class in a Visual Studio .NET–based application.
- The knowledge and skills to use the **PrintPreviewDialog**, **PageSetupDialog**, and **PrintDialog** classes in a Visual Studio .NET–based application to provide user control of the print process.
- The knowledge and skills to use the two-dimensional (2-D) vector and Text drawing capabilities of GDI+ in a Visual Studio .NET–based application.

Scenario

Members of the Northwind Traders sales force need to print purchase order documents while they are at a customer site. The purchase order documents—form number NT-2565P (portrait) and NT-2565L (landscape)—have specific requirements associated with document layout, text formatting, and the appearance of 2-D vector graphics objects. You are an application developer at Northwind Traders. The department that you work in is developing a purchase order application that will be used by the Northwind Traders sales force. You have been assigned the task of completing the code sections of the purchase order application that support printing, The Northwind Traders Legal and Media departments have given you the three requirements tables that describe these forms. The tables are included at the end of this lab.

To complete this task, you must add basic print support to a project, enable users to control the print process by using dialog boxes, and develop the code statements necessary to complete the construction of the print document by using GDI+.

Estimated time to complete this lab: 60 minutes

Exercise 1
Adding Print Support to an Application

In this exercise, you will open two existing Visual Studio .NET projects, create a reference to the **Drawing** and **Drawing2D** namespaces, create a subroutine that handles the **PrintPage** event, develop code that ensures that all pages of a print document are included in a print job, and add support for the **PrintPreviewDialog**, **PageSetupDialog**, and **PrintDialog** dialog boxes to your application. This exercise assesses your knowledge of the print process and your ability to use the **PrintDocument** class and the three dialog boxes to provide the application user with control of the print process.

There are starter and solution files associated with this exercise. Browse to *install_folder*\Labfiles\Lab06_1\Ex01\Starter to find the starter files, and browse to *install_folder*\Labfiles\Lab06_1\Ex01\Solution to find the solution files. If you performed a default installation of the course files, *install_folder* corresponds to C:\Program Files\Msdntrain\2565.

Scenario

The user interface of the purchase order application has been developed and the underlying code is functioning as intended. You have reviewed the application code and the code contained in a custom document printing class that inherits from the **PrintDocument** class. The custom printing class that your department created will be used to print the purchase order forms that are used by Northwind Traders. Most of the code that is used to construct (draw) purchase order documents has already been written. You will now begin adding code to your application and the printing class so that users can print purchase order documents.

The Northwind Traders sales force has requested that the application be capable of printing in either portrait or landscape mode and that page margins be fixed in accordance with the Legal department and Media department requirements for the purchase order document. The sales force would also like to have the option to review the purchase order document with a customer before it is printed.

As the application developer, you will start by opening the purchase order application and the printing class in separate projects and checking to see what code still needs to be added to the two projects to support document printing. Then, you will add support for the **PrintPreviewDialog**. In addition to providing the sales force with an easy way to preview a purchase order before printing, the **PrintPreview** dialog box enables you to view the print document as you develop the code that constructs the document. You will then add support for the **PageSetupDialog** class to your application and create the code that is required to show this dialog box. By checking various page layout settings, you can ensure that the print document is constructed in accordance with the page layout parameters needed by your Legal and Media departments. Because your customer also wants the option to print without previewing the document, you will also add support for the **PrintDialog** class.

Tasks	Additional information
1. Open two instances of Visual Studio .NET. In the first instance, open the Lab06Application.sln file. In the second instance, open the Lab06Class.sln file. To open the solution files, in the Lab06Application and Lab06Class folders, respectively, browse to *install_folder*\Labfiles\Lab06_1\Ex01\Starter. You can open two instances of Visual Studio .NET when you want to work on an application and an external class library at the same time.	**a.** For more information about opening a project file and starting an application, see the following resources: • The Visual Studio .NET Help documentation. For additional information about opening a project file, in Search, select the **Search in titles only** check box, then search by using the phrase **Open Project Dialog Box**. For additional information about starting an application from in Designer, in Index, search by using the phrase **Debugging Windows Applications**.
2. Use the Task List in the Lab06Class.vb file to locate the code section 'TODO: Programmatically reference required namespaces' and then add code statements that reference the **Drawing** and **Drawing2D** namespaces. When you create a reference to a namespace, you can refer to the namespace members without having to fully qualify member names in your code. This makes your code easier to develop and easier to read.	**a.** For more information about the **Drawing** and **Drawing2D** namespaces and why you should use them, see the following resources: • Lesson: Constructing Print Document Content by Using GDI+ in Module 6, "Printing and Reporting in Windows Forms Applications," in Course 2565A, *Developing Microsoft .NET Applications for Windows (Visual Basic .NET).* • The Visual Studio .NET Help documentation. For additional information about creating a reference to a namespace, search by using the phrases **References and the Imports Statement**, **Namespaces** and **Imports Statement**. For additional information about the **Drawing** and **Drawing2D** namespaces, search by using the phrases **System.Drawing** and **System.Drawing.Drawing2D**.

Tasks	Additional information
3. Use the Task List in the Lab06Class.vb file to locate the code section 'TODO: Create the declaration statement for the PrintPage Subroutine' and then create the declaration statement for a subroutine named **Lab06Class_PrintPage** that handles the **PrintPage** event. Add code statements to the subroutine that call the **PrintingEmptyForm2565** and **PrintingContentsForm2565** subroutines. The **PrintPage** subroutine handles all requests for a page of the print document. The PrintPageEventArgs class that is passed to the PrintPage subroutine contains the **Graphics** object on which you construct the print document.	**a.** For more information about the **PrintPage** event and the **PrintPageEventArgs** class, see the following resources: • Lesson: Printing From a Windows Forms Application in Module 6, "Printing and Reporting in Windows Forms Applications," in Course 2565A, *Developing* Microsoft *.NET Applications for Windows (Visual Basic .NET).* • Practice: Adding Print Support to a Windows Forms Application in Module 6, "Printing and Reporting in Windows Forms Applications," in Course 2565A, Developing *Microsoft .NET Applications for Windows (Visual Basic .NET).* • The Visual Studio .NET Help documentation. For additional information about the PrintPage event, search by using the phrases **Creating Standard Windows Forms Print Jobs** and **PrintDocument.PrintPage Event**. For additional information about **the PrintPageEventArgs** class, search by using the phrases **PrintPageEventArgs Class** and **PrintPageEventArgs Members**.
4. Use the Task List in the Lab06Class.vb file to locate the code section 'TODO: Determine if more pages must be printed' and then create a code section that tells the event handler for the **PrintPage** event that there are more pages to print when **currentPurchaseItemNumber** is less than **totalPurchaseItems**, otherwise specify that there are no more pages to print. In Visual Studio .NET, you must create your own programming logic to set the **HasMorePages** property to generate print documents that consist of more than one page.	**a.** For more information about how to specify that there are additional pages to be printed, see the following resources: • Lesson: Printing From a Windows Forms Application in Module 6, "Printing and Reporting in Windows Forms Applications," in Course 2565A, *Developing Microsoft .NET Applications for Windows (Visual Basic .NET).* • Practice: Adding Print Support to a Windows Forms Application in Module 6, "Printing and Reporting in Windows Forms Applications," in Course 2565A, Developing *Microsoft .NET Applications for Windows (Visual Basic .NET).* • The Visual Studio .NET Help documentation. Search by using the phrase **PrintPageEventArgs.HasMorePages Property**.

Tasks	Additional information
5. Rebuild the Lab06Class project, and then, in the Lab06Application project, in Solution Explorer, update the reference to Lab06Class. After you rebuild a class library, ensure that your **applications** reference the new version.	**a.** For more information about referencing an external class, see the following resource: • The Visual Studio .NET Help documentation. Search by using the phrases **Project References**, **Adding and Removing References**, and **Preparing and Managing Builds**.
6. Open the code editor view of MainForm.vb in the Lab06Application project, and configure the Task List to display comments. Using the Task List and TODO comments can help you remember development tasks that must still be done.	**a.** For more information about the code editor view and the Task List, see the following resource: • The Visual Studio .NET Help documentation. For help with the code editor, search by using the phrase **Managing the Code Editor and View**. For help with Task List, search by using the phrase **Task List Views**.
7. Use the Task List to locate the code section 'TODO: Create an instance of the **PrintPreviewDialog** class'. Add code below the comment line that creates an instance of the **PrintPreviewDialog** class named **form2565PreviewDialog**.	**a.** For more information about the **PrintPreviewDialog** class and how to add an instance of this dialog box to your application, see the following resources: • Lesson: Using the Print Preview, Page Setup, and Print Dialogs in Module 6, "Printing and Reporting in Windows Forms Applications," in Course 2565A, *Developing Microsoft .NET Applications for Windows (Visual Basic .NET).* • Practice: Using the PrintPreviewDialog Control in Module 6, "Printing and Reporting in Windows Forms Applications," in Course 2565A, *Developing Microsoft .NET Applications for Windows (Visual Basic .NET).* • The Visual Studio .NET Help documentation. Search by using the phrase **Introduction to the Windows Forms PrintPreviewDialog Control**.

Tasks	Additional information
8. Use the Task List to locate the code section 'TODO: Create an instance of the **PageSetupDialog** class'. Add code below the comment line that creates an instance of the **PageSetupDialog** class named **form2565SetupDialog**. The **PageSetupDialog** class enables users to modify the page settings of a print document. You can use it to test the code that constructs the print document by displaying the print document with various page setting values. You will get a chance to modify page settings later in this lab exercise.	**a.** For more information about adding the **PageSetupDialog** class to an application, see the following resources: • Lesson: Using the Print Preview, Page Setup, and Print Dialogs in Module 6, "Printing and Reporting in Windows Forms Applications," in Course 2565A,*Developing Microsoft .NET Applications for Windows (Visual Basic .NET)*. • Practice: Using the PageSetupDialog Control in Module 6, "Printing and Reporting in Windows Forms Applications," in Course 2565A, Developing *Microsoft .NET Applications for Windows (Visual Basic .NET)*. • The Visual Studio .NET Help documentation. Search by using the phrases Introduction **to the Windows Forms PageSetupDialog Component**, **PageSetupDialog Class**, and **PageSetupDialog Members**.
9. Use the Task List to locate the code section 'TODO: Create an instance of the PrintDialog class'. Add code below the comment line that creates an instance of the **PrintDialog** class named **form2565PrintDialog**.	**a.** For more information about adding support for the **PrintDialog** class to your application, see the following resources: • Lesson: Using the Print Preview, Page Setup, and Print Dialogs in Module 6, "Printing and Reporting in Windows Forms Applications," in Course 2565A, *Developing Microsoft .NET Applications for Windows (Visual Basic .NET)*. • Practice: Using the PageSetupDialog Control in Module 6, "Printing and Reporting in Windows Forms Applications," in Course 2565A, *Developing Microsoft .NET Applications for Windows (Visual Basic .NET)*. • The Visual Studio .NET Help documentation. Search by using the phrases **Introduction to the Windows Forms PrintDialog Component** and **PrintDialog Component**.

Tasks	Additional information
10. Use the Task List to locate the code section 'TODO: Set purchaseItemNumber and purchaseItemCount'. Add code below the TODO comment that assigns a value of **0** to the *MainModule.purchaseItemNumber* variable and assigns the value of the **Count** property of MainModule.mainPOForm.ProductOrderPanel.Controls to the *MainModule.purchaseItemCount* variable. In addition to developing the code logic that determines when **HasMorePages** is **True** or **False**, you must reset the variables that are used to make this determination every time a print document is generated.	**a.** The *purchaseItemNumber* and *purchaseItemCount* variables are passed to the Lab06Class class (inherits from PrintDocument) and used to determine when HasMorePages should be set to **True** or **False**. The *purchaseItemNumber* variable is the current purchase item being printed, and the *purchaseItemCount* variable is the total number of purchase items in the current purchase order.
11. Use the Task List to locate the code section 'TODO: Add support for a full screen preview of the print document'. Add code below the comment line that assigns the **form2565Document** instance of the Lab06Class class to the **Document** property of **form2565PreviewDialog** (the print preview dialog box) and displays the print document by using the full display screen. Implementing support for the print preview dialog box early in the development process enables you to preview the print document as you develop the code that constructs your document.	**a.** For more information about the **PrintPreviewDialog** class and how it can be used in the print process, see the following resources: • Lesson: Using the Print Preview, Page Setup, and Print Dialogs in Module 6, "Printing and Reporting in Windows Forms Applications," in Course 2565A, *Developing Microsoft .NET Applications for Windows (Visual Basic .NET).* • Practice: Using the PrintPreviewDialog Control in Module 6, "Printing and Reporting in Windows Forms Applications," in Course 2565A, *Developing Microsoft .NET Applications for Windows (Visual Basic .NET).* • The Visual Studio .NET Help documentation. Search by using the phrase **Displaying Print Preview in Windows Applications**.

Tasks	Additional information
12. Rebuild and then start the Lab06Application project. Use the **File** menu or the **Print** button on the ToolBar control to demonstrate that you can now display the print preview dialog box. Close the Lab06Application executable file. You can use the **Print Preview** dialog box to verify that the code in your **PrintPage** subroutine is working correctly. Try adding 25 purchase items to a purchase order. The print document should now wrap onto a second page when previewed.	**a.** For more information about building and debugging your applications, and for information about running the Purchase Order application, use the following resources: • Demonstration, Purchase Order Application, in Module 0, "Introduction," in Course 2565A, *Developing Microsoft .NET Applications for Windows (Visual Basic .NET)*. • In the Visual Studio .NET Help documentation, search by using the phrases **Default and Custom Builds** and **Using the Debugger**.
13. Use the Task List to locate the code section 'TODO: Apply the initial page settings'. Add code below the comment line that assigns the *form2565PageSettings* variable to the **PageSettings** property of the **Page Setup** dialog box that you instantiated. The page setup dialog box must be assigned an initial **PageSettings** value before it can be displayed for the first time; otherwise, an error will occur.	**a.** The **form2565PageSettings** object is scoped at the module level so that user-specified settings are maintained between viewings of the **PageSetupDialog** class. **b.** For more information about the **PageSettings** class, see the following resources: • Lesson: Using the Print Preview, Page Setup, and Print Dialogs in Module 6, "Printing and Reporting in Windows Forms Applications," in Course 2565A, *Developing Microsoft .NET Applications for Windows (Visual Basic .NET)*. • Practice: Using the PageSetupDialog Control in Module 6, "Printing and Reporting in Windows Forms Applications," in Course 2565A, *Developing Microsoft .NET Applications for Windows (Visual Basic .NET)*. • The Visual Studio .NET Help documentation. Search by using the phrase **PageSettings Class**.

Tasks	Additional information
14. Use Task List to locate the code section 'TODO: Disable user access to the Margins section of the dialog'. Add code below the comment line that disables user access to the margin settings. Restricting user access to only those page settings that are required will help to eliminate support issues that would be generated when users modify settings in an unpredictable manner.	**a.** For more information about members of the **PageSetupDialog** class, see the following resources: • Lesson: Using the Print Preview, Page Setup, and Print Dialogs in Module 6, "Printing and Reporting in Windows Forms Applications," in Course 2565A, *Developing Microsoft .NET Applications for Windows (Visual Basic .NET).* • Practice: Using the PageSetupDialog Control in Module 6, "Printing and Reporting in Windows Forms Applications," in Course 2565A, *Developing Microsoft .NET Applications for Windows (Visual Basic .NET).* • The Visual Studio .NET Help documentation. Search by using the phrase **PageSetupDialog Members**.
15. Rebuild and then start the Lab06Application project. Use the **File** menu to open the page setup dialog box and change the page orientation from portrait to landscape. Use the print preview dialog box to view the print document. Close the Lab06Application executable file.	**a.** For more information about building and debugging your application, use the following resource: • The Visual Studio .NET Help documentation. Search by using the phrases **Default and Custom Builds** and **Using the Debugger**.
16. Use the Task List to locate the code section 'TODO: Determine if the document should be printed'. Add code statements below the comment line that will send *form2565Document* document to the printer when the application user clicks **OK** to close the print dialog. You must use DialogResult to determine whether the user closed **PrintDialog** by clicking **Cancel** or by clicking **OK**.	**a.** For more information about using **DialogResult**, see the following resources: • Lesson: Using the Print Preview, Page Setup, and Print Dialogs in Module 6, "Printing and Reporting in Windows Forms Applications," in Course 2565A, *Developing Microsoft .NET Applications for Windows (Visual Basic .NET).* • Practice: Using the PageSetupDialog Control in Module 6, "Printing and Reporting in Windows Forms Applications," in Course 2565A, *Developing Microsoft .NET Applications for Windows (Visual Basic .NET).* • The Visual Studio .NET Help documentation Search by using the phrase **Retrieving the Result for Dialog Boxes**.

Tasks	Additional information
17. Rebuild and then start the Lab06Application project. Use the **File** menu to demonstrate that the print dialog box is working as intended. Close the Lab06Application executable file.	**a.** For more information about building and debugging your application, see the following resource: • The Visual Studio .NET Help documentation. Search by using the phrases **Default and Custom Builds** and **Using the Debugger**.
18. Save the changes that you made to your code, and then close both solution files.	Additional information is not necessary for this task.

Exercise 2
Creating Printed Output by Using GDI+

In this exercise, you will create pens, brushes, and fonts and then use them to draw 2-D vector objects and text at specific locations on a print document. This exercise provides you with an opportunity to assess your ability to complete the construction of a print document by using GDI+.

There are starter and solution files associated with this exercise. Browse to *install_folder*\Labfiles\Lab06_1\Ex02\Starter to find the starter files, and browse to *install_folder*\Labfiles\Lab06_1\Ex02\Solution to find the solution files. If you performed a default installation of the course files, *install_folder* corresponds to C:\Program Files\Msdntrain\2565.

Scenario

Initial testing has revealed that the custom printing class does not accurately reproduce the legal and official representation of the organization's purchase order documents—Northwind Traders forms NT-2565P and NT-2565L. To correct this problem, you will review the data contained in the NT-2565P and NT-2565L requirements tables (the tables of data from the Media and Legal Departments that are included after this exercise) and develop GDI+ code statements that produce the required 2-D vector objects and text. You will begin by creating some of the pens, brushes, and fonts required to construct portions of the forms. After that, you will develop the code that draws some of the 2D vector shapes that are used to create the base forms. The last step will be to develop the code used to draw some of the text that appears on the NT-2565P and NT-2565L forms.

Tasks	Additional information
1. In the first instance of Visual Studio .NET, browse to *install_folder*\Labfiles\Lab06_1\Ex02\Starter and open the Lab06Application.sln file. In the second instance, browse to *install_folder*\Labfiles\ Lab06_1\Ex02\Starter and open the Lab06Class.sln file.	**a.** For more information about opening a project file and starting an application, see the following resources: • The Visual Studio .NET Help documentation. For additional information about opening a project file, in Search, select the **Search in titles only** check box, then search by using the phrase **Open Project Dialog Box**. For additional information about starting an application from in Designer, in Index, search by using the phrase **Debugging Windows Applications**.
2. Open the code editor view of the Lab06Class.vb file and use Task List to locate the code section 'TODO: Create the pageBorderPen'. Add code below the comment line that creates a pen named *pageBorderPen* and that has the following characteristics: Color = Gray, width = 3, DashStyle = Dash.	**a.** For more information about creating pens, see the following resources: • Lesson: Constructing Print Document Content Using GDI+ in Module 6, "Printing and Reporting in Windows Forms Applications," in Course 2565A, *Developing Microsoft .NET Applications for Windows (Visual Basic .NET)*. • Practice: How to Construct Print Document Content Using GDI+ in Module 6, "Printing and Reporting in Windows Forms Applications," in Course 2565A, *Developing Microsoft .NET Applications for Windows (Visual Basic .NET)*. • The Visual Studio .NET Help documentation. Search by using the phrases **Pens, Brushes, and Colors**; **Setting Pen Width and Alignment** (in the .NET Framework Developer's Guide) and **Using a Brush to Fill Shapes**.

<table>
<tr><th>Tasks</th><th>Additional information</th></tr>
<tr><td>3. Use the Task List to locate the code section 'TODO: Create the footerBrush'. Add code below the comment line that creates a solid black brush named footerBrush.</td><td>a. For more information about creating brushes, see the following resources:
• Lesson: Constructing Print Document Content Using GDI+ in Module 6, “Printing and Reporting in Windows Forms Applications,” in Course 2565A, Developing Microsoft .NET Applications for Windows (Visual Basic .NET).
• Practice: How to Construct Print Document Content Using GDI+ in Module 6, “Printing and Reporting in Windows Forms Applications,” in Course 2565A, Developing Microsoft .NET Applications for Windows (Visual Basic .NET).
• The Visual Studio .NET Help documentation. Search by using the phrases Pens, Brushes, and Colors; Setting Pen Width and Alignment and Using a Brush to Fill Shapes.</td></tr>
<tr><td>4. Use the Task List to locate the code section 'TODO: Create the footerFont'. Add code below the comment line that creates a font named footerFont and that has the following characteristics: family = Microsoft Sans Serif, emSize = 7.</td><td>a. For more information about creating fonts, see the following resources:
• Lesson: Constructing Print Document Content Using GDI+ in Module 6, “Printing and Reporting in Windows Forms Applications,” in Course 2565A, Developing Microsoft .NET Applications for Windows (Visual Basic .NET).
• Practice: How to Construct Print Document Content Using GDI+ in Module 6, “Printing and Reporting in Windows Forms Applications,” in Course 2565A, Developing Microsoft .NET Applications for Windows (Visual Basic .NET).
• The Visual Studio .NET Help documentation. Search by using the phrases Constructing Font Families and Fonts (in the .NET Framework Developer’s Guide), Fonts and Text (in the .NET Framework Developer’s Guide), and Using GDI+ Managed Classes (in the .NET Framework Developer’s Guide).</td></tr>
</table>

Tasks	Additional information
5. Use the Task List to locate the code section 'TODO: Draw the border of the Customer Address table'. Create the code statements required to draw the border of the customer address table by using the following variables: *sectionOutlinePen*, *customerSectionLeft*, *customerSectionTop*, *customerSectionWidth*, *customerSectionHeight*. GDI+ offers many ways to draw an outlined shape such as a rectangle. As a developer, it is important to consider whether the parameters used to draw a shape can be used again later in your program before you select a drawing method.	**a.** For more information about drawing 2-D vector shapes, see the following resources: • Lesson: Constructing Print Document Content Using GDI+ in Module 6, "Printing and Reporting in Windows Forms Applications," in Course 2565A, *Developing Microsoft .NET Applications for Windows (Visual Basic .NET).* • Practice: How to Construct Print Document Content Using GDI+ in Module 6, "Printing and Reporting in Windows Forms Applications," in Course 2565A, *Developing Microsoft .NET Applications for Windows (Visual Basic .NET).* • The Visual Studio .NET Help documentation. Search by using the phrases **Pens, Lines, and** Rectangles; **Using a Pen to Draw Lines and Rectangles**; and **Graphics Methods**.
6. Use the Task List to locate the code section TODO: Draw a rectangle that defines the margin limits'. Create the code statements required to draw a rectangle that defines the limits of the page by using the following variables: *pageBorderPen, pageLeft, pageTop, pageWidth, pageHeight.*	**a.** For more information about drawing 2-D vector shapes, see the following resources: • Lesson: Constructing Print Document Content Using GDI+ in Module 6, "Printing and Reporting in Windows Forms Applications," in Course 2565A, *Developing Microsoft .NET Applications for Windows (Visual Basic .NET).* • Practice: How to Construct Print Document Content Using GDI+ in Module 6, "Printing and Reporting in Windows Forms Applications," in Course 2565A, *Developing Microsoft .NET Applications for Windows (Visual Basic .NET).* • The Visual Studio .NET Help documentation. Search by using the phrases **Pens, Lines, and Rectangles**; **Using a Pen to Draw Lines and Rectangles**; and **Graphics Methods**.

<table>
<tr><th>Tasks</th><th>Additional information</th></tr>
<tr><td>7. Use the Task List to locate the code section 'TODO: Draw the shaded area of the Purchase Items table'. Create the code statements required to draw the shaded portion of the Purchase Items table by using the following variables: purchaseSectionHeaderRowBackgroundBrush, purchaseSectionLeft, purchaseSectionTop, purchaseSectionWidth, purchaseSectionRowHeight.

When you use filled shapes on a print document, consider how the document will look when it is photocopied or printed by using a gray scale.</td><td>a. For more information about filled shapes, see the following resources:
• Lesson: Constructing Print Document Content Using GDI+ in Module 6, “Printing and Reporting in Windows Forms Applications,” in Course 2565A, Developing Microsoft .NET Applications for Windows (Visual Basic .NET).
• Practice: How to Construct Print Document Content Using GDI+ in Module 6, “Printing and Reporting in Windows Forms Applications,” in Course 2565A, Developing Microsoft .NET Applications for Windows (Visual Basic .NET).
• The Visual Studio .NET Help documentation. For additional information about drawing 2-D filled shapes, search by using the phrases Drawing Lines and Shapes with GDI+ and GDI+ Graphics.</td></tr>
<tr><td>8. Use Task List to locate the code section 'TODO: Draw the horizontal lines inside the Purchase Items table'. Create the code statements required to draw the interior lines by using the following variables: sectionInteriorPen, purchaseSectionLeft, verticalPosition, purchaseSectionRight, verticalPosition.

In addition to using the width and color properties to change the appearance of a line, you should consider using line styles and line caps.</td><td>a. For more information about drawing lines, see the following resources:
• Lesson: Constructing Print Document Content Using GDI+ in Module 6, “Printing and Reporting in Windows Forms Applications,” in Course 2565A, Developing Microsoft .NET Applications for Windows (Visual Basic .NET).
• Practice: How to Construct Print Document Content Using GDI+ in Module 6, “Printing and Reporting in Windows Forms Applications,” in Course 2565A, Developing Microsoft .NET Applications for Windows (Visual Basic .NET).
• The Visual Studio .NET Help documentation. Search by using the phrases Using a Pen to Draw Lines and Rectangles, Drawing a Line with Line Caps, and Using a Pen to Draw Lines and Shapes.</td></tr>
</table>

Tasks	Additional information
9. Use the Task List to locate the code section 'TODO: Draw the footer text'. Create the code statements required to draw the contents of the *printText* variable by using the variables *footerFont*, *footerBrush*, *horizontalPosition*, and *verticalPosition*, where *horizontalPosition* has a value equal to the left margin value of the page and *verticalPosition* has a value equal to the bottom margin value of the page minus the height of the font. By default, text is drawn below and to the right of the position specified in a **DrawString** command.	**a.** For more information about drawing and measuring text, see the following resources: • Lesson: Constructing Print Document Content Using GDI+ in Module 6, "Printing and Reporting in Windows Forms Applications," in Course 2565A, *Developing Microsoft .NET Applications for Windows (Visual Basic .NET).* • Practice: How to Construct Print Document Content Using GDI+ in Module 6, "Printing and Reporting in Windows Forms Applications," in Course 2565A, *Developing Microsoft .NET Applications for Windows (Visual Basic .NET).* • The Visual Studio .NET Help documentation. Search by using the phrases **Drawing Text with GDI+** and **Fonts and Text**.
10. Rebuild the Lab06Class project, reconstruct the reference to the class library in the Lab06Application project, and then view the updated print document by using Lab06Application.	**a.** For more information about building and debugging your application, use the following resource: • The Visual Studio .NET Help documentation. Search by using the phrases **Default and Custom Builds** and **Using the Debugger**.
11. Save your projects, and then close Visual Studio .NET.	Additional information is not necessary for this task.

The following tables provide information required to construct the NT-2565P and NT-2565L forms, which are the official Northwind Traders purchase order documents.

Page Layout Table for Forms NT-2565P and NT-2565L		
Document region/feature	**Size constraint, NT-2565P (portrait)**	**Size constraint, NT-2565L (landscape)**
Top Margin	1.0 inch (25.4 mm)	0.85 inch (21.6 mm)
Left Margin	1.2 inch (30.5 mm)	1.6 inch (40.6 mm)
Right Margin	0.8 inch (20.3 mm)	1.0 inch (25.4 mm)
Bottom Margin	1.0 inch (25.4 mm)	0.7 inch (17.8 mm)
Document Title Area	10% of available height*, full width	Same as NT-2565P
Address Table	25% of available height*, full width	Same as NT-2565P
Purchase Table	62.5% of available height*, full width	Same as NT-2565P
This table is incomplete. The complete **Page Layout Table for Forms NT-2565P and NT-2565L** table would contain additional information required to recreate the NT-2565P and NT-2565L forms. Information has been left out of this table because the additional information is not required to complete the exercises in this lab.		
* The available height is the distance between the top and bottom margins.		

Vector Objects Table for Forms NT-2565P and NT-2565L		
Document region/feature	**Object type**	**Pen/brush details**
Page Border	Rectangle	Dashed line type, 3 point (pt) width, gray
Address Table, border lines	Rectangle	Solid line type, 2 pt width, blue
Address Table, interior lines	Line	Solid line type, 1 pt width, blue
Address Table, 'Ship To' rows	Filled Rectangle	Light-gray brush fill
Purchase Table, border lines	Rectangle	Solid line type, 2 pt width, blue
Purchase Table, interior lines	Line	Solid line type, 1 pt width, blue
Order Item Table, header row	Filled Rectangle	Light-blue brush fill

Font Specification Table for Forms NT-2565P and NT-2565L		
Document region/feature	**Font details (font name, style, point size, and color)**	**Text layout (position in region)**
Company Name	Microsoft Sans Serif, Bold, 16 pt, Blue	Center-left position in Document Title region
Company Address	Microsoft Sans Serif, Regular, 8 pt, Blue	Immediately to the right of, and bottom-aligned to Company Name
Address Table Labels	Microsoft Sans Serif, Regular, 7 pt, Gray	Offset 10% of the font height from the top-left corner of the cell
Address Table Text	Microsoft Sans Serif, Regular, 10 pt, Black	Offset 25% of the font height from the left side of the cell and down 110% of the font height from the top of the cell
Order Item Table Header	Microsoft Sans Serif, Regular, 10 pt, Black	Centered in the cell
Order Item Table Text: Quantity, Unit Price, Discount	Microsoft Sans Serif, Regular, 9 pt, Black	Right justified in the cell with an offset of 25% of the font height
Order Item Table Text: Product Description, Unit Size	Microsoft Sans Serif, Regular, 9 pt, Black	Left justified in the cell with an offset of 25% of the font height

msdn training

Module 7: Asynchronous Programming

Contents

Microsoft

Overview

- The .NET Asynchronous Programming Model
- The Asynchronous Programming Model Design Pattern
- Protecting State and Data in a Multithreaded Environment

Introduction

A well-designed Microsoft® .NET Framework Windows Forms application includes techniques to prevent blocking user interaction.

In this module, you will learn about the how to use the techniques of asynchronous programming and multithreading to avoid blocking the user interface of an application.

Objectives

After completing this module, you will be able to:

- Describe the .NET Framework asynchronous programming model.
- Modify a client application to use built-in .NET Framework support for asynchronous calls to methods.
- Describe how to add explicit support for asynchronous calls to any method.

Lesson: The .NET Asynchronous Programming Model

- What Is Asynchronous Programming?
- Demonstration: Comparing Synchronous and Asynchronous Versions of an Application
- Asynchronous Programming Support in the .NET Framework

Introduction

The .NET Framework provides extensive support for asynchronous calls and multithreading.

In this lesson, you will learn about asynchronous programming and. the NET asynchronous programming model.

Lesson objectives

After completing this lesson, you will be able to:

- Define asynchronous programming.
- List typical scenarios in which asynchronous programming is useful.
- Describe the .NET asynchronous programming model.

What Is Asynchronous Programming?

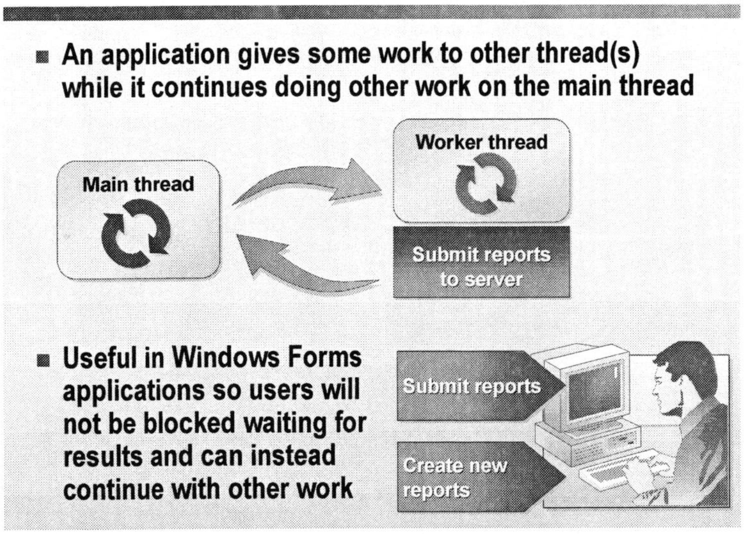

Introduction

One important measure of a Windows Forms application is its timely response to user interaction. One important technique developers have to support responsiveness is asynchronous programming.

Definition

The central idea behind asynchronous programming is to be able to issue method calls to other components and to carry on with other work, without waiting for the operation to complete. The .NET Framework common language runtime provides rich support for asynchronous programming and handles the details of threading and data exchange.

Example of asynchronous scenarios

In a non-programming scenario, consider a painting crew that is painting the rooms in a house that is some distance from town. As they are painting walls of the rooms, the crew chief realizes that they did not bring enough trim paint for the woodwork. The crew chief can tell one of the crew members to go to the paint store to order and wait for more trim paint to be custom mixed to the appropriate color, while the rest of the crew continues to paint the walls. When the crew member finally returns with the trim paint, some members of the crew can switch to painting the woodwork in those rooms where the walls have dried.

There are quite a few scenarios in the programming world that involve potential wait times: requests for file or network input/output (I/O), Web access, and so forth. You can use asynchronous techniques in your applications in these scenarios to allow users to remain productive.

Demonstration: Comparing Synchronous and Asynchronous Versions of an Application

In this demonstration, you will be able to compare the user experience in synchronous and asynchronous versions of the Expense Report application

Introduction

In this demonstration, you see a comparison of the user experience in synchronous and asynchronous versions of the Expense Report application.

Instructions

► **To demonstrate the synchronous behavior of the Expense Report application**

1. Run the synchronous version of the Expense Report application, ExpenseReport.exe, in *install_folder*\Democode\Mod07\Mod07_01\Sync.

> **Note** If you performed a default installation of the course files, *install_folder* corresponds to C:\Program Files\Msdntrain\2565.

2. In the main application window, click the **View Submitted Reports** button.
3. Notice that the application is not responsive while the XML Web service is being called. You can test this by trying to move the main application window, or by trying to minimize the main application window before the expense report list window opens.
4. After the expense report list window opens, close the application.

► To demonstrate the asynchronous behavior of the Expense Report application

1. Run the asynchronous version of the Expense Report application, ExpenseReport.exe, in *install_folder*\Democode\Mod07\Mod07_01\Async.
2. On the main application window, click the **View Submitted Reports** button.
3. Notice that the application is responsive while the XML Web service is being called. You can test this by moving the splitter control in the expense report list window, or by minimizing the main application window.
4. After data is loaded in the expense report list window, close the application.

Asynchronous Programming Support in the .NET Framework

- **A design pattern for asynchronous programming**
  - Used by the .NET Framework to make asynchronous calls uniform across different parts of the framework
  - User-created classes that support asynchronous calls should conform to this design pattern
- **Asynchronous support is provided in many of the logical areas**
  - I/O, sockets, networking, ASP.NET and XML Web services, messaging, and asynchronous delegates
  - Implementation is transparent, call the appropriate methods and let the .NET Framework handle the details

Introduction

The .NET Framework provides a design pattern for asynchronous programming and built-in support for many areas which often involve making complex calls that take a considerable amount of time to complete.

Support provided by the .NET Framework

The .NET Framework provides a design pattern that makes asynchronous calls uniform across the different parts of the .NET Framework.

Classes that include built-in support have a pair of asynchronous methods for each synchronous method they contain. For example, if you want to read from a stream synchronously, you use the **Read** method of the **System.IO.Stream** class. If, however, you want to make the call asynchronously, then you would instead use the **BeginRead** and **EndRead** methods of the **System.IO.Stream** class.

In addition, the .NET Framework makes the details of threading that support asynchronous programming mechanisms largely transparent to the developer.

For more information about using the support provided for asynchronous programming by the .NET Framework in your applications, see the lesson The Asynchronous Programming Model Design Pattern in this module.

Lesson: The Asynchronous Programming Model Design Pattern

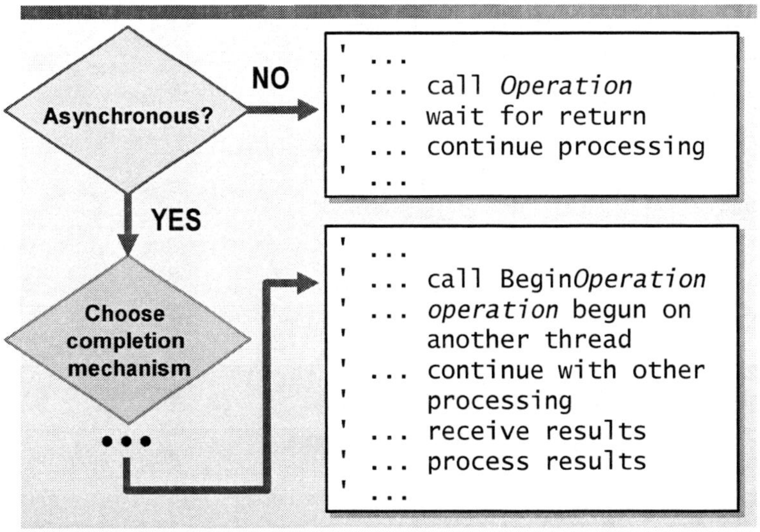

Call Back

Introduction

The asynchronous programming model design pattern provides a consistent and type-safe way to call methods asynchronously. This lesson concentrates on how to make asynchronous calls to classes that contain built-in asynchronous support. In the lesson How to Make Asynchronous Calls to Any Method, you will learn about the additional steps you must take to make asynchronous calls to classes that do not contain built-in asynchronous support.

Lesson objectives

After completing this lesson, you will be able to:

- Describe the asynchronous programming model design pattern.
- List the four ways to be notified of completion and describe appropriate scenarios for each way.
- List the steps for using asynchronous callback as the notification method.
- Modify a client application to use built-in .NET Framework support for asynchronous calls to methods.

Overview of the Asynchronous Programming Model Design Pattern

- **Caller decides whether a particular call should be asynchronous**
- **Asynchronous operation logically split into two parts**
  1. Client begins the operation by calling the Begin*Operation* method
  2. Client notified that operation is complete and receives results

Completion Technique	Comments
Use a callback	Supply a callback delegate, method will be called when operation completes
Poll	Poll the **IAsyncResult** interface's **IsCompleted** property
Call the End*Operation* method	Call the End*Operation* method and block till operation completes
Wait on a handle	Wait on **IAsyncResult** interface's **WaitHandle** property, then call End*Operation* method

Introduction

One of the innovations provided by the asynchronous design pattern is that the caller can decide whether a particular call should be asynchronous.

Beginning the operation

After you determine that you want to make an asynchronous call to one of the classes that provides built-in asynchronous support, you simply make a call to the class's appropriate Begin*Operation* method and determine what method you want to use to complete the call. The call to Begin*Operation* returns an object implementing this **IAsyncResult** interface. Depending on the completion technique used, this object may be used to help complete or get information about the asynchronous operation.

Receiving completion notification and results

You must also determine how you want your application to be notified of the completion of the asynchronous call and to receive the results (if any) of the call.

Callback

When you want to avoid blocking the thread that made the asynchronous call, use a callback method to be notified of the asynchronous call completion.

This is the technique most appropriate when you want to avoid blocking user interaction, for example, in Windows Forms applications, or in other heavily event-driven processing scenarios. For this reason the remainder of this lesson will focus on using this technique.

When you use a callback, you typically call the End*Operation* method, described later in this topic, inside the callback method to retrieve the results of the asynchronous operation.

Polling

If you want to maintain complete control over the flow of the application, then you can use a polling method. When using this technique, you will incur the overhead of manually checking the returned **IAsyncResult** interface's **IsCompleted** property to determine if the call is completed.

This technique is typically not appropriate for event-driven or user interaction scenarios.

EndOperation

The End*Operation* technique can be used when you have a finite amount of work to be done on the main thread that is not dependent on the asynchronous call. After that work is done and your application must receive the results of the asynchronous operation before it can do any further meaningful work, you can call the End*Operation* method to block until the asynchronous operation completes.

Be aware that an End*Operation* might block forever if the asynchronous call never completes due to a network or server failure. Therefore, the *wait on a handle* technique might be more appropriate to use in certain situations.

Wait on a handle

With the *wait on a handle* technique, you can specify a maximum time-out to wait for an asynchronous operation to complete. You can also use the **System.Threading.WaitHandle.WaitAll** method to wait on multiple asynchronous operations and be notified when they have all completed.

For more information about using the polling and wait on a handle techniques, see Module 14, "Threading and Asynchronous Programming in Course 2415B, *Programming with the Microsoft .NET Framework (Microsoft Visual Basic® .NET).*

Using the Design Pattern with an Asynchronous Callback for Completion

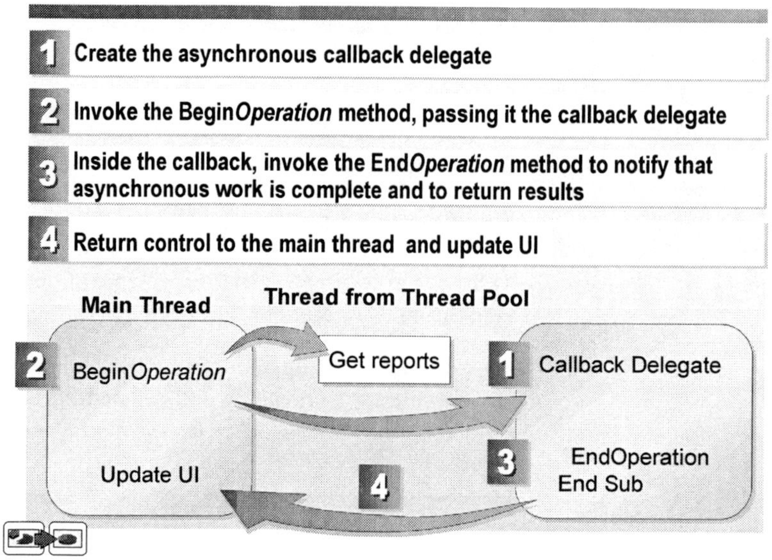

Introduction

Before providing the details of the code used for making an asynchronous call with an asynchronous callback for completion, it is useful to provide an overview of the process.

Process: Using asynchronous callbacks for completion

When you use the callback as the completion technique, there are four main steps in the process:

1. To set up for the asynchronous call, create an asynchronous delegate that points to the callback method you want to have invoked when the asynchronous operation completes.

Definition

A delegate is an object that you can use to call the methods of other objects. In other words, a delegate is an object-oriented, type-safe, secure way to provide the functionality of a function pointer in the .NET Framework.

2. Wherever appropriate in your application, initiate the asynchronous call by invoking the appropriate Begin*Operation* method, passing it the asynchronous delegate.
3. Inside the callback, invoke the appropriate End*Operation* method to retrieve results, if appropriate.
4. Return control to the main thread to update the user interface.

The remaining topics in this lesson provide the programming details related to these steps.

How to Set Up and Initiate the Call

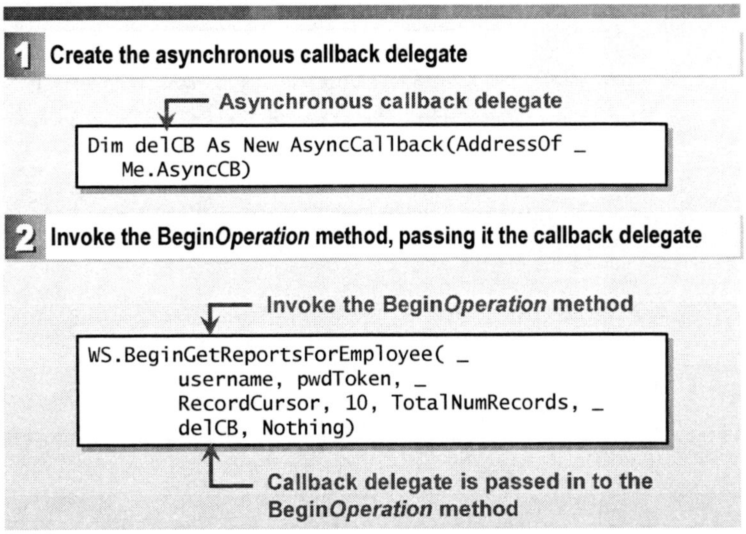

Introduction

An appropriate scenario for using a callback to notify completion and return results of an asynchronous call is calling a method of an XML Web service to obtain information for a Windows Forms application.

Procedure: Setting up and initiating the call

1. Set up the asynchronous call by creating an asynchronous delegate that points to the callback method that you want to have invoked when the asynchronous operation completes, in this case the **AsyncCB** method of the form from which you make the call.

   ```
   Dim delCB As New AsyncCallback(AddressOf Me.AsyncCB)
   ```

   Notice that part of the .NET Framework support provided for asynchronous programming is the **AsyncCallback** delegate class. The signature for a method referred to by an AsyncCallback delegate is as follows:

   ```
   Sub AsyncCB(ByVal result As IAsyncResult)
   ```

   For more information about the **AsyncCallback** delegate, search for AsyncCallback delegate in the Microsoft Visual Studio® .NET Help documentation.

2. Initiate the asynchronous call, by invoking the Begin*Operation* method, in this case **WS.BeginGetReportsForEmployee** and passing it the callback delegate, in this case, **delCB**. Notice that the callback delegate is always passed in as the next to the last parameter.

   ```
   WS.BeginGetReportsForEmployee( _
      username, pwdToken, _
      RecordCursor, 10, TotalNumRecords, _
      delCB, Nothing)
   ```

The final parameter of the **BeginInvoke** method is of type **System.Object** and is for user data. This user data is passed into the callback when the operation is completed in the **AsyncState** property of the **IAsyncResult** parameter of the callback.

The .NET Framework will take care of allocating a thread from the thread pool to run the code in the **GetReportsForEmployee** method and, when it completes, will call the method pointed to by **delCB** (**AsyncCB**).

How to Receive Completion Notification and Results

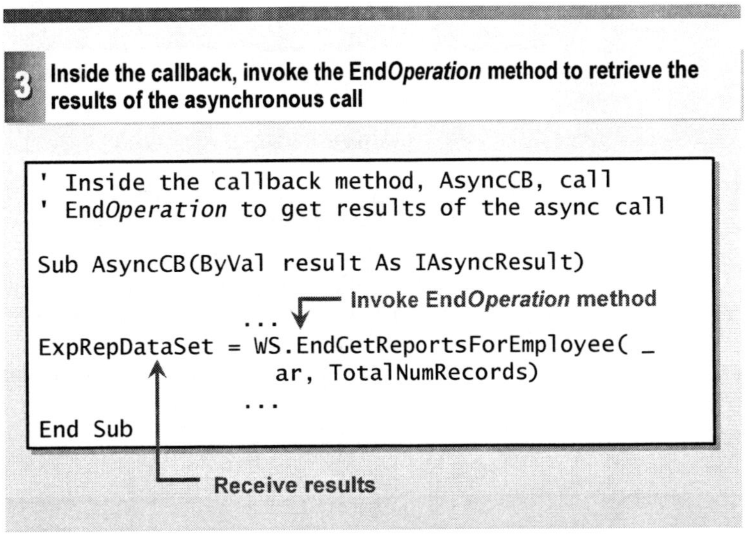

Introduction

After the method that you called asynchronously has completed its work, the .NET Framework calls the asynchronous callback delegate that you designated.

Procedure: Receiving completion notification and results

- Inside the asynchronous callback delegate, call the appropriate End*Operation* method and return any results.

```
' Inside the callback method, AsyncCB, call
' EndOperation to get the results of the async call

Sub AsyncCB(ByVal result As IAsyncResult)
            ...
  ExpRepDataSet = WS.EndGetReportsForEmployee( _
           ar, TotalNumRecords)
            ...
End Sub
```

Exceptions

If the asynchronous operation throws an exception, it will be returned from the call to the End*Operation* method.

How to Return Control to the Main Thread

In Windows Forms applications, any calls to methods or properties for controls on the form must be done on the main thread

4 Return control to the main thread

```
' Switch back to main thread to update the UI
' First, create a MethodInvoker delegate for
' the method to be called
Dim mi As New MethodInvoker(Me.UpdateUI)

' Use the current form's BeginInvoke to
' invoke the delegate
Me.BeginInvoke(mi)
```

Introduction

In Windows Forms applications, any changes to properties for controls on forms must be done on the main thread. Methods and properties for controls cannot be safely accessed from any other thread.

Procedure: Returning control to the main thread

To return control to the main thread:

1. From inside the callback, switch back to the main thread.

   ```
   ' Switch back to main thread to update UI
   ' First, create a MethodInvoker delegate for
   ' the method to be called

   Dim mi As New MethodInvoker(Me.UpdateUI)
   ```

   The .NET Framework provides a **MethodInvoker** delegate class that you can use to call generic methods. In the previous code sample, you create a delegate that refers to the **UpdateUI** method in the current object. The signature for a method referred to by a **MethodInvoker** delegate is as follows.

   ```
   Sub UpdateUI()
   ```

2. Update the user interface.

   ```
   ' Use the current form's BeginInvoke to
   ' invoke the delegate.

   Me.BeginInvoke(mi)
   ```

   This call to the form's **BeginInvoke** method will cause the method referred to by *mi* to be called on the main thread, and therefore update the user interface (UI) safely. By calling the **BeginInvoke** method instead of the **Invoke** method, the worker thread used to make the asynchronous call returns to the thread pool faster, thus avoiding exhaustion of threads in the thread pool.

Animation: Making an Asynchronous Call to an XML Web Service

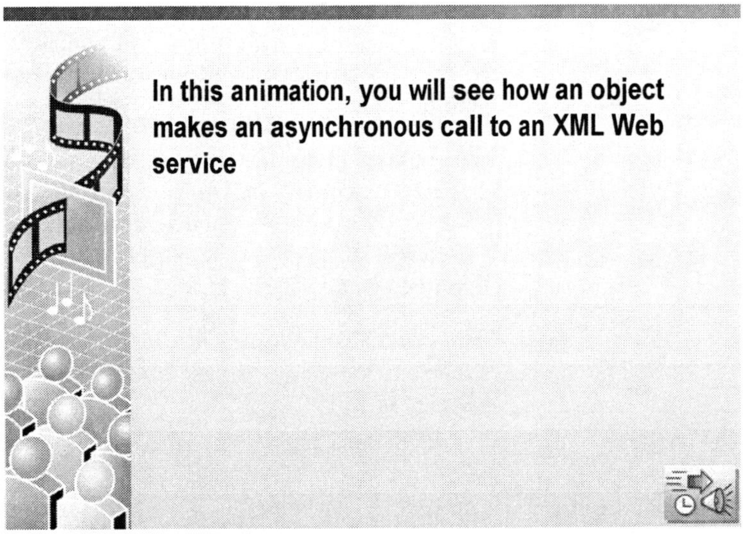

In this animation, you will see how an object makes an asynchronous call to an XML Web service.

A Windows Forms client application calls an XML Web service to retrieve and change information about expense reports. The XML Web service provides a **SubmitReport** method that takes an expense report, validates it, and adds it to the database of expense reports.

When a Web service reference is added to a Microsoft Visual Studio .NET project, a client proxy class for the XML Web service is generated. In addition to the synchronous **SubmitReport** method, the proxy includes the asynchronous **BeginSubmitReport** and **EndSubmitReport** methods.

A callback method named **SubmitReportCallback** is used as the callback method for the asynchronous operation. The asynchronous operation is started by calling the proxy's **BeginSubmitReport** method, passing a delegate object that refers to the callback method. When the **BeginSubmitReport** method is called, it calls the **SubmitReport** method on another thread from the runtime's thread pool and returns immediately to the caller. The client is free to continue executing other code and the user interface remains responsive.

When the **SubmitReport** method completes, the callback method is invoked. The callback method invokes the **EndSubmitReport** method to retrieve the results of the XML Web service call. If the **SubmitReport** method completed successfully, the **EndSubmitReport** method returns the results; otherwise, an exception is thrown in the **EndSubmitReport** method for the callback to handle.

The application displays the results of the XML Web service call by using the **UpdateUI** method. The **UpdateUI** method manipulates controls to show the results. Controls can be called safely only from the application's main thread. The callback method is not executing on the application's main thread, and therefore cannot call the **UpdateUI** method directly.

Instead, it calls the form's thread-safe **BeginInvoke** method, passing it a delegate to the **UpdateUI** method. **BeginInvoke** then executes this method on the main thread.

Practice: Making an Asynchronous Call to an XML Web Service

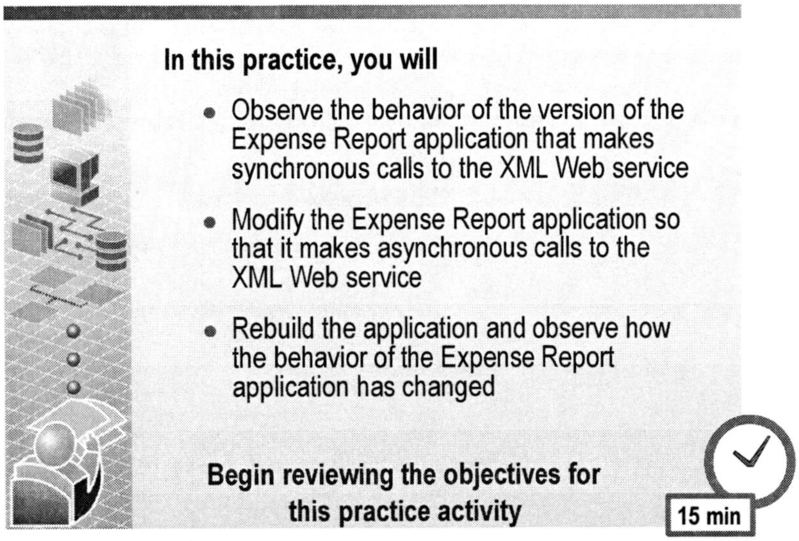

Introduction

In this practice, you will convert a synchronous XML Web service call to an asynchronous XML Web service call.

Instructions

► **Observe the synchronous version of the Expense Report application**

1. Open the Mod07Practice.sln solution file in *install_folder*\Practices\Mod07\Mod07_01\Starter.
2. Open the MainForm.vb file and view the code.
3. Build the project and run the application.
4. Click **Call Web Service**. While the XML Web service call is happening, click the minimize button to try to minimize the application. Notice that the application is not responsive. It will not minimize until the XML Web service call completes.
5. Click **Exit** to quit the application.

► **Modify the Expense Report application to make asynchronous calls**

1. Show TODO comments in the task list.

   To show TODO comments, on the **View** menu, point to **Show Tasks**, and then click **All**.

2. Find the first TODO comment in the code. Add the code to instantiate an **AsyncCallback** delegate that refers to the **WebserviceCallback** method of this class.

```
Dim asyncCB As New AsyncCallback _
    (AddressOf Me.WebserviceCallback)
```

3. Find the next TODO comment. Add the code to begin the call to the XML Web service.

```
WS.BeginGetReportsForEmployee(Nothing, Nothing, _
    0, 10, TotalReports, asyncCB, Nothing)
```

4. Find the next TODO comment and uncomment the line of code after the TODO comment.

5. Find the next two TODO comments. Comment out the rest of the code (the synchronous code) in the method.

6. Find the next TODO comment. Add the code to finish the call to the XML Web service.

```
ExpenseReports = WS.EndGetReportsForEmployee(result, _
   TotalReports)
```

7. Find the next TODO comment. Add the code to instantiate a **MethodInvoker** delegate that points to the **UpdateUI** method of this class.

```
Dim mi As New MethodInvoker(AddressOf Me.UpdateUI)
```

8. Find the next TODO comment. Add the code to call **BeginInvoke** on this form, passing the **MethodInvoker** delegate created in step 6.

```
Me.BeginInvoke(mi)
```

9. Save your files and build the project.

► **Observe how the Expense Report application behavior has changed**

1. Run the application.

2. Click **Call Web Service**. After the message **Async: Calling web service...** appears, try to minimize the window. Notice that the UI is still responsive during the call to the XML Web service.

3. Click **Exit** to quit the application.

4. Set breakpoints in the **CallBtn_Click**, **WebserviceCallback**, and **UpdateUI** methods. Rerun the application to see the flow of control of the asynchronous operation.

Lesson: How to Make Asynchronous Calls to Any Method

- Overview of How to Make Asynchronous Calls to Any Method
- How to Create the Asynchronous Delegate
- How to Initiate the Asynchronous Call
- How to Complete the Asynchronous Call
- How to Return Control to the Main Thread
- Demonstration: Using Asynchronous Delegates

Introduction

It is not necessary for a called object to provide explicit support for asynchronous calls. The .NET Framework provides services required for you to call any method asynchronously.

Lesson objectives

After completing this lesson, you will be able to:

- Describe how to make asynchronous calls to any method.
- Describe techniques to protect state and data in a multithreaded environment.
- Explicitly create and call asynchronous delegates.

Overview of How to Make Asynchronous Calls to Any Method

1 **You must explicitly create and call a delegate for the method that you want to invoke**

2 **Follow the design pattern for asynchronous programming**

- Initiate the call
- Complete the call
- Return data (if applicable) and control to the main thread

Introduction

When you make asynchronous calls to classes that contain built-in support for asynchronous programming, such as XML Web services and stream I/O, the compiler creates asynchronous delegates and their Begin*Operation* and End*Operation* methods for you.

Explicitly create the asynchronous delegate

When you want to asynchronously call methods in classes without built-in support, you must explicitly create and call the delegate for the method that you want to invoke.

Definition

A delegate is an object-oriented, type-safe, secure way to provide the functionality of a function pointer in the .NET Framework. Asynchronous delegates allow you to call a synchronous method in an asynchronous manner.

Follow design pattern for asynchronous programming

After creating the asynchronous delegate, you then follow the same process that you would use for making asynchronous calls to classes with built-in support:

1. Choose the completion mechanism that you want to use and do any setup the completion mechanism requires.
2. Initiate the asynchronous call.
3. Receive the completion notification and any results.
4. Return control to the main thread and update the UI, as appropriate.

Techniques for protecting state and data is covered in the topic How to Protect State and Data in a Multithreaded Environment.

How to Create the Asynchronous Delegate

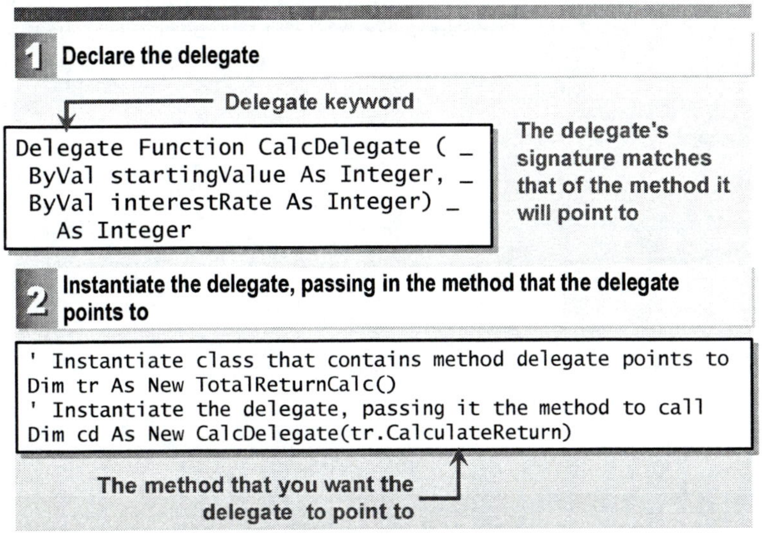

Introduction

After you have explicitly declared an asynchronous delegate, you can use the asynchronous methods of a delegate object created for you by the compiler. The .NET Framework will still make the threading infrastructure necessary for asynchronous programming transparent to you.

Procedure: Declaring the delegate

To declare the delegate, use the **delegate** keyword.

```
Delegate Function CalcDelegate ( _
   ByVal startingValue As Integer, _
   ByVal interestRate As Integer) _
   As Integer
```

The previous code declares a delegate to a method that returns an integer and takes two integers as parameters.

Because Microsoft Visual C#™ and Microsoft Visual Basic .NET compilers support asynchronous delegates, they generate the **Invoke** method and the **BeginInvoke** and **EndInvoke** methods when you declare the delegate.

Use the **Invoke** method if you want to call the target method synchronously.

Use the **BeginInvoke** method to call the target method asynchronously. The runtime queues the request and returns immediately to the caller. The target method will be called on a thread from the thread pool. The original thread that submitted the request is free to continue executing in parallel to the target method, which is running on a thread pool thread.

If a callback has been specified on **BeginInvoke**, it is called when the target method returns. In the callback, the **EndInvoke** method is used to obtain the return value and the in/out parameters. If the callback is not specified on **BeginInvoke**, you can use the other asynchronous design pattern techniques, for example, polling, on the original thread that submitted a request.

Procedure: Instantiating the delegate

Instantiate the class that contains the method that the delegate will point to.

```
Dim tr As New TotalReturnCalc()
```

Then instantiate the delegate, passing in the method it points to.

```
Dim cd As New CalcDelegate(tr.CalculateReturn)
```

How to Initiate the Asynchronous Call

1 Create the delegate to the callback method

2 Call the BeginInvoke method

- When using a callback method, pass in the delegate for the callback method
- Returns an object implementing **IAsyncResult**

Method that will receive the callback notification

```
' create AsyncCB delegate to callback method
Dim cb As New AsyncCallback(Me.ResultsCB)

' call BeginInvoke to asynchronously call the method
Dim ar As IAsyncResult = cd.BeginInvoke(startVal, intRate, _
   cb, Nothing)
```

Callback delegate passed in to BeginInvoke

Introduction

Using a callback method as the completion mechanism is most appropriate for Windows Forms applications. To use the callback method, you must create a delegate to safely invoke it.

Procedure: Creating the delegate to the callback method

To create the delegate that allows you to call the callback method, instantiate an **AsyncCallback** object:

```
Dim cb As New AsyncCallback(Me.ResultsCB)
```

In the code example above, **Me** refers to the object from which you are making the asynchronous call. Alternatively, the method that handles the callback could be in a different object, if necessary for your scenario.

Procedure: Calling the BeginInvoke method

To call the **BeginInvoke** method, pass the callback delegate, named **cb** in the code example, to the **BeginInvoke** method as the second to last parameter.

```
Dim ar As IAsyncResult = cd.BeginInvoke(startVal, intRate, _
   cb, Nothing)
```

The final parameter of the **BeginInvoke** method is of type **System.Object** and is for user data. This user data is passed into the callback when the operation is completed in the **AsyncState** property of the **IAsyncResult** parameter of the callback.

How to Complete the Asynchronous Call

1 Call the EndInvoke method

Returns a return value or a data structure that includes a return value

```
' inside the callback method called ResultsCB
Sub ResultsCB(ByVal ar As IAsyncResult)

   ...
   Dim result As Integer = cd.EndInvoke(ar)
   ...
End Sub
```

Use EndInvoke to return results

2 Update the UI to reflect the results of the operation

When using Windows Forms, this involves returning control back to the main UI thread because Windows Forms can only be safely called from the main thread

---

Introduction

When the asynchronous operation completes, the .NET Framework calls your callback method. Your callback method, in turn, calls the **EndInvoke** method to notify the caller of completion. For Windows Forms applications, you must return control to the main thread before updating the user interface.

Procedure: Calling the EndInvoke method

You can call the **EndInvoke** method to retrieve the results of the operation.

```
Dim result As Integer = cd.EndInvoke(ar)
```

Exceptions

If the asynchronous operation throws an exception, it will be returned from the call to the **EndInvoke** method.

Updating the UI

In Windows Forms applications, you must return control to the main thread before updating the user interface.

How to Return Control to the Main Thread

1 Instantiate a MethodInvoker delegate for the UI update method

```
' Switch back to main thread before updating UI

Dim mi As New MethodInvoker(Me.UpdateUI)
```

2 Asynchronously call the MethodInvoker delegate

```
' Use BeginInvoke to call the MethodInvoker, because
' it returns worker thread to thread pool faster

Me.BeginInvoke(mi)
```

Introduction

As with the design pattern discussed in the previous lesson, you use the **MethodInvoker** delegate to transfer control to the main thread.

Procedure: Instantiating a MethodInvoker delegate

```
Dim mi As New MethodInvoker(Me.UpdateUI)
```

Procedure: Invoking the MethodInvoker delegate asynchronously

```
Me.BeginInvoke(mi)
```

By calling the **UpdateUI** method asynchronously by using **BeginInvoke** instead of **Invoke**, the worker thread used to make the asynchronous call returns to the thread pool faster, thus promoting better application performance.

Notice that this step is only necessary if the UI in a Windows Forms application must be updated. Also notice that all of the steps after creating the delegate are the same in this case as they are in the case in which a delegate is not used.

Demonstration: Using Asynchronous Delegates

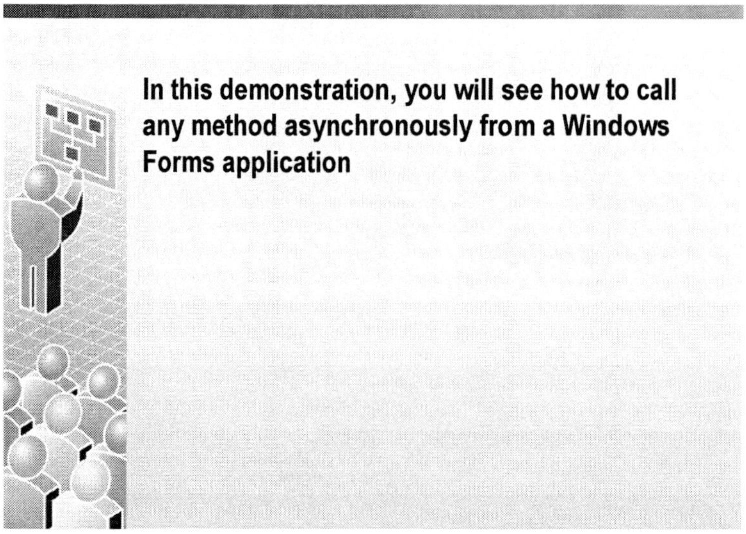

Introduction

In this demonstration, you will see how to call a method asynchronously from a Windows Forms application.

► **To view the code for the application**

1. Open the AsyncDelegates.sln solution file in *install_folder*\Democode\Mod07\Mod07_02\AsyncDelegates.
2. Open the Class1.vb source file and view the code.
3. Notice the **FactorizeDelegate** declaration near the top of the file. This shows an example of a delegate declaration.
4. Notice the **Factorize** method in the **PrimeFactorizer** class. This is the method the delegate will refer to and invoke asynchronously.
5. Notice the **FactorizeNumber** method in the **Simple** class. This is the method that instantiates a **PrimeFactorizer** object, then instantiates a delegate referring to the **Factorize** method in that class. Then it calls **BeginInvoke** on the delegate.
6. Notice the **FactorizedResults** method in the **Simple** class. This is the callback method that is invoked when the asynchronous operation completes.

► **To view the flow of control as the application executes**

1. Set breakpoints at the top of the **Factorize**, **FactorizeNumber**, and **FactorizedResults** methods.
2. Run the application, noticing the flow of control between the three methods mentioned above.

Lesson: Protecting State and Data in a Multithreaded Environment

- How to Protect State and Data in a Multithreaded Environment
- Demonstration: Protecting State and Data in a Multithreaded Environment

Introduction

No synchronization is the default for objects. Therefore, when you use asynchronous programming techniques, you must consider how to protect state and data in this multithreaded environment.

Lesson objective

After completing this lesson, you will be able to describe techniques to protect state and data in a multithreaded environment.

How to Protect State and Data in a Multithreaded Environment

- **Automatic Synchronization**

  Potential overhead incurred
- **Synchronized Code Region**

  Monitor class
- **Manual Synchronization**
  - **Mutex** class
  - **ReaderWriterLock** class
  - **Interlocked.Increment** and **Interlocked.Decrement** methods
- **Design applications to try to minimize synchronization needs**

Introduction

For many Windows Forms applications, little state protection code may be necessary, because most access of object state happens on the main thread. However, this will not be the case for every application. The **System.Threading** namespace provides classes and interfaces for synchronizing access to data to provide thread safety.

Automatic synchronization

You can use the **SynchronizationAttribute** on any class that is derived from **ContextBoundObject** to synchronize all instance methods and fields. All objects in the same context domain share the same lock. Multiple threads are allowed to access the instance methods and fields, but only a single thread is allowed at any one time. Static members are not protected from concurrent access by multiple threads.

Note Using automatic synchronization can incur more overhead than using manual synchronization techniques.

Synchronized code regions

Another technique that you can use is a compiler keyword to synchronize blocks of code, instance methods, and static methods. In Visual Basic .NET, the keyword is **SyncLock**. This keyword uses the **Monitor** class to lock the object.

For example, to synchronize access in a static method:

```
Class Cache

  Public Shared Sub Add(ByRef x As Integer)
      ' method code that doesn't require exclusive access
      SyncLock GetType(Cache)
          ' code requiring exclusive access to static data
      End SyncLock
      ' method code that doesn't require exclusive access
  End Sub
End Class
```

Or, to synchronize access in an instance method:

```
Class Counter

  Public Sub Read(ByVal threadNum As Integer)
      ' method code that doesn't require exclusive access
      SyncLock Me
          ' code requiring exclusive access to instance data
      End SyncLock
      ' method code that doesn't require exclusive access
  End Sub
End Class
```

Manual synchronization

You can use the **Monitor**, **Interlocked**, **Mutex**, **ManualResetEvent**, **AutoResetEvent**, and **ReaderWriterLock** classes to acquire and release a lock to protect global, static, and instance fields and global, static, and instance methods.

Designing applications to minimize synchronization needs

For many UI-based applications, little or no special synchronization code is required. All of the changes of the UI must happen on the main application thread, so this usually forces synchronous access to state information. Also, careful enabling and disabling of UI elements can prevent the application from getting into an undefined state. For example, the Expense Reporting sample application enables and disables buttons as asynchronous XML Web service calls are made to prevent threading related problems. Therefore, no special synchronization code is required in the Expense Reporting application, other than the use of **MethodInvoker** delegates to switch control to the main thread upon completion of asynchronous calls.

For more information about synchronization techniques, see Module 14, "Threading and Asynchronous Programming" in Course 2415B, *Programming with the Microsoft .NET Framework (Microsoft Visual Basic® .NET).*

Demonstration: Protecting State and Data in a Multithreaded Environment

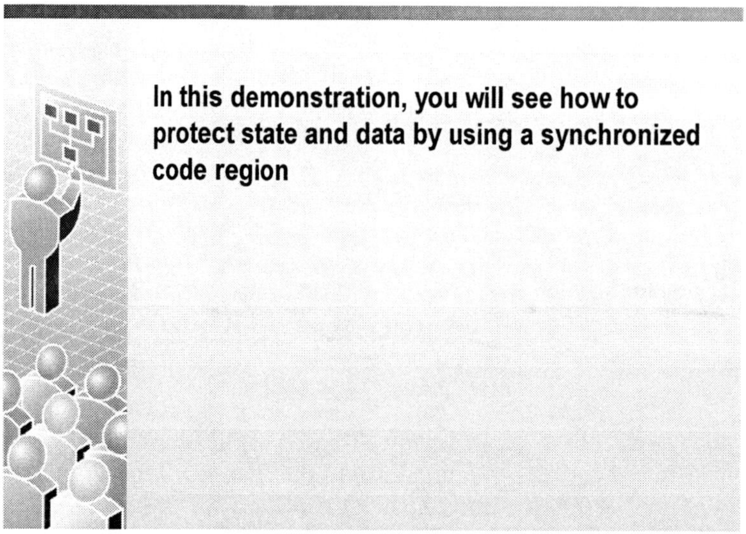

Introduction

In this demonstration, you will see how to protect state and data by using a synchronized code region.

► **To view the code for the ThreadSafety application**

1. Open the ThreadSafety.sln solution file in *install_folder*\Democode\Mod07\Mod07_03\ThreadSafety.
2. Open the Class1.vb source file and view the code.
3. Notice the **Read** method in the **CounterUnsafe** class.

   This method reads the **count** member variable twice, with a delay in between the two readings. If other threads change the value of **count** during that interval, two different values will be read.
4. Notice the **Increment** method in the **CounterUnsafe** class.

   This method increments the **count** variable, with a long delay between when it reads the value of count and writes the updated value of **count**. If other threads try to update the value of **count** during this interval, the value of **count** written by this method overwrites the results of other calls.
5. Notice the **Read** method in the **CounterUsingLock** class.

   This method reads the **count** variable twice, with a delay in between the two readings. However, this method accesses **count** within a **lock** code block, so the value of **count** will not change between the two readings.
6. Notice the **Increment** method in the **CounterUsingLock** class.

   This method increments the **count** variable, with a long delay between when it reads the value of **count** and writes the updated value of **count**. However, this method accesses **count** within a **lock** code block, so the value of **count** cannot be changed while this method accesses it.

▶ **To run the application and view the output**

1. To open the Visual Studio .NET command prompt, click **Start**, point to **All Programs**, point to **Microsoft Visual Studio .NET**, point to **Visual Studio .NET Tools**, and then click **Visual Studio .NET Command Prompt**.
2. Change directories to *install_folder*\Democode\Mod07\Mod07_03\ThreadSafety\bin. Run the application ThreadSafety.exe from the command line.
3. View the output of the test. The output should look similar to the following.

```
Unsafe test:
Start Resource writing (Thread=0) count: 0
Stop  Resource writing (Thread=0) count: 1
Start Resource reading (Thread=1)count: 1
Stop  Resource reading (Thread=1) count: 1
Start Resource writing (Thread=2) count: 1
Stop  Resource writing (Thread=2) count: 2
Start Resource reading (Thread=3)count: 2
Stop  Resource reading (Thread=3) count: 2
Start Resource writing (Thread=4) count: 2
Stop  Resource writing (Thread=4) count: 3
Start Resource reading (Thread=5)count: 3
Start Resource writing (Thread=6) count: 3
Stop  Resource reading (Thread=5) count: 3
Start Resource reading (Thread=7)count: 3
Stop  Resource reading (Thread=7) count: 3
Start Resource writing (Thread=8) count: 3
Stop  Resource writing (Thread=6) count: 4
Start Resource reading (Thread=9)count: 4
Stop  Resource reading (Thread=9) count: 4
Stop  Resource writing (Thread=8) count: 4
All Unsafe threads have completed.
```

(*Code continued on the following page.*)

```
Lock test:
Start Resource writing (Thread=0) count: 0
Stop Resource writing (Thread=0) count: 1
Start Resource reading (Thread=1)count: 1
Stop Resource reading (Thread=1) count: 1
Start Resource writing (Thread=2) count: 1
Stop Resource writing (Thread=2) count: 2
Start Resource reading (Thread=3)count: 2
Stop Resource reading (Thread=3) count: 2
Start Resource writing (Thread=4) count: 2
Stop Resource writing (Thread=4) count: 3
Start Resource reading (Thread=5)count: 3
Stop Resource reading (Thread=5) count: 3
Start Resource writing (Thread=6) count: 3
Stop Resource writing (Thread=6) count: 4
Start Resource reading (Thread=7)count: 4
Stop Resource reading (Thread=7) count: 4
Start Resource writing (Thread=8) count: 4
Stop Resource writing (Thread=8) count: 5
Start Resource reading (Thread=9)count: 5
Stop Resource reading (Thread=9) count: 5
All Lock threads have completed.
```

Note that even though **Increment** was called five times for the unsafe test, the value of the counter never reaches five. Also, the start and stop notifications are interspersed among different threads. In the lock version, the start and stop notifications are paired for each thread, and the counter is correctly incremented to five.

Review

- The .NET Asynchronous Programming Model
- The Asynchronous Programming Model Design Pattern
- Protecting State and Data in a Multithreaded Environment

1. When and why would you use asynchronous programming techniques in an application?

   Lot of interaction

2. In a Windows Forms application, what are the main steps to follow to use the asynchronous programming design pattern with an asynchronous callback for completion?

3. List the four ways to complete an asynchronous call.

4. Why do you need to return control to the main thread before updating the UI in Windows Forms applications?

5. What additional step must you follow to asynchronously call a method of any class?

   must create own delegate

6. If an asynchronous operation throws an exception, when does your code receive the exception?

   pop up in your form
   when your end operation is called

7. What keyword is provided by the Visual Basic .NET language for controlling access by multiple threads to a block of code?

   SyncLock

Lab 7.1: Making Asynchronous Calls to an XML Web Service

Objectives

After completing this lab, you will have demonstrated your ability to:

- Make asynchronous calls by using the .NET Framework asynchronous design pattern.
- Convert synchronous calls to asynchronous calls by using the .NET Framework asynchronous design pattern.
- Use the Visual Studio .NET debugger to follow the flow of asynchronous calls.

Note This lab focuses on the concepts in Module 7, "Asynchronous Programming," in Course 2565A, *Developing Microsoft .NET Applications for Windows (Visual Basic .NET)*. As a result, this lab may not comply with Microsoft security recommendations.

Prerequisites

Before working on this lab, you must have:

- The knowledge and skills to develop a simple Windows Forms application by using a Visual Studio .NET–compatible programming language.
- The knowledge and skills to debug an application by using Visual Studio .NET.
- The knowledge and skills to call XML Web services and make asynchronous calls by using the .NET Framework asynchronous design pattern.

Scenario

The Expense Report application makes numerous calls to an XML Web service. To improve the responsiveness and usability of the application, all of the XML Web service calls should be made asynchronously.

To make the calls asynchronous, you must perform the following tasks:

- Convert the synchronous XML Web service calls to asynchronous calls.
- Write the method that handles the asynchronous callback.
- Write the method that updates the user interface.

In the starter code for this lab, the asynchronous callback method and user interface update method have already been written, and some of the XML Web service calls have already been converted.

In this lab, you will convert the rest of the synchronous XML Web service calls to asynchronous calls and then use the Visual Studio debugger to follow the flow of the asynchronous calls in the resulting code.

Lab Setup

There are starter and solution files associated with this lab. Browse to *install_folder*\Labfiles\Lab07_1\Ex01\Starter to find the starter files, and browse to *install_folder*\Labfiles\Lab07_1\Ex01\Solution to find the solution files. If you performed a default installation of the course files, *install_folder* corresponds to C:\Program Files\Msdntrain\2565.

Estimated time to complete this lab: 45 minutes

Exercise 1
Converting Synchronous Calls to Asynchronous Calls

In this exercise, you will convert some synchronous XML Web service calls to asynchronous calls. You will also use the Visual Studio debugger to view the flow of asynchronous calls and test your application to ensure that it has the expected results.

<table>
<tr><th>Tasks</th><th>Additional information</th></tr>
<tr><td>1. Open the ExpenseReport project in Visual Studio .NET. Browse to install_folder\Labfiles\Lab07_1\Ex01\Starter to find the project files.</td><td>a. For more information about opening a project file and starting an application, see the following resource:
• The Visual Studio .NET Help documentation. For additional information about opening a project file, in Search, select the Search in titles only check box, then search by using the phrase Open Project Dialog Box. For additional information about starting an application in the Designer, in Index, search by using the phrase Debugging Windows Applications.</td></tr>
<tr><td>2. Open the ExpenseReportList source file, and view the code. Refer to the synchronous versions of the calls to see which parameters to pass:
• The first five parameters should be the same.
• The sixth parameter should be the callback delegate.
• The seventh parameter should be Nothing.</td><td>a. See the TODO comments in the code for more detailed information about the tasks that you must perform to convert the synchronous XML Web service calls in the constructor to asynchronous calls.
b. For more information about how to make asynchronous calls, see the following resources:
• Practice: Making an Asynchronous Call to an XML Web Service in Module 7, “Asynchronous Programming,” in Course 2565A, Developing Microsoft .NET Applications for Windows (Visual Basic .NET).
• Lesson: The Asynchronous Programming Model Design Pattern in Module 7, “Asynchronous Programming,” in Course 2565A, Developing Microsoft .NET Applications for Windows (Visual Basic .NET).
• The .NET Framework SDK documentation. For more information about the asynchronous design pattern, search by using the phrase Including Asynchronous Calls.</td></tr>
</table>

Tasks	Additional information
3. View the flow of asynchronous code by setting breakpoints in the **ExpenseReportList** constructor and the **GetReportsCB** and **UpdateReportsUI** methods. **a.** Run the application in the Visual Studio debugger. Click **View Submitted Reports**. Step through the code, and make sure it executes as expected. **b.** Confirm the correct behavior in the user interface by making sure that the expense reports are downloaded asynchronously when a new list window is opened.	**a.** For more information about debugging and controlling the flow of asynchronous calls, see the following resources: • Practice: Making an Asynchronous Call to an XML Web Service in Module 7, "Asynchronous Programming," in Course 2565A, *Developing Microsoft .NET Applications for Windows (Visual Basic .NET)*. This practice contains information about how to debug an asynchronous call. • Lesson: The Asynchronous Programming Model Design Pattern in Module 7, "Asynchronous Programming," in Course 2565A, *Developing Microsoft .NET Applications for Windows (Visual Basic .NET)*. This lesson contains information about the flow of control of an asynchronous call.

msdn® training

Module 8: Enhancing the Usability of Applications

Contents

Microsoft®

Overview

- Adding Accessibility Features
- Adding Help to an Application
- Localizing an Application

Introduction

Enhancing the usability of an application has several benefits. It can help all users to learn how to use an application more quickly and more efficiently in their work. It can also make the application available for wider audiences—from people with disabilities, such as people who are blind or deaf, to worldwide audiences who speak different languages and who come from different cultures.

This module explores the support that is available in the Microsoft® .NET Framework that allows developers to more easily enhance the usability of the applications that they develop.

Objectives

After completing this module, you will be able to:

- Use .NET Framework features to add and enable accessibility features in an application.
- Add support for context-sensitive Help, Help menus, and ToolTips to an application.
- Use localization properties and resource files to create a localized version of a .NET Framework Windows Forms application.

Lesson: Adding Accessibility Features

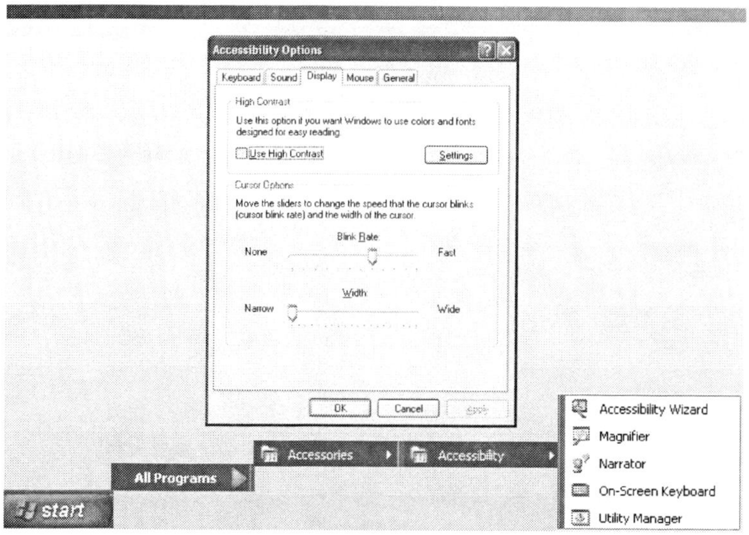

Introduction

By following accessibility design practices and by using support for accessibility features in the .NET Framework, you can make your applications available to your customers or employees with accessibility needs.

This lesson will briefly describe the accessibility support available in the .NET Framework and how to make the forms and controls of your applications accessible. The lesson also covers how to test the application by using Microsoft Narrator, an accessibility utility that is included with the Microsoft Windows® XP operating system.

For more information about supporting accessibility in your applications, refer to the topics under "Accessibility" in the MSDN Library section titled "User Interface Design and Development."

Lesson objectives

After completing this lesson, you will be able to:

- Describe the accessibility support that is available in the .NET Framework.
- Make the forms and controls in your application accessible.
- Test the accessibility of your application.

Accessibility Support in the .NET Framework

- **Accessibility options**

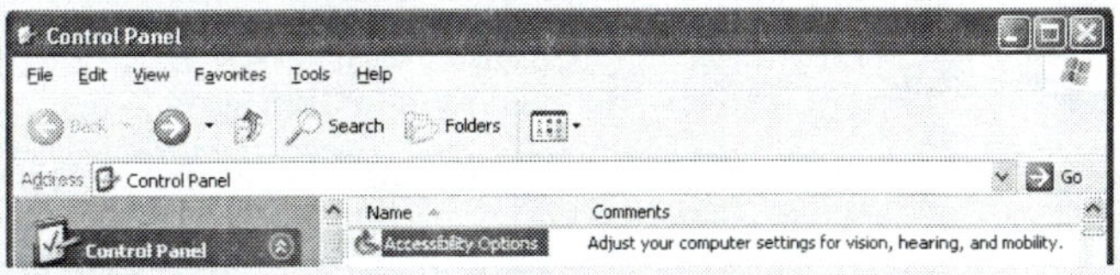

- **Microsoft accessibility aids**
  - Narrator
  - Magnifier
  - On-Screen Keyboard
- **Developers can provide accessibility support by setting properties on forms and controls in their applications**

Introduction

One of the goals for Windows XP was to deliver easier and better customization that caters to specific hearing, vision and mobility needs.

Windows support

The Windows operating system provides several accessibility options that users can set from Control Panel to control interaction with the keyboard, mouse, display, and sounds.

Definition

Accessibility aids are specialized programs and devices that help people with disabilities use computers more effectively. Some accessibility aids are built in to the Windows operating system. There are many types of aids. Some examples include:

- Screen enlargers for people who have low vision.
- Screen readers for people who are blind.
- Voice input utilities for people who control their computers by providing verbal commands to their computers instead of by using the keyboard or mouse.

In this lesson, you will use Narrator—the screen reader included with Windows XP—to demonstrate and test the accessibility properties that you can set on the user interface elements of your applications.

Developer support

For more information about the guidelines for designing accessible applications, see the MSDN Library and the Microsoft Accessibility Web site http://www.microsoft.com/enable/.

Some examples of the guidelines include:

- The application must be compatible with specific system color, size, font, sound, and input settings.

  This provides a consistent user interface (UI) across all applications on the user's system. Users can configure their preferred settings for these elements by using Control Panel.

- Applications must be compatible with the High Contrast display option.

  Users who desire a high degree of screen legibility select the **Use High Contrast** check box on the **Display** tab of the **Accessibility Options** dialog box. When this option is selected, several restrictions are imposed on the application. For example, only system colors that can be selected through Control Panel, or colors set by the user, may be used by the application.

- The application must provide keyboard access to all features.

  This allows the user to interact with the application without requiring a pointing device, such as a mouse.

- Applications must not convey information by sound alone.

  Applications that convey information by sound must provide additional options to express this information. This includes on-screen messages.

Many of the standard user interface elements also have properties that you can set either at design time or programmatically in your applications to provide information for use by accessibility aids.

How to Make Forms and Controls Accessible

1 Set standard properties to values that support accessibility

Text, Font Size, Forecolor, Backcolor, BackgroundImage

2 Set Accessibility properties

At design time or programmatically

Control Property	Description
AccessibleName	Briefly describes and identifies the object. Examples: button or menu item text
AccessibleDescription	Provides greater context for low-vision or blind users
AccessibleRole	Describes the use of the element in the user interface

```
Me.AppExitButton = New System.Windows.Forms.PushButton()
Me.AppExitButton.Text = "E&xit"
AppExitButton.AccessibleRole = _
   System.Windows.Forms.AccessibleRole.PushButton
AppExitButton.AccessibleName = "Exit"
AppExitButton.AccessibleDescription = _
   "Use this button to exit the application"
Me.Controls.Add(Me.AppExitButton)
```

Introduction

The settings of various properties of a control or form can affect how accessible your application will be. Some properties are specifically designed for use by accessibility aids while others are more general properties like **FontSize**.

Properties related to accessibility

This table provides accessibility considerations related to certain properties.

Property	Considerations for accessibility
AccessibleName	This control property briefly describes and identifies the object, such as the text in a button, the name of a menu item or a label displayed next to a text box control. Accessibility aids read the value of this property and report it to the user. For example, this text is read by Narrator and provided to the user audibly.
AccessibleDescription	This control property provides greater context beyond the **AccessibleName** property for low-vision or blind users. You can use this property to describe the visual appearance of the object such as buttons that contain graphics rather than text. Narrator does not read the value of this property, but other accessibility aids may.
AccessibleRole	This control property describes the use of the element in the user interface. For example, button, text box, animation, dialog box, Help balloon, list, and so forth. Leave this set to **(default)** unless you need to provide a more specific description for a custom or composite control.
TabIndex	Creates a sensible navigational path through the form. It is important for controls without intrinsic labels, such as text boxes, to have their associated label immediately precede them in the tab order.

(*continued*)

Property	**Considerations for accessibility**
Text	Use the ampersand (&) character to create access keys. Using access keys is part of providing documented keyboard access to features.
FontSize	If the font size is not adjustable, then it should be set to 10 points or larger. After the form's font size is set, all the controls added to the form thereafter will have the same size.
ForeColor	If this property is set to the default, then the user's color preferences will be used on the form.
BackColor	If this property is set to the default, then the user's color preferences will be used on the form.
BackgroundImage	Leave this property blank to make text more readable.

Setting accessibility properties at design time

At design time, use the Properties window to set the appropriate values for properties for a form or control.

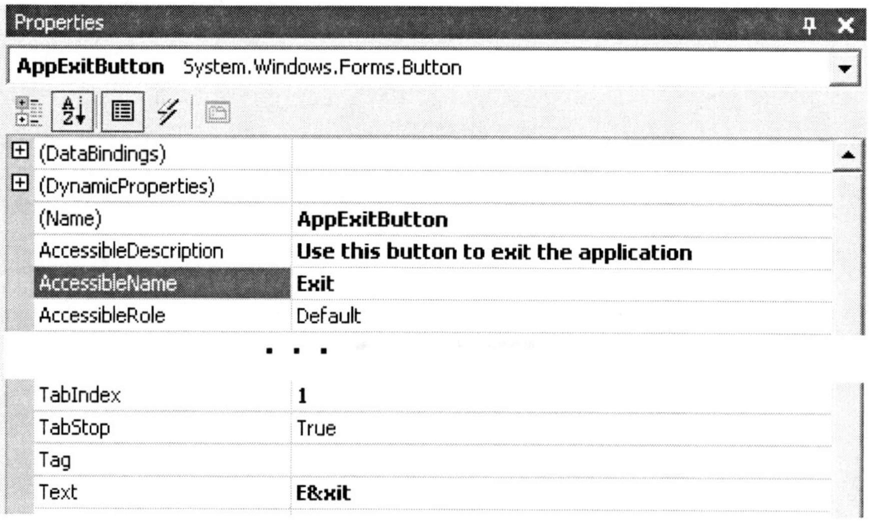

Programmatically setting accessibility properties

You can also set the property values programmatically. In the following code, a button that has the appropriate property values is created and added to a form. The **Me** keyword in the code refers to the form to which the button is added.

```
Me.AppExitButton = New System.Windows.Forms.PushButton()
Me.AppExitButton.Text = "E&xit"
AppExitButton.AccessibleRole = _
   System.Windows.Forms.AccessibleRole.PushButton
AppExitButton.AccessibleName = "Exit"
AppExitButton.AccessibleDescription = _
   "Use this button to exit the application"
Me.Controls.Add(Me.AppExitButton)
```

How to Test Accessibility

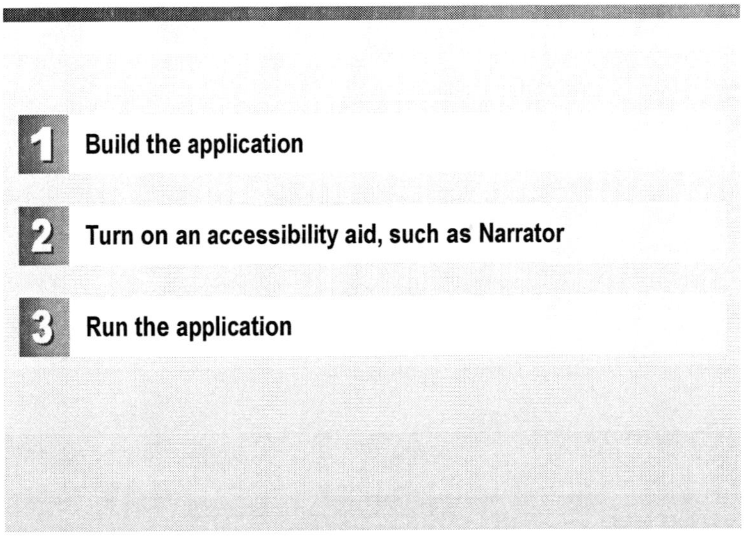

Introduction

After you set the appropriate property values for your user interface elements to support accessibility and build your application, you can use one of the built-in accessibility aids such as Narrator to test the application.

Procedure: Testing the application with Narrator

To test the accessibility features that you added to your application:

1. If you have not already done so, build your application.
2. Set the volume on your computer to a level that is comfortable for you.
3. On the **Start** menu, point to **All Programs**, point to **Accessories**, point to **Accessibility**, and then click **Narrator**.
4. Start your application and navigate the user interface.
5. Notice how Narrator uses the accessibility property information to describe the user interface and your interaction with the application.

Note Notice that Narrator reads the information for one of the controls twice. This is because Narrator automatically reads the information from the control that has focus, then reads the information about the form, and finally reads the information about all the controls that appear on the form.

Practice: Adding Accessibility Support to an Application

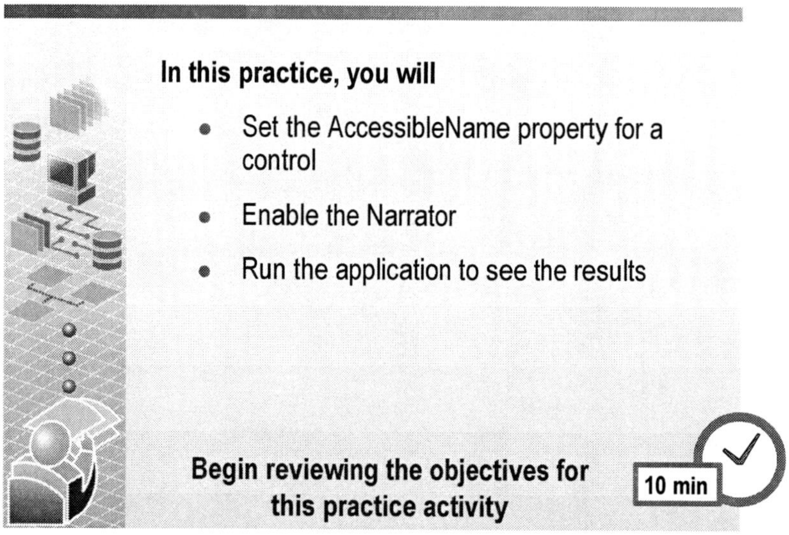

Introduction

In this practice, you will set the **AccessibleName** property for a control in the UsabilityDemo project, enable Narrator, and run the UsabilityDemo application to see the results.

Instructions

► **Add accessibility support to an application**

1. In Microsoft Visual Studio® .NET, open the UsabilityDemo project in *install_folder*\Practices\Mod08\Mod08_01\Starter.

> **Note** If you performed a default installation of the course files, *install_folder* corresponds to C:\Program Files\Msdntrain\2565.

2. Open the UsabilityDemo form.
3. Click **Show Date/Time**.
4. Set the **AccessibleName** property to **Shows the computer's current date and time**.
5. Make sure that the **AccessibleRole** property is set to **Default**.
6. Save your changes and rebuild the project.
7. Set the volume on your computer to a level that is comfortable for you.
8. Start Narrator. On the **Start** menu, point to **All Programs**, point to **Accessories**, point to **Accessibility**, and then click **Narrator**.
9. Run the UsabilityDemo application either from the command prompt or from Windows Explorer.
10. As the application runs, listen to Narrator describe the UsabilityDemo form and the **Show Date/Time** button.

Lesson: Adding Help to an Application

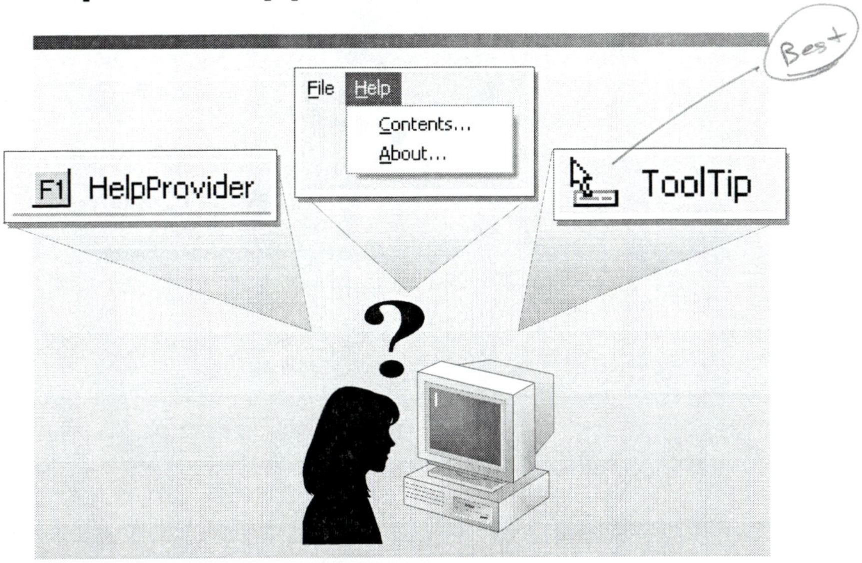

Introduction

Adding Help to your application will make it easier for all users to learn how to use your application more quickly and more efficiently.

Lesson objectives

After completing this lesson, you will be able to:

- Describe the Help support available in the .NET Framework.
- Add Help to an application by adding context-sensitive Help, Help menus, and ToolTips.

Help in the .NET Framework

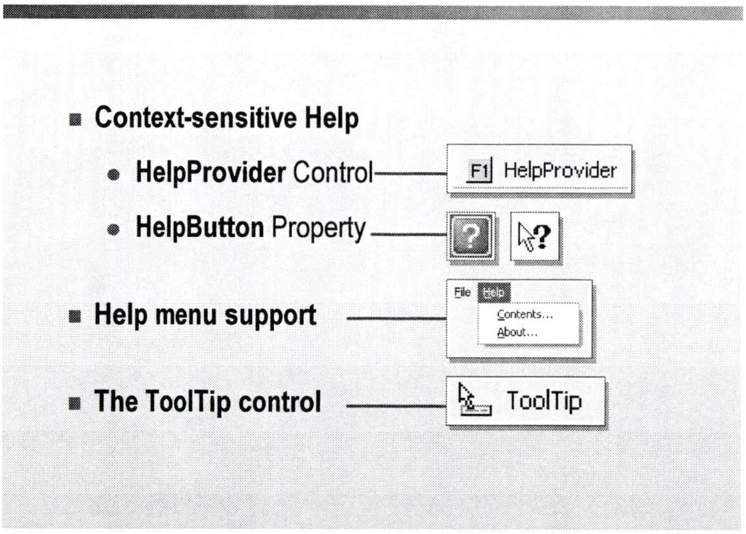

Introduction

The .NET Framework provides support for adding Help to your application by using three main areas:

- Context-sensitive Help
- Help menus
- ToolTips

Adding support for Help at design time

Visual Studio .NET provides several new controls that you can use when developing applications. To provide context-sensitive Help, you can use the **HelpProvider** control and the **HelpButton** property. To create a short Help text string that will appear when a user rests the mouse on a control, you can use the **ToolTip** control. The **HelpProvider** and **ToolTip** controls do not appear on the form. They provide an interface between the controls and the properties that you can set to provide Help and ToolTips.

You can use the **MainMenu** control to add a Help menu to the application to provide easy access to Help topics.

How to Add Context-Sensitive Help for Forms and Controls

1. **Add the HelpProvider control**
   Set the **HelpNamespace** property
2. **Add a HelpButton to the form**
3. **For each control that you want to add Help information set the following properties**
   - **HelpKeyword**
   - **HelpNavigator**
   - **HelpString**
4. **Build and test the application**
   Give a control focus and press F1

Introduction

Context-sensitive Help is the information that is displayed about the user interface element that has focus when the user presses F1 or clicks the **Help** button on a form and then clicks a user interface element.

Adding context-sensitive Help for forms and controls involves several steps.

Procedure: Adding the HelpProvider control

The **HelpProvider** control enables Help in an application.

1. In Visual Studio .NET Design view, use the Toolbox to add a **HelpProvider** control to a form.
2. Associate help text with each control.
   - If you do not set the **HelpNamespace** property of the **HelpProvider** control, then information in the **HelpString** property for the control with focus displays in a small pop-up window near the control.
   - If you do set the **HelpNamespace** property of the **HelpProvider** control to a URL or a file, then when the user presses F1 at run time, the information from the URL or file specified in the **HelpNamespace** property displays.

Procedure: Adding a Help button to the form

When the user clicks the **Help** button on the form at run time and then clicks a control, the text in the **HelpString** property for that control displays.

1. In Visual Studio .NET Design view, set the following properties for the form to which you want to add a **Help** button.
2. Set the **HelpButton** property to **True**.
3. Set the **MaximizeBox** property to **False**.
4. Set the **MinimizeBox** property to **False**.

Set the Help information for each control

In Visual Studio .NET Design view, set the **HelpKeyword**, **HelpNavigator**, and **HelpString** properties for each control for which you want to add Help information.

If you set the **HelpNamespace** property in the **HelpProvider** control to an HTML page and you set the **HelpKeyword** property of a control, the Help system will try to locate an anchor tag in the Help file that has the keyword in it when the F1 key is pressed. For example, if the keyword is **FormHelp**, the Help system will look for <A NAME="FormHelp"> in the target HTML file. Because F1 is now overridden by setting the **HelpNamespace** property to bring up a separate Help file, the **Help** button can be used to mimic the F1 functionality.

The **HelpNavigator** property determines how the keyword is used by the Help system to locate the information the user has requested. This property can take one of the following values.

HelpNavigator property value	Description
AssociateIndex	Specifies that the index for a specified topic is performed in the specified URL.
Find	The search page for the specified URL is displayed.
Index	The index page for the specified URL is displayed.
TableOfContents	The table of contents page for the specified URL is displayed.
KeywordIndex	Specifies a keyword search for and the action to take in the specified URL.
Topic	The topic referenced by the specified URL is displayed.

The **HelpString** property is used for pop-up Help (the Help that is displayed when a user presses F1 when a specific control has focus). If the **HelpNamespace** property on the **HelpProvider** is set, pressing F1 on a Help-enabled control will always bring up the target Help file rather than the pop-up window.

Note If you set the **HelpButton** property on a form to **True** and do not set the **MaximizeBox** and **MinimizeBox** properties to **False**, then the form will display the maximize box and minimize box, but it will not display the Help button.

How to Link Help Topics to a Menu

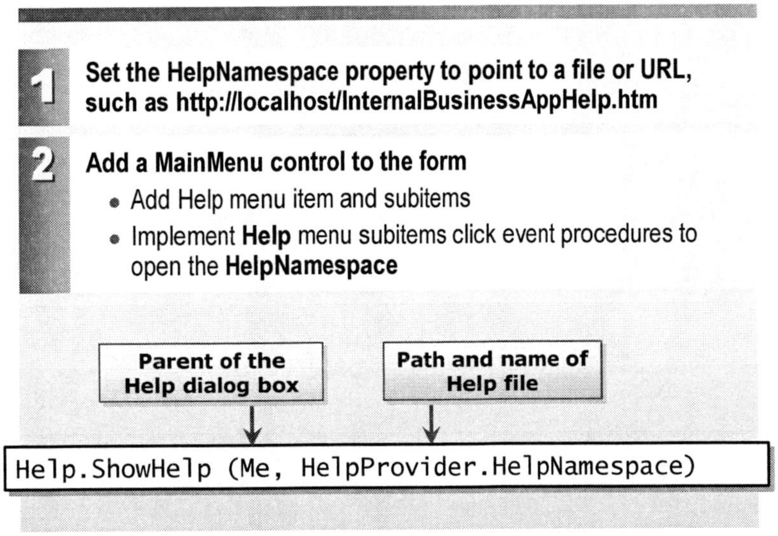

Introduction

You can use the Visual Studio .NET **MainMenu** control to add a menu and submenus to your application.

Procedure: Linking Help topics to a menu

To link Help topics to a menu:

1. In Visual Studio .NET Design view, add the **MainMenu** control to the form.

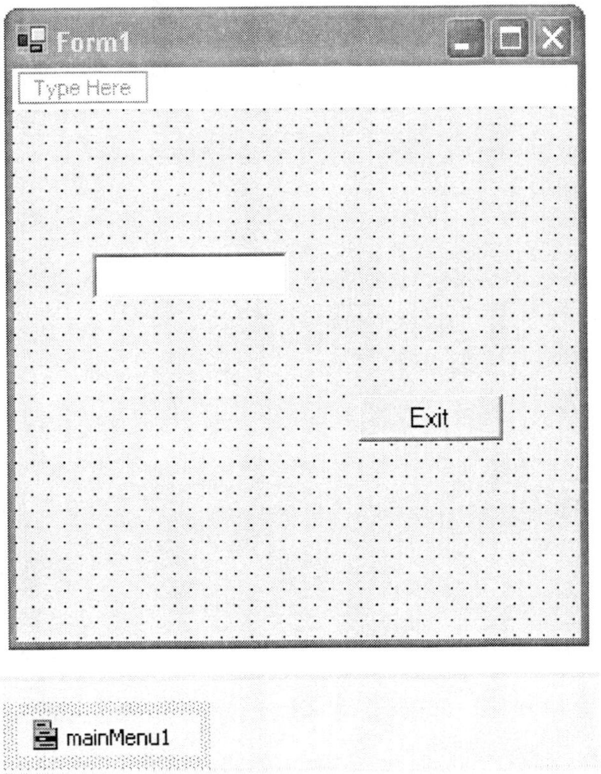

2. Edit the menu to add the **Help** menu and **Help** menu items.

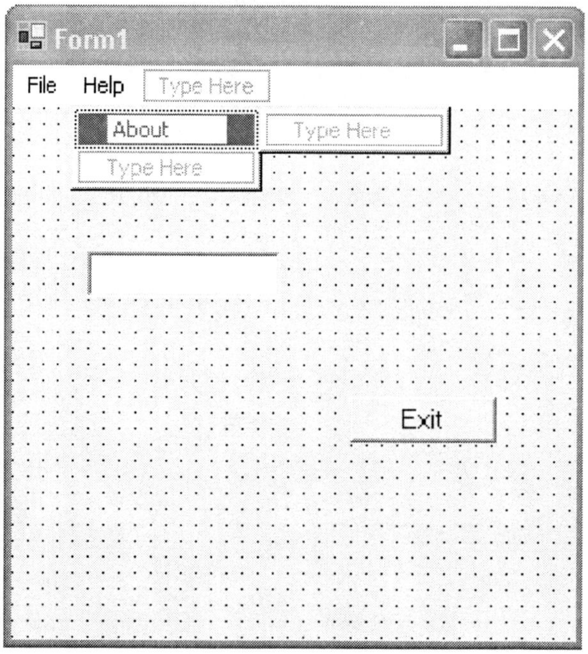

3. When the **Help** menu option is clicked at run time, it fires a click event. In the click event code for the menu item, add code to open the Help file:

```
Help.ShowHelp(Me, HelpProvider.HelpNamespace)
```

In the previous code:

- The first parameter (**Me**) is the control that identifies the parent of the **Help** dialog box. In this case, the form is the parent control of the **Help** dialog box.
- The second parameter (**HelpProvider.HelpNamespace**) is the path and name of the Help file. The URL can be of the form C:\..., file:///..., or http://....

Practice: Adding Help to an Application

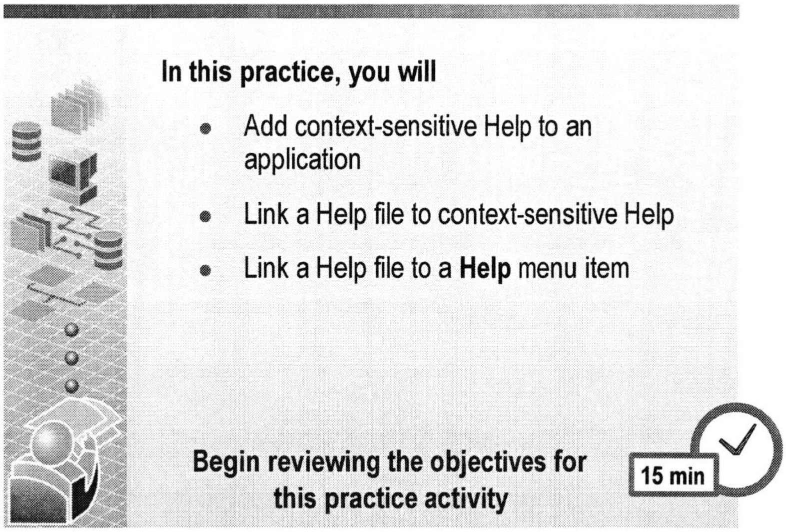

Introduction

In this practice, you will add the **HelpProvider** control to the application and set the **HelpString** property of the **Show Date/Time** button to support context-sensitive Help. Then you will set the **HelpNamespace** property on the **HelpProvider** control and the **HelpKeyword** and **HelpNavigator** properties of the **Show Date/Time** button to support access to Help files. You will also add the **Help** button to the form and complete the code for the **Help** menu to display the Help file.

Instructions

► **Add context-sensitive Help to an application**

1. In Visual Studio .NET, open the UsabilityDemo.sln solution file in *install_folder*\Practices\Mod08\Mod08_02\Starter.
2. Open the UsabilityDemo.vb form in Design view.
3. On the **View** menu, click **ToolBox**.
4. In the **ToolBox**, double-click the **HelpProvider** control to add it to the form.
5. Change the **(Name)** property of the **HelpProvider** to **UsabilityDemoHelpProvider**.
6. Click the **Show Date/Time** button to display its properties.
7. Set the **HelpString on UsabilityDemoHelpProvider** property to **Shows the current date and time in the text box above**.
8. Build and run the application.
9. Tab through the controls until the **Show Date/Time** button has focus.
10. Press F1 to view the context-sensitive Help for the **Show Date/Time** button.

► **Link to a Help file to provide context-sensitive Help**

1. In the UsabilityDemo project, change the **HelpNamespace** property of the **UsabilityDemoHelpProvider** control to **http://localhost/UsabilityDemoHelpFile.htm**.
2. Click the **Show Date/Time** button to display its properties.
3. Set the **HelpKeyword on UsabilityDemoHelpProvider** property to **DateAndTime**.
4. Set the **HelpNavigator on UsabilityDemoHelpProvider** property to **Topic**.
5. Set the **HelpButton** property of the **UsabilityDemo** form to **True**.
6. Set the **MaximizeBox** property of the **UsabilityDemo** form to **False**.
7. Set the **MinimizeBox** property of the **UsabilityDemo** form to **False**.
8. Build and run the application.
9. Tab through the controls until the **Show Date/Time** button has focus.
10. Press F1 to view the topic in the Help file in Microsoft Internet Explorer.
11. Close Internet Explorer.
12. Click the help button in the upper right corner of the window to enable context-sensitive Help.

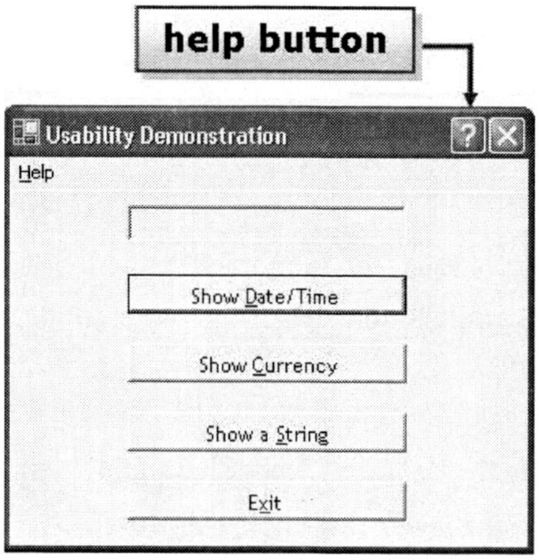

13. Click **Show Date/Time**.

    A small window will appear that explains what the **Show Date/Time** button does.

14. Close the application.

► Link Help to a Help menu in an application

1. In the UsabilityDemo.sln solution file, open the UsabilityDemo.vb form in Design view.
2. Click the **Help** menu to show the items in the menu.
3. Double-click the **Help** menu item in the **Help** menu to display the source code for the **Click** event for the menu item.
4. Show TODO comments in the Task List.

   To show TODO comments, on the **View** menu, point to **Show Tasks**, and then click **All**.
5. Locate the TODO comment in the **Click** event handler for the menu item, and add the following code.

```
' TODO: Call the ShowHelp method to display the
'       help file to the user.
Help.ShowHelp(Me, UsabilityDemoHelpProvider.HelpNamespace)
```

6. Build and run the application.
7. On the **Help** menu, click the **Help** menu item.

   Internet Explorer displays the Help file.

How to Display Help with the ToolTip Control

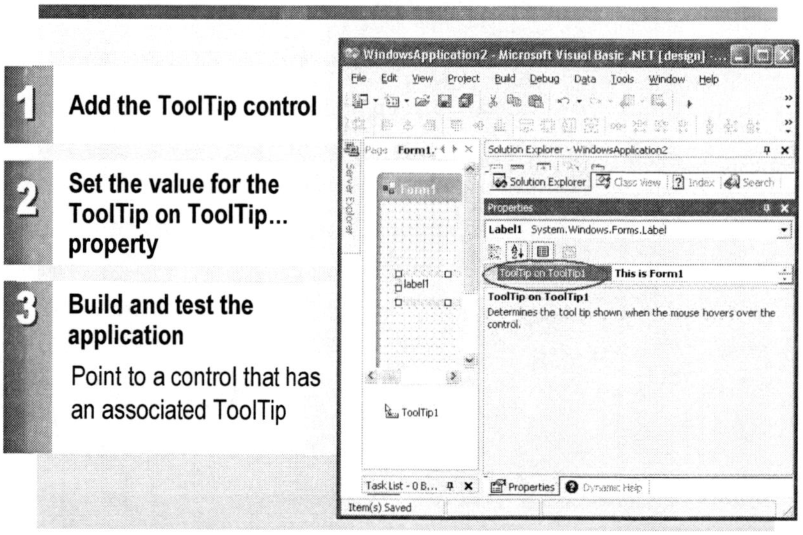

Introduction

To enable ToolTips in an application, you must add a **ToolTip** control to each form.

Procedure: Adding ToolTips to an application

To add ToolTips to an application:

1. In Visual Studio .NET Design view, add a **ToolTip** control to the form.

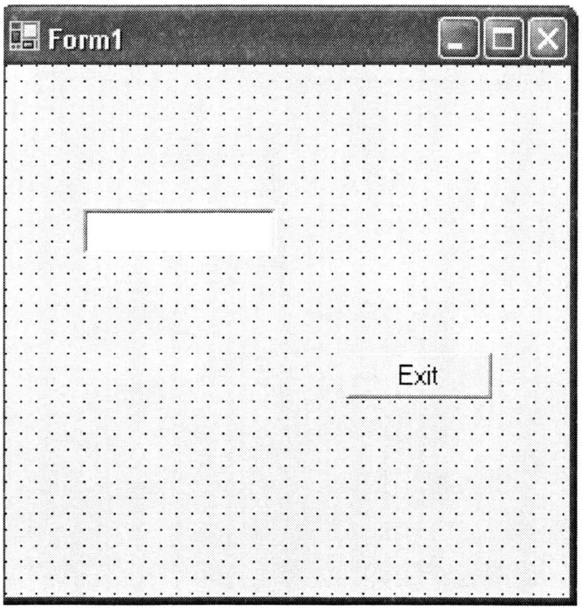

2. Set the appropriate value for the ToolTip in the **ToolTipControlName** Properties window for each control on the form for which you want a ToolTip to display.

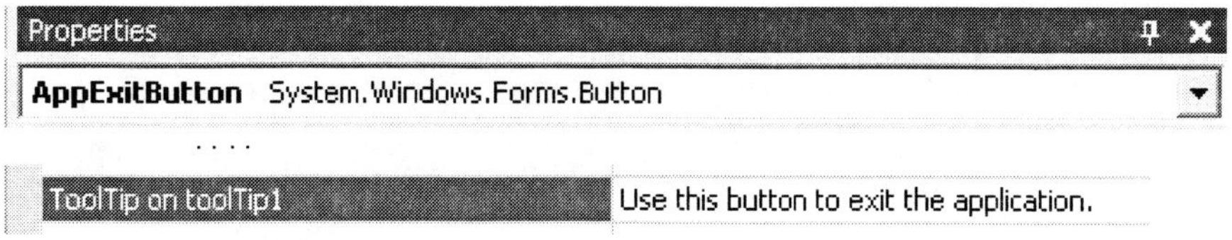

When the user moves the mouse pointer over the control at run time, after a short pause the ToolTip window appears, displaying the text that you set as the value for the **ToolTip on toolTip1** property.

Practice: Adding ToolTips to an Application

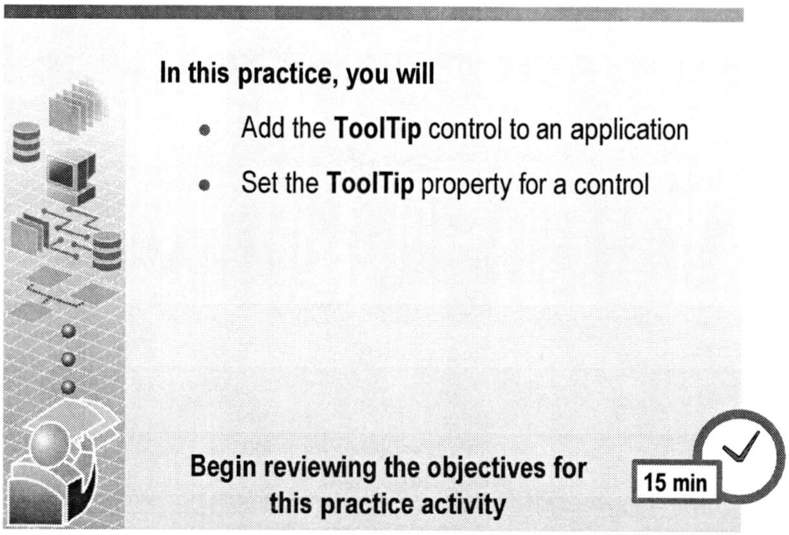

Introduction

In this practice, you will add a **ToolTip** control to the form and set the **ToolTip on UsabilityToolTip** property of the **Show Date/Time** button to a short string. You will then run the application to test whether the ToolTip appears when you point to the button by using the mouse pointer.

Instructions

► **Add ToolTips to an application**

1. In Visual Studio .NET, open the UsabilityDemo.sln solution file in *install_folder*\Practices\Mod08\Mod08_03\Starter.
2. Open the UsabilityDemo form.
3. On the **View** menu, click **ToolBox**.
4. In the ToolBox, double-click the **ToolTip** control to add it to the form.
5. Change the **(Name)** property of the **ToolTip** control to **UsabilityDemoToolTip**.
6. On the menu, click the **Show Date/Time** button to display its properties.
7. Set the **ToolTip on UsabilityToolTip** property of the button to **Displays the current date and time.**
8. Build and run the application.
9. Move the mouse pointer over the **Show Date/Time** button.

   A ToolTip window appears and shows the text that you added.

Lesson: Localizing an Application

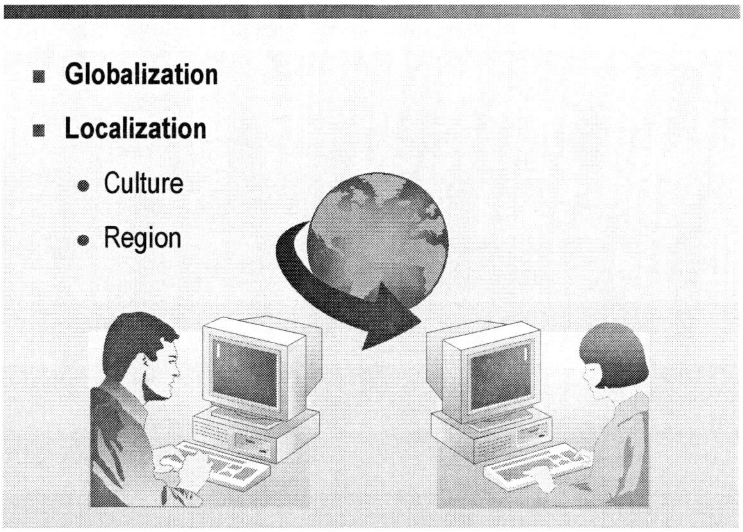

Introduction

When you want to develop applications for use by people who speak various languages and come from various cultures there are two aspects to consider:

- Globalization

  You should build the core functionality of the application without sources that will be localized. By doing this, you are designing applications that can be adapted to different cultures.

- Localization

  You then localize an application for specific cultures and regions by creating translations of resources. *Culture* is "who you are," *region* is "where you are." For example, you can localize an application into English for various regions, such as the United States of America (en-US) and the United Kingdom (en-GB).

  Within culture there are two concepts: current *culture* and current *uiculture*. Culture is for formatting numerics and datetime; uiculture is for retrieving resources by the correct localized language.

Localization support in the .NET Framework

The **CultureInfo** class contains culture-specific information, such as the language, country/region, calendar, and cultural conventions associated with a specific culture. This class also provides the information required for performing culture-specific operations, such as casing, formatting dates and numbers, and comparing strings.

The **CultureInfo** class specifies a unique name for each culture. The name is a combination of a two-letter lowercase culture code associated with a language and, if required, a two-letter uppercase subculture code associated with a country or region. For a list of all the valid culture and region codes, see the topic "CultureInfo Class" in the .NET Framework software development kit (SDK) documentation.

Lesson objectives

After completing this lesson, you will be able to:

- Differentiate between the concepts of globalization and localization of an application.
- Use localization properties and resource files to create a localized version of an application.

Localization in the .NET Framework

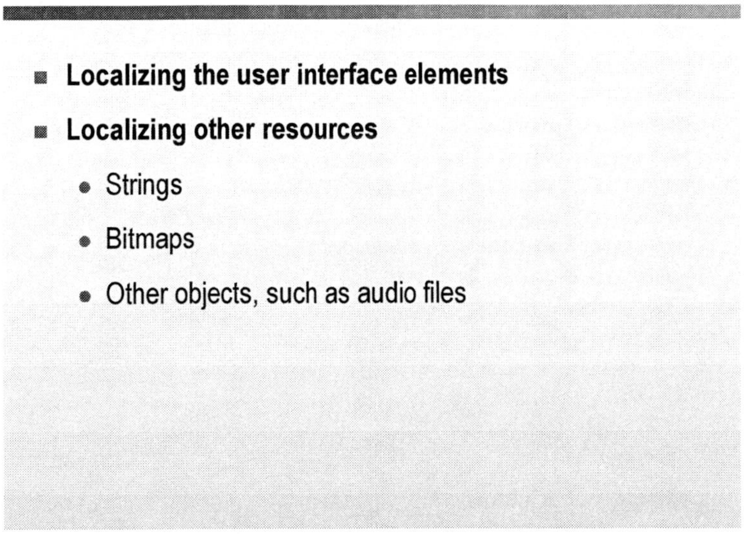

Introduction

Visual Studio .NET provides good support for developers who want to create localized versions of their applications.

Localizing user interface elements

You can set properties on forms and controls to create multiple language versions of the user interface of your application.

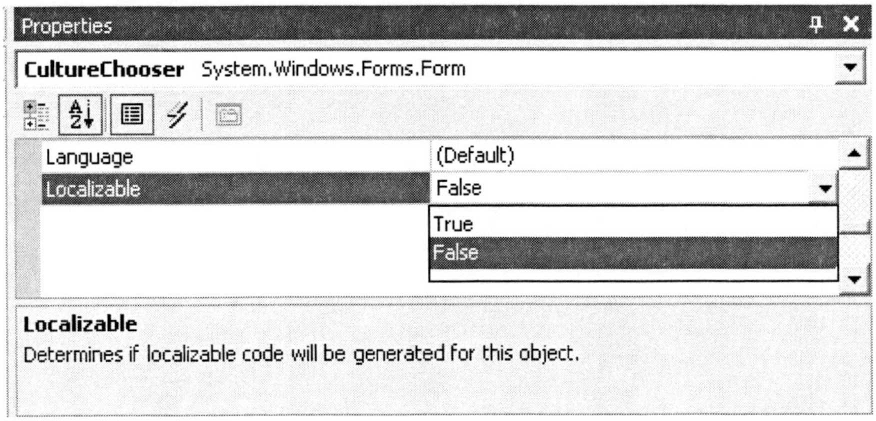

Visual Studio .NET creates and uses resource files to store the information created for each form and control for the different cultures and regions.

When you create multiple language versions of a form, Visual Studio .NET automatically creates resource files to store the localization information. There are two resource files for each language: one for the specific culture and region and one for the overall culture. You can view these files by using Windows Explorer to the view folder for your project.

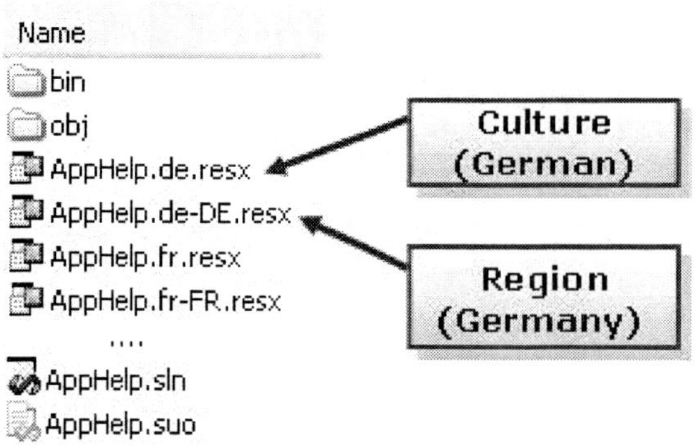

Localizing other resources

When you localize other resources, such as text strings, bitmaps, and so on., you must create resource files manually. To do this, add a new resource file to the project, name it appropriately, and then use the **ResourceManager** object in the .NET Framework to retrieve the appropriate resources at run time.

How to Set Localization Properties

1. Create the default culture version of the form
2. Set the Localizable property of the form to True
3. Set the appropriate value for the Language property of the form
4. Modify the Text property values for the form and controls into the appropriate language
5. Resize and/or reposition each control as needed
6. Build the application

Introduction

Before you localize your application, you must create the initial user interface. Then, test the interface thoroughly for functionality: button clicks, hiding and showing controls, enabling and disabling controls, and so forth. This is the default culture version of the user interface for your application. Set the **Language** property to **(default)** and the **Localizable** property to **False**.

After you have created and tested the UI in the default language, you can then create the other localized versions that your organization's business needs require by setting localization properties and providing new values for the text or other values of the controls.

Procedure: Setting localization properties

To set localization properties on a form:

1. In Visual Studio .NET Design view, select the form that you want to localize.
2. Set the **Localizable** property of the form to **True**.
3. Set the **Language** property of the form to the language into which you want to localize the form.
4. Set the **Text** properties for each control with the correction for that culture.
5. Resize and/or reposition each control, as needed, to fit the localized text.
6. Build and test the application in the appropriate culture.

Each time that you choose another culture to localize to, Visual Studio .NET creates a new resource file for that culture. The data stored in the resource file is XML and includes not only the localized data but also changes made to control positioning and size.

How to Create Localized Resource Files

1 Open an existing project and add an assembly resource file for the appropriate culture

2 Add entries to the resource file with values in the appropriate language for the culture

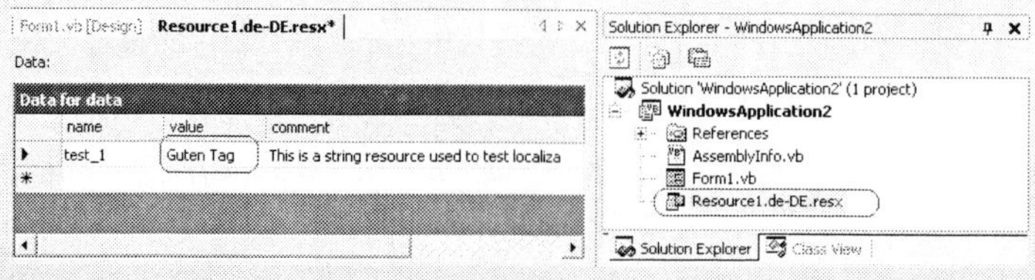

3 Save the file

4 Build the application

Introduction

You can localize text strings associated with your application, such as informational or error messages, by using separate resource files for the various culture and region versions of your application.

Procedure: Creating a localized resource file

To create a localized resource file:

1. In Visual Studio .NET, open the existing project for the application to which you want to add localized strings.
2. On the **Project** menu, click **Add New Item**, and then select the **Assembly Resource File** icon in the Templates pane. Give the file a name that includes the appropriate culture identifier: for example, UsabilityDemoText.de-DE.resx.

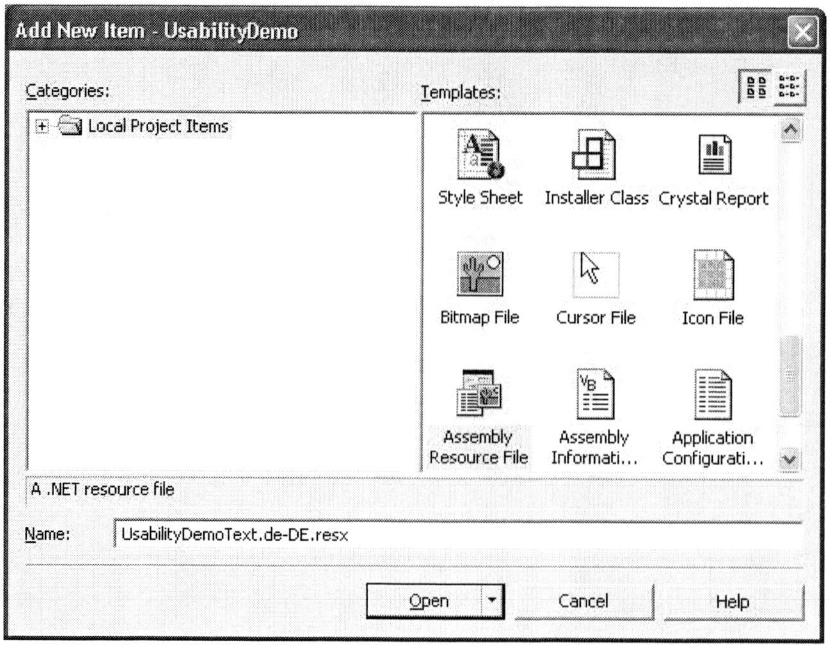

3. Add entries into the resource file, with values in the appropriate language for the culture.

4. Save the file.

   When you create resources files in this manner, they will be listed in the Visual Studio .NET Solution window as part of the project.

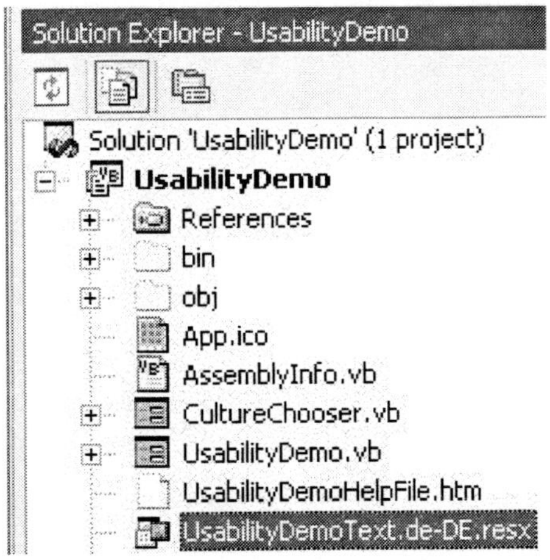

5. Build the application.

   The compiler automatically creates a compiled version (or satellite assembly) for each culture.

Using satellite assembly files

A *satellite assembly* is an assembly that contains only resources. After you build an application that contains multiple resource files for multiple cultures, the resulting satellite assembly names are all the same; however, they are stored in different folders that are named after the culture that they represent. For example, if you build an application called UsabilityDemo with the resource file mentioned in the previous procedure, the resulting satellite assembly would be named UsabilityDemo.resources.dll, and it would be stored in *ApplicationFolder*\bin*culture* (for example, UsabilityDemo\bin\de-DE).

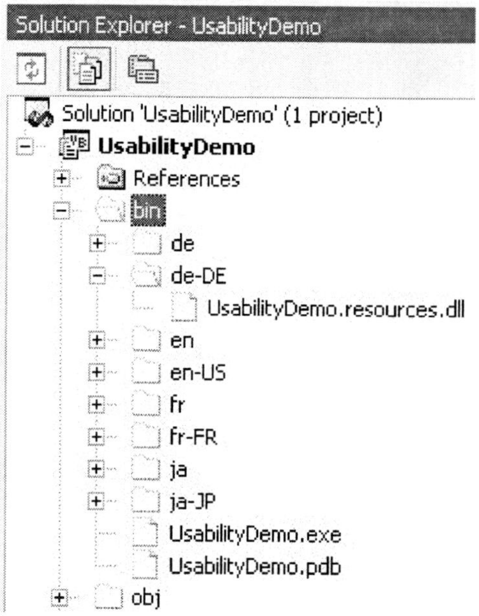

The best reason to use satellite assemblies is the separation of resources from the application. You can build a version of your application with the default culture and release it to the public. At a later time, you can deploy a satellite assembly for each culture that you support. When a culture for your application becomes available, you put it in a separate assembly and make it available to your clients (by using the network, a Web site, or some other media).

Third-party organizations can create resource files by using the Resource File Generator (ResGen.exe) tool that is included with the .NET Framework. You can use this tool to create resource files without having Visual Studio .NET installed. Source files for ResGen must be text files with a file extension of .txt or XML files with the file extension of .resx. ResGen compiles these files into resource files that have the file extension .resource.

For more information about how the .NET Framework searches for resource files, see Module 4, "Assembly Versioning and Satellite Assemblies," in Course 2350A, *Securing and Deploying Microsoft .NET Assemblies* or see the .NET SDK documentation.

How to Change the Locale

The user can change the regional and language options from Control Panel

1. Add code to an application to programmatically set the culture and UICulture for an application to the new value
2. Add code to the application to use a resource manager to extract the elements from the resource file

```
Imports System.Globalization
Imports System.Resources
Imports System.Threading
          ...
Thread.CurrentThread.CurrentUICulture = _
   Thread.CurrentThread.CurrentCulture
          ...
Dim rm As New ResourceManager ("MyNamespace.Resource1", _
   Assembly.GetExecutingAssembly())

MessageBox.Show(rm.GetString("test_1"))
```

Root name of the resource file

Main assembly for the resources

Introduction

After you have resource files with localized strings for the various versions of your application, you can add the code to set the culture of your application to match changes in locale that the user has selected. Then, you can add code to use a resource manager to display strings as appropriate. The .NET Framework ensures that the correct resource file for the culture is used as the source for your text strings.

Procedure: Changing the locale to match the Control Panel settings

To change the locale to match the Control Panel settings:

1. Add the following **using** directives, which are needed to work with culture information:

```
Imports System.Globalization
            ' Defines culture-related
            ' information, such as
            ' the language, the country and
            ' region, calendars in use, format
            ' pattern for dates, currency, and
            ' number, and sort order for strings.

Imports System.Resources
            ' provides classes and interfaces
            ' that allow developers to create, store and
            ' manage various culture-specific resources
            ' used in an application

Imports System.Threading
```

2. Set the thread's User Interface culture based on what is set in Control Panel.

```
Thread.CurrentThread.CurrentUICulture = _
   Thread.CurrentThread.CurrentCulture
```

In this case, the **Thread.CurrentThread.CurrentCulture** property value is taken from the settings in Control Panel. To make the UI use the correct culture, you set the **CurrentUICulture** property value of the current thread.

Note If you want to ensure that your Windows Forms application starts with the culture that is set in the **Regional and Language Options** dialog box in Control Panel, set the **Thread.CurrentThread.CurrentUICulture** property value prior to the call to the **InitializeComponents** method in the startup class constructor.

The resource manager uses the resource fallback process to control how an application retrieves resources. The resource manager uses the **CultureInfo.CurrentUICulture** property to determine which resources to search for and load. If you want to use a different culture than that of the local computer, then you must set this property programmatically in your application. For example, if you set the **Culture.CurrentUICulture** property to **en-GB**, the runtime searches for a satellite assembly that supports the **en-GB** culture. If the **Culture.CurrentUICulture** is not set, the common language runtime sets the culture to that of the local computer.

Because the runtime always searches for the default culture when all other possibilities are exhausted, you should always include a default culture with your applications. The default culture is the only one that is built into the main application assembly. For more information about how the .NET Framework searches for resource files, see Module 4, "Assembly Versioning and Satellite Assemblies," in Course 2350A, *Securing and Deploying Microsoft .NET Assemblies* or the .NET SDK documentation.

Procedure: Accessing localized strings by using a resource manager

To access localized strings by using a resource manager:

1. Add the code to instantiate a resource manager and access resources.

```
Dim rm As New ResourceManager _
   ("MyNamespace.Resource1", _
   Assembly.GetExecutingAssembly())
```

   The first parameter is the root name of the resource file. For example, if the resource file is Resource1.en-EN.resources, the root name is Resource1. The root name of the resource file is qualified with the namespace that contains the resource file. The second parameter is the main assembly for the resources. Because you are in the assembly that is the main assembly, the call to **GetExecutingAssembly()** returns the current assembly's name.

2. Add the code to access the resource and display the localized string.

```
MessageBox.Show (rm.GetString("test_1"))
```

   When you create an instance of the resource manager, it automatically gets the value for the current culture and locates the appropriate resource file. Call **GetString**, passing the name of a specific resource file element, and it will return the value from the correct resource file that matches the current culture setting. If the resource manager cannot locate the appropriate resource file, an exception is thrown. Therefore, any code that uses the resource manager should be wrapped in exception-handling code.

Practice: Localizing an Application

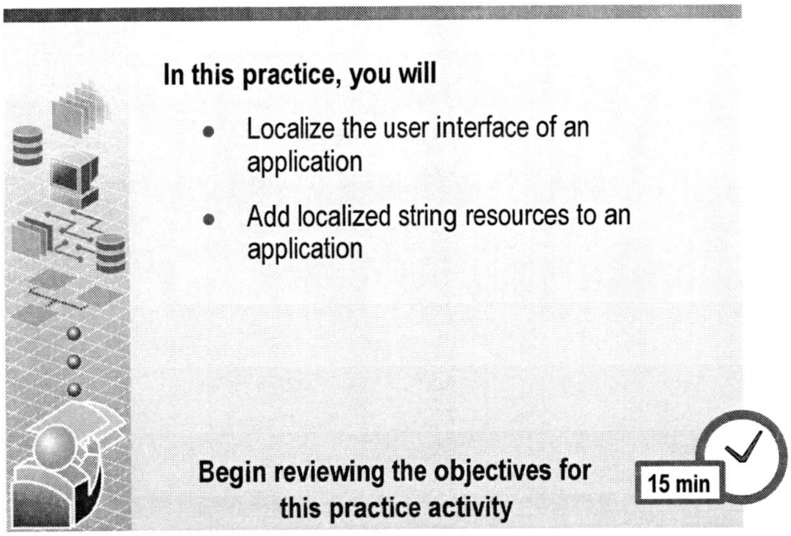

Introduction

In this practice, you will localize the user interface of an application and add localized string resources for an application.

Instructions

► **Localize a form in a Windows Forms application**

1. In Visual Studio .NET, open the UsabilityDemo.sln solution file in *install_folder*\Practices\Mod08\Mod08_04\Starter.
2. Open the UsabilityDemo form.
3. Click the **Show All Files** button in the Solution Explorer window.

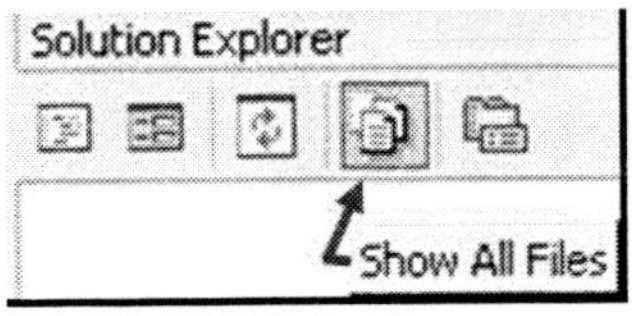

4. Examine the **Localizable** property of the form. Notice that it is set to **True**, which means that the form can be localized.
5. Set the **Language** property of the form to **French (France)**.

   The English version of the form is still displayed, but it can be localized into French. Notice that a set of new resource files for the form can be found under the UsabilityDemo source file in Solution Explorer. These are UsabilityDemo.fr.resx and UsabilityDemo.fr-FR.resx. Both of these files are required for the resource fallback process.
6. Notice that this form has also been localized into German and Japanese.
7. Set the **Text** property of the form to **Démonstration de l'utilisation**.

Note To get the strings for the French version of the form, go to the UsabilityDemoLocalizedStrings.rtf file in *install_folder*\Practices\Mod08\Mod08_04.

8. Set the **Text** property of the menu and menu item to **Aide**.
9. Set the **Text** property of the **Choose a Culture** button to **Choisir une langue**.
10. Set the **Text** property of the **Show Date/Time** button to **Afficher la date/l'heure**.
11. Set the **Text** property of the **Show Currency** button to **Afficher la devise**.
12. Set the **Text** property of the **Show a String** button to **Afficher une chaîne**.
13. Set the **Text** property of the **Exit** button to **Quitter**.

► **Add a string resource file to the application**

1. In Solution Explorer, right-click the **UsabilityDemo** project, select **Add**, and choose **Add New Item**.
2. In the **Add New Item** window, select the **Assembly Resource File** icon in the **Templates** pane.
3. Set the name of the resource file to **UsabilityDemoText.fr-FR.resx**., and then click **Open**.
4. Set the **Name** of the resource string to **SimpleTextString**.
5. Set the **Value** of the resource string to **Voici du texte**.
6. Save and close the resource file.

► **Add code to obtain resource strings**

1. View the UsabilityDemo source file.
2. Show TODO comments in the Task List. To do this, click the **View** menu, point to **Show Tasks**, and then click **All**.
3. Find the first TODO comment in the code. Add the three **Imports** statements to enable support for localization in the application.

```
Imports System.Globalization
Imports System.Resources
Imports System.Threading
```

4. Find the next TODO comment. Declare a **private** resource manager variable.

```
Private RM As ResourceManager
```

5. Find the next TODO comment. Create an object instance of the resource manager. The code is added to the first constructor in the application.

```
RM = New ResourceManager _
  ("UsabilityDemo.UsabilityDemoText", _
  System.Reflection.Assembly.GetExecutingAssembly())
```

6. Find the next TODO comment. Create an object instance of the resource manager. The code is added to the second constructor in the application.

```
RM = New ResourceManager _
  ("UsabilityDemo.UsabilityDemoText", _
  System.Reflection.Assembly.GetExecutingAssembly())
```

7. Find the next TODO comment. Add code to use the resource manager to retrieve the text string from the resource file and display it in the text box.

```
OutputTextBox.Text = RM.GetString("SimpleTextString")
```

8. Find the next TODO comment. Add code to set the current thread's **Culture** and **UICulture** property values to the same culture that the user requested.

```
Thread.CurrentThread.CurrentUICulture = _
   New CultureInfo(ChosenCulture, False)
Thread.CurrentThread.CurrentCulture = _
   New CultureInfo(ChosenCulture, False)
```

9. Save your work.

► **Test the application**

1. Build and run the application.
2. Notice that the only thing that you can do when the application starts is either choose a culture or exit the application. After you choose a culture for the application, the other buttons become available.
3. Click **Choose a Culture**.
4. Select one of the cultures.

   If you don't select any of them, the application uses English as the default.
5. When you click **OK** on the **CultureChooser** form, the **CultureChooser** form disappears and the **UsabilityDemo** form reappears in the correct culture.

Review

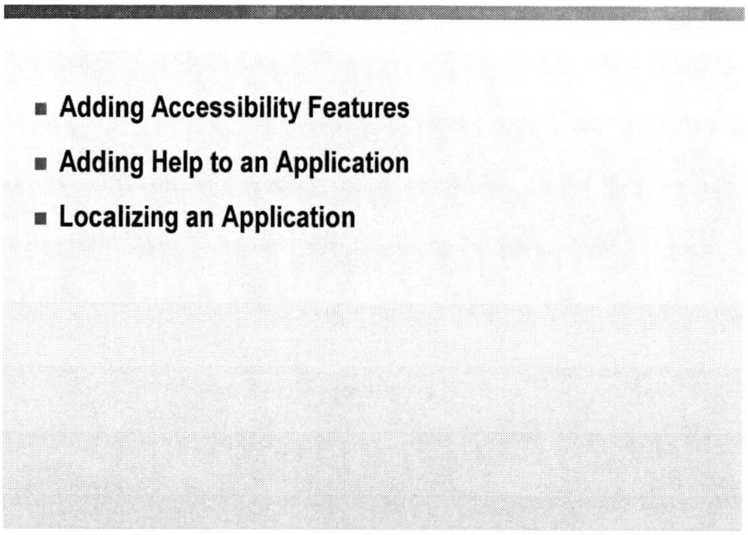

1. What is an accessibility aid? List the accessibility aids that are included with Windows XP.

2. List some guidelines that developers should consider with regard to accessibility when writing an application.

3. What control properties are available to enable accessibility of an application through an accessibility aid? Describe their uses.

4. Describe the purpose of the ampersand (&) character with regard to the text for controls.

5. Describe techniques for adding Help to an application.

6. What is the purpose of the **HelpNamespace** property?

7. When enabling the **HelpButton** property, what must be done to ensure that the **Help** button appears on the form at run time?

8. Where do the **HelpProvider** and **ToolTip** controls appear when they are added to a form?

9. What should be localized when building a Windows application?

10. What properties must be set to localize a form?

11. What is required to change the locale of an application at run time so that it matches the current settings of the computer?

12. Describe the purpose of resource files.

Lab 8.1: Enhancing the Usability of an Application

- Exercise 1: Adding Support for Accessibility
- Exercise 2: Adding Help to an Application
- Exercise 3: Adding ToolTips to an Application
- Exercise 4: Localizing the User Interface of an Application
- Exercise 5: Localizing Resources in an Application

Objectives

After completing this lab, you will have demonstrated your ability to:

- Enhance an application by adding accessibility features.
- Provide user Help and ToolTips in an application.
- Localize the user interface of an application.
- Create and access localized resource files.

Note This lab focuses on the concepts in Module 8, "Enhancing the Usability of Applications," in Course 2565A, *Developing Microsoft .NET Applications for Windows (Visual Basic .NET)*. As a result, this lab may not comply with Microsoft security recommendations.

Prerequisites

Before working on this lab, you must have:

- The knowledge and skills to develop a simple Windows Forms application by using a Visual Studio .NET–compatible programming language.
- The knowledge and skills to modify the properties of controls.
- The knowledge and skills to add accessibility and Help features and to localize an application's user interface and resources by using Visual Studio .NET.

Scenario

The Internal Business Application shell provides a common access point to various internal business applications. The shell must provide accessibility support and Help to users in the organization. In addition, the application must be localized into several languages to support the languages spoken by people of different cultures across the organization.

Supporting accessibility requires that you set control properties and use an accessibility aid such as the Narrator utility included in Windows XP. Including Help as part of the application requires that you use the **HelpProvider** control, set several properties on controls, and add code to the application to provide access to a Help file. To localize the application for specific region and culture combinations requires that each user interface element (form, controls, and so on) and resources found in the source code be localized for the appropriate cultures. In addition, the use of a resource manager is required to retrieve localized resources from resource files.

In this lab, you will add some accessibility support and Help features to the Internal Business Application shell and localize the application for several region and culture combinations.

Estimated time to complete this lab: 60 minutes

Exercise 1
Adding Support for Accessibility

In this exercise, you will update the Internal Business Application shell by adding support for accessibility and testing the application by using the Narrator accessibility aid in Windows XP.

There are starter and solution files associated with this exercise. Browse to *install_folder*\Labfiles\Lab08_1\Ex01\Starter to find the starter files, and browse to *install_folder*\Labfiles\Lab08_1\Ex01\Solution to find the solution files. If you performed a default installation of the course files, *install_folder* corresponds to C:\Program Files\Msdntrain\2565.

Tasks	Additional information
1. Open the InternalBusinessApp project in Visual Studio .NET. Browse to *install_folder*\Labfiles\Lab08_1\Ex01\Starter to find the project.	**a.** For more information about opening a project file and starting an application, see the following resource: • The Visual Studio .NET Help documentation. For additional information about opening a project file, in Search, select the **Search in titles only** check box, then search by using the phrase **Open Project Dialog Box.** For additional information about starting an application in the Designer, in Index, search by using the phrase **Debugging Windows Applications**.
2. Open the AppControlForm form and set the form's **AccessibleName** property to **Internal Business Application Control Panel.**	**a.** For more information about how to add accessibility support to an application, see the following resources: • Practice: Adding Accessibility Support to an Application, in Module 8, "Enhancing the Usability of Applications," in Course 2565A, *Developing Microsoft .NET Applications for Windows (Visual Basic .NET).* • Lesson: Adding Accessibility Features in Module 8, "Enhancing the Usability of Applications," in Course 2565A, *Developing Microsoft .NET Applications for Windows (Visual Basic .NET).* **b.** For more information about writing accessible applications, see the following resource: • The Visual Studio.NET Help documentation. In Search, select the **Search in titles only** check box, then search by using the phrase **Designing Accessible Applications**.

<table>
<tr><th>Tasks</th><th>Additional information</th></tr>
<tr><td>3. Set the AccessibleName property for the buttons. See the following table for the values to give to the AccessibleName property for each button.

<u>Button</u> — <u>Value</u>
Make Travel Plans — Make Travel Plans
Expense Reporting — Expense Reporting
Procurement — Procurement
Exit — Exit the Application</td><td>a. For more information about how to add accessibility support to an application, see the following resources:
• Practice: Adding Accessibility Support to an Application, in Module 8, “Enhancing the Usability of Applications,” in Course 2565A, Developing Microsoft .NET Applications for Windows (Visual Basic .NET).
• Lesson: Adding Accessibility Features in Module 8, “Enhancing the Usability of Applications,” in Course 2565A, Developing Microsoft .NET Applications for Windows (Visual Basic .NET).</td></tr>
<tr><td>4. Enable Narrator.</td><td>a. For more information about how to enable Microsoft Narrator in Windows XP Professional, see the following:
• Practice: Adding Accessibility Support to an Application, in Module 8, “Enhancing the Usability of Applications,” in Course 2565A, Developing Microsoft .NET Applications for Windows (Visual Basic .NET).
• Lesson: Adding Accessibility Features in Module 8, “Enhancing the Usability of Applications,” in Course 2565A, Developing Microsoft .NET Applications for Windows (Visual Basic .NET).</td></tr>
<tr><td>5. Run the application to test the accessibility support. You can log on with the user name mario and the password P@ssw0rd.</td><td>a. For more information about starting an application in the Designer, see the following resource:
• The Visual Studio.NET Help documentation. In Search, select the Search in titles only check box, then search by using the phrase Debugging Windows Applications.</td></tr>
</table>

Exercise 2
Adding Help to an Application

In this exercise, you will update the Internal Business Application shell by adding on-screen Help. When the user presses the F1 key, a Help message that is associated with the control that has focus appears.

There are starter and solution files associated with this exercise. Browse to *install_folder*\Labfiles\Lab08_1\Ex02\Starter to find the starter files, and browse to *install_folder*\Labfiles\Lab08_1\Ex02\Solution to find the solution files. If you performed a default installation of the course files, *install_folder* corresponds to C:\Program Files\Msdntrain\2565.

Tasks	Additional information
1. Open the InternalBusinessApp project in Visual Studio .NET. Browse to *install_folder*\Labfiles\Lab08_1\Ex02\Starter to find the project.	**a.** For more information about opening a project file and starting an application, see the following resource: • The Visual Studio .NET Help documentation. For additional information about opening a project file, in Search, select the **Search in titles only** check box, then search by using the phrase **Open Project Dialog Box**. For additional information about starting an application in the Designer, in Index, search by using the phrase **Debugging Windows Applications**.
2. View the Toolbox, and add the **HelpProvider** control to the AppControlForm form. **a.** Set the **(Name)** property of the **HelpProvider** control to **InternalBusinessAppHelpProvider**. **b.** Set the HelpNamespace property **to http://localhost/InternalBusinessAppHelp.htm**.	**a.** For more information about adding Help to an application, see the following resources: • Practice: Adding Help to an Application in Module 8, "Enhancing the Usability of Applications," in Course 2565A, *Developing Microsoft .NET Applications for Windows (Visual Basic .NET)*. • Lesson: Adding Help to an Application in Module 8, "Enhancing the Usability of Applications," in Course 2565A, *Developing Microsoft .NET Applications for Windows (Visual Basic .NET)*. • The .NET Framework SDK documentation. Search by using the phrase **Introduction to the Windows Forms HelpProvider**.

<table>
<tr><th>Tasks</th><th>Additional information</th></tr>
<tr><td>
3. Select the AppControlForm form. To enable Help on the form, set some of the Help properties. See the following table for the properties and the corresponding values to set.

<table>
<tr><th>Property</th><th>Value</th></tr>
<tr><td>HelpKeyword</td><td>IBA_ControlPanel</td></tr>
<tr><td>HelpNavigator</td><td>Topic</td></tr>
<tr><td>HelpString</td><td>Provides access to the company's internal applications</td></tr>
</table>
</td><td>
a. For more information about adding Help to an application, see the following resources:
• Practice: Adding Help to an Application in Module 8, "Enhancing the Usability of Applications," in Course 2565A, Developing Microsoft .NET Applications for Windows (Visual Basic .NET).
• Lesson: Adding Help to an Application in Module 8, "Enhancing the Usability of Applications," in Course 2565A, Developing Microsoft .NET Applications for Windows (Visual Basic .NET).
• The .NET Framework SDK documentation. In Search, select the Search in titles only check box, then search by using the phrase Introduction to the Windows Forms HelpProvider.
</td></tr>
</table>

<table>
<tr><th>Tasks</th><th>Additional information</th></tr>
<tr>
<td>
4. For each of the controls on the AppControlForm form, set the Help properties to enable Help. Use the following tables to set the appropriate properties for the following controls.
a. Make Travel Plans control
<table>
<tr><th>Property</th><th>Value</th></tr>
<tr><td>HelpKeyword</td><td>IBA_Travel</td></tr>
<tr><td>HelpNavigator</td><td>Topic</td></tr>
<tr><td>HelpString</td><td>Plan a business trip.</td></tr>
</table>
b. Expense Reporting control
<table>
<tr><th>Property</th><th>Value</th></tr>
<tr><td>HelpKeyword</td><td>IBA_Expense</td></tr>
<tr><td>HelpNavigator</td><td>Topic</td></tr>
<tr><td>HelpString</td><td>Log expenses for reimbursement.</td></tr>
</table>
c. Procurement control
<table>
<tr><th>Property</th><th>Value</th></tr>
<tr><td>HelpKeyword</td><td>IBA_Procurement</td></tr>
<tr><td>HelpNavigator</td><td>Topic</td></tr>
<tr><td>HelpString</td><td>Internal Purchasing.</td></tr>
</table>
d. Exit control
<table>
<tr><th>Property</th><th>Value</th></tr>
<tr><td>HelpKeyword</td><td>IBA_Exit</td></tr>
<tr><td>HelpNavigator</td><td>Topic</td></tr>
<tr><td>HelpString</td><td>Exit the Internal Business Application.</td></tr>
</table>
e. Status Bar control
<table>
<tr><th>Property</th><th>Value</th></tr>
<tr><td>HelpKeyword</td><td>IBA_Status</td></tr>
<tr><td>HelpNavigator</td><td>Topic</td></tr>
<tr><td>HelpString</td><td>Network Connection Status</td></tr>
</table>
</td>
<td>
a. For more information about adding Help to an application, see the following resources:
• Practice: Adding Help to an Application in Module 8, “Enhancing the Usability of Applications,” in Course 2565A, Developing Microsoft .NET Applications for Windows (Visual Basic .NET).
• Lesson: Adding Help to an Application in Module 8, “Enhancing the Usability of Applications,” in Course 2565A, Developing Microsoft .NET Applications for Windows (Visual Basic .NET).
• The .NET Framework SDK documentation. In Search, select the Search in titles only check box, then search by using the phrase Introduction to the Windows Forms HelpProvider.
</td>
</tr>
</table>

Tasks	Additional information
5. Add a **Help** button to the AppControlForm form. a. Set the value for the **MaximizeBox** and **MinimizeBox** properties to **False**.	a. For more information about adding Help to an application, see the following resources: • Practice: Adding Help to an Application in Module 8, "Enhancing the Usability of Applications," in Course 2565A, *Developing Microsoft .NET Applications for Windows (Visual Basic .NET).* • Lesson: Adding Help to an Application in Module 8, "Enhancing the Usability of Applications," in Course 2565A, *Developing Microsoft .NET Applications for Windows (Visual Basic .NET).* • The .NET Framework SDK documentation. In Search, select the Search in titles only check box, then search by using the phrase **Introduction to the Windows Forms HelpProvider**.
6. Link the **Help** menu to the Help file.	a. For more detailed information about the tasks that you must perform, see the TODO comments in the code. b. For more information about adding Help to an application, see the following resources: • Practice: Adding Help to an Application in Module 8, "Enhancing the Usability of Applications," in Course 2565A, *Developing Microsoft .NET Applications for Windows (Visual Basic .NET).* • Lesson: Adding Help to an Application in Module 8, "Enhancing the Usability of Applications," in Course 2565A, *Developing Microsoft .NET Applications for Windows (Visual Basic .NET).* • The .NET Framework SDK documentation. In Search, select the **Search in titles only** check box, then search by using the phrase **Introduction to the Windows Forms HelpProvider**.
7. Run the application to test Help.	a. For more information about starting an application in the Designer, see the following resource: • The Visual Studio.NET Help documentation. In Search, select the **Search in titles only** check box, then search by using the phrase **Debugging Windows Applications**.

Exercise 3
Adding ToolTips to an Application

In this exercise, you will update the Internal Business Application shell by adding ToolTips to the AppControlForm form and providing ToolTip text for the controls on the form.

There are starter and solution files associated with this exercise. Browse to *install_folder*\Labfiles\Lab08_1\Ex03\Starter to find the starter files, and browse to *install_folder*\Labfiles\Lab08_1\Ex03\Solution to find the solution files. If you performed a default installation of the course files, *install_folder* corresponds to C:\Program Files\Msdntrain\2565.

Tasks	Additional information
1. Open the InternalBusinessApp project in Visual Studio .NET. Browse to *install_folder*\Labfiles\Lab08_1\Ex03\Starter to find the project.	**a.** For more information about opening a project file and starting an application, see the following resource: • The Visual Studio .NET Help documentation. For additional information about opening a project file, in Search, select the **Search in titles only** check box, then search by using the phrase **Open Project Dialog Box**. For additional information about starting an application in the Designer, in Index, search by using the phrase **Debugging Windows Applications**.
2. View the AppControlForm form in the form designer. **a.** View the Toolbox, and add the **ToolTip** control to the AppControlForm form. **b.** Set the **(Name)** property of the **ToolTip** control to **ApplicationToolTip**.	**a.** For more information about adding ToolTips to an application, see the following resource: • Practice: Adding ToolTips to an Application in Module 8, "Enhancing the Usability of Applications," in Course 2565A, *Developing Microsoft .NET Applications for Windows (Visual Basic .NET)*. • Lesson: Adding Help to an Application in Module 8, "Enhancing the Usability of Applications," in Course 2565A, *Developing Microsoft .NET Applications for Windows (Visual Basic .NET)*. • The .NET Framework SDK documentation. Search by using the phrase **ToolTip Component**.

<table>
<tr><th>Tasks</th><th>Additional information</th></tr>
<tr><td>
3. Set the text for the ToolTip for each of the controls on the AppControlForm form.
a. Use the following table to set the value for the ToolTip on ApplicationToolTip property for each control.
<table>
<tr><th>Control</th><th>Value</th></tr>
<tr><td>Form</td><td>Accesses internal applications.</td></tr>
<tr><td>Make Travel Plans</td><td>Allows you to plan a business trip.</td></tr>
<tr><td>Expense Reporting</td><td>Allows you to submit and check expense reports.</td></tr>
<tr><td>Procurement</td><td>Allows you to purchase items at company rates.</td></tr>
<tr><td>Exit</td><td>Exit the application.</td></tr>
<tr><td>Status bar</td><td>Displays the network connection status.</td></tr>
</table>
</td><td>
a. For more information about adding ToolTips to an application, see the following resources:
• Practice: Adding ToolTips to an Application in Module 8, “Enhancing the Usability of Applications,” in Course 2565A, Developing Microsoft .NET Applications for Windows (Visual Basic .NET).
• Lesson: Adding Help to an Application in Module 8, “Enhancing the Usability of Applications,” in Course 2565A, Developing Microsoft .NET Applications for Windows (Visual Basic .NET).
• The .NET Framework SDK documentation. Search by using the phrase ToolTip Component.
</td></tr>
<tr><td>
4. Run the application to test the ToolTips.
</td><td>
a. For more information about starting an application from within Designer, see the following resource:
• The Visual Studio.NET Help documentation. In Index, search by using the phrase Debugging Windows Applications.
</td></tr>
</table>

Exercise 4
Localizing the User Interface of an Application

In this exercise, you will update the Internal Business Application shell by localizing the AppControlForm form into French.

There are starter and solution files associated with this exercise. Browse to the *install_folder*\Labfiles\Lab08_1\Ex04\Starter to find the starter files, and browse to *install_folder*\Labfiles\Lab08_1\Ex04\Solution to find the solution files. If you performed a default installation of the course files, *install_folder* corresponds to C:\Program Files\Msdntrain\2565.

Tasks	Additional information
1. Open the InternalBusinessApp project in Visual Studio .NET. Browse to *install_folder*\ Labfiles\Lab08_1\Ex04\Starter to find the project.	**a.** For more information about opening a project file and starting an application, see the following resource: • The Visual Studio .NET Help documentation. For additional information about opening a project file, in Search, select the Search **in titles only** check box, then search by using the phrase **Open Project Dialog Box**. For additional information about starting an application in the Designer, in Index, search by using the phrase **Debugging Windows Applications**.
2. View the AppControlForm form in the form designer. Set the **Language** property of the form to **French (France)**.	**a.** For more information about localizing an application, see the following resources: • Practice: Localizing an Application in Module 8, "Enhancing the Usability of Applications," in Course 2565A, *Developing Microsoft .NET Applications for Windows (Visual Basic .NET)*. • Lesson: Localizing an Application in Module 8, "Enhancing the Usability of Applications," in Course 2565A, *Developing Microsoft .NET Applications for Windows (Visual Basic .NET)*. • The .NET Framework SDK documentation. Search by using the phrase **Developing World-Ready Applications**.

<table>
<tr><th>Tasks</th><th>Additional information</th></tr>
<tr>
<td>
3. Change the Text property of each control from English to its equivalent French translation.

a. Use the following table to set the value for Text property for each control.
<table>
<tr><th>Control</th><th>Value</th></tr>
<tr><td>Form</td><td>Tableau de bord des applications</td></tr>
<tr><td>HelpMenu</td><td>Aide</td></tr>
<tr><td>HelpMenuItem</td><td>Aide</td></tr>
<tr><td>AboutMenuItem</td><td>À propos de l'application interne d'entreprise</td></tr>
<tr><td>Expense Reporting</td><td>Notes de frais</td></tr>
<tr><td>Procurement</td><td>Réservation</td></tr>
<tr><td>Exit</td><td>Quitter</td></tr>
</table>
Note: You can copy and paste the French strings from the file install_folder\Labfiles\Lab08_1\Ex04\Starter\InternalBusinessApplicationLocalizedStrings.rtf.
</td>
<td>
a. For more information about localizing an application, see the following resources:
• Practice: Localizing an Application in Module 8, "Enhancing the Usability of Applications," in Course 2565A, Developing Microsoft .NET Applications for Windows (Visual Basic .NET).
• Lesson: Localizing an Application in Module 8, "Enhancing the Usability of Applications," in Course 2565A, Developing Microsoft .NET Applications for Windows (Visual Basic .NET).
• The .NET Framework SDK documentation. Search by using the phrase Developing World-Ready Applications.
</td>
</tr>
<tr>
<td>
4. Add code to the AppControlForm form to set the culture to match the regional and language information that the user has set in Control Panel.
</td>
<td>
a. For more detailed information about the tasks that you must perform, see the TODO comments in the code.

b. For more information about localizing an application, see the following resources:
• Practice: Localizing an Application in Module 8, "Enhancing the Usability of Applications," in Course 2565A, Developing Microsoft .NET Applications for Windows (Visual Basic .NET).
• Lesson: Localizing an Application in Module 8, "Enhancing the Usability of Applications," in Course 2565A, Developing Microsoft .NET Applications for Windows (Visual Basic .NET).
• The .NET Framework SDK documentation. Search by using the phrase Developing World-Ready Applications.
</td>
</tr>
</table>

<table>
<tr><th>Tasks</th><th>Additional information</th></tr>
<tr><td>5. Change the default language for the computer, and test the application.
a. Open Control Panel in Windows XP Professional:
• If you are using Category View in Control Panel, click Date, Time, Language, and Regional Options, and then click Regional and Language Options.
• If you are using Classic View in Control Panel, double-click Regional and Language Options.
b. In the Regional and Language Options dialog box, on the Regional Options tab, in the Standards and formats area, in the list of languages, click French (France).
c. Run the application.</td><td>No additional information is required for this task.</td></tr>
</table>

Exercise 5
Localizing Resources in an Application

In this exercise, you will update the Internal Business Application shell by localizing strings used in the AppControlForm form.

There are starter and solution files associated with this exercise. Browse to the *install_folder*\Labfiles\Lab08_1\Ex05\Starter to find the starter files, and browse to *install_folder*\Labfiles\Lab08_1\Ex05\Solution to find the solution files. If you performed a default installation of the course files, *install_folder* corresponds to C:\Program Files\Msdntrain\2565.

Tasks	Additional information
1. Open the InternalBusinessApp project in Visual Studio .NET. Browse to *install_folder*\Labfiles\Lab08_1\Ex05\Starter to find the project.	**a.** For more information about opening a project file, see the following resource: • The Visual Studio.NET Help documentation. Search by using the phrase **Open Project Dialog Box**.
2. Create a new resource file, and name it AppControlRes.fr-FR.resx.	**a.** For more information about localizing an application, see the following resources: • Practice: Localizing an Application in Module 8, "Enhancing the Usability of Applications," in Course 2565A, *Developing Microsoft .NET Applications for Windows (Visual Basic .NET)*. • Lesson: Localizing an Application in Module 8, "Enhancing the Usability of Applications," in Course 2565A, *Developing Microsoft .NET Applications for Windows (Visual Basic .NET)*. • The .NET Framework SDK documentation. Search by using the phrase **Developing World-Ready Applications**.

<table>
<tr><th>Tasks</th><th>Additional information</th></tr>
<tr><td>
3. Add text in French to the resource file.
a. Use the following table to set the Name and Value elements for each resource string.
<table>
<tr><th>Name</th><th>Value</th></tr>
<tr><td>AppUnavailable Message</td><td>Application non disponible</td></tr>
<tr><td>PermissionDenied Message</td><td>Autorisation refusée</td></tr>
<tr><td>Unauthorized Message</td><td>Vous ne disposez pas des autorisations nécessaires pour utiliser cette application</td></tr>
<tr><td>OfflineMode</td><td>Mode hors connexion</td></tr>
<tr><td>OnlineMode</td><td>Mode connexion</td></tr>
</table>
Note: You can copy and paste the French strings from the file install_folder\Labfiles\Lab08_1\Ex05\Starter\InternalBusinessApplicationLocalizedStrings.rtf.
</td><td>
a. For more information about localizing an application, see the following resources:
<ul>
<li>Practice: Localizing an Application in Module 8, “Enhancing the Usability of Applications,” in Course 2565A, Developing Microsoft .NET Applications for Windows (Visual Basic .NET).</li>
<li>Lesson: Localizing an Application in Module 8, “Enhancing the Usability of Applications,” in Course 2565A, Developing Microsoft .NET Applications for Windows (Visual Basic .NET).</li>
<li>The .NET Framework SDK documentation. Search by using the phrase Developing World-Ready Applications.</li>
</ul>
</td></tr>
<tr><td>
4. Add code to the AppControlForm form to set the culture to match the regional and language information that the user has set in Control Panel.
</td><td>
a. For more detailed information about the tasks that you must perform, see the TODO comments in the code.
b. For more information about localizing an application, see the following resources:
<ul>
<li>Lesson: Localizing an Application in Module 8, “Enhancing the Usability of Applications,” in Course 2565A, Developing Microsoft .NET Applications for Windows (Visual Basic .NET).</li>
<li>The .NET Framework SDK documentation. Search by using the phrase Developing World-Ready Applications.</li>
</ul>
</td></tr>
</table>

Tasks	Additional information
5. Make sure that the default language for the computer is set still to **French (France)** and test the application. a. To change the default language for the computer, open Control Panel in Windows XP Professional: • If you are using Category View in Control Panel, click **Date, Time, Language, and Regional Options**, and then click **Regional and Language Options**. • If you are using Classic View in Control Panel, double-click **Regional and Language Options**. b. In the Regional **and Language Options** dialog box, on the **Regional Options** tab, in the **Standards and formats** area, in the list of languages, click **French (France)**. c. Run the **application**.	No additional information is required for this task.

Course Evaluation

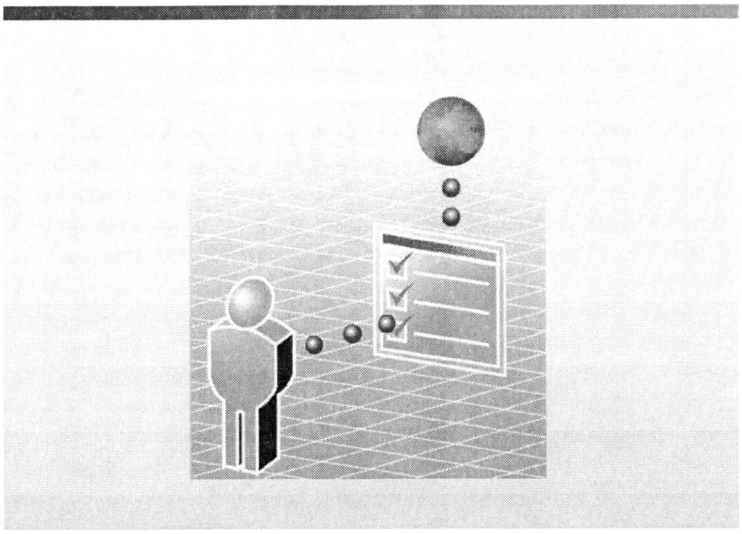

Your evaluation of this course will help Microsoft understand the quality of your learning experience.

At a convenient time before the end of the course, please complete a course evaluation, which is available at http://www.metricsthatmatter.com/survey/.

Microsoft will keep your evaluation strictly confidential and will use your responses to improve your future learning experience.

msdn training

Module 9: Deploying Windows Forms Applications

Contents

Microsoft

Overview

- .NET Assemblies
- Deploying Windows Forms Applications

Introduction

In this module, you will learn about assemblies and the use of strong-named assemblies and the global assembly cache in the Microsoft® .NET Framework. You will also learn how to configure and deploy your .NET applications.

Objectives

After completing this module, you will be able to:

- Use strong-named assemblies in .NET applications.
- Use application configuration files to configure and use Microsoft Windows® Installer 2.0 to package and deploy .NET applications.

Lesson: .NET Assemblies

- What is an Assembly?
- What Are Private Assemblies?
- What Are Strong-Named Assemblies?
- How to Build a Strong-Named Assembly
- How to Call a Strong-Named Assembly
- Demonstration: Viewing Assembly Metadata
- Practice: Calling a Strong-Named Assembly
- How to Install Assemblies into the Global Assembly Cache
- Demonstration: Using the .NET Framework Configuration Tool to Work with the Global Assembly Cache
- Practice: Working with the Global Assembly Cache

Introduction

In this lesson, you will learn about the difference between private and strong-named assemblies, how to build and call strong-named assemblies. You will learn how to install strong-named assemblies in the global assembly cache and why you would want to do so. You will also learn how to use the Fusion Log Viewer (FusLogVw utility) to trace the assembly load process to troubleshoot application activation problems.

Lesson objectives

After completing this lesson, you will be able to:

- Describe the difference between private and strong-named assemblies.
- Build strong-named assemblies and call them from an application.
- Install strong-named assemblies in the global assembly cache.
- Use the FusLogVw utility to trace the assembly load process to troubleshoot application activation problems.

What is an Assembly?

- A functional unit of sharing, versioning, and identity in the .NET Framework
- A unit for which permissions are requested and granted
- Can be shared across .NET applications

Introduction

Applications in the .NET Framework always consist of one or more assemblies.

Definition

An assembly:

- Is a functional unit of sharing, versioning, and identity in the .NET Framework.
- Is a unit for which permissions are requested and granted.
- Can be shared across .NET applications.

In the simplest case, an application can consist of one assembly that contains one managed module with all the code and resources for the application. In most scenarios, however, an application has multiple assemblies, and each assembly may have multiple files. References between assemblies are not resolved until the code making the call is executed. So, all assemblies of an application need not be present at run time. Assemblies, such as localization resources, can be retrieved on demand.

All assemblies are self-describing. Each assembly contains metadata that includes the identity and version of the assembly and the types implemented by that assembly. You can use the Microsoft intermediate language (MSIL) Disassembler (Ildasm.exe) to view the contents of the assembly file. At the command prompt, type the following command:

```
ildasm <assembly name>
```

What are Private Assemblies?

- **Private assemblies**

  Private assemblies are deployed with and used exclusively by a single application
- **Where private assemblies can reside**
  - Default probing process

    Application folder tree
  - Use **Assembly.LoadFrom** for these locations

    Any folder on the local computer

    Any folder on a remote computer

    A URL

```
Dim PrivateAssembly As [Assembly]
PrivateAssembly = Assembly.LoadFrom("C:\PrivateAssembly.dll")
' Obtain a reference to a method known to exist in assembly.
Dim Method As MethodInfo = _
   PrivateAssembly.GetTypes(0).GetMethod("CalculateSum")
```

Introduction

In the .NET Framework, you can create source code by using any programming language that is compatible with the .NET Framework. You then use the corresponding compiler to build a managed module. A managed module is a standard portable executable (PE) file for the Windows operating system that contains MSIL code that is executed by the common language runtime. Managed modules must be packaged in assemblies before they can be executed by the common language runtime, therefore all code written for the .NET Framework must be packaged as an assembly before it can be executed.

Definition

A private assembly is deployed with and used exclusively by a single application. A private assembly is referenced by its simple name. The simple name is defined in the assembly's metadata.

Where private assemblies can reside

When the common language runtime searches for a private assembly, it uses the assembly's simple name to locate the referenced assembly.

When the application is installed, the private assembly is also installed in the same root directory of the application, or in a subdirectory that appears under the root directory of the application.

The probing process for private assemblies can be summarized with the following steps:

1. The runtime obtains the private assembly's simple name from the metadata of the application that is referencing the private assembly.
2. The runtime starts probing first in the application's root directory, next in the assembly's named subdirectory, and then in the assembly's culture subdirectory. For example, if the application MyApp is installed in C:\Program Files\MyApp, the following directories may be searched:

   C:\Program Files\MyApp\MyAssembly.dll.

   C:\Program Files\MyApp\MyAssembly\MyAssembly.dll.

   C:\Program Files\MyApp\MyAssembly.exe.

   C:\Program Files\MyApp\MyAssembly\MyAssembly.exe.

   C:\Program Files\MyApp\de\MyAssembly.dll.

   C:\Program Files\MyApp\de\MyAssembly\MyAssembly.dll.

   C:\Program Files\MyApp\de\MyAssembly.exe.

   C:\Program Files\MyApp\de\MyAssembly\MyAssembly.exe.

To access an assembly that is not in the directory tree of the application, you can use the **Assembly.LoadFrom()** method, providing the location where the assembly can be found. To use **Assembly.LoadFrom()**, you must include the using directive **Imports System.Reflection**. The following code demonstrates how to call **LoadFrom()**:

```
Dim PrivateAssembly As [Assembly]
PrivateAssembly = Assembly.LoadFrom("C:\PrivateAssembly.dll")
' Obtain a reference to a method known to exist in assembly.
Dim Method As MethodInfo = _
PrivateAssembly.GetTypes(0).GetMethod("CalculateSum")
```

What are Strong-Named Assemblies?

- **Strong-named assemblies**

  Strong names identify assemblies uniquely and allow for features that guarantee the assembly is authentic and has not been tampered with
- **Benefits of strong names**
- **Where strong-named assemblies can reside**
- **Where strong-named assemblies should reside**
- **Private assemblies vs. strong-named assemblies**

Introduction

To get many of the benefits assemblies provide, such as sharing by multiple applications on the system, side-by-side versioning, and better support for security and deployment, you must use strong-named assemblies

Definition

The .NET Framework uses strong names to provide a way to identify assemblies uniquely, allowing applications to run with the versions of the strong-named assemblies they were built with. Also, strong-names allow for features to guarantee the assembly is authentic and has not been tampered with.

Strong-named assemblies consist of the assembly's identity, which is:

- The simple text name of the assembly.
- The version number of the assembly.
- The culture information, if it is provided (optional).
- A public key for the client.
- A digital signature.

The tool used to create the assembly generates a hash of the file that contains the assembly's manifest. The private key is used to sign the hash (digital signature). The digital signature is stored in the PE file that contains the manifest for the assembly. The public key is used by the client of the strong-named assembly to decrypt its digital signature.

Benefits of strong names

Strong names guarantee name uniqueness by relying on unique key pairs. No one can generate the same assembly name that you can, because an assembly generated with one private key has a different name than an assembly generated with another private key.

Strong names protect the version lineage of an assembly. A strong name can ensure that no one can produce a subsequent version of your assembly. Users can be sure that a version of the assembly they are loading comes from the same publisher that created the version the application was built with.

Strong names provide a strong integrity check. Passing the .NET Framework security checks guarantee that the contents of the assembly have not been changed since it was built. Note, however, that strong names in and of themselves do not imply a level of trust, such as that provided by a digital signature and the supporting certificate.

Note Strong-named assemblies can only reference other strong-named assemblies.

When you reference a strong-named assembly, you are expecting to get certain benefits, such as versioning and naming protection. If that strong-named assembly then references a private assembly, which does not have these benefits, you lose the benefits you would derive from using a strong-named assembly and revert to dynamic link-library (DLL) conflicts.

Where strong-named assemblies can reside

Strong-named assemblies can reside in:

- An application folder.
- Any folder on the local computer.
- Any folder on a remote computer.
- A URL.
- The global assembly cache.

Where strong-named assemblies should reside

Assemblies shared by multiple applications should be installed in the global assembly cache, a centralized repository. .NET clients can access the same copy of the assembly, which is signed and installed in the global assembly cache. The global assembly cache can handle multiple versions of an assembly, and it's a secure place where assemblies can be stored. If the assembly is not going to be shared, then the assembly should be installed in the application directory tree. Once a strong-named assembly has been installed in the global assembly cache, it is referred to as a shared assembly.

The only differences between a strong-named assembly and a shared assembly are (a) where they are located, and (b) when the integrity/security validation occurs. If the assembly is installed in the global assembly cache, the runtime checks the assembly during the install. If the assembly is not installed in the global assembly cache, the integrity is checked at runtime.

Differences between private and strong-named assemblies

Some key differences between private and strong-named assemblies are listed below.

Private assemblies:

- Can only be installed in an application's directory structure.
- Are referenced only by their simple name.
- Can have version information, but the runtime does not use it.
- Are not installed in the global assembly cache and therefore the runtime will not look in the global assembly cache when probing for the private assembly.

Strong-named assemblies:

- Can be installed in a number of different locations.
- Are referenced by their simple name, culture, version, and public key.
- Contain version information that the runtime checks when loading the assembly.
- Can be installed in the global assembly cache and therefore the runtime will look in the global assembly cache as part of the probing process.
- Can have multiple versions deployed in a side-by-side manner within the global assembly cache.

In addition to the differences and benefits mentioned above, strong-named assemblies can be used instead of private assemblies to provide the following two benefits:

- When the application is built, it is tied to a specific version of the assembly it references. Therefore, a new version of the assembly cannot simply be installed in place of the original assembly because the application will not run.
- When the application runs, the reference strong-named assembly is verified for tampering prior to it being loaded and executed. This prevents any malicious activity that may occur if the assembly being loaded is not the same one that the application was built with.

For more information about both private and strong-named assemblies, see Course 2350A, *Securing and Deploying Microsoft .NET Applications.*

How to Build a Strong-Named Assembly

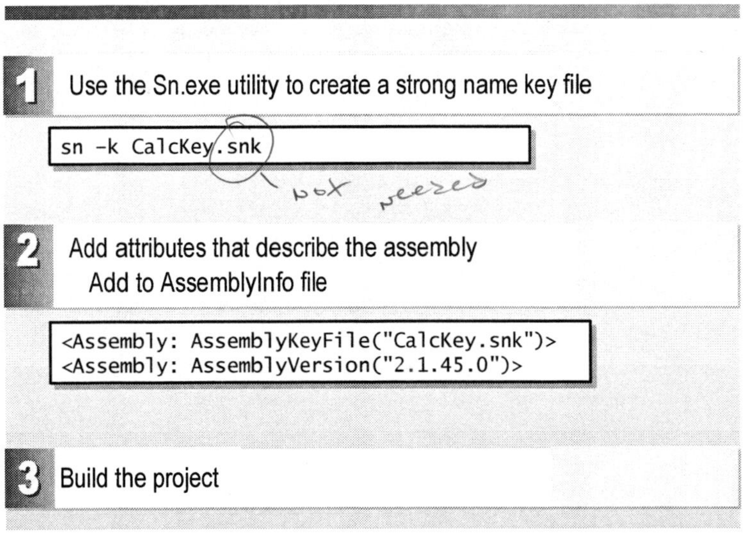

Introduction

To create a strong-named assembly, you need to use a private key to sign the assembly. The public key is included with the assembly to allow client applications to verify the strong name. The public key is automatically included in the assembly when it is signed. For more information about signing an assembly, see Module 10, "Securing Windows Forms Applications," in Course 2565A, *Developing Microsoft .NET Applications for Microsoft Windows (Visual Basic® .NET).*

Procedure: Creating a Strong-Named Assembly

To create a strong-named assembly:

1. Use the SN.exe utility to create a strong name key file.

   The command-line Strong Name tool (Sn.exe) that comes with the .NET Framework is used to build strong-name key files. For example, the following command will build a strong-name key file named CalcKey.snk:

   ```
   sn -k CalcKey.snk
   ```

2. Add the **AssemblyKeyFile** attribute flags and other assembly attributes, as appropriate.

   To create a strong-named assembly, use assembly attributes. An assembly attribute is placed in the AssemblyInfo file that is part of the Microsoft Visual Studio® .NET project. Assembly attributes instruct the compiler to populate certain assembly metadata settings or perform certain actions as defined by the attribute.

3. Build the application.

Examples of assembly attributes

The **AssemblyKeyFile** attribute tells the compiler to create a strong-named assembly and indicates where the key pair can be found. The following example demonstrates the use of the **AssemblyKeyFile** and **AssemblyVersion** attributes (note that the **AssemblyVersion** attribute is not used to force the compile to build a strong-named assembly, but is needed to give the assembly a version number):

```
Imports System.Reflection
 ...
<Assembly: AssemblyKeyFile("CalcKey.snk")>
<Assembly: AssemblyVersion("2.1.45.0")>
```

There are other assembly attributes that can be added to the AssemblyInfo file. For more information about assembly attributes, search on the phrase **assembly-level attributes** in Visual Studio .NET online Help.

How to Call a Strong-Named Assembly

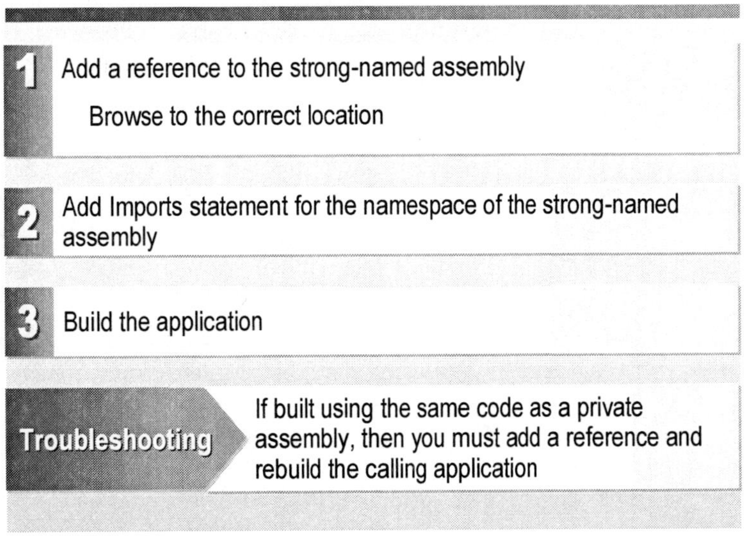

Introduction

Now that you have created a strong-named assembly, how do you call it from an application?

Procedure: Calling a Strong-Named Assembly

To call a strong-named assembly:

1. Add a reference to the strong-named assembly to your project:
   a. In the Visual Studio .NET Solution Explorer, right-click the **References** node.
   b. Click **Add Reference**.

      The **Add Reference** dialog box appears.
   c. Click the **Browse** button to locate the assembly.
   d. When you have selected the correct assembly, click **OK**.
   e. Check the References node in Solution Explorer, to verify that the reference to the assembly has been added.
2. Add an **Imports** statement for the Namespace of the strong-named assembly to the source files that require access to the assembly.
3. Build and run the application.

Troubleshooting

Default binding policy refers to the process by which the runtime locates an assembly based on the binding information contained in the application. An application will be bound to an assembly it was built and tested with, even if a newer version of the assembly is available. Default binding policy is always used unless it is explicitly overridden.

Important If you originally build an application that uses a private assembly and then make a strong-named version of that private assembly, you must add a reference to the strong-named assembly and rebuild the calling application in order for the calling application to use the strong-named version of the assembly.

In the lesson, Deploying Windows Forms Applications, in Module 9, "Deploying Windows Forms Applications" in Course 2565A, *Developing Microsoft .NET Applications for Microsoft Windows (Visual Basic .NET)*, you will learn how you can use application configuration files to override the default binding policy.

Demonstration: Viewing Assembly Metadata

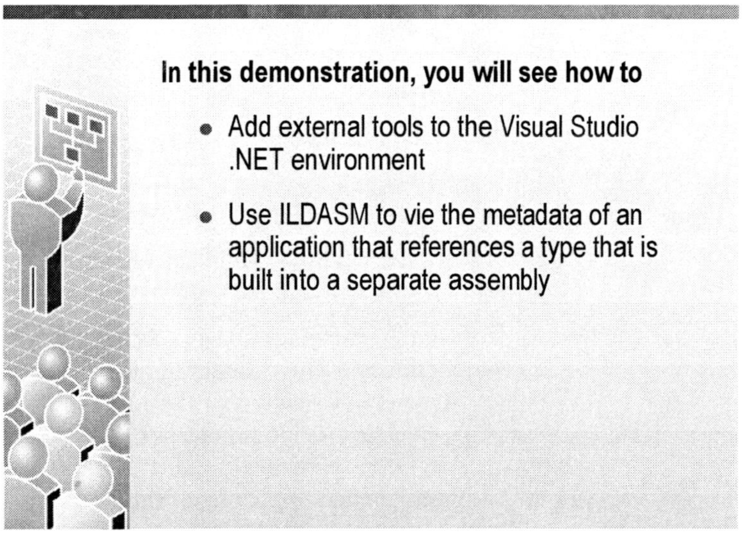

Introduction

In this demonstration, you will see how to add external tools to the Visual Studio .NET environment. You will then see how to view the metadata of an application that references a type that is built into a separate assembly.

Note If you performed a default installation of the course files, *install_folder* corresponds to C:\Program Files\Msdntrain\2565.

Instructions

► **To add ILDASM to the Visual Studio .NET environment**

1. Start Visual Studio .NET.
2. From the **Tools** menu, select **External Tools**.
3. In the **External Tools** dialog box, click **Add**.
4. In the **Title** box type, MSIL Disassembler.
5. Click the **...** button to the right of the **Command** field.
6. In the **Open File** dialog box, browse to C:\Program Files\Microsoft Visual Studio .NET\FrameworkSDK\bin.
7. Select **ildasm.exe** and click **Open**.
8. On the **External Tools** dialog box, click **OK**.
9. View the **Tools** menu again and notice that a menu item for MSIL Disassembler is now available.

▶ **To view the metadata of an assembly**

1. In Visual Studio .NET, click the **Tools** menu and select **MSIL Disassembler**.
2. When the ILDASM window appears, click the **File** menu and then click **Open**.
3. In the **Open** dialog box, browse to *install_folder*\Democode\Mod09\Mod09_01.
4. Select CalculatorEngine.dll and click Open.
5. Notice that the CalculatorEngine.dll node has two sub-nodes, the MANIFEST and the Calculator namespace.
6. Double-click the MANIFEST sub-node. Notice that there is an **.assembly CalculatorEngine** entry in the manifest. Below this reference you will see the **.ver** entry showing what version of CalculatorEngine.dll was built. CalculatorEngine is not a strong-named assembly because there is no public key entry in the manifest. Therefore, even though a version number has been applied to CalculatorEngine.dll, the runtime will not consider it when probing for this assembly when an application that references it is executed.
7. Close the MANIFEST window and ILDASM.
8. Run ILDASM from the Tools menu again on WindowsCalculator.exe.
9. Notice that the WindowsCalculator.exe node also has two sub nodes, the MANIFEST and the WindowsCalculator namespace.
10. Double-click the MANIFEST sub-node.
11. Notice that there is an entry in the manifest called **.assembly extern CalculatorEngine** that contains the version number. This indicates that this reference is to an EXTERNAL assembly—one that is different than WindowsCalculator.exe.

Practice: Calling a Strong-Named Assembly

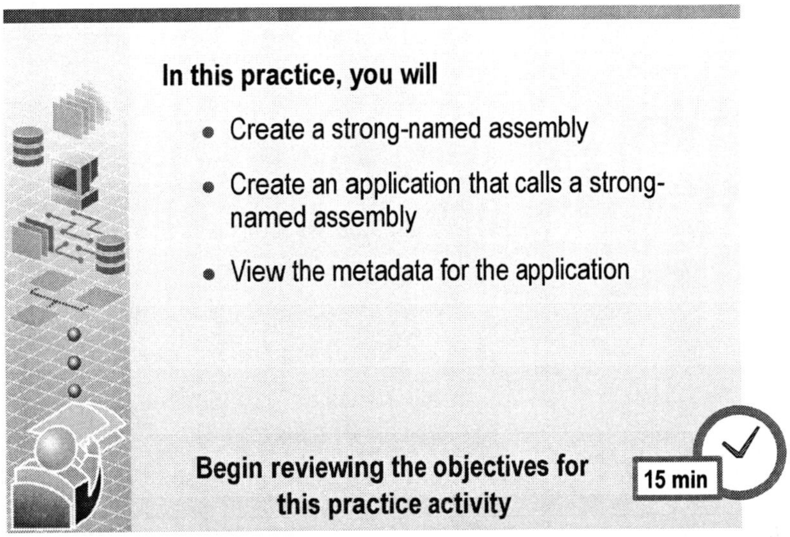

Introduction

In this practice, you will create a strong-name key pair file and reference this file in the CalculatorEngine library. You will then create the WindowsCalculator application so that it references the strong-named assembly. In addition, you will use ILDASM to inspect the metadata of both CalculatorEngine.dll and WindowsCalculator.exe.

Instructions

► **Creating a strong-named assembly**

1. Open a Command Prompt window, by clicking **Start**, pointing to **All Programs**, pointing to **Microsoft Visual Studio .NET**, pointing to **Visual Studio .NET Tools**, and then clicking **Visual Studio .NET Command Prompt**.
2. At the command prompt, change directory to *install_folder*\Practices\Mod09\Mod09_01\Starter\CalculatorEngine.
3. Enter the command **sn –k CalcKey.snk**. This creates a strong-named key file that we can use to build a strong-named assembly.
4. In Visual Studio .NET, open the CalculatorEngine.sln solution file in *install_folder*\Practices\ Mod09\Mod09_01\Starter\CalculatorEngine.
5. Show TODO comments in the Task List.

   To show TODO comments, click the **View** menu, point to **Show Tasks**, and then click **All**.
6. Open the AssemblyInfo.vb file.
7. Locate the first TODO comment. Change the version number from 2.0.1.1 to **3.0.1.1**.

```
<Assembly: AssemblyVersion("3.0.1.1")>
```

8. Locate the next TODO comment. Add a new attribute at the bottom of the file to reference the strong name key pair file.

```
<Assembly: AssemblyKeyFile("CalcKey.snk")>
```

9. Open the Calculator.vb source file.

10. Locate the TODO comment. Change the versionInfo string from v2.0.1.1 to v3.0.1.1.

```
Private Shared versionInfo As String = _
    "Calculator v3.0.1.1"
```

11. Rebuild the assembly and then close Visual Studio.NET.

12. In a Visual Studio .NET Command Prompt window, change directories to *install_folder*\Practices\Mod09\Mod09_01\Starter\CalculatorEngine\bin.

13. At the command prompt, run ILDASM on CalculatorEngine.dll.

```
ildasm CalculatorEngine.dll
```

14. Open the MANIFEST sub-node.

15. Notice that under the **.assembly CalculatorEngine** entry, there is a **.publickey** entry. This indicates that CalculatorEngine is a strong-named assembly.

16. Close the MANIFEST window and ILDASM.

► **Creating an application that references the strong-named assembly**

1. In Visual Studio .NET, open the WindowsCalculator.sln solution file in *install_folder*\Practices\Mod09\Mod09_01\Starter. Rebuild the solution.

2. Run the application and notice that the version number is 3.0.1.1. This is the version number of CalculatorEngine.dll.

3. In a Visual Studio .NET Command Prompt window, change directories to *install_folder*\Practices\ Mod09\Mod09_01\Starter \bin.

4. Run ILDASM on WindowsCalculator.exe by typing the command:

```
ildasm WindowsCalculator.exe
```

5. Open the MANIFEST sub- node. Notice that the **.assembly extern CalculatorEngine** entry has both the version number entry of 3:0:1:1, and a **.publickeytoken** entry. This shows that this application has a reference to an external strong name assembly.

How to Install Assemblies into the Global Assembly Cache

Several tools available for installing assemblies in the global assembly cache

- During development and testing phases, use
  GACUtil.exe
  GACUtil.exe Options
  -i (install)
  -l (list)
  -u (uninstall)
- For deployment, use
  MSCORCFG.msc
  Windows Installer Setup Project

Introduction

The global assembly cache is a machine-wide code cache used for storing one or more versions of an assembly. Storing multiple versions of an assembly in the global assembly cache is called side-by-side deployment. The global assembly cache stores assemblies that can be shared among many applications on the computer.

Assemblies that are deployed in global assembly cache must have a strong name. This is because the global assembly cache has stricter naming rules to ensure that side-by-side deployment and execution is possible. As a result, when you install an assembly in the global assembly cache, the common language runtime verifies that the assembly is unique to any other assembly already installed in the global assembly cache and has not been tampered with. The verification process begins by decrypting the signature of the strong name by using the public key that is included in the assembly. If the signature is not present or the results of decrypting the signature do not match the contents of the assembly, the installation process is terminated.

To install or uninstall an assembly in the global assembly cache, you need to have administrator-level privileges on the computer on which the cache resides. Assemblies should be installed in the global assembly cache by using Windows Installer or by using the .NET Framework configuration tool, Mscorcfg.msc. During development, you can use the Global Assembly Cache tool or Windows Explorer to install your assembly in the global assembly cache for testing purposes. Both of these tools are available for convenience only and should not be used for production deployment.

Using GACUtil.exe

GACUtil.exe is a command line utility that allows you to view and manipulate the contents of the global assembly cache. GACUtil.exe options include:

- /i or –i: installs a strong-named assembly into the global assembly cache.
- /l or –l: lists the contents of the global assembly cache.
- /u or –u: removes one or more assemblies from the global assembly cache.

Using MSCORCFG.msc

The .NET Framework Configuration tool is a Microsoft Management Console (MMC) snap-in that allows you to manage and configure assemblies in the global assembly cache, adjust code access security policy, and adjust remoting services.

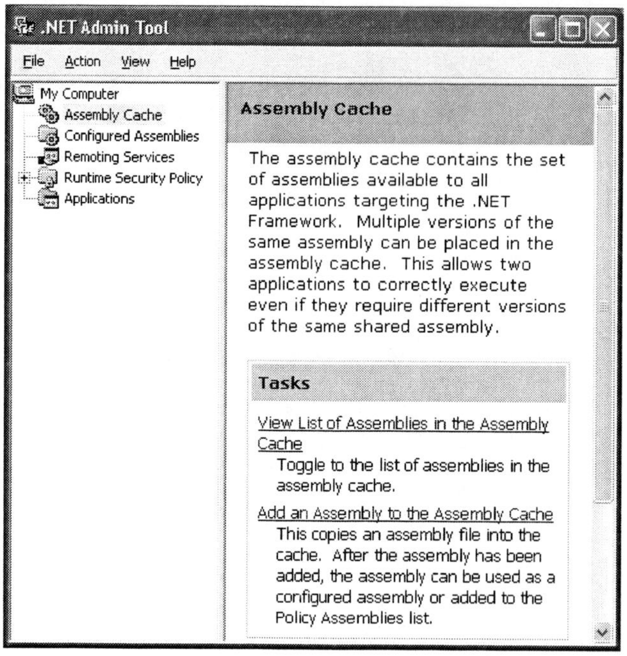

Using a Windows Installer 2.0 setup project

When you create a Microsoft Windows Installer 2.0 setup project for your application, you can add strong-named assemblies to the Global Assembly Cache node of your setup project.

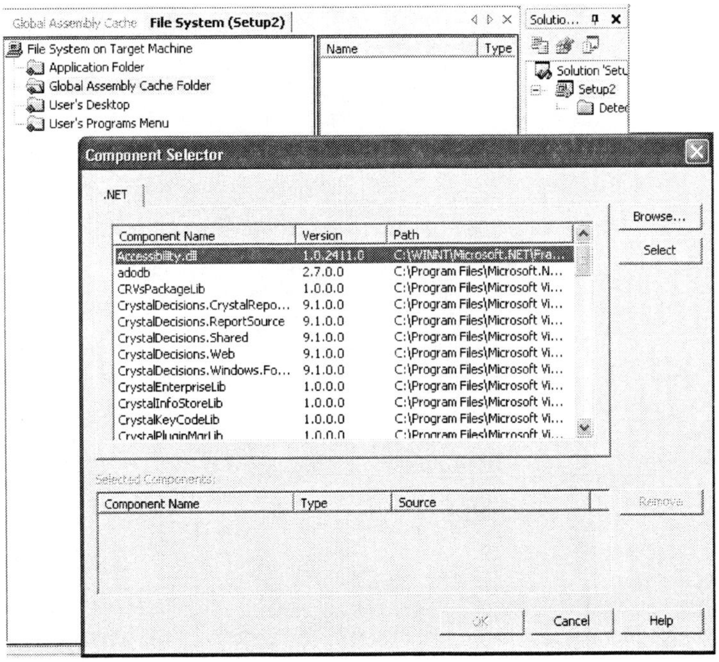

When your application is installed by using the Windows Installer, these strong-named assemblies will be installed into the global assembly cache of the computer where the installed project is run. For more information about setup projects see the lesson, Deploying Windows Forms Applications, in Module 9, "Deploying Windows Forms Applications," in Course 2565A, *Developing Microsoft .NET Applications for Microsoft Windows (Visual Basic .NET).*

Demonstration: Using the .NET Framework Configuration Tool to Work with the Global Assembly Cache

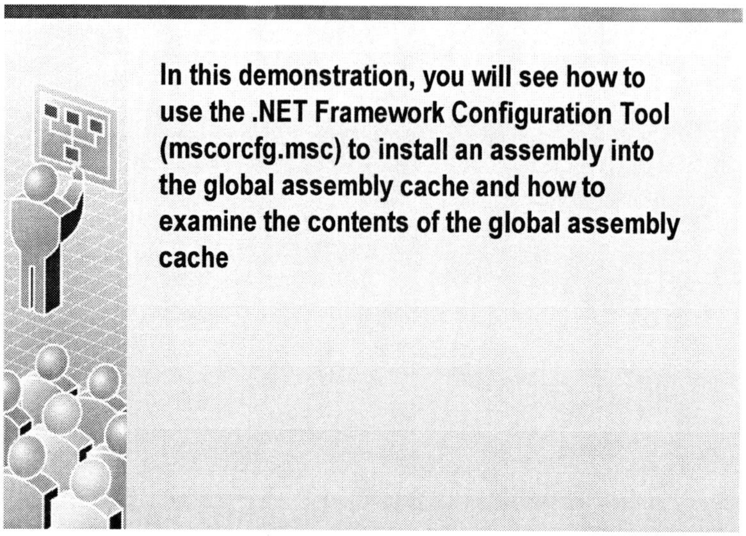

Introduction

In this demonstration, you will see how to use the .NET Framework Configuration Tool (mscorcfg.msc) to install an assembly into the global assembly cache, and how to examine the contents of the global assembly cache.

Instructions

► **To install an assembly into the global assembly cache by using the .NET Framework configuration tool**

1. Run the .NET Framework configuration tool (mscorcfg.msc) by double-clicking the mscorcfg.msc icon on the desktop.
2. In the left pane of the .NET Framework Configuration Tool window, click the **Assembly Cache** node.
3. In the right pane of the .NET Framework Configuration Tool window, click **Add an Assembly to the Assembly Cache**.
4. In the **Add an Assembly** dialog, change folders to *install_path*\Democode\Mod09\Mod09_02.
5. Select CalculatorEngine.dll and click the **Open** button.

► **To use the .NET Framework configuration tool to examine the global assembly cache**

1. In the right pane of the .NET Framework Configuration Tool window, click **View List of Assemblies in the Assembly Cache**.
2. Scroll through the cache list and locate CalculatorEngine. Notice it lists the version, culture, and public key token information as well.

Practice: Working with the Global Assembly Cache

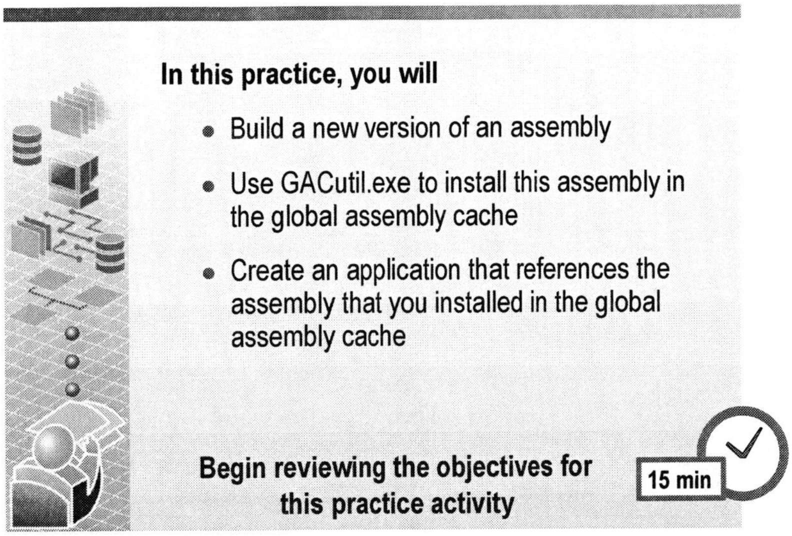

Introduction

In this practice, you will install the CalculatorEngine assembly in the global assembly cache. You will then build the WindowsCalculator application. Prior to running the application, you will remove all the local copies of CalculatorEngine.dll. You will then verify that WindowsCalculator still runs because it finds the correct version of CalculatorEngine in the global assembly cache.

Important During development, you can use the Global Assembly Cache tool (GACUtil) to install your assembly in the global assembly cache for testing purposes. This tool is available for convenience only and should not be used for production deployment. For production environments, assemblies should be installed in the global assembly cache by using Windows Installer or by using the .NET Framework configuration tool, Mscorcfg.msc.

Instructions

► **Building a new version of the CalculatorEngine assembly**

1. In Visual Studio .NET, open the CalculatorEngine.sln solution file in *install_folder*\Practices\Mod09\Mod09_02\Starter\CalculatorEngine.
2. Show TODO comments in the Task List.

   To show TODO comments, click the **View** menu, point to **Show Tasks**, and then click **All**.
3. Open the AssemblyInfo.vb file.
4. Locate the first TODO comment. Change the version number from **3.0.1.1** to **4.0.1.1**.

```
<Assembly: AssemblyVersion("4.0.1.1")>
```

5. Open the Calculator.vb source file.
6. Locate the TODO comment. Change the versionInfo string from **v3.0.1.1** to **v4.0.1.1**.

```
Private Shared versionInfo As String = _
    "Calculator v4.0.1.1"
```

7. Rebuild the library, and then close Visual Studio .NET.

► **Using GACUtil to install an assembly into the global assembly cache**

1. Open the Visual Studio .NET Command Prompt window by clicking **Start** pointing to **All Programs**, pointing to **Microsoft Visual Studio .NET**, pointing to **Visual Studio .NET Tools**, and then clicking **Visual Studio .NET Command Prompt**.
2. Change directories to *install_folder*\Practices\Mod09\Mod09_02\Starter\CalculatorEngine\bin.
3. Install the CalculatorEngine assembly into the global assembly cache by entering the command:

```
gacutil -i CalculatorEngine.dll
```

   You should receive the message Assembly successfully added to the cache.
4. Display the contents of the global assembly cache by entering the command:

```
gacutil -l
```

5. Scroll through the list to find CalculatorEngine. The entry should contain the information "CalculatorEngine, Version=4.0.1.1, Culture-neutral, PublicKeyToken=***, Custom=null".

► Building the application that references the strong-named assembly in the global assembly cache

1. In Visual Studio .NET, open the WindowsCalculator.sln solution file in *install_folder*\Practices\Mod09\Mod09_02\Starter.
2. Expand the References node in the Solution Explorer.
3. Right-click the References node and select **Add Reference**.
4. In the **Add Reference** dialog box, click **Browse** and locate CalculatorEngine.dll in *install_folder*\Practices\Mod09\Mod09_02\Starter\CalculatorEngine\bin. Click **Open** and then click **OK**.
5. Open the CalcUI.vb source file.
6. Show TODO comments in the task list.

   To show TODO comments, click the **View** menu, point to **Show Tasks**, and then click **All**.
7. Locate the TODO comment. Add a **using** directive to access Calculator.

   ```
   Imports Calculator
   ```
8. Build the WindowsCalculator application.
9. In Windows Explorer, rename all local copies of **CalculatorEngine.dll** to **OLD_Calculator.dll**. This would include *install_folder*\Practices\Mod09\Mod09_02\Starter\CalculatorEngine\bin and *install_folder*\Practices\Mod09\Mod09_02\Starter\CalculatorEngine\obj\Debug.
10. In Windows Explorer, browse to *install_folder*\Practices\Mod09\Mod09_02\Starter\bin.
11. Run the application by double-clicking WindowsCalculator.exe. Notice that the WindowsCalculator application still runs even though a local copy of the CalculatorEngine.dll assembly could not be found. This is because the runtime found the correct assembly in the global assembly cache and loaded it.

Lesson: Deploying Windows Forms Applications

- What Are Application Configuration Files?
- Elements of Application Configuration Files
- Element Attributes
- Practice: Creating and Using Application Configuration Files
- Other Configuration Files
- Demonstration: Tracing the Assembly Loading Process
- Packaging and Deploying .NET Applications
- Components of a Windows Installer Setup Project
- How to Create and Use a Windows Installer Setup Project
- Practice: Creating and Using a Windows Installer Deployment Project

Introduction

In this lesson, you will learn how to use application configuration files and Windows Installer 2.0 setup projects to deploy your.NET Framework applications.

Lesson objectives

After completing this lesson, you will be able to:

- Create and use application configuration files for.NET applications.
- Trace the assembly load process to aid in troubleshooting.
- Use Microsoft Windows Installer 2.0 to package and deploy .NET applications.

What are Application Configuration Files?

- **Application configuration files provide a way of overriding the metadata in assemblies without having to rebuild the application**
  - Name: *MyApp*.exe.config
  - Format: XML
  - Location: in the same folder as the application executable file
- **Runtime searches for and examines (if found) application configuration files**
- **Application configuration files allow you to override default treatment regarding application, assembly and policies**
- **Application configuration files contain**
  - Hierarchical elements
  - Some elements have attributes

Introduction

Every assembly and application is versioned in the .NET Framework. Application configuration files provide a way of overriding the metadata in assemblies without having to rebuild the application.

Definition

When an application runs, the .NET Framework common language runtime searches for dependencies that the application needs, such as other assemblies and resource files. This is known as the probing process. As part of the probing process, the runtime searches for and examines (if found) application configuration files. If a file is found, the runtime modifies its probing behavior based on the contents of the configuration file.

Definition

Application configuration files are XML files that contain settings specific to an application. This file contains configuration settings that the common language runtime reads (such as assembly binding policy) when it probes for the application's dependencies. Application configuration files allow you to override the application/assembly version, location of dependent assemblies, the probing process, and any publisher policy that a third-party vendor may have provided

The application configuration file can redirect an application to use a different version of an assembly or look in a different location for an assembly, but the assembly itself must still be built with the same key pair that the application expects. This is because, the runtime will check for tampering when a strong-named assembly is referenced. This helps prevents the use of redirection for malicious intentions, because the perpetrator would have to obtain the key pair to accomplish their task.

Application configuration files reside in the same folder as the executable to which they apply. The naming convention for an application configuration file is *executable_name*.config. For example, if your application is named MyApp.exe, the application configuration file must be named MyApp.exe.config.

Example of an application configuration file

Application configuration files contain hierarchical elements and some of these elements can have attributes. Here is an example of a simple application configuration file.

```
<configuration>
  <runtime>
    <assemblyBinding xmlns="urn:schemas-microsoft-com:asm.v1">
      <dependentAssembly>
        <assemblyIdentity name="CalculatorEngine"
                          publicKeyToken="3a1061701aba2b5b"
                          culture="en-US"/>
        <bindingRedirect oldVersion="3.0.1.1"
                         newVersion="4.0.1.1"/>
        <codeBase version="4.0.1.1"
                  href="file:///C:/Program
Files/MyApplications/WindowsCalculator/CalculatorEngine.dll"/>
      </dependentAssembly>
    </assemblyBinding>
  </runtime>
</configuration>
```

Note The path for the <codeBase> element may differ from the one shown in the example configuration file, depending on where the referenced assembly is located.

Other topics in this lesson provide more information about configuration elements and element attributes.

Elements of Application Configuration Files

```
<configuration>
   <runtime>
       <assemblyBinding>
           <dependentAssembly>
               <assemblyIdentity>
               <bindingRedirect>
               <codeBase>
               <publisherPolicy>
       <probing>
       <publisherPolicy>
   . . .
<configuration>
```

Introduction

Configuration files are structured in a hierarchical fashion beginning with the root <configuration> element. Because the elements and sub elements are well-formed XML, they are case-sensitive.

Application configuration file elements

The table describes the elements that may be included in the configuration file.

Element	Description
<configuration>	The root element of the configuration file, <configuration> indicates that the information that follows the element is used to configure the application. All configuration files must contain the starting and ending configuration elements.
<runtime>	A sub element of <configuration>, <runtime>contains information about assembly binding at run time.
<assemblyBinding>	A sub element of <runtime>, <assemblyBinding> contains information about assembly version redirection and locations of assemblies.
<dependentAssembly>	A sub element of <assemblyBinding>, <dependentAssembly> encapsulates binding policy information, such as the assembly name, the version number, and the assembly's location. This element contains the binding rules for an individual assembly. If binding policy is needed for multiple assemblies, use one <dependentAssembly> element for each assembly.

(continued)

Element	Description
<assemblyIdentity>	A sub element of <dependentAssembly>, <assemblyIdentity> contains identifying information about the assembly. The identity information can include the simple name of the assembly, culture information if it is provided, and a token that maps to a public key.
<bindingRedirect>	A sub element of <dependentAssembly>, <bindingRedirect> redirects the runtime from one assembly version to another.
<codeBase>	A sub element of <dependendAssembly>, <codeBase> specifies where the runtime can find a strong-named assembly.
<probing>	Specifies subdirectories of the application's base directory that might contain assemblies.
<publisherPolicy>	Specifies whether the runtime applies publisher policy. If placed within the <dependentAssembly> element, the <publisherPolicy> element will apply to the specific assembly. If placed within the <assemblyBinding> element, the <publisherPolicy> element will apply to all assemblies referenced by the application.

Element Attributes

Second name for this.
OEM

- <assemblyIdentity>
  - name (required)
  - publicKeyToken (optional)
  - culture (optional)
- <codeBase>
  - version (required)
  - href (required)
- <bindingRedirect>
  - oldVersion (required)
  - newVersion (required)
- <probing>
  - privatePath (required)
- <publisherPolicy>
  - apply (required)

Introduction

Some of the policy configuration elements include attributes that specify additional details for the runtime to use in locating referenced assemblies.

Configuration file element attributes

The table describes the attributes that can be used with certain configuration file elements.

Element	Attribute	Description
<assemblyIdentity>	name:	(required) The simple name of the assembly.
	publicKeyToken	(optional) Value that specifies the strong name of the assembly.
	culture	(optional) String that indicates the language and country/region of the assembly.
<codeBase>	version	(required) Specifies the version of the assembly the codebase applies to. The format of version numbers in .NET is major.minor.build.revision.
	href	(required) Specifies the URL where the assembly is stored.

(continued)

Element	Attribute	Description
<bindingRedirect>	oldVersion	(required) Specifies the version or version range of the assembly that was originally requested.
	newVersion	(required) Specified the version of the assembly to use instead of the originally requested version.
<probing>	privatePath	(required) Contains the directories that the runtime should search for assemblies. The directories specified in privatePath must be subdirectories of the application base directory.
<publisherPolicy>	Apply	(required) Indicates whether publisher policy is applied at runtime. Values are yes and no.

Practice: Creating and Using Application Configuration Files

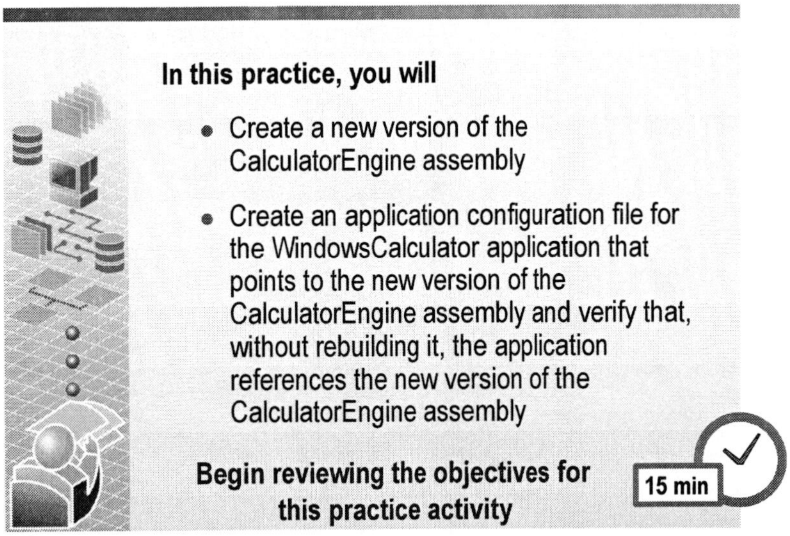

Introduction

In this practice, you will install a new version of the **CalculatorEngine** assembly in the global assembly cache. You will then build an application configuration file for the WindowsCalculator application that points the application to the new version of **CalculatorEngine**. You will not have to rebuild the WindowsCalculator application for it to use the new version of **CalculculatorEngine**.

Instructions

► **Install a new version of the CalculatorEngine assembly into the global assembly cache**

1. Open the Visual Studio .NET Command Prompt window by clicking **Start**, pointing to **All Programs**, pointing to **Microsoft Visual Studio .NET**, pointing to **Visual Studio .NET Tools**, and then clicking **Visual Studio .NET Command Prompt**.
2. Change directories to *install_folder*\Practices\Mod09\Mod09_03\Starter.
3. Delete CalculatorEngine.dll.

   This is version 4.0.1.1, which is the assembly that WindowsCalculator currently references.
4. Copy **CalculatorEngine.dll.v5011** to **CalculatorEngine.dll.**
5. Install the **CalculatorEngine** assembly into the global assembly cache by typing the following command:

   ```
   gacutil -i CalculatorEngine.dll
   ```
   You should receive the message Assembly successfully added to the cache.
6. Display the contents of the global assembly cache by typing the following command:

   ```
   gacutil -l
   ```
7. Scroll through the list to find **CalculatorEngine**. There should be two versions of **CalculatorEngine** in the global assembly cache. One version is 4.0.1.1 and the other is 5.0.1.1.

► **Create an application configuration file for WindowsCalculator**

1. Run the .NET Framework configuration tool (Mscorcfg.msc) by double-clicking the Mscorcfg.msc icon on the desktop.
2. Click the Applications node.
3. Click **Add an Application to Configure**.

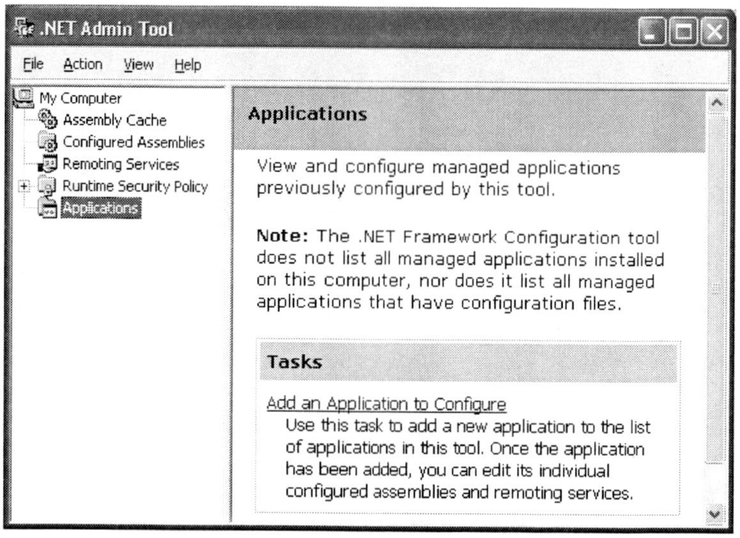

4. In the **Configure an Application** dialog box, click **Other** to locate the assembly.
5. Browse to *install_folder*\Practices\Mod09\Mod09_03\Starter, select **WindowsCalculator.exe**, and then click **Open**.
6. In Mscorcfg.msc, under Applications, expand the WindowsCalculator.exe application node, and then click **Configured Assemblies**.
7. In the right pane, click the **Configure an Assembly** link.
8. In the **Configure an Assembly** dialog box, select **Choose an assembly from the assembly cache**.
9. Click **Choose Assembly**.
10. In the **Choose Assembly from Assembly Cache** dialog box, scroll through the list of assemblies to locate CalculatorEngine version 5.0.1.1. Click **CalculatorEngine**, and then click **Select**.
11. Click **Finish**.

    The CalculatorEngine Properties dialog box appears.

12. Click the **Binding Policy** tab.
13. In the **Requested Version** column, type **4.0.1.1**
14. In the **New Version** column, type **5.0.1.1**
15. Click **Apply**, and then click **OK**.
16. Use Notepad to open *install_folder*\Practices\Mod09\Mod09_03\Starter\WindowsCalculator.exe.config and examine the contents. Notice the <bindingRedirect> tag. Close Notepad.
17. Run the application by double-clicking **WindowsCalculator.exe**. Verify that it uses the new version of the **CalculatorEngine** assembly. The version will be 5.0.1.1.

Other Configuration Files

- Publisher policy
- Machine policy
- Enterprise policy

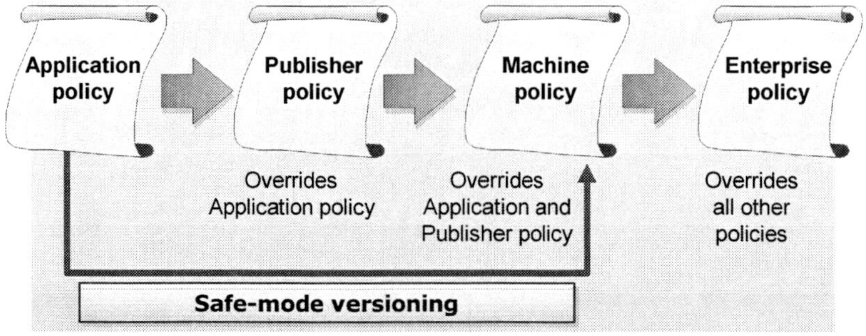

Introduction

There are several other policy levels that can be applied to your application that can override the default binding policy and settings in the application configuration file.

Publisher policy configuration files

Publisher policy configuration files are usually explicitly installed as part of a service pack or program update. For example, when using third-party components, the vendor may provide an updated version as a service pack. As part of the service pack, a publisher policy file is included to redirect applications to use the new version of the component. By default, publisher policy overrides application policy and the metadata that is found in the application's metadata. However, safe-mode versioning is allowed by configuring the application configuration file to ignore the publisher policy file. This is accomplished through the <publisherPolicy> element by setting the apply attribute to **no**.

Machine policy configuration file

The machine configuration file, Machine.config, contains settings that apply to an entire computer. This file is located in the %runtime install path%\Config directory. Putting the settings in the machine configuration file makes your system easier to maintain. For example, if you have a third-party component that both your client and server application uses, or that multiple applications use, it is easier to put the settings for that component in one place. In this case, the machine configuration file is the appropriate place for the settings, so you don't have the same settings in multiple different files. By default, machine policy overrides publisher policy and application policy.

Enterprise policy configuration file

The enterprise policy level affects every computer and user on the network and can only be administered by enterprise or domain administrators. You might consider administering policy on this level when every person in your enterprise uses an application and you want to make sure that it always receives sufficient permissions to run. By default, enterprise policy overrides machine, publisher, and application policy.

Demonstration: Tracing the Assembly Loading Process

In this demonstration, you will see how to use the Fusion Log Viewer (FUSLOGVW) to trace the assembly loading process and solve probing errors

In this demonstration, you will see how to use the Fusion Log Viewer (FUSLOGVW) to trace the assembly loading process and identify assembly loading problems (probing errors).

Important Prior to performing this demonstration, run the Fusion Log Viewer and enable the **Log Failures** checkbox. If you do not do so, the run time will ***not*** log probing errors and the following practice will not work as expected. It is also beneficial to leave tracking of log failures turned on at all times to help you in troubleshooting application problems.

Instructions

► **Run the WindowsCalculator application**

1. In Windows Explorer, browse to *install_folder*\Democode\Mod09\Mod09_03.
2. Double-click **WindowsCalculator.exe** to run the application. Notice that the version number of the CalculatorEngine is 3.0.1.1.

► **Using the configuration file**

1. In Windows Explorer, delete **CalculatorEngine.dll** from *install_folder*\Democode\Mod09\Mod09_03.
2. Rename HoldWindowsCalculator.exe.config to WindowsCalculator.exe.config.
3. Run the application again.

   You should see a System.IO.FileNotFoundException.

▶ To use FUSLOGVW (Fusion Log Viewer) to solve probing errors

1. Open a Visual Studio .NET Command Prompt window.

   To open a Visual Studio .NET Command Prompt window, click **Start**, point to **All Programs**, point to **Microsoft Visual Studio .NET**, point to **Visual Studio .NET Tools**, and then click **Visual Studio .NET Command Prompt**.

2. Run the Fusion Log Viewer by typing the command:

```
fuslogvw
```

3. In the Assembly Binding Log Viewer window, locate the entry that matches the last execution of the WindowsCalculator application and double-click it.

4. Look through the log entries noting the various points at which the runtime attempted to locate the CalculatorEngine assembly and the order in which each attempt was made. The log be will similar to the following:

```
LOG: Processing DEVPATH.
LOG: DEVPATH is not set. Falling through to regular bind.
LOG: Publisher policy file is not found.
LOG: Host configuration file not found.
LOG: Using machine configuration file from
C:\WINDOWS\Microsoft.NET\Framework\v1.0.3705\config\machine
.config.
LOG: Post-policy reference: CalculatorEngine,
Version=3.0.1.1, Culture=neutral,
PublicKeyToken=3d117e8f75e2ae71
LOG: Cache Lookup was unsuccessful.
LOG: Attempting download of new URL
file:///C:/Courses/2565A/CD_Trainer/StudentCD/Democode/Mod0
9/Demo09_03/CalculatorEngine.DLL.
LOG: Attempting download of new URL
file:///C:/Courses/2565A/CD_Trainer/StudentCD/Democode/Mod0
9/Demo09_03/CalculatorEngine/CalculatorEngine.DLL.
LOG: Attempting download of new URL
file:///C:/Courses/2565A/CD_Trainer/StudentCD/Democode/Mod0
9/Demo09_03/CalculatorEngine.EXE.
LOG: Attempting download of new URL
file:///C:/Courses/2565A/CD_Trainer/StudentCD/Democode/Mod0
9/Demo09_03/CalculatorEngine/CalculatorEngine.EXE.
LOG: All probing URLs attempted and failed.
```

▶ Run the executable

1. Rename **CalculatorEngine.dll.v4.0.1.1** to **CalculatorEngine.dll**.
2. Run the WindowsCalculator application once again. Notice that the version number of **CalculatorEngine** is now 4.0.1.1.

Packaging and Deploying .NET Applications

- **Packaging Applications**
  - As a set of executables and DLLs
  - Microsoft Windows Installer 2.0 package
  - Cabinet files
- **Deploying Applications**
  - XCOPY
  - Windows Installer 2.0
  - Code download

Introduction

You have several options for how you package and deploy your .NET applications.

Definitions

Packaging is the act of creating a package that can install your application onto the user's computer.

Deployment is the act of distributing a built application to the computer and setting up the application so it will run correctly.

Packaging Options

This table compares packaging options available for .NET applications.

Packaging Option	Description	Comments
Executables and DLLs	A set of executables and DLLs in the original folder hierarchy in which the application was built.	No packaging is required with .NET applications and assemblies. You can use the EXE and DLL files as they were built.
Windows Installer 2.0	Use Visual Studio .NET to create .msi files for use with the Windows Installer.	This is the standard way of distributing and installing applications that run on the desktop. Other applications can also be deployed by using .msi files. For example, Microsoft ASP.NET applications can be packaged in an .msi file.
Cabinet Files	Use Visual Studio .NET to create cabinet (.cab) files for deployment of a .NET Framework application.	The following restrictions apply when creating the .cab file for .NET compatible applications: • Only one assembly can be stored in a .cab file. The .cab file must have the same name as the file in the assembly that contains the manifest. For example, if the file containing the manifest in the assembly is called MyClasses.dll, then the .cab file must be named MyClasses.cab. • After you have created a .cab file, it can be downloaded by specifying its location by using the <codeBase> element in one of the configuration files.

Deployment Options

This table compares the deployment options available for .NET applications.

Deployment Option	Description	Comments
XCOPY	Because common language runtime applications are self-describing and require no registry entries, you can use XCOPY to copy the application to an appropriate directory. The application can then be run from that directory. You can also use FTP to deploy your application.	Easiest way to install an application. To remove the application from the computer, just delete for directory structure for the application. Installs private and strong-named assemblies only. No shared assemblies can be installed this way.
Windows Installer 2.0	Windows Installer 2.0 can install, repair, or remove Microsoft .NET Framework assemblies in the global assembly cache and in private directories. This is the recommended way to deploy Windows Forms Applications.	Use a Visual Studio .NET setup project to build an .msi file. Installation, repair, and removal of assemblies in the global assembly cache. Install, repair, or remove assemblies in private locations designated for particular applications. Rollback unsuccessful installations, repairs, or removals of assemblies. Install-on-demand strong-named assemblies in the global assembly cache and in private locations designated for particular applications.
Code Download	If you are distributing your application over the Internet or through a corporate intranet, you can download the code to a computer and run the application.	

Components of a Windows Installer Setup Project

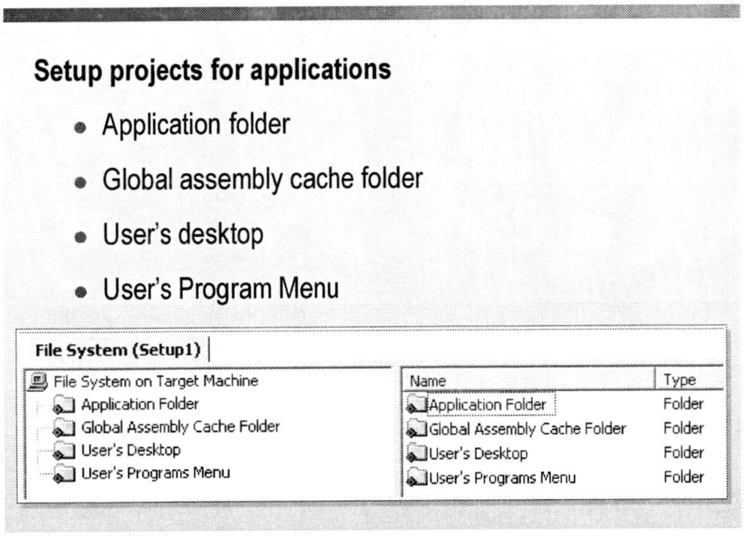

Introduction

By using a Windows Installer setup project you can customize how the application is deployed on the user's computer.

Note Remember to add files from a Release build, not a Debug build, to setup projects.

Components of a Windows Installer setup project

This table describes the uses for the various components of a Windows Installer setup project.

Setup Component	Description
Application folder	The folder used to store the application, for example, C:\Program Files\Manufacturer\Product.
Global Assembly Cache Folder	Use this folder to install shared assemblies. When creating a new setup project, the Global Assembly Cache Folder will not appear in the File Editor by default. To show the Global Assembly Cache Folder, right-click on File System on Target Machine, highlight Add Special Folder, and select Global Assembly Cache Folder.
User's Desktop	Use this folder to install shortcuts on the desktop.
User's Program Menu	Use this folder to install a shortcut in the program menu.

How to Create and Use a Windows Installer Setup Project

1. Create a new setup project in Visual Studio .NET
2. Set project properties as appropriate
3. Add the application files to be installed in the application folder
   - For example, .exe, .dll, and locale files
4. Add icons for your application to the setup project
5. Add any shared assemblies to the Global Assembly Cache folder of the project
6. Build the project
7. In Explorer double-click the setup.exe file created by the setup project to install the application

Introduction

You can use Visual Studio .NET to create a Windows Installer setup project for your application. You can then copy the .msi file to the appropriate computer and double-click the .msi file from the setup project to install your application.

Procedure: Creating and using a Windows Installer setup project

1. Create a new setup project in Visual Studio .NET.

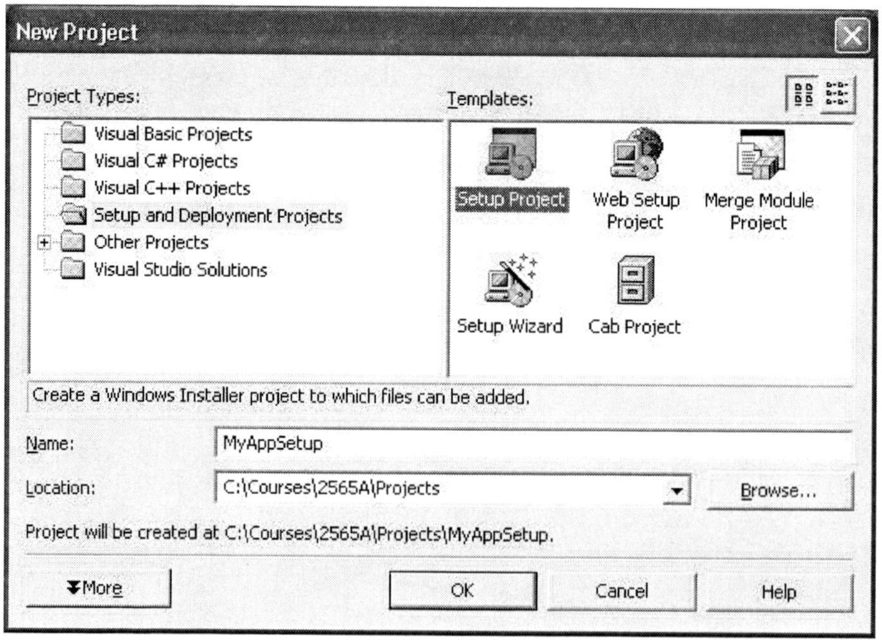

2. Click OK and then set project properties such as **Author**, **Description**, **Manufacturer**, **ManufacturerUrl**, **ProductName**, **Title**, and **Version**.

3. To add the application files to be installed in the application folder, in the **File System** tree, right-click the **Application Folder** then, click **Add**, and then click **Folder** or **File**, as appropriate.

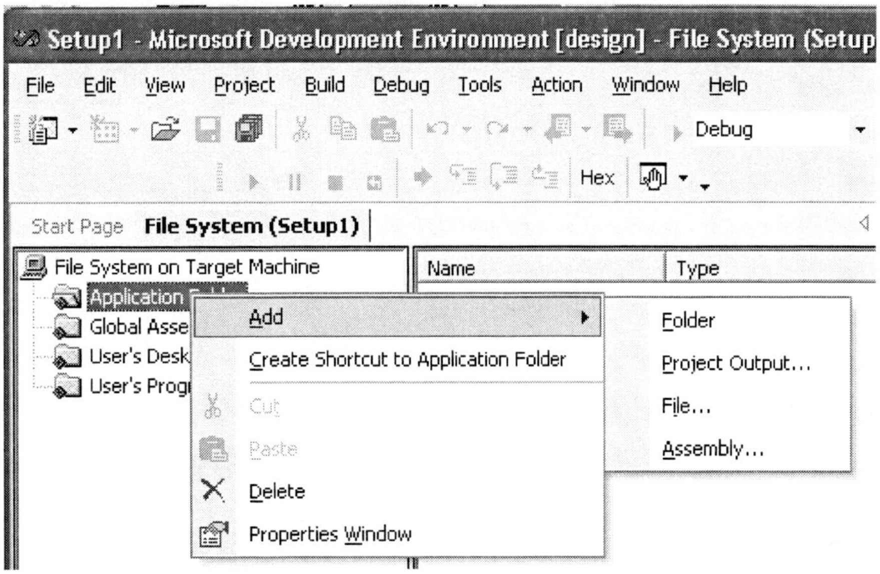

4. Set the **DefaultLocation** property of the Application Folder if you wish to change the location of where the contents of the Application Folder will be installed.

5. To add the icons for your application to the setup project, in the **File System** tree, right-click **User's Desktop** or **User's Program Menu**, and choose **Create Shortcut to User's Desktop** or **Create Shortcut to User's Programs Menu**, as appropriate.

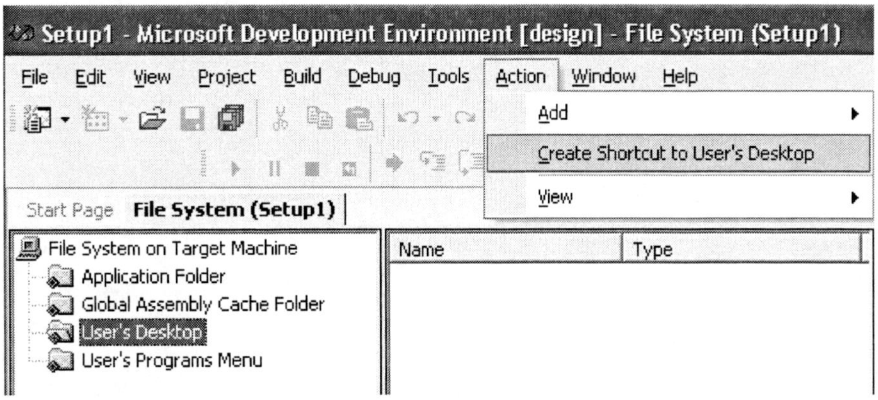

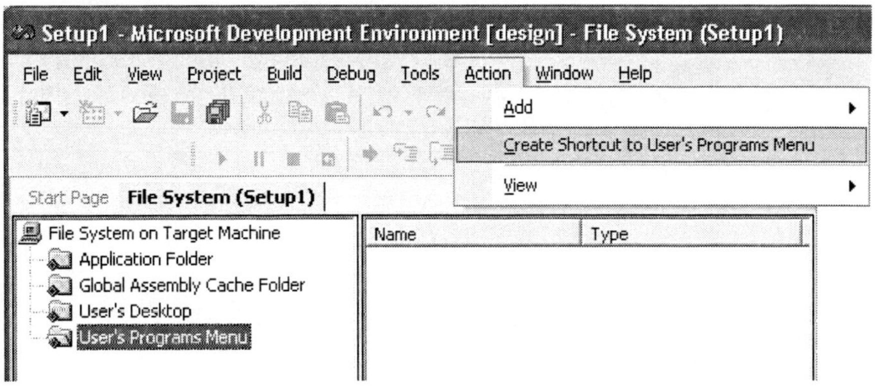

6. To add any shared assemblies to the global assembly cache at setup time (these are strong-named assemblies that will be shared among multiple applications), in the **File System** tree, right-click the **File System on Target Machine** root node, click **Add Special Folder**, and then click **Global Assembly Cache Folder**. Right-click the **Global Assembly Cache Folder**, point to **Add**, and then click **Assembly**. Use the Component Selector to browse and a select any strong-named assemblies you wish to add to the global assembly cache.

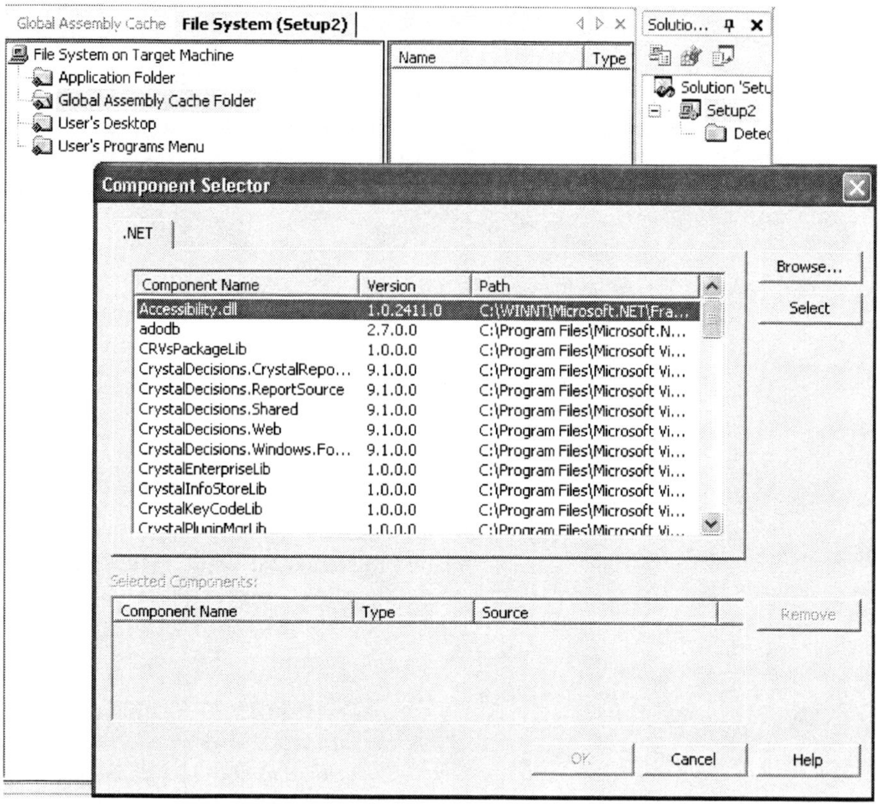

7. Build the setup project.

   The output is an .msi file.

8. In Windows Explorer, locate and double-click **Setup.exe** to install the application on your computer.

Important By default, the .NET framework redistributable library is not included in the deployment project. This library can be added to the deployment project in the event the target machines do not have the .NET Framework already installed. To add the redistributable library, expand the **Detected Dependencies** list in the Solution Explorer window, right-click on **dotnetfxredist_x86_enu.msm**, and clear the **Exclude** option on the shortcut menu.

Practice: Creating and Using a Windows Installer Deployment Project

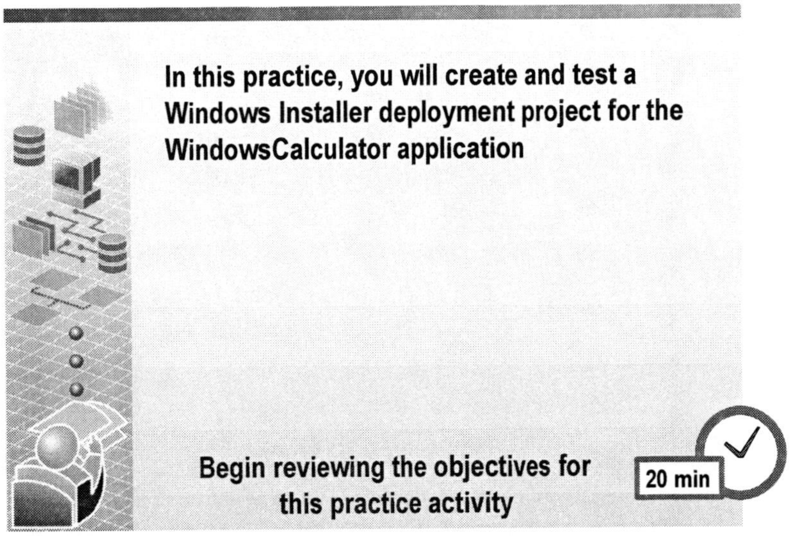

Introduction

In this practice, you will create a Microsoft Installer setup project and add the WindowsCalculator application to the project. You will then test the project to validate that the application installed and works correctly.

Instructions

► **Create the setup project**

1. Start Visual Studio .NET.
2. On the **Start** page, click **New Project**.
3. In the New Project window, in the Project Type pane, click **Setup and Deployment Projects**.
4. In the Templates pane, click **Setup Project**.
5. Set the Location to *install_folder*\Practices\Mod09\Mod09_04\Starter.
6. Set the Name to **WinCalc**. Click **OK** to create the project.
7. In the File System tree, right-click **File System on Target Machine**, click **Add Special Folder**, and then click **Global Assembly Cache Folder**.
8. Right-click **Global Assembly Cache Folder**, click **Add**, and then click **File**.
9. In the **Add Files** dialog box, change folder to *install_folder*\Practices\Mod09\Mod09_04\Starter, and then double-click **CalculatorEngine.dll**.
10. Right-click **Application Folder**, click **Add**, and then click **File**.
11. In the **Add Files** dialog box, double-click **WindowsCalculator.exe**.
12. Right-click **Application Folder**, click **Add**, and then click **File**.
13. In the **Add Files** dialog box, double-click **KEYS03.ICO**.

14. Right-click the **Application Folder**, and then click **Properties Window**. In the Properties window, change the **DefaultLocation** property to **[ProgramFilesFolder]\[ProductName]** by removing the Manufacturer entry. Also, change the **AlwaysCreate** property to **True**.
15. In Solution Explorer, expand **Detected Dependencies**. In the **Detected Dependencies** folder, right-click **CalculatorEngine.dll**, and then click **Exclude**.
16. To create a shortcut for the User's Desktop, select the **Application Folder** again, and then click **WindowsCalculator.exe**.

    When you reach step 24 you will be directed to repeat steps 16 through 22 to create a second shortcut for the **Program** menu.
17. On the **Action** menu, click **Create Shortcut to WindowsCalculator.exe**. Rename the shortcut to **Windows Calculator**.
18. In the Properties window, make sure the **Target** property is set to **WindowsCalculator**.
19. Click on the **Icon** property and select **Browse**.
20. In the **Icon** dialog box, click **Browse**.
21. Select **Application Folder** from the **Look In** dropdown list and click on **KEYS03.ICO**.
22. Click **OK** and then click **OK** in the **Icon** dialog box.
23. Drag the shortcut from the Application Folder to the User's Desktop node.
24. To create a shortcut for the **Program** menu, repeat steps 16 through 22 again to create another shortcut with the same name.
25. Drag the shortcut to the User's Program Menu node.
26. In Solution Explorer, click the **WinCalc** project. In the Properties window, set the following properties to their associated values.

Property	Value
Author	*Your Name*
Manufacturer	*Your Name* or *Your Company's Name*
ProductName	WinCalc
Title	Windows Calculator

27. Save and build the setup project.

► **Install and run the application**

1. In Windows Explorer, browse to *install_folder*\Practices\Mod09\Mod09_04\Starter\WinCalc\Debug.
2. Double-click **Setup.exe** to start the installation of the Windows Calculator application.
3. Click **Next** three times. The application will be installed on the computer.
4. Click **Close** after the application has been installed.
5. View the computer's desktop and double-click the **Windows Calculator** icon.

   The application should start and show that it is using version 6.0.1.1 of the **CalculatorEngine** assembly.
6. Close the Calculator.
7. Click the **Start** button, point to **All Programs**, and then click the **Windows Calculator**.

   The application should run and show that it, too, is using version 6.0.1.1. of the **CalculatorEngine** assembly.
8. Close the Calculator.
9. In Windows Explorer, browse to C:\Program Files\WinCalc.

   You should see the WindowsCalculator.exe file in this folder, but not CalculatorEngine.dll.
10. In Windows Explorer, change directories to C:\WINDOWS\assembly.

    You should see CalculatorEngine version 6.0.1.1 installed in the global assembly cache.

Review

- .NET Assemblies
- Deploying Windows Forms Applications

1. Describe how private assemblies and strong-named assemblies differ.

2. Describe how strong-named assemblies and shared assemblies differ.

3. What is needed to build a strong-named assembly?

4. How is an assembly installed in the global assembly cache?

5. Why would you use an application configuration file?

use newer version

6. You want to redirect the runtime to load version 2.3.4.56 of an assembly that an application needs from D:\CustomAssemblies\MyAssembly.dll. What entry needs to be made in the application configuration file?

7. When would a publisher policy configuration file be used?

8. List the three methods of deploying an application.
   - **Copying the application to a folder on the target machine through the use of XCOPY.**
   - **Using Windows Installer.**
   - **Using .cab files.**

Lab 9.1: Deploying an Application

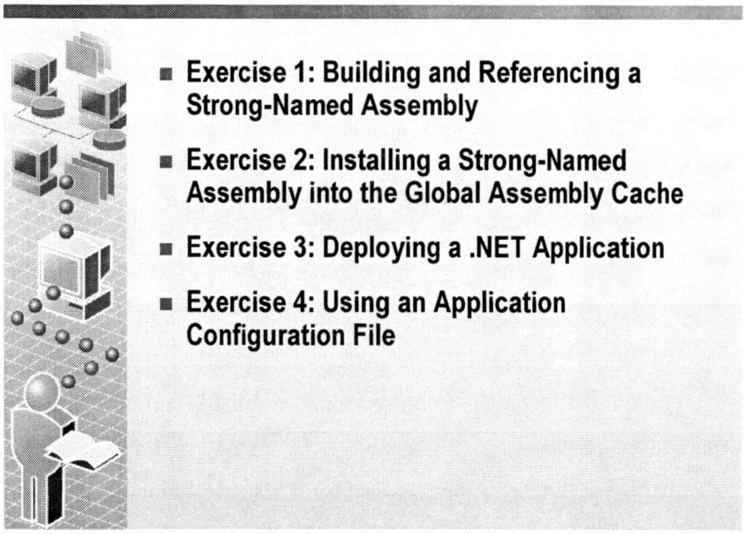

Objectives

After completing this lab, you will have demonstrated your ability to:

- Build a strong-named assembly.
- Build an application that references a strong-named assembly.
- Install a strong-named assembly in the global assembly cache.
- Deploy an application by using Windows Installer.
- Use an application configuration file to cause an application to use a new version of a referenced assembly.

Prerequisites

Before working on this lab, you must have:

- The knowledge and skills to develop a simple Windows Forms application by using a Visual Studio .NET–compatible programming language.
- The knowledge and skills to debug an application by using Visual Studio .NET.
- The knowledge and skills to build strong-named assemblies and applications that reference strong-named assemblies.
- The knowledge and skills to create a .NET setup project to deploy an application.
- The knowledge and skills to create an application configuration file for an application.

Scenario

Many applications that you create for the .NET Framework will require the use of assemblies that are not included with the application assembly. The referenced assembly may be installed into the global assembly cache, or it may reside in a location other than the application's folder.

In this lab, you will create a strong-named assembly and then reference this assembly from an application. You will then deploy the application by using a Setup and Deployment project to build a Windows Installer file. In addition, you will upgrade the strong-named assembly to a new version and modify the application to use the new assembly through the use of application configuration files.

Estimated time to complete this lab: 60 minutes

Exercise 1
Building and Referencing a Strong-Named Assembly

In this exercise, you will use the Expense Reporting application to build a strong-named assembly. You will then use the Internal Business Application shell application to reference the strong-named assembly. You will also use ILDASM to verify that ExpenseReport.DLL is a strong-named assembly.

There are starter and solution files associated with this exercise. Browse to *install_folder*\Labfiles\Lab09_1\Ex01\Starter to find the starter files, and browse to *install_folder*\Labfiles\Lab09_1\Ex01\Solution to find the solution files. If you performed a default installation of the course files, *install_folder* corresponds to C:\Program Files\Msdntrain\2565.

Tasks	Additional information
1. Open the ExpenseReport project in Visual Studio .NET. Browse to *install_folder*\Labfiles\Lab09_1\Ex01\Starter\ExpenseReportApp to find the project files.	**a.** For more information about opening a project file, see the following resource: • The Visual Studio .NET Help documentation. In Search, select the **Search in titles only** check box, then search by using the phrase **Open Project Dialog Box**.
2. Build the expense report project. Keep this instance of Visual Studio .NET open.	**a.** For more information about building an application, see the following resource: • The Visual Studio .NET Help documentation. Search by using the phrase **Preparing and Managing Builds.**
3. Open the InternalBusinessApp project in another instance of Visual Studio.NET. Browse to *install_folder*\Labfiles\Lab09_1\Ex01\Starter\Business Application Shell to find the project files.	**a.** For more information about opening a project file, see the following resource: • The Visual Studio .NET Help documentation. In Search, select the **Search in titles only** check box, then search by using the phrase **Open Project Dialog Box**.
4. Add a reference to the ExpenseReport DLL file.	**a.** For more information about how to add a reference to an assembly by using Visual Studio .NET, see the following resource: • Practice: Working with the Global Assembly Cache in Module 9, "Deploying Windows Forms Applications," in Course 2565A, *Developing Microsoft .NET Applications for Windows (Visual C# .NET)*.
5. Build and test the internal business application. Keep this instance of Visual Studio .NET open.	No additional information is necessary for this task.

Tasks	Additional information
6. Open a Visual Studio .NET Command Prompt window and change directories to the location of InternalBusinessApp.exe. Browse to *install_folder*\Labfiles\Lab09_1\Ex01\Starter\ Business Application Shell\bin to find the executable.	**a.** For more information about how to open a Visual Studio .NET Command Prompt window, see the following resource: • Practice: Calling a Strong-Named Assembly in Module 9, "Deploying Windows Forms Applications," in Course 2565A, *Developing Microsoft .NET Applications for Windows (Visual C# .NET).*
7. Run ILDASM, and view the information for InternalBusinessApp.exe. View the MANIFEST, and note that the reference to the **ExpenseReport** assembly does not include a public key token. Close ILDASM.	**a.** For more information about how to use ILDASM, see the following resources: • Practice: Calling a Strong-Named Assembly in Module 9, "Deploying Windows Forms Applications," in Course 2565A, *Developing Microsoft .NET Applications for Windows (Visual C# .NET).* • The .NET Framework SDK documentation. Search by using the phrase **MSIL Disassembler (Ildasm.exe)**.
8. In a Visual Studio .NET Command Prompt window, change directories to where the ExpenseReport project is located. Browse to *install_folder*\Labfiles\Lab09_1\Ex01\Starter\ ExpenseReportApp to find the project.	**a.** For more information about how to open a command prompt window in Visual Studio .NET, see the following resource: • Practice: Calling a Strong-Named Assembly in Module 9, "Deploying Windows Forms Applications," in Course 2565A, *Developing Microsoft .NET Applications for Windows (Visual C# .NET).*
9. Run the strong-name tool to generate a strong-name key pair file. • Name the strong-name key pair file **ExpenseReport.snk**.	**a.** For more information about SN.EXE, see the following resource: • The .NET Framework SDK documentation. Search by using the phrases **Strong Name Tool (Sn.exe)** and **Creating a Key Pair**.

Tasks	Additional information
10. Switch to the Visual Studio .NET instance in which the ExpenseReport project is open. **a.** Complete the **AssemblyKeyFile** attribute to reference the ExpenseReport.snk key pair file. **b.** Rebuild the ExpenseReport project.	**a.** For more information about how to use ILDASM, see the following resource: • Practice: Calling a Strong-Named Assembly in Module 9, "Deploying Windows Forms Applications," in Course 2565A, *Developing Microsoft .NET Applications for Windows (Visual C# .NET).* **b.** For more information about global attributes and the AssemblyInfo file, see the following resource: • The .NET Framework SDK documentation. Search by using the phrase **Global Attributes**.
11. Switch to the Visual Studio .NET instance in which the InternalBusinessApp project is open. **a.** Rebuild and run the application. **b.** In a Visual Studio .NET Command Prompt window, run ILDASM to view the information for InternalBusinessApp.exe. **c.** View the MANIFEST. Notice that the reference to the ExpenseReport assembly now includes a public key token.	**a.** For more information about how to use ILDASM, see the following resources: • Practice: Calling a Strong-Named Assembly in Module 9, "Deploying Windows Forms Applications," in Course 2565A, *Developing Microsoft .NET Applications for Windows (Visual C# .NET).* • The .NET Framework SDK documentation. Search by using the phrase **MSIL Disassembler (Ildasm.exe)**.

Exercise 2
Installing a Strong-Named Assembly into the Global Assembly Cache

In this exercise, you will update the **ExpenseReport** assembly to version 2.0.1.1 and install it into the global assembly cache. You will then build and run the Internal Business Application to reference the **ExpenseReport** assembly and use ILDASM to verify that the Internal Business Application is referencing the correct version of the **ExpenseReport** assembly.

There are starter and solution files associated with this exercise. Browse to *install_folder*\Labfiles\Lab09_1\Ex02\Starter to find the starter files, and browse to *install_folder*\Labfiles\Lab09_1\Ex02\Solution to find the solution files. If you performed a default installation of the course files, *install_folder* corresponds to C:\Program Files\Msdntrain\2565.

Tasks	Additional information
1. Open the ExpenseReport project in Visual Studio .NET. Update the AssemblyVersion attribute to **"2.0.1.1"** and build the expense report project. Browse to *install_folder*\Labfiles\Lab09_1\Ex02\Starter\ExpenseReportApp to find the project.	**a.** For more information about opening a project file, see the following resource: • The Visual Studio .NET Help documentation. In Search, select the **Search in titles only** check box, then search by using the phrase **Open Project Dialog Box**.
2. Open the InternalBusinessApp project in another instance of Visual Studio.NET. Browse to *install_folder*\Labfiles\Lab09_1\Ex02\Starter\Business Application Shell to find the project.	**a.** For more information about opening a project file, see the following resource: • The Visual Studio .NET Help documentation. In Search, select the **Search in titles only** check box, then search by using the phrase **Open Project Dialog Box**.
3. Add a reference to the ExpenseReport DLL file. Browse to *install_folder*\Labfiles\Lab09_1\Ex02\Starter\ExpenseReportApp\bin to find the DLL.	**a.** For more information about how to add a reference to an assembly using Visual Studio .NET, see the following resource: • Practice: Working with the Global Assembly Cache in Module 9, "Deploying Windows Forms Applications," in Course 2565A, *Developing Microsoft .NET Applications for Windows (Visual C# .NET).*

Tasks	Additional information
4. In Solution Explorer, beneath **References**, click the **ExpenseReport** entry. **a.** Change the **Copy Local** property to **False**. This prevents Visual Studio .NET from copying the ExpenseReport.dll file into the bin folder of the Internal Business Application. **b.** Build the Internal Business Application.	No additional information is necessary for this task.
5. Open a command prompt window in Visual Studio .NET, and change directories to the location where ExpenseReport.dll is located. Browse to *install_folder*\Labfiles\Lab09_1\Ex02\Starter\ExpenseReportApp\bin to find the file.	**a.** For more information about how to open a command prompt window in Visual Studio .NET, see the following resource: • Practice: Calling a Strong-Named Assembly in Module 9, "Deploying Windows Forms Applications," in Course 2565A, *Developing Microsoft .NET Applications for Windows (Visual C# .NET).*
6. Run GACUTIL to install ExpenseReport.dll into the global assembly cache. **a.** View the global assembly cache after installing the **ExpenseReport.dll** assembly. There should be an entry for **ExpenseReport** in the global assembly cache.	**a.** For more information about how to use GACUTIL, see the following resource: • Practice: Working with the Global Assembly Cache in Module 9, "Deploying Windows Forms Applications," in Course 2565A, *Developing Microsoft .NET Applications for Windows (Visual C# .NET).*
7. Run the Internal Business Application.	No additional information is necessary for this task.
8. Open a Visual Studio .NET Command Prompt window and change directories to the location where InternalBusinessApp.exe is located. Browse to *install_folder*\Labfiles\Lab09_1\Ex02\Starter\Business Application Shell\bin to find the executable file.	**a.** For more information about how to open a Visual Studio .NET Command Prompt window, see the following resource: • Practice: Calling a Strong-Named Assembly in Module 9, "Deploying Windows Forms Applications," in Course 2565A, *Developing Microsoft .NET Applications for Windows (Visual C# .NET).*
9. Run ILDASM, and view InternalBusinessApp.exe. • View the MANIFEST. Notice that the reference to the **ExpenseReport** assembly is now to version 2.0.1.1.	**a.** For more information about how to use ILDASM, see the following resources: • Practice: Calling a Strong-name Assembly in Module 9, "Deploying Windows Forms Applications," in Course 2565A, *Developing Microsoft .NET Applications for Windows (Visual C# .NET).* • The .NET Framework SDK documentation. Search by using the phrase **MSIL Disassembler (Ildasm.exe)**.

Exercise 3
Deploying a .NET Application

In this exercise, you will package the Expense Reporting application into a Windows Installer file by using a Setup and Deployment project. You will then install the application on the local computer.

Note The Internal Business Application component of the Expense Reporting application requires that the Expense Report XML Web service be installed on the target computer. This exercise assumes that the Expense Report XML Web service has already been installed on the target computer.

There are solution files associated with this exercise. Browse to *install_folder*\Labfiles\Lab09_1\Ex03\Solution to find the solution files. If you performed a default installation of the course files, *install_folder* corresponds to C:\Program Files\Msdntrain\2565.

Tasks	Additional information
1. Open the InternalBusinessApp project in Visual Studio .NET. Browse to *install_folder*\Labfiles\Lab09_1\Ex03\Starter\Business Application Shell to find the project files.	**a.** For more information about opening a project file, see the following resource: • The Visual Studio .NET Help documentation. In Search, select the **Search in titles only** check box, then search by using the phrase **Open Project Dialog Box**.
2. Build the InternalBusinessApp project. Close the InternalBusinessApp solution, but keep Visual Studio .NET open.	**a.** For more information about building an application, see the following resource: • The Visual Studio .NET Help documentation. Search by using the phrase **Preparing and Managing Builds**.
3. Create a new Setup and Deployment project. Use the template that will create a Windows Installer setup project. • Set the project name to InternalBusinessApplication. • Set the project location to *install_folder***Labfiles\Lab09_1\Ex03\Starter**.	**a.** For more information about how to create a new Setup and Deployment project, see the following resource: • The How to Create and Use a Windows Installer Setup Project topic in Module 9, "Deploying Windows Forms Applications," in Course 2565A, *Developing Microsoft .NET Applications for Windows (Visual C# .NET)*.

Tasks	Additional information
4. Add the global assembly cache folder to the project.	**a.** For more information about how to add the global assembly cache folder, see the following resource: • Practice: Creating and Using a Windows Installer Deployment Project in Module 9, "Deploying Windows Forms Applications," in Course 2565A, *Developing Microsoft .NET Applications for Windows (Visual C# .NET).* **b.** For more information about deploying applications, see the following resources: • Lesson: Deploying Windows Forms Applications in Module 9, "Deploying Windows Forms Applications," in Course 2565A, *Developing Microsoft .NET Applications for Windows (Visual C# .NET).* • The .NET Framework SDK. Search by using the phrase **Deploying Applications**.
5. Add the localized folders to the Application folder. **a.** Right-click Application **folder**, point to **Add**, and select **Folder**. **b.** Create folders with the following names: **de**, **de-DE**, **en**, **en-US**, **fr**, **fr-FR**, **ja**, and **ja-JP**.	**a.** For more information about how to add the Application folder, see the following resource: • Practice: Creating and Using a Windows Installer Deployment Project in Module 9, "Deploying Windows Forms Applications," in Course 2565A, *Developing Microsoft .NET Applications for Windows (Visual C# .NET).* **b.** For more information about deploying applications, see the following resources: • Lesson: Deploying Windows Forms Applications in Module 9, "Deploying Windows Forms Applications," in Course 2565A, *Developing Microsoft .NET Applications for Windows (Visual C# .NET).* • The .NET Framework SDK. Search by using the phrase **Deploying Applications**.
6. Add the InternalBusinessApp.exe file to the Application folder. Browse to *install_folder*\Labfiles\Lab09_1\Ex03\Starter\Business Application Shell\bin to find the InternalBusinessApp.exe file.	**a.** For more information about deploying applications, see the following resources: • Lesson: Deploying Windows Forms Applications in Module 9, "Deploying Windows Forms Applications," in Course 2565A, *Developing Microsoft .NET Applications for Windows (Visual C# .NET).* • The .NET Framework SDK. Search by using the phrase **Deploying Applications**.

Tasks	Additional information
7. Add the ExpenseReport.dll file to the global assembly cache folder. Browse to *install_folder*\Labfiles\Lab09_1\Ex03\Starter\Business Application Shell to find the ExpenseReport.dll.	**a.** For more information about how to add the global assembly cache folder, see the following resource: • Practice: Creating and Using a Windows Installer Deployment Project in Module 9, "Deploying Windows Forms Applications," in Course 2565A, *Developing Microsoft .NET Applications for Windows (Visual C# .NET).* **b.** For more information about deploying applications, see the following resources: • Lesson: Deploying Windows Forms Applications in Module 9, "Deploying Windows Forms Applications," in Course 2565A, *Developing Microsoft .NET Applications for Windows (Visual C# .NET).* • The .NET Framework SDK. Search by using the phrase **Deploying Applications.**
8. Add the localized resource assemblies to their associated folders in the setup project. These folders are the localized folders that you created in step 5. Browse to *install_folder*\Labfiles\Lab09\Ex03\Starter\Business Application Shell\bin to find the folders that contain the localized resource files. The localized resource files are named InternalBusinessApp.resources.dll and can be found in the folders named de, de-DE, en, en-US, fr, fr-FR, ja, and ja-JP under *install_folder*\Labfiles\Lab09_1\Ex03\Starter\Business Application Shell\bin.	**a.** For more information about packaging and deploying resources, see the following resource: • The .NET Framework SDK. Search by using the phrase **Deploying Applications.**
9. Create the directory for the Help file, and add it to the project. **a.** Name the custom folder **IISRoot.** **b.** Set the **DefaultLocation** property of IISRoot to **C:\inetpub\wwwroot.** **c.** Browse to *install_folder*\ Labfiles\Lab09_1\Ex03\Starter\Business Application Shell, find the InternetBusinessAppHelp.htm file, and add it to IISRoot.	**a.** For more information about deploying applications, see the following resources: • Lesson: Deploying Windows Forms Applications in Module 9, "Deploying Windows Forms Applications," in Course 2565A, *Developing Microsoft .NET Applications for Windows (Visual C# .NET).* • The .NET Framework SDK. Search by using the phrase **Deploying Applications.**

<table>
<tr><th>Tasks</th><th>Additional information</th></tr>
<tr><td>10. Set the following project properties.

Property | Value
Author | Contoso, Ltd.
Manufacturer | Contoso, Ltd.
ProductName | International Business Application
Title | International Business Application
Version | 3.0.1

a. When prompted to change the ProductCode and PackageCode properties, click Yes.
b. Set the AlwaysCreate property for the Application folder to True.</td><td>No additional information is necessary for this task.</td></tr>
<tr><td>11. Create the application shortcuts.</td><td>a. For more information about deploying applications, see the following resources:
• Lesson: Deploying Windows Forms Applications in Module 9, "Deploying Windows Forms Applications," in Course 2565A, Developing Microsoft .NET Applications for Windows (Visual C# .NET).
• The .NET Framework SDK. Search by using the phrase Deploying Applications.</td></tr>
<tr><td colspan="2">Warning: A new dependency to ExpenseReport.dll may appear under Detected Dependencies in Solution Explorer. If this occurs, right-click the ExpenseReport.dll dependency, and select Exclude from the context menu. If you do not do this, a copy of the ExpenseReport.dll file will be installed in the target application folder in addition to the global assembly cache, and your application will use the .dll file from the application folder instead of the .dll from the global assembly cache.</td></tr>
<tr><td>12. Build the project, and install the Internal Business Application. Browse to install_folder\ \Labfiles\Lab09_1\Ex03\Starter\ InternalBusinessApplication\Debug to find the Setup.exe file.</td><td>a. For more information about deploying applications, see the following resources:
• Lesson: Deploying Windows Forms Applications in Module 9, "Deploying Windows Forms Applications," in Course 2565A, Developing Microsoft .NET Applications for Windows (Visual C# .NET).
• The .NET Framework SDK. Search by using the phrase Deploying Applications.</td></tr>
<tr><td>13. Test the Internal Business Application.
• Test the different region/culture settings that the application supports.</td><td>a. For more information about deploying applications, see the following resources:
• Lesson: Deploying Windows Forms Applications in Module 9, "Deploying Windows Forms Applications," in Course 2565A, Developing Microsoft .NET Applications for Windows (Visual C# .NET).
• The .NET Framework SDK. Search by using the phrase Deploying Applications.</td></tr>
</table>

Exercise 4
Using an Application Configuration File

In this exercise, you will create an application configuration file that will redirect the Internal Business Application to load a new version of the ExpenseReport.dll file.

There are starter and solution files associated with this exercise. Browse to *install_folder*\Labfiles\Lab09_1\Ex04\Starter to find the starter files, and browse to *install_folder*\Labfiles\Lab09_1\Ex04\Solution to find the solution files. If you performed a default installation of the course files, *install_folder* corresponds to C:\Program Files\Msdntrain\2565.

Tasks	Additional information
1. Open the Visual Studio .NET Command Prompt window and install the ExpenseReport.dll file into the global assembly cache. After the file is installed in the global assembly cache, delete it from the folder. Browse to *install_folder*\Labfiles\Lab09_1\Ex04\Starter to find the ExpenseReport.dll file.	**a.** For more information about how to create application configuration files, see the following resource: • Practice: Creating and Using Application Configuration Files in Module 9, "Deploying Windows Forms Applications," in Course 2565A, *Developing Microsoft .NET Applications for Windows (Visual C# .NET)*. **b.** For more information about configuration files, see the following resources: • Lesson: Deploying Windows Forms Applications in Module 9, "Deploying Windows Forms Applications," in Course 2565A, *Developing Microsoft .NET Applications for Windows (Visual C# .NET)*. • The .NET Framework SDK. Search by using the phrase **Configuration Files**.
2. Run the .NET Configuration Tool, and create a new application configuration file for the InternalBusinessApp.exe application. Change the **BindingRedirect** entry from **3.0.1.1** to **4.0.1.1**. Browse to *install_folder*\Labfiles\Lab09_1\Ex04\Starter to find the InternalBusinessApp.exe file.	**a.** For more information about how to create application configuration files, see the following resource: • Practice: Creating and Using Application Configuration Files in Module 9, "Deploying Windows Forms Applications," in Course 2565A, *Developing Microsoft .NET Applications for Windows (Visual C# .NET)*. **b.** For more information about configuration files, see the following resources: • Lesson: Deploying Windows Forms Applications in Module 9, "Deploying Windows Forms Applications," in Course 2565A, *Developing Microsoft .NET Applications for Windows (Visual C# .NET)*. • The .NET Framework SDK. Search by using the phrase **Configuration Files**.
3. Run the application. • Verify that the application still runs with the new version of ExpenseReport.dll.	No additional information is necessary for this task.

msdn training

Module 10: Securing Windows Forms Applications

Contents

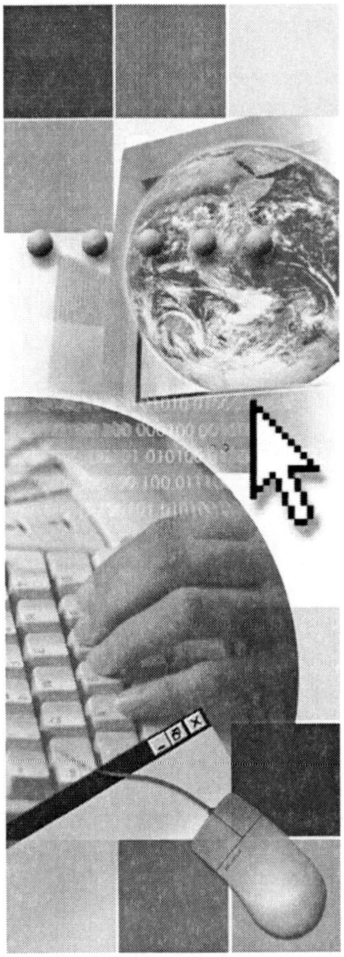

Microsoft

Overview

- Security in the .NET Framework
- Using Code Access Security
- Using Role-Based Security

Introduction

The Microsoft® .NET Framework provides many new features to secure an application.

In this module, you will learn about the .NET Framework security model and learn how to use .NET Framework security features in your applications.

Objectives

After completing this module, you will be able to:

- Describe the .NET Framework security model.
- Use code access security to secure an application.
- Use role-based security to control access to an application.

Lesson: Security in the .NET Framework

- **Security Basics**
- **What is Evidence?**
- **What are Permissions?**
- **How Does Code Access Security Work?**
- **Animation: Code Access Security**
- **What is Role-Based Security?**
- **What is Authentication?**
- **What is Authorization?**

Introduction

The Microsoft Windows® 2000 security model protects a system by preventing unauthorized users from accessing that system. The security model in the .NET Framework protects application code and data from being misused or damaged by other code by enforcing security restrictions on managed code. The .NET Framework security model is based on type safety, code signing, encryption of data, code access security, role-based security, and isolated storage.

In this lesson, you will learn about the .NET Framework security model.

Lesson objectives

After completing this lesson, you will be able to:

- Define evidence and describe its role in the security system in the .NET Framework.
- Define Authentication and Authorization and describe their roles in the security system in the .NET Framework.
- List the major characteristics of code access security and role-based security.
- Describe the .NET Framework security model.

Security Basics

- **Code Access Security**
  Permissions granted to code based on:
  - Evidence
  - Permissions and Permission Sets
  - Security Policy
- **Role-Based Security**
  Permissions granted to users based on:
  - User name
  - Roles

    Windows group(s)

    Generic and custom principals and identities

    Microsoft .NET Passport

Introduction

Two important aspects of the .NET Framework security model are code access security, which controls what resources your code can access, and role-based security, which allows developers to limit which users can run certain parts of an application.

Code access security

The .NET Framework code access security model allows code to use protected resources only if it has permission to do so. This is implemented by using the concept of permissions, which represent the right for code to access protected resources. Evidence about an assembly is used to grant code a set of permissions based on security policy. When code accesses resources to perform a task, a demand for the permissions it needs is made, and the .NET Framework security system determines whether all of the callers to that code have been granted the permissions being demanded.

Role-based security

The .NET Framework includes support for role-based security. This allows code to determine the identity and role membership for the user of an application and make access decisions based on identity.

For more information about building secure applications, see *Writing Secure Code*, by Howard, Michael, and David LeBlanc. Redmond, WA: Microsoft Press, 2002.

What is Evidence?

- **A set of information about the identity and origin of an assembly**
- **Used by the .NET Framework security system at load time to determine the permissions that an assembly receives based on existing security policy**
- **Examples of Items that Make Up Evidence**
  - Strong name signature, code publisher, location, and zone
  - Other custom-defined items
- **Strength of Evidence**

Introduction

The security system uses this evidence about the assembly to determine which permissions to grant it based upon existing security policy.

Definition

Evidence is a set of information about the identity and origin of an assembly.

Examples

Evidence may include:

- The assembly's strong name, consisting of a unique public key, a simple name, and a version.
- The assembly's publisher, from the Microsoft Authenticode® signature.
- The zone from which the assembly originates, such as the local computer, intranet, or Internet zones.
- The location from which the assembly originates, expressed as a URL, universal naming convention (UNC) path, or local computer folder.
- The cryptographic hash of the assembly.

The creator of an assembly can also include custom evidence with the assembly. This custom evidence is evaluated only if security policy is configured to use the custom evidence.

Strength of evidence

Some forms of evidence are stronger than others and can therefore be used to make more far-reaching security policy decisions.

Strong names, for instance, provide an extremely reliable form of evidence, because they are very difficult to falsify unless the publisher's private key has been compromised. Authenticode signatures are also strong forms of evidence.

Conversely, evidence such as an assembly's zone or URL is weaker. Web sites can be hacked, and packets can be tampered with over the Internet. It is a risk to grant permissions based heavily on weaker forms of evidence. However, both strong and weak forms of evidence can be combined in an effective security policy.

What are Permissions?

Code access permissions are the rights to access certain computing resources

- Examples of built-in permission classes
  - UIPermission, PrintingPermission, WebPermission, IsolatedStorageFilePermission

Introduction

Code access permissions represent rights to access certain computing resources.

Example

Actions protected by permissions include reading and writing files on the file system, accessing environment variables, and making calls to ADO.NET for database access.

Built-in code access permission classes

The .NET Framework has many built-in code access permission classes that are designed to protect access to system resources. The .NET Framework uses the built-in permission classes to protect system resources. ~~You, as a developer, do not need to take any further action to use system resources~~, because the .NET Framework will make the appropriate security checks. The built-in permission classes are listed in the following table.

Code access permission class	Resource protected
DirectoryServicesPermission	Directory services
DnsPermission	DNS services
EnvironmentPermission	Environment variables
EventLogPermission	Event logs
FileDialogPermission	File dialog boxes in the UI
FileIOPermission	Files and folders on the file system
IsolatedStorgeFilePermission	Isolated storage
MessageQueuePermission	Message queues
OleDbPermission	Databases accessed by the OLEDB data access provider
PerformanceCounterPermission	Performance counters
PrintingPermission	Printers
ReflectionPermission	Type information at run time
RegistryPermission	Registry

(*continued*)

Code access permission class	Resource protected
SecurityPermission	Execute code, assert permissions, call unmanaged code, skip verification, and other rights
ServiceControllerPermission	Running or stopping services
SocketPermission	Connections to other computers by means of sockets
SqlClientPermission	Databases accessed by the Microsoft SQL Server™ data access provider
UIPermission	Windows and other UI elements
WebPermission	Connections to other computers by means of HTTP

In addition to the built-in permission classes, developers can add new permissions to the security system by implementing custom permissions.

How Does Code Access Security Work?

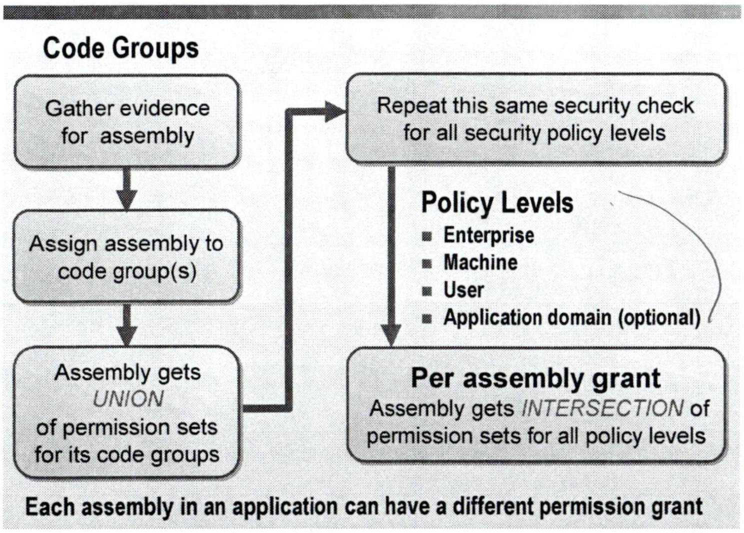

Introduction

The .NET Framework enforces security restrictions on managed code. Every assembly that is loaded is granted a set of permissions by the .NET Framework to access various system resources. A group of permissions is called a *permission set*. These permissions are based on security policy. The security policy uses evidence about an assembly to determine which permissions to grant that assembly. In other words, the .NET Framework uses security policy to map evidence about an assembly to a set of permissions for that assembly.

Code groups

A code group consists of a membership condition and a set of permissions that an assembly might be granted if it meets that membership condition. The runtime evaluates the membership condition specified in the code group against the evidence about the assembly. If the assembly meets the membership condition, it is eligible to be granted the permission set associated with the code group. When an assembly meets the membership conditions for a code group, it is said to be a member of that code group.

As an example, the membership condition for a code group could specify that the publisher of an assembly is Microsoft. Therefore, any assembly published by Microsoft would satisfy the membership condition and be eligible to receive the permission set associated with the code group. This permission set could represent the right to access the C:\temp directory and the USERNAME environment variable, for instance.

An assembly receives the union of permissions for all code groups to which it belongs.

Security policy levels

Security policy is organized into different policy levels: enterprise policy level, machine policy level, user policy level, and an optional application domain policy level.

Security Policy Levels	Description
Enterprise	Enterprise-level policy is specified by the network administrator, and contains a code group hierarchy that applies to all managed code on the entire network.
Machine	Machine-level policy is specified by the local computer administrator, and contains the code group hierarchy that applies to all managed code on the computer.
User	User-level policy contains a code group hierarchy that applies to all managed code run by a particular user. Either the local computer administrator or the user sets user policies.
Application domain (optional)	Application domain policy level is an optional level that provides isolation, unloading, and security boundaries for executing managed code.

A final permission grant is assigned on a per assembly basis, so each assembly in an application can have a different permission grant.

Default security policy

The common language runtime provides a default security policy and uses the following named permission sets to implement that policy:

- Nothing

  Provides code with no permissions. Code cannot run. Under default security policy, code in the untrusted zone gets this permission set.

- Execution

  Provides permission for code to run only. Does not allow code to use any protected resources.

- Internet

  Allows code to execute, to create safe top-level windows and file dialog boxes, to make Web connections to the same site that the assembly originates from, and to use isolated storage with a quota. Under default security policy, all code from the Internet and trusted zones receives this permission set.

Note Service Pack 1 of the .NET Framework changes default security policy for code executed from the Internet zone. Under the new policy, code from the Internet receives no permissions by default.

- LocalIntranet

  Allows code to execute, to create user interface elements without restrictions; to use isolated storage with no quota; to use DNS services; to read the USERNAME, TEMP, and TMP environment variables; to make Web connections to the same site the assembly originates from; and to read files in the same folder as the assembly. Under default security policy, all code from the LocalIntranet zone receives this permission set.

- Everything

  Provides all standard permissions except permission to skip verification.

- FullTrust

  Provides full access to all resources protected by permissions. Under default security policy, all code from the local computer zone receives this permission set.

Animation: Code Access Security

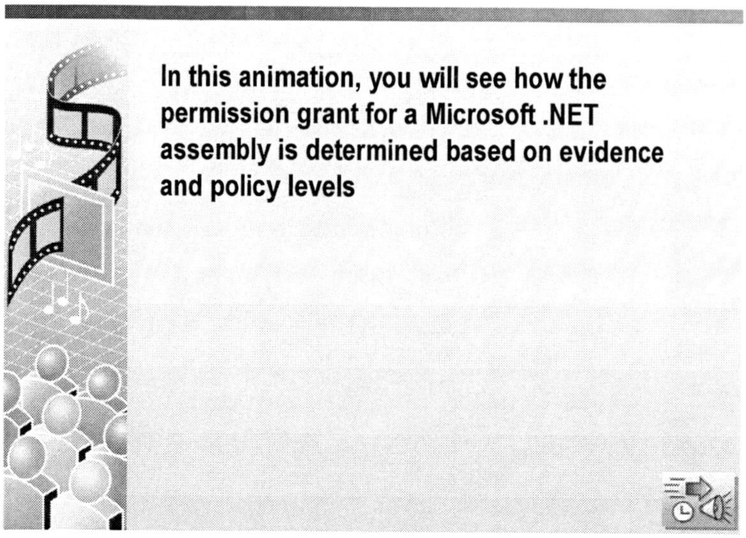

Introduction

In this animation, you will see how the permission grant for a Microsoft .NET assembly is determined based on evidence and policy levels.

Summary

When an assembly is loaded, the common language runtime examines the evidence that the code provides. The permissions that are granted to managed code are determined at the time that the assembly containing that code is loaded.

Policies are represented by a hierarchy of code groups. At the root of the hierarchy of each code group is a group containing all code. This root group has child groups, which in turn may have child groups, and so on. Code that is not a member of a parent code group cannot be a member of any of a child code group in the code group hierarchy. However, code that is a member of a parent code group can also be a member of one or more child code groups.

The runtime uses the evidence about the code to decide which code groups that code belongs to. Code groups specify a set of membership conditions for code. The permission set that the code is assigned at the machine policy level is the union of the permissions that are associated with all of the code groups that the code is a member of.

This procedure is carried out for each policy level and is based on the code's evidence. The runtime computes the intersection of the permission sets that have been assigned to the code at each policy level to determine the final set of permissions that are assigned to the code. For example, if the user policy grants only the permissions that are part of the LocalIntranet permission set, and the machine policy grants the FullTrust permission set, then the final permission set granted is that of LocalIntranet intersected with FullTrust, which is the LocalIntranet permission set.

What is Role-Based Security?

- **Identity**
  - Typically consists of user's log on name
- **Principal**
  - Typically consists of role(s) associated with a user
  - Roles can be

    Microsoft Windows user and group

    \- Or -

    Custom (using generic principals and identities)
- **Authenticated identity generally == identity + principal**

Introduction

A *role-based* security model uses authenticated identity information about the user to make decisions about security authorization. The authenticated identity information typically consists of the user's login name and the roles associated with the user.

Role-based security in the .NET Framework extensively uses two concepts: identities and principals.

Identity

An *identity* encapsulates the user's login name.

Principal

A *principal* encapsulates the user's role membership information.

Role-based security in the .NET Framework allows developers to use Microsoft Windows user and group information, or to do custom authentication and authorization by using generic principals and identities.

What is Authentication?

- **Process of finding and verifying the identity of a user**
- **Done against some authentication authority**

  Examples of authentication mechanisms:

    Operating system (NTLM or Kerberos v. 5)

    .NET Passport

    Application-defined mechanisms

Introduction

Before you determine what a specific user is authorized to do, you must verify the identity of that user.

Definition

Authentication is the process of discovering and verifying the identity of a user by examining the user's credentials, and then validating those credentials against some authority.

Authentication mechanisms

A variety of authentication mechanisms are used today, some of which can be used with .NET Framework role-based security. Examples of commonly used mechanisms include the operating system, Microsoft Passport, and application-defined mechanisms. Specific examples of operating system authentication mechanisms are NTLM authentication and the Kerberos version 5 authentication protocol.

What is Authorization?

- **Process of determining whether a user's request to do something is allowed to proceed**
- **Happens after authentication and is based on the user's authenticated identity**

Introduction

The next step after authentication is authorization.

Definition

Authorization is the process of determining whether a user is allowed to perform a requested action.

Authorization occurs after authentication and uses information about a user's identity and roles to determine what resources that user can access. You can use .NET Framework role-based security to implement authorization.

For more information about how to implement authorization, see Using Role-Based Security in this module.

Lesson: Using Code Access Security

- How to Use Code Access Security
- How to Make Assembly Permission Requests
- Demonstration: Administering Security Policy Settings
- How to Test the Code Access Security of an Application
- Practice: Adding Permission Requests

Introduction

Every application that targets the common language runtime must interact with the runtime's security system. When an application executes, the runtime automatically evaluates it and gives it a set of permissions. Depending on the permissions that the application receives and the resources it uses, it either runs properly or generates a security exception.

The local security settings on a particular computer ultimately determine which permissions code receives. Because these settings can change from computer to computer, you can never be sure that your code will receive sufficient permissions to run. Therefore, every developer must be familiar with code access security concepts to write effective applications targeting the common language runtime.

Interaction with the runtime security system is performed by using imperative and declarative security calls. *Declarative* calls are performed by using attributes; *imperative* calls are performed by using new instances of classes in your code. Some calls can only be performed imperatively, while others can be performed only declaratively. Some calls can be performed in either manner. For more information about imperative security calls and class and method level declarative security calls, see Course 2350A, *Securing and Deploying Microsoft .NET Applications*.

Because most system resources are already protected by built-in permissions, most developers will not need to implement new permissions. Also, the runtime code that accesses these resources already makes the appropriate security checks to make sure calling code has been granted the proper permissions. So, the main task for developers is to document their use of permissions and make sure their code behaves as expected in the security contexts in which it will run. This is done by using permission requests and runtime tools to configure security policy.

In this lesson, you will learn how to implement permission requests in Windows Forms applications.

Lesson objectives

After completing this lesson, you will be able to:

- Make assembly level declarative requests for permissions to access resources.
- Test applications in various security contexts.

How to Use Code Access Security

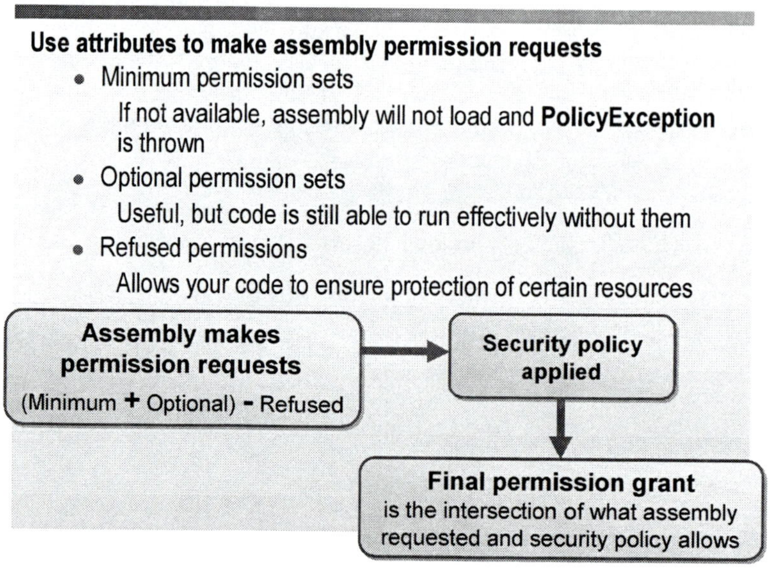

Introduction

Because the NET Framework protects system resources, the major security task for developers is to make permission requests to document the permissions the code uses. In the development phase, adding permission requests allows you to test if your assembly will be able to run successfully in the security contexts in which you expect the application to be deployed.

To make permission requests for an assembly, add attributes to the AssemblyInfo source file of your project. These attributes are then stored in the metadata of an assembly. The assembly permission requests are examined when an assembly is loaded. The .NET Framework proceeds based on the kind of permission request the assembly makes.

Kinds of permission requests

The three kinds of permission requests are:

- Minimum permissions (**RequestMinimum**)

  The permissions in these requests represent the minimum set of permissions that an assembly needs to work effectively. If these permissions are not available to an assembly when it is loaded, the .NET Framework does not execute the code in that assembly and throws a **PolicyException**. A minimum permission request for an assembly documents the required permissions for that assembly. Not making a minimum permission request for an assembly is the equivalent of making a minimum permission request of Nothing.

- Optional permissions (**RequestOptional**)

  The permissions in these requests represent permissions that code can use, but the code is still able to run effectively without them. These permissions are granted to an assembly if they are available to that assembly, but if they are not available, the assembly is still allowed to run. Not making an optional permission request for an assembly is the equivalent of making an optional permission request of FullTrust. If an assembly does not need any optional permissions, it is a best practice to make an optional request for no permissions. This prevents your code from getting any additional permissions from security policy, and forces it to run with least privilege.

- Refused permissions (**RequestRefused**)

  The permissions in these requests represent permissions that code is never to be granted, even if security policy allows them to be granted. Not making a refused permission request is the equivalent of making a refused permission request of Nothing.

Final permission grant

The permissions the assembly actually receives are the result of the following operation:

$FG = SP \cap ((M \cup O) - R)$

Where FG is the final grant, SP is the permission set an assembly receives from security policy, $\cap$ is intersection of sets, M is the minimum permission request, $\cup$ is the union of sets, O is the optional permission request, and R is the refused permission request.

How to Make Assembly Permission Requests

1 Add attributes to the assembly information file

Be sure to include assembly scope on permission request attributes

```
' Add attributes to the AssemblyInfo source file
' Request for a specific permission
<Assembly:UIPermission( _
  SecurityAction.RequestMinimum, _
  Window:=UIPermissionWindow.SafeTopLevelWindows)>

' Request for a permission set
<Assembly:PermissionSet( _
  SecurityAction.RequestMinimum, _
  Name:="LocalIntranet")>
```

Assembly scope

2 Add code to handle security exceptions

CodeExample

Introduction

You can request permissions by adding assembly-level attributes to the AssemblyInfo source file. You can make more than one permission request of a certain kind by using multiple attributes. These attributes vary, depending on the permissions you are requesting. The attribute used to make permission requests is scoped with *assembly* and the **SecurityAction** is **RequestMinimum**, **RequestOptional**, or **RequestRefused**.

Procedure: Making assembly permission requests

To better document your code, place your assembly permission requests in the AssemblyInfo source file.

1. Open the AssemblyInfo.vb source file for the appropriate project and add attributes for permission requests. Be sure to include the assembly scope qualifier to the request, as in the following examples:

Example: Assembly permission request attributes

```
' Add attributes to the AssemblyInfo source file
' Request for a specific permission
<Assembly:UIPermission( _
  SecurityAction.RequestMinimum, _
  Window:=UIPermissionWindow.SafeTopLevelWindows)>

' Request for a permission set
<Assembly:PermissionSet( _
  SecurityAction.RequestMinimum, _
  Name:="LocalIntranet")>
```

The following example makes an optional permission request for no permissions:

```
<Assembly:PermissionSet( _
  SecurityAction.RequestOptional, _
  Unrestricted:=false)]
```

2. If you make any optional permission requests, your code may be granted the permission. However, if it is not, you'll have to add code to handle security exceptions.

Example: Handling security exceptions

```
Imports System.Security
Imports System.IO

Dim fs As FileStream = Nothing

Try
  ' open a file for reading
  fs = New FileStream("C:\log.txt", _
    FileMode.Open, _
    FileAccess.Read)
  ' read from file
  ...
Catch se As SecurityException
  ' display error message
  MessageBox.Show("ExceptionMessage: " + se.Message)
End Try
```

Demonstration: Administering Security Policy Settings

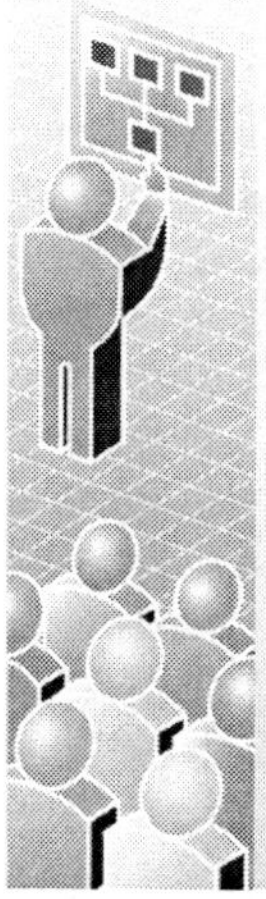

In this demonstration, you will see how to use the .NET Framework Configuration tool (Mscorcfg.msc) to administer security policy settings

Introduction

The .NET Framework configuration Microsoft Management Console (MMC) snap-in provides a graphical interface to modify security policy.

Instructions

► **To view current security policy**

1. Run the .NET Framework Configuration tool (Mscorcfg.msc) by double-clicking the Mscorcfg.msc icon on the desktop.
2. In the console tree, expand the following nodes:
   a. **Runtime Security Policy**
   b. **Machine**
   c. **Code Groups**
   d. **All_Code**

   Point out that these code groups are the children of the root (All_Code) code group for the machine policy level.
3. In the console tree, click the **My_Computer_Zone** code group.
   a. In the details pane, point out that the properties for this code group are shown. These include a description of the code group, the membership condition for the code group, and the permission set granted by the code group.
   b. Point out that the last four code groups under All_Code have been added for testing purposes for the practice and lab in this module.
4. In the console tree, expand the **Internet_Zone** node and point out that it has a child code group that grants access to the same Internet site from which the code originated. This code group will only be evaluated if its parent code group's membership condition is satisfied.
5. In the console tree, right-click the **Internet_Zone** code group, and then click **Properties**. Point out that this dialog box shows the properties for the code group, and also lets you edit them.

6. Click the **Membership Condition** tab, and point out that the membership condition for this code group is Internet zone.
   a. Click the **Condition type** box to show the different conditions available for use in a membership condition.
   b. Select the **Strong Name** condition type, and point out that the parameters for the condition type change.
   c. Click the **Condition type** box and change it back to **Zone**.
7. Click the **Permission Set** tab, and point out that the permission set granted for this code group is the Internet permission set.
   a. Click the **Permission set** box to show the different permission sets available for use, but do not change the permission set. This tab also shows the permissions that make up the Internet permission set.
   b. In the permission list, click **User Interface**, and then click the **View Permission** button. Point out that the **Permission Viewer** dialog box that appears displays the user interface-related permissions that are granted as part of the Internet permission set.
   c. Click **Close** to close the permission viewer dialog box.
   d. Click **Security**, and then click **View Permission**. Point out the security-related permissions that are either granted or denied as part of the Internet permission set.
   e. Click **Close** to close the permission viewer dialog box.
   f. Click **Cancel** to close the **Internet_Zone Properties** dialog box.
8. The default security policy for the user and enterprise policy levels is that all code gets the **FullTrust** permission set.
   a. To show this in the console tree, in the **Runtime Security Policy** node, expand the **Enterprise** and **Code Groups** nodes, and then, in the **Enterprise** hierarchy, click **All_Code**. Point out that it grants FullTrust.
   b. Do the same thing for the **All_Code** node in the **User** hierarchy, pointing out that it looks the same and also grants FullTrust. Explain that code will not get FullTrust based on these policy levels, because the policy grants for the user and enterprise policy levels will be intersected with the policy grant for the machine policy level to determine the final permission grant. Assuming that the machine policy level grants something less than FullTrust when the enterprise and user policy levels are intersected with the machine policy level, an assembly would get the permission set associated with the machine policy level.
   c. Collapse the **Enterprise** and **User** hierarchies before moving to the next step.
9. The snap-in also allows viewing of permission sets.
   a. In the **Machine** node, expand **Permission Sets**. This shows a list of the permission sets for the machine policy level.
   b. Under the **Permission Sets** list, click **Internet**, and point out that the permissions that make up the Internet permission set are shown in the details pane.

► **To add a new code group**

The snap-in can also be used to add new code groups and permission sets.

1. In the **Machine** and **Code Groups** nodes, right-click the **All_Code** node, and then click **New**. The Create Code Group Wizard appears.
2. In the Create Code Group Wizard, in the **Name** box, type **New_Test**. In the description box, type **a new test code group**, and then click **Next**.
3. In the **Condition Type** box, click **URL**. In the **URL** box, type **file:///C:/testfolder/*** and then click **Next**.
4. In the **Use existing permission set** box, click **LocalIntranet**, and then click **Next**.
5. Click **Finish**.
6. In the console tree, right click the **New_Test** code group, and then click **Properties**. On the **General** tab of the **New_Test Properties** dialog box, select the **This policy level will only have the permissions from the permission set associated with this code group** box to set the **Exclusive** attribute. The code group now has an exclusive URL membership condition of **file:///C:/testfolder/***. Any code run from that folder will get the **LocalIntranet** permission set. Click **OK**.
7. In the console tree, right-click the **New_Test** code group, and then click **Delete**. In the **Remove Code Group** dialog box, click **Yes**. Notice that the code group is gone.
8. Close the MMC snap-in.

How to Test the Code Access Security of an Application

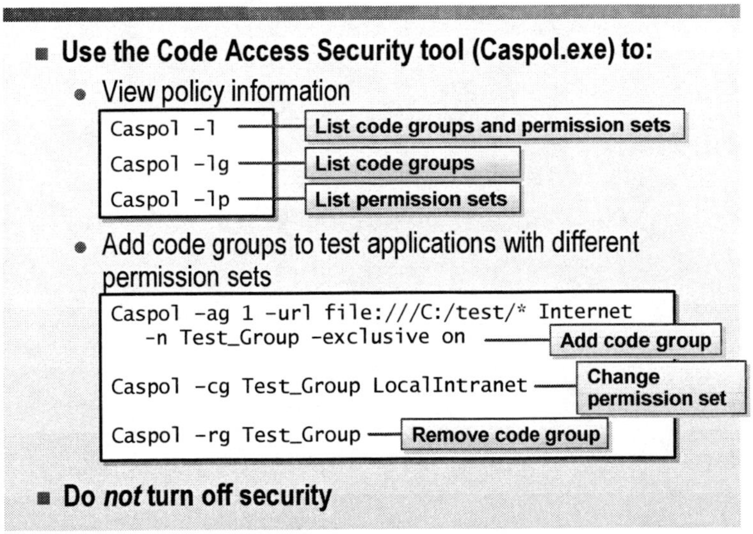

Introduction

The Code Access Security tool (Caspol.exe) is a command-line utility that allows you to view and manipulate security policy. The Code Access Security tool ships with the .NET Framework software development kit (SDK), and it can be used from scripts to configure security.

The Code Access Security tool displays all the available information for the default policy level, which is the machine level. This information includes the code group hierarchy, named permission sets, and assemblies with full trust. To view information about another policy level, you can use a command-line option before any other command-line options to indicate the policy level you wish to view or modify.

The syntax for Caspol.exe is a follows:

```
caspol <option> <args> ...
```

The following table lists the command-line options used in the examples in this topic.

Command-line option	Action or qualifier	Comments
-l	List	Lists all available information for the default policy level, which is the machine level.
-lg	List code groups	Lists the code groups for the default policy level. This is thc most useful option for viewing current security policy.
-lp	List permission sets	Lists named permission sets.
-ag	Add code group	Add a new code group to the default policy level.

(continued)

Command-line option	Action or qualifier	Comments
-url	URL	The code on the slide uses the URL of the assembly as the condition for the code group.
-n	Code group name	The name for the new code group.
-exclusive	Set the policy statement Exclusive flag	This is useful for testing purposes. Any assemblies that meet the code group's condition will get the associated permission set, and only the associated permission set, for this policy level. For example, this can be used to prevent code running on the local machine from automatically being granted the FullTrust permission set.
-cg	Change code group	Change an existing code group.
-rg	Remove code group	Remove an existing code group.

To get information about the command-line options available for Caspol.exe, type the following command:

```
Caspol -help
```

Procedure: Using Caspol.exe to view security policy information

The Code Access Security tool is quick way to view security policy.

1. To list all available information about code groups and permission sets, open the Microsoft Visual Studio® .NET Command Prompt window and type the following command:

   ```
   Caspol -l
   ```
   To open the Visual Studio .NET Command Prompt window, click **Start**, point to **All Programs**, point to **Microsoft Visual Studio .NET**, point to **Visual Studio .NET Tools**, and then click **Visual Studio .NET Command Prompt**.

2. To list code groups, open the Visual Studio .NET Command Prompt window and type the following command:

   ```
   Caspol -lg
   ```
3. To list permission sets, in the Visual Studio .NET Command Prompt window type the following command:

   ```
   Caspol -lp
   ```
4. To reset the current policy level to default security policy, in the Visual Studio .NET Command Prompt window type the following command:

   ```
   Caspol -reset
   ```

By default, all code running on the local computer receives the FullTrust permission set. Often, when testing the security characteristics of your code, it is convenient to have your code run with different permission sets. An easy way to do this is to create a test folder and configure security policy to treat this folder as a different zone.

Procedure: Testing your application by using Caspol.exe

You can also use the Code Access Security tool to set up security context test environments for your applications.

1. Create a folder named **C:\testfolder**.
2. To create a new code group to test an application that you want to run with the Internet permission set, open the Visual Studio .NET Command Prompt window and type the following command:

   ```
   Caspol -ag 1 -url file:///C:/testfolder/* Internet
   -n Test_Group -exclusive on
   ```

   This adds a new exclusive code group at the machine policy level with a URL membership condition of file:///C:/test/* that grants the Internet permission set and is named Test_Group. The code group must be exclusive. This ensures that other code groups that would normally match your assembly are ignored, as in the case of code whose zone is MyComputer, which would usually be granted FullTrust. You can then copy your application to the test directory, and when you run it, it will get the Internet permission set.

   To open the Visual Studio .NET Command Prompt window, click **Start**, point to **All Programs**, point to **Microsoft Visual Studio .NET**, point to **Visual Studio .NET Tools**, and then click **Visual Studio .NET Command Prompt**.

3. To change this code group to test your application against the LocalIntranet permission set, type the following command:

   ```
   Caspol -cg Test_Group LocalIntranet
   ```

4. To remove your test code group by typing the following command:

   ```
   Caspol -rg Test_Group
   ```

Important Do *not* turn off security. The Code Access Security tool has an option that allows you to turn off security. Avoid using this option if at all possible.

Practice: Adding Permission Requests

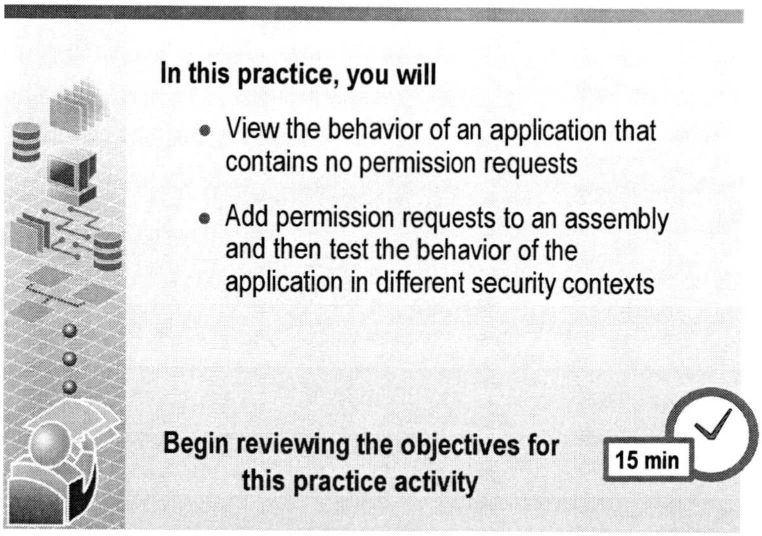

Introduction

In this practice, you will compare the behavior of an application that tries to access various resources under different permission request situations and in different security contexts.

Instructions

► **View application behavior without permission requests**

1. In Visual Studio .NET, open the PermissionRequests.sln solution file in *install_folder*\Practices\Mod10\Mod10_01\Starter.

Note If you performed a default installation of the course files, *install_folder* corresponds to C:\Program Files\Msdntrain\2565.

---

2. Open the PermReqForm.vb form and view its code.
3. Build the project and run the application.
4. Click each of the three buttons at the top of the form and notice that all of the operations succeed.

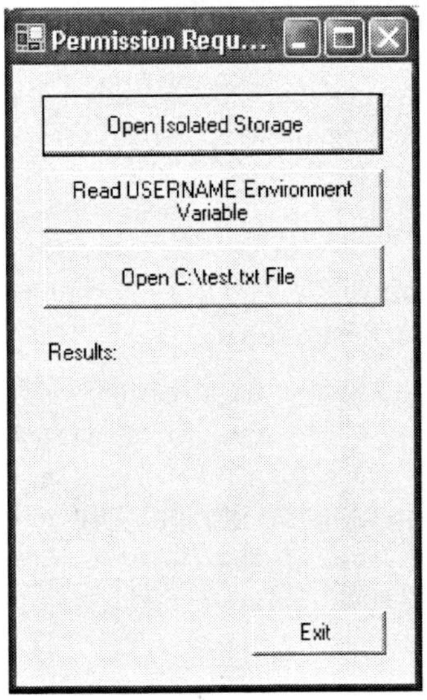

   This happens because the code is running with the **FullTrust** permission set, with no permission request restrictions.

5. Click **Exit** to quit the application.

► **Add permission requests to the application**

1. Open the AssemblyInfo.vb file and find the TODO comment at the bottom of the file. Notice that a minimum permission request for a **UIPermission** has already been added.
2. Add a minimum permission request for the required **IsolatedStorageFilePermission**.

```
<Assembly:IsolatedStorageFilePermission( _
    SecurityAction.RequestMinimum, _
    UsageAllowed:= _
        IsolatedStorageContainment.DomainIsolationByUser)>
```

3. Add a minimum permission request for the required **EnvironmentVariablePermission**.

```
<Assembly:EnvironmentPermission( _
    SecurityAction.RequestMinimum, _
    Read:="USERNAME")>
```

4. Add an optional permission request for no permissions. This prevents the assembly from getting any additional permissions that security policy may allow.

```
<Assembly:PermissionSet(SecurityAction.RequestOptional, _
    Unrestricted:=False)>
```

5. Build the project and run the application.
6. Click **Open Isolated Storage**, and then click **Read USERNAME Environment Variable**. Notice that these two operations succeed. Then click **Open C:\test.txt File**. That operation fails with a security exception, even though the code would normally get the FullTrust permission set. This happens because the optional permission request for no permissions was added to the assembly.
7. Exit the application.
8. In the **AssemblyInfo** file, add a minimum permission request for the required **FileIOPermission**.

```
<Assembly:FileIOPermission( _
    SecurityAction.RequestMinimum, _
    All:="C:\test.txt")>
```

9. Build the project and run the application. Try all three operations that you tried in Step 6. Notice that all three operations succeed now. Click **Exit** to quit the application.

► **Test application behavior in other security contexts**

1. In Windows Explorer, copy the **PermissionRequests.exe** file from *install_folder*\Practices\Mod10\Mod10_01\PermissionRequests\bin to C:\test\LocalIntranet.
2. In the C:\test\LocalIntranet folder, double -click the **PermissionRequests.exe** file to run the application. Notice that an exception window appears, notifying you of a **System.Security.Policy.PolicyException** exception. The application was not able to run because it makes a minimum permission request from permissions that are not granted as part of the **LocalIntranet** permission set. Specifically, the request for permission to read the C:\Test.txt file is not allowed in the **LocalIntranet** permission set.
3. Click **No** to avoid debugging the application.

Lesson: Using Role-Based Security

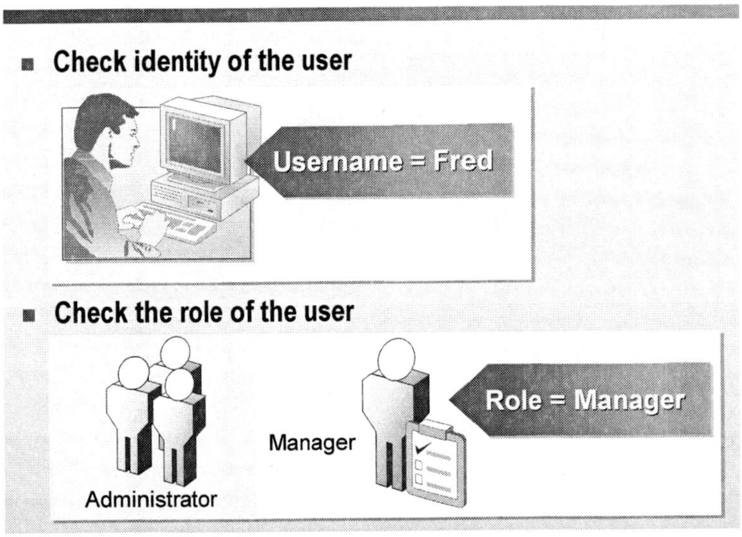

Introduction

Role-based security allows developers to control access to applications based on the user's identity. In this lesson, you will learn how to use the .NET Framework role-based features in your applications.

For more information about role-based security calls, see Course 2350A, *Securing and Deploying Microsoft .NET Applications*.

Lesson objectives

After completing this lesson, you will be able to:

- Use Windows principals and identities to control access to an application.
- Implement custom authentication by using generic principals and identities.

How Role-Based Security Works

- **Authentication and authorization**
- **Identities**
  - Windows identity
  - Generic identity
  - Custom identity
- **Principals**
  - Windows principal
  - Generic principal
  - Custom principal

Introduction

Principal and identity objects are used to access information about the user. You can access information about Windows users and the Windows groups that they belong to by using the **WindowsPrincipal** and **WindowsIdentity** objects. To access user information based on your own custom authentication scheme, you can use the **GenericPrincipal** and **GenericIdentity** objects or implement your own custom principal and identity objects.

Authentication

Before you determine what a specific user is authorized to do, you must verify the identity of that user. *Authentication* is the process of discovering and verifying the identity of a user by examining the user's credentials and then validating those credentials against some authority.

Authorization

The next step after authentication is authorization. *Authorization* is the process of determining whether a user is allowed to perform a requested action. Authorization occurs after authentication and uses information about a user's identity and roles to determine what resources that user can access.

Identities

An identity object encapsulates information about the user or entity being validated, such as the user name and authentication type. The .NET Framework provides three kinds of identity objects:

- Windows identity

  Represents the identity of the user based on a method of authentication that is supported by the Windows operating system. A Windows identity provides the ability to impersonate another user, so resources can be accessed on behalf of that other user. The **WindowsIdentity** class implements this kind of identity.

- Generic identity

  Represents the identity of the user based on a custom authentication method, which is defined by the application. The **GenericIdentity** class implements this kind of identity.

- Custom identity

  Represents an identity that encapsulates custom user information. Any custom identity class must implement the **IIdentity** interface.

All identity classes must implement the **IIdentity** interface. The **IIdentity** interface has three public properties, listed in the following table.

Property	Description
Name	The name of the current user, represented as a string.
IsAuthenticated	A Boolean value indicating whether the user has been authenticated.
AuthenticationType	The type of authentication used, represented as a string.

Principals

A principal object represents the security context under which code is running. This includes the identity of the user, as represented by an associated identity object, and the roles associated with the user.

A role defines a group of related users of an application. For example, a banking application might impose limits on the withdrawal amounts that can be transacted, based on role. In this scenario tellers might be authorized to process withdrawals that are less than a specified amount, while managers might be allowed to process withdrawals above the specified amount.

Role-based security in the .NET Framework supports three kinds of principals.

- Windows principal

  Represents Windows users and their roles. The roles are the Windows groups that the user is a member of. The **WindowsPrincipal** class implements this kind of principal.

- Generic principal

  Represents users and roles that are independent of Windows users and their roles. Essentially, the generic principal is a simple solution for application authentication and authorization. The **GenericPrincipal** class implements this kind of principal.

- Custom principal

  Represents application-specific role information. Any custom principal class must implement the **IPrincipal** interface.

All principal classes implement the **IPrincipal** interface. The **IPrincipal** interface has an **Identity** property that stores the identity object related to the current principal and an **IsInRole** method that determines whether the current principal belongs to the specified role.

A principal object is bound to a call context object in an application domain object. A default call context is always created for each new application domain, so there is always a call context available. When a new thread is created, a call context object is also created for that thread. The principal object reference is automatically copied from the creating thread to the new thread's call context.

How to Create WindowsPrincipal and WindowsIdentity Objects

- **Choice of two techniques**
  - Creating objects for a single validation

```
Dim MyIdentity As WindowsIdentity = _
  WindowsIdentity.GetCurrent()
Dim MyPrincipal As WindowsPrincipal = _
  new WindowsPrincipal(MyIdentity)
```

  - Creating objects for repeated validation

```
AppDomain.CurrentDomain.SetPrincipalPolicy( _
  PrincipalPolicy.WindowsPrincipal)
Dim MyPrincipal As WindowsPrincipal = _
  System.Threading.Thread.CurrentPrincipal
      As WindowsPrincipal
```

CodeExample

Introduction

There are two ways to create **WindowsPrincipal** objects, depending on whether code must repeatedly perform role-based validation or must perform it only once.

Procedure: Creating a WindowsPrincipal object for a single validation

When you must perform role-based validation once, you can call the **WindowsIdentity.GetCurrent** method.

1. Initialize a new instance of the **WindowsIdentity** class by calling the shared **WindowsIdentity.GetCurrent** method.

   In the first example shown on the slide, the **GetCurrent** method queries the current Windows account and places information about that account into the identity object.

2. Create a new instance of the **WindowsPrincipal** class and pass the value of a **WindowsIdentity** object to it.

Procedure: Creating a WindowsPrincipal object for repeated validation

When you must perform role-based validation repeatedly, you can call the **SetPrincipalPolicy** method on the **System.AppDomain** object.

1. Call the shared **SetPrincipalPolicy** method on the **System.AppDomain** object, passing it a **PrincipalPolicy** enumeration value that indicates what the policy should be. Supported values are **NoPrincipal**, **UnauthenticatedPrincipal**, and **WindowsPrincipal**.

2. With the policy set, use the **Thread.CurrentPrincipal** property to retrieve the principal that encapsulates the current Windows user.

The following example creates an instance of a **WindowsIdentity** object and a **WindowsPrincipal** object, and gathers identity and principal information from the objects:

```
Imports System
Imports System.Threading
Imports System.Security.Principal
Class Class1

  Public Shared Sub Main()

      Dim MyIdentity As WindowsIdentity = _
              WindowsIdentity.GetCurrent()
      Dim MyPrincipal As New WindowsPrincipal(MyIdentity)

      'Principal values.
      Dim Name As String = MyPrincipal.Identity.Name
      Dim Type As String = _
         MyPrincipal.Identity.AuthenticationType
      Dim Auth As String = _
         MyPrincipal.Identity.IsAuthenticated.ToString()
      'Identity values.
      Dim IdentName As String = MyIdentity.Name
      Dim IdentType As String = MyIdentity.AuthenticationType
      Dim IdentIsAuth As String = _
         MyIdentity.IsAuthenticated.ToString()
      Dim ISAnon As String = MyIdentity.IsAnonymous.ToString()
      Dim IsG As String = MyIdentity.IsGuest.ToString()
      Dim IsSys As String = MyIdentity.IsSystem.ToString()
      Dim Token As String = MyIdentity.Token.ToString()
      ...
  End Sub
End Class
```

How to Create GenericPrincipal and GenericIdentity Objects

- **Create and initialize a GenericIdentity object**

```
Dim MyIdentity As New GenericIdentity("User1")
```

- **Create and initialize a GenericPrincipal object and attach it to the current thread**

```
Dim MyStringArray(2) As String
MyStringArray(0) = "Manager"
MyStringArray(1) = "Employee"
Dim MyPrincipal As New GenericPrincipal(MyIdentity, _
  MyStringArray)
System.Threading.Thread.CurrentPrincipal = MyPrincipal
```

Introduction

You can use the **GenericIdentity** class in conjunction with the **GenericPrincipal** class to implement role-based security that is independent of the Windows security system. For example, you can prompt a user for a name and password, check them against a database or a Lightweight Directory Access Protocol (LDAP) directory, and then create identity and principal objects based on the values in the database.

Procedure: Implementing role-based security by using GenericIdentity and GenericPrincipal objects

There are three mains steps for implementing role-based security by using **GenericIdentity** and **GenericPrincipal** objects.

1. Create a new instance of the **GenericIdentity** class and initialize it with the name that you want it to hold.
2. Create a new instance of the **GenericPrincipal** class and initialize it with the previously created **GenericIdentity** object and an array of strings that represent the roles that you want associated with this principal. The second example on the slide specifies an array of strings that represent a Manager role and a Teller role. The **GenericPrincipal** object is then initialized with the previous **GenericIdentity** object and the string array.
3. Attach the principal to the current thread, as shown on the slide. Attaching the principal to the current thread is valuable in situations where the principal must be validated several times, it must be validated by other code running in your application, or it must be validated by a **PrincipalPermission** object.

Important The code attaching the principal to the current thread must have been granted the **ControlPrincipal** member of the **SecurityPermission** class to successfully attach the principal to the thread.

Example

The following example creates an instance of a **GenericPrincipal** and a **GenericIdentity**:

```
Imports System
Imports System.Security.Principal
Imports System.Threading
Class Class1

  Public Shared Sub Main()

      ' Prompt user for username and password, and then
      ' authenticate those credentials against a database
      ' or other authority. For this sample, the username
      ' is hard-coded.
      Dim Username As String = "Joe"

      ' Assuming authentication succeeds, create the
      ' GenericIdentity representing the user.
      Dim MyIdentity As New GenericIdentity(Username)

      ' Look up the roles the user belongs to in a database
      ' or other location. For this sample, the roles are
      ' hard-coded.

      Dim MyRoles(2) As String
      MyRoles(0) = "Manager"
      MyRoles(1) = "Teller"

      ' Create the GenericPrincipal representing the user
      ' and associated roles.
      Dim MyPrincipal As New GenericPrincipal(MyIdentity, _
          MyRoles)

      ' Store the principal on the thread, so it can be
      ' retrieved and used by other code.
      Thread.CurrentPrincipal = MyPrincipal
  End Sub
End Class
```

How to Use Principals and Identities to Control Access to an Application

After you have created a principal object

- Use the **Name** property of the principal's identity object to check the user's name

```
' Assume a valid principal is in MyPrincipal
If (String.Compare(MyPrincipal.Identity.Name, _
  "DOMAIN\Fred", True)=0) Then
' Permit access to some code
```

- Use the principal's **IsInRole** method to check role membership

```
' Assume a valid principal is in MyPrincipal
If (MyPrincipal.IsInRole( _
  "DOMAIN\Administrators")) Then
' Permit access to some code
```

Introduction

After you have created a principal object, you can add code to your application to control access to your application based on elements of a user's identity.

Example

You can control access to code based on the user's name, as shown in the first example on the slide. The example the following code uses a case-insensitive string comparison to see if the user's name is DOMAIN\Fred. The first two parameters to the static **String.Compare** method are the strings to be compared, and the third parameter tells the method to do a case-insensitive comparison.

```
' Assume a valid principal is in MyPrincipal
If (String.Compare(MyPrincipal.Identity.Name, _
  "DOMAIN\Fred", True)=0) Then
' Permit access to some code
```

For **WindowsIdentity** objects, the name represents the user's login name, including the domain.

Example

You can check role membership by calling the **IsInRole** method on the principal object, as shown in the second example on the slide. The example on the slide checks if the user belongs to the DOMAIN\Administrators role.

For **WindowsPrincipal** objects, a role maps to a Windows group, including the domain. When checking for membership in built-in Windows groups, you can use the **WindowsBuiltInRole** enumeration. The following example uses a hard-coded string in the call to determine if the user is a member of the built-in Administrators role:

```
MyPrincipal.IsInRole("BUILTIN\Administrators")
```

The code works, but it is not easily localized. The following example uses the **WindowsBuiltInRole** enumeration instead, and is more easily localized:

```
MyPrincipal.IsInRole(WindowsBuiltInRole.Administrator)
```

Note .NET Framework role-based security does not provide access to COM+ roles with these mechanisms. Classes in the **System.EnterpriseServices** namespace must be used to gain access to COM+ role-based security information.

very unsecure

Demonstration: Using Role-based Security to Control Access to an Application

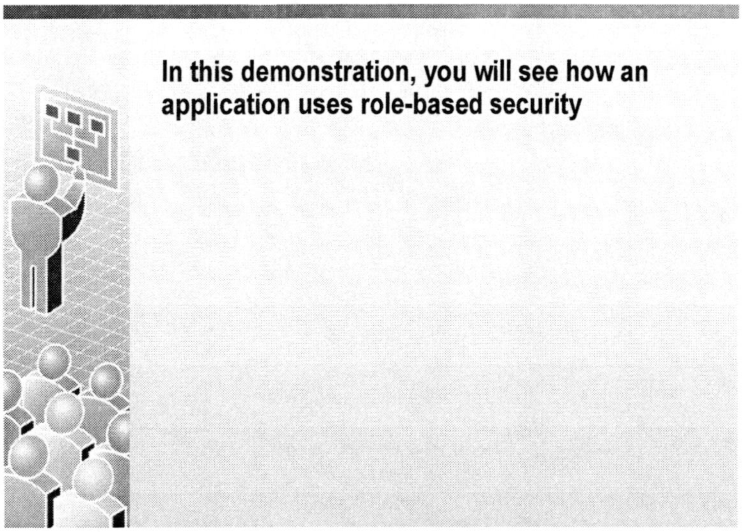

Introduction

In this demonstration, you will see how an application uses role-based security.

Instructions

► **To view code that uses role-based security**

1. Open the RoleBasedSecurity.sln solution file in *install_folder*\Democode\Mod10\Mod10_01\RoleBasedSecurity.
2. Open the RBSForm form and view its code.
3. Note how the current **WindowsPrincipal** is obtained in the **RBSForm** constructor.
4. Set breakpoints in the **CheckUserBtn_Click** and **CheckRoleBtn_Click** methods.
5. Run the application.
6. In the **User Name** box, type your user name, making sure to include the domain, for example, ***computername*\myuser**.
7. Click **Check User Name**.
8. Step through the code in the event handler and note how the user name check is performed. When you are done with the code in this method, press **F5** to continue execution of the application.
9. In the **Role** box, type a role that you are a member of, such as **BUILTIN\Users**.
10. Click **Check Role**.
11. Step through the code in the event handler and note out how the role membership check is performed. Then click **Exit** to quit the application.

Review

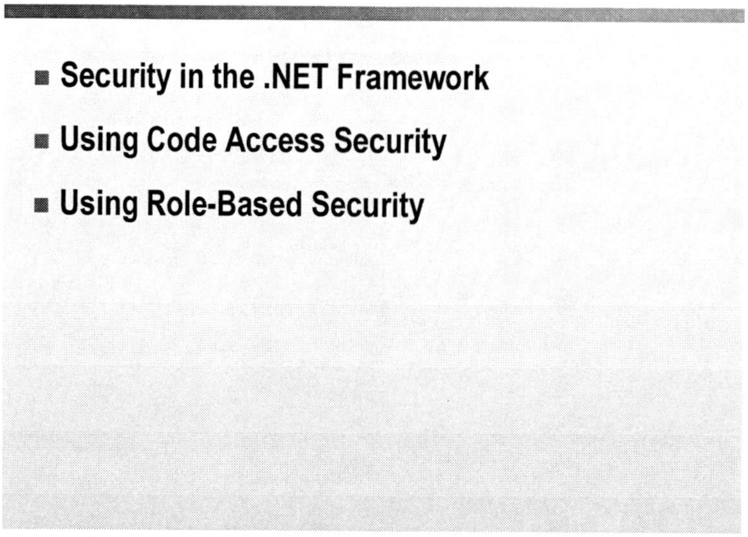

1. What are the two major areas of security in the .NET Framework?

2. How are evidence, security policy, and permissions related?

3. What are the three types of permission requests that you can make?

4. What kind of permissions should you include in a minimum permission request?

5. What are the two ways to configure the security policy to test an application?

.Net Configuration Tool

6. What are authentication and authorization?

7. Describe when you would use a WindowsPrincipal object and when you would use a **CustomPrincipal** object to implement role-based security.

8. What method of the **Principal** class do you use to perform role check?

   IsInRole

9. What are the three main steps to implement role-based security with **GenericIdentity** and **GenericPrincipal** objects in your application?

Lab 10.1: Adding and Testing Permission Requests

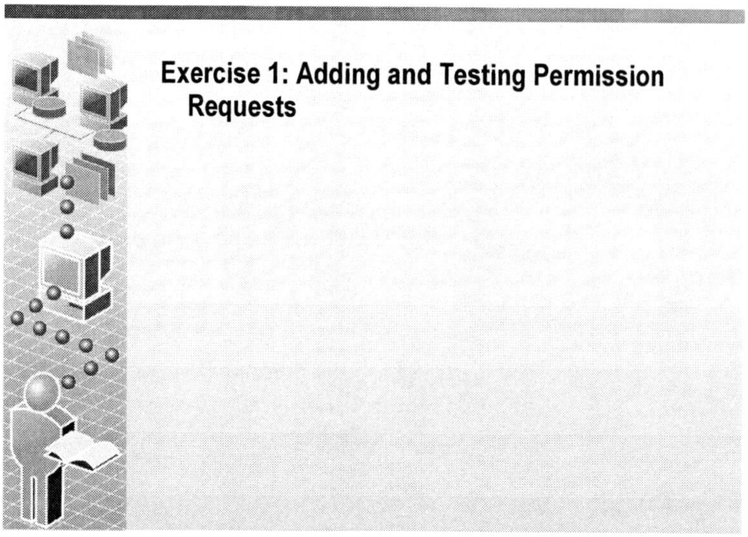

Objectives

After completing this lab, you will have demonstrated your ability to:

- Add assembly permission requests.
- Test an application by running it in different security contexts.

Note This lab focuses on the concepts in Module 10, "Securing Windows Forms Applications," in Course 2565A, *Developing Microsoft .NET Applications for Windows (Visual Basic .NET).* As a result, this lab may not comply with Microsoft security recommendations.

Prerequisites

Before working on this lab, you must have:

- The knowledge and skills to develop a simple Windows Forms application by using a Visual Studio .NET–compatible programming language.
- The knowledge and skills to debug an application by using Visual Studio .NET.
- The knowledge and skills to add permission requests.

Scenario

To follow best practices, you want to document the permissions that your application requires and to run it with the fewest privileges possible. To do this with the .NET Framework security system, you will use permission requests. This will also help you to configure the security policy if you decide to deploy your application in other security contexts.

In this lab, you will add minimum permission requests for the permissions that you need and an optional permission request for no permissions to prevent any additional permissions from being granted to your application.

Lab setup

There are starter and solution files associated with this lab. Browse to *install_folder*\Labfiles\Lab10_1\Ex01\Starter to find the starter files, and browse to *install_folder*\Labfiles\Lab10_1\Ex01\Solution to find the solution files. If you performed a default installation of the course files, *install_folder* corresponds to C:\Program Files\Msdntrain\2565.

Estimated time to complete this lab: 45 minutes

Exercise 1
Adding and Testing Permission Requests

In this exercise, you will add some minimum permission requests to the Expense Report application. You will also test the Expense Report application in different security contexts.

Tasks	Additional information
1. Open the ExpenseReport.sln solution file in Visual Studio .NET. Browse to *install_folder*\Labfiles\Lab10_1\Ex01\Starter to find the project files.	**a.** For more information about opening a project file and starting an application, see the following resource: • The Visual Studio .NET Help documentation. For additional information about opening a project file, in Search, select the **Search in titles only** check box, then search by using the phrase **Open Project Dialog Box.** For additional information about starting an application in the Designer, in Index, search by using the phrase **Debugging Windows Applications.**

2. Open the AssemblyInfo.vb file. Add minimum permission requests for the following permissions:
• Use of all windows.
• Use of Isolated Storage, isolated by domain and user. Use the following syntax (this attribute should appear on a single line—line continuation marks have been omitted for space reasons):
`<Assembly: IsolatedStorageFilePermission( SecurityAction.RequestMinimum, UsageAllowed:=IsolatedStorageContainment.DomainIsolationByUser)>`
• Use of Web access for the Expense Report Web service. Use the following syntax (this attribute should appear on a single line—line continuation marks have been omitted for space reasons):
`<Assembly: WebPermission( SecurityAction.RequestMinimum, Connect:="http://localhost/ExpenseReportWebService/ ExpenseReportWebService.asmx")>`
• Add an optional permission request for no permissions.
	a. For more information about permission requests, see the following resources:
	• Practice: Adding Permission Requests in Module 10, "Securing Windows Forms Applications," in Course 2565A, *Developing Microsoft .NET Applications for* Windows *(Visual Basic .NET).* This practice contains information about how to add the minimum permission request for the use of all windows and the optional permission request for no permissions.
	• Lesson: Using Code Access Security in Module 10, "Securing Windows Forms Applications," in Course 2565A, *Developing Microsoft .NET Applications for Windows (Visual Basic .NET).* This lesson contains information about how to make permission requests.
	• The .NET Framework SDK documentation. In Search, select the **Search in titles only** check box, then search by using the phrase **Requesting Permissions.**

Tasks	Additional information
3. Test the permission requests. **a.** Build and run the application in Visual Studio to make sure it still works. **b.** Copy the ExpenseReport.exe file from the bin(\debug) folder of the project to the C:\Test\LocalIntranet folder. **c.** Double-click the application and attempt to run it. Notice that you get a policy exception.	**a.** In step 3.c., the application will not run because the LocalIntranet permission set limits Web access to the same site that the assembly was downloaded from. If the application were installed on localhost, it would run in the LocalIntranet permission set. **b.** For more information about the default security policy, see the following resources: • Lesson: Using Code Access Security in Module 10, "Securing Windows Forms Applications," in Course 2565A, *Developing Microsoft .NET Applications for Windows (Visual Basic .NET)*. This lesson contains information about configuring the security policy. • The .NET Framework SDK documentation. In Search, select the **Search in titles only** check box, then search by using the phrase **Default Security Policy**.

Course Evaluation

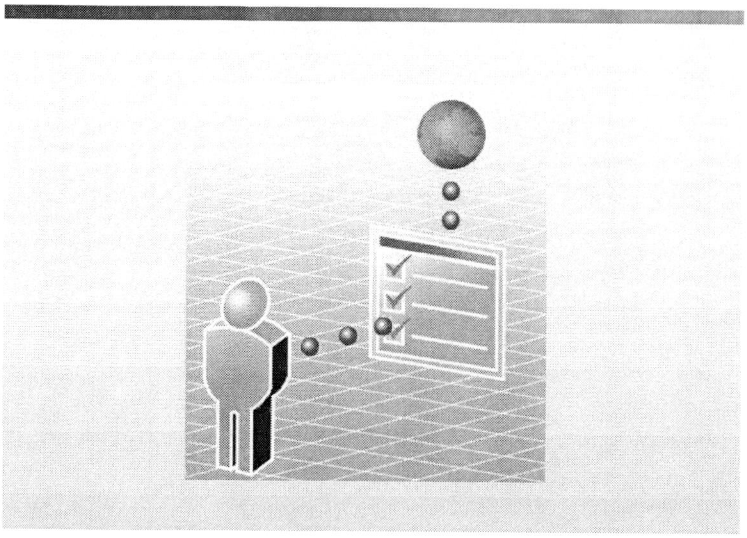

Your evaluation of this course will help Microsoft understand the quality of your learning experience.

To complete a course evaluation, go to http://www.metricsthatmatter.com/survey/.

Microsoft will keep your evaluation strictly confidential and will use your responses to improve your future learning experience.

msdn® training

Appendix A: Using Filled Shapes and Images

Contents

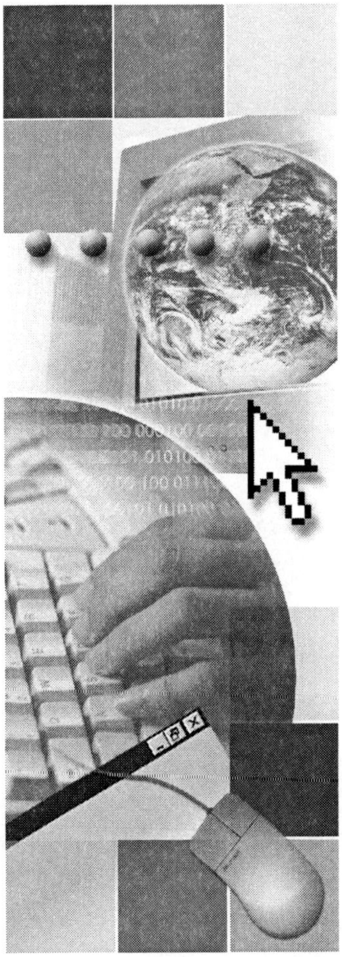

Microsoft®

Overview

- Creating Brushes and Filled Shapes
- Working with Bitmap Images

Introduction

The Microsoft® .NET Framework common language runtime uses an advanced implementation of the Microsoft Windows® graphics design interface (GDI) called GDI+. GDI+ allows you to create graphics, draw text, and manipulate graphical images as objects. GDI+ is designed to offer performance as well as ease of use. You can use GDI+ to render graphical images on Windows Forms and controls as well as on any Graphics object. GDI+ has fully replaced GDI and is now the only way to render graphics programmatically in Windows Forms applications.

Module 6, "Reporting and Printing in Windows Forms Applications," in Course 2565A, *Developing Microsoft .NET Applications for Windows (Visual Basic® .NET)*, introduces the basics of GDI+ and how to draw text and shapes by using the **Graphics** object methods.

In this appendix, you will learn about some more advanced tasks that you can perform with GDI+, such how to create and use additional brush types and manipulate images.

For more information about GDI+ beyond what is included in this appendix, see the Microsoft .NET Framework software development kit (SDK) documentation and *Programming Microsoft Windows with C#,* by Charles Petzold.

Objectives

After completing this module, you will be able to:

- Create and use textured, hatched, and gradient brushes to fill shapes.
- Manipulate bitmap images and use them in a Windows Forms application.

Lesson: Creating Brushes and Filled Shapes

- Types of Brushes for Filled Shapes
- How to Create Solid and Texture Filled Shapes
- How to Create Hatch Filled Shapes
- How to Create a Gradient Filled Shape
- How to Create a Path Gradient Filled Shape
- How to Create Transparent Shapes
- Practice: Creating Brushes and Filled Shapes

Introduction

Two-dimensional (2-D) shapes are vector objects that can be drawn as an outline by using a pen and, in the case of a closed shape, filled by using a brush. Rectangles and ellipses are good examples of closed shapes because they consist of an outline and an interior. Closed shapes can be drawn as either an outline by using a **Draw*xxx*** method or as a filled shape by using a **Fill*xxx*** method.

In this lesson, you will learn how to draw filled shapes by using each of the different types of brushes supported by GDI+.

Lesson objectives

After completing this lesson, you will be able to:

- Draw filled shapes by using GDI+ methods.
- Create hatch filled shapes.
- Create texture filled shapes.
- Create gradient filled shapes.
- Create path gradient filled shapes.
- Create transparent shapes.

Types of Brushes for Filled Shapes

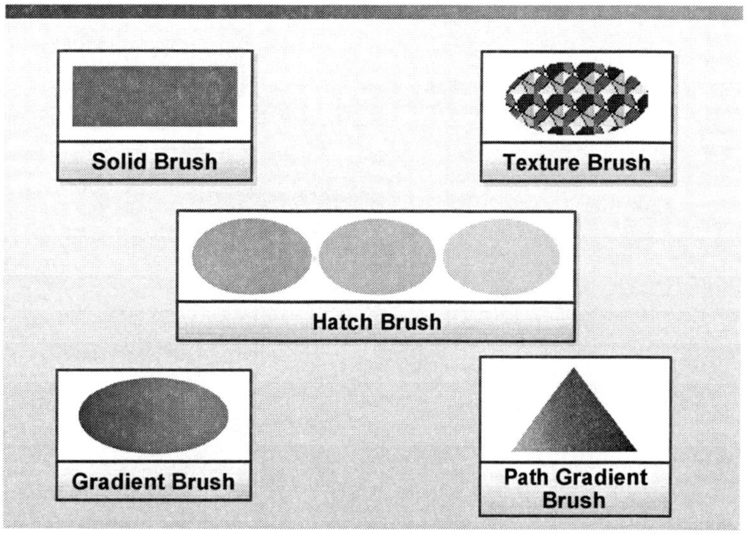

Introduction

Applications use filled shapes for a variety of tasks. Spreadsheet applications, for example, use filled shapes to construct charts and graphs, and drawing and painting applications use filled shapes to enable the user to draw vector objects.

GDI+ provides five brush classes for filling the interiors of closed shapes. The five brush types are **SolidBrush**, **TextureBrush**, **HatchBrush**, **LinearGradientBrush**, and **PathGradientBrush**. All of these classes inherit the members of the **Brush** class.

Solid brushes

The **SolidBrush** is the simplest form of brush and is used to fill a shape with solid color. **SolidBrush** is found in the **System.Drawing** namespace.

Texture brushes

The **TextureBrush** is similar to a solid brush, but uses an image rather than a solid color to fill a shape. With a texture brush, you can fill a shape with any pattern that is available in a bitmap form. **TextureBrush** is found in the **System.Drawing** namespace.

Hatch brushes

The **HatchBrush** enables you to select from more than 50 preset hatch style patterns (enumerations of **HatchStyle**) to fill in a shape. When you fill a shape with a hatch brush, you specify a line color, a background color, and a hatch style. **HatchBrush** is found in the **System.Drawing.Drawing2D** namespace.

Linear gradient brushes

You can use a linear gradient brush to fill a shape with color that changes gradually as you move across the shape horizontally, vertically, or diagonally. **LinearGradientBrush** is found in the **System.Drawing.Drawing2D** namespace.

Path gradient brushes

A path gradient brush provides you with many additional capabilities beyond those of a linear gradient brush. You use a path gradient brush when you want to create a shape that begins with a single color on the inside and gradually changes to one or more other colors along the perimeter of the shape. **PathGradientBrush** is found in the **System.Drawing.Drawing2D** namespace.

How to Create Solid and Texture Filled Shapes

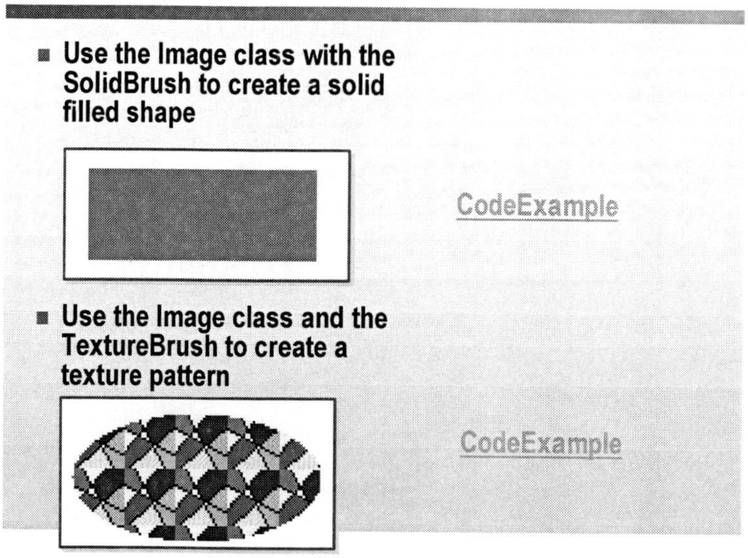

Introduction

You can fill a closed shape with a solid color or a texture by using the **Image** class and the **SolidBrush/TextureBrush** class. Both **SolidBrush** and **TextureBrush** are included in the **System.Drawing** namespace.

Procedure: How to create a solid filled shape

The following example shows how to draw a solid blue ellipse.

```
Dim mySolidBrush As New SolidBrush(Color.Blue)
myGraphics.FillRectangle(mySolidBrush, 0, 0, 120, 40)
```

Procedure: How to create a texture filled shape

The following example fills an ellipse with an image. The code constructs an **Image** object and then passes the address of that **Image** object as an argument to a **TextureBrush** constructor. The last line of the code example statement fills the ellipse with repeated copies of the image.

```
Dim imageFileName As String = "C:\Images\Image01.jpg"
Dim brushImage = New Bitmap(imageFileName)
Dim myImageBrush As New TextureBrush(brushImage)
e.Graphics.FillEllipse(myImageBrush, 0, 0, 120, 40)
```

Note You can also use a brush to draw lines by constructing a pen based on the brush rather than a solid color. For more information about using a brush as the source of a line color, see "Drawing a Line Filled with a Texture" in the .NET Framework SDK documentation.

How to Create Hatch Filled Shapes

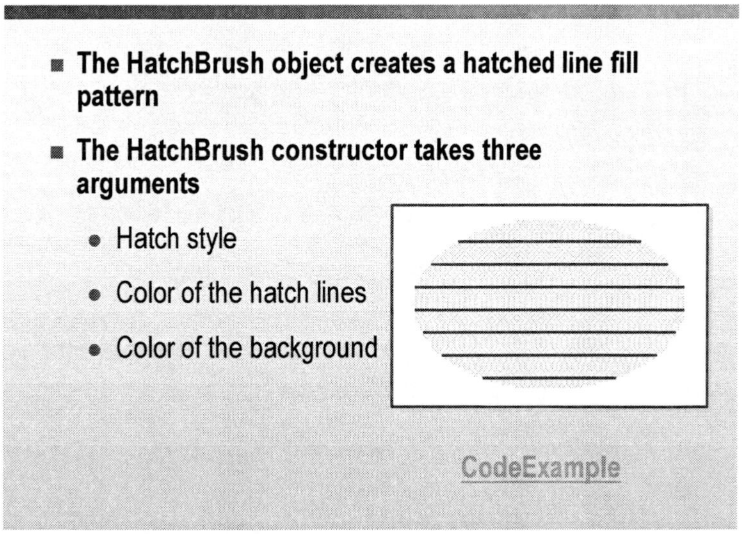

Introduction

A hatch brush allows you to select from a large variety of preset hatched line patterns to fill in a shape.

Each hatch pattern is made from two colors: one for the background and one for the lines that form the pattern over the background. To fill a closed shape with a hatch pattern, use a **HatchBrush** object. **HatchBrush** and **HatchStyle** are included in the **System.Drawing.Drawing2D** namespace.

Procedure

The **HatchBrush** constructor takes three arguments:

- Hatch style
- Color of the hatch lines
- Color of the background

The hatch style argument can be any of the more than 50 values from the **HatchStyle** enumeration, such as **Cross**, **Horizontal**, **OutlinedDiamond**, **Sphere**, **Vertical**, and **ZigZag**.

The following example demonstrates how to fill an ellipse with a horizontal line hatch pattern of red on a cyan background:

```
Imports System.Drawing.Drawing2D
...
Dim myHatchBrush = New HatchBrush( _
    HatchStyle.Horizontal, Color.Red, Color.Cyan)
e.Graphics.FillEllipse(myHatchBrush, 0, 200, 120, 40)
```

How to Create a Gradient Filled Shape

Use a gradient brush to fill a shape with a gradually changing color

```
Dim rect As Rectangle = New Rectangle( _
              hPos, vPos, txtWidth, txtHeight)
Dim myBrush As LinearGradientBrush = New _
    LinearGradientBrush(rect, Color.SeaGreen, _
    Color.BlueViolet, LinearGradientMode.Horizontal)
e.Graphics.DrawString(myText, myFont, myBrush, hPos, _
   vPos)
```

Introduction

You can fill a shape with a gradually changing color by using a gradient brush. For example, you can use a horizontal gradient to fill a shape with color that changes gradually as you move from the left edge of the shape to the right edge.

A linear gradient changes color as you move horizontally, vertically, or diagonally across a closed shape. For creating linear gradients, GDI+ provides a **LinearGradientBrush** which inherits from the **Brush** class and is included in the **System.Drawing.Drawing2D** namespace.

The orientation of a **LinearGradientBrush** (horizontal, vertical, or diagonal) is determined by the orientation of a line connecting the two points used in the construction of the brush. When the brush is constructed by using a rectangle rather than two points, the orientation is determined by the value of either the **LinearGradientMode** parameter or the **angle** parameter.

By default, the color in a linear gradient changes uniformly from one endpoint to another. However, you can customize a linear gradient in many ways. For example, you can create a nonuniform linear gradient or a gradient that begins with one color in the middle and blends into a second color at both ends.

For more information about customizing the appearance of a **LinearGradientBrush**, see "Creating a Linear Gradient and Filling Shapes with a Gradient Brush" in the .NET Framework SDK documentation, or see "LinearGradientBrush Members" in the .NET Framework Class Library.

Procedure: How to create a horizontal linear gradient

The following example draws a string (myText) by using a linear gradient brush. The size of the brush is determined by a rectangle, which is constructed to be the same size as the string when it is drawn on the graphics object.

```
Dim rect As Rectangle = New Rectangle( _
                hPos, vPos, txtWidth, txtHeight)
Dim myBrush As LinearGradientBrush = New _
            LinearGradientBrush(rect, Color.SeaGreen, _
            Color.BlueViolet, LinearGradientMode.Horizontal)
e.Graphics.DrawString(myText, myFont, myBrush, hPos, vPos)
```

Note If the object being drawn with a linear gradient brush extends beyond the size of the brush, the color gradient repeats itself until the entire object is filled.

How to Create a Path Gradient Filled Shape

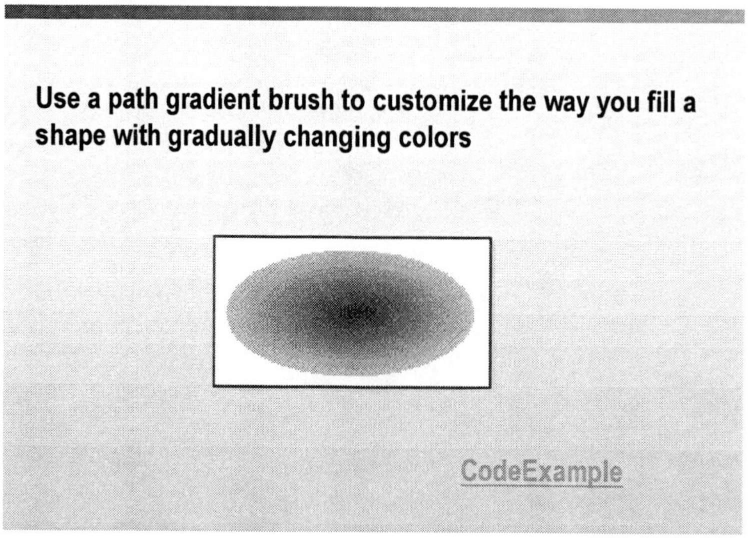

Introduction

The **PathGradientBrush** class enables you to create gradients with more than two colors and additional methods for customizing a gradient fill. For example, you can specify one color for the center of a path and another color for the outside edge. You can also specify separate colors for each of several points along the perimeter of a path.

Procedure: How to fill an ellipse with a path gradient

The following example fills shapes with a path gradient brush. The center color is set to white and the color of the outside edge is set to a predefined color.

```
Dim pgBrush As New PathGradientBrush(pathShape1)
pgBrush.CenterColor = Color.White
pgBrush.SurroundColors = colorsShape1

e.Graphics.FillPath(pgBrush, pathShape1)
```

By default, a path gradient brush does not extend outside the boundary of the path. If you use the path gradient brush to fill a figure that extends beyond the boundary of the path, the area of the object that is outside the path is not filled.

For more information about customizing a PathGradientBrush, see "Creating a Path Gradient" in the .NET Framework SDK documentation.

Procedure: How to set the center point

By default, the center point of a path gradient brush is at the centroid of the path used to construct the brush. You can change the location of the center point by setting the **CenterPoint** property of the **PathGradientBrush** class.

The following example creates a path gradient brush based on an ellipse. The center of the ellipse is at (70, 35), but the center point of the path gradient brush is set to (120, 40).

```
' Create a path that consists of a single ellipse.
Dim path As New GraphicsPath()
path.AddEllipse(0, 0, 140, 70)

' Use the path to construct a brush.
Dim pthGrBrush As New PathGradientBrush(path)

' Set the center point to a location that is not
' the centroid of the path.
pthGrBrush.CenterPoint = New PointF(120, 40)

' Set the color at the center of the path to blue.
pthGrBrush.CenterColor = Color.FromArgb(255, 0, 0, 255)

' Set the color along the entire boundary
' of the path to aqua.
Dim colors As Color() = {Color.FromArgb(255, 0, 255, 255)}
pthGrBrush.SurroundColors = colors

e.Graphics.FillEllipse(pthGrBrush, 0, 0, 140, 70)
```

How to Create Transparent Shapes

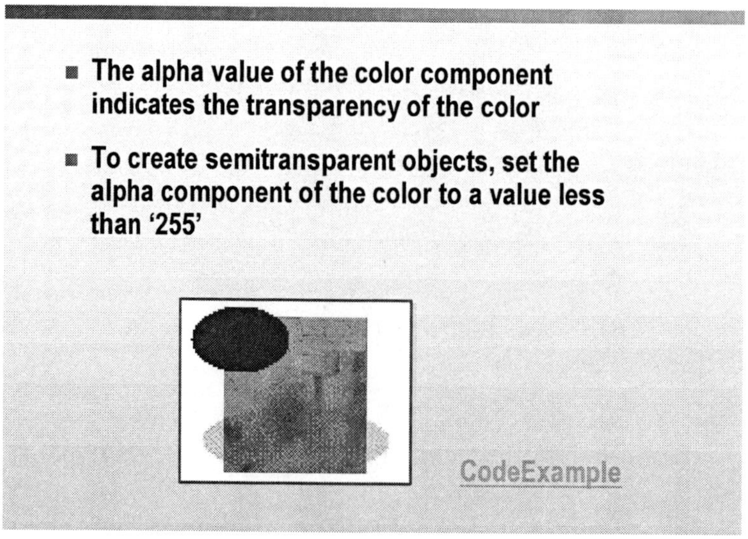

Introduction

In GDI+, a color is a 32-bit value with 8 bits each for alpha, red, green, and blue. The alpha value indicates the transparency of the color—the extent to which the color is blended with the background color. Alpha values range from 0 through 255, where 0 represents a fully transparent color, and 255 represents a fully opaque color.

Procedure

When you fill a shape, you must pass the address of a **Brush** object to one of the fill methods of the **Graphics** class. One parameter of the **SolidBrush** constructor is a **Color** object.

To fill an opaque shape, set the alpha component of the color to 255. To fill a semitransparent shape, set the alpha component to any value from 1 through 254. For a transparent object, set the alpha component value to 0.

When you fill a semitransparent shape, the color of the shape is blended with the colors of the background. The alpha component specifies how the shape and background colors are mixed. Alpha values near 0 place more weight on the background colors, and alpha values near 255 place more weight on the shape color.

The following example draws two ellipses on a textured background. The first ellipse uses an alpha component of 255, so it is opaque. The second ellipse uses an alpha component of 128, so it is semitransparent. Background images can be seen through a semitransparent shape.

```
Dim bitmap As New Bitmap(imageFileName)
e.Graphics.DrawImage(bitmap, 50, 50, bitmap.Width, _
                     bitmap.Height)

Dim opaqueBrush As New SolidBrush(Color.FromArgb(255, _
                     Color.Blue))
Dim semiTransBrush As New SolidBrush(Color.FromArgb(128, _
                     Color.Blue))

e.Graphics.FillEllipse(opaqueBrush, 0, 200, 45, 30)
e.Graphics.FillEllipse(semiTransBrush, 0, 250, 45, 30)
```

Practice: Creating Brushes and Filled Shapes

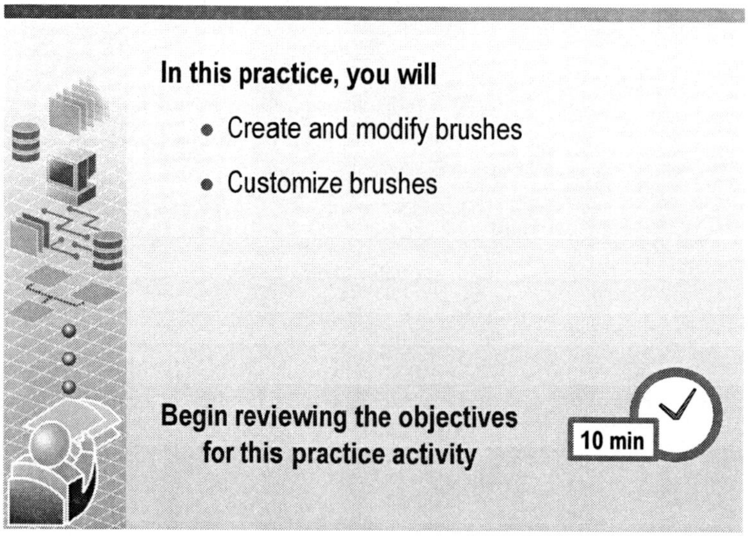

Introduction

You are a software developer at Northwind Traders. You have been asked to create a **Form** class that can be used throughout the company as a splash screen that displays while an application loads.

In this practice, you will work with hatched, textured, gradient, and semitransparent brushes.

Instructions

► Open the practice project file

1. Use Windows Explorer to browse to *install_folder*\Practices\AppendixA\AppendixA_01\Starter.

Note If you performed a default installation of the course files, *install_folder* corresponds to C:\Program Files\Msdntrain\2565.

---

2. Double-click the **Filled Shapes.sln** solution file to open the project.
3. On the **Debug** menu, click **Start**.
4. Click **Show Splash Screen**.

   Identify the brush types used on the splash screen form.

► **Create and modify brushes**

1. Stop the splash screen application, and then open the Code Editor for splashForm.vb.
2. On the **View** menu, point to **Show Tasks**, and then click **Comment**.
3. In the Task List, double-click **TODO: modify TextureBrush**.
4. Enable the code statement that follows the TODO line.
5. In the Task List, double-click **TODO: modify HatchBrush**.
6. Modify the code statement that creates the **HatchBrush** by changing the **HatchStyle** from **LargeCheckerBoard** to **Cross**.
7. In the Task List, double-click **TODO: modify LinearGradientBrush**.
8. Modify the code statement that creates the **LinearGradientBrush** by changing the **LinearGradientMode** from **Vertical** to **Horizontal**.
9. In the Task List, double-click **TODO: create PathGradientBrush**.
10. Add the following code statements below the TODO line.

```
Dim brushShape1 as New PathGradientBrush(pathShape1)
brushShape1.CenterColor = Color.White
brushShape1.SurroundColors = colorsShape1
```

11. In the Task List, double-click **TODO: draw pathShape1**.
12. Add the following code statement below the TODO line.

```
e.Graphics.FillPath(brushShape1, pathShape1)
```

13. Do any of the code statements that you modified or added require a reference to the **Drawing2D** namespace?

____

____

14. On the **Debug** menu, click **Start**.
15. Click **Show Splash Screen**.

    Examine the change to the splash screen form.
16. Close the splash form, and then close the splash screen application.

► **Customize brushes**

1. In the Task List, double-click **TODO: customize the linear gradient brush.**
2. Modify the code statement that uses the **SetBlendTriangularShape** method by changing the value passed to the method from **0.0** to **0.5**.
3. In the Task List, double-click **TODO: enable customizations to the path gradient brush.**
4. Enable the code statement that follows the TODO line.
5. On the **Debug** menu, click **Start**.
6. Click **Show Splash Screen**.

   Examine the change to the splash screen form. If necessary, change the code statements back to their original state, run the application again to see the appearance of the "Purchase Order Application" text and "star-shaped path" before the changes were made, and then reintroduce the changes made in steps 2 and 4 above.
7. Close the splash screen form, and then close the splash screen application.
8. If time permits, experiment with the code used to set the alpha value (transparency) for the path gradient brushes. You can find the appropriate code section by double-clicking **TODO: modify transparency settings for path gradient brushes** in the Task list.

Lesson: Working with Bitmap Images

- What Is a Bitmap Image?
- How to Load and Display an Image
- How to Crop and Scale Images
- How to Rotate, Skew, and Reflect Images
- How to Create Thumbnail Images
- Practice: Working with Bitmap Images

Introduction

Certain kinds of pictures are difficult or impossible to display with the techniques of vector graphics. For example, the pictures on toolbar buttons and the pictures that appear as icons would be difficult to specify as collections of lines and curves. Images of this type are stored as bitmaps, arrays of numbers that represent the colors of individual dots on the screen.

Lesson objectives

After completing this lesson, you will be able to:

- Describe bitmaps and the various file formats for saving bitmaps.
- Load and display bitmaps on screen.
- Crop and scale images.
- Rotate, skew, and reflect images.
- Create thumbnail images.

What Is a Bitmap Image?

- **Bitmap**
  - A bitmap is an array of bits that specify the color of each pixel in a rectangular array of pixels
- **Graphic File Formats**
  - Used for saving bitmaps in disk files
- **Types of Graphic File Formats**
  - BMP, GIF, JPEG, EXIF, PNG, TIFF

Introduction

A *bitmap* is an array of bits that specify the color of each pixel in a rectangular array of pixels. The number of bits devoted to an individual pixel determines the number of colors that can be assigned to that pixel. For example, if each pixel is represented by 4 bits, then a pixel can be assigned one of 16 different colors (2^4 = 16).

Disk files that store bitmaps usually contain one or more information blocks that store information such as the number of bits per pixel, number of pixels in each row, and number of rows in the array. Such a file might also contain a color table (sometimes called a color palette). A color table maps numbers in the bitmap to specific colors.

A bitmap that stores indexes in a color table is called a *palette-indexed* bitmap. Some bitmaps have no need for a color table. For example, if a bitmap uses 24 bits per pixel, that bitmap can store the colors themselves rather than indexes in a color table.

Graphics file formats

There are many standard formats for saving bitmaps in disk files. GDI+ supports the following graphics file formats.

- BMP

  BMP is a standard format used by Windows to store device-independent and application-independent images. BMP files are usually not compressed and therefore are not well suited for transfer across the Internet.

- Graphics Interchange Format (GIF)

  GIF is a common format for images that appear on Web pages. GIFs work well for line drawings, pictures with blocks of solid color, and pictures with sharp boundaries between colors. GIFs are compressed, but no information is lost in the compression process; a decompressed image is exactly the same as the original. GIF files can store only colors with 1, 2, 4, or 8 bits per pixel.

- Joint Photographic Experts Group (JPEG)

  JPEG is a compression scheme that is used for natural scenes such as scanned photographs. Some information is lost in the compression process, but often the loss is imperceptible to the human eye. JPEGs store 24 bits per pixel, so they are capable of displaying more than 16 million colors.

- Exchangeable Image File (EXIF)

  EXIF is a file format used for photographs captured by digital cameras. An EXIF file contains an image that is compressed according to the JPEG specification. An EXIF file also contains information about the photograph (date taken, shutter speed, exposure time, and so on) and information about the camera (manufacturer, model, and so on).

- Portable Network Graphics (PNG)

  The PNG format retains many of the advantages of the GIF format but also provides capabilities beyond those of GIF. Like GIF files, PNG files are compressed with no loss of information. PNG files can store colors with 8, 24, or 48 bits per pixel and grayscales with 1, 2, 4, 8, or 16 bits per pixel. In contrast, GIF files can use only 1, 2, 4, or 8 bits per pixel.

  PNG improves on GIF in its ability to progressively display an image; that is, to display better and better approximations of the image as it arrives over a network connection. PNG files can contain gamma correction and color correction information so that the images can be accurately rendered on a variety of display devices.

- Tagged Image File Format (TIFF)

  TIFF is a flexible and extendable format that is supported by a wide variety of platforms and image-processing applications. TIFF files can store images with an arbitrary number of bits per pixel and can use a variety of compression algorithms. Several images can be stored in a single, multiple-page TIFF file. Information related to the image, such as scanner make, host computer, type of compression, orientation, samples per pixel, and so on can be stored in the file and arranged through the use of tags.

How to Load and Display an Image

- **Use the Bitmap class for working with bitmap images**
- **To load and display a bitmap**
  - Create a **Bitmap** object and pass the name of the image to the **Bitmap** constructor
  - Pass that Bitmap object to the **DrawImage** method of a **Graphics** object

CodeExample

Introduction

GDI+ provides the **Bitmap** class for working with bitmap images. The **Bitmap** class derives from the **Image** class but provides additional methods for loading saving, and manipulating bitmap images.

Procedure

To load a bitmap from a file and display that bitmap on the screen, you use a **Bitmap** object and a **Graphics** object. The **Bitmap** class supports several file formats, including BMP, GIF, JPEG, PNG, and TIFF.

To load and display a bitmap:

1. Create a **Bitmap** object.

   When you create the **Bitmap** object, pass the name of the image file to the **Bitmap** constructor.

2. After you have created a **Bitmap** object, pass that **Bitmap** object to the **DrawImage** method of a **Graphics** object.

   The following example creates a **Bitmap** object from a JPEG file located in the startup folder of the application and then draws the bitmap with its upper-left corner at (60, 10).

```
Dim fileName As String = Application.StartupPath & _
                         "\Bitmap.jpg"
Dim fileImage As New Bitmap(fileName)
e.Graphics.DrawImage(fileImage, 60, 10)
```

How to Crop and Scale Images

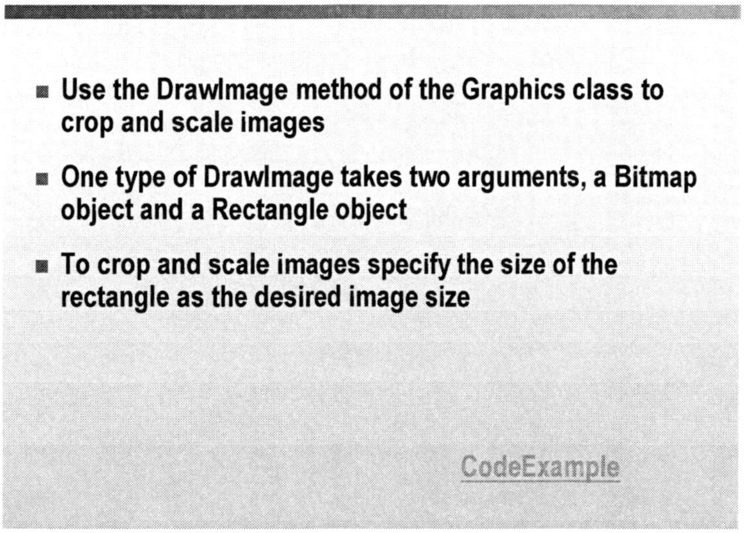

Introduction

The **Graphics** class in GDI+ provides several **DrawImage** methods, some of which have source and destination rectangle parameters that you can use to crop and scale images.

Procedure

One of the **DrawImage** methods receives a **Bitmap** object and uses a **Rectangle** object to specify the size of the drawn image. The rectangle specifies the destination for the drawing operation; that is, it specifies the rectangle in which to draw the image. If the size of the destination rectangle is different from the size of the original image, the image is scaled to fit the destination rectangle. The following example draws an image full scale and then draws the image with scaled coordinates.

```
' draw the original image
e.Graphics.DrawImage(fileImage, 0, 0)

Dim topImage As Single = e.PageBounds.Top
Dim leftImage As Single = e.PageBounds.Left
Dim widthImage As Single = fileImage.Size.Width
Dim heightImage As Single = fileImage.Size.Height

' create a rectangle that can be used to create a
'   scaled version of the original image
Dim scaledCoordinates As New Rectangle(leftImage, _
                        topImage + heightImage, _
                        0.5 * widthImage, _
                        0.5 * heightImage)

' draw a smaller version of the bitmap image by
'    specifying the image and a rectangle
e.Graphics.DrawImage(fileImage, scaledCoordinates)
```

Some overloads of the **DrawImage** method include a source-rectangle parameter as well as a destination-rectangle parameter. The source-rectangle parameter specifies the portion of the original image to draw. The destination rectangle parameter specifies the rectangle in which to draw that portion of the image. If the source rectangle specifies a region of the original image that is smaller than the original image, the image drawn in the destination rectangle will be a cropped version of the original image showing only that portion of the image specified by the source rectangle. If the size of the destination rectangle is different from the size of the source rectangle, the image is scaled to fit the destination rectangle.

How to Rotate, Skew, and Reflect Images

- **To rotate, skew, and reflect an image**
  - Specify destination points for the upper-left, upper-right, and lower-left corners of the original image

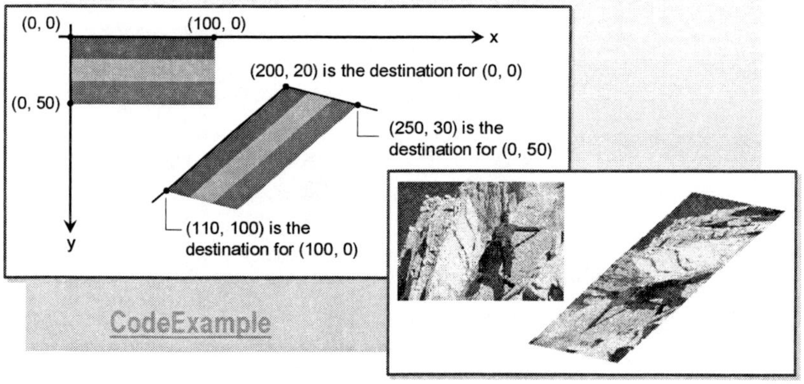

Introduction

You can rotate, skew, and reflect an image by specifying destination points for the upper-left, upper-right, and lower-left corners of the original image.

Procedure

The following code demonstrates how to create the point arrays that can be used to rotate, skew, and reflect an image.

```
' create a set of points that can be used to
' draw a version of the original image
' that is rotated 90 degrees counter-clockwise
'
' upper-left becomes lower-left
' upper-right becomes upper-left
' lower-left becomes lower-right

Dim rotatedCoordinates As Point() = { _
New Point(leftImage, _
topImage + heightImage + widthImage), _
New Point(leftImage, _
topImage + heightImage), _
New Point(leftImage + heightImage, _
topImage + heightImage + widthImage)}
e.Graphics.DrawImage(fileImage, rotatedCoordinates)


' create a set of points that can be used to
' draw a skewed version of the original image
'
' upper-left remains upper-left
' upper-right remains upper-right
' lower-left becomes lower-left + .5 width

Dim skewedCoordinates As Point() = { _
New Point(leftImage, _
topImage + heightImage), _
New Point(leftImage + widthImage, _
topImage + heightImage), _
New Point(leftImage + 0.5 * widthImage, _
topImage + 2.0 * heightImage)}
e.Graphics.DrawImage(fileImage, skewedCoordinates)


' create a set of points that can be used to
' draw a reflected version of the original image
'
' upper-left becomes lower-left + .5 width
' upper-right becomes lower-right +.5 width
' lower-left becomes upper-left

Dim reflectedCoordinates As Point() = { _
New Point(leftImage + 0.5 * widthImage, _
topImage + 2 * heightImage), _
New Point(leftImage + 1.5 * widthImage, _
topImage + 2 * heightImage), _
New Point(leftImage, _
topImage + heightImage)}
e.Graphics.DrawImage(fileImage, reflectedCoordinates)
```

How to Create Thumbnail Images

Create a thumbnail image by calling the GetThumbnailImage method of an Image object

```
Dim fileName As String = Application.StartupPath _
& "\WinForms.jpg"
Dim fileImage As New Bitmap(fileName)
Dim pThumbnail As Image = _
    fileImage.GetThumbnailImage( _
    fileImage.Width / 6, _
    fileImage.Height / 6, _
    Nothing, New IntPtr())

e.Graphics.DrawImage(pThumbnail, 100, 100, _
pThumbnail.Width, pThumbnail.Height)
```

Introduction

A thumbnail image is a small version of an image. You can create a thumbnail image by calling the **GetThumbnailImage** method of an **Image** object.

Procedure

The following code constructs an **Image** object from the file WinForms.jpg. The code creates a thumbnail image that is 1/6 the size of the original. The *callback* and *callbackData* parameters of the **GetThumbnailImage** method are not used in this example.


```
Dim fileName As String = Application.StartupPath _
& "\WinForms.jpg"
Dim fileImage As New Bitmap(fileName)
Dim pThumbnail As Image = _
    fileImage.GetThumbnailImage( _
    fileImage.Width / 6, _
    fileImage.Height / 6, _
    Nothing, New IntPtr())

e.Graphics.DrawImage(pThumbnail, 100, 100, _
pThumbnail.Width, pThumbnail.Height)
```

Practice: Working With Bitmaps

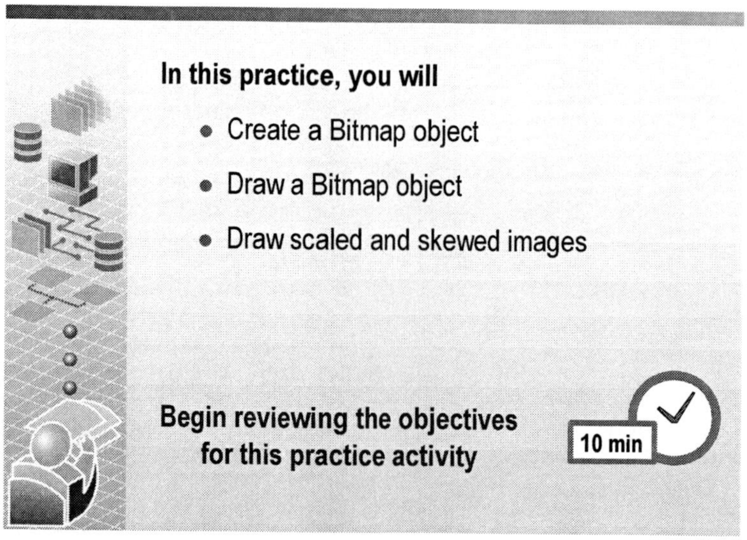

Introduction

You are a software developer at Northwind Traders. One of your current projects requires that you create a routine for opening, modifying, and printing bitmap images.

In this practice, you will draw and preview a bitmap object on a print document, scale the image, skew the image, and examine the code used to create a semitransparent image.

Instructions

► **Open the practice project file**

1. Use Windows Explorer to browse to *install_folder*\Practices\AppendixA\AppendixA_02\Starter.
2. Double-click the Bitmap Images.sln solution file to open the project.
3. Open Form1 in the Code Editor.
4. On the **View** menu, point to **Show Tasks**, and then click **Comment**.

► **Create a Bitmap object**

1. In the Task List, double-click **TODO: create bitmap object**.
2. Add the following code statement below the TODO line.

```
Dim fileImage As New Bitmap(fileName)
```

► **Draw a Bitmap object**

1. In the Task List, double-click **TODO: draw the bitmap image**.
2. Add the following code statement below the TODO line.

```
e.Graphics.DrawImage(fileImage, leftImage, topImage)
```

3. On the **Debug** menu, click **Start**, and then click **Print Preview**.
4. Close the **Print Preview** dialog box and the Bitmap Images application.

▶ Draw scaled and skewed images

1. In the Task List, double-click **TODO: draw a scaled image**.
2. Add the following code statement below the TODO line.

```
e.Graphics.DrawImage(fileImage, scaledCoordinates)
```

3. On the **Debug** menu, click **Start**, and then click **Print Preview**.
4. Close the **Print Preview** dialog box and the Bitmap Images application.
5. In the Task List, double-click **TODO: draw a skewed image**.
6. Add the following code statement below the TODO line.

```
e.Graphics.DrawImage(fileImage, skewedCoordinates)
```

7. On the **Debug** menu, click **Start**, and then click **Print Preview**.
8. Close the **Print Preview** dialog box.
9. Click **Draw semitransparent reflection**, and then click **Print Preview**.
10. Close the **Print Preview** dialog box and the Bitmap Images application.
11. Examine the code used to set up the scaled and skewed versions of the image and the transparency settings.

www.mobilelearning.TV

2354 course #

Notes

Notes

Notes

Notes

Notes

Notes

Notes

Notes

Notes

Notes

MSM2565ACP/C90-03131

0 99751 06461 4